WESTERN CIVILIZATIONS

THEIR HISTORY AND THEIR CULTURE

VOLUME II / THIRTEENTH EDITION

WESTERN CIVILIZATIONS

THEIR HISTORY AND THEIR CULTURE

ROBERT E. LERNER

STANDISH MEACHAM

EDWARD McNALL BURNS

VOLUME II / THIRTEENTH EDITION

W · W · NORTON & COMPANY NEW YORK · LONDON

The Library of Congress has catalogued the one-volume edition as follows:
Lerner, Robert E.
Western civilizations, their history and their culture/Robert E.
Lerner, Standish Meacham, Edward McNall Burns.—13th ed.
p. cm.
Includes bibliographical references and index.
ISBN 0-393-97192-9
1. Civilization, Western. 2. Europe—Civilization. I. Meacham,
Standish. II. Burns, Edward McNall, 1897– . III. Title.
CB245.L47 1998
909'.09812–dc21   97–32338

The text of this book is composed in ITC Stone Serif with the display set in Optima.
Composition by TSI Graphics and manufacturing by Quebecor Hawkins County.
Book design by Jack Meserole

W. W. Norton & Company, Inc., 500 Fifth Avenue, New York, N.Y. 10110
W. W. Norton & Company Ltd., 10 Coptic Street, London WC1A 1PU

http://www.wwnorton.com

ISBN 0–393–97220–8 (pbk.)

2 3 4 5 6 7 8 9 0

For Dietlind and Olivia;
Edith, Louisa, and Samuel

CONTENTS

PART FIVE

THE FRENCH AND INDUSTRIAL REVOLUTIONS AND THEIR CONSEQUENCES

PART SIX

THE WEST AT THE WORLD'S CENTER

PART SEVEN

THE EMERGENCE OF A WORLD CIVILIZATION

CHAPTER 32   PROBLEMS OF WORLD
                CIVILIZATION   1095

LIST OF MAPS

PREFACE

George Orwell once remarked that "keeping the past up to date is a full-time job." This insight seems particularly telling as a result of the startling rush of events during the last few years. "Trends" that seemed so clear only yesterday have turned out to be no trends at all. In addition, dramatic advances in historical scholarship have cast new light on old problems and have placed into prominence subject matters that historians previously had all but ignored. Accordingly we have worked hard to keep the past up to date for this thirteenth edition of *Western Civilizations*. Yet we have always worked within the framework of authorial principles bequeathed to us by E. M. Burns—principles that may have served to make this book a "textbook classic." We offer a history of civilizations—an evolving account of the ways in which human beings have organized their lives in response to changing environments and persistent needs. Thus we complement narrative passages with discussions of ideas and societal institutions, and we draw heavily on pictorial material to give our readers the best impression possible of how our civilizations really looked. We try as well to avoid a tone of disembodied truth, both because we do not believe there is such a thing and because we want to engage and maintain our readers' attention. Our urgent desire is to demonstrate without resorting to cheapness that "first-year history" need not be viewed as a chore but might be welcomed as a source of intellectual excitement, even delight.

Although we have gone over *Western Civilizations* line by line in our effort to keep the past up to date, teachers will wish to know where the most significant changes occur. This bright new edition features full-color maps and illustrations throughout the text and, as an additional pedagogical aid for students, highlighted summary points at the end of each chapter. Toward the goal of keeping the volume within manageable limits we have deleted the material on fossils and paleoanthropology in Chapter 1; rather than beginning with *Homo habilis,* we now begin with *Homo sapiens* and the Ice-Age cave murals. The remainder of Chapter 1 has been substantially rewritten, with revised treatments of cave art, the emergence of food production, and the birth of cities in western Asia. In addition, a prominent new feature of Chapter 1 is a discussion of the central place of cloth production by women in early villages. Another means for holding down the length of the volume has been to reduce the amount of space (hitherto generous) devoted to the details of early religions and wars: the treatment of these subjects has been streamlined in Chapters 2 (Mesopotamia) and 3 (Egypt). In Chapter 4 the narrative of Hebrew political history now opens with the entrance of the Hebrews into Canaan, the period when the biblical account begins to be corroborated by independent evidence.

Chapter 4 also contains a new treatment of Minoan society, with special attention to women's dress.

The major changes in Chapter 5 are as follows: the section on early Greek religion has been shortened; Greek "colonization" is now called Greek expansion; erroneous statements about the electoral system under Clisthenes have been corrected; and there is a revised treatment of the poetess Sappho. In Chapter 6 we have deleted the coverage of the Cynics, Menander, and Hellenistic utopias as being too specialized for an introductory text, and we have revised the discussion of the Hellenistic pastoral. Chapter 7 contains changes in coverage and interpretation in the sections concerning the Roman republican constitution, Roman religion, Roman policy in granting citizenship, and Roman art and architecture. Throughout Parts One and Two we now use the abbreviation B.C.E. (before common era) for designating the time before the birth of Christ.

In Chapter 11 we have added a paragraph on Hildegard of Bingen, and in Chapter 13 we offer substantially revised treatments of Machiavelli, Botticelli, and Michelangelo's *David*. Chapter 14 presents corrected dates for early Portuguese sailings and colonizations of the Atlantic islands, and Chapter 15 contains a new approach to the problem of defining Mannerism.

The principal addition to the chapters on the nineteenth and twentieth centuries has been the introduction of considerable new material on nationalism. Chapter 19, on the French Revolution, now includes a discussion of the way in which warfare—and the idea of an enemy "other"—encouraged a nationalistic spirit throughout Europe. The chapter concludes with an assessment of nationalism as one of the lasting legacies of the revolutionary movement. Chapter 23, "Nationalism and Nation-Building," addresses the subject at considerable length. We argue, as do most recent scholars, that nationalism must be understood as policy as well as sentiment. It was manufactured by governments, "invented" as a way of encouraging loyalty to emerging and increasingly powerful state systems. In Chapter 24, we link nationalism to the rise of imperialism. And in Chapters 26 and 28, we demonstrate the manner in which nationalism fostered xenophobia and the rise of anti-Semitism, fascism, and Nazism.

We have also added material on the history of women, particularly in Chapter 21, where we explore the way in which women defined the public and private spheres of their daily existence. We take note also of the critical role that women played in the success of various early reform movements such as the abolition of slavery. Finally, material in Chapters 31 and 32 has been thoroughly updated, and includes a discussion of such topics as the fragmentation of Eastern Europe following the collapse of the Soviet Union, as well as recent changes on the continent of Africa.

Robert Lerner has been responsible for Chapters 1 through 15 and Chapter 18; Standish Meacham for the rest. As in the past, we have relied on the helpful criticisms and suggestions of fellow teachers. For this edition, we are indebted for reviews provided by George K. Behlmer (University of Washington), Ronald M. Berger (SUNY Oneonta), Michael D. Bess (Vanderbilt University), Maryann E. Brink, James M. Brophy (University of Delaware), Phyllis Culham (U.S. Naval Academy), Jeffrey W. Merrick (University of Wisconsin, Milwaukee), Phillip C. Naylor (Marquette University), John F. Robertson (Central Michigan University), and David R. Shearer (University of Delaware). Robert Lerner is grateful for suggestions from Stephen Harris, Laura May (Northwestern University), Tammy Ruen, Alauddin Samarrai (St. Cloud State University), Nancy Spatz (University of Northern Colorado), and Stephen Wessley (York College of Pennsylvania). Standish Meacham acknowledges the valuable assistance of Steven M. Salzman. At W. W. Norton Steven Forman and Jon Durbin have guided this edition along. Kate Nash resolved crises, gathered illustrations with efficiency and flair, and proved a superb consultant on a wide range of issues. Our editor, Traci Nagle, has throughout provided us with gentle but firm guidance in a way that has made working with her a genuine pleasure.

Robert Lerner
Standish Meacham

WESTERN
CIVILIZATIONS

CHAPTER 15

A CENTURY OF CRISIS FOR EARLY-MODERN EUROPE (c. 1560–c. 1660)

I do not wish to say much about the customs of the age in which we live. I can only state that this age is not one of the best, being a century of iron.
—R. MENTET DE SALMONET, *History of the Troubles in Great Britain* (1649)

What in me is dark
Illumine, what is low raise and support.

—JOHN MILTON, *Paradise Lost*

O N THE NIGHT before St. Bartholomew's Day in August of 1572 the Catholic queen mother of France, Catherine de Medici, authorized the ambush of French Protestant leaders who had come to Paris to attend a wedding. Thereupon, during the hours after midnight, unsuspecting people were awakened and stabbed to death or thrown out of windows. Soon all the targeted Protestants were eliminated, but the killing did not stop because roving bands of Parisian Catholics seized the opportunity of licensed carnage to slaughter at will any enemies they happened upon, Protestant or otherwise. By morning the River Seine was clogged with corpses and scores of bodies hung from gibbets in witness to an event known ever since as the Massacre of St. Bartholomew's Day.

> A massacre in Paris

Had this lamentable incident been an isolated event it hardly would be worth mentioning, but in fact throughout the hundred years from roughly 1560 to roughly 1660 outbreaks of religious mayhem—with Protestants the ruthless killers in certain cases as Catholics were in others—recurred in many parts of Europe. Moreover, to make matters far worse, economic hardships and prolonged wars accompanied religious riots to result in a century of pronounced crisis for European civilization. Granted that Europe's early-modern period of crisis was much less uniform in its nature and extent than the terrible times of the Later Middle Ages, seen from the broadest perspective the period from 1560 to 1660 was western Europe's "iron century"—an age of great turbulence and severe trials.

> A century of crisis

The St. Bartholomew's Day Massacre. A contemporary painting depicts the merciless slaughter of Huguenots in Paris. At the top left (in front of the large gate next to the Seine) the Queen Mother Catherine looks over a pile of naked dead bodies; to the right a Huguenot leader is being pushed out of a window.

ECONOMIC, RELIGIOUS, AND POLITICAL TESTS

Impending crisis

Europe's time of troubles crept up on contemporaries unawares. For almost a century before 1560 most of the West had enjoyed steady economic growth, and the discovery of the New World seemed the basis of greater prosperity to come. Political trends too seemed auspicious, since most western European governments were becoming ever more efficient and providing more internal peace for their subjects. Yet around 1560 thunderclouds were gathering in the skies that would soon burst into terrible storms.

Soaring prices

Although the causes of these storms were interrelated, each may be examined separately, starting with the great price inflation. Nothing like the upward price trend that affected western Europe in the second half of the sixteenth century had ever happened before. The cost of a measure of wheat in Flanders, for example, tripled between 1550 and 1600, grain prices in Paris quadrupled, and the overall cost of living in England more than doubled during the same period. Certainly the twentieth century has seen much more dizzying inflations than this, but since the skyrocketing of prices in the later sixteenth century was a novelty, most historians agree on calling it a "price revolution."

If experts agree on the terminology, however, very few of them agree on the exact combination of circumstances that caused the price revolution, for early-modern statistics are patchy and many areas of economic theory remain under dispute. Nonetheless, for present purposes two explanations for the great inflation may be offered with confidence. The first is demographic. Starting in the later fifteenth century, Europe's population began to mount again after the plague-induced falloff: roughly estimated, there were about 50 million people in Europe around 1450 and 90 million around 1600. Since Europe's food supply remained more or less constant owing to the lack of any noteworthy breakthrough in agricultural technology, food prices inevitably were driven sharply higher by greater demand. Although the prices of manufactured goods did not rise as steeply because there was a greater match between supply and demand, the prices of manufactured items did rise, especially in cases where the supply of agricultural raw materials crucial to the manufacturing process remained relatively inelastic.

Causes of inflation: (1) population increase

Population trends explain much, but since Europe's population did not grow nearly as rapidly in the second half of the sixteenth century as prices, other explanations for the great inflation are still necessary. Foremost among these is the enormous influx of bullion from Spanish America. Around 1560 a new technique of extracting silver from ore made the working of newly discovered mines in Mexico and upper Peru highly practical, soon transforming the previous trickle of silver entering the European economy into a flood. Whereas in the five years from 1556 to 1560 roughly 10 million ducats worth of silver passed through the Spanish entry point of Seville, between 1576 and 1580 that figure had doubled, and between 1591 and 1595 it had more than quadrupled. Inasmuch as most of this silver was used by the Spanish crown to pay its foreign creditors and its armies abroad, or by private individuals to pay for imports from other countries, Spanish bullion quickly circulated throughout Europe, where much of it was minted into coins. This dramatic increase in the volume of money in circulation further fueled the spiral of rising prices. "I learned a proverb here," said a French traveler in Spain in 1603, "everything costs much here except silver."

(2) Influx of silver

Aggressive entrepreneurs and landlords profited most from the changed economic circumstances, while the masses of laboring people were hurt the worst. Obviously, merchants in possession of sought-after goods were able to raise prices at will, and landlords either could profit directly from the rising prices of agricultural produce or, if they did not farm their own lands, could always raise rents. But laborers in country and town were caught in a squeeze because wages rose far more slowly than prices, owing to the presence of a more-than-adequate labor supply. Moreover, because the cost of food staples rose at a sharper rate than the cost of most other items of consumption, poor people had to spend an ever-greater percentage of their paltry incomes on necessities. In normal years they barely managed to survive, but when disasters such as wars or poor harvests drove grain prices out of reach, some of the poor literally

Effects of inflation on the laboring poor

starved to death. The picture that thus emerges is one of the rich getting richer and the poor getting poorer—splendid feasts enjoyed amid the most appalling suffering.

In addition to these direct economic effects, the price inflation of the later sixteenth century had significant political effects as well because higher prices placed new pressures on the sovereign states of Europe. The reasons for this were simple. Since the inflation depressed the real value of money, fixed incomes from taxes and dues in effect yielded less and less. Thus merely to keep their incomes constant governments would have been forced to raise taxes. But to compound this problem, most states needed much more real income than previously because they were undertaking more wars, and warfare, as always, was becoming increasingly expensive. The only recourse, then, was to raise taxes precipitously, but such draconian measures incurred great resentment on the part of subject populations—especially the very poor who were already strapped more than enough by the effects of the inflation. Hence governments faced continuous threats of defiance and potential armed resistance.

Less need be said about the economic stagnation that followed the price revolution because it interfered little with most of the trends just discussed. When population growth began to ease and the flood of silver from America began to abate around 1600, prices soon leveled off. Yet because the most lucrative economic exploitation of the New World began only in the late seventeenth century and Europe experienced little new industrial development, the period from about 1600 to 1660 was at best one of very limited overall economic growth, even though a few areas—notably Holland—bucked the trend. Within this context the rich were usually able to hold their own, but the poor as a group made no advances since the relationship of prices to wages remained fixed to their disadvantage. Indeed, if anything, the lot of the poor in many places deteriorated because the mid-seventeenth century saw some particularly expensive and destructive wars, causing helpless civilians to be plundered by rapacious tax collectors or looting soldiers, or sometimes both.

It goes without saying that most people would have been far better off had there been fewer wars during Europe's iron century, but given prevalent attitudes, newly arisen religious rivalries made wars inevitable. Simply stated, until religious passions began to cool toward the end of the period, most Catholics and Protestants viewed each other as minions of Satan who could not be allowed to live. Worse, sovereign states attempted to enforce religious uniformity on the grounds that "crown and altar" offered each other mutual support and in the belief that governments would totter where diversity of faith prevailed. Rulers on both sides felt certain that religious minorities, if allowed to survive in their realms, would inevitably engage in sedition; nor were they far wrong since militant Calvinists and Jesuits were indeed dedicated to subverting constituted powers in areas where they had not yet triumphed. Thus states tried to extirpate all potential religious resistance, but in the process sometimes provoked civil wars in which each side tended to assume there could be no victory until the other was exterminated. And of course civil wars might become international in scope when one or more foreign powers resolved to aid embattled religious allies elsewhere.

Compounding the foregoing problems were more strictly political ones: namely, while strapped by price trends and racked by religious wars, governments brought certain provincial and constitutional grievances down upon themselves. Regarding the provincial issue, most of the major states of early-modern Europe had been built up by conquests or dynastic unions with the result that many smaller territories had been subjected to rule by foreign governors. At first some degree of provincial autonomy was usually preserved and hence the inhabitants of such territories did not object too much to their annexation. But in the iron century, when governments were making ever-greater financial claims on all their subjects or trying to enforce religious uniformity, rulers customarily moved to destroy all remnants of provincial autonomy in order to implement their financial or religious policies. Naturally the province-dwellers were usually not inclined to accept total subjugation without a fight, so rebellions might break out on combined patriotic and economic or religious grounds. Nor was that all, since most governments seeking money and/or religious uniformity tried to rule their subjects with a firmer hand than before, and thus sometimes provoked armed resistance in the name of traditional constitutional liberties. Given this bewildering variety of motives for revolt, it is by no means surprising that the century between 1560 and 1660 was one of the most turbulent in all European history.

A HALF-CENTURY OF RELIGIOUS WARS

The greatest single cause of warfare in the first half of Europe's iron century was religious rivalry. Indeed, wars between Catholics and Protestants began as early as the 1540s when the Catholic Holy Roman emperor Charles V tried to reestablish Catholic unity in Germany by launching a military campaign against several German princes who had instituted Lutheran worship in their principalities. At times thereafter it appeared as if Charles was going to succeed in reducing his German Protestant opponents to complete submission, but since he was also involved in fighting against France, he seldom was able to devote concerted attention to affairs in Germany. Accordingly, religious warfare sputtered on and off until a compromise settlement was reached in the Religious Peace of Augsburg (1555). This rested on the principle of *cuius regio, eius religio* ("as the ruler, so the religion"), which meant that in those principalities where Lutheran princes ruled, Lutheranism would be the sole state religion, and Catholicism for those with Catholic princes. Although the Peace of Augsburg was a historical milestone inasmuch as Catholic rulers for the first time acknowledged the legality of Protestantism, it boded ill for the future in assuming that no sovereign state larger than a free city (for which it made exceptions) could tolerate religious diversity.

Governmental crises

Religious wars in Germany until the Peace of Augsburg

Jeanne D'Albret

Moreover, in excluding Calvinism it ensured that Calvinists would become aggressive opponents of the status quo.

Even though wars in the name of religion were fought in Europe before 1560, those that raged afterward were far more brutal, partly because the combatants had become more fanatical (intransigent Calvinists and Jesuits customarily took the lead on their respective sides), and partly because the later religious wars were aggravated by political and economic resentments. Since Geneva bordered on France, since Calvin himself was a Frenchman who longed to convert his mother country, and since Calvinists had no wish to displace German Lutherans, the next act in the tragedy of Europe's confessional warfare was played out on French soil. Calvinist missionaries had already made much headway in France in the years between Calvin's rise to power in Geneva in 1541 and the outbreak of religious warfare in 1562. Of the greatest aid to the Calvinist (Huguenot) cause was the conversion of many aristocratic French women to Calvinism because such women often won over their husbands, who in turn maintained large private armies. The foremost example is that of Jeanne d'Albret, queen of the tiny Pyrenean kingdom of Navarre, who brought over to Calvinism her husband, the prominent French aristocrat Antoine de Bourbon, and her brother-in-law, the prince de Condé. Not only did Condé take command of the French Huguenot party when civil war broke out in 1562, but he later was succeeded in this capacity by Jeanne's son, Henry of Navarre, who came to rule all of France at the end of the century as King Henry IV. In addition to aristocrats, many people from all walks of life became Huguenots for a variety of motives, with Huguenot strength greatest in areas of the south that had long resented the dominance of northern rule from Paris. In short, by 1562 Calvinists comprised between 10 and 20 percent of France's population of roughly 16 million, and their numbers were swelling every day.

Since both Catholics and Protestants assumed that France could have only a single *roi, foi,* and *loi* (king, faith, and law), civil war was inevitable, and no one was surprised when a struggle between the Huguenot Condé and the ultra-Catholic duke of Guise for control of the government during a royal minority led in 1562 to a show of arms. Soon all France was aflame. Rampaging mobs, often incited on either side by members of the clergy, ransacked churches and settled local scores. After a while it became clear that the Huguenots were not strong or numerous enough to gain victory, but they were also too strong to be defeated. Hence, despite intermittent truces, warfare dragged on at great cost of life until 1572. Then, during an interval of peace, the cultivated queen mother Catherine de Medici, normally a woman who favored compromise, plotted with members of the Catholic Guise faction to kill all the Huguenot leaders while they were assembled in Paris for the wedding of Henry of Navarre. In the early morning of St. Bartholomew's Day (August 24) most of the Huguenot chiefs were murdered in bed and two to three thousand other Protestants were slaughtered in the streets or drowned in the Seine by Catholic mobs. When word of the Parisian massacre spread to the provinces, some ten thousand more Huguenots were killed in a frenzy of blood lust that swept through France.

The St. Bartholomew's Day episode effectively broke the back of Huguenot resistance, but even then warfare did not cease because the neurotic King Henry III (1574–1589)* tried to play off Huguenots against the dominant Catholic Guise family and because die-hard Huguenots sometimes were able to ally with Catholics revolting against overburdensome taxes or inequities in tax assessments. Only when the politically astute Henry of Navarre succeeded to the French throne as Henry IV (1589–1610), initiating the Bourbon dynasty that would rule until 1792, did civil war finally come to an end. In 1593 Henry abjured his Protestantism in order to placate France's Catholic majority ("Paris is worth a Mass") and then, in 1598, he offered limited religious freedom to the Huguenots by the Edict of Nantes. According to the terms of this proclamation, Catholicism was recognized as the official religion, but Huguenot nobles were allowed to hold Protestant services privately in their castles, other Huguenots were allowed to worship at specified places (excluding Paris and all cities where bishops and archbishops resided), and the Huguenot party was permitted to fortify some towns, especially in the south and west, for military defense if the need arose. Thus, although the Edict of Nantes certainly did not countenance absolute freedom of worship, it nevertheless represented a major stride in the direction of toleration. With religious peace established, France quickly began to recover from decades of devastation, but Henry IV himself was cut down by the dagger of a Catholic fanatic in 1610.

Contemporaneous with the religious warfare in France was equally bitter religious strife between Catholics and Protestants in the neighboring Netherlands, where national resentments gravely compounded religious hatreds. For almost a century the Netherlands (or Low Countries),

Henry IV establishes French religious peace

Habsburg rule in the Netherlands

*Here, as elsewhere, dates following a ruler's name refer to dates of reign.

The Assassination of Henry IV. This contemporary engraving shows Henry seated in an open carriage without any concern for his personal danger while his assassin climbs on the spoke of the carriage wheel to attack him. The entire composition conveys a vivid impression of early-modern Paris.

Philip II of Spain. Titian's portrait shows Philip's resemblance to his father, Charles V, particularly in the protruding lower jaw of the Habsburgs (see p. 477).

Philip II and the Netherlands

The Duke of Alva. The gaunt Spanish general who attempted in vain to extirpate Calvinism in the Netherlands.

comprising modern-day Holland in the north and Belgium in the south, had been ruled by the Habsburg family. Particularly the southern part of the Netherlands prospered greatly from trade and manufacture: southern Netherlanders had the greatest per capita wealth of all Europe, and their metropolis of Antwerp was northern Europe's leading commercial and financial center. Moreover, the half-century-long rule of the Habsburg Charles V (1506–1556) had been popular because Charles, who had been born in the Belgian city of Ghent, felt a sense of rapport with his subjects, and allowed them a large degree of local self-government.

But around 1560 the good fortune of the Netherlands began to ebb. When Charles V retired to a monastery in 1556 (dying two years later) he ceded all his vast territories outside of the Holy Roman Empire and Hungary—not only the Netherlands, but Spain, Spanish America, and close to half of Italy—to his son Philip II (1556–1598). Unlike Charles, Philip had been born in Spain, and thinking of himself as a Spaniard, made Spain his residence and the focus of his policy. Thus he viewed the Netherlands primarily as a potentially rich source of income necessary for pursuing Spanish affairs. (Around 1560 silver was only beginning to flood through Seville.) But in order to tap the wealth of the Netherlands Philip had to rule it more directly than his father had, and such attempts were naturally resented by the local magnates who until then had dominated the government. To make matters worse, a religious storm also was brewing, for after a treaty of 1559 ended a long war between France and Spain, French Calvinists had begun to stream over the Netherlandish border, making converts wherever they went. Soon there were more Calvinists in Antwerp than in Geneva, a situation that Philip II could not tolerate because he was an ardent Catholic who subscribed wholeheartedly to the goals of the Counter-Reformation. Indeed, as he wrote to Rome on the eve of conflict, "rather than suffer the slightest harm to the true religion and service of God, I would lose all my states and even my life a hundred times over because I am not and will not be the ruler of heretics."

Evidence of the complexity of the Netherlandish situation is found in the facts that the leader of resistance to Philip, William the Silent, was at first not a Calvinist and that the territories that ultimately succeeded in breaking away from Spanish rule were at first the most Catholic ones in the Low Countries. William "the Silent," a prominent nobleman with large landholdings in the Netherlands, was in fact very talkative, receiving his nickname from his ability to hide his true religious and political feelings when the need arose. In 1566, when still a nominal Catholic, he and other local nobles not formally committed to Protestantism appealed to Philip to allow toleration for Calvinists. But while Philip momentarily temporized, radical Protestant mobs proved to be their own worst enemy—ransacking Catholic churches throughout the country, methodically desecrating hosts, smashing statuary, and shattering stained-glass windows. Though local troops soon had the situation under control, Philip II nonetheless decided to dispatch an army of ten thousand com-

Europe, c. 1560

manded by the steely Spanish duke of Alva to wipe out Protestantism in the Low Countries forever. Alva's tribunal, the "Council of Blood," soon examined some twelve thousand persons on charges of heresy or sedition, of whom nine thousand were convicted and one thousand executed. William the Silent fled the country, and all hope for a free Netherlands seemed lost.

The revolt of the Netherlands

But the tide turned quickly for two related reasons. First, instead of giving up, William the Silent converted to Protestantism, sought help from Protestants in France, Germany, and England, and organized bands of sea rovers to harass Spanish shipping on the Netherlandish coast. And second, Alva's tyranny helped William's cause, especially when the hated Spanish governor attempted to levy a 10 percent sales tax. With internal

William the Silent seizes the northern Netherlands

509

Protestants Ransacking a Catholic Church in the Netherlands. The "Protestant fury" of 1566 was responsible for the large-scale destruction of religious art and statuary in the Low Countries, provoking the stern repression of Philip II.

disaffection growing, in 1572 William, for tactical military reasons, was able to seize the northern Netherlands even though the north until then had been predominantly Catholic. Thereafter geography played a major role in determining the outcome of the conflict. Spanish armies repeatedly attempted to win back the north, but they were stopped by a combination of impassable rivers and dikes that could be opened to flood out the invaders. Although William the Silent was assassinated by a Catholic in 1584, his son continued to lead the resistance until the Spanish crown finally agreed by a truce in 1609 to stop fighting and thus implicitly recognized the independence of the northern Dutch Republic. Meanwhile, the pressures of war and persecution had made the whole north Calvinistic, whereas the south—which remained Spanish—returned to uniform Catholicism.

Religious strife could thus take the form of civil war, as in France, or war for national liberation, as in the Netherlands. But it could also take the form of warfare between sovereign states, as in the case of the late-sixteenth-century struggle between England and Spain. After narrowly escaping domination by the Catholic Queen Mary and her Spanish husband Philip II, English Protestants rejoiced in the rule of Queen Elizabeth I (1558–1603) and naturally harbored great antipathy toward Philip II and the Counter-Reformation. Furthermore, English economic interests were directly opposed to those of the Spanish. A seafaring and trading people, the English in the later sixteenth century were steadily making inroads into Spanish naval and commercial domination, and were also determined to resist any Spanish attempt to block England's lucrative trade with the Low Countries. But the greatest source of antagonism lay in naval contests in the Atlantic, where English privateers, with the tacit

Antagonism between England and Spain

consent of Queen Elizabeth, could not resist raiding silver-laden Spanish treasure ships. Beginning around 1570, and taking as an excuse the Spanish oppression of Protestants in the Netherlands, English admirals or pirates (the terms were really interchangeable) such as Sir Francis Drake and Sir John Hawkins began plundering Spanish vessels on the high seas. In a particularly dramatic sailing exploit lasting from 1577 to 1580, lust for booty and prevailing winds propelled Drake all the way around the world, to return with stolen Spanish treasure worth twice as much as Queen Elizabeth's annual revenue.

All this would have been sufficient provocation for Philip II to have retaliated against England, but because he had his hands full in the Netherlands he resolved to invade the island only after the English openly allied with the Dutch rebels in 1585. And even then Philip did not act without extensive planning and a sense of assurance that nothing could go wrong. Finally, in 1588 he dispatched an enormous fleet, confidently called the "Invincible Armada," to punish insolent Britannia. After an initial standoff in the English Channel, however, English fireships outmaneuvered the Spanish fleet, setting some Spanish galleons ablaze and forcing the rest to break formation. "Protestant gales" did the rest and a battered flotilla soon limped home with almost half its ships lost.

The defeat of the Spanish Armada was one of the most decisive battles of Western history. Had Spain conquered England it is quite likely that the Spanish would have gone on to crush Holland and perhaps even to

The defeat of the Spanish Armada

The salvation of Protestantism

Left: **The Defeat of the Spanish Armada.** Right: **Queen Elizabeth I.** The contemporary English oil painting of the great sea battle gives only a schematic idea of its turbulence. Note, however, the prominence of the papal insignia (tiara over crossed keys of St. Peter) on the ship in the middle foreground. Englishmen were convinced that had they not defeated the Spanish Armada in 1588 the pope would have planted his banner on their shores. At the right is a typically overblown portrait of Queen Elizabeth, known to her admiring subjects as "Gloriana," standing on a map of England.

destroy Protestantism everywhere. But, as it was, the Protestant day was saved, and not long afterward Spanish power began to decline, with English and Dutch ships taking ever-greater command of the seas. Moreover, in England itself patriotic fervor became intense. Popular even before then, "Good Queen Bess" was virtually revered by her subjects until her death in 1603, and England embarked on its golden "Elizabethan Age" of literary endeavor. War with Spain dragged on inconclusively until 1604, but the fighting never brought England any serious harm and was just lively enough to keep the English people deeply committed to the cause of their queen, their country, and the Protestant religion.

YEARS OF TREMBLING

A new phase of turmoil

With the promulgation of the Edict of Nantes in 1598, the peace between England and Spain of 1604, and the truce between Spain and Holland of 1609, religious warfare tapered off and came to an end in the early seventeenth century. But in 1618 a major new war broke out, this time in Germany. Since this struggle raged more or less unceasingly until 1648 it bears the name of the Thirty Years' War. Far from returning to enduring peace, Spain and France became engaged in the conflict in Germany and in war with each other, and internal resentments in Spain, France, and England flared up in the decade of the 1640s in concurrent outbreaks of uprisings and civil turmoil. As an English preacher said in 1643, "these are days of shaking, and this shaking is universal." He might have added that while in some instances religion remained one of the contested issues, secular disputes about powers of government were now becoming predominant.

The Thirty Years' War

The clearest example is that of the Thirty Years' War, which began in a welter of religious passions as a war between Catholics and Protestants but immediately raised basic German constitutional issues and ended as an international struggle in which the initial religious dimension was almost entirely forgotten. Between the Peace of Augsburg in 1555 and the outbreak of war in 1618, Calvinists had replaced Lutherans in a few German territories, but the overall balance between Protestants and Catholics within the Holy Roman Empire had remained undisturbed. In 1618, however, when a Protestant uprising against Habsburg Catholic rule in Bohemia (not a German territory, yet part of the Holy Roman Empire) threatened to upset the balance, German Catholic forces ruthlessly counterattacked, first in Bohemia and then in Germany proper. Led by Charles V's Habsburg descendant Ferdinand II, who was archduke of Austria, king of Hungary, and from 1619 to his death in 1637, Holy Roman emperor, a German Catholic league seized the military initiative and within a decade seemed close to extirpating Protestantism throughout Germany. But Ferdinand, who was intent on pursuing political goals, imposed firm direct rule in Bohemia in order to build up the strength of his own Austro-Hungarian state, and attempted to revive the faded authority of the Holy Roman Empire in whatever ways he could.

Two Artistic Broadsides from the Thirty Years' War. On the left the German peasantry is ridden by the soldiery; on the right is an allegorical representation of "the monstrous beast of war."

Thus when the Lutheran king of Sweden, Gustavus Adolphus, the "Lion of the North," marched into Germany in 1630 to champion the nearly lost cause of Protestantism, he was welcomed by several German Catholic princes who preferred to see the former religious balance restored rather than stand the chance of surrendering their sovereignty to Ferdinand II. To make matters still more ironic, Gustavus's Protestant army was secretly subsidized by Catholic France, whose policy was then dictated by a cardinal of the Church, Cardinal Richelieu. This was because Habsburg Spain had been fighting in Germany on the side of Habsburg Austria, and Richelieu was determined to resist any possibility of France being surrounded by a strong Habsburg alliance on the north, east, and south. In the event, the military genius Gustavus Adolphus started routing the Habsburgs, but when he fell in battle in 1632, Cardinal Richelieu had little choice but to send ever-greater support to the remaining Swedish troops in Germany, until in 1635 French armies entered the war directly on Sweden's side. From then until 1648 the struggle was really one of France and Sweden against Austria and Spain, with most of Germany a helpless battleground.

The result was that Germany suffered more from warfare in the terrible years between 1618 and 1648 than it ever did before or after until the twentieth century. Several German cities were besieged and sacked nine or ten times over, and soldiers from all nations, who often had to sustain themselves by plunder, gave no quarter to defenseless civilians. With plague and disease adding to the toll of outright butchery, some parts of Germany lost more than half their populations, although it is true that others went relatively unscathed. Most horrifying was the loss of life in the final four years, when the carnage continued unabated even while

Gustavus Adolphus at the Battle of Leipzig. This engraving celebrates a victory won by the king of Sweden in 1631. One of the angels trumpets "German freedom," but the city of Leipzig is partly in flames and the Thirty Years' War would continue mercilessly for another seventeen years.

peace negotiators had already arrived at broad areas of agreement and were dickering over subsidiary clauses.

Nor did the Peace of Westphalia, which finally ended the Thirty Years' War in 1648, do much to vindicate anyone's death, even though it did establish some abiding landmarks in European history. Above all, from the international perspective, the Peace of Westphalia marked the reemergence of France as the predominant power on the continental European scene, replacing Spain—a position France was to hold for two centuries more. In particular, France moved its eastern frontier directly into German territory by taking over large parts of Alsace. As for strictly internal German matters, the greatest losers were the Austrian Habsburgs, who were forced to surrender all the territory they had gained in Germany and to abandon their hopes of using the office of Holy Roman Emperor to dominate central Europe. Otherwise, something very close to the German status quo of 1618 was reestablished, with Protestant principalities in the north balancing Catholic ones in the south, and Germany so hopelessly divided that it could play no united role in European history until the nineteenth century.

Still greater losers from the Thirty Years' War than the Austrian Habsburgs were their Spanish cousins, for Spain had invested in the struggle vast sums it could not afford and ceased being a great power forever after. The story of Spain's swift fall from grandeur is almost like a Greek tragedy in its relentless unfolding. Despite the defeat of the "Invincible Armada" in 1588, around 1600 the Spanish empire—comprising all of the Iberian peninsula (including Portugal, which had been annexed by Philip II in 1580), half of Italy, half of the Netherlands, all of Central and South America, and even the Philippine Islands—was still the mightiest power

The Peace of Westphalia

The decline of Spain

514

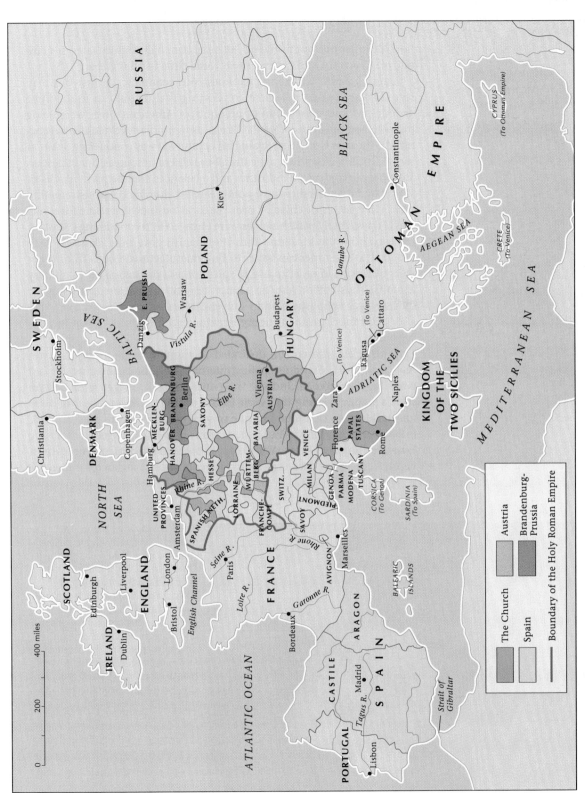

Europe at the End of the Thirty Years' War, 1648

not just in Europe but in the world. Yet a bare half-century later this empire on which the sun never set had come close to falling apart.

Spain's greatest underlying weakness was economic. At first this may seem like a very odd statement considering that in 1600, as in the three or four previous decades, huge amounts of American silver were being unloaded on the docks of Seville. Yet as contemporaries themselves recognized, "the new world that Spain had conquered was conquering Spain in turn." Lacking either rich agricultural or mineral resources, Spain desperately needed to develop industries and a balanced trading pattern as its rivals England and France were doing. But the dominant Spanish nobility had prized ideals of chivalry over practical business ever since the medieval days when Spanish nobles were engaged in reconquering Christian territory from the Muslims. Thus the Spanish governing class was only too glad to use American silver to buy manufactured goods from other parts of Europe in order to live in splendor and dedicate itself to military exploits. Thus bullion left the country as soon as it entered, virtually no industry was established, and when the influx of silver began to decline after 1600 the Spanish economy remained with nothing except increasing debts.

Nonetheless, the crown, dedicated to supporting the Counter-Reformation and maintaining Spain's international dominance, would not cease fighting abroad. Indeed, the entire Spanish budget remained on such a warlike footing that even in the relatively peaceful year of 1608 four million out of a total revenue of seven million ducats were paid for military expenditures. Thus when Spain became engaged in fighting France during the Thirty Years' War it overextended itself. The clearest visible sign of this was that in 1643 French troops at Rocroi inflicted a

The Recapture of Bahía. The Spanish constantly had to defend their overseas holdings from the Dutch. In 1625 a Spanish fleet recaptured the Brazilian port of Bahía, taken by the Dutch the year before. This Spanish propaganda painting combines realism and allegory by showing Spain's governing minister, the count of Olivares, proudly pointing to a painting of King Philip IV, while the returning inhabitants of Bahía nurse a wounded soldier.

The Escorial. Philip II of Spain ordered the building between 1563 and 1584 of this somber retreat—part royal residence, part monastery—on an isolated spot, well removed from Madrid. Conceived on a grid-iron plan to honor the grid-iron martyrdom of St. Lawrence (on whose feast day Philip had won a decisive victory against the French), the Escorial symbolizes for many the Spanish crown's dedication to the ideals of the Counter-Reformation as well as its attempt to impose rationalized central government on the outlying provinces of the Spanish Empire. Some observers will note that it is the model for a racetrack in Kentucky—Churchill Downs.

stunning defeat on the famed Spanish infantry, the first time that a Spanish army had been overcome in battle since the reign of Ferdinand and Isabella. Worse still was the fact that by then two territories belonging to Spain's European empire were in open revolt.

In order to understand the causes of these revolts one must recognize that in the seventeenth century the governing power of Spain lay entirely in Castile. After the marriage of Isabella of Castile and Ferdinand of Aragon in 1469, geographically central Castile emerged as the dominant partner in the Spanish union, becoming even more dominant when Castile conquered the Muslim kingdom of Granada in southern Spain in 1492 and took over Portugal in 1580. In the absence of any great financial hardships, semi-autonomous Catalonia (the most fiercely independent part of Aragon) endured Castilian hegemony. But in 1640, when the strains of warfare induced Castile to limit Catalan liberties in order to raise more money and men for combat, Catalonia revolted and drove off Castilian governors. Immediately afterward the Portuguese learned of the Catalan uprising and revolted as well, followed by southern Italians who revolted against Castilian viceroys in Naples and Sicily in 1647. At that point only the momentary inability of Spain's greatest external enemies, France and England, to take advantage of its plight saved the Spanish Empire from utter collapse. Nothing if not determined, the Castilian government quickly put down the Italian revolts and by 1652 also brought Catalonia to heel. But Portugal retained its independence, and by the Peace of the Pyrenees, signed with France in 1659, Spain in effect conceded that it would entirely abandon its ambition of dominating Europe.

> Internal revolts against the Castilian government

Spain and France compared

A comparison between the fortunes of Spain and France in the first half of the seventeenth century is highly instructive because some striking similarities existed between the two countries, but in the end differences turned out to be most decisive. Spain and France were of almost identical territorial extent, and both countries had been created by the same process of accretion. Just as the Castilian crown had gained Aragon in the north, Granada in the south, and then Portugal, so the kingdom of France had grown by adding on such diverse territories as Languedoc, Dauphiné, Provence, Burgundy, and Brittany. Since the inhabitants of all these territories cherished traditions of local independence as much as the Catalans or Portuguese, and since the rulers of France, like those of Spain, were determined to govern their provinces ever more firmly—especially when the financial stringencies of the Thirty Years' War made ruthless tax-collecting urgently necessary—a direct confrontation between the central government and the provinces in France became inevitable, just as in Spain. But France weathered the storm whereas Spain did not, a result largely attributable to France's greater wealth and the greater prestige of the French crown.

The reign of Henry IV

In good times most French people, including those from the outlying provinces, tended to revere their king. Certainly they had excellent reason to do so during the reign of Henry IV. Having established religious peace in 1598 by the Edict of Nantes, the affable Henry, who declared that there should be a chicken in every French family's pot each Sunday, set about to restore the prosperity of a country devastated by four decades of civil war. Fortunately France had enormous economic resiliency, owing primarily to its extremely rich and varied agricultural resources. Unlike Spain, which had to import food, France normally was able to feed itself, and Henry's finance minister, the duke of Sully, quickly saw to it that France could feed itself once more. Among other things, Sully distributed throughout the country free copies of a guide to recommended farming techniques and financed the rebuilding or new construction of roads, bridges, and canals to help expedite the flow of goods. In addition, Henry IV was not content to see France rest its economic development on agricultural wealth alone; instead he ordered the construction of royal factories to manufacture luxury goods such as crystal glass and tapestries, and he also supported the growth of silk, linen, and woolen cloth industries in many different parts of the country. Moreover, Henry's patronage allowed the explorer Champlain to claim parts of Canada as France's first foothold in the New World. Thus Henry IV's reign certainly must be counted as one of the most benevolent in all French history.

Cardinal Richelieu

Far less benevolent was Henry's *de facto* successor as ruler of France, Cardinal Richelieu (1585–1642), yet Richelieu fully managed to maintain France's forward momentum. The cardinal, of course, was never the real king of France—the actual title was held from 1610 to 1643 by Henry IV's ineffectual son Louis XIII. But as first minister from 1624 to his death in 1642 Richelieu governed as he wished, and what he wished most of all was to enhance centralized royal power at home and expand French influence in the larger theater of Europe. Accordingly, when Huguenots rebelled against restrictions placed on them by the Edict of Nantes, Richelieu put them down with an iron fist and emended the Edict in 1629 by depriving them of all their political and military rights. Since his armed campaigns against the Huguenots had been very costly, the cardinal then moved to gain more income for the crown by abolishing the semi-autonomy of Burgundy, Dauphiné, and Provence so that he could introduce direct royal taxation in all three areas. Later, to make sure all taxes levied were efficiently collected, Richelieu instituted a new system of local government by royal officials known as *intendants* who were expressly commissioned to run roughshod over any provincial obstructionism. By these and related methods Richelieu made French government more centralized than ever and managed to double the crown's income during his rule. But since he also engaged in an ambitious foreign policy directed against the Habsburgs of Austria and Spain, resulting in France's costly involvement in the Thirty Years' War, internal pressures mounted in the years after Richelieu's death.

A reaction against French governmental centralization manifested itself in a series of revolts between 1648 and 1653 collectively known as "the slingshot tumults," or in French, the *Fronde*. By this time Louis XIII had been succeeded by his son Louis XIV, but because the latter was still a boy, France was governed by a regency consisting of Louis's mother, Anne of Austria, and her paramour Cardinal Mazarin. Considering that both were foreigners (Anne was a Habsburg and Mazarin originally an Italian adventurer named Giulio Mazarini), it is not surprising that many of their subjects, including some extremely powerful nobles, hated them. Moreover, nationwide resentments were greater still because the costs of war and several consecutive years of bad harvests had brought France temporarily into a grave economic plight. Thus when cliques of nobles expressed their disgust with Mazarin for primarily self-interested reasons, they found much support throughout the country, and uncoordinated revolts against the regency flared on and off for several years.

France, however, did not come close to falling apart. Above all, the French crown itself, which retained great reservoirs of prestige owing to a well-established national tradition and the undoubted achievements of Henry IV and Richelieu, was by no means under attack. On the contrary, neither the aristocratic leaders of the *Fronde* nor the commoners from all ranks who joined them in revolt claimed to be resisting the young king but only the alleged corruption and mismanagement of Mazarin. Some of the rebels, it is true, insisted that part of Mazarin's fault lay in his pursuit of Richelieu's centralizing, antiprovincial policy. But since most of the aristocrats who led the *Fronde* were merely "outs" who wanted to be "in," they often squabbled among themselves—sometimes even arranging agreements of convenience with the regency or striking alliances with France's enemy, Spain, for momentary gain—and proved completely unable to rally any unified support behind a common program. Thus when Louis XIV began to rule in his own name in 1651 and pretexts

Cardinal Richelieu. A contemporary portrait emphasizing the cardinal's austere bearing.

The *Fronde*

French absolutism triumphant

for revolting against "corrupt ministers" no longer existed, all opposition was soon silenced. As so often happens, the idealists and poor people paid the greatest price for revolt: in 1653 a defeated leader of popular resistance in Bordeaux was broken on a wheel, and not long afterward a massive new round of taxation was proclaimed. Remembering the turbulence of the *Fronde* for the rest of his life, Louis XIV resolved never to let his aristocracy or his provinces get out of hand again and ruled as the most effective royal absolutist in all of French history.

Compared to the civil disturbances of the 1640s in Spain and France, those in England proved the most momentous in their results for the history of limited government. Whereas all that the revolts against Castile accomplished was the achievement of Portuguese independence and the crippling of an empire that was already in decline, and all that happened in France was a momentary interruption of the steady advance of royal power, in England a king was executed and barriers were erected against royal absolutism.

England around 1600 was caught up in a trend toward the growth of centralized royal authority characteristic of all western Europe. Not only had Henry VIII and Elizabeth I brought the English Church fully under royal control, but both monarchs employed so-called prerogative courts wherein they could proceed against subjects in disregard of traditional English legal safeguards for the rights of the accused. Furthermore, although Parliament met regularly during both reigns, members of Parliament were far less independent than they had been in the fifteenth century: any parliamentary representative who might have stood up to Henry VIII would have lost his head, and almost all parliamentarians admired Elizabeth enough to abide by her policies. Thus when the Stuart dynasty succeeded Elizabeth, the last of the Tudors, it was only natural that the Stuarts would try to increase royal power still more. And indeed they might have succeeded had it not been for their ineptness and an extraordinary combination of forces ranged against them.

Lines of contention were drawn immediately at the accession of Elizabeth's nearest relative, her cousin James VI of Scotland, who in 1603 retained his Scottish crown but also became king of England as James I (1603–1625). Homely but vain, addled but erudite, James fittingly was called by Henry IV of France "the wisest fool in Christendom," and presented the starkest contrast to his predecessor. Whereas Elizabeth knew how to gain her way with Parliament without making a fuss about it, the schoolmasterish foreigner insisted on lecturing parliamentarians that he was semi-divine and would brook no resistance: "As it is atheism and blasphemy to dispute what God can do, so it is presumption and high contempt in a subject to dispute what a king can do." Carrying these sentiments further, in a speech to Parliament of 1609 he proclaimed that "kings are not only God's lieutenants on earth . . . but even by God Himself they are called gods."

That such extreme pretentions to divine authority would arouse strong opposition was a result even James should have been able to foresee, for

The case of England

Henry VIII and Elizabeth I increase royal power

James I. "The wisest fool in Christendom."

the English ruling groups were still intensely committed to the theory of parliamentary controls on the crown. Yet not just theory was at stake, for the specific policies of the new king antagonized large numbers of his subjects. For example, James insisted upon supplementing his income by modes of money-raising that had never been sanctioned by Parliament, and when the leaders of that body remonstrated, he angrily tore up their protests and dissolved their sessions. Worse, he interfered with the freedom of business by granting monopolies and lucrative privileges to favored companies. And, worst of all in the eyes of most patriotic Englishmen, James quickly put an end to the long war with Spain and refused thereafter to become involved in any foreign military entanglements. Today many of us might think that James's commitment to peace was his greatest virtue; certainly his pacifism was justifiable financially since it spared the crown enormous debts. But in his own age James was hated particularly for his peace policy because it made him seem far too friendly with England's traditional enemy, Spain, and because "appeasement" meant leaving seemingly heroic Protestants in Holland and Germany in the lurch.

Although almost all English people (except for a small minority of clandestine Catholics) objected to James I's pacific foreign policy, those who hated it most were a group destined to play the greatest role in overthrowing the Stuarts, namely, the Puritans. Extremist Calvinistic Protestants, the Puritans believed that Elizabeth I's religious compromises had not broken fully enough with the forms and doctrines of Roman Catholicism. Called Puritans from their desire to "purify" the English Church of all traces of Catholic ritual and observance, they most vehemently opposed the English "episcopal system" of church government by bishops. But James I was as committed to retaining episcopalianism as the Puritans were intent on abolishing it because he viewed royally appointed bishops as one of the pillars of a strong monarchy: "No bishop, no king." Since the Puritans were the dominant faction in the House of Commons and many Puritans were also prosperous merchants who opposed James's monopolistic policies and money-raising expediencies, throughout his reign James remained at loggerheads with an extremely powerful group of his subjects for a combination of religious, constitutional, and economic reasons.

Nonetheless, James survived to die peacefully in bed in 1625, and had it not been for mistakes made by his son Charles I (1625–1649), England might have gone the way of absolutist France. Charles held the same inflated notions of royal power and consequently was quickly at odds with the Puritan leaders of Parliament. Soon after his accession to the throne Charles became involved in a war with France and needed revenue desperately. When Parliament refused to make more than the customary grants, he resorted to forced loans from his subjects, punishing those who failed to comply by quartering soldiers in their homes or throwing them into prison without a trial. In reaction to this, Parliament forced the Petition of Right on the king in 1628. This document declared all taxes not

Causes of antagonism to James I

The Puritans

Charles I

Charles I. This portrait by Van Dyck vividly captures the ill-fated monarch's arrogance.

voted by Parliament illegal, condemned the quartering of soldiers in private houses, and prohibited arbitrary imprisonment and the establishment of martial law in time of peace.

Angered rather than chastened by the Petition of Right, Charles I soon resolved to rule entirely without Parliament—and nearly succeeded. From 1629 to 1640 no Parliaments were called. During this "eleven years' tyranny," Charles's government lived off a variety of makeshift dues and levies. For example, the crown sold monopolies at exorbitant rates, revived highly antiquated medieval financial claims, and admonished judges to collect the stiffest of fines. Though technically not illegal, all of these expedients were deeply resented. Most controversial was the collection of "ship money," a levy taken on the pretext of a medieval obligation of English seaboard towns to provide ships (or their worth in money) for the royal navy. Extending the payment of ship money from coastal towns to the whole country, Charles threatened to make it a regular tax in contravention of the Petition of Right, and was upheld in a legal challenge of 1637 brought against him on these grounds by the Puritan squire John Hampden.

By such means the king managed to make ends meet without the aid of taxes granted by Parliament. But he became ever more hated by most of his subjects, above all the Puritans, not just because of his constitutional and financial policies but also because he seemed to be pursuing a course in religion that came much closer to Catholicism than to Calvinism. Whether the English Puritans would have risen up in revolt on their own is a moot question, but they were ultimately emboldened to do so by a chain of events beginning with a revolt in Scotland. The uprising in Scotland of 1640 against the policy of an English king was not unlike those in Catalonia and Portugal of the same year against the Spanish crown except that the Scottish rising was not just nationalistic but also explicitly religious in nature. Like his father, Charles believed in the adage "no bishop, no king" and hence foolhardily decided to introduce episcopalian church government into staunchly Presbyterian Scotland. The result was armed resistance by Charles's northern subjects and the first step toward civil war in England.

In order to obtain the funds necessary to punish the Scots, Charles had no other choice but to summon Parliament and soon found himself the target of pent-up resentments. Knowing full well that the king was helpless without money, the Puritan leaders of the House of Commons determined to take England's government into their own hands. Accordingly, they not only executed the king's first minister, the earl of Strafford, but they abolished ship money and the prerogative courts that ever since the reign of Henry VIII had served as instruments of arbitrary rule. Most significantly, they enacted a law forbidding the crown to dissolve Parliament and requiring the convening of sessions at least once every three years. After some indecision, early in 1642 Charles replied to these acts with a show of force. He marched with his guard into the House of Commons and attempted to arrest five of its leaders. All of them escaped, but an open conflict between crown and Parliament could no longer be avoided. Both parties collected troops and prepared for an appeal to the sword.

These events initiated the English Civil War, a conflict at once political and religious, which lasted from 1642 to 1649. Arrayed on the royal side were most of England's most prominent aristocrats and largest landowners, who were almost all "high-church" Anglicans. Opposed to them, the followers of Parliament included smaller landholders, tradesmen, and manufacturers, the majority of whom were Puritans. The members of the king's party were commonly known by the aristocratic name of Cavaliers. Their opponents, who cut their hair short in contempt for the fashionable custom of wearing curls, were derisively called Roundheads. At first the royalists, having obvious advantages of military experience, won most of the victories. In 1644, however, the parliamentary army was reorganized, and soon afterward the fortunes of battle shifted. The Cavalier forces were badly beaten, and in 1646 the king was compelled to surrender.

Civil war: the Cavaliers vs. the Roundheads

The struggle would now have ended had not a quarrel developed within the parliamentary party. The majority of its members, who had allied with the Presbyterian Scots, were ready to restore Charles to the throne as a limited monarch under an arrangement whereby a uniform Calvinistic Presbyterian faith would be imposed on both Scotland and England as the state religion. But a radical minority of Puritans, commonly known as Independents, distrusted Charles and insisted upon religious toleration for themselves and all other non-Presbyterian Protestants. Their leader was Oliver Cromwell (1599–1658), who had risen to command the Roundhead army. Taking advantage of the dissension within the ranks of his opponents, Charles renewed the war in 1648, but after a brief campaign was forced to surrender. Cromwell now resolved to end the life of "that man of blood," and, ejecting all the Presbyterians from Parliament by force of arms, obliged the remaining so-called Rump Parliament to vote an end to the monarchy. On 30 January 1649 Charles I was beheaded; a short time later the hereditary House of Lords was abolished, and England became a republic.

Charles I is beheaded

Oliver Cromwell

But founding a republic was far easier than maintaining one, and the new form of government, officially called a Commonwealth, did not last long. Technically the Rump Parliament continued as the legislative body, but Cromwell, with the army at his command, possessed the real power and soon became exasperated by the attempts of the legislators to perpetuate themselves in office and to profit from confiscating the wealth of their opponents. Accordingly, in 1653 he marched a detachment of troops into the Rump Parliament and saying "Come, I will put an end to your prating," ordered the members to disperse. Thereby the Commonwealth ceased to exist and was soon followed by the "Protectorate," or virtual dictatorship established under a constitution drafted by officers of the army. Called the Instrument of Government, this text was the nearest approximation of a written constitution England has ever had. Extensive powers were given to Cromwell as "lord protector" for life, and his office

From republic to dictatorship

was made hereditary. At first a Parliament exercised limited authority in making laws and levying taxes, but in 1655 its members were abruptly dismissed by Cromwell. Thereafter the government became a thinly disguised autocracy, with Cromwell now wielding a sovereignty even more absolute than any the Stuart monarchs would have dared to claim.

Given the choice between a Puritan military dictatorship and the old royalist regime, when the occasion arose England unhesitatingly opted for the latter. Above all, years of Calvinistic austerities such as the prohibition of any public recreation on Sundays—then the worker's only holiday—had discredited the Puritans, making most people long for the milder Anglicanism of the original Elizabethan settlement. Thus not long after Cromwell's death in 1658, one of his generals seized power and called for elections for a new Parliament which met in the spring of 1660 and proclaimed as king Charles I's exiled son, Charles II. With the reign of Charles II (1660–1685) Anglicanism was immediately restored, but by no means the same was true for untrammeled monarchical power. Rather, stating with characteristic good humor that he did not wish to "resume his travels," Charles agreed to respect Parliament and observe the Petition of Right. Of greatest constitutional significance was the fact that all the legislation passed by Parliament immediately before the outbreak of the Civil War, including the requirement to hold Parliaments at least once every three years, remained as law. Thus in striking contrast to absolutist France, England became a limited monarchy. Putting its constitutional struggles behind it after one brief further test in the late seventeenth century, the realm of England would soon live up to the poet Milton's prediction of "a noble and puissant nation rousing herself like a strong man after sleep."

QUESTS FOR LIGHT OUT OF DARKNESS

Caught up in economic uncertainty, religious rivalries, and political turmoil, many Europeans between 1560 and 1660 understandably cast about for emotional or intellectual resolutions of their most pressing problems. Sometimes, as in the case of the great witchcraft delusion, this quest led merely to an intensification of hysteria. But in the case of more dispassionate reflections, the search for ways of resolving Europe's crises led to some of the most enduring statements of moral and political philosophy of all time.

In seeking to explain belief in witchcraft, historians agree that the idea itself took shape toward the end of the Middle Ages. Peasant culture throughout the Middle Ages included belief in the possibilities of sorcery. In other words, most simple rural people assumed that certain unusual individuals could practice good, or "white" magic in the form of healing, divination for lost objects, and fortune-telling, or perhaps also evil, "black" magic that might, for example, call up tempests or ravage crops. Yet only in the fifteenth century did learned authorities begin to insist on theological grounds that black magic could be practiced only as a result of pacts with the devil. Naturally, once this belief became accepted, judicial officers soon found it urgent to prosecute all "witches" who practiced black magic because warfare against the devil was paramount to Christian society and "the evil one" could not be allowed to hold any sway. Accordingly, in 1484 Pope Innocent VIII ordered papal inquisitors to root out alleged witchcraft with all the means at their disposal, and the pace of witch hunts gained momentum in the following decades. Nor were witch trials curtailed in areas that broke with Rome, for Protestant reformers believed in the insidious powers of Satan just as much as Catholics did. Indeed, Luther himself once threw an inkpot at a supposed apparition of the devil, and Calvin saw Satan's evil workings wherever he looked. Thus both urged that alleged witches be tried more peremptorily and sentenced with less leniency than ordinary criminals, and persecutions of innocent people continued apace in Protestant as well as Catholic lands.

Yet the outbreak of a real mania for catching and killing "witches" did not begin until about 1580. Therefore it can only be supposed that the witchcraft hysteria was connected in some way with Europe's general crisis—all the more since it continued for about as long as the age of crisis itself (until roughly 1660) and was most severe in just those localities where warfare or economic dislocation was most intense. In such places, whenever crops failed or cattle sickened people assumed that a "witch"— usually a defenseless old woman—was responsible, and rushed to put her to death. If not always old, the victims were most frequently women, no doubt in part because preachers had encouraged their flocks to believe that evil had first come into the world with Eve and in part because men

Witchcraft hysteria and the European crisis

Supposed Witches Worshiping the Devil in the Form of a Billy-Goat. In the background other "witches" ride bareback on flying demons. This is one of the earliest visual conceptions of witchcraft, dating from around 1460.

Burning of Witches at Dernberg in 1555. From a sixteenth-century German pamphlet denouncing witchcraft.

in authority felt psychologically most ambivalent about members of the opposite sex. Pure sadism certainly cannot have been the original motive for such proceedings, but once trials began, horrendous sadism very often was unleashed. Thus old women, young girls, and sometimes even mere children might be brutally tortured by having needles driven under their nails, fires placed at their heels, or their legs crushed under weights until marrow spurted from their bones, in order to make them confess to having had filthy orgies with demons. The final death toll will never be known, but in the 1620s there was an average of one hundred burnings a year in the German cities of Würzburg and Bamberg, and around the same time it was said the town square of Wolfenbüttel "looked like a little forest, so crowded were the stakes."

The end of the hysteria

Why persecution quickly ended in the years immediately after 1660 will remain a matter for scholarly speculation. Aside from the fact that better times returned to most of Europe around then, probably the best explanation is that shortly after 1660 educated magistrates began to adhere to a mechanistic view of the universe. In other words, once the leaders of society came to believe that storms and epidemics arose from natural rather than supernatural causes, they ceased to countenance witch hunts.

Montaigne

Fortunately, other attempts of Europeans between 1560 and 1660 to master the darkness around them were not in themselves so dark. Indeed, one of the most "enlightened" of all European moral philosophers was the Frenchman Michel de Montaigne (1533–1592), who wrote during the height of the French wars of religion. The son of a Catholic father and a Huguenot mother of Jewish ancestry, the well-to-do Montaigne retired from a legal career at the age of thirty-eight to devote himself to a life of leisured reflection. The *Essays* that resulted were a new literary form originally conceived as "experiments" in writing (the French *essai* simply means "trial"). Because they are extraordinarily well written as well as being searchingly reflective, Montaigne's *Essays* ever since have ranked securely among the most enduring classics of French literature and thought.

Although the range of subjects of the *Essays* runs a wide gamut from "The Resemblance of Children to Their Fathers" to "The Art of Conversing," two main themes are dominant. One is a pervasive skepticism. Making his motto *"Que sais-je?"* (What do I know?), Montaigne decided that he knew very little for certain. According to him, "it is folly to measure truth and error by our own capacities" because our capacities are severely limited. Thus, as he maintained in one of his most famous essays, "On Cannibals," what may seem indisputably true and proper to one nation may seem absolutely false to another because "everyone gives the title of barbarism to everything that is not of his usage." From this Montaigne's second main principle followed—the need for tolerance. Since all people think they know the perfect religion and the perfect government, no religion or government is really perfect and consequently no belief is worth fighting for to the death.

Michel de Montaigne

If the foregoing description makes Montaigne sound surprisingly modern, it must be emphasized that he was by no means a rationalist. On the contrary, he believed that "reason does nothing but go astray in everything," and that intellectual curiosity "which prompts us to thrust our noses into everything" is a "scourge of the soul." Moreover, concerning practical affairs Montaigne was a fatalist who thought that in a world governed by unpredictable "fortune" the best human strategy is to face the good and the bad with steadfastness and dignity. Lest people begin to think too highly of their own abilities, he reminded them that "sit we upon the highest throne in the world, yet we do sit upon our own behinds." Nonetheless, despite his passive belief that "fortune, not wisdom,

Montaigne's fatalism

Rhinoceros and Unicorn. Sixteenth-century books of naturalism depicted "newly discovered" animals, some of which were real and others of which were figments of the imagination. (In fact a rhinoceros is hardly a less improbable creature than a unicorn.) Uncertain of absolute truth and falsity, Montaigne concluded that what seemed true one day might be cast into doubt tomorrow.

Jean Bodin

rules the life of mankind," the wide circulation of Montaigne's *Essays* did help combat fanaticism and religious intolerance in his own and subsequent ages.

If Montaigne sought refuge from the trials of his age in skepticism, tolerance, and resigned dignity, his contemporary, the French lawyer Jean Bodin (1530–1596), looked for more light to come out of darkness from the powers of the state. Like Montaigne, Bodin was particularly troubled by the upheavals caused by the religious wars in France—he had even witnessed the frightful St. Bartholomew's Day Massacre of 1572 in Paris. But instead of shrugging his shoulders about the bloodshed, he resolved to offer a political plan to make sure turbulence would cease. This he did in his monumental *Six Books of the Commonwealth* (1576), the earliest fully developed statement of governmental absolutism in Western political thought. According to Bodin, the state arises from the needs of collections of families, but once constituted should brook no opposition, for maintaining order is paramount. Whereas writers on law and politics before him had groped toward a theory of governmental sovereignty, Bodin was the first to offer a succinct definition; for him, sovereignty was "the most high, absolute, and perpetual power over all subjects," consisting principally in the power "to give laws to subjects without their consent." Although Bodin acknowledged the theoretical possibility of government by aristocracy or democracy, he assumed that the nation-states of his day would be ruled by monarchs and insisted that such monarchs could in no way be limited, either by legislative or judicial bodies, or even by laws made by their predecessors or themselves. Expressing the sharpest opposition to contemporary Huguenots who were saying (in contravention of the original teachings of Luther and Calvin) that subjects had a right to resist "ungodly princes," Bodin maintained that a subject must trust in the ruler's "mere and frank good will." Even if the ruler proved a tyrant, Bodin insisted that the subject had no warrant to resist, for any resistance would open the door "to a licentious anarchy which is worse than the harshest tyranny in the world." Since in his own day Bodin knew much "licentious anarchy" but had hardly any notion of how harsh the "harshest tyranny" could be, his position is somewhat understandable. Yet in the next century his *Commonwealth* would become the grounds for justifications of an increasingly oppressive French royal absolutism.

John Milton and the Levellers

Quite understandably, just as the French civil wars of the sixteenth century provoked a variety of responses, so did the English Civil War of the seventeenth. Drawing on a tradition of resistance to untrammeled state power expressed by French Huguenots and earlier English parliamentarians and Puritans, the great English Puritan poet John Milton enunciated a stirring defense of freedom of the press in his *Areopagitica* (1644). Similarly bold upholders of libertarianism were a party of Milton's Puritan contemporaries known as Levellers, the first exponents of democracy in the West since the ancient Greeks. Organizing themselves as a pressure group within Cromwell's army in the later 1640s when Charles I's monarchy seemed clearly doomed, the Levellers—who derived their name from their advocacy of equal political rights for all classes—agitated in favor of a parlimentary republic based on nearly universal male suffrage. For them, servants and other wage-laborers had no right to vote because they formed part of their employer's "family" and allegedly were represented by the family head. Moreover, the Levellers did not even deign to argue about women's rights. Otherwise, however, in the immortal words of one of their spokesmen, they argued that "the poorest He that is in England hath a life to live as the greatest He, and therefore . . . every man that is to live under a government ought first by his own consent to put himself under that government." But since Oliver Cromwell, who believed that the only grounds for suffrage was sufficient property, would have none of this, once Cromwell assumed virtually dictatorial powers the Leveller party disintegrated. More radical still were the communalist Diggers, so called from their attempts to cultivate common lands in 1649. Claiming to be "true Levellers," the Diggers argued that true freedom lies not in votes, but "where a man receives his nourishment," and hence argued for the redistribution of property. Cromwell, however, dispersed them quickly, and thus the Diggers have merely historical interest as vanguards of movements to come.

Far to the other extreme of the libertarian Puritans was the political philosopher Thomas Hobbes (1588–1679), whose reactions to the English Civil War led him to become the most forceful advocate of unrestrained state power of all time. Like Bodin, who was moved by the events of St. Bartholomew's Day to formulate a doctrine of political absolutism, Hobbes was moved by the turmoil of the English Civil War to do the same in his classic of political theory, *Leviathan* (1651). Yet Hobbes differed from Bodin in several respects. For one, whereas Bodin assumed that the absolute sovereign power would be a royal monarch, the more radical Hobbes, writing without any respect for tradition in Cromwell's England two years after the beheading of a king, thought the sovereign could be any ruthless dictator whatsoever. Then too, whereas Bodin defined his state as "the lawful government of families" and hence did not believe that the state could abridge private property rights because families could not exist without property, Hobbes's state existed to rule over atomistic individuals and thus was licensed to trample over both liberty and property.

But the most fundamental difference between Bodin and Hobbes lay in the latter's uncompromisingly pessimistic view of human nature. Hobbes posited that the "state of nature" that existed before civil government came into being was a condition of "war of all against all." Since man naturally behaves as "a wolf" toward man and increasing fear of violent death in the state of nature makes human life "solitary, poor, nasty, brutish, and short," people for their own good at some purely theoretical point in time surrender their liberties to a sovereign ruler in exchange for his agreement to keep the peace. Having granted away their liberties, subjects have no right whatsoever to seek them back, and the sovereign can tyrannize as he likes—free to oppress his charges in any way other than to

The Title Page of Hobbes's *Leviathan*

Hobbes's pessimism

kill them, an act that would negate the very purpose of his rule. It is a measure of the relentless logic and clarity of Hobbes's abstract exposition that his *Leviathan* is widely regarded as one of the four or five greatest political treatises ever written, for practically nobody really likes what he says. Indeed, even in his own age Hobbes's views were vastly unpopular—libertarians detested them for obvious reasons, and royalists hated them as much because Hobbes was contemptuous of dynastic claims based on blood lineage and rationalized absolutist rule not on the grounds of powers granted from God, as most royalists did, but on powers surrendered by society. Yet because many important thinkers felt compelled to argue against Hobbes, he had enormous influence, if only in provoking the responses of others.

Perhaps the most moving attempt to bring light out of pervasive darkness was that of the seventeenth-century French moral and religious philosopher Blaise Pascal (1623–1662). Pascal began his career as a mathematician and scientific rationalist. A modern computer language has been named for him because he constructed the first calculating machine. (He did this when he was nineteen years old.) But at age thirty Pascal abandoned science as the result of a conversion experience and became a firm adherent of Jansenism, a puritanical faction within French Catholicism. From then till his death he worked on a highly ambitious philosophical-religious project meant to persuade doubters of the truth of Christianity by appealing simultaneously to their intellects and their emotions. Unfortunately, because of his premature death all that came of this was his *Pensées* (Thoughts), a collection of fragments and short informal pieces about religion written with great literary power. In these he argued that faith alone could show the way to salvation and that "the heart has its reasons of which reason itself knows nothing." Pascal's *Pensées* express the author's own sense of terror and anguish in the face of evil and eternity, but make the awe itself a sign of the existence of God. Individuals today will be moved by this work in varying degrees according to their own convictions, but few of any persuasion will dispute Pascal's proposition that "man knows he is wretched; he is therefore wretched because he is so; but he is very great because he knows it."

Blaise Pascal

LITERATURE AND THE ARTS

The combined wretchedness and greatness of humanity may be taken as the theme for the extraordinary profusion of towering works of literature and art produced during western Europe's period of crisis from 1560 to 1660. Of course not every single writing or painting of the era expressed the same message. During a hundred years of extraordinary literary and artistic creativity, works of all genres and sentiments were produced, ranging from the frothiest farces to the darkest tragedies, the serenest still lifes to the most grotesque scenes of religious martyrdom. Nonetheless, the greatest writers and painters of the period all were moved by a realization of the ambiguities and ironies of human existence not unlike that expressed in different ways by Montaigne and Pascal. They all were fully aware of the horrors of war and human suffering so rampant in their day, and all were directly or indirectly aware of the Protestant conviction that men are "vessels of iniquity," but they also inherited a large degree of Renaissance affirmativeness, and most of them accordingly preferred to view life on earth as a great dare.

From the host of remarkable writers who flourished during what was probably the most extraordinary century in the entire history of western European poetry and drama, we may take the very greatest: Cervantes, the Elizabethan dramatists—Shakespeare to the fore—and John Milton. Although Miguel de Cervantes (1547–1616) was not strictly speaking either a poet or a dramatist, his masterpiece, the satirical romance *Don Quixote,* exudes great lyricism and drama. The plot recounts the adventures of a Spanish gentleman, Don Quixote of La Mancha, who has become slightly unbalanced by constant reading of chivalric epics. His mind filled with all kinds of fantastic adventures, he sets out at the age of fifty upon the slippery road of knight-errantry, imagining windmills to be glowering giants and flocks of sheep to be armies of infidels whom it is his duty to rout with his spear. In his distorted fancy he mistakes inns for castles and serving girls for courtly ladies on fire with love. Set off in contrast to the "knight-errant" is the figure of his faithful squire, Sancho Panza. The latter represents the ideal of the practical man, with his feet on the ground and content with the modest but substantial pleasures of eating, drinking, and sleeping. Yet Cervantes clearly does not wish to say that the realism of a Sancho Panza is categorically preferable to the "quixotic" idealism of his master. Rather, the two men represent different facets of human nature. Without any doubt, Don Quixote is a devastating satire on the anachronistic chivalric mentality that would soon help hasten Spain's decline. But for all that, the reader's sympathies remain with the protagonist, the man from La Mancha who dares to "dream the impossible dream."

Directly contemporaneous with Cervantes were the English Elizabethan dramatists who collectively produced the most glorious age of theater known in the Western world. Writing after England's victory over the Spanish Armada, when national pride was at a peak, all exhibited great exuberance but none was by any means a facile optimist. In fact a strain of reflective seriousness pervades all their best works, and a few, like the tragedian John Webster (c. 1580–c. 1625), who "saw the skull beneath the skin," were if anything morbid pessimists. Literary critics tend to agree that of a bevy of great Elizabethan playwrights the most outstanding were Christopher Marlowe (1564–1593), Ben Jonson (c. 1572–1637), and, of course, William Shakespeare (1564–1616). Of the three, the fiery Marlowe, whose life was cut short in a tavern brawl before he reached the age of thirty, was the most youthfully energetic. In

Miguel de Cervantes

Elizabethan drama

William Shakespeare. Portrait made for the First Folio edition of his works, 1623.

Shakespeare's three periods: (1) confidence

plays such as *Tamburlaine* and *Doctor Faustus* Marlowe created larger-than-life heroes who seek and come close to conquering everything in their path and feeling every possible sensation. But they meet unhappy ends because, for all his vitality, Marlowe knew that there are limits on human striving, and that wretchedness as well as greatness lies in the human lot. Thus though Faustus asks a reincarnated Helen of Troy, conjured up by Satan, to make him "immortal with a kiss," he dies and is damned in the end because immortality is not awarded by the devil or found in earthly kisses. In contrast to the heroic tragedian Marlowe, Ben Jonson wrote corrosive comedies that expose human vices and foibles. In the particularly bleak *Volpone* Jonson shows people behaving like deceitful and lustful animals, but in the later *Alchemist* he balances an attack on quackery and gullibility with admiration for resourceful lower-class characters who cleverly take advantage of their supposed betters.

Incomparably the greatest of the Elizabethan dramatists, William Shakespeare was born into the family of a tradesman in the provincial town of Stratford-on-Avon. His life is enshrouded in more mists of obscurity than the careers of most other great people. It is known that he left his native village, having gained little formal education, when he was about twenty, and that he drifted to London to find employment in the theater. How he eventually became an actor and still later a writer of plays is uncertain, but by the age of twenty-eight he had definitely acquired a reputation as an author sufficient to excite the jealousy of his rivals. Before he retired to his native Stratford about 1610 to spend the rest of his days in ease, he had written or collaborated in writing nearly forty plays, over and above 150 sonnets and two long narrative poems.

As everyone knows, Shakespeare's plays rank as a kind of secular Bible wherever the English language is spoken. The reasons lie not only in the author's unrivaled gift of expression, and in his scintillating wit, but most of all in his profound analysis of human character seized by passion and tried by fate. Shakespeare's dramas fall rather naturally into three groups. Those written during the playwright's earlier years are characterized by a sense of confidence. They include a number of history plays, which recount England's struggles and glories leading up to the triumph of the Tudor dynasty; the lyrical romantic tragedy *Romeo and Juliet;* and a wide variety of comedies including the magical *Midsummer Night's Dream* and Shakespeare's greatest creations in the comic vein—*Twelfth Night, As You Like It,* and *Much Ado about Nothing.* Despite the last-named title, few even of the plays of Shakespeare's early, lightest period are "much ado about nothing." Rather, most explore with wisdom as well as wit fundamental problems of psychological identity, honor and ambition, love and friendship. Occasionally they also contain touches of deep seriousness, as in *As You Like It,* when Shakespeare has a character pause to reflect that "all the world's a stage, and all the men and women merely players" who pass through seven "acts" or stages of life.

Such touches, however, never obscure the restrained optimism of Shakespeare's first period, whereas the plays from his second period are far darker in mood. Apparently around 1601 Shakespeare underwent a crisis during which he began to distrust human nature profoundly and to indict the whole scheme of the universe. The result was a group of dramas characterized by bitterness, frequent pathos, and a troubled searching into the mysteries of things. The series begins with the tragedy of indecisive idealism represented by *Hamlet,* goes on to the cynicism of *Measure for Measure* and *All's Well That Ends Well,* and culminates in the cosmic tragedies of *Macbeth* and *King Lear,* wherein characters assert that "life's but a walking shadow . . . a tale told by an idiot, full of sound and fury signifying nothing," and that "as flies to wanton boys are we to the gods; they kill us for their sport." Despite all this gloom, however, the plays of Shakespeare's second period generally contain the dramatist's greatest flights of poetic grandeur.

(2) Crisis

Although *Macbeth* and *Lear* suggest an author in the throes of deep depression, Shakespeare managed to resolve his personal crisis and end his dramatic career with a third period characterized by a profound spirit of reconciliation. Of the three plays (all idyllic romances) written during this final period, the last, *The Tempest,* is the greatest. Here ancient animosities are buried and wrongs are righted by a combination of natural and supernatural means, and a wide-eyed, youthful heroine rejoices on first seeing men with the words "O brave new world, that has such people in it!" Here, then, Shakespeare seems to be saying that for all humanity's trials life is not so unrelentingly bitter after all, and the divine plan of the universe is somehow benevolent and just.

(3) Reconciliation

Though less versatile than Shakespeare, not far behind him in eloquent grandeur stands the Puritan poet John Milton (1608–1674). The leading publicist of Oliver Cromwell's regime, Milton wrote the official defense of the beheading of Charles I as well as a number of treatises justifying Puritan positions in contemporary affairs. But he was also a man full of contradictions who loved the Greek and Latin classics at least as much as the Bible. Hence he could write a perfect pastoral elegy, *Lycidas,* mourning the loss of a dear friend in purely classical terms. Later, when forced into retirement by the accession of Charles II, Milton, though now blind, embarked on writing a classical epic, *Paradise Lost,* out of material found in Genesis concerning the creation of the world and the fall of man. This magnificent poem, which links the classical tradition to Christianity more successfully than any literary work written before or since, is surely one of the greatest epics of all time. Setting out to "justify the ways of God to man," Milton in *Paradise Lost* first plays "devil's advocate" by creating the compelling character of Satan, who defies God with boldness and subtlety. But Satan is more than counterbalanced in the end by the real "epic hero" of *Paradise Lost,* Adam, who learns to accept the human lot of moral responsibility and suffering, and is last seen leaving Paradise with Eve, the world "all before them."

John Milton. From the first edition of his poems, 1645.

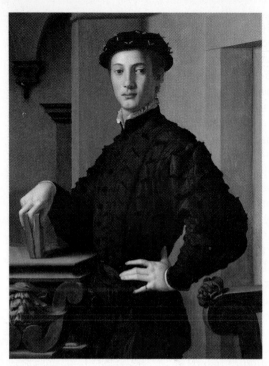

Portrait of a Young Man, by Bronzino (1503–1572). Bronzino was a Florentine Mannerist painter who preferred the "objective" representation of oddities. Notice the carefully chiseled grotesques at the bottom and the young man's wandering left eye. The numerous contrasts between light and shade and the large number of vertical surfaces in the background contribute to a sense of surrealism.

"Mannerism": Pontormo and Bronzino

Fray Felix Hortensio Paravicino, by El Greco (c. 1541–1614). More restrained in composition than most of the artist's other work, this portrait nonetheless communicates a sense of deep spiritual intensity.

The ironies and tensions inherent in human existence also were portrayed with eloquence and profundity by several immortal masters of the visual arts who flourished during the "century of crisis." The dominant goal in Italian and Spanish painting during the first half of this period, the years between about 1540 and 1600, was to fascinate the viewer with special effects. This goal, however, was achieved by means of two entirely different styles. (Confusingly, both styles are sometimes referred to as "Mannerism.") The first was based on the style of the Renaissance master Raphael but moved from that painter's gracefulness to a highly self-conscious elegance bordering on the bizarre and surreal. Representatives of this approach were the Florentines Pontormo (1494–1557) and Bronzino (1503–1572). Their sharp-focused portraits are flat and cold, yet strangely riveting.

The other extreme was theatrical in a more conventional sense—highly dramatic. Painters who followed this approach were indebted to Michelangelo but went much farther than he did in emphasizing shadowy contrasts, restlessness, and distortion. Of this second group, the two most outstanding were the Venetian Tintoretto (1518–1594) and the Spaniard El Greco (c. 1541–1614). Combining aspects of Michelangelo's style with the traditionally Venetian taste for rich color, Tintoretto produced an enormous number of monumentally large canvases devoted to religious subjects that still inspire awe with their broodingly shimmering light and gripping drama. More emotional still is the work of Tintoretto's disciple, El Greco. Born Domenikos Theotokopoulos on the Greek island of Crete, this extraordinary artist absorbed some of the stylized elongation

The Crucifixion, by Tintoretto (1518–1594). This Venetian master of Mannerism combined typically Venetian richness of color with an innovative concern for movement and emotion.

Saint Andrew and St. Francis, by El Greco. A striking exemplification of the artist's penchant for elongation as well as his profound psychological penetration.

The Laocoön, by El Greco. An extreme example of Manneristic stress on restlessness and distortion. Note that the Spanish painter here drew for inspiration on the famous Hellenistic sculpture group shown on p. 145.

shown on p. 145.

"Mannerism": Tintoretto and El Greco

characteristic of Greco-Byzantine icon painting before traveling to Italy to learn color and drama from Tintoretto. Finally he settled in Spain, where he was called "El Greco"—Spanish for "the Greek." El Greco's paintings were too strange to be greatly appreciated in his own age, and even now they appear so unbalanced as to seem the work of one almost deranged. Yet such a view slights El Greco's deeply mystical Catholic fervor as well as his technical achievements. Best known today is his transfigured land-scape, the *View of Toledo,* with its somber but awesome light breaking where no sun shines. But equally inspiring are his swirling religious scenes and several of his stunning portraits in which gaunt, dignified Spaniards radiate a rare blend of austerity and spiritual insight.

The Baroque style

The dominant artistic school of southern Europe from about 1600 until the early 1700s was that of the Baroque, a school not only of paint-ing but of sculpture and architecture. The Baroque style retained aspects of the dramatic and the irregular (the word "Baroque" itself comes from the Portuguese for a rough pearl), but it avoided seeming bizarre or over-heated and aimed above all to instill a sense of the affirmative. The main reason for this was that Baroque art in all genres was most often propa-gandistic. Originating in Rome as an expression of the ideals of the Counter-Reformation papacy and the Jesuit order, Baroque architecture in particular aimed to gain adherence for a specific worldview. Similarly, Baroque painting often was done in the service of the Counter-Reforma-tion Church, which at its high tide around 1620 seemed everywhere to be on the offensive. When Baroque painters were not celebrating Counter-

View of Toledo, by El Greco. Light breaks where no sun shines. One of the most awesomely mysterious paintings in the entire Western tradition.

The Calling of St. Matthew, by Caravaggio
(1565–1609). Among the earliest of the great Baroque
painters, Caravaggio specialized in contrasts of light
and shade (*chiaroscuro*), and preferred to conceive of
religious scenes in terms of everyday life. Here Christ
(extreme right), whose halo is the only supernatural
detail in the composition, enters a tavern to call
St. Matthew (pointing doubtfully at himself) to his
service.

Left: **David**, by Bernini (1598–1680). Whereas the earlier conceptions of David by the
Renaissance sculptors Donatello and Michelangelo were reposeful (see pp. 433 and 434),
the Baroque sculptor Bernini chose to portray his young hero at the peak of physical exertion. Right: **The Ecstasy of St. Theresa**, by Bernini. As David is seen at the peak of
bodily exertion, St. Theresa is shown at the peak of spiritual transport.

Reformation ideals, most of them worked in the service of monarchs who sought their own glorification.

Indubitably the most imaginative and influential figure of the original Roman Baroque was the architect and sculptor Gianlorenzo Bernini (1598–1680), a frequent employee of the papacy who created one of the most magnificent celebrations of papal grandeur in the sweeping colonnades leading up to St. Peter's Basilica. Breaking with the serene Renaissance classicism of Palladio, Bernini's architecture retained the use of classical elements such as columns and domes, but combined them in ways meant to express both aggressive restlessness and great power. In addition Bernini was one of the first to experiment with church facades built "in depth"—building frontages not conceived as continuous surfaces but that jutted out at odd angles and seemingly invaded the open space in front of them. If the purpose of these innovations was to draw the viewer emotionally into the ambit of the work of art, the same may be said for Bernini's aims in sculpture. Harking back to the restless motion of Hellenistic statuary—particularly the Laocoön group—and building on tendencies already present in the later sculpture of Michelangelo, Bernini's statuary emphasizes drama and incites the viewer to respond to it rather than serenely to observe.

Since most Italian Baroque painters lacked Bernini's artistic genius, to view the very greatest masterpieces of southern European Baroque painting one must look to Spain and the work of Diego Velázquez (1599–1660). Unlike Bernini, Velázquez, a court painter in Madrid just when Spain hung on the brink of ruin, was not an entirely typical exponent of the Baroque style. Certainly many of his canvases display a characteristically Baroque delight in motion, drama, and power, but Velázquez's best work is characterized by a more restrained thoughtfulness than is usually found in the Baroque. Thus his famous *Surrender of Breda* shows muscular horses and splendid Spanish grandees on the one hand, but un-Baroque humane and deep sympathy for defeated, disarrayed troops on the other. Moreover, Velázquez's single greatest painting, *The Maids of Honor,* done around 1656 after Spain's collapse, radiates thoughtfulness rather than drama and is one of the most probing artistic examinations of illusion and reality ever executed.

Southern Europe's main northern rival for artistic laurels in the "iron century" was the Netherlands, where three extremely dissimilar painters all explored the theme of the greatness and wretchedness of man to the fullest. The earliest, Peter Brueghel (c. 1525–1569), worked in a vein related to earlier Netherlandish realism. But unlike his predecessors, who favored quiet urban scenes, Brueghel exulted in portraying the busy, elemental life of the peasantry. Most famous in this respect are his rollicking *Peasant Wedding* and *Peasant Wedding Dance,* and his spacious *Harvesters,* in which guzzling and snoring fieldhands are taking a well-deserved break from their heavy labors under the noon sun. Such vistas give the impression of uninterrupted rhythms of life, but late in his career Brueghel became appalled by the intolerance and bloodshed he witnessed during

The Church of S. Carlo alle Quattro Fontane, Rome. Built by Bernini's contemporary Francesco Borromini in 1665, the facade of S. Carlo well exemplifies the frontage "in depth" characteristic of Baroque architecture.

Brueghel

Pope Innocent X, by Velázquez (1599–1660). A trenchant portrait with an evident debt to Raphael's Julius II (see p. 419).

The Surrender of Breda, by Velázquez. Celebrating a Spanish victory over the Dutch in an early phase of the Thirty Years' War, the Spanish lances point proudly skyward in contrast to the desolate Dutch smoke, but the Spanish commander displays magnanimity for the defeated enemy.

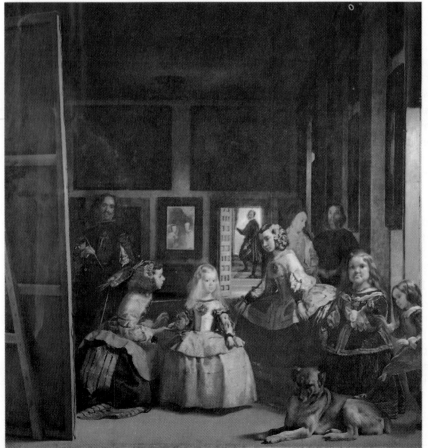

The Maids of Honor, by Velázquez. The artist himself is at work on a double portrait of the king and queen of Spain (who may be seen in the rear mirror), but reality is more obvious in the foreground in the persons of the delicately impish princess, her two maids, and a misshapen dwarf. The twentieth-century Spanish artist Picasso gained great inspiration from this work.

The Massacre of the Innocents, by Brueghel (c. 1525–1569). This painting shows how effectively art can be used as a means of social commentary. Many art historians believe that Brueghel was tacitly depicting the suffering of the Netherlands at the hands of the Spanish in his own day.

The Harvesters, by Brueghel. Brueghel chose to depict both the hard work and the recreation of the peasantry.

Rubens

**Rubens's Portrait of his Son
Nicholas.**

Rembrandt

the time of the Calvinist riots and the Spanish repression in the Netherlands and expressed his criticism in an understated yet searing manner. In *The Blind Leading the Blind,* for example, we see what happens when ignorant fanatics start showing the way to each other. More powerful still is Brueghel's *Massacre of the Innocents,* which from a distance looks like a snug scene of a Flemish village buried in snow. In fact, however, heartless soldiers are methodically breaking into homes and slaughtering babies, the simple peasant folk are fully at their mercy, and the artist—alluding to a Gospel forgotten by warring Catholics and Protestants alike—seems to be saying "as it happened in the time of Christ, so it happens now."

Vastly different from Brueghel was the Netherlandish Baroque painter Peter Paul Rubens (1577–1640). Since the Baroque was an international movement closely linked to the spread of the Counter-Reformation, it should offer no surprise that Baroque style was extremely well represented in just that part of the Netherlands which, after long warfare, had been retained by Spain. In fact, Rubens of Antwerp was a far more typical Baroque artist than Velázquez of Madrid, painting literally thousands of robust canvases that glorified resurgent Catholicism or exalted second-rate aristocrats by portraying them as epic heroes dressed in bearskins. Even when Rubens's intent was not overtly propagandistic he customarily reveled in the sumptuous extravagance of the Baroque manner, being perhaps most famous today for the pink and rounded flesh of his well-nourished nudes. But unlike a host of lesser Baroque artists, Rubens was not entirely lacking in subtlety and was a man of many moods. His gentle portrait of his son Nicholas catches unaffected childhood in a moment of repose, and though throughout most of his career Rubens had celebrated martial valor, his late *Horrors of War* movingly portrays what he himself called "the grief of unfortunate Europe, which, for so many years now, has suffered plunder, outrage, and misery."

In some ways a blend of Brueghel and Rubens, the greatest of all Netherlandish painters, Rembrandt van Rijn (1606–1669), defies all attempts at facile characterization. Living across the border from the Spanish Netherlands in staunchly Calvinistic Holland, Rembrandt belonged to a society that was too austere to tolerate the unbuckled realism of a Brueghel or the fleshy Baroque pomposity of a Rubens. Yet Rembrandt managed to put both realistic and Baroque traits to new uses. In his early career he gained fame and fortune as the painter of biblical scenes that lacked the Baroque's fleshiness but retained its grandeur in their swirling forms and stunning experiments with light. In this early period too Rembrandt was active as a realistic portrait painter who knew how to flatter his self-satisfied subjects by emphasizing their Calvinistic steadfastness, to the great advantage of his purse. But gradually his prosperity faded, apparently in part because he grew tired of flattering and definitely because he made some bad investments. Since personal tragedies also mounted in the painter's middle and declining years his art inevitably became far more pensive and sombre, but it gained in dignity, subtle lyricism, and

The Horrors of War, by Rubens (1577–1640). The war god Mars here casts aside his mistress Venus and threatens humanity with death and destruction. In his old age Rubens took a far more critical view of war than he did for most of his earlier career.

The Triumph of the Eucharist, by Rubens. A typical Baroque work, this painting proclaims the victory of the Cross and the Eucharistic Chalice, symbols of Counter-Reformation Catholicism.

The Polish Rider, by Rembrandt (1606–1669). Unlike Titian's equestrian Charles V (see p. 477), Rembrandt's rider is reflective and hence more humane.

Aristotle Contemplating the Bust of Homer, by Rembrandt. One of the greatest painters' view of one of the greatest of philosophers caught up by the aura of one of the greatest poets.

Self-Portrait, by Judith Leyster (1609–1660). Leyster was a Dutch contemporary of Rembrandt who pursued a successful career as an artist during her early twenties, before she married. Respected in her own day, she was all but forgotten for centuries thereafter.

awesome mystery. Thus his later portraits, including those of himself, are imbued with introspective qualities and a suggestion that only the half is being told. Equally moving are explicitly philosophical paintings such as *Aristotle Contemplating the Bust of Homer,* in which the supposedly earthbound philosopher seems spellbound by the otherworldly luminous radiance of the epic poet, and *The Polish Rider,* in which realistic and Baroque elements merge into a higher synthesis portraying a pensive young man setting out fearlessly into a perilous world. Like Shakespeare, Rembrandt knew that life's journey is full of perils, but his most mature paintings suggest that these can be mastered with poetry and courage.

SUMMARY POINTS

- Economic hardships, prolonged wars, and religious riots combined to produce a century of pronounced crisis in Europe from about 1560 to about 1660.

- Dramatic price inflation, caused in part by growing populations and influx of silver from Spanish South America, devastated the laboring poor and reduced the resources of governments.

- Conflicts between Catholics and Protestants led to civil war in France and England, a war for the independence of the Netherlands, and a war on the high seas between England and Spain.

The Thirty Years' War was at first a religious war between Catholics and Protestants in Germany but gradually turned into an international struggle for hegemony in Europe in which France replaced Spain as the mightiest European power.

- Political philosophers responded to the turmoil of the age with prescriptions for government that ranged from the libertarianism sought by some Huguenots and Puritans to the absolutism advocated by Jean Bodin and Thomas Hobbes.

- Extraordinary works of literature and art were produced between 1560 and 1660, including the plays of William Shakespeare, the poems of John Milton, and the paintings of El Greco, Brueghel, and Rembrandt.

SELECTED READINGS

Aston, T. H., ed., *Crisis in Europe: 1560–1660,* London, 1965. A collection of highly valuable essays.

Braudel, Fernand, *The Mediterranean and the Mediterranean World in the Age of Philip II,* 2 vols., New York, 1972. One of the most brilliant history books of our age. Treats life in the Mediterranean regions in the second half of the sixteenth century with particular emphasis on how geography determines the course of human history.

Chute, Marchette, *Shakespeare of London,* New York, 1949. The best popular biography.

Dean, Leonard F., ed., *Shakespeare: Modern Essays in Criticism,* rev. ed., New York, 1967. A variety of scholarly appraisals.

Dunn, Richard S., *The Age of Religious Wars, 1559–1715,* 2d ed., New York, 1979. The best college-level text on this period. Extremely well written.

Elliott, John H., *Imperial Spain, 1469–1716,* London, 1963. A splendid work of synthesis.

———, *Europe Divided: 1559–1598,* London, 1968. An extremely lucid narrative of complex events.

———, *Richelieu and Olivares,* New York, 1984. Brilliant comparative history setting off similarities and differences between seventeenth-century France and Spain.

Elton, G. R., *England under the Tudors,* 3d ed., London, 1991. Engagingly written and authoritative.

Frame, Donald, *Montaigne: A Biography,* New York, 1965. By far the best study in English.

Fraser, Lady Antonia, *Cromwell: The Lord Protector,* London, 1973. A popular biography.

Held, Julius S., and Donald Posner, *17th and 18th Century Art: Baroque Painting, Sculpture, Architecture,* New York, 1979. The most complete introductory review of the subject in English.

Hibbard, Howard, *Bernini,* Baltimore, 1965. The basic study in English of this central figure of Baroque artistic activity.

Hill, Christopher, *The Century of Revolution: 1603–1714,* 2d ed., New York, 1982. A valuable survey of English developments that holds narrative to a minimum and stresses economic and social trends.

Hirst, Derek, *Authority and Conflict: England, 1603–1658,* London, 1986. Integrates recent interpretations. The best survey out of several available.

Kahr, Madlyn M., *Velázquez: The Art of Painting,* New York, 1976.

Kamen, Henry, *The Iron Century: Social Change in Europe, 1559–1660,* rev. ed., New York, 1976. One of the most detailed and persuasive statements of the view that there was a "general crisis" in many different aspects of European life.

Le Roy Ladurie, Emmanuel, *Carnival in Romans,* New York, 1979. A close-up view of social turmoil in France in 1580.

Levack, Brian P., *The Witch-Hunt in Early Modern Europe,* 2d ed., New York, 1995.

Mattingly, Garrett, *The Armada,* Boston, 1959. Fascinating narrative; thoroughly reliable and reads like a novel.

Monter, E. William, ed., *European Witchcraft,* New York, 1969. Selected readings with fine introductions by one of the world's leading experts.

Parker, Geoffrey, *The Dutch Revolt,* rev. ed., Ithaca, N.Y., 1989. The standard survey in English on the revolt of the Netherlands.

———, *Europe in Crisis: 1598–1648,* Brighton, Sussex, 1980. A primarily political narrative of war and revolution in Europe exclusive of England.

Pennington, D. H., *Seventeenth-Century Europe,* London, 1970. An extremely thorough and reliable survey that follows the conventional periodization of treating a century bounded by the round numbers 1600 and 1700.

Pierson, Peter, *Philip II of Spain,* London, 1975. An absorbing attempt to study Philip's personality and actions in terms of the dominant assumptions of his age.

Rabb, Theodore K., *The Struggle for Stability in Early Modern Europe,* New York, 1975. A stimulating essay arguing that a shift from crisis to stability took place around 1660.

Roots, Ivan, ed., *Cromwell, A Profile,* New York, 1973. A collection of readings on problems in interpretation; complements Fraser.

Rosenberg, Jakob, *Rembrandt: Life and Work,* rev. ed., Ithaca, N.Y., 1980.

Russell, Conrad, *The Crisis of Parliaments: English History, 1509–1660,* New York, 1971. The best survey covering this broad range of time.

Shearman, John, *Mannerism,* Baltimore, 1967. Treats trends in late-sixteenth-century architecture and sculpture as well as Manneristic painting.

Steinberg, S. H., *The Thirty Years' War and the Conflict for European Hegemony, 1600–1660,* New York, 1966. The best scholarly account.

Stone, Lawrence, *The Causes of the English Revolution, 1529–1642,* New York, 1972. A judicious analysis by one of the foremost social historians of our age.

Thomas, Keith, *Religion and the Decline of Magic,* London, 1971. A marvelously insightful broad-gauged study of popular belief in England.

Walzer, Michael, *The Revolution of the Saints: A Study in the Origins of Radical Politics,* Cambridge, Mass., 1965. An attempt by a political scientist to demonstrate that English Puritanism was the earliest incarnation of modern political radicalism.

Wedgwood, C. V., *William the Silent,* London, 1944. A laudatory and urbanely written biography.

Cervantes, Miguel de, *Don Quixote,* tr. Walter Starkie, New York, 1957.

Hobbes, Thomas, *Leviathan,* abridged by F. B. Randall, New York, 1964.

Montaigne, Michel de, *Essays,* tr. J. M. Cohen, Baltimore, 1958.

Pascal, Blaise, *Pensées,* French-English ed., H. F. Stewart, London, 1950.

Sprenger, Jakob, and H. Kramer, *The Malleus Maleficarum,* tr. M. Summers, 2d ed., London, 1948. A frightful yet fascinating work, the *Malleus* ("The Hammer of Witches") was the most frequently used handbook of early-modern witchcraft prosecutors.

CHAPTER 16

THE ECONOMY AND SOCIETY
OF EARLY-MODERN EUROPE

We ought to esteem and cherish those trades which we have in remote or far countries, for besides the increase in shipping and mariners thereby, the wares also sent thither and received from thence are far more profitable unto the kingdom than by our trades near at hand.

—THOMAS MUN, *England's Treasure by Foreign Trade,* 1630

In nearly every state in Europe citizens are divided into the three orders of nobles, clergy, and people. . . . Even Plato, although he intended all his citizens to enjoy an equality of rights and privileges, divided them into the three orders of guardians, soldiers and labourers. All this goes to show that there never was a commonwealth, real or imaginary, even if conceived in the most popular terms, where citizens were in truth equal in all rights and privileges. Some always have more, some less than the rest.

—JEAN BODIN, *Six Books of the Commonwealth,* 1570

A NY STUDY of early-modern European society must concern itself with change, with the factors that in the two hundred years after 1600 were powerful enough to produce the political upheaval of the French Revolution and the economic stimulus for the Industrial Revolution. Arguably, the most profound change during that period was economic. By the latter part of the eighteenth century, the freebooting overseas expansionism that had begun in the sixteenth century with the Spanish *conquistadores* had ended with Europe at the center of a vast system of worldwide trade. Commerce on this increasingly global scale had given birth to institutions fashioned for its support, and had altered patterns of living among those caught up in its overpowering dynamic. Banks and joint-stock companies financed international commercial ventures. New urban workshops responded to the intensified demand for manufactured goods. As international banking developed into a highly sophisticated profession, its practitioners became powerful. As urban workshops imposed new conditions and habits, the urban artisan was forced to bend uncomfortably to unfamiliar demands.

European society as a whole found bending no more comfortable. Change was imposed upon national communities that, in many cases, were still defined according to the hierarchies of the Middle Ages: landlord

Economic change

New economic realities and old social forms

549

and peasant, nobleman and serf. Each order was expected to acknowledge its inherent obligations and responsibilities, as each was assumed to be part of an organic and divinely sanctioned communal whole. Where, within this preordained structure, was the independent commercial entrepreneur or the dispossessed laborer supposed to fit? Tension of this sort between old forms and new realities was further exacerbated by the general crisis that we analyzed in the preceding chapter. Change produced by economic expansion and dislocation occurred against the background of civil and religious turmoil that tore much of Europe to pieces in the seventeenth century, and against an equally disruptive cycle of demographic swings caused by warfare and disease, by good weather one year, bad weather—and hence famine—the next. Those were the changes closest to the lives of most Europeans, the men and women still bound to the land, for whom, as the French historian Pierre Goubert has observed, "death was at the center of life, just as the graveyard was at the center of the village." The concerns of this chapter are thus both the economic and social circumstances that produced change over a period of almost two hundred years, and the habits and traditions that were making change complex and difficult.

LIFE AND DEATH: PATTERNS OF POPULATION

No facts better illustrate the degree to which the two hundred years of European history between 1600 and 1800 were subject to chance and change than those having to do with life and death—patterns of population, as they imprinted themselves across the early-modern period.

The threat of famine

The pattern of life for most Europeans centered on the struggle to stay alive. They lived and worked within a subsistence economy, considering themselves extremely fortunate if they could grow or earn what it took to survive. In most instances their enemy was not an invading army, but famine; it is not surprising that one's well-being was measured simply by one's girth. At least once a decade, climatic conditions—usually a long period of summer rainfall—would produce a devastatingly bad harvest, which in turn would result in widespread malnutrition often leading to serious illness and death. A family might survive for a time by eating less, but eventually, with its meager stocks exhausted and the cost of grain high, the human costs would mount. The substitution of grass, nuts, and tree bark for grain on which the peasants depended almost entirely for nourishment was as inadequate for them as it appears pathetic to us.

Population crises

Widespread crop failures occurred at fairly regular intervals—the worst in France, for example, about every thirty years (1597, 1630, 1662, 1694). They helped to cause the series of population crises that are the outstanding feature of early-modern demographic history. Poor harvests and the high prices produced by a scarcity of grain meant not only undernourishment and possible starvation, but increasing unemployment: with fewer crops to be harvested, more money was spent on food and, consequently,

Left: **A Plague Hospital in Vienna.** The efforts to contain outbreaks of plague by gathering the sick in establishments such as this and burying the dead on the site proved unsuccessful. Right: **A Physician's Mask.** This German device containing smelling salts in its curved beak was designed to combat the plague, which physicians incorrectly believed was spread by poisonous vapors.

less on manufactured goods. The despair such conditions could easily breed would in turn contribute to a postponement of marriage and of births, and thus to a population decline. The patterns of marriages and births revealed in local parish registers indicate that throughout Europe the populations of individual communities rose and fell dramatically in rhythm with the fortunes of the harvest.

An undernourished population is a population particularly susceptible to disease. Bubonic plague ravaged seventeenth-century Europe. Severe outbreaks occurred in Seville in 1649, in Amsterdam in 1664, and in London the following year. By 1700 it had all but disappeared; it last appeared in western Europe in a small area of southern France in 1720, though Moscow suffered an outbreak as late as 1771. Despite the gradual retreat of the plague, however, other diseases took a dreadful toll, in an age when available medical treatment was little more than crude guesswork, and in any event, beyond the reach of the poor. Epidemics of dysentery, small-pox, and typhus occurred with savage regularity. As late as 1779, more than 100,000 people died of dysentery in the French province of Brittany. Most diseases attacked rich and poor impartially. Water supplies in towns and in the country were contaminated by heedless disposal of human waste and by all manner of garbage and urban filth. Bathing, feared at one time as a method of spreading disease, was by no means a weekly habit, whatever the social status of the household. Samuel Pepys, a prosperous servant of the crown in seventeenth-century London, recorded in his diary that his housemaid was in the habit of picking the lice from his scalp, that he took his first bath only after his wife had taken hers and

Health and sanitation

"Summer Amusement: Bugg Hunting." In this joking treatment of one of the facts of everyday life the bedbugs meet sudden death in a full chamber pot.

Population growth

experienced the pleasures of cleanliness, and that he had, on occasion, thought nothing of using the fireplace in his bedroom as a toilet, the maid having failed to provide him with a chamberpot. If such was Pepys's attitude toward hygiene and sanitation, imagine that of the poverty-stricken peasant, and the threat to health implicit in such attitudes.

The precariousness of life helped encourage most men and women in early-modern Europe to postpone marriage until their mid- to late twenties, by which time they hoped not only to have survived but also to have accumulated sufficient resources to establish a household. Young couples lived on their own, and not, as in societies elsewhere, as part of "extended" families of three generations. Since a son could not inherit until his father died, he was compelled to establish himself independently, and to postpone starting his own family until he had done so. Though historians have failed to find a clear explanation for this pattern of later marriages, it may have resulted from a growing desire on the part of younger men and women for a higher standard of living. Late marriage helped to control the birth rate. Once married, however, a couple generally produced their first child within a year. Although subsequent children appeared with annual or biennial regularity, long periods of breastfeeding, which tends to reduce the mother's fertility, and near poverty went some way toward limiting childbirth.

Until the middle of the eighteenth century, populations continued to wax and wane according to the outbreak of warfare, famine, and disease. From about 1750 on, however, there was a steady and significant population increase, with almost all countries experiencing major growth. In Russia, where territorial expansion added further to the increases, the population rate may have tripled in the second half of the eighteenth century. Gains elsewhere, while not usually as spectacular, were nevertheless significant. The population of Prussia doubled; Hungary's more than

Eighteenth-Century Sanitation. "Nightmen" moved through city streets after dark emptying the refuse of privies.

tripled; and England's population, which was about 5.5 million in 1700, reached 9 million in 1800. France, already in 1700 the most heavily populated country in Europe (about 20 million), added another 6 million before 1790. Spaniards multiplied from 7.6 million in 1717 to 10.5 million in 1797. Although reasons for the population increase remain something of a mystery, historians are inclined to agree that it was the cumulative result of a decrease in infant mortality and a very gradual decline in the death rate, due in large measure to an equally gradual increase in the food supply. Better transportation facilitated the shipment of food over greater distances. Land clearances, particularly in England, and in Prussia and Russia, where territories were opened to colonization, provided an essential ingredient for increased production. New staples—the potato and maize—supplemented the diets of the very poor. And although evidence here is only fragmentary, it appears that whereas the climate of seventeenth-century Europe was abnormally bad, that of the succeeding hundred years was on the whole favorable.

Population increase brought with it new problems and new attitudes. For example, in France, it meant pressure on the land, as more peasants attempted to wring survival from an overpopulated countryside. The consequence was migration from the country to the city. The decline in the death rate among infants—along with an apparent increase in illegitimacy at the end of the eighteenth century—created a growing population of unwanted babies among the poor. Some desperate women resorted to infanticide, though since children murdered at birth died without benefit of baptism, the crime was stigmatized as especially heinous by the Church as well as by society in general. More often, babies were abandoned at the doors of foundling hospitals. As an English benefactor of several such institutions, Jonas Hanway, remarked in 1766, "it is much less difficult to the human heart and the dictates of self-preservation to drop a child than to kill it." In Paris during the 1780s from seven to eight thousand children were being abandoned out of a total of thirty thousand new births. Paradoxically, some historians now argue that during this same period the decrease in infant and child mortality encouraged many parents to lavish care and affection on their offspring in a way that they had not when the repeated early deaths of their sons and daughters had taught them the futility of that emotional bond.

Although somewhere between 80 and 90 percent of the population lived in small rural communities, towns and cities were coming to play an increasingly important role in the life of early-modern Europe. One must speak of the "rise" of towns and cities with caution, however, since the pace of urbanization varied greatly across the Continent. Russia remained almost entirely rural: only 2.5 percent of its population lived in towns in 1630, and that percentage had risen by only 0.5 percent by 1774. In Holland, on the other hand, 59 percent of the population was urban in 1627 and 65 percent in 1795.

The total number of urban dwellers did not vary markedly after the end of the sixteenth century, when there were approximately 200 cities

New problems and attitudes

The "rise" of towns and cities

Shifts in urban population

in Europe with a population of over 10,000. What did change between 1600 and 1800 was, first, the way in which those cities were distributed across the map, concentrated increasingly in the north and west; and second, the growing proportion of very large cities to the whole. The patterns of trade and commerce had much to do with these shifts. Cities like Hamburg in Germany, Liverpool in England, Toulon in France, and Cadiz in Spain grew by about 250 percent between 1600 and 1750. Amsterdam, the hub of early-modern international commerce, increased from 30,000 in 1530 to 115,000 in 1630 and 200,000 by 1800. Naples, the busy Mediterranean port, went from a population of 300,000 in 1600 to nearly half a million by the late eighteenth century. Where goods were traded, processed, and manufactured, fleets built and provisioned, people flocked to work. An eighteenth-century commentator noted that the laborers in Paris were "almost all foreigners"—that is, men and women born outside the city: carpenters from Savoy, water carriers from Auvergne, porters from Lyons, stonecutters from Normandy, wigmakers from Gascony, shoemakers from Lorraine.

Ebb and flow of urban growth

As some cities expanded, others stagnated or declined as a result of commercial changes. Norwich, in England, grew at the expense of older industrial centers on the English Channel when the manufacture of woolen goods shifted north. The population of the important German market center of Frankfurt declined during and after the Thirty Years' War, when difficulties of communication and the general instability caused by frequent military campaigns diverted much of its former business to Amsterdam.

Growth of administrative centers

The most spectacular urban population growth occurred in the administrative capitals of the increasingly centralized nations of Europe. By the middle of the eighteenth century, Madrid, Berlin, and St. Petersburg all had populations of over 100,000. London grew from 674,000 in 1700 to 860,000 a century later. Paris, a city of approximately 180,000 in 1600, increased to over half a million by 1800. Berlin grew from a population of 6,500 in 1661, to 60,000 in 1721, to 140,000 in 1783. Its increase was due in part to the fact that successive Prussian rulers undertook to improve its position as a trade center by the construction of canals that linked it with Breslau and Hamburg. Its population rose as well, however, because of the marked increase in Prussian army and bureaucratic personnel based in the capital city. Of the 140,000 citizens of Berlin in 1783, approximately 65,000 were state employees or members of their families.

THE DYNAMICS OF AGRICULTURE AND INDUSTRY

Traditional techniques yield to innovation

The dramatic shifts in population we have been tracing were in some cases the cause, in others the effect, of equally important changes occurring in agriculture and industry. Throughout most of the two-hundred-year period under review, agricultural production was generally carried on according to traditional techniques that kept the volume of produc-

The Open-Field System in Northern France, 1738. Note the subdivision of large tracts into narrow strips, often owned by different proprietors.

tion low; yet by the end of the eighteenth century, tradition in some areas had yielded to innovation, with the result that production was increasing dramatically.

Most of the agricultural regions of seventeenth-century Europe consisted of open fields. In the north, these fields were usually large sections of land, divided into long, narrow strips; in the south, the strips tended to reflect the more irregular shape of local landscapes. Although one or two rich proprietors might own as much as three-fourths of the land in an open-field village, that land did not make up one solid block. Instead it was made up of a great many plots, seldom contiguous, within the various open fields that surrounded the village. Landholding was further complicated by local usage. In France, for example, a *seigneur* might own a group of estates (*seigneury*) whose boundaries were not contiguous with any one parish. A parish, in turn, might be dependent on more than one *seigneur*. A property owner's *desmesne*—which he worked with hired laborers for his own direct profit—and his tenant farms—those that he leased out to peasants—all consisted of bits and pieces of land that lay alongside other bits and pieces that belonged to other landowners—very often small peasant proprietors. Each large open field thus resembled a patchwork quilt. Under these circumstances, in order for the fields to be cultivated with any degree of efficiency, all the "patches" had to be planted with the same crop, and sown, cultivated, and harvested together.

The open-field system

The inefficiency inherent in the management of a multitude of plots by many farmers was a price small peasant proprietors were willing to pay in return for the social utility of communal decision-making and the right to graze livestock on common land. Once landlords, particularly in England and Holland, began to compete for markets as capitalist agricultural entrepreneurs, however, they looked for ways to overcome the inefficiency of traditional practices, so as to improve the yield on their land.

Enclosure

By the end of the eighteenth century a great many English and Dutch landlords had resolved the problem of low production by adopting a full range of innovative farming techniques, the most drastic of which was the enclosure of open fields to allow for more systematic and therefore more productive farming. "Enclosure" was the term for land reorganization within a traditional village community. The earliest enclosures in England took place in the fifteenth and sixteenth centuries and entailed the conversion of lands into fenced-off sheep meadows. Because of the great profits to be accrued from wool, some landlords converted common pastures that hitherto had supported peasant livestock into their own preserves for sheep-raising, thus threatening the livelihood of entire peasant communities.

Absolute vs. common property rights

Enclosure was more easily accomplished in those countries—England most notably—where there was a system of absolute property rights and wage labor. Where the tradition of "common" rights to grazing and foraging was strong, as in France, landlords found it far more difficult to impose a new economic order. In France, as well, a large peasantry owned small plots of land outright, adding up to approximately one-third of all agricultural land. It had neither an interest in nor the financial capacity for change. Monarchs tended to oppose enclosure since it promised to enrich further a rival noble class. In seventeenth-century France the monarchy needed an economically stable peasantry to support its expanding tax programs, and therefore worked to secure peasants in the customary tenure of their farms. Thus defended, the peasants were better able to resist effectively attempts at enclosure launched by large landholders. English property owners were more fortunate, taking advantage of the absence of royal opposition during the Cromwellian period to enclose on a broad scale.

Scientific farming

The really dramatic enclosure movement in England took place, however, at the end of the early-modern period, between 1710 and 1810. Landlords began to engage in the practice of "scientific farming." They realized that by introducing new crops and farming methods they could reduce the amount of land kept fallow and bring in higher yields and thus higher profits. The most important new crops with which landowners experimented were clover, alfalfa, and related varieties of leguminous plants. These reduced fertility much less than cereal grains and helped to improve the quality of the soil by gathering nitrogen and making the ground more porous. Another new crop that had a similar effect was the turnip. The greatest propagandist for the planting of this unattractive vegetable was Viscount Charles Townshend (1674–1738), a prominent aristocrat and politician, who toward the end of his life gained the nickname of "Turnip" Townshend because of his dedication to the use of the turnip in new crop-rotation systems.

Clover, alfalfa, and turnips not only helped do away with fallow lands; they also provided excellent winter food for animals, thereby aiding the production of more and better livestock. More livestock also meant more manure. Accordingly, intensive manuring became another way in which scientific farmers could eliminate the need for fallow land. Other improvements in farming methods introduced in the period were more intensive hoeing and weeding, and the use of the seed drill for planting grain. The latter eliminated the old wasteful method of sowing grain by hand, much of it remaining on top to be eaten by birds.

Enclosure was a change that had major social consequences where it occurred. Village life under the open-field system was communal to the extent that decisions as to which crops were to be grown where and when had to be arrived at jointly. Common land afforded the poor not only a place to tether a cow, to fish, or to gather firewood, but to breathe at least a bit of the air of social freedom. Enclosure cost villagers their modest freedoms, as well as the traditional right to help determine how the community's subsistence economy was to be managed. Cottagers (very small landholders) and squatters, who had over generations established a customary right to the use of common lands, were reduced to the rank of landless laborers.

On the Continent, except for Holland, there was nothing comparable to the English advance in scientific farming. Nor, with the notable exception of Spain, was there a pronounced enclosure movement as in England and the Low Countries. Yet despite that fact, European food production became increasingly capitalistic in the seventeenth and eighteenth centuries. Landlords leased farms to tenants and reaped profits as rent. Often they allowed tenants to pay rent in the form of half their crops. This system of sharecropping was most prevalent in France, Italy, and Spain. Farther east, in Prussia, Poland, Hungary, and Russia, landowners continued to rely on unpaid serfs to till the land. But wherever the scale of production and marketing was altered to increase profits, it brought change in its wake.

The eighteenth century saw the introduction of two crops from the New World, maize (Indian corn) and the potato, which eventually resulted in the provision of a more adequate diet for the poor. Since maize can be grown only in areas with substantial periods of sunny and dry weather, its cultivation spread through Italy and the southeastern part of the Continent. Whereas an average ear of grain would yield only about four seeds for every one planted, an ear of maize would yield about seventy or eighty. That made it a "miracle" crop, filling granaries where they had been almost empty before. The potato was an equally miraculous innovation for the European North. Its advantages were numerous: potatoes could be grown on the poorest, sandiest, or wettest of lands where

Improved Farming. The title page of one of many agricultural tracts available to farmers interested in improving their output.

The increasingly capitalistic basis of European agriculture

Introduction of maize and potatoes

nothing else could be raised; they could be fitted into the smallest of patches. Raising potatoes even in small patches was profitable because the yield of potatoes was extraordinarily abundant. Finally, the potato provided an inexpensive means of improving the human diet. It is rich in calories and contains many vitamins and minerals. Northern European peasants initially resisted growing and eating potatoes. Clergymen taught them to fear the plant because it is not mentioned in the Bible. Some claimed that it transmitted leprosy. Still others insisted that it was a cause of flatulence, a property acknowledged by a French authority on diet in 1765, although the writer added, "What is a little wind to the vigorous organs of the peasants and workers?" Yet in the course of the eighteenth century the poor grew accustomed to the potato, although sometimes after considerable pressure. Frederick the Great compelled Prussian peasants to cultivate potatoes until the crop achieved acceptance and became a staple throughout much of northern Germany. By about 1800 the average north German peasant family ate potatoes as a main course at least once a day.

Agriculture was not the only commercial enterprise in early-modern rural Europe. Increasingly, manufactured goods—particularly textiles—were being produced in the countryside, as entrepreneurs battled to circumvent artisanal and guild restrictions that limited production in urban manufacturing centers. Unfettered rural industry was a response to the constantly growing demand of new markets created by the increase in regional, national, and international commerce. Entrepreneurs made use of the so-called putting-out system to address this demand and to reap large profits. Unhampered by guild regulations, which in medieval times had restricted the production and distribution of textiles to maintain price levels, merchants would buy up a stock of raw material, most often wool or flax, which they would then "put out," or supply, to rural workers for carding (combing the fibers) and spinning. Once spun, the yarn or thread was collected by the merchant and passed to rural weavers, who wove it into cloth. Collected once more, the material was processed by other workers at bleaching or dyeing shops and collected for a final time by the entrepreneur who then sold it either to a wholesaler or directly to retail customers.

Although the putting-out phenomenon—or, as it is often referred to, the process of *proto-industrialization*—occurred throughout Europe, it was usually concentrated regionally. Most industrial areas specialized in the production of particular commodities, based on the availability of raw materials. Flanders was a producer of linens; Verviers (in present-day Belgium) of woolens; Silesia of linens. As markets—regional, national, and international—developed, these rural manufacturing areas grew accordingly. Industries employed homeworkers by the thousands. A major mid-eighteenth-century textile firm in Abbeville, France, provided work to 1,800 in central workshops but to 10,000 in their own homes. One of the largest woolen manufacturers in Linz, Austria, in 1786 was employing 35,000, of whom more than 29,000 were domestic spinners.

Rural manufacturing: the putting-out system

Regional specialization

Rural workers accepted this system of manufacture as a means of staving off poverty or possible starvation in years of particularly bad harvests. Domestic textile production involved the entire family. Even the youngest children could participate in the process of cleaning the raw wool. Older children carded. Wives and husbands spun or wove. Spinning, until the invention of the jenny at the end of the eighteenth century (see p. 729), was a far more time-consuming process than weaving, which had been speeded considerably by the Englishman John Kay's early-eighteenth-century invention of the fly-shuttle, a mechanical device that automatically returned the shuttle to its starting place after it had been "thrown" across the loom.

In addition to providing extra income, the putting-out system brought other advantages to rural homeworkers. They could regulate the pace of their labor to some degree, and could abandon it altogether when farm work was available during the planting and harvest seasons. Their ability to work at home was a mixed blessing, however, for conditions in cottages that were wretchedly built and poorly ventilated were often exceedingly cramped and unpleasant, especially when workers were compelled to accommodate a bulky loom within their already crowded living quarters. But domestic labor, however unpleasant, was preferable to work away from home in a shop, where conditions might be even more oppressive under the watchful eye of an unsympathetic master. There were also advantages for the merchant-entrepreneur, who benefited not only

Family production

Advantages of putting-out

Left: **"Rustic Courtship."** This detail from an etching (1785) by the English satirist Thomas Rowlandson suggests the advantages of doorstep domestic industry: natural lighting, improved ventilation, and a chance to converse with visitors. Work under these self-paced conditions, though usually long and hard, was carried on to a personal rhythm. Right: **Artisan and Family**, by Gerard ter Borch. This seventeenth-century wheelwright, though a skilled artisan, is nevertheless depicted as living in a house whose condition suggests near-poverty. Sickness, a bad harvest, unemployment—any of these might easily drive him and his family over the edge.

from the absence of guild restrictions, but from the fact that none of his capital was tied up in expensive equipment. (Spinners usually owned their spinning wheels; weavers either owned or rented their looms.) Governments appreciated the advantages of the system too, viewing it as one way to alleviate the ever-present problem of rural poverty. The French abolished the traditional privileges of urban manufacturers in 1762, acknowledging by law what economic demand had long since established: the widespread practice of unrestricted rural domestic production. By that time, proto-industrialization prevailed not only in northern France, but in the east and northeast of England, in Flanders, and in much of northern Germany—all areas where a mixed agricultural and manufacturing economy made economic sense to those engaged in it as entrepreneurs and producers.

Later generations, looking back nostalgically on the putting-out system, often compared it favorably to the factory system that displaced it. Life within the system's "family economy" was seldom other than hard, however. While workers could set their own pace to some extent, they remained subject to the demands of small, often inexperienced entrepreneurs who, misjudging their markets, might overload spinners and weavers with work at one moment, then abandon them for lack of orders the next. Though it often kept families from starvation, the system did little to mitigate the monotony and harshness of their lives. Its pressures are crudely if eloquently expressed in an English ballad in which the weaver husband responds to his wife's complaint that she has no time to sit at the "bobbin wheel," what with the washing and baking and milking she must do. No matter, the husband replies. She must "stir about and get things done./ For all things must aside be laid,/ when we want help about our trade."

Quality of life under the family system

Textiles were not the only manufactured goods produced in the countryside. In France, for example, metal-working was as much a rural as an urban occupation, with migrant laborers providing a work force for small, self-contained shops. In various parts of Germany, the same sort of unregulated domestic manufacturing base prevailed: in the Black Forest for clock-making, in Thuringia for toys. English production of iron grew fivefold from the mid-sixteenth to the late seventeenth century. The phenomenon of proto-industrialization increased demand for raw materials. Pressure on timber reserves for fuel led to widespread deforestation, with a resulting exploitation of coal reserves, particularly in the Rhineland, England, and the south Netherlands. In 1550 the English mined 200,000 tons of coal. By 1800 that figure had risen to 3 million.

Other rural manufacturing activities

Rural industry flourished despite the fact that for most of the early-modern period transportation systems remained rudimentary. In all but a very few cases, roads were little more than ill-defined tracks, full of holes as much as four feet deep, and all but impassable in the rain, when carts and carriages might stay mired in deep ruts for days. One of the few paved roads ran from Paris to Orléans, the main river port of France, but that was a notable exception. In general, no one could travel more than

Rudimentary transportation systems

Outside an Inn, by Thomas Rowlandson. Coaching inns brought the outside world into the lives of isolated villagers. Note the absence of any clearly defined roadway.

12 miles an hour—"post haste" at a gallop on horseback—and speed such as that could be achieved only at the expense of fresh horses at each stage of the ride. In the late seventeenth century, a journey of 60 miles over good roads could be accomplished in twenty-four hours, provided that the weather was fair. To travel by coach from Paris to Lyons, a distance of approximately 250 miles, took ten days. Merchants ran great risks when they shipped perishable goods. Breakables were not expected to survive for more than 15 miles. Transportation of goods by boat along coastal routes was far more reliable than shipment overland, though in both cases the obstacle of excessive tolls was frequently inhibiting. In 1675, English merchants calculated that it was cheaper to ship coal 300 miles by water than to send it 15 miles overland, so impassable were the roads to heavy transport. Madrid, without a river, relied upon mules and carts for its supplies. By the mid-eighteenth century, the city required the services of over half a million mules and 150,000 carts, all forced to labor their way into town over rugged terrain. In 1698, a bronze statue of Louis XIV was sent on its way from the river port of Auxerre, southeast of Paris, to the town of Dijon. The cart in which it was dispatched was soon stuck in the mud, however, and the statue remained marooned in a wayside shed for twenty-one years, until the road was improved to the point that it could continue its belated journey.

Gradually in the eighteenth century transportation improved. The French established a Road and Bridge Corps of civil engineers, with a separate training school, in 1747. Work began in the 1670s on a series of canals that eventually linked the English Channel to the Mediterranean. In England, private investors, spearheaded by that inveterate canal-builder the duke of Bridgewater, constructed a network of waterways and turnpikes tying provincial towns to each other and to London. With improved roads came stagecoaches, feared at first for their speed and recklessness much as automobiles were feared in the early twentieth century.

Transportation improvements

The Duke of Bridgewater Canal

People objected to being crowded into narrow carriages designed to reduce the load pulled by the team of horses. "If by chance a traveller with a big stomach or wide shoulders appears," an unhappy passenger lamented, "one has to groan or desert." But improvements such as stagecoaches and canals, much as they might increase the profits or change the pattern of life for the wealthy, meant little to the average European. Barges plied the waterways from the north to the south of France, but most men and women traveled no farther than to their neighboring market town, on footpaths or on rutted cart tracks eight feet wide, which had served their ancestors in much the same way.

Urban manufacturing centers

That industry flourished to the extent it did, despite the hazards and inefficiencies of transport, is a measure of the strength of Europe's ever-increasing commercial impulse. Rural proto-industrialization did not prevent the growth of important urban manufacturing centers. In northern France, many of the million or so men and women employed in the textile trade lived and worked in cities such as Amiens, Lille, and Rheims. The eighteenth-century rulers of Prussia made it their policy to develop Berlin as a manufacturing center, taking advantage of an influx of French Protestants to establish the silk-weaving industry there. Even in cities, however, work was likely to be carried out in small shops, where anywhere from five to twenty journeymen labored under the supervision of a master to manufacture the particular products of their craft. Despite the fact that manufacturing was centered in homes and workshops, by 1700 these industries were increasing significantly in scale as many workshops grouped together to form a single manufacturing district. Textile industries led this trend, but it was true as well of brewing, distilling, soap and candle-making, tanning, and the manufacturing of various chemical substances for the bleaching and dyeing of cloth. These and other industries might often employ several thousand men and women congregated together into towns—or larger communities of several towns—all dedicated to the same occupation and production.

Techniques in some crafts remained much as they had been for centuries. In others, however, inventions changed the pattern of work as well as the nature of the product. Knitting frames, simple devices to speed the manufacture of textile goods, made their appearance in England and Holland. Wire-drawing machines and slitting mills, the latter enabling nailmakers to convert iron bars into rods, spread from Germany into England. Mechanically powered saws were introduced into shipyards and elsewhere across Europe in the seventeenth century. The technique of calico printing, the application of colored designs directly to textiles, was imported from the Far East. New and more efficient printing presses appeared, first in Holland and then elsewhere. The Dutch invented a machine called a "camel," by which the hulls of ships could be raised in the water so that they could be more easily repaired.

New machinery and techniques

Innovations of this kind were not readily accepted by workers. Labor-saving machines such as mechanical saws threw men out of work. Artisans, especially those organized into guilds, were by nature conservative, anxious to protect not only their restrictive "rights," but the secrets of their trade. Often, too, the state would intervene to block the widespread use of machines if they threatened to increase unemployment. The Dutch and some German states, for example, prohibited the use of what was described as a "devilish invention," a ribbon-loom capable of weaving sixteen or more ribbons at the same time. Sometimes the spread of new techniques was curtailed by states in order to protect the livelihood of powerful commercial interest groups. On behalf of both domestic textile manufacturers and importers of Indian goods, calico printing was for a time outlawed in both France and England. The cities of Paris and Lyons and several German states banned the use of indigo dyes because they were manufactured abroad.

Adverse reaction to changing machinery and processes

Changes that occurred in trade, commerce, agriculture, and industry, though large-scale phenomena, nevertheless touched individual men and women directly. Enclosure stripped away customary rights. An English cottager by 1780 might well have lost his family's age-old right to tether a cow on the common, which was now an enclosed and "scientifically" manured corn field. Markets developed to receive and transmit goods from around the world altered the lives of those whose work now responded to their rhythms. A linen weaver in rural Holland in 1700, whose peasant father had eked out a meager living from his subsistence farm, now supplemented his income by working for an Amsterdam entrepreneur, and paid progressively less for his food as a result of the cheap grain imported to the Low Countries across the Baltic Sea from eastern Europe. A carpenter in an early-eighteenth-century Toulon shipyard lost his job when his employer purchased a mechanical saw that did the work of five men. A sailor on one of the ships built in that Toulon shipyard died at sea off the French colony of Martinique, an island of which he had never heard, at a distance so far from home as to be inconceivable to

The human implications of change

those who mourned his death when they learned of it months later. Meanwhile, in vast areas of southern and eastern Europe, men and women led lives that followed the same patterns they had for centuries, all but untouched by the changes taking place elsewhere. They clung to the life they knew, a life which, if harsh, was at least predictable.

THE COMMERCIAL REVOLUTION

Capitalism defined

Hand in hand with changes in agriculture and industry came an alteration in the manner in which commerce was organized and trade conducted. So extensive were changes in these areas over the course of two hundred years that it is accurate to speak of them as comprising a commercial revolution. The early-modern world of commerce and industry grew increasingly to be governed by the assumptions of capitalism and mercantilism. Reduced to its simplest terms, *capitalism* is a system of production, distribution, and exchange, in which accumulated wealth is invested by private owners for the sake of gain. Its essential features are private enterprise, competition for markets, and business for profit. Generally it involves the wage system as a method of payment of workers—that is, a mode of payment based not on the amount of wealth workers create, but rather upon their willingness to compete with one another for jobs. Capitalism represented a direct challenge to the semi-static economy of the medieval guilds, in which production and trade were—in theory, at least—conducted for the benefit of society and with only a reasonable charge for the service rendered, instead of unlimited profits. Capitalism is a system designed to encourage commercial expansion beyond the local level, on a national and international scale. Guildmasters had neither the money (capital) to support nor the knowledge to organize and direct commercial enterprises beyond their own towns. Activity on that wider scale demanded the resources and expertise of wealthy and experienced entrepreneurs. The capitalist studied patterns of international trade. He knew where markets were and how to manipulate them to his advantage.

The medieval origins of mercantilism

Capitalism is a system designed to reward the individual. In contrast, *mercantilist* doctrine emphasized direct governmental intervention in economic policy to enhance the general prosperity of the state and to increase political authority. Mercantilism was by no means a new idea. It was in fact a variation on the medieval notion that the populace of any particular town was a community with a common wealth, and that the economic well-being of such communities depended on the willingness of that populace to work at whatever task God or their rulers assigned them to benefit the local community as a whole. The mercantilism of the seventeenth and eighteenth centuries translated this earlier concept of community as a privileged, but regimented, economic unit from the level of towns to the level of the entire state. The theory and practice of mercantilism reflected the expansion of state power. Responding to the needs of war, rulers enforced mercantilist policies, often by increasingly autocratic methods, certain that the needs of the state must take precedence over those of individuals.

Mercantilist theory held that a state's power depended on its actual, calculable wealth. The degree to which a state could remain self-sufficient, importing as little as necessary while exporting as much as possible, was the clearest gauge not only of its economic prosperity but of its power. This doctrine had profound effects on state policy. First, it led to the establishment and development of overseas colonies. Colonies, mercantilists reasoned, would, as part of the national community, provide it with raw materials, including precious metals in some instances, which would otherwise have to be obtained outside the community. Second, the doctrine of mercantilism inspired state governments to encourage industrial production and trade, both sources of revenue that would increase the state's income.

Although most western European statesmen were prepared to endorse mercantilist goals in principle, the degree to which their policies reflected those goals varied according to national circumstance. Spain, despite its insistence on closed colonial markets and its determination to amass a fortune in bullion, never succeeded in attaining the economic self-sufficiency that mercantilist theory demanded. But mercantilism, which appealed at least in theory to the rulers in Madrid, had little attraction for the merchants of Amsterdam. The Dutch recognized that the United Provinces were too small to permit them to achieve economic self-sufficiency. Throughout the seventeenth and eighteenth centuries the Dutch remained dedicated in principle and practice to free trade, often investing, contrary to mercantilist doctrine, in the commercial enterprises of other countries and promoting national prosperity by encouraging the rest of Europe to rely upon Amsterdam as a hub of international finance and trade.

Capitalism and mercantilism represented a coming together of theories and practices imposed often sporadically and seldom systematically by entrepreneurs and governments during the early-modern period. The result over time, however, produced important consequences for individuals as well as for nations and regions. Laboring men and women frequently found themselves the victims of the policies and programs of those who, either as individuals or state functionaries, managed and controlled dynamic, expansionist national economies. For example, capitalists could afford to invest in large quantities of manufactured goods, and if necessary, hold them unsold until they could command a high price, favorable to them but damaging to the budget of humbler consumers. Mercantilism persuaded policy-makers to discourage domestic consumption, since goods purchased on the home market reduced the goods available for export. Government policy was thus to keep wages low, so that laborers would not have more money to spend than it took to provide them with basic food and shelter.

Together, governments and entrepreneurs designed new institutions that facilitated the expansion of global commerce during the seventeenth and eighteenth centuries to effect the commercial revolution of early-modern Europe. While local and regional markets continued to flourish,

Mercantilism in theory

Mercantilism in practice

Effects of capitalism and mercantilism on individuals

International centers and commercial routes

international centers such as Antwerp, Amsterdam, and London became hubs for a flourishing and complex system of international trade. An increasing number of European men and women grew dependent upon the commerce that brought both necessities and luxuries into their lives. The eighteenth-century essayist Joseph Addison sang the praises of the beneficient merchant prince: "There are not more useful members in the Commonwealth," he wrote. "They distribute the gifts of nature, find work for the poor, and wealth to the rich, and magnificence to the great."

Elements of the commercial
revolution: (1) increased capital

Enterprise on this new scale depended on the availability of capital for investment. And that capital was generated primarily by a long-term, gradual increase in agricultural prices throughout much of the period. Had that increase been sharp, it would probably have produced enough hunger and suffering to retard rather than stimulate economic growth. Had there been no increase, however, the resulting stagnation produced by marginal profits would have proved equally detrimental to expansion. Agricultural entrepreneurs had surplus capital to invest in trade; bankers put that surplus to use to expand their commercial enterprises. Together, capitalist investors and merchants profited.

(2) The rise of banking

Banks played a vital role in the history of this expansion. Strong religious and moral disapproval of lending money at interest meant that banking had enjoyed a dubious reputation in the Middle Ages. Because the Church did come to allow profit-making on commercial risks, however, banks in Italy and Germany were organized during the fourteenth and fifteenth centuries, most notably by the Medici family in Florence and the Fugger family in Augsburg. The rise of these private financial

A Square in Seventeenth-Century Amsterdam. This contemporary painting emphasizes the central role independent merchants, consumers, and trade played in Dutch city life.

houses was followed by the establishment of government banks, reflecting the mercantilist goal of serving the monetary needs of the state. The first such institution, the Bank of Sweden, was founded in 1657. The Bank of England was established in 1694, at a time when England's emergence as a world commercial power guaranteed that institution a leading role in international finance. The growth of banking was necessarily accompanied by the adoption of various aids to financial transactions on a large scale, further evidence of a commercial revolution. Credit facilities were extended and payment by check introduced, thereby encouraging an increase in the volume of trade, since the credit resources of the banks could now be expanded far beyond the actual amounts of cash in their vaults.

International commercial expansion called forth larger units of business organization. The prevailing unit of production and trade in the Middle Ages was the workshop or store owned by an individual or a family. Partnerships were also quite common, in spite of the grave disadvantage of unlimited liability of each of its members for the debts of the entire firm. Obviously neither of these units was well adapted to business involving heavy risks and a huge investment of capital. The attempt to devise a more suitable business organization resulted in the formation of *regulated companies,* which were associations of merchants banded together for a common venture. Members did not pool their resources but agreed merely to cooperate for their mutual advantage and to abide by certain definite regulations.

(3) Changes in business organization: (a) regulated companies

The commercial revolution was facilitated in the seventeenth century when the regulated company was largely superseded by a new type of organization at once more compact and broader in scope. This was the *joint-stock company,* formed through the issuance of shares of capital to a considerable number of investors. Those who purchased the shares might or might not take part in the work of the company. Whether they did or not, they were joint owners of the business and therefore entitled to share in its profits in accordance with the amount they had invested. The joint-stock company of the early-modern period is best understood not so much as a conscious precursor of capitalist endeavor but as a pragmatic attempt at commercial expansion by both individuals and the state, its structure dictated by present opportunity and circumstance. Initially, for example, the Dutch United East India Company, one of the earliest joint-stock ventures, had expected to pay off its investors ten years after its founding in 1602, much as regulated companies had. Yet when that time came, the directors recognized the impossibility of the plan. By 1612, the company's assets were scattered—as ships, wharves, warehouses, and cargoes—across the globe. As a result, the directors urged those anxious to realize their profits to sell their shares on the Amsterdam exchange to other eager investors, thereby ensuring the sustained operation of their enterprise and, in the process, establishing a practice of continuous financing that was soon to become common.

(b) joint-stock companies

While most of the early joint-stock companies were founded for commercial ventures, some were organized later in industry. A number of the

(c) chartered companies

The Lyons Stock Exchange. Built in 1749, the stylish and impressive facade of the structure bespeaks the prominent role of commerce in French society.

outstanding trading combinations were also *chartered companies*. They held charters from the government granting a monopoly of the trade in a certain locality and conferring extensive authority over the inhabitants, and were thus an example of the way capitalist and mercantilist interests might coincide. Through a charter of this kind, the British East India Company undertook the exploitation of vast territories on the Indian subcontinent, and remained virtual ruler there until the end of the eighteenth century.

(d) partnership between state and commerce

In most European countries, and particularly in France, government and commerce generally worked to promote each other's interests. The exception was the Dutch, who almost exclusively put their capital to work not for the state but for the rest of Europe. In time of war, governments called upon commercial capitalists to assist in the financing of their campaigns. When England went to war against France in 1689, for example, the government had no long-range borrowing mechanism available to it; during the next quarter-century the merchant community, through the Bank of England, assisted the government in raising over £170 million and in stabilizing the national debt at £40 million. In return, trading companies used the war to increase long-distance commercial traffic at the expense of their French enemy, and exerted powerful pressure on the government to secure treaties that would work to their advantage.

(4) A money economy

A final important feature of the commercial revolution was the development of a more efficient money economy. Money had been used widely since the revival of trade in the eleventh century. Nevertheless, there were few coins with a value that was recognized other than locally; no country could be said to have had a uniform monetary system. The growth of trade and industry in the commercial revolution accentuated the need for more stable and uniform monetary systems. The problem was solved by the adoption by every important state of a standard system of money to be used for all transactions within its borders. Much time elapsed, however, before the reform was complete.

The economic institutions just described never remained static, but rather existed in a continuously volatile state of development. This volatility, in turn, had a direct effect on the lives of individual men and women. One major result of overseas expansion, for example, was the severe inflation caused by the increase in the supply of silver that plagued Europe at the end of the sixteenth century. Price fluctuations, in turn, produced further economic instability. Businessmen were tempted to expand their enterprises too rapidly; bankers extended credit so liberally that their principal borrowers, especially noblemen, often defaulted on loans. In both Spain and Italy, wages failed to keep pace with rising prices, which brought severe and continuing hardships to the lower classes. Impoverishment was rife in the cities, and bandits flourished in the rural areas.

> Inflation caused by increased availability of silver

Speculative greed could, and sometimes did, threaten to bring a nation to its knees. Though feverish speculation characterized the early-modern period as a whole, the most notorious bouts of that particular economic disease occurred in the early eighteenth century. The so-called South Sea Bubble was the result of deliberate inflation of the value of stock of the South Sea Company in England, whose offer to assume the national debt led to unwarranted confidence in the company's future. When buoyant hopes gave way to fears, investors made frantic attempts to dispose of their shares for whatever they would bring. The crash that came in 1720 was the inevitable result.

> The South Sea Bubble

During the years when the South Sea Bubble was being inflated in England, the French were engaged in a similar wave of speculative madness. In 1715 a Scotsman by the name of John Law persuaded the regent of France to adopt his scheme for paying off the national debt through the issuance of paper money and to grant him the privilege of organizing the Mississippi Company for the colonization and exploitation of Louisiana. As happened in England, stock prices soared in response to an alluring but basically unrealistic scheme. Stories were told of butchers and tailors who made fortunes from their few initial shares. Ultimately, however, panic set in, and in 1720 the Mississippi Bubble burst in a wild panic.

> The Mississippi Bubble

COLONIZATION AND OVERSEAS TRADE

The institutions of the commercial revolution—banks, credit facilities, joint-stock companies, monetary systems—were designed specifically to assist both capitalist entrepreneurs and mercantilist policy-makers in the development and exploitation of trade. Despite the existence of increasingly profitable European commercial routes and centers, the most visible

> Spanish colonization

evidence of the economic expansionism of early-modern Europe were the overseas colonies and trading posts developed and exploited during the seventeenth and eighteenth centuries. Following the exploits of the *conquistadores,* the Spanish established colonial governments in Peru and in Mexico, which they controlled from Madrid in proper mercantilist fashion by a Council of the Indies. The governments of Philip II and his successors were determined to defend their monopoly in the New World. They issued trading licenses only to Spanish merchants; exports and imports passed only through the port of Seville (later the more navigable port of Cadiz), where they were registered at the government-operated Casa de Contratación, or customs house. In their heyday, Spanish traders circled the globe. Because of the lucrative market for silver in East Asia, they found it well worth their while to establish an outpost in far-off Manila in the Philippines, where Asian silk was exchanged for South American bullion. The silk was then shipped back to Spain by way of the Mexican ports of Acapulco and Veracruz. The search for gold and silver was accompanied by the establishment of permanent colonies in Central and South America and on the east and west coasts of North America in what are now the states of Florida and California.

Spain's predominance did not deter other countries from attempting to win a share of the treasure for themselves. Probably the boldest challengers were the English, and their leading buccaneer the "sea dog" Sir Francis Drake, who three times raided the east and west coasts of Spanish America and who, in 1587, the year before the Armada set sail on its ill-fated voyage north, "singed the beard of the Spanish king" by attacking the Spanish fleet at its anchorage in Cadiz harbor. Yet despite dashing heroics of that sort, the English could do no more than dent the Spanish trade.

English colonists sought profits elsewhere by establishing agricultural settlements in North America and the Caribbean basin. Their first permanent, though ultimately unsuccessful, colony was Jamestown, in Virginia, founded in 1607. Over the next forty years, 80,000 English emigrants sailed to over twenty autonomous settlements in the New World. In this instance, however, religious freedom, as well as economic gain, was often the motive of the settlers. The renowned band of "pilgrim fathers" that landed on the New England shores in 1620 was but one of a large number of dissident groups, both Protestant and Catholic, that sought to escape attempts to impose religious conformity. Religion also played a role in the efforts of the Spanish to colonize Central and South America, and of the French to penetrate the hinterlands of North America. Roman Catholic Jesuit missionaries, intent upon the conversion of native Americans to Christianity, joined fur traders in journeys across the continent to the Great Lakes and the Mississippi.

Both England and France were quick to extract profit from their expanding colonial empires. England's agricultural colonies were producing crops in high demand throughout Europe. The success of colonial planters encouraged the governments of both Oliver Cromwell and

Challenges to Spanish
predominance

English colonization

The growth of English colonial
regulation

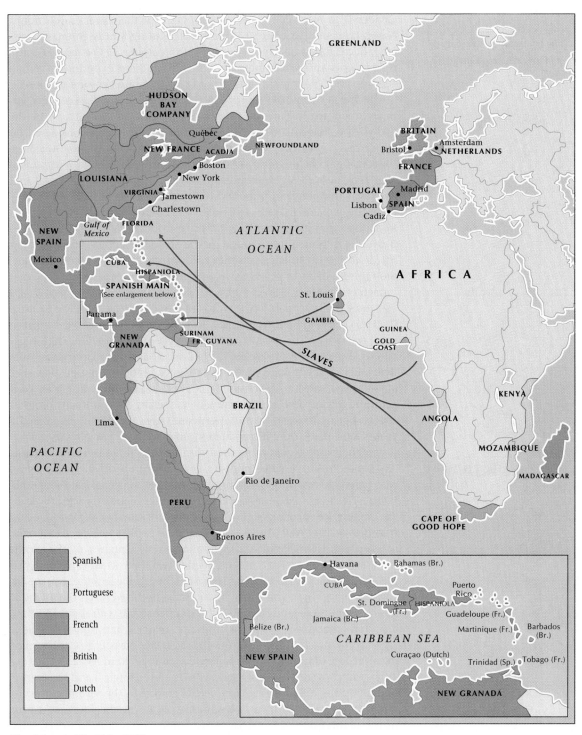

The Atlantic World in 1713

Charles II to intervene in the management of their overseas economy. Navigation acts, passed in 1651 and 1660, and rigorously enforced thereafter, decreed that all exports from English colonies to the mother country be carried in English ships, and forbade the direct exporting of certain "enumerated" products directly from the colonies to Continental ports.

Sugar and tobacco

The most valuable of those products were sugar and tobacco. Sugar, virtually unknown in Europe earlier, had become a popular luxury by the end of the sixteenth century. Where once it had been considered no more than a medicine, one observer now noted that the wealthy were "devouring it out of gluttony." Sugarcane was grown in the West Indies after 1650 in ever-larger amounts. In the eighteenth century, the value of the sugar that England imported from its small island colonies there—Barbados, Jamaica, St. Kitts, and others—exceeded the value of its imports from the vast subcontinents of China and India. Although the tobacco plant was imported into Europe by the Spaniards about fifty years after the discovery of America, another half-century passed before Europeans took up the habit of smoking. At first the plant was believed to possess miraculous healing powers and was referred to as "divine tobacco" and "our holy herb nicotian." (The word "nicotine" derives from the name of the French ambassador to Portugal, Jean Nicot, who brought the tobacco plant to France.) The practice of smoking was popularized by English explorers, especially by Sir Walter Raleigh, who had learned to smoke while living among the Indians of Virginia. It spread rapidly through all classes of European society. Governments at first joined the Church in condemning the use of tobacco because of its socially and spiritually harmful effects, but by the end of the seventeenth century, having realized the profits to be made from its production, they were encouraging its use.

The French in America

French colonial policy matured during the administration of Louis XIV's mercantilist finance minister, Jean Baptiste Colbert (1619–1683), who perceived of overseas expansion as an integral part of state economic policy. He organized joint-stock companies to compete with those of the English. He encouraged the development of lucrative sugar-producing colonies in the West Indies, the largest of which was St. Domingue (present-day Haiti). France also dominated the interior of the North American continent. Frenchmen traded furs and preached Christianity to the Indians in a vast territory that stretched from Acadia and the St. Lawrence River in the northeast to Louisiana in the west. Yet the financial returns from these lands were hardly commensurate with their size. Furs, fish, and tobacco were exported to home markets, but not in sufficient amounts to match the profits from the sugar colonies of the Caribbean or from the line of trading posts the French maintained in India.

The Dutch in the Far East

The Dutch were even more successful than the English and the French in establishing a flourishing commercial empire in the seventeenth century. They succeeded in establishing a colony on the southern tip of Africa at the Cape of Good Hope. Far more important, however, were their commercial adventurings in South Asia. Their joint-stock East India Company, founded in 1602, rivaled its English counterpart in Asia, gain-

The Dutch East India Company Warehouse and Timber Wharf at Amsterdam. The substantial warehouse, the stockpiles of lumber, and the company ship under construction in the foreground illustrate the degree to which overseas commerce could stimulate the economy of the mother country.

ing firm control of Sumatra, Borneo, and the Moluccas, or Spice Islands, and driving Portuguese traders from an area where they had heretofore enjoyed an undisturbed commercial dominion. The result was a Dutch monopoly in pepper, cinnamon, nutmeg, mace, and cloves. The Dutch also secured an exclusive right to trade with the Japanese, and maintained outposts in China and India as well. In the Western Hemisphere, their achievements were less spectacular. Following a series of trade wars with England, they surrendered their North American colony of New Amsterdam (subsequently renamed New York) in 1667, retaining Surinam, off the northern coast of South America, as well as the islands of Curaçao and Tobago in the West Indies in compensation.

The fortunes of these commercial empires rose and fell in the course of the seventeenth and eighteenth centuries. The Spanish, mired in persistent economic stagnation and embroiled in a succession of expensive wars and domestic rebellions, were powerless to prevent losses to their empire. Their merchant marine, once a match for cunning pirate-admirals like Drake, was by the middle of the seventeenth century unable to protect itself from attack by its more spirited commercial rivals. In a war with Spain in the 1650s, the English captured not only the island of Jamaica but treasure ships lying off the Spanish harbor of Cadiz. Further profit was obtained by bribing Spanish customs officials on a grand scale. During the second half of the century, two-thirds of the imported goods sold in Spanish colonies were smuggled in by Dutch, English, and French traders. By 1700, though Spain still possessed a colonial empire, it was one that lay at

The decline of the Spanish commercial empire

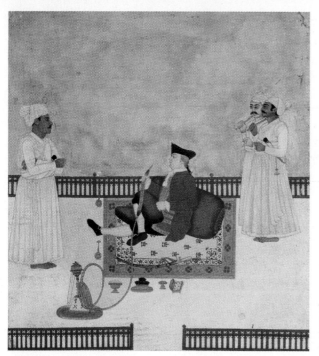

The Rewards of Commercial Exploitation. An English employee of the East India Company enjoying his ease and his opium, as depicted by an eighteenth-century Indian artist.

the mercy of its more dynamic rivals. A brief revival of its fortunes under more enlightened leadership in the mid-eighteenth century did nothing to prevent its ultimate eclipse.

English trade with Portugal and its colonies

Portugal, too, found it impossible to prevent foreign penetration of its colonial economies. The English worked diligently and successfully to win commercial advantages there. They obtained concessions to export woolens duty-free into Portugal itself in return for similar preferential treatment for Portuguese wines. (The notorious affection of the English upper class for port wine dates from the signing of the Treaty of 1703.) English trade with the mother country led in time to English trade with the Portuguese colony of Brazil, and indeed to the opening of commercial offices in Rio de Janeiro.

Anglo-French rivalry

During the eighteenth century, however, a growing Anglo-French rivalry in India stole the commercial spotlight from the Dutch spice monopoly in the Far East. The French and English East India Companies employed mercenaries to establish and expand trading areas such as Madras, Bombay, and Pondichéry. By exploiting indigenous industries, European capitalists continued to increase the flow of fine cotton textiles, tea, and spices, which passed through these commercial depots on their way to Europe. The struggle for worldwide economic dominance reached a peak in the mid-eighteenth century (see pp. 628–629). At that time the Anglo-French rivalry in India was resolved in England's favor. As a sign of France's defeat, in 1769 the French East India Company was dissolved.

Despite the commercial importance of India, however, patterns of world trade came increasingly to be dominated by western routes that had developed in response to the lucrative West Indian sugar industry, and to the demand for slaves from Africa to work the plantations in the Caribbean. Here England again eventually assumed the lead. Typically, a ship might begin its voyage from New England with a consignment of rum and sail to Africa, where the rum would be exchanged for a cargo of slaves. From the west coast of Africa the ship would then cross the South Atlantic to the sugar colonies of Jamaica or Barbados, where slaves would be traded for molasses, which would make the final leg of the journey to New England, where it would be made into rum. A variant triangle might see cheap manufactured goods move from England to Africa, where they would be traded for slaves. Those slaves would then be shipped to Virginia and exchanged for tobacco, which would be shipped to England and processed there for sale in Continental markets. Other eighteenth-century trade routes were more direct: the Spanish, French, Portuguese, and Dutch all engaged in the slave trade between Africa and Central and South America; the Spanish attempted, in vain, to retain a mercantilist monopoly on direct trade between Cadiz and their South American colonies; others sailed from England, France, or North America to the Caribbean and back again. And of course trade continued to flourish between Europe and the Near and Far East. But the triangular western routes, dictated by the grim economic symbiosis of sugar and slaves, remained dominant.

The cultivation of sugar and tobacco depended on slave labor, and as demand for those products increased, so did the traffic in black slaves, without whose labor those products could not be raised or harvested. At the height of the Atlantic slave trade in the eighteenth century, somewhere between 75,000 and 90,000 blacks were shipped across the Atlantic yearly: 6 million in the eighteenth century, out of a total of over 9 million for the entire history of the trade. About 35 percent went to English and French Caribbean plantations, 5 percent (roughly 450,000) to North America, and the rest to the Portuguese colony of Brazil and to Spanish colonies in South America. Although run as a monopoly by various governments in the sixteenth and early seventeenth centuries, in its heyday the slave trade was open to private entrepreneurs who operated ports on the West African coast. Traders exchanged cheap Indian cloth, metal goods, rum, and firearms with African slave merchants in return for their human cargo. Already disoriented and degraded by their capture at the hands of rival tribes, black men, women, and children were packed by the hundreds into the holds of slave ships for the gruesome "middle passage" across the Atlantic (so called to distinguish it from the ship's voyage from Europe to Africa, and from the slave colony back to Europe again). Shackled to the decks, without sanitary facilities, the black "cargo" suffered horribly; the mortality rate, however, remained at about 10 or 11 percent, not much higher than the rate for a normal sea voyage of one hundred days or more. Since traders had to invest as much as £10 per slave in their enterprise, they ensured that their consignment would reach its destination in good enough shape to be sold for a profit.

Increasing dominance of western trade routes

The slave trade

How Slaves Were Stowed Aboard Ship during the Middle Passage. Men were "housed" on the right; women on the left; children in the middle. The human cargo was jammed onto platforms six feet wide without sufficient headroom to permit an adult to sit up. This diagram is from evidence gathered by English abolitionists and depicts conditions on the Liverpool slave ship *Brookes*.

High profits from slaves

Female Slave Being Whipped. After capture by rival tribes, black men, women, and children could expect further suffering, both during the middle passage and after reaching their final destinations.

The trade was risky, dependent on a good wind and fair weather, and competition was increasingly keen. Yet profits could run high, occasionally as much as 300 percent. Demand for slaves remained constant throughout the eighteenth century. By the 1780s, there were more than 500,000 slaves on the largest French plantation island, St. Domingue, and 200,000 or more on the English counterpart, Jamaica. Those numbers reflected the expanding world market for slave-grown crops. As long as there was a market for the crops cultivated by slaves—as long as the economy relied to the extent it did upon slave labor—governments would remain unwilling to halt the system that, as one Englishman wrote in 1749, provided "an unexhaustible fund of wealth to this nation."

Apologists for the slave trade argued that though there was reason to rejoice that slavery had been banished from the continent of Europe (forgetting, apparently, the extent to which it continued to exist east of the Elbe in the form of serfdom), it remained a necessity in other parts of the world. Not until the very end of the eighteenth century did Europeans begin to protest the ghastly traffic. Public pressure, first from Quakers and then from others motivated by either religious or humanitarian zeal, helped put an end to the trade in England in 1807, and to slavery itself in British colonies in 1833. Slavery in French colonies was abolished in 1793, but only after slaves had risen in massive revolt on St. Domingue. Elsewhere, in Latin and North America, slavery lasted well into the nineteenth century—in the United States, until the Civil War of 1861–1865. The racism it promulgated has lasted until the present day.

The slave trade was an integral part of the history of the dramatic rise of English and French commerce during the eighteenth century. French colonial trade, valued at 25 million livres in 1716, rose to 263 million livres in 1789. In England, during roughly the same period, foreign trade increased in value from £10 million to £40 million, the latter amount more than twice that for France. These figures suggest the degree to which statecraft and private enterprise were bound to each other. If merchants depended on their government to provide a navy to protect and defend their overseas investments, governments depended equally on entrepreneurship, not only to generate money to build ships, but to sustain the trade upon which national power had come to rely so heavily.

LIFE WITHIN A SOCIETY OF ORDERS

Despite the economic and demographic shifts that were occurring in early-modern Europe, society remained divided into traditional orders or ranks. The changes we have been concerned with occurred against the continuity of long-accepted social divisions based upon birth and occupation. As circumstances altered, the fluid patterns of economic reorganization clashed with older, rigid assumptions about the place of men and women within a preordained—to many, a divinely ordained—social hierarchy. Jean Bodin, the French philosopher, wrote in 1570 that the division of the citizenry into "the three orders of nobles, clergy and people" was no more than natural. "There never was a commonwealth, real or imaginary, where citizens were in truth equal in all rights and privileges. Some always have more, some less than the rest." And some had none.

Most would have recognized infinitely subtle subdivisions among and between the three orders Bodin specified. Ranks were demarcated by rights and privileges. "Freedom" was understood as one such privilege, as a benefit, bestowed not upon all men and women but upon special groups whose position "freed" them to do certain things others could not do, or freed them from the burden of doing certain things that were required of others. An English landowner was, because of the position his property conferred upon him, privileged, and therefore "free," to participate directly in the election of his government. A French nobleman was privileged, and therefore "free," to avoid the heavy burden of taxation levied upon the unprivileged orders. A German tailor who had served out his seven-year apprenticeship was free to set up his own shop for profit, something an unapprenticed man was not traditionally "at liberty" to do, no matter what his degree of skill with needle and thread. The master tailor's position conferred his freedom, just as the position of aristocrat and property owner conferred theirs.

The members of the higher orders attempted at all times to live their lives in a particular style that accorded with their rank. The nobility was taught from birth to consider itself above and apart from the rest of society. Merchants and manufacturers were just as insistent upon maintaining the traditional marks of privilege that separated them from artisans and peasants. Sumptuary laws decreed what could be worn and by whom. An edict promulgated in the German principality of Brunswick in 1738, for example, forbade servant girls to use silk dress materials, to wear gold or silver ornaments, or shoes of anything but plain black leather. A similar seventeenth-century law in the Polish city of Posen prohibited the wives of burghers from wearing capes or long hair. Style was not simply a matter of current whim. It was a badge of status and was carefully adhered to as such. An aristocratic lady powdered her hair and rouged her cheeks as a

Orders, privilege, and freedom

The meaning of "freedom"

The theater of a society of orders

Middle-Class Fashion. In this seventeenth-century portrait of a Dutch burgomaster and his family, the patriarch and his wife are wearing the costume of an earlier generation, while the children are clothed in the current style. All display the opulence characteristic of their prosperous class.

sign that she was an aristocrat. Life within a society of orders demanded a certain degree of theatricality, especially from those at the top of the social hierarchy. Aristocrats "acted" their part in a calculatedly self-conscious way. Their manner of speech, their dress, the ceremonial sword they were privileged to wear, the title by which they were addressed—these were the props of a performance that constantly emphasized the distinctions between those above and those below. Noble families lived in castles, chateaux, or country houses whose size and antiquity were a further proclamation of superiority. When they built new mansions, as the *nouveau riche* capitalist English gentry did in the eighteenth century, they made certain their elaborate houses and spacious private parks declared their newfound power. The English politician Robert Walpole had an entire village moved to improve the view from his grand new residence.

The nobility

The vast majority of men and women defined and understood social hierarchy in terms of the rural communities in which they lived. At the head of those communities, in all likelihood, stood a representative of the noble elite. The nobility probably numbered about 3 percent of the total population of Europe. The percentage was higher in Russia, Poland, Hungary, and Spain; lower in Germany, France, and England. Ownership of a landed estate was proof of one's elevated rank. Generally speaking, the more land one possessed, the higher one stood within the social hierarchy. In Hungary, five noble families owned about 14 percent of the entire country; the greatest of these, Prince Esterházy, controlled the lives of more than half a million peasants. Most noblemen were not nearly so

Gala Dinner at Schoenbrunn Palace in Vienna. Given on the occasion of Joseph II's wedding, this banquet was an example of the extravagance this Hapsburg monarch believed suitable to the occasion.

rich and powerful. Some, indeed, could rely on little more than inherited privilege to distinguish themselves from peasants.

Tradition had it that noble service meant military service; yet, as we shall see, that tradition—like so many others—was increasingly breached during the early-modern period. Noble title was granted by a monarch, in theory for service to the state. But such service was more and more frequently defined as nonmilitary, as support, financial and political, for the expanding apparatus of local and central government. The pattern of noble life varied considerably from country to country. In England and Prussia, the nobility tended to reside on its estates; in south and west Germany, and in France, they were more likely to leave the management of their estates to stewards and to live at the royal court or in cities. Despite the traditional assumption that noblemen need not, and therefore must not, soil their aristocratic reputation by commercial dealing, by the end of the eighteenth century they were involving themselves in increasing numbers in a variety of entrepreneurial enterprises. Some exploited mineral deposits on their estates; others invested in overseas trade. In France, two of the four largest coal mines were owned and operated by noblemen, while the duke of Orléans was an important investor in the newly established chemical dye industry. In eastern Europe, because there were few middle-class merchants, noblemen frequently undertook to market their agricultural produce themselves.

Nobility and commerce

579

An "open" nobility

The peasantry

Peasant subordination in eastern
Europe

The position of the peasantry

In no country was the nobility a completely closed order. Men who proved of use to the crown as administrators or lawyers, men who amassed large fortunes as a consequence of judicious—and often legally questionable—financial transactions, moved into the ranks of the nobility with increasing frequency during the late seventeenth and eighteenth centuries. Joseph II of Austria was making financiers into noblemen by the dozen in the late eighteenth century. In France, it was possible to attain nobility through the purchase of expensive offices from the crown. Membership could be purchased in the legal nobility of the "robe," headed by members of the thirteen provincial *parlements* whose function it was to record, and thereby sanction, the laws of the kingdom, and to adjudicate cases appealed from lower courts.

Land ownership brought the nobility into direct relationship with the peasants and laborers who worked the land and over whose lives their masters exercised dominion. The status of the peasantry varied greatly across the face of rural Europe. In the east—Russia, Poland, Hungary, and in parts of Germany beyond the Elbe—the desire for profit in agriculture and the collusion of the state with the nobility led to the growth of a "second serfdom," a serf system much stronger than that which had existed during the Middle Ages. In East Prussia, serfs often had to work from three to six days a week for their lord, and some had only late evening or night hours to cultivate their own lands.

Peasants throughout eastern Europe found their destinies controlled in almost all respects by their masters. Noble landlords dispensed justice in manorial courts and even ruled in cases to which they were themselves interested parties. These men were a combination of sheriff, chief magistrate, and police force in one, able to sentence their "subjects" to corporal punishment, imprisonment, exile, or in many cases death, without right of appeal. Peasants could not leave their land, marry, or learn a trade unless permitted to do so by their lord. In Russia, where half the land was owned by the state, peasants were bound to work in mines or workshops if their masters so ordered, and could be sold to private owners. Although Russian peasant serfs were said to possess a "legal personality" that distinguished them from slaves, the distinction was obscured in practice. They lived as bound to their masters as had their great-grandfathers.

In western Europe, the position of the peasantry reflected the fact that serfdom had all but disappeared by the sixteenth century. Peasants might theoretically own land, although the vast majority were either tenants or laborers. Hereditary tenure was in general more secure than in the east; peasants could dispose of their land and had legal claim to farm buildings and implements. Although far freer than their eastern European counterparts, the peasantry of western Europe still lived to a great degree under the domination of landowners. They were in many cases responsible for the payment of various dues and fees: an annual rent paid to landlords by those who might otherwise own their land outright; a special tax on recently cleared land; a fee, often as much as one-sixth of the assessed value of the land, collected by the manorial lord whenever peasant property changed hands; and charges for the use of the lord's mill, bakery, or wine press. In France, peasants were compelled to submit to the *corvée,* a requirement that they labor for several weeks a year maintaining local roads. Even access to the often questionable justice meted out in the manorial courts, which endured throughout the early-modern period in almost all of western Europe, was encumbered with fees and commissions. To many peasants, however, the most galling badge of their inferiority was their inability to hunt within the jurisdiction of their landlord's manor. The slaughter of game was a privilege reserved to the nobility, a circumstance generating sustained resentment on the part of a population that looked upon deer and pheasant not as a symbol of aristocratic status but as a necessary supplement to its meager diet. Noble landlords rarely missed an opportunity to extract all the money they could from their peasants while constantly reminding them of the degree to which their destiny was controlled by the lord of the manor.

Despite their traditional subservience, however, western European peasants found themselves caught up directly in the process of economic change. The growth of centralized monarchies intensified the states' need for income, with the result that peasants were more burdened than ever with taxes and required services. They responded by accepting a new role as wage-earners in an expanding market economy, some as agricultural day laborers on enclosed estates, others as part of the work force in expanding rural industries. A few were genuinely independent, literate, influential members of the communities where they lived, owning not only land but considerable livestock. In France, some acted as intermediaries between their landlords, from whom they leased several large farms, and the sharecroppers who actually worked the land. Most, however, were far less fortunate. Those with claim to a small piece of property usually worked it into infertility in the course of one or two generations as they scrambled to make it produce as much as possible.

Poor peasants often lived, contrary to the biblical injunction, by bread alone—two pounds a day if they were lucky, the dark dough a mixture of wheat and rye flour. According to region, bread was supplemented by peas and beans, beer, wine, or, far less often, skimmed milk. Peasant houses usually contained no more than one or two rooms, and were constructed of wood, plastered with mud or clay. Roofs were most often thatched with straw, which was used as fertilizer when replaced, and provided fodder for animals at times of scarcity. Furnishings seldom consisted of more than a table, benches, pallets for sleeping, a few earthenware plates, and simple tools—an axe, a wooden spade, a knife.

Peasant women tended livestock and vegetables, and managed the dairy, if there was one. Women went out as field workers, or worked at home knitting, spinning, or weaving in order to augment the family income. A popular seventeenth-century poem has a laborer's wife lamenting her lot with a refrain that has echoed down the ages: ". . . my labor is hard,/ And all my pleasures are debarr'd;/ Both morning, evening, night and noon,/ I am sure a woman's work is never done."

A French Peasant. Tattered and overworked, this peasant farmer is shown feeding his livestock as the tax collector at his door relieves him of all of his profits.

Peasant bread and board

Peasant women

Market Scene, by Jean Michelin. Peasant women and children bringing produce to a nearby market town.

Urban living conditions

The spread of proto-industrialization broke down the previously sharp demarcations between town and country, between the life lived inside a city's medieval walls and that lived outside. Suburbs merged urban and rural existence. In some, textile workers labored. In others, families of fashion took their ease, creating an environment "where the want of London smoke is supplied by the smoke of Virginia tobacco," as one Englishman remarked wryly. Houses in areas inhabited by the wealthy were increasingly built of brick and stone, which replaced the wood, lath, and plaster of the Middle Ages. This change was a response to the constant danger of fire. The great fire of London in 1666, which destroyed three-quarters of the town—12,000 houses—was the largest of the conflagrations that swept cities with devastating regularity. Urban dwellings of the laboring poor remained firetraps. Workers' quarters were badly overcrowded; entire families lived in one-room accommodations in basements and attics that were infested with bugs and fleas.

Urban society: the bourgeoisie

Urban society was, like its rural counterpart, a society of orders. In capital cities, noble families occupied the highest social position, as they did in the countryside, living a parasitic life of conspicuous consumption. The majority of cities and towns were dominated by a nonnoble *bourgeoisie.* That French term originally designated a burgher or townsman who was a long-term, resident property owner or leaseholder and taxpayer. By the eighteenth century it had come to mean a townsman of some means who aspired to be recognized as a person of local importance and evinced a willingness to work hard, whether at counting-house or government office, and a desire to live a comfortable, if by no means extravagant, existence. A bourgeois gentleman might derive his income from rents; he might, as well, be an industrialist, banker, merchant, lawyer, or physician.

If he served in the central bureaucracy, he would consider himself the social superior of those provincials whose affairs he administered. Yet he would himself be looked down upon by the aristocracy, many of whom enjoyed thinking of the bourgeoisie as a class of vulgar social climbers, often conveniently forgetting their own commercial origins a generation or two previously. The French playwright Molière's comedy *The Bourgeois Gentleman* (1670) reflected this attitude, ridiculing the manners of those who were trying to ape their betters. "Bourgeois," another French writer observed, "is the insult given by noblemen to anybody they deem slow-witted or out of touch with the court." The bourgeoisie usually constituted about 20 to 25 percent of a town's population. As its economic elite, these men were almost always its governing elite as well.

Throughout the early-modern period, there was considerable movement into and out of the urban bourgeoisie. Prosperous tradesmen and successful small-time commercial entrepreneurs might see their offspring rise in station, particularly if they married well. At the same time, those who made their money in trade could purchase land, and by paying fees to their king, gain the right to an ennobling office. In seventeenth-century Amiens, a major French textile center, the upper bourgeoisie deserted trade and derived the majority of its income from land or bonds. Where the bourgeoisie thrived, it more often than not did so as the result of a burgeoning state or regional bureaucracy.

Next within the urban hierarchy was a vast middle range of shopkeepers and artisans. Many of the latter continued to learn and then to practice their crafts as members of guilds, which in turn contained their own particular ascending order of apprentice, journeyman, and master, thus preserving the pervasive principle of hierarchy. Throughout the early-modern period, however, commercial expansion threatened the rigid hierarchy of the guild structure. The expense and curtailed output resulting from restrictive guild practices met with serious opposition in big cities such as Paris and London, and in the industrial hinterlands of France and Germany, where expanding markets called for cheaper and more readily available goods. Journeymen tailors and shoemakers in increasing numbers set up shops without benefit of mastership and produced cheaper coats and shoes in defiance of guild regulations. In the silk workshops of Lyons, both masters and journeymen were compelled to labor without distinction of status for piece rates (wages paid per finished article, rather than per hour) set by merchandising middlemen and far below an equitable level in the opinion of the silk workers. Artisans like these, compelled to work for low wages at the behest of profiteering middlemen, grew increasingly restive. In France and Germany, journeymen's associations had originated as social and mutual-aid organizations for young men engaged in "tramping" the country to gain experience in their trade. In some instances, however, these associations fostered the development of a trade consciousness that led to strikes and boycotts against masters and middlemen over the issues of wages and working conditions. An imperial law passed in Germany in 1731 deprived the associations of their

The "**Bon Ton.**" This English cartoon mocks the rage for French fashion and illustrates the affluence of a middle class able to afford the changing dictates of fashion.

Urban society: shopkeepers and artisans

Urban society: the poor

Attitudes toward poverty

The treatment of paupers

right to organize, and required journeymen to carry a certificate of identification as testimony of their respectability during their travels.

At the bottom of urban society was a mass of semi-skilled and unskilled workers: carters and porters; stevedores and dockers; water carriers and sweepers; seamstresses, laundresses, cleaners, and domestic servants. These men and women, like their rural counterparts, lived on the margins of life, constantly battling the trade cycles, seasonal unemployment, and epidemics that threatened their ability to survive. A number existed in shanties on the edge of towns and cities. In Genoa, the homeless poor were sold as galley slaves each winter. In Venice, the poor lived on decrepit barges under the city's bridges. A French ordinance of 1669 ordered the destruction of all houses "built on poles by vagabonds and useless members of society." Deprived of the certainty of steady work, these people were prey not only to economic fluctuations and malevolent "acts of God," but to a social system that left them without any "privilege" or "freedom" whatsoever.

Attitudes toward poverty varied from country to country. Most localities extended the concept of orders to include the poor: "the deserving"—usually orphans, the insane, the aged, the infirm; and "the undeserving"—able-bodied men and women who were out of work or who, even though employed, could not support themselves and their families. The authorities tended to assume in the latter case that poverty was the result of personal failings; few made a connection between general economic circumstances and the plight of the individual poor. For the deserving, private charitable organizations, such as those in France founded by the order of St. Vincent de Paul and by the Sisters of Charity, provided assistance. For the undeserving, there was harsh treatment at the hands of the state whose concern to alleviate extreme deprivation arose more from a desire to avert public disorder than from motives of human charity. Food riots were common occurrences. In times of scarcity the French government frequently intervened to reduce the price of grain, hoping thereby to prevent an outbreak of rioting. Yet riots nevertheless occurred. When property damage resulted, the ringleaders were generally severely punished, usually by hanging. The remainder of the crowd was often left untouched by the law, a fact suggesting the degree to which governments were prepared to tolerate rioting itself as a means of dealing with the chronic consequences of poverty.

Poverty remained a central and intractable problem for the governments of all European countries. Poor vagrants were perceived as a serious threat to social tranquillity. They were therefore frequently rounded up at harvest time to keep them from plundering the fields. Vagrants and other chronically unemployed persons were placed in poorhouses where conditions were little better than those in prisons. Often the very young, the very old, the sick, and the insane were housed together with hardened criminals. Poor relief in England was administered parish by parish in accordance with a law passed in 1601. Relief was tied to a "law of settlement," which stipulated that paupers might receive aid only if still resid-

Hanging Thieves. This seventeenth-century engraving is designed to teach a lesson. Troops stand by and priests bless the condemned criminals as they are executed by the dozen. "At last," the engraver's caption reads, "these infamous lost souls are hung like unhappy fruit."

ing in the parish of their birth. An unemployed weaver who had migrated fifty miles in search of work could thus expect assistance only if he returned home again. In the late eighteenth century, several European countries established modest public works programs in an attempt to relieve poverty by reducing unemployment. France, for example, undertook road-building projects in the 1770s under the auspices of its progressive finance minister, Turgot. But generally speaking, indigence was perceived not as a social ill for which a remedy might be sought, but as an indelible stigma demarking those at the bottom of society.

European social institutions reflected the patterns of hierarchy. Nowhere was this more apparent than in the field of education. One barrier—a knowledge of Latin—separated nobles and a fair number of scholars and professionals from the commercial middle ranks; a second—the ability to read and write—separated the middle from the rest. Noblemen were generally educated by private tutors; though they might attend university for a time, they did so not in preparation for a profession but to receive further educational "finishing." Indeed during the late seventeenth and eighteenth centuries, universities more or less surrendered intellectual leadership to various academies established with royal patronage by European monarchs to enhance their own reputations as well as to encourage the advancement of science and the arts: the Royal Society of London, founded by Charles II in 1660; the French Academy of Sciences, a project upon which Louis XIV lavished a good deal of ostentatious attention; and the Berlin Royal Academy of Science and Letters, patronized by Frederick the Great of Prussia in the eighteenth century. Few noblemen had the interest or the intelligence to participate in the activities of these august organizations, which were not, in any case, teaching institutions. Far better suited to their needs and inclinations was "the grand tour,"

Education in a society of orders: the nobility

often of many months' duration, which led the nobleman through the capitals of Europe, and during which he was expected to acquire a kind of international *politesse*. One observer, commenting on the habits of young English noblemen abroad, remarked, "they game; purchase pictures, mutilated statues, and mistresses to the astonishment of all beholders."

Training for government service

Endowed, fee-charging institutions for the training of a governmental elite existed in France (the *collège*) and Spain (the *colegio mayor*) and in Germany and Austria (the *gymnasium*). Here the emphasis was by no means on "practical" subjects such as modern language or mathematics, but on the mastery of Greek and Latin translation and composition, the intellectual badge of the educated elite. An exception was the Prussian University of Halle, designed to teach a professional elite; a contemporary described that institution as teaching only what was "rational, useful, and practical."

Education for the middle orders

Male children from the middle orders destined to enter the family business or profession as a rule attended small private academies where the curriculum included the sort of "useful" instruction ignored in the *collèges* and *gymnasia*. Female children, from both the upper and the middle orders, were almost invariably educated at home, receiving little more than rudimentary instruction in gentlewomanly subjects such as modern language, belles lettres, and music, if from the noble ranks; and a similar, if slightly more practical training, if from the bourgeoisie.

Education for the poor

No European country undertook the task of providing primary education to all its citizens until the middle of the eighteenth century, when Frederick the Great in Prussia and the Habsburg monarchs Maria Theresa and her son Joseph II in Austria instituted systems of compulsory attendance. Available evidence suggests that their results fell far short of expectation. An early-nineteenth-century survey from the relatively enlightened Prussian province of Cleves revealed dilapidated schools, poorly attended classes, and an incompetent corps of teachers. Educational conditions were undoubtedly worse in most other European communities.

Increasing literacy

Though modern scholars can make no more than educated guesses, it appears certain that literacy rates increased considerably in the seventeenth and eighteenth centuries; in England, from one in four males in 1600 to one in two by 1800; in France, from 29 percent of the male population in 1686 to 47 percent in 1786. Literacy among women increased as well, though their rate of increase generally lagged behind that of men: only 27 percent of the female population in France was literate in 1786. Naturally, such rates varied according to particular localities and circumstances, and from country to country. Literacy was higher in urban areas that contained a large proportion of artisans. In rural eastern Europe, literacy remained extremely low (20–30 percent) well into the nineteenth century. Notwithstanding state-directed efforts in Prussia and Austria, the rise in literacy was largely the result of a growing determination on the part of religiously minded reformers to teach the poor to read and write as a means of encouraging obedience to divine and secular authority. A

Establishing the French Academy of Sciences and the Foundation of the Observatory, by Henri Testelin. This painting, which shows Louis XIV as patron, testifies to his enthusiastic support of the Academy.

Sunday-school movement in eighteenth-century England and similar activities among the Christian Brotherhood in France are clear evidence of this trend.

Though the majority of the common people were probably no more than barely literate, they possessed a flourishing culture of their own. Village life, particularly in Roman Catholic countries, centered about the church, to which men and women would go on Sundays not only to worship but to socialize. Much of the remainder of their day of rest would be devoted to participation in village games. Religion provided the opportunity for association and for a welcome break from the daily work routines. Pilgrimages to a nearby shrine, for example, would include a procession of villagers led by one of their number carrying an image of the village's patron saint and accompanied by drinking, dancing, and picnicking. In towns, Catholics joined organizations called "confraternities" in France, Italy, Austria, and the Netherlands, which provided mutual aid and a set of common rituals and traditions centered upon a patron saint. Religious community was expressed as well in popular Protestant movements that arose in the eighteenth century: Pietism on the Continent and Methodism in England. Both emphasized the importance of personal salvation through faith and the potential worth of every human soul regardless of station. Both therefore appealed particularly to people whose position within the community had heretofore been presumed to be without

Popular culture

Vauxhall Gardens, by Thomas Rowlandson. This London scene suggests the degree to which men and women from different social orders came together for sport, drinking, and adventure.

Carnival and other amusements

any value. Though Methodism's founder, John Wesley (1703–1791), preached obedience to earthly authority, his willingness to rely on working men and women as preachers and organizers gave them a new sense of personal importance.

Popular culture often combined in one event traditions that were part religious, part secular, and, indeed, part pagan. One such occasion was Carnival, that vibrant pre-Lenten celebration indigenous not only to Mediterranean Europe but to Germany and Austria as well. Carnival represented an opportunity for common folk to cast aside the burdens and restraints imposed upon their order by secular authority. Performances and processions celebrated a "world turned upside down," a theme popular throughout much of Europe from the Later Middle Ages, which appealed to commoners for a variety of ambiguous psychological reasons, but in large part, certainly, as a way of avenging symbolically the economic and social oppression under which they lived. For a few days, the oppressed played the role of the oppressor and rulers were made to look like fools and knaves. In parades, men dressed as kings walked barefoot while peasants rode on horseback or in carriages; the poor threw pretend money to the rich. These occasions, although emphasizing social divisions, worked to hold communities to a common cultural center, since, through most of the early-modern period, both rich and poor celebrated together, as they did on major religious holidays. Annual harvest festivals, once sponsored by the Church, were increasingly secular celebrations of release from backbreaking labor, punctuated by feasting, drinking, sporting, and lovemaking. Fairs and traveling circuses brought something of distant places and people into lives bound to one spot. The

French Tavern. Often located outside the city limits so as to avoid the payment of municipal taxes, taverns such as this provided a gathering place for workers to drink, gossip, and relax after the day's labors. The tavern also served as a convenient place for public readings and for airing common grievances.

drudgery of everyday life was also relieved by horse races, cock fights, and bear baiting. Taverns played an even more constant role in the daily life of the village, providing a place for men to gather over tobacco and drink and indulge in gossip and gambling.

Laboring men and women depended on an oral tradition of myth, legend, and superstition to steady their lives and give them point and purpose. Stories in books sold at fairs by peddlers were passed on by those who could read. They told of heroes and saints, and of kings like Charlemagne whose paternal concern for his common subjects led him into battle against his selfish nobility. Belief in villains matched belief in heroes. Witchcraft, as we have seen, was a reality for much of the period. So was Satan. So was any supernatural force, whether for good or evil, that could help them make sense of a world in which they, more than any, were victims of events beyond their control.

Though increasingly secularized, popular customs, celebrations, and beliefs remained a stabilizing force in early-modern Europe. They were the cultural expression of that social order to which the vast majority of Europeans belonged. Popular culture in the main tended to reinforce the traditions and assumptions of order and hierarchy. Peasants and urban workers worshiped saints and venerated heroic rulers, thereby accepting the authority of the established, ordered society of which they were a part. They were seldom satisfied with their lot, yet they were as seldom willing to question the social structure they saw as a bulwark against the swift changes so often surrounding them. Popular culture helped to bind men and women to what civilization had been, as capitalism and mercantilism impelled them in the direction of what it would become.

Stability and change

589

SUMMARY POINTS

- Until the mid-eighteenth century, warfare, famine, and disease curbed population growth. After about 1750, however, most western European countries saw steady and significant population growth, particularly in cities where trade, commerce, and administration attracted laborers.

- Agriculture and industry saw gradual technical improvements in the seventeenth and eighteenth centuries, such as scientific farming and the "putting-out" system of craft production, that improved efficiency and increased output.

- Commerce and industry grew increasingly capitalistic and mercantilistic in the 1600s and 1700s. Cooperation between businesses and governments allowed national economies to expand and international trade to flourish.

- The overseas colonies and trading posts developed by European powers during the seventeenth and eighteenth centuries were evidence of economic expansion and mercantilist policies. The Spanish, French, English, and Dutch competed for trading advantages in North, Central, and South America, the Caribbean, and the Far East. Agricultural industries in the Americas fueled demand for African slaves.

- Early-modern European society was rigidly ordered, giving rights and privileges to those of higher social rank and very little to those of lower rank. Popular customs, celebrations, and beliefs reinforced the traditions of hierarchy.

SELECTED READINGS

Blum, Jerome, *Lord and Peasant in Russia,* Princeton, 1961. A good study of Russian society.

Braudel, F., *The Structures of Everyday Life: The Limits of the Possible,* New York, 1981. A survey of the material conditions of life; profusely illustrated.

Burke, Peter, *Popular Culture in Early Modern Europe,* London, 1978. Synthesizes work on the period between 1500 and 1800; fascinating.

M. L. Bush, ed., *Social Orders and Social Classes in Europe since 1500,* New York, 1992. Essays on a broad range of subjects, including the Church, tenant rights, and the concept of class.

Cipolla, Carlo M., *Before the Industrial Revolution: European Society and Economy, 1000–1700,* 3d ed., New York, 1994. Wide-ranging and full of deft observations.

Darnton, Robert, *The Great Cat Massacre and Other Episodes in French Cultural History,* New York, 1984. Fascinating explorations into early-modern French mentalities.

————, *The Literary Underground of the Old Regime,* Cambridge, 1982. An examination of the world of popular writers, sellers of illegal books, and the literary underworld of eighteenth-century Paris.

Davis, David Brion, *The Problem of Slavery in Western Culture,* Ithaca, N.Y., 1966. A brilliant analysis of Western attitudes and assumptions.

Davis, Natalie Z., *Society and Culture in Early Modern France,* Stanford, 1975. Eight scintillating essays by a pioneer in the use of anthropological methods for the study of early-modern European history.

Davis, Ralph, *The Rise of the Atlantic Economies,* Ithaca, N.Y., 1973. A thorough analysis of early-modern trade and commerce.

De Vries, Jan, *The Economy of Europe in an Age of Crisis, 1600–1750,* New York, 1976. A survey of the emerging capitalist economies of early-modern Europe.

Doyle, William, *The Old European Order, 1660–1800,* 2d ed., New York, 1992. An excellent general survey with chapters on population, trade, social orders, and public affairs.

Forster, Robert, *The Nobility of Toulouse in the Eighteenth Century,* Baltimore, Md., 1960. A careful analysis of the extent and nature of aristocratic power.

Foucault, M., *The History of Sexuality: An Introduction,* Vol. I, New York, 1978. Useful material on the early-modern period.

Fraser, Antonia, *The Weaker Vessel,* New York, 1984. Includes discussion of the role of women in the English Civil War.

Gibson, Wendy, *Women in Seventeenth-Century France,* New York, 1989. A thorough survey of women's lives and work.

Houston, R. A., *Literacy in Early Modern Europe: Culture and Education, 1500–1800,* New York, 1988. A valuable analysis of the various types of educational institutions and who did—and did not—attend them.

Hufton, Olwen H., *The Poor of Eighteenth-Century France, 1750–1789,* Oxford, 1974. One of the first studies of a preindustrial "underclass."

Inikori, Joseph E., and Stanley Engerman, eds., *The Atlantic Slave Trade: Effects on Economies, Societies, and Peoples in Africa, the Americas, and Europe,* Durham, N.C., 1992. An outstanding collection of thoughtful and well-researched essays emphasizing the complexity and enormity of the slave trade and its wide and profound effects.

Kaplow, Jeffry, *The Names of Kings: The Parisian Laboring Poor in the Eighteenth Century,* New York, 1972. A valuable study of the urban poor.

Laslett, Peter, *The World We Have Lost,* 2d ed., New York, 1971. Analyzes the nature of rural society in early-modern England.

Le Roy Ladurie, Emmanuel, *The Peasants of Languedoc,* Urbana, Ill., 1974. A classic on peasant life and demography.

Levine, David, *Family Formation in an Age of Nascent Capitalism,* New York, 1977. A thoughtful treatment of patterns of social formation.

Lougee, Carolyn C., *Le Paradis des Femmes: Women, Salons, and Social Stratification in Seventeenth-Century France.* Princeton, 1976. Women's role in the intellectual life of the old regime.

Mousnier, R., *Peasant Uprisings in Seventeenth-Century France, Russia and China,* New York, 1970. A comparative analysis.

Parry, J. H., *The Age of Reconnaissance,* Berkeley, 1981. The role of the colonies in the economy and politics of early-modern Europe.

Postma, Johannes, *The Dutch in the Atlantic Slave Trade, 1600–1815,* New York, 1990. A thoroughly documented examination of the critical Dutch role in the expansion of the Atlantic slave trade from a small undertaking to a trade with global dimensions.

Ranum, Orest, *Paris in the Age of Absolutism,* New York, 1968. A useful view of urban life.

Rich, E. E., and C. H. Wilson, eds., *The Cambridge Economic History of Europe:* Volume 5, *The Economic Organization of Early Modern Europe,* New York, 1977. An indispensable guide to the study of the period's economy and society.

Roche, Daniel, *The People of Paris: An Essay in Popular Culture in the Eighteenth Century,* Dover, N.H., 1986. Livelihood and concerns of ordinary Parisians.

Sabean, David, *Power in the Blood: Popular Culture and Village Discourse in Early-Modern Germany,* New York, 1984. A reconstruction of the collective mind of a German village over the course of two centuries.

Schama, Simon, *The Embarrassment of Riches: An Interpretation of Dutch Culture in the Golden Age,* New York, 1988. A full-bodied analysis of the God-fearing yet materially inclined Dutch.

Stone, Lawrence, *The Family, Sex and Marriage in England, 1500–1800,* New York, 1977. An important, controversial book that argues important changes in attitudes over the course of three centuries.

Wilson, Charles, *England's Apprenticeship, 1603–1763,* 2d ed., London, 1984. A reliable economic survey.

Wrigley, E. A., *Population and History,* New York, 1969. A good introduction to family history.

SOURCE MATERIALS

Barnett, G. E., ed., *Two Tracts by Gregory King,* Baltimore, 1936. An introduction to the work of the modern world's first real statistician.

Goubert, Pierre, *The Ancien Régime: French Society, 1600–1750,* London, 1973. Particularly strong in its descriptions of rural life. Includes selections from illuminating documents.

Ménétra, Jacques Louis, *Journal of My Life,* trans. Arthur Goldhammer, intr. Daniel Roche, 1986. The autobiography of a Parisian glazier who played checkers with Rousseau and was an eyewitness to the Revolution.

Northrup, David, ed., *The Atlantic Slave Trade,* Lexington, Mass., 1994. A judicious collection of primary and secondary source materials that examines the entire sweep of the trade, from beginnings to the fight for abolition.

Young, Arthur, *Travels in France during the Years 1787, 1788, 1789,* London, various editions. Vivid observations by an English traveler.

CHAPTER 17

THE AGE OF ABSOLUTISM
(1660–1789)

There are four essential characteristics or qualities of royal authority.

First, royal authority is sacred.

Second, it is paternal.

Third, it is absolute.

Fourth, it is subject to reason.

   —JACQUES BOSSUET, *Politics Drawn from the Very Words of Holy Scripture*

T
HE PERIOD FROM the assumption of personal rule by Louis XIV of France (1661) until the French Revolution (1789) is known as the age of absolutism. The label is accurate if we define *absolutism* as the conscious attempt by state sovereigns—sometimes successful; more often not—to extend their legal and administrative power over their subjects, and over the vested interests of the social and economic orders in which those subjects were ranked. The dates are suggestive in that for the period as a whole the activities of French monarchs most clearly expressed the intentions of absolutist government. Yet both the dates and the label need to be treated with some caution. We have already noted that from about 1500 on, a general trend to make the state more powerful had manifested itself in England and on the Continent. Sixteenth-century kings saw in Protestantism a way of asserting the sovereignty of their states over the power of the papacy and the aristocracy. And political thinkers such as Jean Bodin were championing absolutist theory in their writings well before Louis XIV assumed personal rulership of France. By establishing the French monarchs as prototypical early-modern rulers, we risk ignoring other modes of centralized government instituted by the rulers of Prussia, Russia, and Austria. And we exclude the crucially important exception of England, where after 1688, absolutist tendencies gave way to oligarchy.

Absolutism defined

The term "absolutism" needs qualification. As practiced by western European eighteenth-century rulers, absolutism was not despotism. They did not understand it as a license for untrammeled and arbitrary rule, such as that practiced by Oriental potentates. Despite the best efforts of these European monarchs to consolidate their authority, they could not issue irresponsible decrees and achieve lasting compliance. Aristocrats,

Absolutism qualified

churchmen, merchants, and entrepreneurs remained strong enough within their respective orders to ensure that kings and queens would need to justify the actions they took. Moreover, rulers tended to respect not only the strength of their political adversaries but the processes of law; they quarreled openly and broke with tradition only under exceptional circumstances. No matter how "absolute" monarchs might wish to be, they were limited as well by rudimentary systems of transportation and communication from interfering with any degree of consistency and efficiency in the daily lives of their subjects.

The relationship between state power and economic innovation

Although the emphasis in this chapter is largely upon political, diplomatic, and military events, absolutism cannot be fully understood without relating it to the commercial and industrial trends we have just analyzed. Tariff legislation, industrial regulations, wars of trade, currency manipulation, tax laws—all were useful tools in the construction of a new economic order. And all were tools that could be employed only by a strongly centralized state. Governments might take active steps to manage production and exportation, as the English did when they imposed the Navigation Acts in 1660, which restricted imports to material transported on English ships or those of their country of origin, and required colonial goods to pass through English ports before being sold elsewhere. Other governments (the French, for example), in their determination to finance expanding bureaucratic and military establishments, imposed new taxes and exacted an increasingly high price for the privileges they meted out. The state's expanding financial demands placed considerable pressure on both urban middle orders and peasantry to make more money. And the result of that pressure, in turn, was entrepreneurship and wage labor.

Bearing in mind, then, the important symbiotic relationship between state power and economic innovation, we shall, in this chapter, measure the extent of royal power throughout Europe in the late seventeenth and eighteenth centuries, examine the varieties of absolutism as instituted and practiced by different monarchs, and take note of the way in which the centralization of power contributed to the rise of an international state system.

THE APPEAL AND JUSTIFICATION OF ABSOLUTISM

Absolutism's appeal

Absolutism appealed to many Europeans for the same reason that mercantilism did. In theory and practice, it expressed a desire for an end to the constant alarms and confusions of Europe's "iron century." The French religious wars, the Thirty Years' War in Germany, and the English Civil War all had produced great turbulence. The alternative, domestic order, absolutists argued, could come only with strong, centralized government. Just as mercantilists maintained that economic stability would result from regimentation, so absolutists contended that social and political harmony would be realized when subjects recognized their duty to obey their divinely sanctioned rulers.

Absolutist monarchs insisted, in turn, upon *their* duty to teach their subjects, even against their will, how to order their domestic affairs. As Margrave Karl Friedrich, eighteenth-century ruler of the German principality of Baden, expressed it: "We must make them, whether they like it or not, into free, opulent and law-abiding citizens." Looking back to the seventeenth-century wars that had torn Europe apart, rulers can be excused for believing that absolutism's promise of stability and prosperity— "freedom and opulence"—presented an attractive as well as an imperative alternative to disorder. Louis XIV of France remembered the *Fronde* as a threat to the welfare of the nation that he had been appointed by God to rule wisely and justly. When marauding Parisians entered his bedchamber one night in 1651 to discover if he had fled the city with Mazarin, Louis saw the intrusion as a horrid affront not only to his own person, but to the state. Squabbles among the nobility and criticisms of royal policy in the Paris Parlement during his minority left him convinced that he must exercise his powers and prerogatives rigorously if France was to survive and prosper as a great European state.

In order to achieve that objective, absolutist monarchs worked to control the disposition of the state's armed forces, the administration of its legal system, and the collection and distribution of its tax revenues. This ambitious goal required an efficient bureaucracy that owed its primary allegiance not to some social or economic order with interests antithetical to the monarchy, but to the institution of the monarchy itself. One hallmark of absolutist policy was its determination to construct a set of institutions strong enough to withstand, if not destroy, the privileged interests that had hindered royal power in the past. The Church and the nobility, the semiautonomous regions, and the would-be independent representative bodies (the English Parliament and the French Estates-General) were all obstacles to the achievement of strong, centralized monarchical government. And the history of absolutism is, as much as anything, the history of the attempts of various rulers to bring these institutions to heel.

In those major European countries where Roman Catholicism still remained the state religion—France, Spain, and Austria—successive monarchs throughout the eighteenth century made various attempts to "nationalize" the Church and its clergy. We have already noted the way in which in the fifteenth and sixteenth centuries popes had conceded certain powers to the temporal rulers of France and Spain. Later absolutists, building on those earlier precedents, wrested further power from the Church in Rome. Even Charles III, the devout Spanish king who ruled from 1759 to 1788, pressed successfully for a papal concordat granting the state control over ecclesiastical appointments, and established his right to sanction the proclamation of papal bulls.

Powerful as the Church was, it did not rival the nobility as an opponent of a centralized state. Monarchs combatted the noble orders in various ways. Louis XIV attempted to control the ancient French aristocracy by

The duties of the monarch

Goals of absolute monarchs: army, administration, and revenue

Absolutism and the control of the Church and its clergy

Absolutism and the control of the noble orders

depriving it of political power while increasing its social prestige. Peter the Great, the talented and erratic tsar of early eighteenth-century Russia, co-opted the nobility into government service. Later in the century, Catherine II struck a bargain whereby in return for the granting of vast estates and a variety of social and economic privileges such as exemption from taxation, the Russian nobility virtually surrendered the administrative and political power of the state into the empress's hands. In Prussia under Frederick the Great, the army was staffed by nobles; here again, as in Peter's Russia, was a case of co-option. Yet in late-eighteenth-century Austria, the Emperor Joseph II adopted a policy of confrontation rather than accommodation, denying the nobility exemption from taxation and deliberately blurring the distinctions between nobles and commoners.

Struggle between local and central power

These struggles between monarchs and nobles had implications for the additional struggle between local privileges and centralized power. Absolutists in France waged a constant and never entirely successful war against the autonomy of provincial institutions, often headed by nobles, much as Spanish rulers in the sixteenth century had battled independent-minded nobles in Aragon and Catalonia. Prussian rulers intruded into the governance of formerly "free" cities, assuming police and revenue powers over their inhabitants. These various campaigns, constantly waged and usually successful for a time, were evidence of the nature of absolutism and of its continuing success.

Theoretical apologists for absolutism

Absolutism had its theoretical apologists as well as its able practitioners. In addition to the political philosophies of men such as Bodin, defenders of royal power could rely on treatises such as Bishop Jacques Bossuet's *Politics Drawn from the Very Words of Scripture* (1708), written during the reign of Louis XIV, to sustain the case for extended monarchical control. Bossuet argued that absolute government was not the same as arbitrary government, since God, in whom "all strength and all perfection were united," was united as well with the person of the king. "God is holiness itself, goodness itself, and power itself. In these things lies the majesty of God. In the image of these things lies the majesty of the prince." It followed that the king was answerable to no one but God himself, and that the king was as far above other mortals as God was above the king. "The prince, as prince, is not regarded as a private person; he is a public personage, all the state is in him. . . . As all perfection and all strength are united in God, all the power of individuals is united in the Person of the prince. What grandeur that a simple man should embody so much." What grandeur indeed! Bossuet's treatise was the most explicit and extreme statement of the theory of the divine right of kings, the doctrine that James I had tried to foist upon the English. Unlikely as it may sound to modern ears, the political philosophy of Bossuet was comforting to men and women in the upper orders of society who craved peace and stability after a century or more of international and domestic turmoil, who found themselves embarked upon bold economic adventures that required a strong and stable polity, and who realized that absolutism might well require their collaboration and therefore bring them gain.

Bishop Jacques Bossuet

The Château of Versailles. Dramatically expanded by Louis XIV in the 1660s from a hunting lodge to the principal royal residence and the seat of government, the château became a monument to the international power and prestige of the Grand Monarch.

THE ABSOLUTISM OF LOUIS XIV

Examine a portrait of Louis XIV (1643–1715) in court robes; it is all but impossible to discern the human being behind the facade of the absolute monarch. That facade was carefully and artfully constructed by Louis, who recognized, perhaps more clearly than any other early-modern ruler, the importance of theater as a means of establishing authority. Well into the eighteenth century, superstitious commoners continued to believe in the power of the king's magic "touch" to cure disease. Louis and his successors manipulated the theater of their sovereignty so as to enhance their position as divine-right rulers endowed with God-like powers and far removed from common humanity.

Absolutism as theater: Louis XIV

The advantages of strategic theater were expressed most clearly in Louis's palace at Versailles, the town outside of Paris to which he moved his court. The building itself was a stage upon which Louis attempted to mesmerize the aristocracy into obedience by his performance of the daily rituals of absolutism. The main facade of the palace was a third of a mile

Louis XIV's opulence

in length. Inside, tapestries and paintings celebrated French military victories and royal triumphs. In the vast gardens outside, statues of Apollo, god of the sun, recalled Louis's claim to be the "Sun King" of the French. Noblemen vied to attend him when he arose from bed, ate his meals (usually stone-cold, having traveled the distance of several city blocks from royal kitchen to royal table), strolled in his gardens, or rode to the hunt. As Louis called himself the Sun King, so his court was the epicenter of his royal effulgence. Its glitter, in which France's leading nobles were required by their monarch to share, was deliberately manufactured so as to blind them to the possibility of disobedience to the royal will. Instead of plotting some sort of minor treason on his estate, a marquis enjoyed the pleasure of knowing that on the morrow he was to be privileged to engage the king in two or three minutes of vapid conversation as the royal party made its stately progress through the vast palace halls (whose smells were evidence of the absence of sanitation facilities and of the seamy side of absolutist grandeur).

Louis understood this theater as part of his duty as sovereign, a duty

Louis XIV on his duties

that he took with utmost seriousness. Though far from brilliant, he was hard-working and conscientious. Whether or not he actually remarked *"L'état, c'est moi"* (I am the State), he believed himself personally responsi-

One of the Fountains in the Gardens at Versailles. The grounds as well as the palace were part of the backdrop for the theater of absolutism.

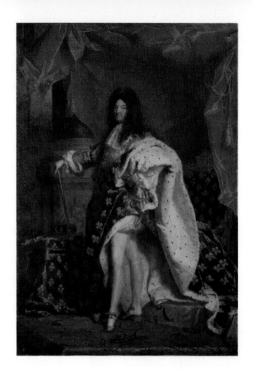

Louis XIV, the Sun King. This portrait by Rigaud illustrates the degree to which absolute monarchy was defined in terms of studied performance.

ble for the well-being of his subjects. "The deference and the respect that we receive from our subjects," he wrote in a memoir he prepared for his son on the art of ruling, "are not a free gift from them but payment for the justice and the protection that they expect from us. Just as they must honor us, we must protect and defend them."

Louis defined this responsibility in absolutist terms: as a need to concentrate royal power so as to produce general domestic tranquillity. While taming the nobility, he conciliated the upper bourgeoisie by enlisting its members to assist him in the task of administration. He appointed them as intendants, responsible for the administration and taxation of the thirty-six *generalités* into which France was divided. Intendants usually served outside the region where they were born, and were thus unconnected with the local elites over which they exercised authority. They held office at the king's pleasure, and were clearly "his" men. Other administrators, often from families newly ennobled as a result of administrative service, assisted in directing affairs of state from Versailles. These men were not actors in the theater of Louis the Sun King; they were the hard-working assistants of Louis the royal custodian of his country's welfare. Much of the time and energy of Louis's bureaucrats were expended on the collection of taxes, necessary above all in order to finance the large standing army on which France's ambitious foreign policy depended. Absolutism, it must never be forgotten, was a mechanism designed to assist ambitious monarchs in their determination to increase their power through conquest. In addition to the *taille,* or land tax, which increased

The administration of French absolutism: intendants and revenue throughout the seventeenth century and upon which a surtax was levied as well, the government introduced a *capitation* tax (head tax), payable by all, and pressed successfully for the collection of indirect taxes such as those on salt (the *gabelle*) and on wine and tobacco. Since the nobility was exempt from the *taille,* its burden fell most heavily on the peasantry, whose periodic local revolts Louis easily crushed.

Curbing regional power

Regional opposition—and indeed regionalism generally—was curtailed, but by no means eliminated, during Louis's reign. Although intendants and lesser administrators came from afar, did not speak the local dialect, and ignored local custom, they were generally obeyed. The semiautonomous outer provinces of Brittany, Languedoc, and Franche-Comté (several of the territories known collectively as the *pays d'états*) suffered the crippling of their provincial Estates. To put an end to the power of regional *parlements,* Louis decreed that members of those bodies that refused to register his laws would be summarily exiled. The Estates-General, the national French representative assembly last summoned in 1614 during the troubled regency that followed the death of Henry IV, did not meet again until 1789.

Louis XIV's religious policies

Louis was equally determined, for reasons of state and of personal conscience, to impose religious unity upon the French. That task proved to be difficult and time-consuming. The Huguenots were not the only source of theological heterodoxy. Quietists and Jansenists—both claiming to represent the "true" Roman faith—battled among themselves for adherents to their particular brand of Catholicism. Quietists preached retreat into personal mysticism that emphasized a direct relationship between God and the individual human heart. Such doctrine, dispensing as it did with the intermediary services of the Church and of the orthodox authority those services represented, was suspect in the eyes of absolutists wedded to the doctrine of *un roi, une loi, une foi* (one king, one law, one faith). Jansenism—a movement named for its founder Cornelius Jansen, a seventeenth-century bishop of Ypres—challenged the authority of the state church with an unorthodox doctrine of predestination, proclaiming the salvation of no more than an elected few. Louis persecuted Quietists and Jansenists, offering them the choice of recanting or of prison and exile. Against the Huguenots he waged an even sterner war. Protestant churches and schools were destroyed; Protestant families were forced to convert. In 1685, Louis revoked the Edict of Nantes, the legal foundation of the toleration Huguenots had enjoyed since 1598. French Protestants were thereafter denied civil rights, and their clergy was exiled. Thousands of religious refugees fled France for England, Holland, the Protestant states of Germany, and America, where their particular professional and artisanal skills made a significant contribution to economic prosperity. (The silk industries of Berlin and of Spitalfields, an urban quarter of London, were established by Huguenots.)

Colbert's economic policies

Louis's drive for unification and centralization was assisted by his ability to rely upon increased revenues. Those revenues were largely the result of policies and programs initiated by Jean Baptiste Colbert (1619–1683), the country's finance minister from 1664 until his death. Colbert was an energetic and committed mercantilist who believed that until France could put its fiscal house in order it could not achieve economic greatness. He tightened the process of tax collection, and he eliminated wherever possible the practice of tax farming, the system whereby collection agents were permitted to withhold a certain percentage of what they gathered for themselves. When Colbert assumed office, only about 25 percent of the taxes collected throughout the kingdom was reaching the treasury. By the time he died, that figure had risen to 80 percent.

Colbert's efforts were not limited to managing the public debt and wringing the inefficiencies out of the tax system, however. During this period the state also merchandised government positions and privileges on an increasing scale. Judgeships, mayoralities, and other public offices were sold, and guilds purchased the right to enforce trade regulations. The state extracted direct profit from every office it created and every privilege it controlled, demonstrating once again the way in which economy and politics were inextricably intertwined.

As a mercantilist, Colbert did all he could to increase the nation's income by means of protection and regimentation. Tariffs he imposed in 1667 and 1668 were designed to discourage the importation of foreign goods into France. He invested in the improvement of France's roads and waterways. And he used state money to promote the growth of national industry, in particular the manufacture of goods such as silk, lace, tapestries, and glass, which had long been imported. Yet Colbert's efforts to achieve national economic stability and self-sufficiency could not withstand the insatiable demands of Louis XIV's increasingly expensive wars. Indeed, by the end of Louis's reign, the limitations of his absolutist ambitions were strikingly evident. As we shall see, his aggressive foreign policy lay in ruins. The country's finances were enfeebled by the economic demands that policy exacted. Colbert himself foreshadowed Louis's ultimate failure when he lectured him in 1680, "Trade is the source of public finance and public finance is the vital nerve of war. . . . I beg your Majesty to permit me only to say to him that in war as in peace he has never consulted the amount of money available in determining his expenditures."

Jean Baptiste Colbert

Colbert as mercantilist

ABSOLUTISM IN CENTRAL AND EASTERN EUROPE, 1660–1720

Whatever success Louis XIV did enjoy as an absolute monarch was in part the result of his own abilities, and of those of his advisers. Yet it was due as well to the fact that he could claim to stand as the supreme embodiment of the will of all of his people. Despite its internal division into territories and orders that continued to claim some right to independence, France was already unified before the accession of Louis XIV and possessed a sense of itself as a nation. In this, it differed from the empires,

Absolutism and national unity

kingdoms, and principalities to the east, where rulers faced an even more formidable task than did Louis as they attempted to weld their disparately constructed monarchies into a united, centralized whole. The Thirty Years' War had delivered a final blow to the pretensions of the Holy Roman Empire, which the French philosopher Voltaire dubbed neither holy, Roman, nor an empire. Power, in varying degrees, passed to the over three hundred princes, bishops, and magistrates who governed the assorted states of Germany throughout the remainder of the seventeenth and eighteenth centuries.

Absolutism in the German states

Despite the minute size of their domains, many of these petty monarchs attempted to establish themselves as absolutists in miniature, building lesser versions of Louis XIV's Versailles. They remodeled cities to serve as explicit expressions of their power. Broad avenues led to monumental squares and eventually to the grand palace of the monarch. Medieval cities had masked the inequalities of the social order in their crowded, twisted streets and passageways, where different social ranks often lived jumbled together in close physical proximity. Absolutist capital cities, in contrast, celebrated inequality, their planning and architecture purposely emphasizing the vast distance separating the ruler from the ruled. European absolutists followed the French example by maintaining standing armies and paying for their expensive pretensions by tariffs and tolls that severely hampered the development of any sort of economic unity within the region as a whole. Although these rulers often prided themselves on their independence from imperial control, in many instances they were client states of France. A sizable portion of the money Louis devoted to the conduct of foreign affairs went to these German princelings. States like Saxony, Brandenburg-Prussia, and Bavaria, which were of a size to establish themselves as truly independent, were not averse to forming alliances against their own emperor.

The absolutism of Frederick William of Brandenburg

Most notable among these middle-sized German states was Brandenburg-Prussia, whose emergence as a power of consequence during this period was the result of the single-minded determination of its rulers, principally Frederick William, elector of Brandenburg from 1640 to 1688, whose abilities have earned him the title of "Great Elector." The rise of Brandenburg-Prussia from initial insignificance, poverty, and devastation in the wake of the Thirty Years' War resulted from three basic achievements that can be credited to the Great Elector. First, he pursued an adroit foreign policy that enabled him to establish effective sovereignty over the widely dispersed and underdeveloped territories under his rule: Brandenburg, a large but not particularly productive territory in north-central Germany; Prussia, a duchy to the east that was dangerously exposed on three sides to Poland; and a sprinkling of tiny states—Cleves, Mark, and Ravensberg—to the west. By siding with Poland in a war against Sweden in the late 1650s, the Great Elector obtained the Polish king's surrender of nominal overlordship in East Prussia. And by some crafty diplomatic shuffling in the 1670s, he secured his western provinces from French interference by returning Pomerania, captured in a recent war, to France's Swedish allies.

Frederick William's second achievement was the establishment of a large standing army, the primary instrument of his diplomatic successes. By 1688, Brandenburg-Prussia had 30,000 troops permanently under arms. That he was able to sustain an army of this size in a state with comparatively limited resources was a measure of the degree to which the army more than repaid its costs. It ensured the elector and his successors absolute political control by fostering obedience among the populace, an obedience they were prepared to observe if their lands might be spared the devastation of another Thirty Years' War.

The third factor contributing to the emergence of the Great Elector's state as an international power was his imposition of an effective system of taxation and his creation of a government bureaucracy to administer it. Here he struck an important bargain with the powerful and privileged landlords (*Junkers*) without whose cooperation his programs would have had no chance of success. In return for an agreement that allowed them to reduce their peasant underlings to the status of serfs, the Junkers gave away their right to oppose a permanent tax system, provided, of course, that they were made immune from the payment of taxes themselves. (As in other European countries, taxes in Prussia fell most heavily on the peasantry.)

Henceforth, the political privileges of the landlord class diminished; secure in their right to manage their own estates as they wished, the Junkers were content to surrender management of the Hohenzollern possessions into the hands of a centralized bureaucracy. Its most important department was a military commissariat, whose functions included not only the dispensing of army pay and matériel, but the development of industries to manufacture military equipment. Frederick William's success

The establishment of a large standing army

Taxation and bureaucracy: bargaining with the Junkers

The Junkers and the army

Prussians Swearing Allegiance to the Great Elector at Königsberg, 1663. The occasion upon which the Prussian estates first acknowledged the overlordship of their ruler. This ceremony marked the beginning of the centralization of the Prussian state.

was due primarily to his ability to gain the active cooperation of the Junker class, something he needed even more than Louis XIV needed the support of the French nobility. Without it, Frederick William could never have hammered together a state from the disparate territories that were his political raw material. To obtain it, he used the army, not only to maintain order, but as a way of co-opting Junker participation. The highest honor that could befall a Brandenburg squire was commission and promotion as a military servant of the state.

The Habsburg Empire

Like the Prussian rulers, the Habsburg monarchs were confronted with the task of transforming four different regions into a cohesive state. In the case of Austria, this effort was complicated by the fact that these areas were ethnically and linguistically diverse: the southernmost Germanic lands that roughly make up the present-day state of Austria; the northern Czech- (Slavic-) speaking provinces of Bohemia and Moravia; the German-speaking Silesia, inherited in 1527; and Hungary (where the Magyar population spoke a non-Slavic, Finno-Ugric language), also acquired in 1527 but largely lost to Turkish invasion just a few years afterward. For the next 150 years the Habsburgs and the Turks vied for control of Hungary. Until 1683 Turkish pashas ruled three-fourths of the Magyar kingdom, extending to within eighty miles of the Habsburg capital of Vienna. In 1683 the Turks beseiged Vienna itself, but were repulsed by the Austrians, assisted by a mixed German and Polish army under the command of King John Sobieski of Poland. This victory was a prelude to the Habsburg reconquest of virtually all of Hungary by the end of the century.

Bargaining with Bohemia and Moravia

The task of constructing an absolutist state from these extraordinarily varied territories was tackled with limited success by the seventeenth-century Habsburg emperors Ferdinand III (1637–1657) and Leopold I (1658–1705). Most of their efforts were devoted to the establishment of productive agricultural estates in Bohemia and Moravia, and to taming the independent nobility there and in Hungary. Landlords were encouraged to farm for export and were supported in this effort by a government decree that compelled peasants to provide three days of unpaid *robot* service per week to their masters.* For this support, Bohemian and Moravian landed elites exchanged the political independence that had in the past expressed itself in the activities of their territorial legislative Estates.

Problems with the Hungarian nobility

Habsburg rulers tried to effect this same sort of bargain in Hungary as well. But there the tradition of independence was stronger and died harder. Hungarian (or Magyar) nobles in the west claimed the right to elect their king, a right they eventually surrendered to Leopold in 1687. But the central government's attempts to reduce the country further by administering it through the army, by granting large tracts of land to German aristocrats and settlers, and by persecuting non-Catholics were almost total failure. The result was a powerful nobility that remained fiercely determined to retain its traditional constitutional and religious

---

*The English usage of the term *robot* derives from the Czech designation of a serf.

"liberties." The Habsburg emperors could boast that they too, like absolutists elsewhere, possessed a large standing army and an educated (in this case, German-speaking) bureaucracy. But the exigencies imposed by geography and ethnicity kept them at some distance from the absolutist goal of a unified, centrally controlled and administered state.

Undoubtedly the most dramatic episode in the history of early-modern absolutist rule was the dynamic reign of Tsar Peter I of Russia (1682–1725). Peter's accomplishments alone would clearly have earned him his history-book title, Peter the Great. But his imposing height—he was nearly seven feet tall—as well as his mercurial personality—jesting one moment, raging the next—certainly helped. Peter is best remembered as the tsar whose policies brought Russia into the world of western Europe. Previously the country's rulers had set their faces firmly against the West, disdaining a civilization at odds with the Eastern Orthodox culture that was their heritage, while laboring to keep the various ethnic groups—Russians, Ukrainians, and a wide variety of nomadic tribes—within their ever-growing empire from destroying not only each other but the tsarist state itself. Since 1613 Russia had been ruled by members of the Romanov dynasty, who had attempted with some success to restore political stability following the chaotic "time of troubles" that had occurred after the death of the bloodthirsty, half-mad Tsar Ivan (the Terrible) in 1584. Tsar Alexis I (1645–1676) took a significant step toward unification in 1654 when he secured an agreement with the Ukrainians to incorporate that portion of the Ukraine lying east of the Dneiper River into the Muscovite state. But the early Romanovs were faced with a severe threat to this unity and their rule between 1667 and 1671, when a Cossack leader (the Russian Cossacks were semiautonomous bands of peasant cavalrymen) named Stenka Razin led much of southeastern Russia into rebellion. Stenka Razin's uprising found widespread support from serfs who had been oppressed by their masters as well as from non-Russian tribes in the lower Volga area who longed to cast off the domination of Moscow. But ultimately Tsar Alexis and the Russian nobility whose interests were most at stake were able to raise an army capable of defeating Razin's zealous but disorganized bands. Before the rebellion was finally crushed, more than 100,000 rebels had been slaughtered.

These campaigns were but a prelude to the deliberate and ruthless drive to absolutist power launched by Peter after he overthrew the regency of his half-sister Sophia and assumed personal control of the state in 1689. Within ten years he had scandalized nobility and clergy alike by traveling to Holland and England to recruit highly skilled foreign workers and to study the craft of shipbuilding. Upon his return he distressed them still further by declaring his intention to Westernize Russia and initiating this campaign by cutting off the "Eastern" beards and flowing sleeves of leading noblemen at court. Determined to "civilize" the nobility, he published a book of manners which forbade spitting on the floor and eating with one's fingers, and encouraged the cultivation of the art of polite conversation between the sexes.

Russian absolutism

Peter the Great. An eighteenth-century mosaic.

Peter Cutting a Nobleman's Beard. In this Russian woodcut Peter the Great is portrayed as a diminutive pest.

Much as Peter wished to consider himself a westerner, his particular brand of absolutism differed from that of other contemporary monarchs. As we have seen, the autocracy imposed by Ivan III in the fifteenth century had a decidedly Eastern cast. Peter was the willing heir to much of that tradition. He considered himself above the law and thus his own absolute master to a degree that was alien to the absolutist theories and traditions of the Habsburgs and Bourbons. Autocrat of all the Russias, he ruled despotically, with a ferocious individual power that western European rulers did not possess. Armed with such arbitrary power in theory, and intent on realizing its full potential in practice, Peter set out to turn Russia toward the West and to modernize his state. He would brook no opposition.

Confronted with a rebellion among the *streltsy,* the politically active, elite corps of the army who were most opposed to his innovations and who favored the restoration of his half-sister to the throne, Peter reacted with a savagery that astonished his contemporaries. Roughly 1,200 suspected conspirators were summarily executed, many of them gibbeted outside the walls of the Kremlin, where their bodies remained for months as a graphic reminder of the fate awaiting those who would dare to challenge his absolute authority. Applying a lesson from the West, Peter proceeded to create a large standing army recruited from the ranks of the peasantry and scrupulously loyal to the tsar. One of every twenty males was conscripted for lifelong service. He financed his army, as did other absolutists, by increasing taxes, with their burden falling most heavily on the peasantry. To equip his new military force, he fostered the growth of the iron and munitions industries. Factories were built and manned by peasant laborers whose position was little better than that of slaves. Serfs

Peter the Great's Execution of the Streltsy. This contemporary print shows scores of corpses gibbeted outside the walls of the Kremlin. Peter kept the rotting bodies on display for months to discourage his subjects from opposing his efforts to Westernize Russian society.

were also commandeered for other public works projects, such as road and canal building, necessary for the modernization of the state.

In an effort to further consolidate his absolute power, he replaced the Duma—the nation's rudimentary national assembly—with a rubber-stamp senate, and appointed a procurator, or agent, dependent directly on him, to manage the affairs of the tradition-bound Russian Orthodox Church, which essentially became an extension of the state. At the same time, Peter was fashioning new, larger, and more efficient administrative machinery to cope with the demands of his modernization program. Although he preferred to draw into the bureaucracy "new" men, whose loyalty to the tsar would be unerring, he was compelled to rely upon the services of the noble—or *boyar*—class as well, rewarding them by increasing their control over their serfs. Nevertheless, membership in his new bureaucracy did not depend on birth. One of his principal advisers, Alexander Menshikov, began his career as a cook and finished as a prince. Bureaucratic status replaced noble rank as the key to power. The administrative machinery devised by Peter furnished Russia with its ruling class for the next two hundred years.

Peter the Great's Eurocentric worldview also manifested itself in his foreign policy, as witnessed by his bold drive to gain a Russian outlet on the Baltic Sea. Previous battles with the Turks to secure a port on the Black Sea, and thus a southern passage to the West, had failed. Now he engaged in a war with Sweden's meteoric soldier-king Charles XII (1697–1718), who devoted most of his reign to campaigns in the field against the Danes, the Poles, and the Russians. By defeating Charles decisively at the battle of Poltava in 1709, Peter was able to secure his window to the West. He promptly outdid his absolutist counterparts in Europe, who had moved their courts to the outskirts of their capital cities, by moving the Russian capital from Moscow to an entirely new city on the Gulf of Finland. An army of serfs was employed to erect the baroque city of St. Petersburg around a palace intended to imitate and rival Louis XIV's Versailles.

Not surprisingly, Peter's drastic programs met with concerted resistance. Resentment smoldered under his imposing hand, even within the palace. His son Alexis, who had dared to declare himself opposed to his father's innovations, became a rallying point for the forces of resistance to the tsar and his policies, and died under torture inflicted at his father's command in 1718. Upon Peter's death in 1725, *boyar* determination to undo his reforms surfaced during the succession struggle. There followed a series of ineffective tsars, creatures of the Palace Guard, thus allowing the resentful nobles to rescind many of his reforms. In 1762, the crown passed to Catherine II, a ruler whose ambitions and determination were equal to those of her august predecessor.

Peter the Great of Russia, Leopold I of Austria, Frederick William of Brandenburg-Prussia, and above all Louis XIV of France: these were the "great" seventeenth-century absolutists. Elsewhere, the fortunes of absolutism fared far less well. The ineffectual, weak-minded Spanish monarch

The St. Petersburg Palaces. This first of six versions of the Winter Palace (left) was erected in 1711. It quickly proved to be too modest for Peter's needs. Within a decade he had created a far more elaborate complex called Peterhof (right), complete with fountains fashioned after those of Versailles.

Charles II found himself besieged by rebellions in Portugal and Sicily. In 1668, after years of fighting, he was forced to recognize Portuguese independence. In Sweden, Charles X and Charles XI managed to extend their territories at the expense of the Danes and to quell the independence of the aristocracy by confiscating their fiefdoms. During the reign of Charles XII, however, that legacy was dissipated by an adventurous but ultimately unproductive foreign policy. In Poland, the opposition of the landed gentry—or *szlachta*—to any form of centralized government produced a political stalemate that amounted to little more than anarchy. Foreign powers took advantage of this situation to intervene in Polish affairs and, in the eighteenth century, to carve up the country and distribute it among themselves.

THE ENGLISH EXCEPTION

The policies of Charles II

But what of England, which had experienced a taste of absolutist centralization under the Tudors and early Stuarts, and indeed under Oliver Cromwell, but which possessed in its Parliament the longest tradition and most highly developed form of representative government in western Europe? England's political history in the late seventeenth century provides the most striking contrast to Continental absolutism. Charles II (son of the beheaded Charles I), who returned from exile and ascended the throne in 1660, was initially welcomed by most English men and women. He pledged himself not to reign as a despot, but to respect Parliament and to observe Magna Carta and the Petition of Right, for he admitted that he was not anxious to "resume his travels." His delight in the unbuttoned moral atmosphere of his court and the culture it supported (risqué plays, dancing, and marital infidelity) mirrored a public desire to forget the restraints of the puritan past. The wits of the time suggested that Charles, "that known enemy to virginity and chastity," played his role as the father of his country to the fullest. However, as Charles's admiration of things French grew to include the absolutism of Louis XIV, he came to be regarded as a threat to more than English womanhood by a great many powerful Englishmen. However anxious to restore the monarchy, they were not about to surrender their traditional rights to another Stuart autocrat. By the late 1670s, the country found itself divided politically into those who supported the king (called by their opponents "Tories," a popular nickname for Irish Catholic bandits) and those opposed to him (called by their opponents "Whigs," a similar nickname for Scottish Presbyterian rebels).

As the new party labels suggest, religion remained an exceedingly divisive national issue. Charles was sympathetic to Roman Catholicism, even to the point of a deathbed conversion in 1685. He therefore opposed the stiff code of ecclesiastical regulations, known as the Clarendon Code, which had reestablished Anglicanism as the official state religion and which penalized Catholics and Protestant dissenters. In 1672, Charles suspended the Clarendon Code, although the public outcry against this action compelled him to retreat. This controversy, and rising opposition to the probable succession of Charles's ardent Roman Catholic brother James, led to a series of Whig electoral victories between 1679 and 1681. But Charles found that increased revenues, plus a secret subsidy he was receiving from Louis XIV, enabled him to govern without resort to Parliament, to which he would otherwise have had to go for money. In addition to ignoring Parliament, Charles further infuriated and alarmed Whig politicians by arranging the execution of several of their most prominent leaders on charges of treason, and by remodeling local government in

Charles suspends Clarendon Code

Charles II of England

such a way as to make it more dependent on royal favor. Charles died in 1685 with his power enhanced, but he left behind him a political and religious legacy that was to be the undoing of his successor.

James II was the very opposite of his brother. A zealous Catholic convert, he alienated his Tory supporters, all of whom were of course Anglicans, by dismissing them in favor of Roman Catholics, and by once again suspending the penal laws against Catholics and dissenters. His stubbornness, as one historian has remarked, made it all but impossible for him to take "yes" for an answer. Whereas Charles had been content to defeat his political enemies, James was determined to humiliate them. Like Charles, James interfered in local government, but his appointments were so personally distasteful and so mediocre as to arouse active opposition. James made no attempt to disguise his Roman Catholicism. He publicly declared his wish that all his subjects might be converted, and paraded papal legates through the streets of London. When, in June 1688, he ordered all Anglican clergymen to read his decree of toleration from their pulpits, seven bishops refused and were clapped into prison on charges of seditious libel. At their trial, however, they were declared not guilty, to the vast satisfaction of the English populace.

The trial of the bishops was one event that brought matters to a head. The other was the birth of a son in 1688 to James and his second wife, the Roman Catholic daughter of the duke of Modena. This male infant, who was to be raised a Catholic, replaced James's much older Protestant daughter Mary as heir to the British throne. Despite a rumor that the baby boy was an imposter smuggled into the royal bedchamber in a warming pan, political leaders of both parties were prepared not only to believe in the legitimacy of the child but to take active steps to prevent the possibility of his succession. A delegation of Whigs and Tories crossed the Channel to Holland with an invitation to Mary's husband William of Orange, the *stadholder* or chief executive of the United Provinces and the great-grandson of William the Silent. William was asked to cross to England with an invading army to restore English religious and political freedom. As leader of a Continental coalition determined to thwart Louis XIV's expansionist policies, he accepted, welcoming the chance such a move represented to bring England into active opposition to the French (see p. 614).

William III

William's "conquest" was a bloodless coup. James fled the country in 1688, thereby allowing Parliament to declare the throne vacant and clearing the way for the accession of William and Mary as joint sovereigns of England. A Bill of Rights, passed by Parliament and accepted by the new king and queen in 1689, reaffirmed English civil liberties such as trial by jury, habeas corpus (guaranteeing the accused a speedy trial), and the right of petition and redress, and established that the monarchy was subject to the law of the land. An Act of Toleration, passed in 1689, granted dissenters the right to worship, though not the right to full political protection. In 1701, with the son of the exiled James II now reaching maturity in France, an Act of Succession ordained that the English throne was to pass first to Mary's childless sister Anne, who ruled from 1702 to 1714, and then to George, elector of the German principality of Hanover, who was the great-grandson of James I. The connection was a distant one, but the Hanoverian dynasty was Protestant, and George reputed to be a capable enough ruler. The act was further evidence of the degree to which Parliament could dictate its terms. Henceforth, all English sovereigns were to be communicants of the Church of England. If foreign born, they could not engage England in the defense of their native land, nor leave the country, without Parliamentary consent.

The events of 1688 and 1689 were soon referred to by the English as "the Glorious Revolution." Glorious for the English in that it occurred without bloodshed (although James is reputed to have been suffering from a nosebleed at the moment of crisis). Glorious, too, for defenders of Parliamentary prerogative. Although William and Mary and their royal successors continued to enjoy a large measure of executive power, after 1688 no king or queen attempted to govern without Parliament, which met annually from that time on. Parliament strengthened its control over the collection and expenditure of public money. Future sovereigns were henceforth unable to conduct the country's business without recourse to the House of Commons for the funds to do so. Glorious, finally, for advocates of the civil liberties now guaranteed within the Bill of Rights.

A "glorious" revolution?

Yet 1688 was not all glory. It was a revolution that consolidated the position of large property holders, local magnates whose political and economic power base in their rural constituencies and on their estates had been threatened by the interventions of Charles II and James II. If it was a revolution, it was one designed to restore the *status quo* on behalf of a wealthy social and economic order that would soon make itself even wealthier as it drank its fill of government patronage and war profits. And it was a revolution that brought nothing but misery to the Roman Catholic minority in Scotland, which joined with England and Wales in the union of Great Britain in 1707, and the Catholic majority in Ireland where, following the Battle of the Boyne in 1690, repressive military forces imposed the exploitive will of a self-interested Protestant minority upon the Catholic majority.

1688 as a defense of status quo

Although the "Glorious Revolution" was an expression of immediate political circumstance, it was a reflection as well of anti-absolutist theories that had risen in the late seventeenth century to challenge the ideas of writers such as Bodin, Hobbes, and Bossuet. Chief among these opponents of absolutism was the Englishman John Locke (1632–1704), whose *Two Treatises of Civil Government,* written prior to the revolution, though published in 1690, was used to justify the events of the previous two years. Locke maintained that originally all humans had lived in a theoretical state of nature in which absolute freedom and equality prevailed, and in which there was no government of any kind. The only law was the law of nature, which individuals enforced for themselves in order to protect their natural rights to life, liberty, and property. It was not long, however, before they began to perceive that the inconveniences of the state of

Defense of 1688: the political theories of John Locke

nature greatly outweighed its advantages. With individuals attempting to enforce their own rights, confusion and insecurity were the unavoidable results. Accordingly, the people agreed among themselves to establish a civil society, to set up a government, and to surrender certain powers to it. But they did not make that government absolute. The only power they conferred upon it was the executive power of the law of nature. Since the state was nothing but the joint power of all the members of society, its authority could "be no more than those persons had in a state of nature before they entered into society, and gave it up to the community." All powers not expressly surrendered were reserved to the people themselves. If the government exceeded or abused the authority explicitly granted in the political contract, it became tyrannical; the people then had the right to dissolve it or to rebel against it and overthrow it.

Locke condemned absolutism in every form. He denounced despotic monarchy, but he was no less severe in his strictures against the absolute sovereignty of parliaments. Though he defended the supremacy of the law-making branch, with the executive primarily an agent of the legislature, he nevertheless refused to concede to the representatives of the people an unlimited power. Arguing that state government was instituted among people for the preservation of property, he denied the authority of any political agency to invade the natural rights of a single individual. The law of nature, which embodied these rights, was an automatic limitation upon every branch of the government. Locke's theoretical defense of political liberties emerged in the late eighteenth century as an important element in the intellectual background of the American and French Revolutions. In 1688, however, it served a far less radical purpose. The landed magnates responsible for the exchange of James II for William and Mary could read Locke as an apologia for their conservative revolution. James II, rather than protecting their property and liberties, had encroached upon them; hence they had every right to overthrow the tyranny he had established and to replace it with a government that would, by ensuring their rights, defend their interests.

Locke and limited sovereignty

John Locke

WARFARE AND DIPLOMACY: THE EMERGENCE OF A STATE SYSTEM

The emergence of new state interests

To the extent that absolute monarchs succeeded in attaining their goals of unification and centralization, their states took shape as individual, identifiable political and economic entities. Often, it is true, the interests of a monarch might clash with those of the country over which he ruled. Bourbon kings and Habsburg emperors worried about the future of their family dynasties to the detriment of the future of France or Austria. And religion, the factor that had torn Europe apart in the preceding century, remained an international issue in 1700. But increasingly, both dynasty and religion were superseded by newer "interests"—commerce and international balance and stability.

The result was the emergence of a state system. Although the achievements of various monarchs were limited, they were significant enough to encourage diplomats to speak more commonly than in the past of the "interests" of a particular state, as if that state somehow had a corporate personality of its own, and of the way in which those interests might coincide or conflict with the interests of another state. What followed was a significant redefinition of the aims and calculations of diplomacy and warfare.

The organization of diplomatic bureaucracies was a major accomplishment of absolutist monarchies. Had most foreign ministers and ambassadors read the Dutchman Hugo Grotius's treatise on *The Law of War and Peace* (1625), they would have agreed with him about the necessity of establishing a body of rules that would help to bring reason and order to relations between governments. In practice, of course, reason and order gave way to bribery and improvisation. Yet the rationalization of diplomatic processes and the establishment of foreign ministries and embassies in European capitals, with their growing staffs of clerks and ministers, reflected a desire to bring order out of the international chaos that had gripped Europe during the early seventeenth century. International relations in the late 1600s was, among other things, a history of diplomatic coalitions, an indication of the degree to which negotiation was now a weapon in the armory of the absolutist state.

Warfare, however, continued to play an integral and almost constant role in the international arena. The armies of the period grew dramatically. When Louis XIV acceded to power in 1661, the French army numbered 20,000 men; by 1688, it stood at 290,000; by 1694, 400,000. These armies were increasingly professional organizations, controlled directly by the state, and under the command of trained officers recruited from

Emergence of state system

The growth of diplomacy

The growth of professional armies

The Capture of Cambrai by Louis XIV in 1677. This print illustrates the tactics of siege warfare as practiced by early-modern armies. Louis is shown receiving an emissary from the city, whose walls have been breached by siege guns.

the nobility. In Prussia, common soldiers were mostly conscripts; in other European countries they were volunteers, either native or foreign, though often "volunteers" in no more than name, having been coerced or tricked into service. Increasingly, however, enlistment was perceived by common soldiers as an avenue to a career, one that included the possibility of promotion to corporal or sergeant, and in the case of France, the promise of a small pension at the end of one's service. However recruited, common soldiers became part of an increasingly elaborate and efficient fighting force. Above all, they were made to understand the dire consequences of disobedience, breaking rank, or desertion. Soldiers were expected to obey instantly and unquestioningly. Failure to do so resulted in brutal punishment, often flogging, sometimes execution. Drill, not only on the battlefield but on the parade ground, in brilliant, elaborate uniforms and intricate formations, was designed to reduce individuals to automaton-like parts of an army whose regiments were moved across battlefields as a chess player moves pawns across the board—and with about the same concern for loss of human life.

The foreign policies of Louis XIV

The patterns of international relations during the period from 1660 to 1715 show European monarchs making use of the new machinery of diplomacy and warfare to resolve the conflicting interests of dynasty, stability, and commerce. At the center of that pattern, as at the center of Europe, stood Louis XIV. From 1661 until 1688, in a quest for glory, empire, and even revenge, he waged war across his northern and eastern frontiers on the pretext that the lands in question belonged both to the Bourbons and to the French by tradition, by former treaty, or by dynastic inheritance. His aggressively expansionist policies, alarming to other European rulers, led William of Orange, in 1674, to form an anti-French coalition with Austria, Spain, and various smaller German states. Yet Louis continued to push his frontiers eastward, invading territories that had been Germanic for centuries, and capturing Strassburg in 1681 and Luxembourg in 1684. Louis's seizure of Strassburg (subsequently called Strasbourg by the French), completing the conquest of the German-speaking province of Alsace begun in 1634 by Richelieu, irreversibly incorporated the seeds of a Franco-German animosity centered on this region that would bear bitter fruit in the great wars of the nineteenth and twentieth centuries. A second coalition, the so-called League of Augsburg (1686), which comprised Holland, Austria, Sweden, and further German allies, was only somewhat more successful than the first.

Europe on the verge of war

These allies were concerned above all to maintain some sort of European balance of power. They feared an expansionist France would prove insatiable, as it pressed its boundaries farther and farther into Germany and the Low Countries. Louis, mistakenly expecting that William would be forced to fight an English army under James to establish his right to his new throne and would therefore be too preoccupied to devote his full attention to developments on the Continent, kept up the pressure. In September 1688 he invaded the Palatinate and occupied the city of Cologne. The following year the French armies crossed the Rhine and continued their eastward drive, burning Heidelberg and committing numerous atrocities throughout the middle Rhine area. Aroused at last to effective action, the League of Augsburg, led by William and now including in addition to its original members both England and Spain, engaged Louis in a war that was to last until 1697.

The major campaigns of this War of the League of Augsburg were fought in the Low Countries. William managed to drive an army under his predecessor, James II, from Ireland in 1690; from that point on, he took command of the allied forces on the Continent. By 1694 Louis was pressed hard, not only by his allied foes, but by a succession of disastrous harvests that crippled France. Fighting remained stalemated until a treaty was signed at Ryswick in Holland in 1697, which compelled Louis to return most of France's recent gains, except for Alsace, and to recognize William as the rightful king of England.

War of the League of Augsburg

Ryswick did nothing, however, to resolve the dynastic tangle known as the Spanish Succession. Since Charles II of Spain had no direct heirs, and since he appeared to be on his deathbed in 1699, European monarchs and diplomats were obsessed by the question of who would succeed to the vast domain of the Spanish Habsburgs: not only Spain itself, but also its overseas empire, as well as the Spanish Netherlands, Naples, Sicily, and other territories in Italy. Both Louis XIV and Leopold I of Austria were married to sisters of the decrepit, unstable Charles; and both, naturally, eyed the succession to the Spanish inheritance as an exceedingly tempting dynastic plum. Yet it is a measure of the degree to which even absolutists were willing to keep their ambitions within bounds that both Leopold and Louis agreed to William's suggestion that the lion's share of the Habsburg lands should go to six-year-old Joseph Ferdinand, the prince of Bavaria, who was Charles II's grandnephew. Unfortunately, in 1699 the child died. Though the chances of war increased, William and Louis were prepared to bargain further and arranged a second treaty that divided the Spanish empire between Louis's and Leopold's heirs. Yet at the same time, Louis's diplomatic agents in Madrid persuaded Charles to sign a will in which he stipulated that the entire Spanish Habsburg inheritance should pass to Louis's grandson Philip of Anjou. This option was welcomed by many influential Spaniards, willing to endure French hegemony in return for the protection France could provide to the Spanish empire. For a time, Louis contemplated an alternative agreement that would have given France direct control of much of Italy. When Charles finally died in November 1700, Louis decided to accept the will. As if this was not enough to drive his former enemies back to war, he sent troops into the Spanish Netherlands and traders to the Spanish colonial empire, while declaring the late James II's son—the child of the warming-pan myth—the legitimate king of England.

The problem of the Spanish
Succession

Once it was clear to the allies that Louis intended to treat Spain as if it were his own kingdom, they again united against him in the cause of balance and stability. William died in 1702, just as the War of the Spanish Succession was beginning. His position as first general of the coalition

War: the battle of Blenheim

passed to two brilliant strategists, the Englishman John Churchill, duke of Marlborough, and his Austrian counterpart Prince Eugene of Savoy, an upper-class soldier of fortune who had been denied a commission by Louis. Under their command the allied forces engaged in battle after fierce battle in the Low Countries and Germany, including an extraordinary march deep into Bavaria, where the combined forces under Marlborough and Eugene smashed the French and their Bavarian allies decisively at Blenheim (1704). While the allies pressed France's armies on land, the English navy captured Gibraltar and the island of Minorca, thus establishing a strategic and commercial foothold in the Mediterranean, and helping to open a fourth major military theater in Spain itself.

The War of the Spanish Succession was a "professional" war that tested the highly trained armies of the combatants to the fullest. At the battle of Malplaquet in northeastern France in 1709, 80,000 French soldiers faced 110,000 allied troops. Though Marlborough and Eugene could claim to have won that battle, in that they forced the French to retreat, they suffered 24,000 casualties, twice those of the French. Neither Malplaquet nor other such victories brought the allies any closer to their final goal, which now appeared to be not the containment, but the complete destruction of the French military force. Queen Anne of England (Mary's sister and William's successor), once Marlborough's staunchest defender, grew disillusioned with the war and fired her general.

More than war weariness impelled the combatants toward negotiation, however. The War of the Spanish Succession had begun as a conflict about the balance of power in Europe and the world. Yet dynastic changes had by 1711 compelled a reappraisal of allied goals. Leopold I had died in 1705. When his elder son and successor Joseph I died in 1711, the Austrian monarchy fell to Leopold's youngest son, the Archduke Charles, who had been the allies' candidate for the throne of Spain. With Charles now the Austrian and the Holy Roman Emperor as Charles VI (1711–1740), the prospect of his accession to the Spanish inheritance conjured up the ghost of Charles V and threatened to give him far too much power. International stability therefore demanded an end to hostilities and diplomatic negotiation toward a solution that would reestablish some sort of general balance.

The Treaty of Utrecht settled the conflict in 1713 by redistributing territory and power in equitable portions. No one emerged a major winner or loser. Philip, Louis's grandson, remained on the throne of Spain, but Louis agreed that France and Spain would never be united under the same ruler. Austria gained territories in the Netherlands and Italy. The Dutch, victims of French aggression during the war, were guaranteed protection of their borders against future invasion. The English retained Gibraltar and Minorca, as well as territory in America (Newfoundland, Acadia, Hudson Bay) and in the Caribbean (St. Kitts). Perhaps most valuable of all, the English extracted the *asiento* from Spain, which gave them the right to supply Spanish America with African slaves. The settlement reflected the degree to which new interests had superseded old. Balance of power and stability among states were the major goals of the negotiations, goals that reflected a departure from the world of seventeenth-century turmoil when religion had been a major factor in international conflict. The eventual "winners" were undoubtedly the English, whose dynastic concerns were limited to a general acceptance of the Hanoverian settlement, and who could therefore concentrate their efforts on amassing overseas territories that would contribute to the growth of their economic prosperity and hence their international power.

ENLIGHTENED ABSOLUTISM AND LIMITED MONARCHY IN THE EIGHTEENTH CENTURY

Eighteenth-century absolutism was a series of variations on the dominant themes composed in the previous century by Louis XIV. That it has earned itself the historical distinction of "enlightened" absolutism suggests that those variations were of some consequence. Eighteenth-century rulers backed their sovereign claims not in the language of divine right, but in terms of their determination to act, as Frederick the Great of

"Enlightened" absolutism

The Age of Absolutism

Louis XV

Prussia declared, as "first servant of the state." That phrase meant not so much service to the people as it did service to the goal of further strengthening the authority of the state over institutions that sought to challenge its corporate well-being. Enlightened rulers moved to curtail the privileges of old institutions. The Roman Catholic Church, for example, was compelled to suffer the expulsion of the Jesuits from most Catholic countries. Customary laws benefiting particular orders or interests were reformed. To strengthen the state community, innovative policies in the areas of taxation, economic development, and education were instituted. As we shall see in Chapter 18, rational schemes of this sort reflected the spread of Enlightenment ideals as manifested in the writings of thinkers such as Beccaria, Diderot, and Voltaire. (The last was, in fact, a guest at Frederick's court for several years.) Assisting enlightened "first servants" in the implementation of these changes was a growing cadre of lesser servants: bureaucrats, often recruited from the nobility, but once recruited, expected to declare primary allegiance to their new master, the state. Despite innovation, "enlightened" absolutists continued to insist, as their predecessors had, that state sovereignty rested with the monarchy. Authority remained their overriding concern, and to the extent that they combatted efforts by the estates of their realms to dilute that authority, they declared their descent from their seventeenth-century forebears.

Louis XIV's successors, his great-grandson Louis XV (1715–1774) and that monarch's grandson Louis XVI (1774–1792), were unable to sustain the energetic drive toward centralization that had taken place under the Sun King. Indeed, during his last years, while fighting a desperate defensive war against his allied enemies, Louis XIV had seen his own accomplishments begin to crumble under the mounting pressure of military expenses. His heir was only five years old when he assumed the throne. As he grew up, Louis XV displayed less single-minded determination than had his great-grandfather to act the role of Sun King. The heroic, Baroque grandeur of the main palace at Versailles yielded to the Rococo grace of the Grand and Petit Trianons, pleasure pavilions built by Louis XV in the palace gardens.

During the minority of Louis XV, the French *parlements,* those courts of record responsible for registering royal decrees, enjoyed a resurgence of power which they retained throughout the century. No longer tame adjuncts of absolutist governmental machinery as they had been under Louis XIV, these bodies now proclaimed themselves the protectors of French "liberties." In 1770, encouraged by his chancellor René Maupeou, Louis XV issued an edict effectively ending the right of *parlements* to reject decrees. Protest on the part of the magistrates resulted in their imprisonment or banishment. The *parlements* themselves were replaced by new courts charged not only with the responsibility of rubber-stamping legislation but also with administering law more justly and less expensively. When Louis XVI ascended the throne in 1774, his ministers persuaded him to reestablish the *parlements* as a sign of his willingness to conciliate his trouble-making aristocracy. This he did, with the result that government—particularly the management of finances—developed into a stalemated battle.

Stalemate was what the Prussian successors to Frederick William, the Great Elector, were determined to avoid. Frederick I (1688–1713), the Great Elector's immediate successor, enhanced the appearance and cultural life of Berlin. As the Roman numeral by his name attests, he also succeeded in bargaining his support to the Austrians during the War of the Spanish Succession in return for the coveted right to style himself king. (The Austrian monarch was the Holy Roman Emperor and therefore had the right to create kings.)

Frederick William I (1713–1740), cared little for the embellishments his father had made to the capital city. His overriding concern was the building of a first-rate army. So single-minded was his attention to the military that he came to be called "the sergeant king." Military display became an obsession. His private regiment of "Potsdam Giants" was composed exclusively of soldiers over six feet in height. The king traded musicians and prize stallions for such choice specimens and delighted in marching them about his palace grounds. Frederick William I's success as the builder of a military machine can be measured in terms of numbers: 30,000 men under arms when he came to the throne; 83,000 when he died twenty-seven years later, commander of the fourth-largest army in Europe, after France, Russia, and Austria. Since he could hardly count on volunteers, most of his soldiers were conscripts, drafted from the peasantry for a period of years and required to attend annual training exercises lasting three months. Conscription was supplemented by the kidnapping of forced recruits in neighboring German lands. To finance his army, Frederick William I increased taxes and streamlined their collection through the establishment of a General Directory of War, Finance, and Domains. In 1723, he instituted a system of administration by boards, hoping thereby to eliminate individual inefficiency through collective responsibility and surveillance. In addition, he created an inspectorate to uncover and report to him the mistakes and inefficiencies of his officialdom. Even then, he continued to supervise personally the implementation of state policy while shunning the luxuries of court life; for him, the "theater" of absolutism was not the palace but the office, which placed him at the helm of the state and the army. Perceiving the resources of the state to be too precious to waste, he pared costs at every turn to the point where, it was said, he had to invite himself to a nobleman's table in order to enjoy a good meal.

A hard, unimaginative man, Frederick William I had little use for his son, whose passion was not the battlefield but the flute, and who admired French culture as much as his father disdained it. Not surprisingly, young Frederick rebelled; in 1730, when he was eighteen, he ran away from court with a friend. Apprehended, the companions were returned to the king, who welcomed the fledgling prodigal with something other than a fatted calf. Before Frederick's eyes, he had the friend executed. The grisly lesson took. Thenceforward Frederick, though he never surrendered

The achievements of Frederick I of Prussia

Frederick William I builds first-rate army

Frederick William I

The apprenticeship of Frederick the Great

Frederick the Great and Voltaire. Although Frederick offered asylum to the French philosophe, this "enlightened despot" did not permit his intellectual pursuits to interfere with matters of state.

his love of music and literature, bound himself to his royal duties, living in accordance with his own image of himself as "first servant of the state," and earning himself history's title of Frederick the Great.

Frederick William I's zealous austerity and his compulsion to build an efficient army and administrative state made Prussia a strong state. Frederick the Great (1740–1786), building on the work of his father, raised his country to the status of a major power. As soon as he became king in 1740, Frederick mobilized the army his father had never taken into battle and occupied the poorly protected Austrian province of Silesia to which Prussia had no legitimate claim. Although he had earlier vowed to make morality rather than expediency the hallmark of his reign, he seemingly had little difficulty in sacrificing his youthful idealism in the face of an opportunity to make his Prussian state a leading power. The remaining forty-five years of his monarchy were devoted to the consolidation of this first bold stroke.

Such a daring course required some adjustments within the Prussian state. The army had to be kept at full strength, and to this end, Frederick staffed its officer corps with young noblemen. In expanding the bureaucracy, whose financial administration kept his army in the field, he relied on the nobility as well, reversing the policy of his father, who had recruited his civil servants according to merit rather than birth. But Frederick was not one to tolerate mediocrity; he fashioned the most highly professional and efficient bureaucracy in Europe. The degree to which both army and bureaucracy were staffed by the nobility is a measure of

The seizure of Silesia

The nobility in the army and the bureaucracy

his determination to secure the unflagging support of the most privileged order in his realm, in order to ensure a united front against Prussia's external foes.

Frederick's domestic policies reflected that same strategy. In matters where he ran no risk of offending the nobility, he followed his own rationalist bent, prohibiting the torture of accused criminals, putting an end to the bribing of judges, and establishing a system of elementary schools. He encouraged religious toleration, declaring that he would happily build a mosque in Berlin if he could find enough Muslims to fill it. (Yet he was strongly anti-Semitic, levying special taxes on Jews and making efforts to close the professions and the civil service to them.) On his own royal estates he was a model "enlightened" monarch. He abolished capital punishment, curtailed the forced labor services of his peasantry, and granted them long leases on the land they worked. He fostered scientific forestry and the cultivation of new crops. He opened new lands in Silesia and brought in thousands of immigrants to cultivate them. When wars ruined their farms, he supplied the peasants with new livestock and tools. Yet he never attempted to extend these reforms to the estates of the Junker elite, since to have done so would have alienated that social and economic group upon which Frederick was most dependent.

Although the monarchs of eighteenth-century Austria eventually proved themselves even more willing than Frederick the Great to undertake significant social reform, the energies of Emperor Charles VI (1711–1740) were concentrated on guaranteeing the future dynastic and territorial integrity of the Habsburg lineage and domain. Without a male heir, Charles worked to secure the right of his daughter Maria Theresa to succeed him as eventual empress. By his death in 1740 Charles had managed to persuade not only his subjects but all the major European powers to accept his daughter as his royal heir—a feat known as the "pragmatic sanction." Yet his painstaking efforts were only partially successful. As we have seen, Frederick the Great used the occasion of Charles's death to seize Silesia. The French, unable to resist the temptation to grab what they could, joined the coalition against the new empress, Maria Theresa (1740–1780).

With most of her other possessions already occupied by her enemies, Maria Theresa appealed successfully to the Hungarians for support. The empress was willing to play the role of the wronged woman when, as on this occasion, it suited her interests to do so. Hungary's vital troops combined with British financial assistance enabled her to battle Austria's enemies to a draw, although she never succeeded in regaining Silesia. The experience of those first few years of her reign persuaded Maria Theresa, who was both capable and tenacious, to reorganize her dominions along the tightly centralized lines characteristic of Prussia and France. Ten new administrative districts were established, each with its own "war commissar" appointed by and responsible to the central administration in Vienna—an Austrian equivalent of the French intendant. Property taxes were increased to finance an expanded army, which was modernized and

Frederick the Great as an enlightened absolutist

Charles VI and the "pragmatic sanction"

Maria Theresa of Austria. The empress was a formidable monarch and a match for Frederick the Great.

Maria Theresa: adversity and centralization

professionalized so as to remain on a par with the military establishments of the other great powers. Centralization, finances, army: once more those three crucial elements in the formula of absolute rule came into play.

Reform did not stop there, however. Together Maria Theresa and her son Joseph II, with whom she ruled jointly from 1765 to 1780, and who then succeeded her for another ten years, instituted a series of significant social reforms. Although both mother and son were devout Roman Catholics, they moved to assert their control over the Church, removing the clergy's exemption from taxation and decreeing the state's ability to block the publication of papal bulls in Austria. In 1773, following the papal suppression of the Jesuits, they used the order's assets to finance a program of state-wide primary education. Although the General Schools Ordinance of 1774 never achieved anything like a universally literate population, it did succeed in educating hundreds of thousands, and in financing not only schools for children but schools as well for those who taught the children. Joseph followed these reforms with an "Edict on Idle Institutions" in 1780, which resulted in the closing of hundreds of monastic houses, whose property went to support charitable institutions now under state control. These reforms and others—liberalization of punishment for criminal offenses, a relaxation of censorship, the abolishing of serfdom and feudal dues, and an attempt to eradicate superstition by curbing the practice of pilgrimages and celebration of saint's days—made Joseph more enemies than friends, among both the noble elite and the common people. "Enlightened" though Joseph II was, how-

Edict of Tolerance. An illustration from a pamphlet depicting Joseph II of Austria as an enlightened monarch.

ever, he nevertheless remained a staunch absolutist, as concerned with the maintenance of a strong army and an efficient bureaucracy as with the need to educate his peasantry. Joseph's brother Leopold II, who succeeded him in 1790, attempted to maintain the reformist momentum. His death two years later and the accession of his reactionary son Francis II (1792–1835) put an end to liberalizing experiments.

Unlike Joseph II, Catherine the Great of Russia (1762–1796) felt herself compelled to curry the favor of her nobility by involving them directly in the structure of local administration, by exempting them from military service and taxation, and probably most important, by granting them absolute control over the serfs on their estates. Her policy grew out of her strong ties to powerful nobles and her involvement in the conspiracy that led to the assassination of her husband, Tsar Peter III, the last of a series of weak rulers who followed Peter the Great. Catherine was herself a German, and prided herself on her devotion to Western principles of government. Ambitious to establish a reputation as an intellectual and enlightened monarch, she corresponded with French philosophers, wrote plays, published a digest of William Blackstone's *Commentaries on the Laws of England,* and began a history of Russia. Her contributions to social reform did not extend much beyond the founding of hospitals and orphanages, and the expression of a pious hope that someday the serfs might be liberated. Although she did summon a commission in 1767 to codify Russian law, its achievements were modest: a minor extension of religious toleration, a slight restriction of the use of torture by the state. Catherine's interest in theories of reform did, however, stimulate the development of a social conscience among certain gentry intellectuals, foreshadowing a more widespread movement in the nineteenth century.

Any plans Catherine may have had for improving the lot of the peasants, however, were abruptly cancelled after their frustration with St. Petersburg's centralization efforts erupted in a violent peasant-serf rebellion in 1773–1774. Free peasants in the Volga valley region found themselves compelled to provide labor services to nobles sent by the crown to control them, Cossacks were subjected to taxation and conscription for the first time, and factory workers and miners were pressed into service in the state's industrial enterprises. These and other disparate but dissatisfied groups, including serfs, united under the rebel banner of Emelyan Pugachev, an illiterate Cossack who claimed to be the late Tsar Peter III. The hapless Peter, who had spoken as a reformer in life, in death became a larger-than-life hero for those opposed to the determined absolutism of his successor. As Pugachev marched, he encouraged his followers to strike out not only against the empress but also against the nobility and the church. More than 1,500 landlords and priests were murdered, and the ruling classes were terrified as the revolt spread. While Catherine's forces initially had little success against the rebel army, the threat of famine plagued Pugachev's advance and finally led to disarray among his troops. Betrayed in 1774, he was captured and taken in an iron cage to Moscow, where he was tortured and killed. Catherine responded to this uprising

Catherine as an "enlightened" monarch

Catherine the Great

The Pugachev rebellion

Emelyan Pugachev Shackled and Encaged after His Capture

George I of Britain

with further centralization and tightening of aristocratic authority over the peasantry.

The brutal suppression and punishment of the rebels reflected the ease with which the German-born Catherine took to the despotic authoritarianism that characterized Russian absolutism. At the same time, Catherine continued the work of Peter the Great in introducing Russia to Western ideas; she came to terms with the nobility in a way that brought stability to the state; and she made the country a formidable power in European affairs by extending its boundaries to include not only most of Poland but also lands on the Black Sea.

Eighteenth-century monarchs shared a desire to pursue policies that would mark their regimes as befitting a world that was leaving obscurantism and fanaticism behind. They were determined to press ahead with the task, begun by their seventeenth-century predecessors, of building powerful, centralized states by continuing to attempt the elimination or harnessing of the ancient privileges of still-powerful noble orders and provincial estates. The notion of a limited monarchy, in which power was divided between local and central authorities and shared by monarchs, nobles, and legislative assemblies, struck them as a dangerous anachronism. Yet as the century progressed, they found that conviction challenged by the emergence of England, under limited monarchy, as the world's leading commercial and naval power.

England (or Britain, as the country was called after its union with Scotland in 1707) prospered as a state in which power was divided between the king and Parliament. This division of political power was guaranteed by a constitution which, though unwritten, was grounded in common law and strengthened by precedent and by particular legal settlements such as those that had followed the restoration of the Stuarts in 1660 and the overthrow of James II in 1688. The Hanoverians George I (1714–1727) and his son George II (1727–1760) were by no means political nonentities. Though George I could not speak English, he could converse comfortably enough with his ministers in French. The first two Georges made a conscientious and generally successful effort to govern within their adopted kingdom. They appointed the chief ministers who remained responsible to them for the creation and direction of state policy. Yet because Parliament, after 1688, retained the right to legislate, tax, and spend, its powers were far greater than those of any European parlement, estate, or diet. During the reign of the first two Hanoverians, politics was on most occasions little more than a struggle between factions within the Whig party, composed of wealthy—and in many cases newly rich—landed magnates who were making fortunes in an expanding economy based on commercial and agricultural capitalism.

The Tories, because of their previous association with the Stuarts, remained political "outs" for most of the century. To the Whigs, national politics was no longer a matter of clashing principles. Those principles had been settled—to their satisfaction—in 1688. Nor was politics a matter of legislating in the national interest. Britain was governed locally, not

The House of Commons. Despite its architectural division into two "sides," the House was composed of men of property whose similar economic interests encouraged them to agree on political fundamentals.

Local government

from the center as in an absolutist state. Aristocrats and landed gentry administered the affairs of the particular counties and parishes in which their estates lay, as lords lieutenant, as justices of the peace, as overseers of the poor, unhampered, to a degree unknown on the Continent, by legislation imposed uniformly throughout the kingdom. The quality of local government varied greatly. Some squires were as "allworthy" as Henry Fielding's fictional character of that name in the novel *Tom Jones*. Others cared for little beyond the bottle and the hunt. A French traveler noted in 1747 that the country gentleman was "naturally a very dull animal" whose favorite after-dinner toast was "to all honest fox hunters in Great Britain." These men administered those general laws that did exist—the Poor Law, game laws—which were drawn in such a way as to leave their administrators wide latitude, a latitude that they exercised in order to enhance the appearance of their own local omnipotence. Thus in Britain there was no attempt to pass a law establishing a state-wide system of primary education. Centralizing legislation of that sort, the hallmark of absolutist states, was anathema to the British aristocracy and gentry. They argued that education, if it was to be provided, should be provided at their expense, in village schoolrooms by schoolmasters in their employ. Those instructors would make it their business to teach their pupils not only rudimentary reading, writing, and figuring, but the deferential behavior that bespoke the obligation of the poor to their rich benefactors.

Robert Walpole as chief minister

As the Church of England catechism had it, they were "to do their duty in that station of life unto which it shall please God to call them."

Politics, then, was neither first principles nor national legislation. It was "interest" and "influence," the weaving of a web of obligations into a political faction powerful enough to secure jobs and favors—a third secretaryship in the foreign office from a minister, an Act of Enclosure from Parliament. The greatest master of this game of politics was Robert Walpole (1676–1745), who was Britain's leading minister from the early 1720s until 1742. Walpole is sometimes called Britain's first prime minister, a not entirely accurate distinction, since officially that position did not exist until the nineteenth century. Prime minister or not, he wielded great political power. He took advantage of the king's frequent absences in Hanover to assert control over the day-to-day governance of the country. He ruled as chief officer of his cabinet, a small group of like-minded politicians whose collective name derived from the room in which they met. In time the cabinet evolved into the policy-making executive arm of the British political system; Britain is governed today by cabinet and Parliament, the cabinet being composed of leading politicians from the majority party in Parliament.

Walpole and the nature of British politics

Walpole was a member of a Norfolk gentry family who had risen to national prominence on the fortune he amassed while serving as paymaster-general to the armed forces during the War of the Spanish Succession. Adept at bribery and corruption, he used his ability to reward his supporters with appointments to ensure himself a loyal political following. By the end of his career, grossly fat and stuffed seemingly with the profits of his years in office, he was being depicted by cartoonists and balladeers as Britain's most accomplished robber. "Little villains must submit to Fate,"

Left: **Sir Robert Walpole with Members of His Cabinet.** Right: **A Portrait of Walpole**

lamented a typical lampoon, "while great ones do enjoy the world in state." Walpole was no more corrupt, however, than the political process over which he presided. Most seats in Parliament's lower House of Commons were filled by representatives from boroughs that often had no more than two or three dozen electors. Hence it was a relatively simple task to buy votes, either directly or with promises of future favors. Walpole cemented political factions together into an alliance that survived for about twenty years. During that time, he worked to ensure domestic tranquillity by refusing to press ahead with any legislation that might arouse national controversy. He withdrew what was perhaps his most innovative piece of legislation—a scheme that would increase excise taxes and reduce import duties as a means of curbing smugglers—in the face of widespread popular opposition.

Other Whig politicians succeeded Walpole in office in the 1740s and 1750s, but only one, William Pitt, later elevated to the House of Lords as the earl of Chatham, commanded public attention as Walpole had. George III (1760–1820), who came to the throne as a young man in 1760, resented the manner in which he believed his royal predecessors had been treated by the Whig oligarchy. Whether or not, as legend has it, his mother fired his determination with the constant injunction "George, be king!" he began his reign convinced that he must assert his rightful prerogatives. He dismissed Pitt and attempted to impose ministers of his own choosing on Parliament. King and Parliament battled this issue of prerogative throughout the 1760s. In 1770, Lord North, an aristocrat satisfactory to the king and with a large enough following in the House of Commons to ensure some measure of stability, assumed the position of first minister. His downfall occurred a decade later, as a result of his mismanagement of the overseas war that resulted in Britain's loss of its original thirteen North American colonies. A period of political shuffling was followed by the king's appointment, at the age of twenty-three, of another William Pitt, Chatham's son, and this Pitt directed Britain's fortunes for the next twenty-five years—a political reign even longer than Walpole's. Although the period between 1760 and 1780 witnessed a struggle between crown (as the king and his political following were called) and Parliament, it was a very minor skirmish compared with the titanic constitutional struggles of the seventeenth century. Britain saw the last of absolutism in 1688. What followed was the mutual adjustment of the two formerly contending parties to a settlement both considered essentially sound.

George III: the battle over prerogative

WAR AND DIPLOMACY IN THE EIGHTEENTH CENTURY

The history of European diplomacy and warfare after 1715 is one in which the twin goals of international stability and economic expansion remained paramount. The fact that those objectives often conflicted with each other set off further frequent wars, in which the ever-growing

The Seven Years' War

standing armies of absolutist Europe were matched against each other and in which the deciding factor often turned out to be not Continental military strength, but British naval power. The major conflict at mid-century, known as the Seven Years' War in Europe and the French and Indian War in North America, reflects the overlapping interests of power balance and commercial gain. In Europe, the primary concern was balance. Whereas in the past France had seemed the major threat, now Prussia loomed—at least in Austrian eyes—as a far more dangerous interloper. Under these circumstances, in 1756 the Austrian foreign minister, Prince Wenzel von Kaunitz, effected the so-called diplomatic revolution, which put an end to the enmity between France and Austria, and resulted in a formidable threat to the Prussia of Frederick the Great. Frederick, meanwhile, was taking steps to protect his flanks. While anxious not to arouse his French ally, he nevertheless signed a neutrality treaty with the British, who were concerned with securing protection for their sovereign's Hanoverian domains. The French read Frederick's act as a hostile one, and thus fell all the more readily for Kaunitz's offer of an alliance. The French indeed perceived a pressing need for trustworthy European allies, since they were already engaged in an undeclared war with Britain in North America. By mid-1756 Kaunitz could count France, Russia, Sweden, and several German states as likely allies against Prussia. Rather than await retribution from his enemies, Frederick invaded strategic but neutral Saxony and then Austria itself, thus once again playing the role of aggressor.

Shifting power balances

The configurations in this diplomatic gavotte are undoubtedly confusing. They are historically important, however, because they indicate the way in which the power balance was shifting, and the attempts of European states to respond to those shifts by means of new diplomatic alliances. Prussia and Britain were the volatile elements: Prussia on the Continent; Britain overseas. The war from 1756 to 1763 in Europe centered upon Frederick's attempts to prevent the dismemberment of his domain at the hands of the French-Austrian-Russian alliance. Time and again the Prussian army's superiority and Frederick's own military genius frustrated his enemies' attacks. Ultimately, Prussia's survival against these overwhelming odds—"the miracle of the House of Brandenburg"—was ensured by the death of the Tsarina Elizabeth (1741–1762), daughter of Peter the Great, and by the accession of Peter III (1762), whose admiration for Frederick was as great as was his predecessor's hostility. Peter withdrew from the war, returning the conquered provinces of East Prussia and Pomerania to his country's erstwhile enemy. The peace that followed, though it compelled Frederick to relinquish Saxony, recognized his right to retain Silesia, and hence put an end to Austria's hope of one day recapturing that rich prize.

The British navy as key to victory

Overseas, battles occurred not only in North America but in the West Indies and in India, where Anglo-French commercial rivalry had resulted in sporadic, fierce fighting since the 1740s. Ultimate victory would go to that power possessing a navy strong enough to keep its supply routes

The Battle of Québec, 1759. Most often remembered for the fact that the British and French commanders, Generals Wolfe and Montcalm, were killed on the bluffs above the St. Lawrence River (the Plains of Abraham), this battle was most notable for the success of the British amphibious assault, a measure of Britain's naval superiority.

open—that is, to Britain. Superior naval forces resulted in victories along the North American Great Lakes, climaxing in the Battle of Québec in 1759 and the eventual surrender of all of Canada to the British. By 1762 the French sugar islands, including Martinique, Grenada, and St. Vincent, were in British hands. Across the globe in India, the defeat of the French in the Battle of Plassey in 1757 and the capture of Pondichéry four years later made Britain the dominant European presence on the subcontinent. In the Treaty of Paris in 1763, which brought the Seven Years' War to an end, France officially surrendered Canada and India to the British, thus affording them an extraordinary field for commercial exploitation.

The success of the British in North America in the Seven Years' War was itself a major cause of the war that broke out between the mother country and her thirteen North American colonies in 1775. To pay for the larger army the British now deemed necessary to protect their vastly expanded colonial possessions, they imposed unwelcome new taxes on the colonists. The North Americans protested that they were being taxed without representation. The home government responded that, like all British subjects, they were "virtually" if not actually represented by the present members of the House of Commons. Colonists thundered back that the present political system in Britain was so corrupt that no one but the Whig oligarchs could claim that their interests were being looked after.

Meanwhile the British were exacting retribution for rebellious acts on the part of colonists. East India Company tea shipped to be sold in

"Taxation without representation . . ."

The American Revolution

Boston at prices advantageous to the company was dumped in Boston Harbor. The port of Boston was thereupon closed, and representative government in the colony of Massachusetts curtailed. The British garrison clashed with colonial civilians. Colonial "minutemen" formed a counterforce. By the time war broke out in 1775, most Americans were prepared to sever ties with Britain and declare themselves an independent nation, which they did the following year. Fighting continued until 1781 when a British army surrendered to the colonists at Yorktown to the tune of a song entitled "A World Turned Upside Down." The French, followed by Spain and the Netherlands, determined to do everything possible to inhibit the further growth of Britain's colonial empire, had allied themselves with the newly independent United States in 1778. A peace treaty signed in Paris in 1783 recognized the sovereignty of the new state. Though the British lost direct control of their former colonies, they reestablished their transatlantic commercial ties with America in the 1780s. Indeed, the brisk trade in raw cotton between the slave-owning southern states and Britain made possible the industrial revolution in textiles that began in the north of England at this time, and that carried Britain to worldwide preeminence as an economic power in the first half of the nineteenth century. This ultimately profitable arrangement lay in the future. At the time, the victory of the American colonists seemed to contemporary observers to right the world balance of commercial power, which had swung so far to the side of the British. In this instance, independence seemed designed to restore stability.

Poland and the balance of power in eastern Europe

In eastern Europe, however, the very precariousness of Poland's independence posed a threat to stability and to the balance of power. As an independent state, Poland functioned, at least in theory, as a buffer among the major central European powers—Russia, Austria, and Prussia. Poland was the one major central European territory whose landed elite had successfully opposed introduction of absolutist centralization and a consequent curtailment of its "liberties." The result, however, had not been anything like real independence for either the Polish nobility or the country as a whole. Aristocrats were quite prepared to accept bribes from foreign powers in return for their vote in elections for the Polish king. And their continued exercise of their constitutionally guaranteed individual veto (the *liberum veto*) in the Polish Diet meant that the country remained in a perpetual state of weakness that made it fair game for the land-hungry absolutist potentates who surrounded it.

The first partition of Poland

In 1764 Russia intervened to influence the election of King Stanislaus Poniatowski, an able enough nobleman who had been one of Catherine the Great's lovers. Thereafter Russia continued to meddle in the affairs of Poland—and of Turkey as well—often protecting both countries' Eastern Orthodox Christian minority. When war finally broke out with Turkey in 1769, resulting in large Russian gains in the Balkans, Austria made known its opposition to further Russian expansion, lest it upset the existing balance of power in eastern Europe. In the end Russia was persuaded to acquire territory in Poland instead, by joining Austria and Prussia in a gen-

Dividing the Royal Cake. A contemporary cartoon showing the monarchs of Europe at work carving up a hapless Poland.

eral partition of that country's lands. Though Maria Theresa opposed the dismemberment of Poland, she reluctantly agreed to participate in the partition in order to maintain the balance of power, an attitude that prompted a scornful Frederick the Great to remark, "She weeps, but she takes her share." According to the agreement of 1772, Poland lost about 30 percent of its kingdom and about half of its population.

Following this first partition, the Russians continued to exercise virtual control of Poland. King Stanislaus, however, took advantage of a new Russo-Turkish war in 1788 to press for a more truly independent state with a far stronger executive than had existed previously. A constitution adopted in May 1791 established just that; but this rejuvenated Polish state was to be short-lived. In January 1792, the Russo-Turkish war ended, and Catherine the Great pounced. Together the Russians and Prussians took two more enormous bites out of Poland in 1793, destroying the new constitution in the process. A rebellion under the leadership of Thaddeus Kosciuszko, who had fought in America, was crushed in 1794 and 1795. A final swallow by Russia, Austria, and Prussia in 1795 left nothing of Poland at all. After this series of partitions of Poland, each of the major powers was a good deal fatter; but on the international scales by which such things were measured, they continued to weigh proportionately the same.

The second and third partitions of Poland

The final devouring of Poland occurred at a time when the Continent was once again engaged in a general war. Yet this conflict was not just another military attempt to resolve customary disputes over commerce or problems of international stability. It was the result of violent revolution that had broken out in France in 1789, that had toppled the Bourbon dynasty there, and that threatened to do the same to other monarchs across Europe. The second and third partitions of Poland were a final bravura declaration of power by monarchs who already feared for their heads. Henceforth, neither foreign nor domestic policy would ever again be dictated as they had been in absolutist Europe by the convictions and determinations of kings and queens alone. Poland disappeared as Europe fell to pieces, as customary practice gave way to new and desperate necessity.

Though absolutism met its death in the years immediately after 1789, the relevance of its history to that of the modern world is greater than it might appear. First, centralization provided useful precedents to nineteenth-century state-builders. Modern standing armies—be they made up of soldiers or bureaucrats—are institutions whose origins rest in the age of absolutism. Second, absolutism's centripetal force contributed to an economic climate that gave birth to industrial revolution. Factories built to produce military matériel, capitalist agricultural policies designed to provide food for burgeoning capital cities, increased taxes that drove peasants to seek work in rural industries: these and other programs pointed to the future. Third, in their constant struggle to curb the privileges of nobility and oligarchy, absolute monarchs played out one more act in a drama that would continue into the nineteenth century. French nobles, Prussian junkers, and Russian boyars all bargained successfully to retain their rights to property and its management while surrendering to some degree their role as governors. But as long as their property rights remained secure, their power was assured. The French Revolution would curb their power for a time, but they were survivors. Their adaptability, whether as agricultural entrepreneurs or as senior servants of the state, ensured their order an important place in the world that lay beyond absolutism.

SUMMARY POINTS

- Absolutism, in part a response to the turmoil and insecurity of the late sixteenth and early seventeenth centuries, was instituted by the European monarchs Louis XIV of France, Peter the Great of Russia, Leopold I of Austria, and Frederick William of Brandenburg-Prussia through such means as the development of bureaucracies beholden to the crown, the co-optation of the nobility, and the weakening of the Church and local institutions.

- In England, the system of limited monarchy and representative government survived royal attempts to rule absolutely.

- The European balance of power became the preeminent international issue in the late 1600s and the early 1700s. Concerns over the expanding power of the French and Spanish rulers led to the War of the League of Augsburg (1688–1697) and the War of the Spanish Succession (1702–1714).

- The "enlightened absolutists" of the eighteenth century made some gestures toward more lenient policies, but they nevertheless ruled as absolutists, increasing their own power by raising large standing armies.

- Shifting power balances and the imperatives of economic expansion set off increasingly frequent wars between the Western powers, including the Seven Years' War (1756–1763), which established Britain as the preeminent naval and commercial power in Europe, and the Russo-Turkish War (1769–1792), during and after which Poland was divided among several powers.

SELECTED READINGS

Anderson, M. S., *Peter the Great*, 2d ed., London, 1995. A good, thorough biography.

———, *War and Society in Europe of the Old Regime, 1618–1789*, New York, 1988. An extensive survey that addresses the relationships between war and the societies of early-modern Europe.

Avrich, Paul, *Russian Rebels, 1600–1800*, New York, 1972. A study of revolts against absolutist power.

Baxter, Stephen, *William III and the Defense of European Liberty, 1650–1702*, New York, 1966. The best study of the Dutchman who became England's king.

Beales, Derek, *Joseph II*, New York, 1987. Now the standard biography of this "enlightened" despot.

Brewer, John, *Party Ideology and Popular Politics at the Accession of George III*, New York, 1976. A revisionist interpretation of political alignments and party.

Briggs, Robin, *Early Modern France, 1560–1715*, 2d ed., New York, 1997. A survey that includes sections on social and cultural, as well as political, history.

Burke, Peter, *The Fabrication of Louis XIV*, New Haven, Conn., 1992. A study of the manner in which the king created his self-image.

Carsten, F. L., *The Origins of Prussia*, Westport, Conn., 1954. The standard account of Prussia's rise and of the achievement of the Great Elector.

Churchill, Winston S., *Marlborough*, New York, 1968. An abridged edition of Churchill's magnificently written biography of his ancestor.

Corvisier, André, *Armies and Societies in Europe, 1494–1789*, Bloomington, Ind., 1979. Focuses on the French army.

Dukes, Paul, *The Making of Russian Absolutism: 1613–1801*, 2d ed., New York, 1990. A survey that focuses on the increasing power of the state.

Dunn, Richard S., *The Age of Religious Wars, 1559–1715*, 2d ed., New York, 1979. A detailed and up-to-date survey, useful for the history of late seventeenth- and early eighteenth-century absolutism.

Fraser, Antonia, *Royal Charles: Charles II and the Restoration,* New York, 1979. A readable, reliable life of the king and his times.

Goubert, Pierre, *Louis XIV and Twenty Million Frenchmen,* New York, 1972. A valuable study, the starting point for an understanding of the Sun King's reign.

Hatton, Ragnhild, *Europe in the Age of Louis XIV,* New York, 1969. Thoughtful interpretation of the period; excellent illustrations.

Herr, Richard, *The Eighteenth Century Revolution in Spain,* Princeton, 1958. The best introduction to Spain in this period.

Holborn, Hajo, *The Age of Absolutism,* New York, 1964. The best survey for Germany. Second volume of Holborn's *History of Modern Germany.*

Hufton, Owen H., *Europe: Privilege and Protest, 1730–1789,* Ithaca, N.Y., 1980. Focuses on the growth of central state power.

Lewis, W. H., *The Splendid Century: Life in the France of Louis XIV,* New York, 1953. A delightfully written survey.

Mettam, Roger, *Power and Faction in Louis XIV's France,* Cambridge, 1988. A study that discusses the powers that Louis did not control at court.

Palmer, R. R., *The Age of the Democratic Revolution: A Political History of Europe and America, 1760–1800,* Vol. I, Princeton, 1964. Argues in favor of a general European aristocratic reaction prior to 1789.

Plumb, John H., *Sir Robert Walpole,* 2 vols., Boston, 1956, 1961. A well-written, sympathetic biography of England's leading eighteenth-century politician.

Riasanovsky, Nicholas V., *A History of Russia,* 5th ed., Oxford, 1993. A useful introduction.

Ritter, Gerhard, *Frederick the Great: A Historical Profile,* Berkeley, 1968. A readable biography.

Rudé, George, *Europe in the Eighteenth Century: Aristocracy and the Bourgeois Challenge,* New York, 1972. A survey that stresses social stratification and tension.

Speck, W. A., *Stability and Strife: England, 1714–1760,* Cambridge, Mass., 1977. A good survey.

Vierhaus, Rudolph, *Germany in the Age of Absolutism,* New York, 1988. A synthesis of recent historiography on the growth and spread of absolutism.

Wangermann, Ernst, *The Austrian Achievement, 1700–1800,* London, 1973. A suggestive introductory survey.

Wolf, John B., *Louis XIV,* New York, 1968. The standard biography in English.

Woloch, Isser, *Eighteenth-Century Europe: Tradition and Progress, 1715–1789,* New York, 1982. A thoughtful, well-organized survey.

SOURCE MATERIALS

Locke, John, *Two Treatises of Government.* (Many editions.) The argument against absolutism.

Saint-Simon, Louis, *Historical Memoirs.* (Many editions.) A brilliant source for evidence about life at the court of Louis XIV.

CHAPTER 18

THE SCIENTIFIC REVOLUTION AND THE ENLIGHTENMENT

This is the age wherein philosophy comes in with a spring-tide. . . . Methinks I see how all the old rubbish must be thrown away, and the rotten buildings be overthrown, and carried away with so powerful an inundation.

—HENRY POWER, *Experimental Philosophy* (1663)

Enlightenment is humanity's departure from its self-imposed immaturity. Immaturity is the inability to use one's intellect without the guidance of others. This immaturity is self-imposed when its cause is not a lack of intelligence but a failure of determination and courage to think without the guidance of someone else. Dare to know! This then is the slogan of the Enlightenment.

—IMMANUEL KANT, *What Is Enlightenment?* (1784)

T HE YEARS BETWEEN roughly 1660 and 1789, which witnessed the prevalence of absolutism in western Europe, witnessed as well the most important mutation in all of European intellectual and cultural history to occur between the Middle Ages and the present. Just as the sweep of fresh winds can greatly change the weather, so in the last few decades of the seventeenth century the sweep of new ideas led to a bracing change in Europe's "climate of opinion." For purposes of analysis it is convenient to refer to two phases within the larger period: the triumph of the scientific revolution in the second half of the seventeenth century and the age of "Enlightenment" which followed for most of the eighteenth century. But without any doubt the same intellectual winds that swept into Europe during the later seventeenth century prevailed for well over a hundred years. Indeed, their influence is still felt today.

How did the new intellectual climate differ from the old? Concentrating on essentials, three points may be stressed. First, whereas medieval, Renaissance, and Reformation thinkers all assumed that past knowledge was the most reliable source of wisdom, the greatest thinkers from the seventeenth century onward rejected any obeisance to ancient authority and resolved to rely on their own intellects to see where knowledge would lead them. Making their motto "dare to know," they stressed the autonomy of science and the free play of the mind in ways unheard of in the West since the golden age of Greece. Second, the new breed of thinkers believed strongly that knowledge was valueless if it could not be put to use. For a

New ideas: 1660–1789

Changes in intellectual environment

Plato, an Aristotle, or a St. Thomas Aquinas alike, the greatest wisdom was the most abstract wisdom since such wisdom helped to turn the human mind away from all earthly "corruptibility" and supposedly brought happiness by its sheer resemblance to timeless divinity. But after the change in Europe's climate of opinion in the late seventeenth century, all knowledge without practical value was belittled and thinkers from every realm of intellectual endeavor aimed directly or indirectly at achieving "the relief of man's estate." Finally, the new climate of opinion was characterized by the demystification of the universe. Up until the mid-seventeenth century, most people, learned and unlearned, assumed that the universe was driven and inhabited by occult forces that humans could barely understand and surely never control unless they were magicians. But around 1660 a mechanistic worldview swept away occultism, and pixies became consigned to the realm of children's storybooks. Thereafter nature was believed to work like the finest mechanical clock—consummately predictable and fully open to human understanding.

Causes of change

Why such a dramatic change in basic patterns of thought took place when it did will long remain a subject for speculation. Certainly the prior Scholastic stress on human rationality and the Renaissance reacquisition of classical Greek texts helped to bring European thought to a scientific threshold. Probably the most direct causes of the intellectual mutations, however, were the twin challenges to conventional assumptions introduced in the sixteenth century by the discovery of the New World and the realization that the earth revolves around the sun rather than vice versa, for neither the Bible nor ancient science allowed room for what one bewildered contemporary called "new islands, new lands, new seas, new peoples, and what is more, a new sky and new stars." At first many thinkers, daunted by all this novelty, experienced a sense of intellectual crisis. Some took refuge in skepticism, others in relativism, and others in a return to blind faith. Speaking for several generations, the poet John Donne lamented in 1611 that "new philosophy calls all in doubt, the element of fire is quite put out, the sun is lost, and the earth, and no man's wit can well direct him where to look for it. . . . 'tis all in pieces, all coherence gone." But just as Europe surmounted its early-modern political crisis around 1660, so did it surmount its intellectual one, above all because the last stages of a profound scientific revolution gave a new, completely convincing "coherence" to things. As Alexander Pope wrote in the early eighteenth century, almost as if in response to Donne, "Nature and Nature's Law's lay hid in night:/God said, Let Newton Be! and all was light."

THE SCIENTIFIC REVOLUTION

Even though Europe did not begin to resolve its intellectual crisis until about 1660, the groundwork for that resolution was prepared earlier in the seventeenth century by four great individuals—Kepler, Galileo,

Bacon, and Descartes. Kepler and Galileo—both practicing scientists—have been discussed earlier; suffice it here to say that they removed all doubts about the Copernican heliocentric theory of the solar system and helped lead the way to Sir Isaac Newton's theory of universal gravitation. As for Bacon and Descartes, their main achievements were not in the realm of original scientific discovery but rather in propagating new attitudes toward learning and the nature of the universe.

Sir Francis Bacon (1561–1626), lord chancellor of England, was also an extremely influential philosopher of science. In Bacon's view, expressed most fully in his *Novum Organum* (New instrument) of 1620, science could not advance unless it departed entirely from the inherited errors of the past and established "progressive stages of certainty." For Bacon this meant proceeding strictly on the basis of empirical knowledge (knowledge gained solely by the senses) and by means of the "inductive method," meaning the arrival at truth by proceeding upward from particular observations to generalizations. Insisting that "the corruption of philosophy by superstition and an admixture of theology . . . does the greatest harm," and that thinking people thus should be "sober-minded, and give to faith that only which is faith's," Bacon advocated the advancement of learning as a cooperative venture proceeding by means of meticulously recorded empirical experiments. Unlike the arid speculations of the past, collective scientific research and observation would produce useful knowledge and result in bettering the human lot. Much of Bacon's ideology is vividly evoked in the cover illustration of his *Novum Organum,* wherein intrepid ships venture out beyond the Pillars of Hercules (Straits of Gibraltar) onto a fathomless sea in pursuit of unknown but great things to come.

Title Page of Bacon's *Novum Organum*. Underneath the ship sailing out into the ocean is a quotation from the Book of Daniel: "Many shall venture forth and science shall be increased."

Bacon's later contemporary, the French philosopher René Descartes (1596–1650), agreed with him on two points: that all past knowledge should be discarded, and that the worth of any idea depended on its usefulness. Yet Descartes otherwise proposed some very different approaches to science, for unlike the empiricist Bacon, Descartes was a rationalist and a champion of mathematics. In his *Discourse on Method* (1637), Descartes explained how, during a period of solitude, he resolved to submit all inherited doctrines to a process of systematic doubting because he knew that the "strangest or most incredible" things had previously been set down in learned books. Taking as his first rule "never to receive anything as a truth which [he] did not clearly know to be such," he found himself doubting everything until he came to the recognition that his mere process of thought proved his own existence ("I think, therefore I am"). Thereupon making rationality the point of departure for his entire philosophical enterprise, Descartes rebuilt the universe on largely speculative grounds that differed in almost every detail from the universe conceived by the Greeks, yet conformed fully to the highest principles of human rationality as expressed in the laws of mathematics. That most of his theories were not empirically verifiable did not trouble him at all, because he was confident that "natural processes almost always depend on parts so small that they utterly elude our senses."

René Descartes

Descartes' influence

A Diagram Illustrating Cartesian Principles. Descartes maintained that the pineal gland, seen here at the back of the head, transmitted messages from the eyes to the muscles in purely mechanical fashion. But the pineal gland was also the link between the material body and the nonmaterial human mind. From the 1677 edition of Descartes' *De Homine.*

The English and French traditions

Predictably, the details of Descartes' scientific system are now regarded as mere curiosities, but the French philosopher nonetheless was enormously influential in contributing to the advance of science and in creating a new climate of opinion, for several reasons. First of all, even though his systematic doubting did not succeed in establishing any solid new scientific truths, it did contribute to the discrediting of all the faulty science of the ancients. Then too, Descartes' stress on mathematics was salutary because mathematics has indeed proven to be an indispensable handmaiden to the pursuit of natural science. But undoubtedly Descartes' single most influential legacy was his philosophy of dualism, according to which God created only two kinds of reality—mind and matter. In Descartes' view, mind belonged to man alone, and all else was matter. Thus he insisted that all created existence beyond man—organic and inorganic alike—operated solely in terms of physical laws, or the interplay of "extension and motion." In other words, for Descartes every single entity from the solar system to the realm of animals and plants was a self-operating machine propelled by a force arising from the original motion given to the universe by God. Indeed, Descartes thought that man himself was a machine—although, in this sole exception, a machine equipped with a mind. From this it followed that the entire universe could be studied objectively, without any aid from theology or appeals to the occult. Moreover, all apparent attributes of matter, such as light, color, sound, taste, or smell, which had no "extension" were to be classified as mere subjective impressions of the human mind unfit for proper scientific analysis. Based on such assumptions the pursuit of science could be dispassionate as never before.

Roughly speaking, for about a century after the work of Bacon and Descartes the English scientific community was Baconian and the French Cartesian (a name given to followers of Descartes). This is to say that the English concentrated primarily on performing empirical experiments in many different areas of physical science leading to concrete scientific advances, whereas the French tended to remain more oriented toward mathematics and philosophical theory. Among the numerous great seventeenth-century English laboratory scientists were the physician William Harvey (1578–1657), the chemist Robert Boyle (1627–1691), and the biologist Robert Hooke (1635–1703). Pursuing the earlier work of Vesalius and Servetus, but daring, unlike them, to practice vivisection, Harvey was the first to observe and describe the circulation of the blood through the arteries and back to the heart through the veins. Similarly committed to empirical experiment, Boyle used an air pump to establish "Boyle's law"—namely, that under constant temperature the volume of a gas decreases in proportion to the pressure placed on it. Boyle also was the first chemist to distinguish between a mixture and a compound (wherein the chemical combination occurs), and accomplished much to discredit alchemy. As for Hooke, although he conducted research in astronomy and physics as well as biology, he is best known for having used the microscope to discover the cellular structure of plants. Meanwhile, in

France, Descartes himself pioneered in analytical geometry, Blaise Pascal worked on probability theory and invented a calculating machine before his conversion to religion, and Pierre Gassendi (1592–1655) sought to demonstrate the truth of the atomic theory. Also within the French realm of thought was the Dutch Jew Baruch Spinoza (1632–1677), a philosopher who tried to apply geometry to ethics and believed that he advanced beyond Descartes by interpreting the universe as being composed of a single substance—simultaneously God and nature—instead of two.

The dichotomy between English Baconianism and French Cartesianism, however, breaks down when one approaches the man commonly considered to have been the greatest scientist of all time, Sir Isaac Newton (1642–1727). A highly unattractive personality in his daily conduct—being secretive, petty, and vindictive—Newton was nonetheless a towering genius who drew on both the Baconian and Cartesian heritages. For example, following Bacon, and in the sharpest opposition to Descartes, Newton refused to dismiss the phenomenon of light as a mere subjective impression of "mind." Instead, by means of laboratory experiments he demonstrated that light behaves differently when filtered through different media, and hence offered an interpretation of light as a stream of particles that solidly established optics as an empirical branch of physics. Yet, on the other hand, Newton thoroughly approved of Descartes' stress on mathematics, and once in a burst of purely theoretical inspiration discovered one of modern mathematics' most basic tools, the calculus.

Of course Newton's supreme accomplishment lay in his formulation of the law of universal gravitation, which, as expressed in his monumental Latin *Principia Mathematica* (Mathematical principles of natural philosophy) of 1687, integrated Copernican astronomy with Galileo's physics. In the *Principia* Newton broached the two major scientific questions of his day: (1) What keeps the heavy earth in motion? (before Copernicus the earth had been thought immobile), and (2) Why do terrestrial bodies tend to fall to the earth's center whereas planets stay in orbital motion? (Before Copernicus the planets were thought to be embedded in crystalline spheres moved by angels or "divine intelligences.") In the early seventeenth century Kepler had already suggested the possibility of mutual attractions between all bodies in the solar system that kept the earth and other planets moving, but the Cartesians attacked this explanation as being too occult since attraction over space left out the crucial Cartesian ingredient of matter. Disregarding these Cartesian doubts because he saw no alternative, Newton returned to consider Kepler's theory of mutual attractions, and uniting Baconian observations with Cartesian mathematics, arrived at a single law of universal gravitation according to which "every particle of matter in the universe attracts every other particle with a force varying inversely as the square of the distance between them and directly proportional to the product of their masses." Since this law was verified by experience in both terrestrial and celestial realms, there could be no doubt that it explained all motion. Indeed, Newton's law was so reliable that it was employed immediately to predict the ebb and flow of

Isaac Newton

Sir Isaac Newton

Newton's law of gravitation

tides. Later, in 1846, astronomers, noting irregularities in the motion of the planet Uranus, were able to deduce on Newtonian grounds the presence of the more distant planet Neptune before Neptune was actually located with the aid of high-power telescopes.

Historians of science consider Newton's law of gravity to be "the most stupendous single achievement of the human mind," finding that "no other work in the whole history of science equals the *Principia* either in originality and power of thought or in the majesty of its achievement." Certainly the publication of the *Principia* was the crowning event of the scientific revolution because it confirmed the most important astronomical and physical theories previously set forth by Copernicus, Kepler, and Galileo, and resolved beyond quarrel the major disputes that Copernicus's heliocentric theory had created. Needless to say, scientific work did not thereafter come to a standstill. Quite to the contrary, since Newton's accomplishment proved inspirational to researchers in many other fields, scientific work advanced steadily after 1687. But a fundamental reconception of the nature of the physical universe had been made, and thinkers in all areas could proceed with their work confident that science rather than superstition was the new order of the day.

THE FOUNDATIONS OF THE ENLIGHTENMENT

Although the presuppositions for the Enlightenment were set by the triumph of the scientific revolution in the late seventeenth century, the Enlightenment itself was an eighteenth-century phenomenon, lasting for close to the entire century until certain basic Enlightenment postulates were challenged around 1790 by the effects of the French Revolution and the new movement of romanticism. Of course not every thinker who lived and worked in the eighteenth century was equally "enlightened." Some, such as the Italian philosopher of history G. B. Vico (1668–1744), were opposed to almost everything the Enlightenment stood for, and others, most notably Jean-Jacques Rousseau, accepted certain Enlightenment values but sharply rejected others. Moreover, patterns of Enlightenment ideology tended to vary from country to country and to change in each country over the course of the century. Yet, despite these qualifications, most thinkers of the eighteenth century definitely shared the sense of living in an exciting new intellectual environment in which "the party of humanity" would prevail over traditionalism and obscurantism by dint of an unflinching commitment to the primacy of the intellect.

Most Enlightenment thought stemmed from three basic premises: (1) the entire universe is fully intelligible and governed by natural rather than supernatural forces; (2) rigorous application of "scientific method" can answer fundamental questions in all areas of inquiry; and (3) the human race can be "educated" to achieve nearly infinite improvement. The first two of these premises were products of the scientific revolution and the third primarily an inheritance from the psychology of John Locke.

Regarding the substitution of a natural for a supernatural worldview, explanations must start with the euphoria that greeted Isaac Newton's discovery of a single law whereby all motion in the heavens and earth became intelligible and predictable. If Newton could deal so authoritatively and elegantly with motion, it seemed to follow that all nature is governed neither by mysterious divine intervention nor by caprice, but by humanly perceivable universal laws. Hence most serious thinkers from about 1690 to 1790 became inveterate opponents of belief in miracles, and considered all varieties of revealed religion to be not just irrelevant to the pursuit of science, but positively antithetical to it. This is not to say that the Enlightenment abandoned belief in the existence of God: to the contrary, only the smallest number of Enlightenment thinkers were atheists, and very few even were avowed agnostics. Rather, most adhered to a religious outlook known as Deism, which assumed that God existed but, having once created a perfect universe, no longer took an active interest in it. Expressed in the language of the Deists themselves, God was the "divine clockmaker" who, at the beginning of time, constructed a perfect timepiece and then left it to run with predictable regularity. Most Deists continued to attend the churches of their ancestors (either Protestant or Catholic) from time to time, but they made little secret of their doubts about the efficacy of ritual and spoke out against all forms of religious intolerance.

As for the second Enlightenment premise, the accomplishments of the scientific revolution inspired a deep sense of assurance that "scientific method" was the only valid means for pursuing research in all areas of human inquiry. By scientific method Enlightenment thinkers usually meant the dispassionate, empirical observation of particular phenomena in order to arrive at general laws. Given the acknowledged triumph of

Confidence in scientific method

The Study of an Amateur Scientist. This late-seventeenth-century aristocratic dilettante collected all sorts of specimens from the natural world. The mounting of his crocodile must have offered some challenge.

Newtonian physics, it is not surprising that around 1700 western Europe was struck by a virtual mania for applying scientific method in studying all the workings of nature. Since most scientific work was still simple enough to be understood by amateurs without the benefit of years of specialized education, European aristocrats and prosperous people in all walks of life began to dabble in "research"—buying telescopes, chasing butterflies, or building home laboratories in the hope of participating in some new scientific breakthrough. Writing in 1710, the English essayist Joseph Addison satirized such pursuits by imagining a will written by one "Sir Nicholas Gimcrack," an earnest amateur who left his "recipe for preserving dead caterpillars" to his daughters, his "rat's testicles" to a "learned and worthy friend," and who disinherited his son for "having spoken disrespectfully of his little sister," whose mortal remains Sir Nicholas kept near his desk in "spirits of wine." Of course most of the aristocratic "Gimcracks" never progressed beyond pickling, but their enthusiasm for following the latest developments in scientific research led them to patronize the work of truly gifted scientists and contributed to creating an atmosphere wherein science was prized as humanity's greatest attainment.

The scientific method applied to human concerns

Inevitably, in turn, such an atmosphere was conducive to an assumption that became dominant in the course of the eighteenth century—that scientific method was the only proper means for studying human affairs as well as natural phenomena. Since the world of physical nature seemed well on the way to being mastered, Enlightenment thinkers considered it mere common sense that the world of human nature could soon be mastered as well by scientific means. Thus students of religion started collecting myths from numerous different traditions, not to find any occult truth in them, but to classify their common traits and learn the steps by which humanity supposedly freed itself from superstition. Similarly, historians collected evidence to learn the laws governing the rise and fall of nations, and students of politics compared governmental constitutions to arrive at an ideal and universally applicable political system. In other words, as the English poet Alexander Pope stated in his *Essay on Man* of 1733, "the science of human nature [may be] like all other sciences reduced to a few clear points," and Enlightenment thinkers became determined to learn exactly what those "few clear points" were.

John Locke's psychology and human perfectibility

It must be stressed, however, that if most thinkers of the Enlightenment supposed that the empirical study of human conduct could reduce society's working to a few laws, most also believed that human conduct was not immutable but highly perfectible. In this they were inspired primarily by the psychology of John Locke (1632–1704), who was not only a very influential political philosopher, as we have seen, but also the formulator of an extremely influential theory of knowledge. In his *Essay Concerning Human Understanding* (1690) Locke rejected the hitherto dominant assumption that ideas are innate, maintaining instead that all knowledge originates from sense perception. According to Locke, the human mind at birth is a "blank tablet" (in Latin, *tabula rasa*) upon which nothing is inscribed; not until the infant begins to experience things, that is, to perceive the external world with its senses, is anything registered on its mind. From this point of departure, Enlightenment thinkers concluded that environment determines everything. For example, in their view, if some aristocrats were better than ordinary mortals it was not because they had inherited any special knowledge or virtues, but only because they had been better trained. It therefore followed that all people could be educated to become the equals of the most perfect aristocrats, and that there were no limits to the potential for universal human progress. Indeed, a few Enlightenment thinkers became so optimistic as to propose that all evil might be eradicated from the world, since whatever evil existed was not the result of some divine plan but only the product of a faulty environment that humans had created and humans could change.

THE WORLD OF THE PHILOSOPHES

France, the dominant country in eighteenth-century Europe, was the center of the Enlightenment movement, and thus it is customary to refer to the leading exponents of the Enlightenment, regardless of where they lived, by the French term *philosophe,* meaning "philosopher." In fact the term "philosophe" is slightly misleading inasmuch as hardly any of the philosophes—with the exceptions, to be seen, of David Hume and Immanuel Kant—were really philosophers in the sense of being highly original abstract thinkers. Rather, most were practically oriented publicists who aimed to reform society by popularizing the new scientific interpretation of the universe and applying dispassionate "scientific method" to a host of contemporary problems. Since they sought most of all to gain converts and alter what they regarded as outmoded institutions, they shunned all forms of expression that might seem incomprehensible or abstruse, priding themselves instead on their clarity, and occasionally even expressing their ideas in the form of stories or plays rather than treatises.

General characteristics of the philosophes

By common consent the prince of the philosophes was the Frenchman born François Marie Arouet, who called himself Voltaire (1694–1778). Virtually the personification of the Enlightenment, much as Erasmus two centuries earlier had embodied Christian humanism, Voltaire commented on an enormous range of subjects in a wide variety of literary forms. Probably his greatest single accomplishment lay in championing the cause of English empiricism in previously Cartesian France. Having as a young man been exiled to England for the crime of insulting a pompous French nobleman, Voltaire returned after three years a thorough and extremely persuasive convert to the ideas of Bacon and Locke. Not only did this mean that he persuaded other French thinkers to accept Newton's empirically verifiable scientific system in place of Descartes's unverifiable one, but he also encouraged them to be less abstract and theoretical in all their intellectual inclinations and more oriented toward the solving of everyday problems. To be sure, throughout the eighteenth

Voltaire, by Houdon

Voltaire

century France's intellectual world remained more rationalistic than England's, but Voltaire's lifelong campaign on behalf of empiricism nonetheless helped make French thinkers more practically oriented than before.

Voltaire's social views

Continually engaged in commenting on contemporary problems himself, Voltaire was an ardent spokesman for civil liberties. In this regard his battlecry was *Écrasez l'infâme*—"crush infamy"—meaning by "infamy" all forms of repression, fanaticism, and bigotry. In his own words, he believed that "the individual who persecutes another because he is not of the same opinion is nothing less than a monster." Accordingly, he wrote an opponent a line that forever after has been held forth as the first principle of civil liberty: "I do not agree with a word you say, but I will defend to the death your right to say it." Of all forms of intolerance Voltaire hated religious bigotry most of all because it seemed based on silly superstitions: "the less superstition, the less fanaticism; and the less fanaticism, the less misery." In addition to attacking religious repression, Voltaire also frequently criticized the exercise of arbitrary powers by secular states. In particular, he thought that the English parliamentary system was preferable to French absolutism and that all states acted criminally when their policies resulted in senseless wars. "It is forbidden to kill," he maintained sardonically, "therefore all murderers are punished unless they kill in large numbers and to the sound of trumpets."

Candide

Although Voltaire exerted the greatest effect on his age as a propagandist for the basically optimistic Enlightenment principle that by "crushing infamy" humanity could take enormous strides forward, the only one of his works still widely read today, the satirical story *Candide* (1759), is atypically subdued. Writing not long after the disastrous Lisbon earthquake of 1755, in which more than 20,000 lives were lost for no apparent reason, Voltaire drew back in this work from some of his earlier faith that mankind by its own actions could limitlessly improve itself. Lulled into false security concerning what life has in store for him by the fatuous optimism of his tutor, Dr. Pangloss, the hero of the story, Candide, journeys through the world only to experience one outrageous misfortune after another. Storms and earthquakes are bad enough, but worse still are wars and rapacity caused by uncontrollable human passions. Only in the golden never-never land of "Eldorado" (clearly a spoof of the perfect world most philosophes saw on the horizon), where there are no priests, law courts, or prisons, but unlimited wealth and a "palace of sciences . . . filled with instruments of mathematics and physics," does Candide find temporary respite from disaster. Being a naturally restless mortal, however, he quickly becomes bored with Eldorado's placid perfection and leaves for the renewed buffetings of the real world. After many more lessons in "the school of hard knocks," he finally learns one basic truth by the end of the story: settling down on a modest farm with his once-beautiful but now hideously disfigured wife, he shrugs when Dr. Pangloss repeats for the hundredth time that "this is the best of all possible worlds," and replies, "that's as may be, but we must cultivate our garden." In other words, according to Voltaire, life is not perfect and probably never will be, but humans will succeed best if they ignore vapid theorizing and buckle down to unglamorous but productive hard work.

In addition to Voltaire, the most prominent French philosophes were Montesquieu, Diderot, and Condorcet. The baron de Montesquieu (1689–1755) was primarily a political thinker. In his major work, *The Spirit of Laws* (1748), Montesquieu sought to discover the ways in which differing environments and historical and religious traditions influence governmental institutions. Finding that unalterable differences in climates and geographic terrains affect human behavior, and hence governmental forms, Montesquieu throughout much of *The Spirit of Laws* seems to be saying that external conditions force humans to behave in different ways and that there is nothing they can do about this. But ultimately he was an idealist who preferred one particular political system, the English, and hoped that all nations might overcome whatever environmental handicaps they faced to imitate it. For him, the greatest strength of the English system was that it consisted of separate and balanced powers—executive, legislative, and judicial: thus it guaranteed liberty inasmuch as no absolute sovereignty was given to any single governing individual or group. This idealization of "checks and balances" subsequently influenced many other Enlightenment political theorists and played a particularly dominant role in the shaping of the United States Constitution in 1787.

Unlike Voltaire, who was not a very systematic thinker, and Montesquieu, who wrote in a somewhat ambiguous and primarily reflective mode, the most programmatic of the philosophes was Denis Diderot (1713–1784). As a young firebrand Diderot was clapped into solitary confinement for his attacks on religion and thereafter he worked under the ever-present threat of censorship and imprisonment. Yet throughout his life he never shrank from espousing a fully materialistic philosophy or criticizing what he considered to be backwardness or tyranny wherever he found it. Although, like Voltaire, Diderot wrote on a wide range of

Montesquieu's *The Spirit of Laws*

Montesquieu

Diderot and the *Encyclopedia*

A Laboratory, from Diderot's *Encyclopedia*. Each printed number refers to a detailed discussion in the text. Note the far greater stress on practical instruction here than in the illustration of the amateur scientist's study shown on p. 641.

Diderot. A contemporary portrait by Van Loo.

subjects in numerous different forms, including stories and plays, he exerted his greatest influence as the organizer of and main contributor to an extremely ambitious publishing venture, the *Encyclopedia*. Conceived as a summation and means for dissemination of all the most advanced contemporary philosophical, scientific, and technical knowledge, with articles written by all the leading philosophes of the day (including Voltaire and Montesquieu), the *Encyclopedia* first appeared between 1751 and 1772 in installments totaling seventeen large volumes and eleven more of illustrative plates. Whereas modern encyclopedias serve primarily as reference works, Diderot thought of his *Encyclopedia* as a set of volumes that people would read at length rather than merely using to look up facts. Therefore he hoped that it would "change the general way of thinking." Above all, by popularizing the most recent achievements in science and technology, Diderot intended to combat "superstition" on the broadest front, aid the further advance of science, and thereby help alleviate all forms of human misery. Dedicated to the proposition that all traditional beliefs had to be reexamined "without sparing anyone's sensibilities," he certainly would have excoriated all "irrational" religious dogmas openly if left to himself. But since strict censorship made explicitly antireligious articles impossible, Diderot thumbed his nose at religion in such oblique ways as offering the laconic cross-reference for the entry on the Eucharist, "see cannibalism." Not surprisingly, gibes like this aroused storms of controversy when the early volumes of the *Encyclopedia* appeared. Nonetheless, the project was not only completed in the face of prominent opposition, but as time went on the complete work became so popular that it was reprinted several times and helped spread the ideas of the philosophes not just in France but all over Europe.

One of the youngest of the contributors to the *Encyclopedia*, the marquis de Condorcet (1743–1794) is customarily termed "the last of the philosophes" because his career, and the philosophes' activities in general, was cut short by the excesses of the French Revolution. In his early career Condorcet gained prominence as a brilliant mathematician, but he is best known as the most extreme Enlightenment exponent of the idea of progress. Already in the late seventeenth century, particularly as the result of the triumphs of science, several thinkers began arguing that the intellectual accomplishments of their own day were superior to any of the past and that greater intellectual progress in the future was inevitable. But since it was less clear to some that modern literature was superior to the Greek and Latin classics, around 1700 an argument raged concerning the relative claims of "ancients" and "moderns" wherein so able a critic as the English writer Jonathan Swift could regard what he called the "battle of the books" as a standoff. In the eighteenth century, however, the conviction grew that the present had advanced in all aspects of human endeavor beyond the accomplishments of any earlier time, and that the future was bound to see unlimited further progress on all fronts. Condorcet's *Outline of the Progress of the Human Mind* (1794) was the ultimate expression of this point of view. According to Condorcet, progress in the past had not been uninterrupted—the Middle Ages had been an especially retrogressive era—but, given the victories of the scientific revolution and Enlightenment, indefinite and uninterrupted progress in the future was assured. Venturing into prophecy, Condorcet confidently stated not only that "as preventive medicine improves . . . the average human life-span will be increased and a more healthy and stronger physical constitution guaranteed," but that "the moment will come . . . when tyrants and slaves . . . will exist only in history or on the stage." Ironically, even while Condorcet was writing such optimistic passages he was hiding out from the agents of the French Revolution, who in fact soon counted him among the victims of their "reign of terror."

One other French thinker of the eighteenth century, Jean-Jacques Rousseau (1712–1778), must be considered here, for even though Rousseau was an "outsider" who quarreled with the philosophes and contradicted many of their assumptions, he was still inescapably part of their world. Rousseau's central concerns were similar to those of Voltaire and Diderot: the reform of society, the dissemination of useful knowledge, the search for freedom. Like the philosophes, he despised inherited privilege and believed optimistically that a just and moral society could be created by "crushing the infamy" of tyrannical and repressive government. Yet Rousseau's proposals for creating a just society, which he customarily expressed with the deepest passion, were founded on an almost mystical respect for "nature" as opposed to reason and thus differed greatly from those of his primarily rationalistic allies. Considered a boor and almost a madman in his own day, Rousseau was a forerunner of the French Revolution, nineteenth-century romanticism, and perhaps (although this is debatable) twentieth-century totalitarianism.

Jean-Jacques Rousseau

The two fields in which Rousseau exerted the greatest influence were those of education and political theory. Rousseau's treatise on education, *Émile* (1762), is the ultimate source of all "progressive" pedagogy. Here he laid down as a maxim that "the first impulses of nature are always right." Accordingly, he insisted that children should not be treated as miniature or incomplete adults, but must be allowed their own natural development proper to children. In practice this meant that they were not to be subjected to discipline and drilling; instead they should be encouraged to employ their keen youthful sense impressions and healthy young bodies to discover useful knowledge by themselves and "learn by doing." It was pointless to force a child to reason since reason is the human faculty that develops last. Teaching from books was postponed until adolescence since "books teach us only to talk about things we do not know." Ultimately such education was designed to create moral and useful citizens, those who would be inclined to do good and serve society by engaging in useful vocations. For women, however, it meant staying at home and being "useful" to men, since Rousseau was convinced that this was nature's plan for the female sex.

Rousseau's *Émile*

Rousseau's most important treatise on politics, *The Social Contract,* came out in the same year as *Émile,* 1762, and complemented it in its aim

The Social Contract

of creating a moral society. Here the author argued that humans were "born free." In the state of nature, that is, all had been equal (although we have seen that Rousseau believed women inferior to men) until the institution of private property led owners to protect their property by creating intruments of repression: law, police, slavery. To remedy this situation, Rousseau proposed the altogether new solution of government by the "general will." Supreme authority should be held by all the people, acting in collective assemblies rather than through institutions of representative democracy, whose rule would be absolute and indivisible. The people would act together as legislators, executors, and judges, and in doing so would become transformed into more than the sum of their parts. With the "general will" thus creating a "moral and collective person," individuals would surrender all their rights to the collectivity, yet they would be perfectly free since the general will inevitably would be just and would express their own will. In case any individuals became determined to resist the general will, they would be forced to obey, or, as Rousseau stated the matter, they would be "forced to be free." It has frequently been observed that the ideals of *The Social Contract* were distilled thirty years later in the French Revolution's slogan of "liberty, equality, fraternity." The obvious paradox lies in the fact that the emphasis on liberty and equality looks forward to institutions of modern democracy, but the emphasis on fraternity (the individual sinking into the mass) has ominous undertones of totalitarianism.

Beyond France, philosophes in other countries also made significant contributions to the Enlightenment legacy. After France, the most "enlightened" country of Europe was Great Britain, where the most noteworthy philosophes were Gibbon, Hume, and Adam Smith. Edward Gibbon (1737–1794) was a man of letters and historian whose *Decline and Fall of the Roman Empire* (1776–1788) remains among the two or three most widely read history books of all time. Scintillatingly written, the *Decline and Fall* covers Roman and Byzantine history from Augustus to the fall of Constantinople in 1453. According to Gibbon, the Roman Empire was brought down by "the triumph of barbarism [i.e., the Germanic invasions] and religion [i.e., Christianity]," but the Europe of his day was no longer "threatened with a repetition of those calamities." For him the rise of Christianity was the greatest calamity because "the servile and pusillanimous reign of the monks" replaced Roman philosophy and science with a credulity that "debased and vitiated the faculties of the mind." Certainly Gibbon's antireligious bias vitiated the quality of his own work. He is therefore read today not so much for his particular opinions as for his trenchant character portrayals and above all for his devastating wit.

The Scotsman David Hume (1711–1776), on the other hand, was a truly penetrating philosopher. Dedicated like most Enlightenment thinkers to challenging preconceived opinions, Hume pushed skepticism so far in his major work, *An Enquiry Concerning Human Understanding* (1748), that he undermined all assurance that anyone knew anything for certain. Starting with the assumption that human knowledge derives

Edward Gibbon

David Hume

from sense data alone rather than from abstract reason—that "nothing is in intellect which was not first in sense"—Hume proposed that we have no way of ascertaining whether such knowledge really corresponds to objective truths lodged in the real world. Once he arrived at such extreme skepticism, Hume also proposed a philosophy of relativistic ethics: if we know nothing for certain, then there can be no absolute moral laws, and we must decide on proper courses of action from their contexts. Yet, as skeptical as Hume was, he was by no means cynical; rather, he enthusiastically joined in Voltaire's campaign to crush "infamy," or what Hume called "stupidity, Christianity, and ignorance," on the grounds that it is preferable to voyage amidst a sea of uncertainties than to dwell in a forest of supernatural shadows.

The most practically oriented of the leading British philosophes was the Scottish economist Adam Smith (1723–1790), whose landmark treatise *The Wealth of Nations* (1776) is recognized as the classic expression of "laissez-faire" economics. Strongly opposed to mercantilism—that is, any governmental intervention in economic affairs—Smith maintained that the prosperity of all could best be obtained by allowing individuals to pursue their own interests without competition from state-owned enterprises or legal restraints. The term "laissez-faire" comes from the French expression *laissez faire la nature* (let nature take its course), and Smith's advocacy of laissez-faire economic doctrine reveals how deeply indebted he was to the Enlightenment's idealization of both nature and human nature. In other words, espousing "the obvious and simple system of natural liberty," Smith believed that just as the planets revolve harmoniously in their orbits and are prevented from bumping into each other by the invisible force of gravity, so humans can act harmoniously even while pursuing their selfish economic interests if only "the invisible hand" of competitive, free-market forces is allowed to balance equitably the distribution of wealth. Ironically, although Smith thought of himself as the champion of the poor against the economic injustices inherent in state-supported mercantile privileges, his laissez-faire doctrine later became the favored theory of private industrial entrepreneurs who exploited the poor as much if not more than mercantilistic governments ever did. Nevertheless, Smith's free-market economics, as will be seen in subsequent chapters, certainly represented the wave of the future.

Adam Smith

Beccaria

Elsewhere in Europe the circulation of Enlightenment ideas was by no means as widespread as in France and Britain, owing either to stiffer resistance from religious authorities, greater vigilance of state censors, or the lack of sufficient numbers of prosperous educated people to discuss and support progressive thought. Yet, outside the Papal States, at least a few prominent philosophes flourished in virtually every country in western Europe. In Italy, for example, the Milanese jurist Cesare Beccaria (1738–1794) argued in the same spirit as the French philosophes against arbitrary powers that oppressed humanity. In his most influential writing, *On Crimes and Punishments* (1764), Beccaria attacked the prevalent view that judicial punishments should represent society's vengeance on

Instruments of Torture. The rack and the thumbscrew, from an official Austrian governmental handbook. Beccaria's influence helped phase out the use of such instruments by around 1800.

Kant's practical philosophy

the malefactor, asserting instead that no person has the right to punish another unless some useful purpose is served. For Beccaria, the only legitimate purpose for punishing crimes was the deterrence of other crimes. This granted, he argued for the greatest possible leniency compatible with deterrence, because enlightened humanitarianism dictated that humans should not punish other humans any more than is absolutely necessary. Above all, Beccaria eloquently opposed the death penalty, then widely inflicted throughout Europe for the most trivial offenses, on the grounds that it was no deterrent and set the bad example of public officials presiding over murder rather than striving to deter it. *On Crimes and Punishments* was so favorably received that it was quickly translated into a dozen languages. Owing primarily to its influence, most European countries by around 1800 abolished torture, reserved the death penalty for capital crimes, and made imprisonment rather than any form of maiming the main form of judicial punishment.

The most representative German philosophe was the literary critic and dramatist Gotthold Lessing (1729–1781), who wrote with great eloquence of the need for tolerance. In his play *Nathan the Wise* (1779) Lessing led the audience to see that nobility of character has no relation to religious affiliations, and in his *Education of the Human Race* (1780) he maintained that the development of each of the world's great religions, Christianity included, was simply a step in the spiritual evolution of humanity, which would soon move beyond religion entirely toward pure rationality. The living model for Lessing's dramatic hero "Nathan the Wise" was his friend the German Jewish sage Moses Mendelssohn (1729–1786), another philosophe who urged tolerance—in his case by writing a history of Judaism—but who also argued in favor of the immortality of the soul.

Far more difficult to classify is the greatest German philosopher of the eighteenth century—indeed one of the greatest philosophers of any nation of any time—Immanuel Kant (1724–1804). An unworldly intellectual who lived out his life in the Prussian city of Königsberg, far from the Enlightenment's French center of gravity, Kant addressed his two masterworks, *The Critique of Pure Reason* (1781) and *The Critique of Practical Reason* (1788), to criticizing fashionable Enlightenment skepticism as represented most persuasively by David Hume. One of Kant's positions concerning reality and knowledge went so far against the grain of standard Enlightenment assumptions that it can hardly be called "Enlightened" at all. Namely, he maintained, in the spirit of Platonism, that the existence of a realm of absolute reality consisting of what he termed "things in themselves" cannot be doubted even though this realm remains unknowable to humans. Kant's assumption of absolute but unknowable truth, which implicitly opened philosophy to mystery, was to prove extremely attractive to his German philosophical successors in the nineteenth century, collectively known as "Idealists," but it ill accorded with his own age's stress on scientific verifiability.

In fact, however, Kant did not propose to build an action-oriented system on the basis of his assumed world of "things in themselves"; to the contrary, the bulk of his practical philosophy was more typically Enlightened. Aiming to counteract Hume's skepticism in a second way, he proposed that even though everyday knowledge begins in sense experience, the data of our senses is ordered by our rational minds in the here-and-now world of space and time in such a way as to provide us with reliable knowledge of appearances, or of what Kant called "phenomena." In other words, Kant believed that humans could gain sufficient truth on a daily basis by a combination of sense and reason. Hence he insisted, much like Voltaire, that humans should use their learning faculties to inquire about nature, and, having done so, to improve upon it. Regarding ethics, Kant avoided the extremes of fixing upon conduct arbitrarily according to supernatural divine commandments or relativistically according to changing circumstances. Instead he maintained that if pure reason could neither prove nor disprove the existence of God, practical reason tells us that in the idea of God there exists a notion of moral perfection toward which all must strive. Thus we should always endeavor to act consistently with what Kant called the "categorical imperative": to act as if one's actions were to become a universal law of nature. Kant's principle of the categorical imperative proposed greater moral inflexibility than most philosophes thought realistic in view of the realities of everyday existence, yet it remained reconcilable with the basic Enlightenment worldview inasmuch as it rested on human rather than supernatural determinations.

Immanuel Kant

In taking final stock of the Enlightenment movement, historians customarily raise two major questions. One is whether the philosophes were mere elitists who had no influence on the masses. Certainly, if one studies the sales figures of the philosophes' books or membership lists of eighteenth-century learned societies one finds that the philosophes' immediate audience consisted of aristocrats, government officials, prosperous merchants, and a scattering of members of the higher clergy. To some degree this class bias lay beyond the philosophes' control, for many of the poorer people throughout eighteenth-century Europe remained illiterate, and most of the masses in southern and southeastern Europe—literate and illiterate alike—lived under the sway of an extremely conservative Roman Catholic hierarchy that was determined to keep them ignorant of the philosophes' ideas by means of the strictest censorship. Yet it is also true that many of the philosophes, despite their avowed commitment to clarity, wrote over the heads of most laboring people, and many did not even seek a lower-class audience because they feared that, if taken too far by the "uncouth" masses, their ideas might provoke open revolution. Typical philosophe elitism is well expressed in Gibbon's praise of imperial Roman religious policy, whereby "the various modes of worship . . . were all considered by the people as equally true, by the philosopher as equally false, and by the magistrate as equally useful." Tradition also relates that whenever Voltaire discussed religion with his philosophe friends, he dismissed the servants so that they would not overhear any subversive remarks. Given this prevalent attitude, it is less surprising that Enlightenment ideas hardly percolated down to the

The audience of the philosophes

masses than that they did have some effect on popular beliefs in France and Britain. For example, research on religious practices in southern France demonstrates that from 1760 to 1790 fewer and fewer people of all classes requested that masses be said for their souls after death. Apparently, then, some servants were overhearing the philosophes' drawing-room conversations after all.

The philosophes' commitment to
social reform

The other major question often asked about the Enlightenment is whether the philosophes were not hopelessly impractical "dreamers rather than doers." Without ignoring the clear vein of utopianism in Enlightenment thought, the answer to this must surely be no. Admittedly, most philosophes were far more optimistic about the chances of human perfectibility than most people are today, after the total wars and gas ovens of the twentieth century. Yet even the most optimistic did not expect utopian miracles to occur overnight. Rather, almost all the philosophes were committed to agitating for piecemeal social reforms that they believed would culminate, step by inevitable step, in a new world of enlightenment and virtue. Often such agitation did lead to significant changes in the conduct of practical affairs, and in at least one case, that of the American Revolution, Enlightenment ideas were the main source of inspiration for constructing a fully new political system. Moreover, sometimes even when Enlightenment propagandizing did not have any immediate practical impact, it did help to accomplish change in the future. For example, many philosophes condemned slavery on humanitarian or utilitarian grounds, thereby initiating a process of discussion that led cumulatively to the triumph of abolitionism throughout the West in the nineteenth century. In short, then, it is impossible to deny that the philosophes as a class were among the most practical-minded and influential intellectuals who ever lived.

THE ONWARD MARCH OF SCIENCE

Biology

Although several of the philosophes were natural scientists as well as publicists, it is preferable to treat the progress of eighteenth-century science separately because science, being highly international, is best broached by means of a topical rather than geographical method of review. The three scientific areas that witnessed the greatest progress from around the time of Newton to the end of the eighteenth century were descriptive biology, electricity, and chemistry. Regarding the first, four great pioneers in the use of newly invented high-power microscopes made enormous advances in observing small creatures and plant and cell structures during the last decades of the seventeenth century—the Italian Marcello Malpighi (1628–1694), the Englishman Robert Hooke, and two Dutchmen, Jan Swammerdam (1637–1680) and Antony van Leeuwenhoek (1632–1723). Perhaps most fundamental was the work of the last, a self-taught scientist who discovered bacteria and wrote the first description of human sperm. Building on such accomplishments as well as on numerous observations of his own, the Swedish botanist Karl von Linné (1707–1778)—commonly known by his Latinized name, Linnaeus—formulated the basic system of plant and animal classification that remains in use today. In the "Linnaean Order" there are three realms—animal, vegetable, and mineral—and within the first two there are classes, "genera" and species. Furthermore, in Linnaeus's system every plant and animal is given two scientific Latin names—the first denoting the genus and the second the species. For example, robins are called *Planesticus migratorius:* the migrating species of the genus *Planesticus.*

Rivaling Linnaeus in eighteenth-century biology was the French naturalist Georges Buffon (1707–1788), whose massive *Natural History,* appearing in forty-four volumes from 1749 to 1778, was most advanced in its recognition of the close relationship between humans and other primates. Completely ignoring the biblical version of creation, yet never quite bringing himself to accept the full implications of a theory that located human origins in some form of evolution, Buffon admitted the possibility that the entire range of organic forms had descended from a single species and thus was a precursor of the evolutionism of Charles Darwin.

Georges Buffon

As opposed to developments in descriptive biology, where basic work hardly began before 1660, the "founding father" in the field of electricity was active well before the period under discussion. Around 1600 the Englishman William Gilbert discovered the magnetic properties of lodestones and introduced the word *electricity* into the language (*elektron* is the Greek word for "amber," and Gilbert had observed that amber rubbed on fur will attract paper or straw). Yet because Gilbert worked before the triumph of mechanistic thought, he believed magnetism to be a purely occult force and therefore did not even dream of machines that could generate or harness electricity. Starting in the late seventeenth century, on the other hand, scientists from many different countries progressively began to master the science of electricity as we now know it. In 1672 the German Otto von Guericke published results of experiments wherein he generated electricity; in 1729 the Englishman Stephen Gray demonstrated that electricity could be conducted by means of threads and that certain other substances resisted conducting; and in 1745 a team of scientists at the Dutch University of Leyden invented a method for storing electricity in the "Leyden jar." In 1749 by using a kite-string to conduct lightning the American Benjamin Franklin charged a Leyden jar from a thunderstorm and thus was able to conclude that lightning and electricity are identical. This recognition allowed Franklin to invent the lightning rod, which saves houses from being destroyed by lightning during storms and is one of the best examples of the link between scientific theory and life-enhancing practice.

Electricity

Benjamin Franklin as the God of Electricity, by Benjamin West

Probably the greatest theoretical breakthrough made in the second half of the eighteenth century lay in the field of chemistry, which had been languishing for about a century after the work of Robert Boyle. The reason for this delay lay mostly in the wide acceptance of errors concerning such

Chemistry

matters as heat, flame, air, and the phenomenon of combustion. The most misleading error was the so-called phlogiston theory, based on the idea that "phlogiston" was the substance of fire. When an object burned, phlogiston was supposed to be given off and the remaining ash was said to be the "true" material. In the second half of the eighteenth century important discoveries were made that discredited this theory and cleared the way for a real understanding of basic chemical reactions. In 1766 the Englishman Henry Cavendish reported the discovery of a new kind of gas obtained by treating certain metals with sulfuric acid. He showed that this gas, now known as hydrogen, would not of itself support combustion and yet would be rapidly consumed by a fire with access to the air. In 1774 oxygen was discovered by another Englishman, the Unitarian minister Joseph Priestley. He found that a candle would burn with extraordinary vigor when placed in the new gas—a fact that indicated clearly that combustion was not caused by any mysterious principle or substance in the flame itself. A few years after this discovery, Cavendish demonstrated that air and water, long supposed to be elements, are respectively a mixture and a compound, the first being composed principally of oxygen and nitrogen, and the second of oxygen and hydrogen.

The final blow to the phlogiston theory was administered by the Frenchman Antoine Lavoisier (1743–1794), widely regarded as the greatest scientist of the eighteenth century, who lost his life in the French Revolution. Lavoisier proved that both combustion and respiration involve oxidation, the one being rapid and the other slow. He provided the names for oxygen and hydrogen and demonstrated that the diamond is a form of carbon. But undoubtedly his greatest accomplishment was his discovery of the law of the conservation of mass. He found evidence that "although matter may alter its state in a series of chemical actions, it does not change in amount; the quantity of matter is the same at the end as at the beginning of every operation, and can be traced by its weight." This "law" has, of course, been modified by later discoveries regarding the structure of the atom and the conversion of some forms of matter into energy. It is hardly too much to say, however, that as a result of Lavoisier's genius chemistry became a true science.

Despite the notable scientific advances of the seventeenth and eighteenth centuries, the development of physiology and medicine progressed rather slowly during the same period for several reasons. One was the inadequate preparation of physicians, many of whom had begun their professional careers with little more training than apprenticeship under an older practitioner. Another was the common disrepute in which surgery was held as a mere trade, like that of a barber or blacksmith. Perhaps the most serious of all was the prejudice against dissection of human bodies for use in anatomical study. As late as 1750 medical schools that engaged in this practice were in danger of destruction by irate mobs. Despite these obstacles some progress was still possible. About 1670 Malpighi and Leeuwenhoek confirmed William Harvey's discovery of the circulation of the blood by observing the actual flow of blood

Antoine Lavoisier

Lavoisier's Apparatus for the Decomposition of Air

Comparative slowness of medical progress

through the network of capillaries connecting the arteries and veins. At approximately the same time an eminent physician of London, Thomas Sydenham, proposed a new theory of fever as a natural process by which diseased material is expelled from the system.

Medical progress during the eighteenth century was somewhat more rapid. Among the noteworthy achievements were the discovery of blood pressure, the founding of histology or microscopic anatomy, and the development of the autopsy as an aid to the study of disease. But the chief milestones of medical advancement in this period were the adoption of inoculation and the development of vaccination for smallpox. Knowledge of inoculation came originally from the Near East, where it had long been employed by the Muslims. Information concerning its use was relayed to England in 1717 through the letters of Lady Mary Wortley Montagu, wife of the British ambassador to Turkey. The first systematic application of the practice in the Western world, however, was due to the efforts of the American Puritan minister Cotton Mather, who implored the physicians of Boston to inoculate their patients in the hope of curbing an epidemic of smallpox that had broken out in 1721. Thereafter inoculation had some success in saving lives, but the practice understandably was widely resisted because smallpox inoculation guaranteed the patient one bout with the disfiguring disease before inducing further immunity to it. Only in 1796 did the Englishman Edward Jenner, noticing that milkmaids always seemed to have clear complexions, conclude that in contracting the virus of cowpox from their daily occupation, milkmaids gained immunity to smallpox. Hence inoculation of humans with the deadly smallpox virus appeared unnecessary, and Jenner introduced *vaccination* (from *vacca*—Latin for "cow"), employing the mild cowpox virus instead. Once vaccination proved both harmless and marvelously effective, the vast possibilities opened up for the elimination of contagious diseases appeared to confirm the Enlightenment belief in the ability of science to make nature's laws work for the betterment of the human condition.

Inoculation and vaccination

CLASSICISM AND INNOVATION IN ART AND LITERATURE

Although the spirit of the scientific revolution and the Enlightenment was reflected in certain great artistic monuments, there were no simple, one-to-one correspondences between intellectual and artistic trends in the late seventeenth and eighteenth centuries. Artists and writers responded to a great variety of influences in addition to the new scientific view of the universe: national stylistic traditions, religious demands, differing political and sociological contexts, and, not least, the internal dynamics of artistic evolution within any given creative field. It is best, then, to look at certain major trends without forcing the explanations for them all to fit the same mold.

Manifold influences on artistic trends

French classicism

As we have seen earlier, the dominant style in European art between about 1600 and the early 1700s was the Baroque. But a few countries resisted the dominance of Baroque influences—particularly France, Holland, and England. The French resistance was primarily nationalistic in inspiration. Since Baroque style was closely associated with the tastes of the Spanish and Austrian Habsburgs, against whom the French were fighting throughout most of the seventeenth and early eighteenth centuries, it seemed inappropriate for France to admit cultural inferiority by imitating the style of its political rivals. In opposition to the exuberant Baroque, then, French artists and architects cultivated restrained classicism. Some of the best earlier examples of this are the canvases of seventeenth-century France's greatest painter, Nicolas Poussin (1594–1665), whose reposeful scenes from classical mythology, governed by the artist's programmatic commitment to "things well ordered," stand in the sharpest contrast to the swirling contortions of Poussin's Baroque contemporary, Rubens.

Classicism of the Louvre

"Well-ordered" classicism continued to be the preferred style in France during the reign of Louis XIV (1651–1715) for three reasons. First of all, Louis in particular was determined to make sure that France cultivated its own characteristic national style for reasons of state. Second, Louis's own stylistic preferences tended toward the grand and sober. And third, the symmetrical qualities of classicism seemed to complement best the highly symmetrical natural order then being posited in France by Cartesian philosophers and scientists. Thus when Louis XIV decided to renovate his palace of the Louvre, the leading Baroque architect of the day, Bernini, submitted plans, but these were rejected in favor of those of a native Frenchman who emphasized severe classical monumentality. Later, when Louis erected his splendid new palace at Versailles, Baroque architectural features were introduced. Yet the Baroque of Versailles was a very restrained Baroque that emphasized massive symmetry rather than the jutting angles and startling curves favored by Bernini.

Landscape with the Burial of Phocion, by Nicolas Poussin (1594–1665). An outstanding example of the classical style in painting. As opposed to the Baroque stress on swirling movement, here there is practically no movement at all. Instead, nature is conceived in rigorously geometrical terms to convey a sense of permanence. Note too the presence of ancient classical buildings, making it seem as if the past is enduring.

The Finding of Moses, by Poussin. The artist has included a pyramid in the background (right) as a token of verisimilitude, but otherwise his scene appears to be set in ancient Rome. Note the stress on monumentality and perpendicular lines.

In the other leading countries that resisted the Baroque, Holland and England, there can be little doubt that artistic preferences had religious as well as nationalistic causes. Since Holland and England were Protestant, they naturally preferred to limit Baroque influences emanating from Rome and the Catholic Spanish Netherlands. We have seen that the greatest seventeenth-century Dutch painter, Rembrandt, developed his own highly personal style, which employed Baroque elements whenever he deemed them appropriate. Rembrandt's slightly later Dutch contemporary, Jan Vermeer (1632–1675), however, eliminated the Baroque entirely in painting the serenest realistic indoor genre scenes, as did most other seventeenth-century Dutch genre, landscape, and portrait painters. Similarly, the dominant stylistic commitment in England, after a brief flirtation with the Baroque during the reign of the Catholic-leaning Charles II, was to a classicizing restraint. Thus the most prominent of all English architects, Christopher Wren (1632–1723), did not hesitate to borrow Baroque elements when fitting, but emphasized classicism in his columns and domes, most notably in his masterwork, St. Paul's Cathedral (built from 1675 to 1710). More classical still was the "Palladian revival," which dominated English architecture in the first half of the eighteenth century. In this period numerous country houses commissioned by the landed gentry imitated the Renaissance master Palladio's serenely classical and highly symmetrical Villa Rotonda, just as that building had imitated the Roman Pantheon. Indeed, so many English town houses built in the fashionable resort spa of Bath around 1740 imitated Palladian models that Bath was soon called, after Palladio's main area of activity, "the English Vicenza."

East Entrance of the Louvre, Paris. Built by the French architect Claude Perrault between 1667 and 1670, this facade is an excellent example of the rigorously classical style patronized by Louis XIV.

Left: **St. Peter's Basilica with Colonnade, Rome.** Right: **St. Paul's Cathedral, London.** The sweeping colonnade in front of St. Peter's was designed by the Baroque architectural master Bernini in 1656. Such showy effects were not to the taste of the English architect Christopher Wren, who in designing St. Paul's hewed more closely to the classicism implicit in the Renaissance style of the Vatican Basilica itself. Wren's "English answer to St. Peter's," however, makes classical columns even more prominent than they were in the Vatican. Note how Wren drew inspiration from Perrault's classical Louvre facade (p. 657) in designing St. Paul's second-level elevation.

Classicism in French literature

As classicism was the prevalent style in seventeenth-century French art, so too did it prevail in literature. This can be seen most clearly in the tragedies of Pierre Corneille (1606–1684) and Jean Racine (1639–1699). Both of these playwrights took as their subjects the heroes and heroines of classical mythology and history, such as Medea, Pompey, Andromache, and Phaedra, and both strove as well to imitate the theoretical and structural principles of the classical Greek tragedians. Similarly, the great French writer of comedies, Jean Baptiste Molière (1622–1673), was so

Chiswick House. Built near London around 1725, this country house initiated an English Palladian fad that had its echoes in Thomas Jefferson's Monticello, and later still in the Jefferson Memorial. Note how the design imitates Palladio's Villa Rotonda (see p. 436), just as that building itself was modeled on the Roman Pantheon (see p. 184).

committed to symmetrical formalism as to have his characters speak in rhyming couplets. Yet, unlike Corneille and Racine, Molière set the action of his plays in the present because he believed that "the business of comedy is to represent in general all the defects of men and especially of the men of our time." Accordingly, his work was also highly satirical. In *Tartuffe,* for example, he pilloried religious hypocrisy, and in *The Bourgeois Gentleman* he mocked the vulgar pretentiousness of the social climber. Yet for all his satire, Molière had a measure of sympathy for the trials of human existence, rising to his greatest profundity in *The Misanthrope,* a play that pokes fun at a person who hates society but that also shows that

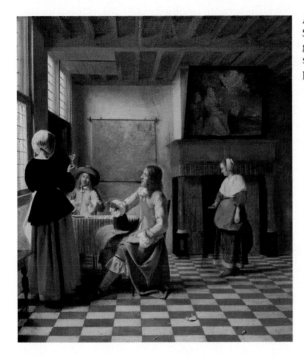

A Dutch Interior, by Pieter de Hooch (c. 1629–c. 1679). Seventeenth-century Dutch painters excelled at indoor genre compositions bathed in light. The restraint of the scene itself stands in contrast to the melodramatic Baroque painting in the background.

The Painter in his Studio, by Jan Vermeer (1632–1675). The model is posing as Clio, the muse of history, and thus stands for the timeless fame of painting. The fact that the source of light is concealed by the curtain may perhaps be understood to mean that the artist works essentially by the interior illumination of his mind.

Classicism in English literature

the character has excellent reasons for his alienation. Thus mixing sympathy and occasional melancholy with wit and searing scorn, Molière was perhaps the most gifted European dramatist after Shakespeare.

As in France, in England artistic classicism was paralleled by literary classicism, which flourished in England from about 1660 to 1760. In fact, the English writers of this period expressly called themselves "Augustans." This they did for two reasons: first, the restoration of royalty in 1660 after the English Civil War seemed to presage an age of peace and civility similar to the one installed by Augustus after civil war in ancient Rome; and second, the favored poetic models of the English Augustans were the Augustan Romans—Virgil, Horace, and Ovid. Still another reason why English literary taste became resolutely classical in the later seventeenth century was that the France of Louis XIV had enormous influence in setting fashions throughout Europe, and the English did not wish to be the slightest bit out of date in following the French lead. Finally, as in France, classicism appeared to be the one available style that came closest to being dispassionately "scientific." In other words, just when the English leisured classes were celebrating the triumphs of Newtonianism and endeavoring to make their own contribution to scientific advance by collecting natural specimens or gazing through telescopes, they patronized a form of writing that seemed to resemble Newtonian methods and laws in stressing simplicity, clarity, and symmetry.

Jonathan Swift and Alexander Pope

Of the numerous members of the English Augustan school, the most outstanding were the prose writer Jonathan Swift (1667–1745) and the poet Alexander Pope (1688–1744). The former, a scathing satirist, was atypical of Augustan thinking in his pessimism concerning the potentialities of human nature: in Swift's masterpiece, *Gulliver's Travels,* humans at one point are dismissed as "the most pernicious race of little odious vermin that nature ever suffered to crawl upon the surface of the earth." Yet Swift's prose is fully Augustan in its economy and clarity; as opposed to earlier flowery stylists, Swift insisted on locating, as he said, "proper words in proper places." As for Pope, he was thoroughly Augustan in both style and thought—almost to a fault. A consistent exponent in highly regular rhyming verse of the naturalistic doctrines of the Enlightenment, Pope in such didactic poems as his *Essay on Man* and his *Essay on Criticism* held that humans must study and imitate nature if they were to bring any semblance of order into their affairs. Most necessary for mankind, in Pope's view, was unblinking self-knowledge, which the poet believed could be obtained apart from theology or metaphysics. Summing up the secularistic spirit of his age, Pope responded to Milton's earlier poetic resolve to "justify the ways of God to man" in his most famous couplet: "Know then thyself, presume not God to scan;/the proper study of Mankind is Man."

Rococo painting

As impressive as numerous artistic and literary productions of French and English classicism may have been, the classical movement self-evidently was not highly innovative. Two entirely separate developments of the eighteenth century, on the other hand, emphasized greater originality—namely, the emergence of the Continental Rococo style in art, and the rise of the English novel. Regarding the former, the basic explanation for the emergence of Rococo art and architecture was the sense of relaxation experienced in France at the coming of peace and at the death of Louis XIV in 1715. Whereas the prolonged War of the Spanish Succession had begun to exhaust the country, and whereas Louis in his declining years had become ever more puritanical and ever more determined to enforce his own severe tastes and standards on everyone else, around 1715 the leisured classes of the nation breathed a deep sigh of relief. This reaction, not surprisingly, resulted in an artistic pendulum swing from classical severity to a cheerful abandonment that goes by the name of Rococo style. In painting, the earliest and most gifted Rococo artist was Antoine Watteau (1684–1721), who was influenced more by the Baroque artist Rubens than by any other single source, but who replaced Rubens's massiveness with airy French elegance and grace. Watteau was admitted into the French Academy of Fine Arts in 1717 for his masterpiece, *The Embarkation for Cythera,* even though none of the members would have dreamed of admitting him two years earlier. Moreover, since the Academy had no formal classification for the *Embarkation*—which merely showed graceful people having a dreamily good time—it invented one for the purpose: *fêtes galantes,* best translated as "stylish revels." At least Watteau's revellers were clothed; the figures in the paintings of his Rococo successors

Le Mezzetin, by Antoine Watteau (1684–1721). Mezzetin was a popular character from Italian comedy. In portraying him in a relaxed pose Watteau succeeded in conveying a sense of dreamy elegance.

The Embarkation for Cythera, by Watteau. This epoch-making painting broke with the severity of Poussin in favor of a greater stress on motion and lushness. No two art historians agree upon exactly what it means, but the evocation of dreamy pleasure is unmistakable.

Marriage à la Mode, by William Hogarth (1697–1764). A satirical look at the arranged marriage: the financial needs of the nobleman and the social aspirations of his middle-class counterpart dominate the negotiations.

François Boucher (1703–1770) and Jean-Honoré Fragonard (1732–1806) were usually half naked and displayed in postures that went well beyond sensuality in the direction of frank eroticism.

Most of the rest of Europe was too strait-laced to imitate the lasciviousness of French Rococo painting, but French Rococo architecture soon became the dominant style throughout the Continent and remained such for most of the eighteenth century. The reasons for this were, first, that the French architects who pioneered in Rococo building in the years shortly after 1715 took Baroque principles for their standards in replacing classical ones, thereby setting themselves in tune with the rest of their Continental contemporaries; and second, that Rococo building design featured curvaceous elegance and thus appealed greatly to the vain European aristocrats who commissioned the major architectural projects of the day.

Perhaps the easiest way to characterize the Rococo building style is to call it the "champagne of Baroque" or "Baroque with a French accent." Both Baroque and Rococo buildings emphasize dynamic movement, but whereas Baroque style exudes force and passion, the Rococo communicates a sense of delicacy and playfulness. Most amazing to initial viewers of Rococo interiors is how light and airy they are: as opposed to Baroque interiors, which are generally sombre, Rococo interiors have walls and ceilings painted in white, gold, and pink. Among the leading European Rococo buildings are the Hôtel de Soubise in Paris, the pavilion known as the Zwinger in Dresden, the jewel-box Vierzehnheiligen Church near

French Rococo architecture

Rococo and Baroque compared

Left: **Madame de Pompadour,** by François Boucher (1703–1770). A characteristically frilly and lightly erotic French Rococo portrait. Madame de Pompadour, King Louis XV's mistress, was a patroness of arts and letters, and for a time the virtual ruler of France. Right: **A Reclining Nude,** by Boucher. The viewer is left to ponder the significance of the fallen flower.

Two German Rococo Interiors. The Vierzehnheiligen Church near Bamberg (left) and the Wieskirche near Munich (right) are the two foremost works of German Rococo interior decoration.

Bamberg, and the Cuvilliès theater in Munich, which is still used for performances of eighteenth-century operas and plays. Although Rococo art and architecture unquestionably allowed great play for the imagination, from the long-term perspective of art history the Rococo style was an end rather than a beginning inasmuch as it represented the final phase of the Baroque.

In contrast, the only really new development in the artistic and literary history of the Enlightenment period that had a promising future was the emergence of the novel. In treating the rise of the novel in eighteenth-century England it must be stressed that the English novel was not invented out of nothing. To the contrary, works of prose fiction known as romances had been composed in classical antiquity and throughout western Europe from the twelfth century onward. Indeed, one European romance—Cervantes's *Don Quixote*—atypically had many of the characteristics of the modern novel. Moreover, in France, where the word *roman* means both "romance" and "novel," prose fictions were written without interruption from the Middle Ages to the recognizably modern novels of the nineteenth-century writers Balzac and Flaubert. Nevertheless, there were such major differences between the best English prose fictions of the eighteenth century and all that came before (other than *Don Quixote*) as to make it possible to say that the modern novel was invented in eighteenth-century England.

The best way of characterizing the difference between the romance and the novel is that the former is patently a fabrication, whereas the latter (allowing a few inevitable exceptions) purports to be a reliable account of how humans behave. Assuming that a judge in a court of law were asked to accept the testimony of a romance as evidence for trying a case, he would have to throw it out and declare a mistrial because romances generally have little sense of verisimilitude, being written in an ornate style and recounting the adventures of clearly imaginary characters—usually from the mythical or semi-mythical past—who find themselves in preposterous situations. But the testimony of a novel might stand up as excellent legal evidence, for in the novel, from the eighteenth-century English examples onward, experiences seem unique, plots and settings fully believable, and the manner of presentation dispassionately straightforward.

Two explanations may be offered for the emergence of the novel in eighteenth-century England. One is that the ideals of the Enlightenment unquestionably created the most conducive atmosphere for novel writing insofar as the "scientific," methodical study of human experience was widely regarded as the order of the day. Yet, because Enlightenment thinking predominated in France even more than in England, it remains to be asked why England in particular was the modern novel's first home. The answer to this appears to relate to the distinctive nature of the English reading public. Specifically, England had a much larger nonaristocratic reading audience than France because of England's greater involvement in trade and industry; this class preferred novels to romances because novels were written in a gripping rather than "elevated" style, and the action of the novel's more prosaic characters seemed more relevant to common, nonaristocratic experience. As will also presently be seen, it was by no means irrelevant to the novelistic form in England that the majority of novel readers were not men but women.

By common consent the three most influential novelists of eighteenth-century England were Daniel Defoe (1660–1731), Samuel Richardson (1689–1761), and Henry Fielding (1707–1754). All three portrayed recognizable, nonaristocratic characters doing their best to make their way in a perilous world, unaffected by any hint of divine intervention for good or ill. In the novels of Defoe and Richardson the narrator is usually a character who participates in the action and thus knows the "truth" of one side directly but of course cannot be expected to understand every other character's point of view. On the other hand, in Fielding's *Tom Jones* an "omnipotent narrator" stands apart from the action, and accordingly has a fuller view of it, but seems by his obtrusive presence to be creating a rather more artificial fiction.

Tom Jones is the only eighteenth-century English novel universally considered to be an enduring classic of world literature, but at the very beginning of the next century the technical achievements of Defoe, Richardson, and Fielding were refined by Jane Austen (1775–1817), whose *Pride and Prejudice* and *Emma* represent for many readers the height of novelistic perfection. That a woman should emerge around 1800 as a greater writer of novels than most men was almost inevitable, above all because early-modern European fiction writing was one of the very few areas of creative expression wherein society easily tolerated female contributions. Indeed, in seventeenth-century France the most widely read authors of romances—Madeleine de Scudéry and the countess de La Fayette—were women, and later in England Fanny Burney (1752–1840), Ann Radcliffe (1764–1823), and Maria Edgeworth (1767–1849) all wrote novels of great popularity and considerable distinction before Jane Austen went to work. Moreover, since the English novel-reading public was predominantly female, women readers understandably were particularly interested in characteristically female problems as seen from a feminine angle, a subject matter and perspective that Jane Austen bountifully provided. But of course Austen would not rank, as she does, among the handful of greatest novelists who ever lived had she been narrowly parochial in her views or lacking in extraordinary artistic skill. Rather, men as well as women can delight in her dry, ironic wit and admire her insight into human nature. Moreover, Jane Austen's technical accomplishments may well represent novelistic skills at their pinnacle. In particular, in compromising between Defoe's and Richardson's first-person narrator and Fielding's omnipotent third-person one by the use of a third-person narrator who remains unobtrusive and pursues events primarily from the point of view of a central character, Jane Austen created a delicate balance between subjectivity and objectivity that may well never have been surpassed.

Defoe, Richardson, and Fielding

Jane Austen and the perfection of the novel

Innovation in Baroque and
classical music

The title of one of the most genial of eighteenth-century symphonic compositions, Haydn's *Surprise* symphony, can be applied to the music of the entire age, for eighteenth-century music is continually full of surprises. Indeed, in contrast to developments in contemporary art and literature, where innovation was comparatively rare, the eighteenth century was the most fertile period of invention in all of western European musical history. Probably the major explanation for this is that early-modern composers, unlike artists and writers, did not have to concern themselves about how much they would borrow from the music of classical antiquity because the principles of ancient musical composition were virtually unknown. More free than painters and poets to strike out on their own, early-modern composers invented form after form in two successive major styles, the Baroque and the so-called classical, treating their listeners to surprise after surprise.

Claudio Monteverdi

Baroque music, like Baroque art and architecture, emerged around 1600 in Italy as an artistic expression of the Counter-Reformation. Yet from the beginning Baroque composers were perforce more inventive than their artistic counterparts, having no equivalent of columns and domes with which to work. The first important figure in the history of Baroque music was the Italian Claudio Monteverdi (1567–1643), who reacted against the highly intricate Renaissance polyphonic style of his major predecessor, Palestrina. Pursuing the Baroque goal of dramatic expressiveness, Monteverdi found that deep human emotions were difficult to convey when members of a chorus were singing against each other as they did in the music of the late Renaissance, and that dramatic intensity becomes greatest when music is combined with theater. Having no classical models to draw upon, Monteverdi thus virtually single-handedly invented a new musical form, that of opera. In addition, to lend his opera singers greater emotional power than they would have had if they had sung alone, Monteverdi wrote instrumental accompaniments so forceful that they have earned him the title of "the father of instrumentation." Since Monteverdi's new form of opera fully suited the spirit of his times, within a generation operas were performed in all the leading cities of Italy. Staged within magnificent settings, and calling upon the talents of singers, musicians, dramatists, and stage designers, opera expressed as clearly as any art form the dedication of Baroque artistic style to grandeur, drama, and display.

The two greatest Baroque
composers

With the notable exception of the Englishman Henry Purcell (1659–1695), no enduringly great composers worked in the second half of the seventeenth century. Nonetheless, many imaginative musicians began to create new forms during this period, most notably the instrumental forms of the sonata and the concerto. Moreover, whatever lull there may have been in the composition of masterpieces was more than compensated for in the last phase of the Baroque era by the appearance of Bach and Handel, two of the greatest composers of all time. Born in the same year very near each other in northern Germany, Johann Sebastian Bach (1685–1750) and George Frederick Handel (1685–1759) had very different musical personalities and very different careers. Bach was an intensely pious introvert who remained in the backwaters of provincial Germany all his life and wrote music of the utmost individuality, whereas Handel was a public-pleasing cosmopolitan whose music is more accessible than Bach's in its robust affirmativeness. Despite these differences, however, both Bach and Handel were distinctly late-Baroque stylists in their commitment to writing music of the deepest expressiveness.

Anyone who has any familiarity with classical music can identify in a moment a work of Bach even if he or she has never heard it before because Bach's music is so extraordinarily individualistic. This, however, does not mean that it is in any way predictable, for part of Bach's individuality lay in his very unpredictability. Combining an uncanny imagination and capacious intellect with heroic powers of discipline and an ability to produce music of the greatest genius on demand, Bach was an extremely prolific composer in the entire gamut of contemporary forms (excluding opera), from unaccompanied instrumental pieces to enormous works for vocal soloists, chorus, and orchestra. As a church musician in Leipzig for most of his mature career, Bach's professional duty was to provide new music regularly for Sunday and holiday services. Therefore much of his work consists of religious cantatas (over two hundred surviving), motets, and passions. One might think that the mere requirement to write such music on schedule might have made it routine and lifeless, but Bach, an ardent Protestant who was entirely unaffected by the secularism of the Enlightenment, seems to have written each one of his church pieces with such fervor that the salvation of the world appears to hang on every note. Not content with expressing himself in spiritual music alone, Bach also gloried in creating joyous concertos and suites for orchestra, and succeeded in composing the purest of "pure music"—extraordinarily subtle and complex fugues for keyboard in which the capacity of the human mind for apprehending abstraction appears to approach the celestial.

Johann Sebastian Bach

Bach

Much unlike the provincial, inner-directed Bach, Handel was a man of the world who sought primarily to establish rapport with large, secular audiences. After spending his early creative years in Italy, where he mastered Italian Baroque compositional techniques, Handel established himself in London. There he tried at first to make a living by composing Italian operas, but since the highly florid Baroque operatic style proved too foreign for more staid English tastes, Handel eventually realized that he would never survive unless he turned to some more salable genre. This he found in the oratorio—a variety of music drama intended for performance in concert form. Marking a transition from the spiritual to the secular, Handel's oratorios were usually set to biblical stories but featured very worldly music, replete with ornate instrumentation and frequent flourishes of drums and trumpets. (Some music historians refer to Handel's "big bow-wow" manner.) These highly virile and heroic works

George Frederick Handel

Handel

succeeded in packing London's halls full of prosperous English people who interpreted the victories of the ancient Hebrews in such oratorios as *Israel in Egypt* and *Judas Maccabaeus* as implicit celebrations of England's own burgeoning national greatness. Of course Handel's music was not for one time but for all, as is demonstrated by the fact that his greatest oratorio, *The Messiah,* is sung widely throughout the English-speaking world every Christmas and its stirring "Hallelujah Chorus" certainly remains the most popular single choral piece in the entire classical repertory.

Although only a few decades separated the activity of Bach and Handel from that of their greatest eighteenth-century successors, the Austrians Joseph Haydn (1732–1809) and Wolfgang Amadeus Mozart (1756–1791), the two pairs appear worlds apart because their compositional styles are utterly different. Whereas Bach and Handel were among the last and certainly the greatest composers of Baroque music, Haydn and Mozart were the leading representatives of the succeeding "classical" style. The latter term is slightly confusing because classicism in music had nothing to do with imitating music written in classical antiquity. Rather, the musical style that prevailed in Europe in the second half of the eighteenth century is called *classical* because it sought to imitate classical principles of order, clarity, and symmetry—in other words, to sound as a Greek temple looked. Moreover, composers of the classical school innovated in creating music that adhered rigorously to certain structural principles. For example, all classical symphonies have four movements, and all open with a first movement in "sonata form," characterized by the successive presentation of theme, development, and recapitulation. Undoubtedly the spread of the ideals of the Enlightenment influenced the development of the classical style, yet there were elements of elegant aristocratic Rococo influence at work as well, for the music of the classical era cus-

Two Contemporary Representations of Mozart. On the left is the child prodigy, aged seven; on the right the composer in his twenties wearing a badge of honor of an Italian musical society that he won at age fourteen.

tomarily has a lightness and gaiety about it that is most reminiscent of Rococo pastels.

Certainly the tastes of the same European aristocrats who commissioned Rococo buildings determined the personal fortunes of most composers in the second half of the eighteenth century, for these composers no longer had any interest in gaining a livelihood by writing church music as Bach had done, and as yet had no large concert-hall public (Handel's London audience being exceptional). The perils of struggling for a living by composing music in the later eighteenth century can be seen best in the sad career of the sublime genius Mozart. As a phenomenal child prodigy, the young Mozart—who began composing at four, started touring Europe as a keyboard virtuoso at six, and wrote his first symphony at nine—was the darling of the aristocracy. The Austrian empress Maria Theresa embraced him and the pope made him "Knight of the Golden Spur." But as soon as Mozart reached puberty he was no longer a curiosity and, owing partly to his rather cantankerous personality, proved unable to gain steady employment in the service of any single wealthy aristocrat. In lieu of that, he strove to support himself as a freelance composer and keyboard performer in Vienna, but could make ends meet only with the greatest difficulty. Although he spent every year of his mature life in bountiful productivity, he had to live from hand to mouth until he died at the age of thirty-five from the effects of an undiagnosed wasting disease. Only a handful of people attended the funeral of one of the greatest creative artists of all time, and he was buried in a pauper's grave. Given these appalling circumstances, it is perfectly amazing that Mozart's music is characteristically sunny and serene. Only rarely did he write in a minor key, and even when he did so, he usually paired a melancholy work with an exuberantly joyful one, as if to demonstrate almost defiantly that the trials of his personal life had no effect on his art.

Haydn's career provides an instructive contrast. Knowing much better how to take care of himself, "Papa Haydn" spent most of his life in the comfortable employment of the Esterházys, an extremely wealthy Austro-Hungarian aristocratic family that maintained its own private orchestra. But this security entailed the indignity of wearing the Esterházy livery, like any common butler. Only toward the end of his life, in 1791, did Haydn, now famous, strike out on his own by traveling to London, where for five years (excluding a brief interval) he supported himself handsomely by writing for a paying public, as Handel once did, rather than for private patrons. The fact that London alone was able to provide opportunities for earning a commercial livelihood to two foreigners is clearly indicative of the city's unusual status in the eighteenth century as one of the few localities where there was a mass market for culture. In this regard London represented the wave of the future, for in the nineteenth century serious music would definitely leave the aristocratic salon for the urban concert hall all over Europe. It may also be noted that whereas in deeply aristocratic Austria Haydn was obliged to wear servants' livery, in London he was greeted as a creative genius—one of the earliest composers to be regarded as such even though poets and painters had been celebrated as

Mozart

Haydn in London. While he worked in the pay of the Esterházy family, Haydn was little more than a high-level servant. In London, on the other hand, he was portrayed as an inspired genius with a preoccupied look in his eye.

Haydn

Original announcement for Mozart's *Don Giovanni*. The advertisement is full of information about the opera, except the name of the person who wrote it. Mozart's name appears once in tiny letters, subordinated even to the name of the librettist, Da Ponte. It is a crowning irony that *Don Giovanni* was probably the greatest opera written by the man who is often considered the greatest operatic composer of all time.

geniuses long before. Thus Haydn's *Miracle* symphony, written for performance in a London concert hall, is called that because during one performance a chandelier came crashing down and many would have been killed had it not been for the fact that the entire audience had moved up as close as possible to get a better view of the "genius" Haydn, who was conducting.

Haydn's stay in London foreshadowed the future in still another way, for the music he wrote on that occasion was wholly secular, as opposed to the semi-religious oratorios of Handel. Indeed, the music of the entire classical era was predominantly secular, as most music would remain until the present, and this secular writing advanced primarily on three fronts— opera, chamber music, and orchestral composition. In the field of opera, an important innovator of the classical period was Christoph Willibald von Gluck (1714–1787), who emphasized the necessity for dramatic action at a time when Monteverdi's many successors had made opera much too static. But by far the greatest operatic composer of the era was Mozart, whose *Marriage of Figaro, Don Giovanni,* and *The Magic Flute* remain among the most magnificent and best-loved operas of all time. As for the realm of chamber music (music written for small instrumental ensembles), the classical era was a most fertile age, for the genre of the string quartet was invented at the beginning of the period and was soon brought to the fullest fruition in the quartets of both Haydn and Mozart.

Yet probably the most impressive invention of the classical era was the symphony—so to speak the novel of music—for the symphony has since proven to be the most versatile and popular of all classical musical forms. Although not the very first writer of symphonies, Haydn is nonetheless usually termed the "father of the symphony" because in over one hundred works in the symphonic form—and preeminently in his last twelve symphonies, which he composed in London—Haydn formulated the most enduring techniques of symphonic composition and demonstrated to the fullest extent the symphony's creative potential. Yet Mozart's three last symphonies (out of his total of forty-one) are generally regarded as greater even than those of Haydn, for the grace, variety, and utter technical perfection of these works are beyond comparison. Mere words cannot do justice to any of the marvelous musical creations of the eighteenth century, yet it may confidently be stated in conclusion that if just one or two of Mozart's musical compositions had survived instead of literally hundreds, they alone would be enough to place the century among the most inspired ages in the entire history of the human creative imagination.

SUMMARY POINTS

- Seventeenth-century scientists and thinkers such as Francis Bacon, René Descartes, Isaac Newton, and John Locke fundamentally shifted science toward objectivity, empirical observation, and a predictable, understandable view of the universe and of human nature.

- The leading exponents of the Enlightenment, called philosophes, emphasized rationality, practicality, and progressive thinking and imagined a world characterized by morality, human perfection, and ideal government.

- Biology, electricity, and chemistry saw the greatest scientific advances during the eighteenth century, such as the development of the Linnaean classification system, the conduction of electricity, the discovery of hydrogen and oxygen, and the development of inoculation and vaccination to combat disease.

- Art and literature during the late seventeenth and eighteenth centuries reflected some influences from Enlightenment ideas, and generally displayed an appreciation for classical order and symmetry. The novel emerged as a major new genre.

- The order, clarity, and symmetry of classical art was echoed in the classical music of the late eighteenth century, perfected above all by Haydn and Mozart. The opera and the symphony were developed during the classical era.

The Scientific Revolution
and the Enlightenment

Baker, Keith, *Condorcet: From Natural Philosophy to Social Mathematics,* Chicago, 1975. Advances the view that Condorcet's greatest significance lies in his attempt to create a quantifiable social science rather than in his theory of historical progress.

Baumer, Franklin L., *Modern European Thought: Continuity and Change in Ideas, 1600–1950,* New York, 1978. An extraordinarily fine intellectual history, organized around major themes rather than the work of individuals.

Becker, Carl L., *The Heavenly City of the Eighteenth-Century Philosophers,* New Haven, 1932. Advances the thesis that the philosophes were just as impractical in their commitment to abstract secular rationalism as the medieval Scholastics were in their theological rationalism. Witty and stimulating but widely regarded as out of date in its views.

Briggs, Robin, *The Scientific Revolution of the Seventeenth Century,* New York, 1969. A very brief but extremely valuable survey, with a documentary appendix.

Bronowski, J., and Bruce Mazlish, *The Western Intellectual Tradition, from Leonardo to Hegel,* New York, 1960. A superb, old-fashioned intellectual history, which serves as an excellent complement to Baumer for the seventeenth and eighteenth centuries.

Bukofzer, Manfred F., *Music in the Baroque Era,* New York, 1947.

Butterfield, Herbert, *The Origins of Modern Science, 1300–1800,* London, 1949. As important for its discussion of Newton's breakthrough regarding gravity and the impact of the scientific revolution on the Enlightenment as it is for its discussion of the Renaissance period.

Chartier, Roger, *The Cultural Origins of the French Revolution,* Durham, N.C., 1991. A cultural history of "de-Christianization."

Darnton, Robert, *The Business of Enlightenment: A Publishing History of the Encyclopédie, 1775–1800,* Cambridge, Mass., 1979. A masterful and fascinating blend of intellectual, social, and business history.

Gay, Peter, *The Enlightenment: An Interpretation;* Vol. 1, *The Rise of Modern Paganism;* Vol. 2, *The Science of Freedom,* New York, 1966–1969. A cross between an interpretation and a survey. Emphasizes the philosophes' sense of identification with the classical world and takes a generally positive view of their accomplishments. Contains extensive annotated bibliographies.

Goodman, Dena, *The Republic of Letters: A Cultural History of the French Enlightenment,* Ithaca, N.Y., 1994. Novel in its attention to the role of literary women.

Hall, A. Rupert, *The Revolution in Science: 1500–1750,* 3d ed., New York, 1983. The best place to look for clear accounts of specific scientific accomplishments.

Hampson, Norman, *The Enlightenment,* Baltimore, 1968. Probably the best shorter introduction.

Hazard, Paul, *The European Mind: The Critical Years (1680–1715),* New Haven, 1953. A basic and indispensable account of the changing climate of opinion that preceded the Enlightenment.

Hildesheimer, Wolfgang, *Mozart,* New York, 1982. Widely regarded as the most literate and thought-provoking biography now available of any major musical figure.

Levey, Michael, *Rococo to Revolution: Major Trends in Eighteenth-Century Painting,* New York, 1966.

Shryock, Richard H., *The Development of Modern Medicine: An Interpretation of the Social and Scientific Factors Involved,* London, 1948. Fascinating reading and still the basic work on the subject.

Shklar, Judith, *Montesquieu,* Oxford, 1987.

Summerson, John, *Architecture in Britain, 1530–1830,* 9th ed., New Haven, Conn., 1971. The best introduction to Wren and English Palladianism.

Wade, Ira O., *The Intellectual Development of Voltaire,* Princeton, 1969. A magnificent synthesis that stresses how Voltaire's "English experience" provided the cornerstone for all his subsequent thought.

Waterhouse, Ellis K., *Painting in Britain, 1530–1790,* 4th ed., Baltimore, 1979. Very good on eighteenth-century developments.

Watt, Ian P., *The Rise of the Novel,* London, 1957. The basic work on the innovative qualities of the novel in eighteenth-century England.

Westfall, R. S., *Never at Rest: A Biography of Isaac Newton,* New York, 1980. Illuminates all aspects of Newton's scientific accomplishment.

SOURCE MATERIALS

Beccaria, Cesare, *An Essay on Crimes and Punishments,* with a Commentary by M. de Voltaire, Stanford, 1953. A reprint of the original English translation of 1767.

Gibbon, Edward, *The Portable Gibbon: The Decline and Fall of the Roman Empire,* ed. D. A. Saunders, New York, 1952. A convenient abridgment.

Rousseau, J.-J., *Political Writings,* ed. A. Ritter, New York, 1987.

Voltaire, *The Portable Voltaire,* ed. B. R. Redman, New York, 1949. An excellent anthology including the complete *Candide.*

PART FIVE

THE FRENCH AND INDUSTRIAL REVOLUTIONS AND THEIR CONSEQUENCES

N O TWO EVENTS more profoundly altered the shape of Western civilization than the French and Industrial Revolutions. "Modern" history begins with their occurrence. The major happenings of the nineteenth and early twentieth centuries—the spread of middle-class liberalism and economic success; the decline of the old, landed aristocracies; the growth of class consciousness among urban workers—all had their roots in these two revolutions.

The French and Industrial Revolutions took place at about the same time and affected many of the same people—though in different ways and to varying degrees. Together they resulted in the overthrow of absolutism, mercantilism, and the last vestiges of manorialism. Together they produced the theory and practice of economic individualism and political liberalism. And together they ensured the growth of class consciousness and the culmination of those tensions between the middle and working classes that imparted new vitality to European history after 1800.

Each revolution, of course, produced results peculiarly its own. The French Revolution encouraged the growth of nationalism and its unattractive stepchild, authoritarianism. The Industrial Revolution compelled the design of a new, urban social order. Yet despite their unique contributions, the two revolutions must be studied together and understood as the joint progenitors of Western history in the nineteenth and early twentieth centuries.

Calico Printing in a Lancashire Cotton Mill, 1834

THE FRENCH AND INDUSTRIAL REVOLUTIONS AND THEIR CONSEQUENCES

	Politics	Science & Industry	Economics & Society	Arts & Letters
				Romantic movement (1690–1850)
1770		James Watt's steam engine patented (1769) Spinning jenny patented (1770)		Ludwig van Beethoven (1770–1827)
	Louis XVI (1774–1792) American War of Independence (1775–1783)			
		Beginning of factory system (1780s)		
	French Revolution begins (1789) Declaration of the Rights of Man (1789)		Jeremy Bentham, *The Principles of Morals and Legislation* (1789)	
			Utilitarianism (1790–1870) Edmund Burke, *Reflections on the Revolution in France* (1790)	Johann von Goethe, *Faust* (1790–1831)
	Declaration of Pillnitz (1791) France declared a republic (1792) The Terror (1793–1794)	Cotton gin invented (1793)	Thomas Paine, *The Rights of Man* (1791–1792)	
		Edward Jenner develops smallpox vaccine (1796)		
	Treaty of Campo Formio (1797) Napoleon declared first consul of France (1799)		Thomas Malthus, *An Essay on the Principle of Population* (1798)	William Wordsworth, *Lyrical Ballads* (1798)
1800	Treaty of Lunéville (1801) Napoleon declared first consul for life (1802) Napoleon crowns himself emperor of the French (1804) Napoleonic Code (1804) Continental System established (1806)			
	Reforms of Stein and Hardenberg, Prussia (1808)			G. W. Hegel, *Phenomenology of the Spirit* (1807) J. G. Fichte, *Addresses to the German Nation* (1808)
	Napoleon's invasion of Russia (1812)		Louis Blanc (1811–1882)	

THE FRENCH AND INDUSTRIAL REVOLUTIONS AND THEIR CONSEQUENCES

Politics	Science & Industry	Economics & Society	Arts & Letters	
Napoleon abdicates (1814) Congress of Vienna (1814–1815) Battle of Waterloo (1815)				
		Founding of Prussian Zollverein (1818)		
"Peterloo Massacre," England (1819) Congress of Verona (1822) Monroe Doctrine (1823) "Decembrist" Revolt, Russia (1825)	First railway, England (1825)			1825
Greek independence (1829) Revolution in France (1830) "Young Italy" (1831) Reform Bill of 1832, England Slavery abolished, British colonies (1833) Poor law reform, England (1834) Chartist movement, England (1838–1848)			Honoré de Balzac, *The Human Comedy* (1829–1841) Eugène Delacroix, *Liberty Leading the People* (1830)	
Corn Laws repealed, England (1846) Revolutions in Europe (1848) Second Republic, France (1848) Frankfurt Assembly, Germany (1848–1849)		John Stuart Mill, *Principles of Political Economy* (1848)	Pre-Raphaelite Brotherhood formed (1848)	
Reign of Louis Napoleon (1851–1870) Crimean War (1854–1856)			Richard Wagner, *The Ring of the Nibelung* (1854–1874) Charles Dickens, *Hard Times* (1854) Gustave Flaubert, *Madame Bovary* (1857)	1850
Unification of Italy (1858–1866) Civil War, United States (1861–1865) Otto von Bismarck's acces- sion to power (1862)		Emancipation of the serfs, Russia (1861)		
Parliamentary Reform Bill, England (1867) Franco-Prussian War (1870)	Union Pacific railroad, United States (1869)			

CHAPTER 19

THE FRENCH REVOLUTION

Men are born, and always continue, free and equal in respect of their rights.
Civil distinctions, therefore, can be founded only on public utility. The nation
is essentially the source of all sovereignty; nor can any individual, or any body
of men, be entitled to any authority which is not expressly derived from it.
—"The Declaration of the Rights of Man and
of the Citizen," 1789

I N 1789, one European out of every five lived in France. And most Europeans, French or not, who thought beyond the boundaries of their own immediate concerns, perceived of France as the center of European civilization. It followed, therefore, that a revolution in France would immediately command the attention of Europe, and would from the first assume far more than mere national significance. Yet the French Revolution attracted and disturbed men and women for reasons other than the fact that it was French. Both its philosophical ideals and its political realities mirrored attitudes, concerns, and conflicts that had occupied the minds of educated Europeans for several decades. When the revolutionaries pronounced in favor of liberty, they spoke not only with the voice of the eighteenth-century philosophes, but with that of the English aristocracy in 1688 and the American revolutionaries of 1776.

Significance of the French Revolution

Absolutism was increasingly the bane of a wide spectrum of thoughtful opinion and passionate feeling within the societies of continental Europe. Aristocrats resented monarchical inroads upon their ancient freedoms. Entrepreneurs who had welcomed mercantilist interference on their behalf in the past now found themselves chafing under absolutist constraints on their economic independence. Peasants fiercely resented what seemed to them the never-ceasing demands of central government upon their limited—often impoverished—resources. Nor were resentments focused exclusively upon absolutist monarchs. They existed as well between country and city dwellers, between rich and poor, overprivileged and underprivileged. The tensions that in the end mounted to the point of revolutionary explosion in France were widespread across the Continent, where elements from top to bottom of society confronted each other in uneasy hostilities that varied in intensity but reflected a common mistrust and uncertainty.

Resentments and tension

Why a revolution?

Until fairly recently, many historians argued that the French Revolution must be understood in terms of class conflict. Grounding their case on the economic and political theories of the nineteenth-century philosopher Karl Marx (see p. 878) these interpreters, strongly influenced by the work of the twentieth-century French scholar Georges Lefebvre, concluded that a rising bourgeoisie, having accumulated wealth and position for several centuries, and inspired by the ideology of Enlightenment philosophers and economists, overthrew the remaining vestiges of an aristocratic order that, despite its declining economic power, nevertheless retained its social and political predominance.

French society

Continuing scholarly investigation has now persuaded most historians to modify, if not entirely discard, this bold thesis. Certainly, to understand the origins of the French Revolution, one must first analyze the nature of the fabric of late-eighteenth-century French society. Yet recent studies appear to prove that far from a society in which the bourgeoisie was pitted against the aristocracy, French society was increasingly controlled in all its aspects by an "order" that was an amalgam of aristocratic, professional, and—to a lesser degree—entrepreneurial elements. To comprehend the Revolution, one must thus comprehend the nature of this dominant segment of French society, and of its serious discontents with the government of Louis XVI.

Ill-defined borders between noble and non-noble

The social borders between noble and non-noble were ill-defined. The French nobility was accessible to those who could pay the price of an ennobling office. Approximately two-thirds of the eighteenth-century French nobility had acceded to its status since 1600, and close to 50,000 new nobles were created between 1700 and 1789. Here, then, was an order dependent for its vigor upon a constant infusion of talent and economic power from the non-noble yet wealthy "third estate." (The French denominated their society into three estates: the clergy—first estate; the nobility—second estate; and the remainder—third estate.)

Mirabeau family as example

The case of the family of that important revolutionary figure Honoré Gabriel Riqueti, the comte de Mirabeau, well illustrates the point. Mirabeau's ancestors had been sixteenth-century merchants. In 1570, however, one of them had purchased the seigneury of Mirabeau. In the following century another bought himself the title of marquis. Despite its commercial origins, the family had acquired positions in the French army. Mirabeau, a lawyer, also held a commission in the cavalry that his grandfather once commanded. Aristocrats spoke of a distinction between the nobility of the sword (*noblesse d'épee*) and of the robe (*noblesse de robe*), the former supposedly of a more ancient and distinguished lineage derived from military service, the latter aristocrats by reason of their purchase of administrative or judicial office (hence the "robe"). Yet the example of the Mirabeau family illustrates how illusory the distinction between robe and sword was in many cases.

A Gentleman of the Third Estate with His Family. A contemporary engraving that illustrates the respectability the third estate wished to see translated into political power.

Noble families by no means disdained investment in trade and commerce. Most industry was financed by noblemen, who also invested heavily in banking and placed their money at risk in such enterprises as ship-owning, the slave trade, mining, and metallurgy. The bulk of their wealth, nevertheless, was what one historian has labeled "proprietary," that is, tied to land, urban properties, purchased offices, and the like. This form of wealth was not the exclusive province of the nobility, however. Proprietary wealth was preferred as a secure investment by rich members of the third estate. Throughout the century, this "bourgeois" wealth was constantly being transformed into "noble" wealth as its owners were transformed into noblemen. Clearly, then, one cannot speak of a separate class consciousness among this economically important bourgeois group. Its members recognized themselves as different from and often opposed to the mass of men and women beneath them who worked with their hands—the populace. But they identified closely with the values of a nobility to which they frequently aspired.

At the same time, however, hostilities and frictions within the middle orders and between bourgeois and noble were both real and important. Less prosperous lawyers—and there were an increasing number of them—were jealous of the privileged position of a favored few in their profession. The escalating price of office, and hence of ennoblement, produced tensions between noncommercial members of the third estate and

Proprietary wealth

Hostilities and friction

the very rich in trade and commerce, by and large the only group able to afford the degree of social advancement to which many more aspired. Not surprisingly, down-at-the-heels nobility resented the success of rich, *arriviste* upstarts whose income allowed them the luxury of life in the grand style that was denied to those nobles long on pedigree but short of cash. Yet though these fissures existed, they did not inhibit the members of the dominant order from attacking with mounting vehemence a government and an economy that were not serving its interests.

Role of literacy and dissemination of ideas

The dominant order aired its frustrations in public debate among a growing audience of literate men and women. Book production reached a peak in 1788; periodicals and newspapers appeared in greater numbers; the first Paris daily was published in 1777. The *parlements,* France's powerful courts of record, used journals to identify themselves as defenders of a national political community threatened by the attempts of ministers to impose their despotic will. Although ideas may not have "caused" the Revolution, they played a critical role in giving shape and substance to the discontent experienced by so many, particularly among the literate middle orders. The political theories of Locke, Voltaire, Montesquieu, and Condorcet appealed to both discontented nobility and bourgeoisie: Voltaire, because of his general execration of privileged institutions; Condorcet because of his belief in progress; Locke and Montesquieu because of their defense of private property and limited sovereignty. Montesquieu's ideas were especially congenial to the dominant order, which read his doctrine of checks and balances as a defense of *parlements* as the constituted bodies that would provide a check to despotism.

The physiocrats

The campaign for change was fueled by another group of libertarian thinkers, economic theoreticians called "physiocrats" in France. Their proposals were grounded in the ideas of the Enlightenment, particularly the notion of a universe governed by mechanistic laws. They argued that production and distribution of wealth were subject to laws as predictable and ultimately salutary as the laws of physics. Those laws would function beneficially, however, only if agriculture and trade were freed from mercantilist regulations. They urged the government to lift its controls on the price of grain, for example, which had been imposed to keep the cost of bread low but which had not accomplished that goal. By allowing the laws of supply and demand to determine the market price, the government would encourage farmers to grow a crop that was more profitable to them, and an increase in supply would thus eventually reduce the cost to consumers.

French economy ailing

Whether or not members of the dominant order were prepared to accept the prescriptions of the physiocrats, they could agree with their diagnosis: that the state of the French economy was seriously ailing. French men and women were suffering increasingly from severe economic depression. A general price rise during much of the eighteenth century, which permitted the French economy to expand by providing capital for investment, worked hardship on the peasantry and on urban tradesmen and laborers, who found their purchasing power considerably reduced.

Their plight deteriorated further at the end of the 1780s, when poor harvests encouraged landlords to extract even larger sums from their dependents in order to compensate for a sharp decline in profits, and when the high price of bread generated desperation among the urban poor. In 1788 families found themselves spending more than 50 percent of their income on bread, which comprised the bulk of their diet; the following year the figure rose to as much as 80 percent. Poor harvests contributed to a marked reduction in demand for manufactured goods; families had little money to spend for anything other than food. Peasants could no longer rely on the system of domestic industry to help them make ends meet, since they were receiving so few orders for the textiles and other articles they were accustomed to making at home. Many left the countryside for the cities, hoping to find work there, only to discover that urban unemployment was far worse than in rural areas. Evidence indicates that between 1787 and 1789 the unemployment rate in many parts of urban France was as high as 50 percent.

Those peasants who remained behind found themselves increasingly embittered by the financial obligations imposed upon them by landlords, church, and state: a tithe and levy on farm produce owed to the Church; fees, called *banalités,* for the use of a landlord's facilities—a mill or a wine press, for example; fees, as well, to the landlord when land changed hands. In addition, peasants were forced to pay a disproportionate share of both direct and indirect taxes—the most onerous of which was the *gabelle,* or salt tax—levied by the government. (For some time the production of salt had been a state monopoly; every individual was required to buy at least seven pounds a year from the government works. The result was a commodity whose cost was often as much as fifty or sixty times its actual value.) Further grievances stemmed from the requirement that

Peasant financial obligations

Pre-Revolutionary Propaganda, 1788–1789. These prints support the popular view that the third estate was carrying the burden of national taxation on its shoulders while the privileged orders enjoyed the fruits of the peasant's labors, tax-free.

peasants work to maintain public roads (the *corvée*) and from the hunting privileges accorded the nobility, which for centuries had regarded the right to indulge in the diversions of the chase, to the exclusion of all others, as a distinctive badge of their order.

Inefficient tax collection and disbursal

The country's financial position was further weakened by an inefficient system of tax collection and disbursal. Not only was taxation tied to differing social status, it varied as well from region to region—some areas, for example, were subject to a much higher *gabelle* than others. The myriad special circumstances and exemptions that prevailed made the task of collectors all the more difficult. Those collectors were in many cases so-called tax farmers, members of a syndicate that loaned the government money in return for the right to collect taxes and to keep for itself the difference between the amounts it took in and the amounts it loaned. The system of disbursal was at least as inefficient as was revenue collection. Instead of one central agency, there were several hundred private accounts, a fact that made it impossible for the government to keep accurate track of its assets and liabilities. The financial system all but broke down completely under the increased expenses brought on by French participation in the American Revolution. The cost of servicing the national debt of approximately 4 billion livres in the 1780s consumed 50 percent of the nation's budget.

Weaknesses in administrative structure

Not only were there problems with the economy, there were also weaknesses in France's administrative structure, ultimately the responsibility of the country's absolutist monarch, Louis XVI (1774–1792). Anxious to serve his people in "enlightened" ways, Louis wished to improve the lot of the poor, to remove torture, and to shift the burden of taxation onto the richer classes. Yet he lacked the capacity to manage his own government and thereby to put into effect these reforms. Well-intentioned but ineffectual, his attempts at reform ultimately undermined his own authority. His appointment of outsiders such as Anne Robert Jacques Turgot, a philosopher, physiocrat, and former provincial intendant, and Jacques Necker, a Swiss Protestant banker, as finance ministers aroused opposition among traditionalist factions within the court. He allowed his wife, the young yet strong-willed Marie Antoinette—daughter of Austria's Maria Theresa—a free hand to dispense patronage among her friends. The result was constant intrigue and frequently reshuffled administrative alliances at Versailles. In consequence, although the intendants, administrative representatives of the central government, possessed considerable power, in theory they found that power too often circumscribed by rivalries and indecision among those to whom they reported. Their administrative effectiveness was further undermined by the fact that they shared authority with provincial governors, local military authorities, and, in a third of the provinces—the *pays d'états*—with local tax-levying bodies.

Louis XVI

Also weakening the country's administrative structure was the continuing battle waged between the central government and the provincial *parlements*. As we have noted, the *parlements* had reasserted their indepen-

France under the Ancien Régime. Compare with the map on p. 693.

dence during the early years of the reign of Louis XV. Throughout the century they had grown increasingly insistent upon what they began to call their "constitutional" rights—in reality, their traditional habit of opposing legislation that did not serve the interests of their members. When Louis XVI pressed for new taxes to be levied on the nobility as well as on the rest of the community after the expensive Seven Years' War, the *parlements* successfully blocked the proposal, insisting upon their right to exemption from major national taxes. In the mid-1770s this episode was reenacted when Turgot, at that time Louis XVI's principal financial

Battle between central government and provincial *parlements* minister, attempted to combat the government's indebtedness through a series of reforms that included the curtailing of court expenses, the abolition of the *corvée* in favor of a small tax on landowners and the abolition of certain guild restrictions in order to stimulate manufacturing. These innovations were steadfastly opposed by the Paris *parlement,* whose members claimed that Turgot was trampling upon ancient prerogatives and privileges—as indeed he was.

Louis XVI's indecisiveness

In the end, however, it was not this opposition that doomed Turgot's plan, for the king was persuaded to make use of his power to overrule the Paris *parlement.* Rather the plan failed because the King withdrew his support for Turgot, who fell victim to court intrigue and was dismissed. *Parlements,* though jealous of their prerogatives, could not indefinitely inhibit the reforms of a determined monarch. Inhibition occurred because of Louis XVI's indecisiveness as supreme governor of France. And it was this indecisiveness that those within the dominant order found increasingly intolerable. By 1788, a weak monarch, together with a chaotic financial situation and severe social tensions, had brought absolutist France to the edge of political disaster.

THE DESTRUCTION OF THE ANCIEN RÉGIME

Financial crisis

The inability of Louis XVI and his government to resolve the country's financial crisis was the immediate cause of the Revolution. In 1787 and 1788 the king's principal ministers, Charles de Calonne and Loménie de Brienne, attempted to institute a series of reforms to stave off bankruptcy. To meet the mounting deficit, they proposed new taxes, notably a stamp duty and a direct tax on the annual produce of the soil.

Demands for constitutional reforms

Hoping to persuade the nobility to agree to these reforms, the king summoned an Assembly of Notables (last called in 1626) from among the aristocracy. Far from acquiescing, however, this group used the financial emergency to attempt to extract major constitutional reforms. Most important, they insisted that any new tax scheme must have the approval of the Estates-General, representative of the three estates of the realm, and that the king had no legal authority to arrest and imprison arbitrarily. The dominant order, its patience with delay and inefficiency at an end, was speaking as English aristocrats had in 1688, and American revolutionaries had in 1775.

Estates-General summoned

Economic hardship *and* financial chaos in the end compelled Louis XVI in the summer of 1788 to summon the Estates-General (which had not met since 1614) to meet in May of the following year. His action appeared to many as the only solution to France's deepening problems. Long-term grievances and short-term hardships had produced bread riots across the country in the spring of 1789. Looting in Brittany, Flanders, Provence, and elsewhere was accompanied by demands for price-fixing that would bring the cost of bread down to a level the populace could afford. Fear that the forces of law and order were collapsing irrevocably and that the populace might take matters into its own hands spurred the delegates to the Estates-General to a sense of their responsibilities and destiny. Each of the three orders elected its own deputies—the third estate indirectly through local assemblies. These assemblies were charged as well with the responsibility of drawing up lists of grievances—*cahiers des doléances*—further contributing to the general determination that the Estates-General must work to perform mighty change.

The delegates of the third estate, though elected by assemblies chosen in turn by artisans and peasants, were representative of the interests and outlook of what we have called the dominant order. Only 13 percent were men of business. About 25 percent were lawyers; 43 percent were government officeholders of some sort. Thus, despite initial disagreements between members of the second and third estates, once the Estates-General convened there remained within that body a strong sense of common grievance and common purpose.

Estates-General representative of the dominant order

The major area of disagreement between the second and third estates stemmed from the tradition that each estate meet and vote as a body. In the past, this had generally meant that the first and second estates had combined to defeat the third. Now the third estate made it clear it would not tolerate such an arrangement. Its leaders demanded that the three orders should sit together and vote as individuals. More important, it insisted that the representatives of the third estate should be double the number of the first and second.

Doubling of third estate

During the months prior to May 1789, the question of "doubling the third" was fiercely debated. After having opposed the reform initially, in December 1788 the king agreed to it. His unwillingness to take a strong stand from the first and his continuing vacillation on the matter of voting procedures cost him support he might otherwise have obtained from the third estate. Shortly after the opening of the Estates-General at Versailles in May 1789, the representatives of the third estate, angered by the king's attitude, took the revolutionary step of leaving the body and declaring themselves the National Assembly. "What Is the Third Estate?" asked the radical clergyman Abbé Emmanuel Sieyès, one of the most articulate spokesmen for a new order, in his famous pamphlet of January 1789. The answer he gave then—"everything"—was the answer the third estate itself gave when it constituted itself the National Assembly of France. Now the middle-class lawyers and businessmen of the third estate acted on that belief. Locked out of the Estates-General meeting hall on June 20, the commoners and a handful of sympathetic nobles and clergymen moved to a nearby indoor tennis court.

Abbé Emmanuel Sieyès

Here, under the leadership of the volatile, maverick aristocrat Mirabeau and the clergyman Sieyès, they bound themselves by a solemn oath not to separate until they had drafted a constitution for France. This Oath of the Tennis Court, on June 20, 1789, can be seen as the beginning of the French Revolution. By claiming the authority to remake the government in the name of the people, the Estates-General was not merely protesting against the rule of Louis XVI but asserting its right to act as the highest

The beginning of revolution

The Tennis Court Oath, by Jacques Louis David (1748–1825). In the hall where royalty played a game known as *jeu de paume* (similar to tennis) leaders of the Revolution swore to draft a constitution. In the center of this painting, standing on the table, is Jean Bailly, president of the National Assembly. Seated at the table below him is Abbé Sieyès. Somewhat to the right of Sieyès, with both hands on his chest, is Robespierre. Mirabeau stands in the right foreground with a hat in his left hand.

sovereign power in the nation, a notion increasingly appealing to many of the nobility as well. On June 27 the king virtually conceded this right by ordering the remaining delegates of the privileged classes to meet with the third estate as members of the National Assembly.

The first stage of the Revolution

The first stage of the French Revolution extended from June 1789 to August 1792. During most of this period the destiny of France was in the hands of the National Assembly. In the main, this stage was moderate, its actions dominated by the leadership of liberal nobles and equally liberal men of the third estate. Yet three events in the summer and fall of 1789 furnished evidence that the Revolution was to penetrate to the very heart of French society, ultimately touching both the urban populace and the rural peasants.

Municipal revolution and the fall of the Bastille

News of the occurrences of late spring 1789 had spread quickly across France. From the very onset of debates on the nature of the political crisis, public attention was high. It was roused not merely by interest in matters of political reform, however, but also by the economic crisis that, as we have seen, brought the price of bread to astronomical heights. Belief was widespread that the aristocracy and king were together conspiring to punish an upstart third estate by encouraging scarcity and high prices. Rumors circulated in Paris during the latter days of June 1789 that the king was about to stage a reactionary coup d'état. The electors of Paris (those who had voted for the third estate) feared not only a counter-revolution but the actions of the Parisian poor, who had been parading through the streets and threatening violence. These electors were workshop masters, craftspeople, shopkeepers, petty tradespeople, the men and women who would soon come to be called *sans-culottes*—so called because the men did not wear upper-class breeches. They formed a provisional municipal government and organized a militia of volunteers to maintain order. Determined to obtain arms, they made their way on July 14 to the Bastille, an ancient fortress where guns and ammunition were stored. Built in the Middle Ages, the Bastille had served as a prison for many years, but was no longer much used. Nevertheless, it symbolized hated royal authority. When crowds demanded arms from its governor, he at first procrastinated and then, fearing a frontal assault, opened fire, killing ninety-eight of the attackers. The crowd took revenge, capturing the fortress (which held only

The Fall of the Bastille, July 14, 1789. A contemporary engraving celebrating the heroic actions of the citizenry of Paris.

seven prisoners—five common criminals and two lunatics) and decapitating the governor. At the same time the *sans-culottes* were establishing a revolutionary municipal government in Paris, similar groups assumed control in other cities across France. This series of events—dramatized by the fall of the Bastille—was the first to demonstrate the commitment of the common people to revolutionary change.

The "Great Fear"

The second popular revolt occurred in the countryside, where the peasants were suffering the direct effects of economic privation. They too expected a monarchical and aristocratic counter-revolution. Eager for news from Versailles, their anticipation turned to fear when they began to understand that the Revolution might not address itself to their determination to put an end to the burdens of manorial taxation. Frightened and uncertain, peasants began attacking and burning manor houses, occasionally in an attempt to discover grain hoards, but almost always to seek out and destroy records of manorial obligations. News of these attacks instilled in other peasants a terror that rural brigands were loose across the countryside. This "Great Fear," as historians have labeled it, simply compounded the confusion abroad in rural areas throughout the summer, while strengthening the belief of deputies at Versailles that law and order were fast vanishing from the realm.

The "October Days"

The third instance of popular uprising, the "October Days" of 1789, was brought on by economic crisis. This time Parisian women from the market district, angered by the price of bread and fired by rumors of the king's continuing unwillingness to cooperate with the Assembly, marched to Versailles on October 5 and demanded to be heard. Not satisfied with its reception by the Assembly, the crowd broke through the

The Departure of the Women of Paris for Versailles, October 1789. A handbill depicting a critical event in the course of the Revolution.

gates to the palace, calling for the king to return to Paris. On the afternoon of the following day the king yielded. The National Guard, sympathetic to the agitators, led the crowd back to Paris, the procession headed by a soldier holding aloft a loaf of bread on his bayonet.

In each of the three cases, these popular uprisings decidedly affected the course of political events as they were unfolding at Versailles. The storming of the Bastille helped persuade the king and nobles to treat the National Assembly as the legislative body of the nation. The "Great Fear" inspired an equally great consternation among the debaters in the Assembly. On August 4, ecclesiastical tithes and the *corvée* were formally abolished. The hunting privileges of the nobles were ended. Exemption from taxation and monopolies of all kinds were eliminated as contrary to natural equality. The ultimate effect of these reforms was to obliterate the remnants of feudalism. One week later, the Assembly abolished the sale of offices, thereby sweeping away one of the fundamental institutions of the old regime.

Following the destruction of privilege the Assembly turned its attention to preparing a charter of liberties. The result was the Declaration of the Rights of Man and of the Citizen, issued in September 1789. Property was declared to be a natural right, along with liberty, security, and "resistance to oppression." Freedom of speech, religious toleration, and liberty of the press were declared inviolable. All citizens were guaranteed equality of treatment in the courts. No one was to be imprisoned or otherwise punished except in accordance with due process of law. Sovereignty was affirmed to reside in the people, and officers of the government were made subject to deposition if they abused the powers conferred upon them. These were not new ideas. They represented a consensus expressed in the *cahiers des doléances* and in the Enlightenment tracts read and approved by members of the dominant order.

The king's return to Paris during the October Days confirmed the reforms already underway and guaranteed further liberalization along lines decreed by the majority in the Assembly. In November 1789, the National Assembly resolved to confiscate the lands of the Church and to use them as collateral for the issue of *assignats,* interest-bearing notes that eventually circulated as paper money. The Assembly hoped—vainly, as it turned out—that this device would resolve the country's inflationary crisis. In July of the following year the Civil Constitution of the Clergy was enacted, providing that all bishops and priests should be elected by the people and should be subject to the authority of the state. Their salaries were to be paid out of the public treasury, and they were required to swear allegiance to the new legislation. The secularization of the Church also involved a partial separation from Rome. The aim of the Assembly was to make the Catholic Church of France a truly national and civil institution with no more than a nominal subjection to the papacy.

Response to this clerical revolution was mixed. Because the Church had enjoyed a privileged position during the old regime, it had earned

Achievements of the first stage:
(1) the destruction of privilege

(2) Declaration of the Rights of Man

(3) Secularization of the Church

An Assignat

Response to secularization

itself the hatred of many who resented its tolerance of clerical abuses and its exploitation of vast monastic land holdings. Bishops and other members of the higher clergy had often held several ecclesiastical appointments at the same time, had paid scant attention to their duties, and had led far from spiritual lives. Exempt from taxes itself, the Church had not hesitated to extract all it could from the peasantry. And its control of the country's educational system made it a target for those men and women who, influenced by Enlightenment thinkers like Voltaire, had turned against the doctrines of Roman Catholicism. On the other hand, the practice of centuries had made the parish church and priest into institutions of great local importance. Peasants found it very difficult to shed habits of deference and respect overnight. The dramatic changes embodied in the Civil Constitution of the Clergy thus encountered considerable resistance in some parts of rural France, and eventually helped to strengthen the forces of counter-revolution.

(4) Constitution of 1791

Not until 1791 did the National Assembly manage to complete its primary task of drafting a new constitution for the nation. The constitution as it finally emerged gave eloquent testimony to the position now held by the dominant order. The government was converted into a limited monarchy, with the supreme power virtually a monopoly of the well-to-do. Although all citizens possessed the same civil rights, the vote was allowed only to those who paid a certain amount in taxes. About half the adult males in France made up this latter category of "active" citizen. Yet even their political power was curtailed, for they were to vote for electors, whose property ownership qualified them for that position. Those electors, in turn, chose department officials and delegates to the National— or, as it was henceforth to be called, Legislative—Assembly. The king was deprived of the control he had formerly exercised over the army and local governments. His ministers were forbidden to sit in the Assembly, and he was shorn of all powers over the legislative process except a suspensive veto, which in fact could be overridden by the issuance of proclamations.

(5) Economic and governmental changes

The economic and governmental changes the National Assembly adopted were as much a reflection of the power of the dominant order as were its constitutional reforms. To raise money, it sold off Church lands, but in such large blocks that peasants seldom benefited from the sales as they had expected to. To encourage the growth of unfettered economic enterprise, guilds and trade unions were abolished. To rid the country of authoritarian centralization and of aristocratic domination, local governments were completely restructured. France was divided into eighty-three equal departments. All towns henceforth enjoyed the same form of municipal organization. All local officials were locally elected. This reorganization and decentralization expressed a belief in the necessity of individual liberty and freedom from ancient privilege. As such these measures proclaimed, as did all the work of the Assembly, that the "winners" of this first stage of the Revolution were the men and women of the dominant order.

France: The Revolutionary Departments after 1789. The map, when compared with that on p. 685, illustrates the degree to which government was rationalized following the Revolution.

A NEW STAGE: POPULAR REVOLUTION

Their triumph did not go unchallenged, however. In the summer of 1792, the Revolution entered a second stage, which saw the downfall of moderate leaders from the dominant order and their replacement by radical republicans claiming to rule on behalf of the common people. Three major factors accounted for this abrupt and drastic alteration in the course of events. First, the politically literate lower classes grew

The second stage:
(1) disappointment of the common people

disillusioned as they perceived that the Revolution was not benefiting them. The uncontrolled free-enterprise economy of the government resulted in constantly fluctuating and generally rising prices. These increases particularly exasperated those elements of the Parisian population that had agitated for change in preceding years. Urban rioters demanded cheaper bread, while their advocates called for governmental control of the ever-growing inflation. Their leaders also articulated the frustrations of a mass of men and women who felt cheated by the constitution. Despite their major role in the creation of a new regime, they found themselves deprived of any effective voice in its operation.

(2) Lack of effective national leadership

A second major reason for the change of course was a lack of effective national leadership during the first two years of the Revolution. Louis XVI remained the weak, vacillating monarch he had been prior to 1789. Though outwardly prepared to collaborate with the leaders of the Assembly, he proved no more than a victim of events. He was compelled to support measures personally distasteful to him, in particular the Civil Constitution of the Clergy. He was thus sympathetic to the plottings of the queen, who was in correspondence with her brother Leopold II of Austria. Urged on by Marie Antoinette, Louis agreed to attempt an escape from France in June 1791, in hopes of rallying foreign support for counter-revolution. The members of the royal family managed to slip past their palace guards in Paris, but they were apprehended near the border at Varennes and brought back to the capital. Though the Constitution of 1791 declared France a monarchy, after Varennes that declaration was more fiction than fact. From that point on, Louis was little more than a prisoner of the Assembly. The leadership of that body remained in the hands of Mirabeau until his death in 1791. Yet he was a less-than-satisfactory leader. An outstanding orator, possessed of the insight of a statesman, he was nevertheless mistrusted by many revolutionaries because of his dissolute, aristocratic youth and his notorious venality. Nor, despite his continued support of a strong constitutional monarchy, did he enjoy the confidence of the king. Even with his shortcomings, Mirabeau was the most effective leader among the moderate constitutionalists, a group that generally failed to capitalize on its opportunities.

(3) The revolution abroad

The third major reason for the dramatic turn of affairs was the fact that after 1792 France found itself at war with much of the rest of the Continent. From the outset of the Revolution, men and women across Europe had been compelled, by the very intensity of events in France, to take sides in the conflict. In the years immediately after 1789, the Revolution in France won the enthusiastic support of a wide range of politically committed intellectuals, merchants, men of commerce, and artisans. The English poet William Wordsworth, later to become disillusioned by the course of revolutionary events, recalled the rapture of his initial mood: "Bliss was it in that dawn to be alive. . . ." His sentiments were echoed across the Continent by poets and philosophers, among the latter the German Johann Gottfried von Herder (see p. 815), who declared the Revolution the most important historical moment since the Reformation. Political societies in Britain proclaimed their allegiance to the principles of the new revolution, often quite incorrectly seeing it as nothing more than a French version of the far less momentous events of 1688. In the Low Countries, a "patriot" group organized strikes and plotted a revolution of its own against dominant merchant oligarchies. Political revolutionaries in western Germany and anticlericals in Italy welcomed the possibility of invasion by the French as a means of achieving radical change within their own countries.

Others opposed the course of the Revolution from the start. Exiled nobles, who had fled France for the haven of sympathetic royal courts in Germany and elsewhere, did all they could to stir up counter-revolutionary sentiment. The distressed clamoring of these emigrés, along with the plight of Louis XVI and his family, aroused the sympathy, if not at first the active support, of European defenders of absolutism and privilege. In Britain the cause was strengthened by the publication in 1790 of Edmund Burke's *Reflections on the Revolution in France*. A Whig politician who had sympathized with the American revolutionaries, Burke nevertheless attacked the Revolution in France as a monstrous crime against the social order. He argued that by remodeling their government as they had, the French had turned their backs on both human nature and history. Men and women were not constitutional abstractions, endowed with an objective set of natural rights, as the Declaration of the Rights of Man had insisted. Rights—and duties as well—were the consequence of the individual histories of the countries into which men and women were born. Those histories bound people to the past and entailed a commitment to the future, as well as the present. Hence they had no right to remake their country and its institutions without reference to the past or concern for the future, as Burke insisted the French had. Their failure to pay proper respect to tradition and custom had destroyed the precious fabric of French civilization woven by centuries of national history.

Counter-revolution: Burke

Edmund Burke

Burke's famous pamphlet, in which he painted a romantic and highly inaccurate picture of the French king and queen, helped arouse sympathy for the counter-revolutionary cause. It is questionable, however, whether that sympathy would have turned to active opposition had not the French soon appeared as a threat to international stability and the individual ambitions of the great powers. It was that threat which led to war in 1792, and which kept the Continent in arms for a generation. This state of war had a most important impact on the formation of political and social attitudes during this period in Europe. Once a country declared war with France, its citizens could no longer espouse sympathy with the Revolution without paying severe consequences. Those who continued to support the Revolution, as did a good many among the artisan and tradespeople class, were persecuted and punished for their beliefs. To be found in Britain, for example, possessing a copy of Thomas Paine's revolutionary tract *The Rights of Man* (1791–1792), a pro-revolutionary response to Burke's *Reflections,* was enough to warrant imprisonment. As the moderate nature of the early Revolution turned to violent extension, entrepreneurs and men of commerce eagerly sought to live down their

French perceived as threat to international stability

Thomas Paine

radical sentiments of a few years past. The wars against revolutionary France came to be perceived as a matter of national survival; to ensure internal security, it seemed that patriotism demanded not only a condemnation of the French but of French ideas as well.

The first European states to express public concern about events in revolutionary France were Austria and Prussia. They were not anxious to declare war; their interests at the time centered upon the division of Poland between themselves. Nevertheless, they jointly issued the Declaration of Pillnitz in August 1791, in which they avowed that the restoration of order and of the rights of the monarch of France was a matter of "common interest to all sovereigns of Europe." The leaders of the French government at this time were a moderate faction, but they were afraid of losing political support in France. They pronounced the Declaration of Pillnitz a threat to national security, hoping that enthusiasm for a war would unite the French and result also in enthusiasm for their continued rule. They were aided in their scheme by the activities of monarchists both within and outside France, whose plottings and pronouncements could be made to appear an additional threat, though to a greater extent than they actually were. On April 20, 1792, the Assembly declared war against Austria and Prussia.

Almost all of the various political factions in France welcomed the war. The political leadership expected that its aggressive policy would solidify the loyalty of the people to their regime. Reactionaries hailed the intervention of Austria and Prussia as the first step in the undoing of all that had happened since 1789. Extremists hoped that initially the French would suffer reverses that would discredit the government and the monarchy, and thus hasten the advent of a more radical regime in France and the triumph of people's armies and revolutionary ideals across Europe. As the radicals hoped, the forces of the French met serious reverses. By August 1792 the allied armies of Austria and Prussia had crossed the frontier and were threatening to capture Paris. A fury of rage and despair seized the capital. Many believed that the military disasters had been the result of treasonable dealings with the enemy by the king and his conservative followers. On August 10, Parisian rioters, organized by their radical leadership, attacked the royal palace, killing the king's guards and driving him to seek refuge in the meeting hall of the Assembly. At the same time, radicals seized the municipal government in Paris, replacing it with a revolutionary Commune under their control. The Commune successfully demanded that the Assembly suspend the king from his duties and hand him and his family over for imprisonment. Here began a second and far more extreme French Revolution.

From this point, the country's leadership passed into the hands of an egalitarian-minded segment of the third estate. These new leaders soon came to be known as *Jacobins,* the name of the political club to which they belonged. Although their headquarters was in Paris, their membership extended throughout France. They proclaimed themselves enemies of the country's former political leaders, the *Girondins,* so called after the department of the Gironde, which was centered about the commercial

Jacobins and Girondins. The key of the Jacobin club is carried into the Convention, symbolizing the passing of the leadership from the Girondins to the Jacobins.

hub of Bordeaux. By so labeling their political foes, the Jacobins hoped to paint them as defenders of the selfish commercial classes, and to proclaim themselves patriotic spokesmen for the populace. Yet recent analysis suggests that although the Girondins were more generally opposed to Paris and to violence than the Jacobins, there was not that much to distinguish between the two groups. Many so-called Girondins were in fact members of Jacobin clubs. And both groups contained large numbers of professionals—government officeholders and lawyers in the main—though an increasing number of artisans joined Jacobin clubs as the movement grew.

Neither the Girondins nor the Jacobins were a tightly organized party. Among the latter, a group that sat in the upper-left-hand seats of the legislative chamber and that therefore adopted "The Mountain" as their political name, came to rule the decisions of the Legislative Assembly and to dominate the politics of France. One of their first actions was to call for an election by universal suffrage of delegates to a national convention, whose task would be to draft and enact a new and republican constitution. The king's flight to Varennes had ensured that the monarchy would cease to bind the nation together; the Convention's work set the seal on the rapid movement toward republicanism that Louis's attempted escape had begun. This Convention became the effective governing body of the country for the next three years. It was elected in September 1792, at a time when disturbances across France reached a new

The convention

The Execution of Louis XVI. A revolutionary displays the king's head moments after it is severed by the guillotine in January 1793.

height. The so-called September massacres occurred when patriotic Paris mobs, hearing a rumor that political prisoners were plotting to escape from their prisons, responded by hauling them before hastily convened tribunals and sentencing them to swift execution. More than one thousand supposed enemies of the Revolution were killed in less than a week. Similar riots engulfed Lyons, Orléans, and other French cities.

The king beheaded

When the newly elected Convention met in September, its membership was far more radical than that of its predecessor, the Assembly, and its leadership was determined to demand an end to the monarchy and the death of Louis XVI. On September 21, the Convention declared France a republic. In December it placed the king on trial, and in January he was condemned to death by a narrow margin. The heir to the grand tradition of French absolutism met his end bravely as "Citizen Louis Capet," beheaded by the guillotine, the frightful mechanical headsman that had become the symbol of revolutionary fervor.

Domestic reforms

Meanwhile, the Convention turned its attention to the enactment of further domestic reforms. Among its most significant accomplishments over the next three years were the abolition of slavery in French colonies;

the prohibition of imprisonment for debt; the establishment of the metric system of weights and measures; and the repeal of primogeniture, so that property might not be inherited exclusively by the oldest son but would be divided in substantially equal portions among all immediate heirs. The Convention also supplemented the decrees of the Assembly in abolishing the remnants of manorialism and in providing for greater freedom of economic opportunity for commoners. The property of enemies of the Revolution was confiscated for the benefit of the government and the lower classes. Some great estates were broken up and offered for sale to poorer citizens on relatively easy terms. The indemnities hitherto promised to the nobles for the loss of their privileges were abruptly cancelled. To curb the rise in the cost of living, maximum prices for grain and other necessities were fixed by law, and merchants who profiteered at the expense of the poor were threatened with the guillotine. Still other measures of reform dealt with religion. An effort was made to abolish Christianity and to substitute the worship of Reason in its place. In accordance with this purpose a new calendar was adopted, dating the year from the birth of the republic (September 22, 1792) and dividing the months in such a way as to eliminate the Christian Sunday. Later, this cult of Reason was replaced by a Deistic religion dedicated to the worship of a Supreme Being and to a belief in the immortality of the soul. Finally, in 1794, the Convention decreed simply that religion was a private matter, that Church and state would therefore be separated, and that all beliefs not actually hostile to the government would be tolerated.

Much of this program, particularly that which involved the managing of the economy—regulating, price-fixing, requisitioning—was by no means representative of Jacobin political conviction. It was the consequence, rather, of desperate political necessity, and of the pressure Jacobin leaders experienced at the hands of the urban *sans-culottes*. More than anything else, the *sans-culottes* demanded cheap food. In three years after 1790, prices had risen in a crippling way: wheat by 27 percent, beef by 136 percent, potatoes by 700 percent. While the government imposed its maximums in Paris, rioters there and elsewhere attacked those they perceived to be hoarders and war profiteers. Left to its own economic inclinations, the Jacobin leadership would have pursued policies in line with liberal, reformist thinking that had challenged absolutist centralization and control. Yet the dire circumstances of Continental warfare and domestic turmoil left the leadership with no choice but to acquiesce to *sans-culottes* demands.

Pressure from urban *sans-culottes*

While effecting a political revolution in France, the Convention's leadership at the same time accomplished an astonishingly successful reorganization of its armies. By February 1793, Britain, Holland, Spain, and Austria were in the field against the French. Britain's entrance into the war was dictated by both strategic and economic reasons. The British feared French penetration into the Low Countries directly across the Channel; they were also concerned that French expansion might pose a serious threat to Britain's own growing economic hegemony around the globe.

The revolutionary wars

Sans-Culottes Feeding Europe with the Bread of Liberty. In this cartoon justifying Europe's declaration of war against revolutionary France, Holland, Germany and Prussia, Britain, Savoy, and the papacy are shown as threatened by the French *sans-culottes*.

The allied coalition, though united only in its desire to contain this puzzling, fearsome revolutionary phenomenon, was nevertheless a formidable force. To counter it, the French organized an army that was able to win engagement after engagement during these years. In August 1793, the revolutionary government imposed a levy on the entire male population capable of bearing arms. Fourteen hastily drafted armies were flung into battle under the leadership of young and inexperienced officers. What they lacked in training and discipline they made up for in improvised organization, mobility, flexibility, courage, and morale. (In the navy, however, where skill was of paramount importance, the revolutionary French never succeeded in matching the performance of the British.) In 1793–1794, the French armies preserved their homeland. In 1794–1795, they occupied the Low Countries, the Rhineland, parts of Spain, Switzerland, and Savoy. In 1796, they invaded and occupied key parts of Italy and broke the coalition that had arrayed itself against them.

These achievements were not without their price, however. To ensure their accomplishment, the rulers of France resorted to a bloody authoritarianism that has come to be known as the Terror. Although the Convention succeeded in 1793 in drafting a new democratic constitution based upon male suffrage, it deferred its introduction because of wartime emergency. Instead, the Convention prolonged its own life year by year, and increasingly delegated its responsibilities to a group of twelve leaders known as the Committee of Public Safety. By this time the Girondins had lost all influence within the Convention. Complete power had passed to the Jacobins, who proclaimed themselves disciples of Jean-Jacques

The dictatorship of the Committee of Public Safety

Rousseau and champions of the common man, arguing that the sort of "democratic absolutism" they were imposing accorded with Rousseau's notions of the sovereign state and the general will.

Foremost among the political leadership were Jean Paul Marat, Georges Jacques Danton, and Maximilien Robespierre, the latter two members of the Committee of Public Safety. Jean Paul Marat was educated as a physician, and by 1789 had already earned enough distinction in that profession to be awarded an honorary degree by St. Andrews University in Scotland. Almost from the beginning of the Revolution he stood as a champion of the common people. He opposed nearly all of the assumptions of his more moderate colleagues in the Assembly, including the idea that France should pattern its government after that of Great Britain, which he recognized to be oligarchic in form. Soon made a victim of persecution and forced to take refuge in unsanitary sewers and dungeons, he persevered in his efforts to rouse the people to a defense of their rights. His exposure to infection left him with a chronic skin affliction from which he could find relief only through frequent bathing. In 1793 he was stabbed through the heart during one of these soothing respites by Charlotte Corday, a young fanatic. In contrast with Marat, Georges Jacques Danton did not achieve prominence until the Revolution was three years old. But, like Marat, he directed his activities toward goading the masses into rebellion. Elected a member of the Committee of Public Safety in 1793, he had much to do with organizing the Terror. As time went on, however, he wearied of ruthlessness and displayed a tendency to compromise that gave his opponents in the Convention their opportunity. In April 1794 Danton was sent to the guillotine. Upon mounting the scaffold he is reported to have said, "Show my head to the people; they do not see the like every day."

The radical leaders

Georges Jacques Danton

The Death of Marat. This painting by the French artist David immortalized Marat. The bloody towel, the box, and the tub were venerated as relics of the Revolution.

Maximilien Robespierre

The ruthless suppression of enemies of the state

The most famous and perhaps the greatest of the radical leaders was Maximilien Robespierre. Born of a family reputed to be of Irish descent, Robespierre was trained for the law and speedily achieved modest success as an advocate. He adopted the belief that the philosophy of Rousseau held the one great hope of salvation for all mankind. To put this philosophy into practice he was ready to employ any means that would bring results, regardless of the cost to himself or to others. This passionate loyalty to a gospel that exalted the masses eventually won him a following. In 1791 he was accepted as the oracle of the Jacobin Club. Later he became president of the National Convention and a member of the Committee of Public Safety. Though he had little or nothing to do with originating the Terror, he was nevertheless responsible for enlarging its scope. He came to justify ruthlessness as a necessary and therefore laudable means to revolutionary progress.

The years of the Terror were years of stern dictatorship in France. Pressed by foreign enemies from without, the Committee faced sabotage from both the political Right and Left at home. In June 1793, responding to the need for absolute political control, leaders of the Mountain, allied with Parisian radicals, purged the Convention of moderates by means of militant and intimidating political rallies. France was now a one-party state. The purge was one important cause of a royalist counter-revolution that same year that broke out in the western area of the Vendée. The peasantry there had remained generally loyal to Church and king. Government attempts to conscript troops into the revolutionary armies fanned long-smoldering resentments into open rebellion. By the summer, the peasant forces there, led by noblemen in the name of a Royal Catholic Grand Army, posed a serious threat to the Convention. Meanwhile, Girondists helped fuel rebellions in the great provincial cities of Lyons, Bordeaux, and Marseilles. This harvest of the policies of the National Assembly was bitter fruit to the Committee. At the same time they met with the scornful criticism of revolutionaries even more radical than themselves. This latter group, known as the *enragés,* was led by the journalist Jacques Hébert and threatened to topple not only the government but the country itself by its crusades. Determined to stabilize France, whatever the necessary cost, the Committee dispatched commissioners into the countryside to suppress the enemies of the state. During the period of the Terror, from September 1793 to July 1794, the most reliable estimates place the number of executions as high as 25,000 to 30,000 in France as a whole, less than 20,000 of whom were condemned by the courts. In addition, approximately 500,000 were incarcerated between March 1793 and August 1794. The victims were by no means all aristocrats. Anyone who appeared to threaten the republic, no matter what his or her social or economic position, was at risk. Far more peasants and laborers than noblemen and women were killed. Among those executed was Marie Antoinette ("The Widow Capet"). When some time later the Abbé Sieyès was asked what he had done to distinguish himself during the Terror, he responded dryly, "I lived."

Meeting of a Revolutionary Committee of Surveillance during the Terror. Note the presence of women and children at the proceedings.

Several points need to be made concerning this "second" French Revolution. First, for a time revolutionary fervor affected the everyday life of French men, women, and children in a remarkably direct way. The city-based *sans-culottes* imposed their style of dress on their fellow citizens. Workers' trousers replaced the breeches that until now were a sartorial badge of the middle classes and the nobility. A red cap, said to symbolize freedom from slavery, was all-but-required headgear, wigs having vanished. Men and women addressed each other as "citizen" or "citizeness." Bowing, along with the kissing of a woman's hand, were considered reactionary gestures. Public life was marked by ceremonies designed

The results of the Committee's rule: (1) a new popular culture

The Guillotine in Paris. The mechanical executioner before and after the fall of the blade.

to celebrate the triumph of a new way of living and thinking. Perhaps the most famous was the "Festival of Reason" sponsored by the radical Paris city government in November 1793. An explicit attack upon Catholicism, the ceremony was held inside the venerable Cathedral of Notre Dame, where a mountain was constructed, symbolizing the all-powerful ruling party. Atop the mountain a temple, adorned with the motto "to philosophy," housed a troop of maidens, dressed in white and crowned with laurel. At the appropriate moment, they descended the mount while the audience sang a hymn that, in the words of an admiring contemporary commentator, "expressed natural truths and not mystical and chimerical adulations." As a finale a woman dressed as Liberty emerged from the temple to receive the homage of the crowd. The fact that Liberty was a real person and not a statue was an indication of the desire on the part of the festival's organizers to abolish the tradition and habits of Catholic idolatry. Though radicals and *sans-culottes* were a minority, and an urban minority as well, they were a remarkably powerful cultural force, whose influence far outweighed their numbers.

(2) Centralization

A second point worth making concerning the radical Revolution of 1792–1793 is that it dramatically reversed the trend toward decentralization that had characterized the reforms of the Assembly. In addition to dispatching its own commissioners from Paris to quell provincial insurrection, the Committee published a *Bulletin des loix*, to inform all citizens what laws were to be enforced and obeyed. And it replaced local officials, some of them still royalist in sympathy, with "deputies on mission," whose task was to conscript troops and generate patriotic fervor. When these deputies appeared too eager to act independently, they were in turn replaced by "national agents," with instructions to report directly to the Committee.

(3) Industrial transformation slowed

Third, by fostering the interests of the less economically powerful the Committee significantly retarded the pace of industrial transformation in France. Through policies that helped the peasant, the small craftsman, and the shopkeeper to acquire property, the government during this "second" Revolution encouraged the entrenchment of a class at once devoted to the principle of republicanism while unalterably opposed to a large-scale capitalist transformation of the economy of France.

(4) A national identity forged

Finally, and most importantly, the domestic and foreign policies pursued with such ruthlessness by the Committee undoubtedly fostered among French men and women a sense of themselves as part of a newly forged nation. The Revolution had eroded the strength of those traditional institutions—church, guild, parish—that had for centuries given people a common bond. In their place now stood patriotic organizations and a culture that insisted upon loyalty to one national cause. Thanks to increasing literacy among the middle and lower orders, and to a publishing industry responsive to that increase, public opinion had been a potent force even before 1789—had indeed helped bring the Revolution into being. Now, four years later, public opinion reflected a total commitment to a new and readily identifiable national interest in the service of a revolutionary ideal.

Patriotic Women's Club. The members of this patriotic club wear "constitutional bonnets" to show their support for the Revolution and the reforms of the Convention.

The realization that the rest of Europe was determined to stifle that ideal—the powerful sense among the revolutionaries of a malevolent "other"—unquestionably strengthened French national identity. The fact that recruits in the armies drafted to battle that "other" were treated as heroic citizens rather than as expendable cannon-fodder helped breed in them, and in the populace more generally, a sense of themselves as a special people, bound to a state defined by its common citizenship and to a community that was becoming the new French nation.

The enemy "other"

The Committee of Public Safety, though able to save France, could not save itself. It failed to put a stop to inflation, thereby losing the support of those commoners whose dissatisfactions had helped bring the Convention to power. The long string of military victories convinced growing numbers that the Committee's demands for continuing self-sacrifice, as well as its insistence upon the necessity of the Terror, were no longer justified. By July 1794, the Committee was virtually without allies. On July 27 (9 Thermidor, according to the new calendar) Robespierre was shouted down by his enemies while attempting to speak on the floor of the Convention. Desperate, he tried to rally loyal Jacobins to his defense and against the Convention. The following day, along with twenty-one fellow conspirators, he met his death as an enemy of the state on the guillotine. Now the only remaining leaders in the Convention were men of moderate sympathies, who, as time went on, inclined toward increasing conservatism. Much of the work of the radicals was undone. The law of maximum prices and the law against "suspects" were both repealed. Political prisoners were freed, the Jacobins driven into hiding, and the Committee of Public Safety shorn of its absolute powers. The new situation made possible the return of priests, royalists, and other emigrés from abroad to add the weight of their influence to the conservative trend.

The third stage: the Thermidorian reaction

In 1795 the National Convention adopted a new constitution, which lent the stamp of official approval to the victory of the prosperous classes.

The constitution granted suffrage to all adult male citizens who could read and write. They were permitted to vote for electors, who in turn would choose the members of the legislative body. In order to be an elector, one had to be the proprietor of a farm or other establishment with an annual income equivalent to at least one hundred days of labor. The drafters of the constitution thus ensured that the authority of the government would actually be derived from citizens of considerable wealth. Since it was not practicable to restore the monarchy, lest the old aristocracy also come back into power, executive authority was vested in a board of five men known as the Directory, chosen by the legislative body. The new constitution included not only a bill of rights but also a declaration of the *duties* of the citizen. Conspicuous among the latter was the obligation to bear in mind that "it is upon the maintenance of property . . . that the whole social order rests."

The reign of the Directory has not enjoyed a good historical press. The collection of *nouveaux riches* speculators and profiteers who rose to prominence as they labored to make a good thing for themselves out of the war was not a particularly attractive crew. They were lampooned as ostentatious and vulgar *"incroyables"* and *"merveilleuses"*—outrageously overdressed men and underdressed women. But however anxious they were to live down the self-denying excesses of the past several years by self-indulgent excesses of their own, they were in no mood to see the major accomplishments of the Revolution undone. They had no difficulty in disposing of threats from the Left, despite their failure to resolve that bugbear of all revolutionary governments, inflation and rising living costs. When in 1796 the radical "Gracchus" Babeuf* launched a campaign to abolish private property and parliamentary government, his followers were arrested and either executed or deported.

To dispatch threats from the Right was not so easy. Elections in March 1797—the first free elections held in France as a republic—returned a large number of constitutional monarchists to the councils of government. Leading politicians, among them some who had voted for the execution of Louis XVI, took alarm. With the support of the army, the Directory in September 1797 annulled most of the election results of the previous spring. Its bold coup did little, however, to end the nation's political irresolution. Two years later, after a series of further abortive uprisings and purges, and with the country still plagued by severe inflation, the Directors were desperate. This time they called their brilliant young general Napoleon Bonaparte to their assistance.

Bonaparte's first military victory in 1793, the recapture of Toulon from royalist and British forces, had earned him promotion from captain to brigadier general at the age of twenty-four. Though arrested as a terrorist following the fall of Robespierre, he was subsequently patronized by Viscount Paul Barras, a Directory politician. Bonaparte had gained further

---

*Called "Gracchus" after the Roman tribune Gaius Gracchus, a hero of the people.

public fame and the gratitude of the Directory when on October 4, 1795 (13 Vendémiaire, new calendar), he had delivered what he called a "whiff of grapeshot" that saved the Convention from attack by opponents of the new constitution. Since that time he had registered a remarkable series of victories in Italy, which had resulted in Austria's withdrawal from the war. Most recently, he had attempted to defeat Britain by attacking its colonies in Egypt and the Near East. Despite initial successes on land, Bonaparte eventually found himself trapped by the British, following the defeat of the French fleet by Admiral Horatio Nelson at Abukir Bay in 1798. A year of further fighting had brought Bonaparte no nearer decisive victory in North Africa.

It was at this point that the call came from the Directory. Bonaparte slipped away from Egypt and appeared in Paris, already having agreed to participate in a coup d'état with the leading director, that former revolutionary champion of the third estate, the Abbé Sieyès. On November 9, 1799 (18 Brumaire), Bonaparte was declared a "temporary consul." He was the answer to the prayers of the Directory: a strong, popular leader who was not a king. Sieyès, who had once declared for revolution in the name of the third estate, now declared for counter-revolution in the name of virtual dictatorship: "Confidence from below, authority from above." With those words Sieyès pronounced the end of the revolutionary period.

The Eighteenth Brumaire. A detail from a painting by Bronchet depicting Napoleon as the man of the hour.

NAPOLEON AND EUROPE

Few men in Western history have compelled the attention of the world as Napoleon Bonaparte did during the fifteen years of his rule in France. And few men have succeeded as he has in continuing to live on as myth in the consciousness, not just of his own country, but of all Europe. Napoleon's early career illustrates the degree to which the Revolution facilitated the rise of able men. Son of a provincial Corsican nobleman, he attended the *école militaire* in Paris, graduating an officer and a gentleman. Because the Revolution had abolished the purchase of military office, he rose beyond the rank of major, a position to which in prerevolutionary France he would have been restricted, given his inability to pay the price of a regimental command.

Napoleon's early career

Napoleon possessed a mind congenial to the ideas of the Enlightenment—creative, imaginative, and ready to perceive things anew. His primary interests were history, law, and mathematics. His particular strengths as a leader lay in his ability to conceive of financial, legal, or military plans and then to master their every detail; his capacity for inspiring others, even those initially opposed to him; and his belief in himself as the destined savior of the French. That last conviction eventually became the obsession that led to Napoleon's undoing. But supreme self-confidence was just what the French government had recently lacked. Napoleon believed both in himself and in France. That latter belief was

Napoleon's abilities

the tonic France now needed, and Napoleon proceeded to administer it in liberally revivifying doses.

During the years from 1799 to 1804, Napoleon ruled under the title of first consul, but in reality as a dictator. Once again, France was given a new constitution. Though the document spoke of universal male suffrage, political power was retained, by the now familiar means of indirect election, in the hands of entrepreneurs and professionals. Recognizing, however, that his regime would derive additional substance if it could be made to appear the government of the people of France, Bonaparte instituted what has since become a common authoritarian device: the plebiscite. The voters were asked to approve the new constitution and did so by the dishonestly achieved and loudly proclaimed vote of 3,011,107 in favor, 1,567 opposed.

Although the constitution provided for a legislative body, that body could neither initiate nor discuss legislation. The first consul made use of a Council of State to draft his laws, but in fact the government depended on the authority of one man. Bonaparte had no desire to undo the major egalitarian reforms of the Revolution. He reconfirmed the abolition of estates, privileges, and local liberties, thereby reconfirming as well the notion of a meritocracy, of "careers open to talent." Through centralization of the administrative departments, he achieved what no recent French regime had yet achieved: an orderly and generally fair system of taxation. His plan, by prohibiting the type of exemptions formerly granted the nobility and clergy, and by centralizing collection, enabled him to budget rationally for expenditures and consequent indebtedness. In this way he reduced the inflationary spiral that had entangled so many past governments. Napoleon's willingness to proceed against the decentralizing tendencies of the earlier years of the Revolution marked him as a student of the absolutist policies of the Bourbons as well as an admirer of the egalitarian reforms of his more immediate predecessors. He replaced the elected officials and local self-government instituted in 1789 with centrally appointed "prefects" and "subprefects" whose administrative duties were defined in Paris, where local government policy was made as well.

Napoleon's most significant accomplishment was his completion of the educational and legal reforms begun during the revolutionary period. He ordered the establishment of *lycées* (high schools) in every major town and a school in Paris for the training of teachers. To supplement these changes, Napoleon brought the military and technical schools under state control and founded a national university to exercise supervision over the entire system. Like almost all his reforms, this one proved of particular benefit to the middle class; so did the new legal code promulgated in 1804. The Napoleonic Code, as the new body of laws was called, reflected two principles that had threaded their way through all the constitutional changes since 1789: uniformity and individualism. The code made French law uniform, declaring past customs and privileges forever abolished. By underscoring in various ways a private individual's right to property, by authorizing new methods for the drafting of contracts, leases, and stock companies, and by once again prohibiting trade unions, the code worked to the benefit of the dominant order, that elite drawn from all three former estates, which, if it included entrepreneurs and men of commerce, was composed primarily of men whose economic base remained the land.

To accomplish these reforms Napoleon called upon the most talented men available to him, regardless of their past political affiliations. He admitted back into the country emigrés of all political stripes. His two fellow consuls—joint executives, but in name only—were a regicide of the Terror and a bureaucrat of the old regime. His minister of police had been an extreme radical republican; his minister of foreign affairs was the opportunist aristocrat Charles Talleyrand. The work of political reconciliation was assisted by Napoleon's 1801 concordat with the pope, which reunited Church and state. Though the action disturbed former anti-Church Jacobins, Napoleon, ever the pragmatist, believed the reconciliation of Church and state necessary for reasons both of domestic harmony and of international solidarity. According to the terms of the concordat, the pope received the right to depose French bishops and to discipline the French clergy. At the same time, the Vatican agreed to lay to rest any claims against the expropriation of former Church lands. Hereafter, that property would remain unchallenged in the hands of its new middle-class rural and urban proprietors. In return, the clergy was guaranteed an income from the state. The concordat did nothing to revoke the principle of religious freedom established by the Revolution. Although the Roman Catholic clergy received state money, so did Protestant clergy.

(3) Reconciliation

Coronation of Napoleon and Josephine, by David. Napoleon crowned himself and his wife and assumed the title of Napoleon I, Emperor of France.

Napoleon crowns himself emperor

Anti-French alliances

Treaty of Lunéville

Napoleon's reforms in Europe

Napoleon's agreement won him the support of those conservatives who had feared for France's future as a godless state. To prove to the old Jacobins, in turn, that he remained a child of their revolution, he invaded the independent state of Baden in 1804 to arrest and then execute the duke of Enghien, a relative of the Bourbons, whom Napoleon falsely accused of a plot against his life. (Three years before he had deported more than one hundred Jacobins on a similar charge, but with no permanent political repercussions.) The balancing act served only to increase Napoleon's general popularity. By 1802 the people of France had accepted him as "consul for life." In 1804, they rejoiced when, borrowing ceremony from the absolutist past, he crowned himself Emperor Napoleon I in the Cathedral of Notre Dame in Paris.

Across the boundaries of France, the nations of Europe had watched, some in admiration, others in horror, all in astonishment, at the phenomenon that was Napoleon. A coalition of European powers—principally Austria, Prussia, and Britain—had fought France from 1792 until 1795 in hopes of maintaining European stability. In 1795, Prussia retired from the fray, financially exhausted and at odds with Austria. In 1797, the Austrians, defeated by Bonaparte in northern Italy, withdrew as well, signing the Treaty of Campo Formio, which ceded to France territories in Belgium, recognized the Cisalpine Republic, which Bonaparte had established in Italy, and agreed to France's occupation of the left bank of the Rhine.

By the following year, Britain was left to fight the French alone. In 1798 it formed a second coalition, this one with Russia and Austria. The results did not differ significantly from those of the first allied attempt to contain France. Russia and Austria had no success in driving the French from Italy; the French likewise failed to break Britain's advantage at sea. By 1801, the coalition was in tatters, Russia having withdrawn two years previously. The Treaty of Lunéville, signed in 1801 by France and Austria, confirmed the provisions of Campo Formio; in addition, the so-called Batavian, Helvetian, Cisalpine, and Ligurian republics—established by Napoleon from territories in the Low Countries, Switzerland, Italy, and Piedmont—were legitimized. The Austrians also acquiesced to a general redrawing of the map of Germany, which resulted eventually in an amalgamation of semi-independent states under French domination into the Confederation of the Rhine. The following year Britain, no longer able to fight alone, settled with the French as well, returning all the territories it had captured in overseas colonial engagements except Trinidad and Ceylon.

Under Napoleon's reign, the territories of central Europe underwent a revolution. This revolution was a thorough governmental reorganization, one that imposed the major egalitarian reforms of the French Revolution upon lands outside the borders of France, while building a French empire. Most affected were territories in Italy (the "Kingdom of Italy" as it was now called); Germany (the Confederation of the Rhine, including the newly formed Kingdom of Westphalia); Dalmatia (the Illyrian provinces); and Holland. (Belgium had been integrated directly into the

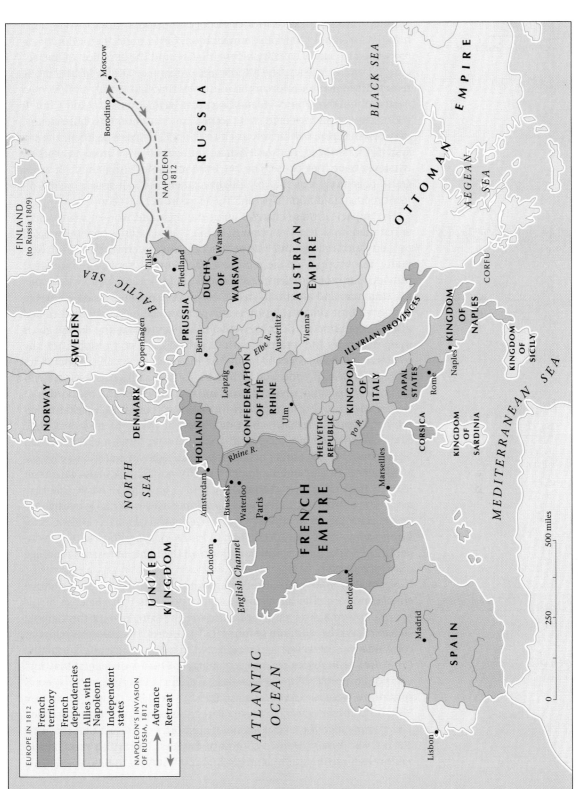

The Empire of Napoleon at Its Greatest Extent

EUROPE IN 1812

- French territory
- French dependencies
- Allies with Napoleon
- Independent states

NAPOLEON'S INVASION OF RUSSIA, 1812

→ Advance
⇢ Retreat

RUSSIA

OTTOMAN EMPIRE

BLACK SEA

AEGEAN SEA

FINLAND (to Russia 1809)

SWEDEN

NORWAY

BALTIC SEA

Moscow

Borodino

NAPOLEON 1812

Tilsit

DUCHY OF WARSAW

Warsaw

Friedland

PRUSSIA

Berlin

AUSTRIAN EMPIRE

Vienna

Austerlitz

Elbe R.

ILLYRIAN PROVINCES

CORFU

KINGDOM OF NAPLES

KINGDOM OF SICILY

Naples

DENMARK

Copenhagen

Leipzig

CONFEDERATION OF THE RHINE

Ulm

HELVETIC REPUBLIC

KINGDOM OF ITALY

Po R.

PAPAL STATES

Rome

CORSICA

KINGDOM OF SARDINIA

HOLLAND

Amsterdam

Rhine R.

Marseilles

NORTH SEA

UNITED KINGDOM

London

English Channel

Brussels

Waterloo

Paris

FRENCH EMPIRE

Bordeaux

Madrid

SPAIN

Lisbon

ATLANTIC OCEAN

MEDITERRANEAN SEA

0   250   500 miles

empire.) Into all these territories Napoleon introduced a carefully organized, deliberate system of administration, based upon the notion of careers open to talent, equality before the law, and the abolition of ancient customs and privileges. The Napoleonic program of reform in the empire represented an application of the principles that had already transformed postrevolutionary France. Manorial courts were liquidated, and Church courts abolished. Provinces were joined into an enormous bureaucratic network that reached directly back to Paris. Laws were codified, the tax system modernized, and everywhere individuals were freed to work at whatever trade they chose. The one freedom denied throughout this new grand hegemony was that of self-government: i.e., all governmental direction emanated from Paris, and therefore from Napoleon.

The impact of these changes upon the men and women who experienced them was clearly enormous. In those principalities previously ruled by petty princelings and minor despots—the patchwork state of Germany, for example, or the repressive Kingdom of Naples—reforms that provided for more efficient, less corrupt administration, a more equitable tax structure, and an end to customary privileges were welcomed by the majority of inhabitants. Business and professional men, who had chafed against economic restrictions, were quick to appreciate the license given them to trade and practice with a new degree of freedom. Yet the Napoleonic presence was by no means an unmixed blessing. Vassal states shared the task of contributing heavily to the maintenance of the emperor's war machine. Levies of taxes and of manpower, and the burden of supporting armies of occupation in their own countries, constantly reminded Germans, Italians, and Dutch that the price of reform was high. Nor were the changes shaped to accommodate local tradition. When Napoleon received complaints that his legal code ran counter to customary practices in Holland, he haughtily retorted, "The Romans gave their laws to their allies; why should not France have hers adopted in Holland?" It was this arrogance, symbolized in the eyes of many by the self-coronation of 1804, that led the German composer Ludwig van Beethoven to revoke the dedication of his *Eroica* symphony to Napoleon, declaring, "Now he, too, will trample on all the rights of man and indulge only his ambition."

Napoleon's motives in introducing radical political and administrative changes were hardly altruistic. He understood that the defense of his enormous domain depended on efficient government and the rational collection and expenditure of funds for his armies. His boldest attempt at consolidation, however, a policy forbidding the importation into the Continent of British goods, proved a failure. This "Continental System," established in 1806, was designed as a strategic measure in Napoleon's continuing economic war against Britain. Its purpose was to destroy Britain's commerce and credit—to starve it economically into surrender. The system failed for several reasons. Foremost was the fact that throughout the war Britain retained control of the seas. The British naval blockade of the Continent, implemented in 1807, served, therefore, as an ef-

Impact of Napoleon's changes

The Continental System

The Handwriting on the Wall. This English cartoon conjures up the biblical Feast of Belshazzar with a vice-ridden Paris, as the new Babylon, doomed to destruction. Headed by a crazed Napoleon and a grotesque Josephine, the banquet table offers a meal including the head of George III, the Tower of London, and the Bank of England.

fective counter to Napoleon's system. While the empire labored to transport goods and raw materials overland to avoid the British blockade, the British worked with success to develop a lively trade with South America. Internal tariffs were a second reason for the failure of the system. Europe remained divided into economic camps, fortified against each other by tariffs, and at odds with each other as they attempted to subsist on nothing more than what the Continent could produce and manufacture. The final reason for the system's collapse was the fact that the Continent had more to lose from these policies than Britain did. Trade-stagnated ports and manufacturing centers grumbled as unemployment rose.

The Continental System was Napoleon's first serious mistake. As such it was one of the causes of his ultimate downfall. A second cause of Napoleon's decline was his constantly growing ambition and increasing sense of self-importance. Napoleon's goal was a Europe modeled after the Roman Empire. The symbols of his empire—reflected in painting, architecture, and the design of furniture and clothing—were deliberately Roman in origin. But Napoleon's Rome was without question imperial, dynastic Rome. The triumphal columns and arches he had erected to commemorate his victories recalled the ostentatious monuments of the Roman emperors. He made his brothers and sisters the monarchs of his newly created kingdoms, which Napoleon controlled from Paris while their mother allegedly sat at court, anxiously wringing her hands and repeating to herself, "If only it lasts!" In 1809 he divorced his first wife, the Empress Josephine, alleging her childlessness, and ensured himself a successor of royal blood by marrying Marie Louise, daughter of Francis I, of the monarchically respectable house of Habsburg. Even his admirers began to question if Napoleon's empire was not simply a larger, more efficient, and, therefore, ultimately more dangerous absolutism than the monarchies of the eighteenth century.

A new Roman empire

The Empress Josephine

Madame Recamier, by David. David was the exponent of a new classicism during and after the French Revolution. The couch, the lamp, and the costume are copied from Rome and Pompeii.

Early French victories

War had broken out again in 1805, with the Russians, Prussians, Austrians, and Swedes joining the British in an attempt to contain France. But to no avail; Napoleon's military superiority led to defeats, in turn, of all three Continental allies. The Battle of Austerlitz, in December 1805, a mighty triumph for the French against the combined forces of Austria and Russia, became a symbol of the emperor's apparent invincibility. Subsequent victories in the following years—against the Prussians at Jena in 1806, the Russians at Friedland in 1807, and the Austrians at Wagram in 1809—increased the conviction on the part of Europe that it had no choice but to acquiesce in Napoleon's grand Continental design. The British admiral Horatio Nelson's naval victory at Trafalgar in 1805, which broke the maritime power of France, was perceived at the time by Napoleon's friends and foes alike as no more than a temporary check to his ambitions.

Invasion of Spain

In 1808, Napoleon invaded Spain as a first step toward the conquest of Portugal, which had remained a stalwart ally of the British. Napoleon was determined to bring the Iberian peninsula into the Continental System. Although he at first promised the senile Spanish king Charles IV that he would cede a part of Portugal to Spain, Napoleon proceeded to overthrow Charles and installed his brother Joseph Bonaparte on the throne. Napoleon then imposed a series of reforms upon the Spanish, similar to those he had instituted elsewhere in Europe. But he reckoned without two factors that led to the ultimate failure of his Spanish mission: the presence of British forces under Sir Arthur Wellesley (later the duke of Wellington), and the determined resistance of the Spanish people. They particularly detested Napoleon's interference in the affairs of the Church, actively opposing his ending of the Inquisition and his abolition of a number of monastic establishments. Together with the British, the Spanish maintained a concerted effort to drive Napoleon from their country, often employing guerrilla warfare to do so. Though at one point Napoleon himself took charge of his army, he could not achieve anything more than temporary victory. The Spanish campaign was the first indication that Napoleon could be beaten. As such, it helped to promote a spirit of anti-Napoleonic defiance that encouraged resistance elsewhere.

A second stage in Napoleon's downfall began with the disruption of his alliance with Russia. As an agricultural country, Russia had suffered a severe economic crisis when it was no longer able, as a result of the Continental System, to exchange its surplus grain for British manufactures. The consequence was that Tsar Alexander I began to wink at trade with Britain and to ignore or evade the protests from Paris. By 1811 Napoleon decided that he could endure this flouting of the Continental System no longer. Accordingly, he collected an army of six hundred thousand (only a third of whom were native Frenchmen) and set out in the spring of 1812 to punish the tsar. The project ended in disaster. The Russians refused to make a stand, drawing the French farther and farther into the heart of their country. They permitted Napoleon to occupy their ancient capital of Moscow. But on the night of his entry, a fire of suspicious origin broke out in the city, leaving little but the blackened walls of the Kremlin palaces to shelter the invading troops. Hoping that the tsar would eventually surrender, Napoleon lingered amid the ruins for more than a

The Russian debacle

The Retreat from Russia. In this painting the horrors of the Russian winter can be seen.

month, finally deciding on October 19 to begin the homeward march. The delay was a fatal blunder. Long before he had reached the border, the terrible Russian winter was upon his troops. Swollen streams, mountainous drifts of snow, and bottomless mud slowed the retreat almost to a halt. To add to the miseries of bitter cold, disease, and starvation, mounted Cossacks rode out of the blizzard to harry the exhausted army. Each morning the miserable remnant that pushed on left behind circles of corpses around the campfires of the night before. On December 13 a few thousand broken soldiers crossed the frontier into Germany—a small fraction of what had once been proudly styled the *Grande Armée*. The lives of nearly three hundred thousand soldiers on both sides of the conflict had been sacrificed in Napoleon's Russian adventure.

Defeat and abdication of Napoleon

Following the retreat from Russia, the anti-Napoleonic forces took renewed hope. United by a belief that they might at last succeed in defeating the emperor, Prussia, Russia, Austria, Sweden, and Britain renewed their attack. Most of the fighting during this so-called war of liberation took place in Germany. The climax of the campaign occurred in October 1813 when, at what was thereafter known as the Battle of the Nations, fought near Leipzig, the allies handed the French a resounding defeat. Meanwhile, allied armies won significant victories in the Low Countries and Italy. By the beginning of 1814, they had crossed the Rhine into France. Burdened with an inexperienced army of raw youths, Napoleon retreated to Paris, continuing, despite constant setbacks, to urge the French people to further resistance. On March 31, Tsar Alexander I of Russia and King Frederick William III of Prussia made their triumphant entry into Paris. Napoleon was forced to abdicate unconditionally, and was sent into exile on the island of Elba, off the Italian coast.

Napoleon's return and final defeat

Less than a year later he once more set foot on French soil. The allies had in the interim restored the Bourbon dynasty to the throne, in the person of Louis XVIII, brother of Louis XVI.* Despite his undoubted administrative abilities, the less-than-charismatic Louis could not fill the void left by Napoleon's abdication. Not surprisingly when the former emperor staged his escape from Elba, his fellow countrymen once more rallied to his side. By the time Napoleon reached Paris, he had generated enough support to cause Louis to flee the country. The allies, meeting in Vienna to conclude peace treaties with the French, were stunned by the news of Napoleon's return. They dispatched a hastily organized army to counter the emperor's typically bold offensive push into the Low Countries. There, at the battle of Waterloo, fought on June 18, 1815, Napoleon suffered defeat for the final time. Shipped off to the bleak island of St. Helena in the South Atlantic, the once-mighty emperor, now the exile Bonaparte, lived out a dreary existence writing self-serving memoirs until his death in 1821.

*Louis XVII, the young son of the executed king and queen, had died under mysterious circumstances in the hands of his revolutionary captors in 1795.

Extrait du Moniteur, du mardi 12 Avril 1814.

ACTE D'ABDICATION
de l'Empereur NAPOLÉON.

Les puissances alliées ayant proclamé que l'empereur Napoléon était le seul obstacle au rétablissement de la paix en Europe, l'empereur Napoléon, fidèle à son serment, déclare qu'il renonce, pour lui et ses héritiers, aux trônes de France et d'Italie, et qu'il n'est aucun sacrifice personnel, même celui de la vie, qu'il ne soit prêt à faire à l'intérêt de la France.

Fait au palais de Fontainebleau, le 11 avril 1814.

Signé, NAPOLÉON.

Pour copie conforme,

Dupont (de Nemours), secrétaire-général du gouvernement provisoire.

Cérémonial pour la réception de S. A. R. Monsieur, frère du Roi.

Lorsque le Gouvernement provisoire aura été instruit du moment de l'arrivée de S. A. R., le cortège qui doit aller à la rencontre du prince, se rassemblera au palais des Tuileries, dans la salle du Conseil-d'État.

Le cortège marchera dans l'ordre suivant :

Le général comte Dessolles, l'état-major et un détachement de la garde nationale.

Les préfets de département et de police, les maires et le conseil municipal;

Les maréchaux et les officiers-généraux;

Les maîtres des cérémonies;

(2)

Le Gouvernement provisoire, entouré par les officiers de la garde nationale et par les guides à cheval de la même garde;

Un détachement de la gendarmerie à cheval;

Le cortège marchera au milieu d'une haie formée par la garde nationale.

Le général Dessolles se portera avec l'état-major et un détachement de la Garde nationale, à cinq cents pas hors de la barrière, pour escorter S. A. R.

S. A. R. sera reçue à la barrière, mais en dedans de la ville; elle sera complimentée par le président du Gouvernement provisoire et par le préfet du département.

A l'entrée de S. A. R. dans Paris, il sera tiré plusieurs salves d'artillerie.

Le cortège se remettra en marche dans l'ordre suivant.

L'état-major et le détachement de la Garde nationale.

Les préfets, les maires et le conseil municipal.

Les maîtres des cérémonies.

Le gouvernement provisoire;

S. A. R. entourée des maréchaux, des généraux de l'armée et des officiers supérieurs de la garde nationale;

Les officiers de la suite de S. A. R.

Le détachement de la gendarmerie;

Le cortège conduira S. A. R. à la Métropole, où le clergé sera réuni pour la recevoir; la garde nationale occupera les postes de la Métropole.

Il sera chanté un *Te Deum* et un *Domine salvum fac Regem.*

Le cortège conduira ensuite S. A. au palais des Tuileries;

Le détachement de la Garde nationale désigné pour garder le palais sera en bataille dans la cour; les tambours battront au champ à l'arrivée du prince.

Les membres du Gouvernement provisoire, les maréchaux et les maîtres des cérémonies accompagneront S. A. R. jusqu'à ses appartements qui auront été préparés d'avance.

Napoleon's Abdication Proclamation, 1814

Napoleon's legacy was an impressive one. His administrative and legal reforms remained in place after his fall. The Napoleonic legal code persisted not only in France but in the Low Countries, Prussia, and various other German states. The institutions introduced during his reign—centralized bureaucracy, police, and educational systems—became part of the machinery of government and society in many parts of nineteenth-century Europe.

To appreciate the larger impact of the Revolution and the Napoleonic era on Western civilization, one must trace the ideas and institutions it fostered as they worked their way into the history of nineteenth- and twentieth-century Europe and America. Liberty—the concept of individual rights and responsibilities as embodied in popular democratic politics—was a notion dear to those who made the French Revolution, and one that remained embodied in the reforms it produced. So was equality—the notion of legal parity, of rational laws applied evenhandedly to all, regardless of birth or position. National identity was the era's third legacy. It was bred in the hearts of the French people, as we have already observed, when their citizen armies repelled attacks against their newly won freedoms. It spread throughout Europe in response to subsequent Jacobin and Napoleonic aggression. The French did not hesitate to champion their revolutionary principles abroad. They proclaimed as universal truths the sovereignty of the nation and the rights

Napoleon's legacy

The legacy of the Revolution and the Napoleonic era

and duties of citizenship. Their enemies, thus taught to define citizenship anew, responded with a growing sense of their own commonality. The threat of annihilation had aroused in the French a sense of themselves as a patriotic nation. Now, in German and Italian principalities, a similar response occurred. Men and women, under the domination of an alien emperor and his unwelcome satraps, grew increasingly conscious of an identity of their own. These three concepts—liberty, equality, and nationality—were no longer merely ideas; as laws and as a new way of addressing life, they rested at the center of European reality.

THE VIENNA SETTLEMENT

Congress participants

The European powers that met at the Congress of Vienna in 1814 to draw up a permanent peace settlement for Europe labored to produce an agreement that would as nearly as possible guarantee international tranquility. At the same time, however, they were by no means unwilling to advance the claims of their own countries to new territories, though such claims threatened conflict, or even war. Although the principal decisions of the congress were made by representatives of the major powers, it was attended by an array of dignitaries from almost all the principalities of Europe. No fewer than six monarchs attended: the tsar of Russia, the emperor of Austria, and the kings of Prussia, Denmark, Bavaria, Sweden, and Württemberg. Britain was represented by Lord Castlereagh and the duke of Wellington. From France came the subtle intriguer Talleyrand, who had served as a bishop under Louis XVI, as foreign minister at the court of Napoleon, and who now stood ready to espouse the cause of reaction.

The dominant roles at the Congress of Vienna were played by Tsar Alexander I (1801–1825) and by the Austrian diplomat Klemens von Metternich. Because Napoleon's defeat had left Russia the most powerful Continental state, the dynamic but baffling tsar played a leading role in the negotiations. Reared at the court of Catherine the Great, he had imbibed Jacobin doctrines from his French tutor, along with notions of absolutist authority from his military-minded father, Tsar Paul. In 1801 he succeeded his murdered father and for the next two decades disturbed the dreams of his fellow sovereigns by becoming the most liberal monarch in Europe. But the chief effect of his voluble expressions of devotion to "liberty" and "enlightenment" was to frighten conservatives into suspecting a plot to extend his power over all of Europe. He was accused of intriguing with Jacobins everywhere to substitute an all-powerful Russia for an all-powerful France.

Tsar Alexander I

The most commanding figure at the congress was Metternich, born at Coblenz in the Rhine valley, where his father was Austrian ambassador at the courts of three small German states. As a student at the University of Strasbourg the young Metternich witnessed mob violence connected with the outbreak of the French Revolution, and to this he attributed his life-

Metternich

long hatred of political innovation. He had been active in fomenting discord between Napoleon and Tsar Alexander, after the two became allies in 1807, and had played some part in arranging the marriage of Napoleon to the Austrian archduchess Marie Louise. Metternich once declared himself an admirer of spiders, "always busy arranging their houses with the greatest of neatness in the world." At the Congress of Vienna, he attempted at every turn to arrange international affairs with equal neatness, to suit his own diplomatic designs. His two great obsessions were hatred of political and social change and fear of Russia. Above all, he feared revolutions inspired by the tsar for the sake of establishing Russian supremacy in Europe. For this reason he favored moderate terms for France in its hour of defeat, and was ready at one time to sponsor the restoration of Napoleon as emperor of the French under the protection and overlordship of the Habsburg monarchy.

Klemens von Metternich

The basic idea that guided the work of the Congress of Vienna was the principle of *legitimacy*. This principle was invented by Talleyrand as a device for protecting France against drastic punishment by its conquerors, but it was ultimately adopted by Metternich as a convenient expression of the general policy of reaction. Legitimacy meant that the dynasties of Europe that had reigned in prerevolutionary days should be restored to their thrones, and that each country should regain essentially the same territories it had held in 1789. In accordance with this principle Louis XVIII was recognized as the "legitimate" sovereign of France; the restoration of Bourbon rulers in Spain and the Two Sicilies was also confirmed. France was compelled to pay an indemnity of 700 million francs to the victorious allies, but its boundaries were to remain essentially the same as in 1789.

The principle of legitimacy

To ensure that the French would not soon again overrun their boundaries, however, a strong barrier was erected to contain them. The Dutch

Ball on the Occasion of the Congress of Vienna, 1814. Europe's nobility gathered in Vienna to restore monarchical rule following the defeat of Napoleon.

Europe after the Congress of Vienna, 1815

Republic, conquered by the French in 1795, was restored as the Kingdom of the Netherlands, with the house of Orange as its hereditary monarchy. To its territory was added that of Belgium, formerly the Austrian Netherlands, with the hope that this now substantial power would serve to discourage any future notions of French expansion. For the same reason the German left bank of the Rhine was ceded to Prussia, and Austria was established as a major power in northern Italy.

The principle of legitimacy was not extended to Germany, however. There, despite pleas from rulers of the sovereign bits and pieces that had existed before 1789, the great powers agreed to reduce the number of states and principalities from over 300 to 39, linked together into the loose German Confederation under the honorary presidency of Austria. Fear of an aggressive Russia led the other European nations to support the maintenance—as an anti-Russian bulwark—of the kingdoms of Bavaria, Württemberg, and Saxony. At the same time, however, Tsar Alexander was demanding that Poland, partitioned into virtual extinction by Russia, Austria, and Prussia in the 1790s, be reconstituted a kingdom with himself as its constitutional monarch. Prussia was prepared to agree with this scheme, provided that it be allowed to swallow Saxony. National avarice for territorial expansion rapidly eclipsed legitimacy as a guiding principle in these negotiations. Metternich, horrified at the double threat thus presented to Austria by Prussia and Russia, allied himself with Talleyrand and Castlereagh, both of whom secretly agreed to go to war against Russia and Prussia, if necessary, in order to prevent them from consummating their Polish-Saxon deal. A compromise was eventually reached, giving to Russia the major part of Poland and to Prussia a part of Saxony. Britain, no less anxious than the other victorious powers to gain compensation for its long years at war, received territories principally under French dominion in South Africa and South America and the island of Ceylon, thus adding further to its commercial empire.

The arbiters of Vienna turned their backs on the three powerful legacies of the revolutionary and Napoleonic eras: liberty, equality, and nationality. They perceived these ideas as subversive to the order at last reimposed on a Europe exhausted by war. The predominant emotion at the congress was undoubtedly fear—a fear of any further international crisis that might overthrow the settlement. Another war, King Leopold of the Belgians observed, would be "a conflict of principles"—a conflict, that is, sparked by that unholy trinity of liberty, equality, and nationality. And "from what I know of Europe," he continued, "such a conflict would change her form and overthrow her whole structure."

Fear of liberty, equality, nationality

Hence the principle of legitimacy. Legitimacy, as expressed in the treaties that concluded the Congress of Vienna, emerged as the latter-day expression of the principles of balance and stability that had shaped diplomacy during the eighteenth century. The age of absolutism had witnessed the emergence of an international state system dedicated to those principles. By enshrining them in their settlement, the diplomats at Vienna ensured that such a state system would be part of the legacy passed to their nineteenth-century successors.

Triumph of the state system

SUMMARY POINTS

- By 1788, severe social tensions, an ailing and inefficient economy, and a weak monarch had brought absolutist France to the edge of political disaster.

- During the first stage of the Revolution, which lasted from June 1789 to August 1792, age-old privileges were abolished, the Church was secularized, individual rights and the sovereignty of the people were proclaimed, and the king and his ministers were stripped of real power. The well-to-do dominant order emerged as the true power in this stage.

- Other European powers saw the Revolution as a threat to international order and stability, leading to war in 1792. Initial defeats for France ushered in the second stage of the Revolution, led by radical republicans claiming to rule on behalf of the common people.

- The Terror (1793–1794) was a year-long period of bloody authoritarianism during which 25,000–30,000 people were executed and 500,000 were imprisoned. After the leaders of the Terror were deposed, the government was placed in the hands of an authoritarian five-person Directory (1795–1799), which squelched its opposition but failed to resolve the problem of inflation.

- Napoleon Bonaparte, who ruled as a dictator from 1799 until 1814, re-centralized government and tax collection and promulgated a new set of laws, the Napoleonic Code. After conquering much of the Continent, he imposed similar reforms across Europe. His "Continental System" failed to break the British and contributed to his defeat by allied Prussian, Russian, Austrian, Swedish, and British forces.

- The revolutionary and Napoleonic eras fostered the ideas of liberty, equality, and national identity in Europe. At the Congress of Vienna these principles were abondoned in favor of the principle of legitimacy in re-establishing the monarchies and the international system that had prevailed before the French Revolution.

SELECTED READINGS

Applewhite, Harriet B., and Darline G. Levy, eds., *Women and Politics in the Age of the Democratic Revolution,* Ann Arbor, 1990. Essays cover women's activities in France, Britain, the Netherlands, and the United States.

Bergeron, Louis, *France under Napoleon,* Princeton, 1981. Concentrates on the era of Napoleon rather than the man.

Bosher, J. F., *The French Revolution,* New York, 1989. A new interpretation that sees the revolutionary struggle driven by socially mixed and transient groupings.

Breunig, Charles, *The Age of Revolution and Reaction, 1789–1850,* 2d ed., New York, 1989. A well-written survey.

Bruun, Geoffrey, *Europe and the French Imperium, 1799–1814,* Westport, Conn., 1983. Describes the impact of Napoleon upon Europe.

Cobb, Richard, *The People's Armies,* New Haven, 1987. Analysis of the para-military fighting units of the *sans culottes*.

Cobban, Alfred, *The Social Interpretation of the French Revolution,* Cambridge, Eng., 1964. A penetrating critique of the radical interpretation of the Revolution, more important for its questions than for its conclusions.

Connelly, Owen, *Napoleon's Satellite Kingdoms,* New York, 1965. Analysis of the experience of European kingdoms under Napoleonic rule.

Doyle, William, *Origins of the French Revolution*, 2d ed., New York, 1988. A revisionist historian surveys recent research on the political and social origins of the Revolution and identifies a new consensus.

Forrest, Alan, *The French Revolution and the Poor*, New York, 1981. An account that argues the poor fared little better under revolutionary governments than under the *ancien régime*.

Geyl, Pieter, *Napoleon: For and Against*, rev. ed., New Haven, 1964. The ways in which Napoleon was interpreted by French historians and political figures.

Goodwin, Albert, *The Friends of Liberty: The English Democratic Movement in the Age of the French Revolution*, Cambridge, Mass., 1979. Detailed, subtle analysis of English reform movements.

Greer, Donald, *The Incidence of the Terror during the French Revolution: A Statistical Interpretation*, Cambridge, Mass., 1935. An important study that reveals that the lower classes suffered most during the Terror, rather than the nobility or the clergy.

Hampson, Norman, *A Social History of the French Revolution*, London, 1963. Deals with institutional development.

Hunt, Lynn, *Politics, Culture, and Class in the French Revolution*, Berkeley, 1984. An analysis of the interaction between political events and sociocultural phenomena out of which grew a new culture of democracy and republicanism.

Jones, P. M., *The Peasantry in the French Revolution*, Cambridge, Eng., 1988. The Revolution's impact on the countryside.

Kissinger, Henry, *A World Restored: Metternich, Castlereagh, and the Problems of Peace, 1812–1822*, Boston, 1957. By the former U.S. secretary of state, an admirer of Metternich.

Landes, Joan B., *Women and the Public Sphere in the Age of the French Revolution*, Ithaca, N.Y., 1988. Discusses the revolutionaries' exclusionary policy toward women.

Lefebvre, Georges, *The Coming of the French Revolution*, Princeton, 1947. An excellent study of the causes and early events of the Revolution.

———, *The French Revolution*, 2 vols., New York, 1962–1964. An impressive synthesis by the greatest modern scholar of the Revolution.

———, *The Great Fear of 1789*, New York, 1973. The best account of the rural disturbances.

McManners, John, *The French Revolution and the Church*, New York, 1969. Describes the impact of revolutionary anticlericalism upon the French Church.

Markham, Felix, *Napoleon*, New York, 1966. An excellent study.

Nicolson, Harold, *The Congress of Vienna: A Study in Allied Unity, 1812–1822*, New York, 1946. An excellent and very readable history, written by a British diplomat.

Palmer, R. R., *The Age of the Democratic Revolution: A Political History of Europe and America, 1760–1800*, 2 vols., Princeton, 1964. Impressive for its scope; places the French Revolution in the larger context of a worldwide revolutionary movement.

———, *Twelve Who Ruled: The Year of the Terror in the French Revolution*, Princeton, 1958. Excellent biographical studies of the members of the Committee of Public Safety; demonstrates that Robespierre's role has been exaggerated.

Rosenberg, Hans, *Bureaucracy, Aristocracy, and Autocracy: The Prussian Experience, 1660–1815*, Frankfurt, 1958. Contains useful information on the Napoleonic period.

Rudé, George, *The Crowd in the French Revolution*, Westport, Conn., 1986. An important monograph that analyzes the composition of the crowds that participated in the great uprisings of the Revolution.

Schama, Simon, *Citizens: A Chronicle of the French Revolution,* New York, 1989. An interesting although controversial treatment of the French Revolution.

Soboul, Albert, *The Sans-Culottes: The Popular Movement and Revolutionary Government, 1793–1794,* Garden City, N.Y., 1972. An outstanding example of "history from below"; analyzes the pressures upon the Convention in the year of the Terror.

Sutherland, D. M. G., *France, 1789–1815: Revolution and Counterrevolution,* Oxford, 1986. Particularly useful in the area of local opposition to revolutionary change.

Thompson, J. M., *Robespierre and the French Revolution,* London, 1953. An excellent short biography.

Tilly, Charles, *The Vendée: A Sociological Analysis of the Counter-Revolution of 1793,* Cambridge, Mass., 1964. An important economic and social analysis of the factors that led to the reaction in the Vendée.

Tocqueville, Alexis de, *The Old Regime and the French Revolution,* Garden City, N.Y., 1955. Originally written in 1856, this remains a classic analysis of the causes of the French Revolution.

Williams, Gwyn A., *Artisans and Sans-Culottes,* New York, 1969. Comparative history of English and French popular movements.

Woloch, Isser, *The New Regime: Transformations of the French Civic Order, 1789–1820,* New York, 1994. The fate of revolutionary civic reform.

SOURCE MATERIALS

Boyer, John W., and Julius Kirshner, eds., *University of Chicago Readings in Western Civilization,* Vol. 7, *The Old Regime and the French Revolution,* 1987. The most useful collection of documents.

Burke, Edmund, *Reflections on the Revolution in France,* London, 1790. (Many editions.) The great conservative statement against the Revolution and its principles.

Levy, Darline Gay, Harriet B. Applewhite, and Mary D. Johnson, eds., *Women in Revolutionary Paris, 1789–1795,* Champaign, Ill., 1979. Women participants in the activities of the Revolution.

Paine, Thomas, *The Rights of Man,* 1791. (Many editions.) Paine's eloquent response to Burke's *Reflections* resulted in his conviction for treason and banishment from England.

Pernoud, G., and S. Flaisser, eds., *The French Revolution,* New York, 1960. Contains eyewitness reports.

Sieyès, Abbé, *What Is the Third Estate?* 1789. (Many editions.) The most important political pamphlet in the decisive year 1789.

Walter, Jakob, *The Diary of a Napoleonic Foot Soldier,* New York, 1991. Provides a harrowing account of the Russian campaign.

Walzer, Michael, ed., *Regicide and Revolution: Speeches at the Trial of Louis XVI,* New York, 1974. Contains a thoughtful introduction.

CHAPTER 20

THE INDUSTRIAL REVOLUTION

Providence has assigned to man the glorious function of vastly improving the productions of nature by judicious culture, of working them up into objects of comfort and elegance with the least possible expenditure of human labor—an undeniable position which forms the basis of our Factory System.

—ANDREW URE, *The Philosophy of Manufactures*

THERE HAVE BEEN MANY revolutions in industry during the history of Western civilization, and there will undoubtedly be many more. Periods of rapid technological change are often called revolutions, and justifiably so. But historically there is one Industrial Revolution. Occurring during the hundred years after 1780, it witnessed the first breakthrough from a largely rural, handicraft economy to one dominated by urban, machine-driven manufacturing. Moreover, technological changes and new production methods triggered social and political upheavals that had revolutionary consequences for human society.

The uniqueness of the revolution

The fact that it was a European revolution was not accidental. Although in the mid-eighteenth century Europe was still a predominantly agricultural continent, although the majority of its people remained illiterate and destined to live out impoverished lives within sight of the place they were born—despite these conditions, which in our eyes might make Europe appear "underdeveloped," it was of course no such thing. European merchants and men of commerce were established as the world's foremost manufacturers and traders. Rulers relied upon this class of men to provide them the wherewithal to maintain the economies of their states, both in terms of flourishing commercial activity and of victorious armies and navies. Those men, in turn, had for the most part extracted from their rulers the understanding that the property they possessed, whether invested in land or commerce or both, was theirs outright. That understanding, substantiated by the written contracts that were replacing unwritten, long-acknowledged custom, helped persuade merchants, bankers, traders, and entrepreneurs that they lived in a world that was stable, rational, and predictable. Believing the world was so, they moved out into it with self-confidence and in hopes of increasing their own, and their country's, prosperity. Only in Europe does one find these presuppositions and this class of men in the eighteenth century; only through the activities of such people could the Industrial Revolution have taken place.

Why a European revolution? (1) The commercial class

(2) Expanding markets

These capitalists could not have prospered without an expanding market for their goods. The existence of this market explains further why it was in Europe that the Industrial Revolution took place. Ever since the beginning of the seventeenth century, overseas commercial exploration and development had been opening new territories to European trade. India, Africa, North and South America—all had been woven into the pattern of European economic expansion. The colonies and commercial dependencies took economic shape at Europe's behest. Even the new United States had not been able to declare its economic independence. Whatever commercial and industrial design Europe might devise, all would be compelled to accommodate themselves to Europe's demands.

(3) Population growth

A third factor helping to ensure that the revolution would occur in Europe was the significant population growth that occurred throughout western Europe in the eighteenth century (see pp. 552–553). Increasing populations, along with overseas expansion, provided an ever-growing market for manufactured goods. It furnished, as well, an adequate pool—eventually a surplus—of laboring men, women, and children to work in the manufacture of those goods either at home or in factories.

Qualifications to the concept of "revolution"

Two important facts have inclined historians to qualify the concept of "revolutionary" industrial change. First, the existence of a thriving commercial class, expanding markets, and increasing populations prior to the Industrial Revolution suggests that the changes we are about to analyze had important antecedents. We have already noted, for example, the manner in which proto-industrialization was transforming rural areas into sizable manufacturing regions in the seventeenth and eighteenth centuries (see p. 558). Second, the Industrial Revolution did not take place everywhere in Europe—or even in any single country—at the same time and at the same pace. Beginning in northern England and western Scotland in the late eighteenth century, it spread gradually region by region, country by country across Europe. Unlike the French Revolution, whose history can be measured by a decade, the Industrial Revolution occurred over the span of at least a century.

THE INDUSTRIAL REVOLUTION IN BRITAIN

Why in Britain? (1) An economy of abundance

It was in Britain that the Industrial Revolution first took hold. Britain's economy had progressed further than that of any other country in the direction of abundance. In simplest terms, fewer people had to struggle just to remain alive, more people were in a position to sell a surplus of the goods they produced to an increasingly expanding market, and more people had enough money to purchase the goods that market offered. British laborers, though poorly paid, enjoyed a higher standard of living than their Continental counterparts. They ate white bread, not brown, and meat with some regularity. Because a smaller portion of their income was spent on food, they might occasionally have some to spare for articles that were bought rather than homemade.

The Corn Exchange, 1842. This London
exchange was evidence of the abundance of
both food and capital in Britain during the
time of the Industrial Revolution.

Further evidence of this increasing abundance was the number of bills
for the enclosure of agricultural land passed by a British Parliament sympathetic to capitalism during the last half of the eighteenth century. The
enclosure of fields, pastures, and waste lands into large fenced tracts of
land under the private ownership and individual management of capitalist landlords meant an increased food supply to feed an increasing and
increasingly urban population. Yet another sign of Britain's abundance
was its growing supply of surplus capital, derived from investment in
land or commerce, and available to finance new economic enterprises.
London, already a leading center for the world's trade, served as a headquarters for the transfer of raw material, capital, and manufactured products. Portugal alone channeled as much as £50,000 in Brazilian gold per
week into London. Thus British capitalists had enough money on hand
to underwrite and sustain an industrial revolution.

But the revolution required more than money. It required habits of
mind that would encourage investments in enterprises that were risky,
but that represented an enormous potential for gain. In Britain, far more
than on the Continent, the pursuit of wealth was perceived to be a worthy end in life. The nobility of Europe had, from the period of the Renaissance, cultivated the notion of "gentlemanly" conduct, in part to hold
the line against social encroachments from below. The British aristocrats,
whose privileges were meager when compared with those of Continental
nobles, had never ceased to respect men who made money; nor had they
disdained to make whatever they could for themselves. Their scramble to

Abundance of food and capital

(2) Climate of opinion

enclose their lands reflected this sympathy with aggressive capitalism. Below the aristocracy, there was even less of a barrier separating the world of urban commerce from that of the rural gentry. Most of the men who pioneered as entrepreneurs in the early years of the Industrial Revolution sprang from the minor gentry or yeoman farmer class. Men from this sort of background felt themselves free to rise as high as their abilities might carry them on the social and economic ladder.

Respect for financial success

Eighteenth-century Britain was not by any means free of social snobbery: lords looked down upon bankers, as bankers looked down upon artisans. But a lord's disdain might well be tempered by the fact of his own grandfather's origins in the counting-house. And the banker would gladly lend money to the artisan if convinced that the artisan's invention might make them both a fortune. The British, as a nation, were not afraid of business. They respected the sensible, the practical, and the financially successful. Robinson Crusoe, that desert island entrepreneur, was one of their models. In the novel (1719) by Daniel Defoe, the hero had used his wits to master nature and become lord of a thriving economy. His triumph was not diminished because it was a worldly triumph; far from it. "It is our vanity which urges us on," declared the economist Adam Smith, whose writings encouraged capitalist investment in manufacturing. And thank God, Smith implied, for our blessed vanity! An individual's desire to show himself a worldly success worked to produce prosperity for the country as a whole.

(3) Expanding markets

Britain's eighteenth-century prosperity was based upon expanding markets both at home and abroad for whatever goods it manufactured. The British were voracious consumers. By the mid-eighteenth century, yearly fashions were setting styles not only for the very rich but for a growing middle-class clientele as well. "Nature may be satisfied with little," one London entrepreneur declared. "But it is the wants of fashion and the desire of novelties that causes trade." The country's small size and the fact that it was an island encouraged the development of a nationwide domestic market that could respond to increasing demand. The absence of a system of internal tolls and tariffs, such as existed on the Continent, meant that goods could be moved freely to the place where they could fetch the best price. This freedom of movement was assisted by a constantly improving transportation system. Parliament in the years just before the Industrial Revolution passed acts to finance turnpike building at the rate of forty per year; the same period saw the construction of canals and the further opening up of harbors and navigable streams. Unlike the government of France, whose cumbrous mercantilist adventures as often as not thwarted economic growth, the British Parliament believed that the most effective way in which it could help businessmen was to assist them in helping themselves.

Overseas expansion

If domestic markets promised steady growth, foreign markets promised greater returns—along with greater risks. Expansion was assisted by a favorable political climate: some members of Parliament were businessmen themselves; others had invested heavily in commerce; hence their eagerness to encourage by statute the construction of canals, the establishment of banks, and the enclosure of common lands. And hence their insistence, throughout the eighteenth century, that Britain's foreign policy respond to its commercial needs. At the end of every major eighteenth-century war, Britain wrested overseas territories from its enemies. At the same time, Britain was penetrating hitherto unexploited territories, such as India and South America, in search of further potential markets and resources. In 1759, over one-third of all British exports went to the colonies; by 1784, if we include the newly established United States, that figure had increased to one-half. Export production increased by 80 percent between 1750 and 1770, while production for domestic consumption gained just 7 percent over the same period. The British possessed a merchant marine capable of transporting goods across the world, and a navy practiced in the art of protecting its commercial fleets. By 1780 Britain's markets, together with its fleet and its established position at the center of world trade, combined to produce a potential for expansion so great as to compel the Industrial Revolution.

British entrepreneurs and inventors grasped the opportunity by revolutionizing the production of cotton textile goods. Although fewer cotton goods were made in eighteenth-century Britain than woolen goods, the extent of cotton manufacture by 1760 was such as to make cotton more than an infant industry. Tariffs prohibiting the importation of East Indian cottons, imposed by Parliament to stimulate the sale of woolen goods, had instead served to spur the manufacture of domestic cottons. Thus the revolution, when it did occur, took place in an already well-established industry. Yet without the invention of some sort of machinery that would improve the quality and at the same time dramatically increase the quantity of spun cotton thread, the necessary breakthrough would not have come. John Kay's 1733 invention of the fly shuttle, which greatly speeded the process of weaving, only made the bottleneck in the prior process of spinning more apparent. The problem was solved by the invention of a series of comparatively simple mechanical devices, the most important of which was the spinning jenny, invented by James Hargreaves, a carpenter and hand-loom weaver, in 1764 (patented 1770). The spinning jenny, named after the inventor's wife, was a compound spinning wheel, capable of producing sixteen threads at once. The threads it spun were not strong enough, however, to be used for the longitudinal fibers, or warp, of cotton cloth. It was not until the invention of the water frame by Richard Arkwright, a barber, in 1769, that quantity production of both warp and woof (latitudinal fibers) became possible. The water frame, along with the spinning mule invented by Samuel Crompton in 1779, which combined the features of both the jenny and the frame, solved the problems that had heretofore curtailed the output of cotton textiles. They increased the mechanical advantage over the spinning wheel enormously. From six to twenty-four times the amount of yarn could be spun on a jenny as on the wheel; by the end of the century two to three hundred times as much could be produced on the mule. Just as important,

The cotton industry

Richard Arkwright

The cotton gin

Location of mills

Growth of factories

The extent of the cotton trade

the quality of the thread improved not only in terms of strength but also of fineness.

Once these machines came into general use, the revolution proceeded apace. Cotton suited the mule and the jenny because it was a tougher thread than wool; as such cotton was a fiber that could withstand the rough treatment it received at the mechanical hands of the crude early machines. In addition, the supply of cotton was expandable in a way that the supply of wool was not. The cotton gin, invented by the American Eli Whitney in 1793, separated seeds from fiber mechanically, thereby making cotton available at a lower price. The invention kept America's slave plantations profitable, and meant that supply would meet increased demand.

The first machinery was cheap enough to allow spinners to continue to work at home. But as it increased in size it was more and more frequently housed not in the cottages of individual spinners, but in workshops or mills located near water that could be used to power the machines. Eventually, with the further development of steam-driven equipment, the mills could be built wherever it might suit the entrepreneur—frequently in towns and cities in the north of England.

The transition from home to factory industry was of course not accomplished overnight. Cotton yarn continued to be spun at home at the same time that it was being produced in mills. Eventually, however, the low cost of building and operating a large plant, plus the efficiency realized by bringing workers together under one roof, meant that larger mills more and more frequently replaced smaller workshops. By 1851, three-fifths of those employed in cotton manufacture worked in medium- to large-size mills. Weaving remained a home industry until the invention of a cheap, practical power loom convinced entrepreneurs that they could save money by moving the process from home to mill. Hand-loom weavers were probably the most obvious victims of the Industrial Revolution in Britain. Their unwillingness to surrender their livelihood to machinery meant that they continued to work for less and less—by 1830, no more than a pitiful six shillings a week. In 1815 they numbered about 250,000; by 1850, there remained only 40,000; by 1860, only 3,000.

British cotton textiles flooded the world market from the 1780s. Here was a light material, suitable for the climates of Africa, India, and the more temperate zones of North America. Here was a material cheap enough to make it possible for millions who had never before enjoyed the comfort of washable body clothes to do so. And here was material fine enough to tempt the rich to experiment with muslins and calicos in a way they had not done before. Figures speak eloquently of the revolutionary change wrought by the expanding industry. In 1760, Britain exported less than £250,000 worth of cotton goods; by 1800 it was exporting over £5 million worth. In 1760, Britain imported 2.5 million pounds of raw cotton; in 1787, 22 million pounds; in 1837, 366 million pounds. By 1800, cotton accounted for about 5 percent of the national income of the country; by 1812, from 7 to 8 percent. By 1815, the export of cotton

Cotton Mill in Lancashire, 1834. Above: Women and girls prepare the cotton by carding, drawing, and roving the fibers. Below: Cotton thread is woven into cloth on a spinning mule.

Calico Printing in a Lancashire Cotton Mill, 1834

textiles amounted to 40 percent of the value of all domestic goods exported from Great Britain. Although the price of manufactured cotton goods fell dramatically, the market expanded so rapidly that profits continued to increase.

Unlike the changes in the textile industry, those occurring in the manufacture of iron were not great enough to warrant their being labeled revolutionary. Yet they were most significant. Britain's abundant supply of coal, combined with its advanced transportation network, allowed the British, from the middle of the eighteenth century, to substitute coal for wood in the heating of molten metal. A series of discoveries made fuel savings possible, along with a higher quality of iron and the manufacture of a greater variety of iron products. Demand rose sharply during the war years at the end of the eighteenth century. It remained high as a result of calls for plant machinery, agricultural implements, and hardware; it rose dramatically with the coming of railways in the 1830s and 1840s. Britain was exporting 571,000 tons of iron in 1814; in 1852, it exported 1,036,000 tons out of a world total of almost 2,000,000—more iron than was made by all the rest of the world combined.

The need for more coal required the mining of deeper and deeper veins. In 1711, Thomas Newcomen had devised a crude but effective steam engine for pumping water from mines. Though of value to the coal industry, it was of less use in other industries since it wasted both fuel and power. In 1763, James Watt, a maker of scientific instruments at the Uni-

The iron industry

The steam engine

versity of Glasgow, was asked to repair a model of the Newcomen engine. While engaged in this task he conceived the idea that the machine would be greatly improved if a separate chamber were added to condense the steam, eliminating the need to cool the cylinder. He patented his first engine incorporating this device in 1769. Watt's genius as an inventor was not matched by his business ability. He admitted that he would "rather face a loaded cannon than settle a disputed account or make a bargain." As a consequence, he fell into debt in attempting to place his machines on the market. He was rescued by Matthew Boulton, a wealthy hardware manufacturer from Birmingham. The two men formed a partnership, with Boulton providing the capital. By 1800 the firm had sold 289 engines for use in factories and mines. The replacement of water by steam power was a slow process: in 1850 more than a third of the power used in woolen manufacture and an eighth of that used in cotton was still produced by water. Nevertheless, there is no question that without the steam engine there could have been no industrial expansion on the scale that we have described.

Other industries experienced profound changes during the hundred years of the Industrial Revolution. Many of those changes came in response to the growth of textile manufacture. The chemical industry, for example, developed new methods of dyeing and bleaching, as well as improved methods of production in the fields of soap and glassmaking. Production of goods increased across the board as profits from the boom in manufacturing increased the demand for new and more sophisticated articles. Such trades as pottery and metalware expanded to meet demands, in the process adopting methods that in most instances reduced cost and speeded manufacture.

To understand fully the nature of the Industrial Revolution in Britain one must not lose sight of two important factors. The first is that dramatic as the revolution was, it happened over a period of two or three generations, at varying paces in different industries in different parts of

The Triumph of Steam and Electricity, 1897. Technological advances made during the reign of Queen Victoria.

Other advances

The limits of the Industrial Revolution

The Steam Hammer, from a painting by James Nasmyth. This steam-powered machine was used to beat out ingots of white-hot metal into strips.

Old Hetton Colliery, Sunderland, England. Designed by the engineer Thomas Hair about 1840, this large mine was typical of those built to meet the increased demand for coal. Note the railways that connected the mines with the sea.

the country. Some men and women continued to work at home, much as their grandfathers and grandmothers had. Old tools and old methods were not immediately replaced by new ones, any more than populations fled the countryside overnight for the city. Second, the revolution was accomplished from a very limited technological and theoretical base. Except in the chemical industry, change was not the result of scientific research. It was the product of empirical experimentation—in some cases, of little more than creative tinkering. To say this is not to disparage the work of men such as Arkwright, Hargreaves, Watt, and their like. It is to suggest, however, the reason why Britain, without a national system of education on any level, was nonetheless able to accomplish the revolution it did. Nor are these remarks intended to belittle the magnitude of the change. What occurred in Britain was a revolution because of the way in which it reshaped the lives, not just of the British, but of people across the globe. By responding as it did to the demands of its apparently insatiable markets, Britain made a revolution every bit as profound and long-lasting as that which occurred simultaneously in France.

THE INDUSTRIAL REVOLUTION ON THE CONTINENT

Reasons for delay: (1) lack of transport and raw materials

The Industrial Revolution came in time to the Continent, but not to any important degree before about 1830. As we have seen, manufacturing in eighteenth-century France and Germany clustered in regions whose proximity to raw materials, access to markets, and traditional attachment to particular skills had resulted in their development as industrial centers. Flanders and Normandy in France, and Saxony in Germany were centers for the manufacture of woolen cloth; Switzerland, southern Germany,

The Industrial Revolution

and Normandy, of cottons; Wallonia (the area around Liège in Belgium), the Marne valley, and Silesia in Germany, of iron. Yet for a variety of reasons, these areas failed to experience the late-eighteenth-century breakthrough that occurred in Britain. Nor were they capable at first of imitating Britain's success, once they began to perceive the great economic advantages that Britain's pronounced lead was bringing it. There were a number of reasons for the delay of Continental industrialization. Whereas Britain's transportation system was highly developed, those of France and Germany were not. France was far larger than Britain, its rivers were not as easily navigable, its seaports were farther apart. Central Europe was so divided into tiny principalities, each with its own set of tolls and tariffs, as to make the transportation of raw materials or manufactured goods over any considerable distance impractical. France itself imposed regulations that thwarted easy shipments. In addition, the Continent was not as blessed with an abundance of raw materials as Britain. France, the Low Countries, and Germany imported wool. Continental Europe lacked an abundant supply of the fuel that was the new source of industrial energy. Few major coal deposits were known to exist, while the ready availability of timber discouraged exploration that might have resulted in its discovery.

(2) Lack of entrepreneurial spirit

After the French Revolution, middle-class Europeans, though free in theory to rise as high on the social and economic ladder as they might aspire, appear largely to have remained content to make only enough money to sustain a modest-size business. The motivation of the middle class was as often social as it was economic: to ensure the continuity of a family rather than to produce increasing quantities of goods. Furthermore, capital was not as readily available on the Continent as in Britain. In France, again, the retarded development of agricultural capitalism, due to the tenacious economic perseverance of small peasant landholders, limited the supply of savings, both for investment in industry and for expenditure on manufactured goods, and also limited the mobility of labor. Nor was the entrepreneurial spirit that compelled Britishers to drive competitors to the wall as highly developed in France and Germany in the years after 1815. Exhausted by the competitiveness of war, and fearful of the disruptions that war brought in its train, Continental businessmen resisted new methods of manufacturing and selling.

(3) Effect of wars

The Continent did not simply stand idle, however, as Britain assumed its industrial lead. The pace of mechanization was increasing in the 1780s. But the French Revolution and the wars that followed disrupted growth that might otherwise have taken place. Battles fought on French, German, and Italian soil destroyed factories and machinery. Although ironmaking increased to meet the demands of the wars, techniques remained what they had been. Commerce was badly hurt both by British destruction of French merchant shipping and by Napoleon's Continental System. Probably the revolutionary change most beneficial to industrial advance in Europe was the removal of previous restraints on the movement of capital and labor—for example, the abolition of trade guilds, and the reduction of tariff barriers across the Continent. On balance, however, the revolutionary and Napoleonic wars clearly thwarted industrial development on the Continent, while at the same time intensifying it in Britain.

A number of factors combined to produce a climate more generally conducive to industrialization on the Continent after 1815. Population continued to increase, not only throughout Europe, but in those areas now more and more dependent upon the importation of manufactured goods—Latin America, for example. European increases, which doubled the populations of most countries between 1800 and 1850, meant that the Continent would now have a growing number of producers and consumers. More people did not necessarily mean further industrialization. In Ireland, where other necessary factors were absent, more people meant less food. But in those countries with an already well-established commercial and industrial base—France and Germany, for example—increased population did encourage the adoption of the technologies and methods of production that were transforming Britain.

Stimuli of industrialization after 1815: (1) population rise

Transportation improved in western Europe both during and following the Napoleonic wars. The Austrian Empire added over 30,000 miles of roads between 1830 and 1847; Belgium almost doubled its road network in the same period; France built, in addition to roads, 2,000 miles of canals. In the United States, where industrialization was occurring at an increasingly rapid rate after 1830, road mileage jumped from 21,000 miles in 1800 to 170,000 in 1856. When these improvements were combined with the introduction of rail transport in the 1840s, the resulting increase in markets available to all Western countries encouraged them to introduce methods of manufacturing that would help meet new demands.

(2) Improved transportation

Governments played a more direct role in the process of industrialization on the Continent than in Britain. Napoleon's rationalization of French and imperial institutions had introduced Europe to the practice of state intervention. His legal code, which guaranteed freedom of contract and facilitated the establishment of joint-stock enterprises, encouraged other rulers to provide a similar framework for commercial expansion. In Prussia, lack of private capital necessitated state operation of a large proportion of that country's mines. In no European country but Britain would railways be built without the financial assistance of the state. In the private sector more attention was given on the Continent than in Britain to the need for artificial stimulation to produce industrial change. It was in Belgium that the first joint-stock investment bank—the Société Générale—was founded, an institution designed to facilitate the accumulation of ready capital for investment in industry and commerce. Europeans were also willing for the state to establish educational systems whose aim, among others, was to produce a well-trained elite capable of assisting in the development of industrial technology. What Britain had produced almost by chance, the Europeans began to reproduce by design.

(3) Centralization

Until the Continent produced its own technicians it was compelled to rely on British expertise. But the pace of Continental, and also American, industrialization, even after 1815, remained far slower than in Britain

The lack of technicians

because of Britain's natural reluctance to see its methods of production pirated by others. British industrialists believed it their patriotic duty to prevent the exportation of their techniques, although they were more than willing to raid the Continent for technological experts: Matthew Boulton imported skilled workers from Vienna and Sweden. Continental entrepreneurs likewise argued that it was patriotism, not profit, that inspired them to compete with the British. "Our reasons for building our factory were exactly those which made you oppose it," a German firm wrote to Boulton; "that is patriotic zeal."

The textile industry

The growth of the textile industry in Europe was patterned by the circumstances of the Napoleonic wars. The supply of cotton to the Continent had been interrupted, thanks to the British blockade, but the military's greater demand for woolen cloth meant that expansion occurred more rapidly in the woolen than in the cotton industry. By 1820, the spinning of wool by machine was the common practice on the Continent; weaving, however, was still accomplished largely by hand. Regional centers for the production of wool were located around Rheims and in Alsace in France; in what is now Belgium; and in Saxony and Silesia in Germany. All possessed, at least in some measure, the various elements necessary to the successful growth and development of a regional economic system: transportation, resources, markets, technology, and labor supply. Mechanization was retarded because manual labor was cheap, and by the important fact that since Britain's market was so large, Continental profits too often depended upon the manufacture of some particular specialty not made in England, and therefore without broad commercial appeal.

A German Textile Factory, 1848. This is an unusually large manufacturing facility for this period on the Continent.

Silk Weavers of Lyons, 1850. The first significant working-class uprisings in nineteenth-century France occurred in Lyons in 1831 and 1834. Note the domestic character of the working conditions.

In the area of heavy industry on the Continent, the picture was much the same as in textiles: i.e., gradual advances in the adoption of technological innovation against a background of more general resistance to change. Here, however, because change came later than in Britain, it coincided with an increased demand for various goods that had come into being as a result of industrialization and urbanization: iron pipe, much in use by mid-century in cities for gas, water, and drainage; metal machinery, now replacing earlier wooden prototypes. Consequently, the iron industry took the lead over textiles on the Continent, accompanied by an increase, where possible, in the production of coal. Coal was scarce, however; in the Rhineland, wood was still used to manufacture iron. The result was an unwillingness on the part of entrepreneurs to make as extensive use of the steam engine as they might have otherwise; it used too much fuel. In France, as late as 1844, hydraulic (i.e., water-driven) engines were employed far more often for the manufacture of iron than were steam engines. One further problem hampered the development of Continental heavy industry during the first half of the nineteenth century: British competition forced Continental machine construction firms to scramble for whatever orders they could get. This need to respond to a variety of requests meant that it was difficult for firms to specialize in a single product. The result was a lack of standardization, and continued production to order, when rationalization and specialization would have resulted in an increased volume of production.

Heavy industry

THE COMING OF RAILWAYS

By about 1840, then, Continental countries, and to some degree the United States, were moving gradually along the course of industrialization traced by Britain, producing far more than they had, yet nothing like as much as their spectacular pacesetter. Within the next ten years, the

Railways as a stimulus to the European and American economies

The New Railway Age. Left: Stephenson's *Rocket.* A reconstruction of the railway engine built by George Stephenson in 1829. Right: "The Railway Juggernaut of 1845." A cartoon from the British humor magazine *Punch* satirizing speculation—often financially disastrous—in railway stocks.

coming of the railways was to alter that situation. Though Britain by no means lost its lead, the stimulus generally provided to Western economies by the introduction of railway systems throughout much of the world carried the Continent and America far enough and fast enough to allow them to become genuine competitors with the British.

Railways as goods carriers

Railways came into being in answer to two needs. The first was the obvious desire on the part of entrepreneurs to transport their goods as quickly and cheaply as possible across long distances. Despite already mentioned improvements in transportation during the years before 1830, the movement of heavy materials, particularly coal, remained a problem. It is significant that the first modern railway was built in England in 1825 from the Durham coal field of Stockton to Darlington, near the coast. "Tramways"—parallel tracks along which coal carts were pulled by horses—had long been in use at pitheads to haul coal short distances. The Stockton-to-Darlington railway was a logical extension of this device, designed to answer the transportation needs produced by constantly expanding industrialization. The man primarily responsible for the design of the first steam railway was George Stephenson, a self-made engineer who had not learned to read until he was seventeen. He talked a group of investors from northern England into the merits of steam traction and was given full liberty to carry out his plans. The locomotives on the Stockton-Darlington line traveled at fifteen miles per hour, the fastest rate at which machines had yet moved people overland.

Railways as an investment opportunity

Railways were also built in response to other than purely industrial needs: specifically, the need for capitalists to invest their money.

Britishers such as those who had made sizable fortunes in textiles, once they had paid out workers' wages and plowed back substantial capital in their factories, retained a surplus profit for which they wanted a decent yet reliable return. Railways provided them with the solution to their problem. Though by no means as reliable as had been hoped, railway investment proved capable of more than satisfying the capitalists' demands. No sooner did the first combined passenger and goods service open in 1830, on the Liverpool-to-Manchester line, than plans were formulated and money pledged to extend rail systems throughout Europe, the Americas, and beyond. In 1830, there were no more than a few dozen miles of railway in the world. By 1840, there were over 4,500 miles; by 1850, over 23,000. The English contractor Thomas Brassey, the most famous, but by no means the only one of his kind, built railways in Italy, Canada, Argentina, India, and Australia.

The railway boom accelerated industrialization generally. Not only did it increase enormously the demand for coal and for a variety of heavy manufactured goods—rails, locomotives, carriages, signals, switches—but by enabling goods to move faster from factory to salesroom, railways decreased the time it took to sell those goods. Quicker sales meant, in turn, a quicker return on capital investment, money that could then be reinvested in the manufacture of more goods. Finally, by opening up the world market as it had never been before, the railway boom stimulated the production of such a quantity of material goods as to ensure the rapid completion of the West's industrialization.

Thomas Brassey

Consequences of railway development

American Railway Scene in Pennsylvania. This advertisement by Currier & Ives suggests the benefits of the rail industry, such as more reliable mail delivery and the comfort of the Pullman Hotel, and conveys the fervid railway mania that swept Europe and America.

A Steam-Driven Coach, one of the marvels of the new industrial age, but soon an irrelevance once the railways were built.

The building of a railway line was an undertaking on a scale infinitely greater than the building of a factory. Railway construction required capital investment beyond the capacity of any single individual. In Britain, a factory might be worth anywhere from £20,000 to £200,000. The average cost of twenty-seven of the more important railway lines constructed between 1830 and 1853 was £2 million. The average labor force of a factory ranged from 50 to 300. The average labor force of a railway, after construction, was 2,500. Because a railway crossed the property of a large number of individual landowners, each of whom would naturally demand as much remuneration as he thought he could get, the planning of an efficient and economical route was a tricky and time-consuming business. The entrepreneur and contractor had to concern themselves not only with the purchase of right-of-way. They also contended with problems raised by the destruction of sizable portions of already existing urban areas, to make room for stations and switching yards. And they had to select a route that would be as free as possible of the hills and valleys that would necessitate the construction of expensive tunnels, cuts, and embankments. Railway-builders ran tremendous risks. Portions of most lines were subcontracted at fixed bids to contractors of limited experience. A spate of bad weather might delay construction to the point where builders would be lucky to bring in the finished job within 25 percent of their original bid. Of the thirty major contractors on the London-to-Birmingham line, ten failed completely.

If the business of a contractor was marked by uncertainty, that of the construction worker was characterized by back-breaking labor. The "navvies," who built railways not only throughout Britain but around the world, were a remarkable breed. Their name derived from "navigator," a term applied to the construction workers on Britain's eighteenth-century canals. The work that they accomplished was prodigious. Because there is little friction between a train's wheels and its tracks, it can transport heavy loads easily. But lack of friction ceases to be an advantage when a train has to climb or descend a grade, thereby running the risk of slippage. Hence the need for comparatively level roadbeds; and hence the need for laborers to construct those tunnels, cuts, and embankments that would keep the roadbeds level. Navvies worked in gangs, whose migrations throughout the countryside traced the course of railway development. They were a rough lot, living in temporary encampments, often with women who were not their wives. The Irish navvies were a particularly tough breed. A sign posted by local residents in Scotland in 1845 warned that if all the Irish navvies were not "off the ground and out of the country" in a week, they would be driven out "by the strength of our armes and a good pick shaft."

The magnitude of the navvies' accomplishment was extraordinary. In Britain and in much of the rest of the world, mid-nineteenth-century railways were constructed almost entirely without the aid of machinery. An assistant engineer on the London-to-Birmingham line, in calculating the magnitude of that particular construction, determined that the labor involved was the equivalent of lifting 25 billion cubic feet of earth and

Railway Navvies. Without the aid of machinery, the burden of building Britain's railways fell on the backs of men such as these.

The magnitude of the accomplishment

Construction of the London-to-Birmingham Railway, London, 1838. This drawing of the building of retaining walls in a new railway cut evokes the chaos created by railway construction within urban areas.

The Dresden Railway Station. Railways had the power to alter the architecture of the city, producing new and dramatic urban spaces.

stone one foot high. This he compared with the feat of building the Great Pyramid, a task he estimated had involved the hoisting of some 16 billion tons. But whereas the building of the pyramid had required over 200,000 men and had taken twenty years, the construction of the London-to-Birmingham railway was accomplished by 20,000 men in less than five years. Translated into individual terms, a navvy was expected to move an average of twenty tons of earth per day. Railways were laid upon an almost infinite base of human muscle and sweat.

INDUSTRIALIZATION AFTER 1850

Britain still the leader

In the years between 1850 and 1870, Britain remained very much the industrial giant of the West. But France, Germany, Belgium, and the United States assumed the position of challengers. In the iron industry, Britain's rate of growth during these years was not as great as that of either France or Germany (5.2 percent for Britain, as against 6.7 percent for France and 10.2 percent for Germany). But in 1870 Britain was still producing half the world's pig iron; 3.5 times as much as the United States, more than 4 times as much as Germany, and more than 5 times as much as France. Although the number of cotton spindles increased from 5.5 to 11.5 million in the United States between 1852 and 1861, and by significant but not as spectacular percentages in European countries, Britain in 1861 had 31 million spindles at work in comparison with France's 5.5 million, Germany's 2 million, Switzerland's 1.3 million, and Austria's 1.8 million.

Continuing European advance

Most of the gains experienced in Europe came as a result of continuing changes in those areas we have come to recognize as important for sustained industrial growth: transport, commerce, and government policy. The improved transportation systems that resulted from the spread of railways helped encourage an increase in the free movement of goods. International monetary unions were established, and restrictions removed on international waterways such as the Danube. The Prussian Zollverein, or tariff union, an organization designed to facilitate internal free trade, was established in 1818 and was extended over the next twenty years to include most of the German principalities outside Austria. Free trade went hand in hand with further removal of barriers to entering trades and to practicing business unhampered by restrictive regulation. The control that guilds and corporations had over artisan production was abolished in Austria in 1859 and in most of Germany by the mid-1860s. Laws against usury, most of which had ceased to be enforced, were officially abandoned in Britain, Holland, Belgium, and in many parts of Germany. Governmental regulation of mining was surrendered by the Prussian state in the 1850s, freeing entrepreneurs to develop resources as they saw fit. The formation of investment banks proceeded apace, encouraged by an important increase in the money supply, and therefore an easing of credit, following the opening of the California gold fields in 1849.

A further reason for increased European production was the growing trade in raw materials. Wool and hides imported from Australia helped diminish the consequences of the cotton shortage suffered after the outbreak of the United States Civil War and the Union blockade of the American South. Other importations—guano from the Pacific, vegetable oils from Africa, pyrites (sulfides) from Spain—stimulated the scale of food production and both altered and increased the manufacture of soap, candles, and finished textiles. Finally, discoveries of new sources of coal, particularly in the Pas-de-Calais region of France and in the Ruhr valley in Germany, had dramatic repercussions. Production of coal in France rose from 4.4 million to 13.3 million tons between 1850 and 1869; during the same years, German production increased from 4.2 million to 23.7 million tons.

Industrialization in eastern and southern Europe after mid-century proceeded at a much slower pace than in western Europe. This was in part a result of the fact that many eastern regions played an increasingly specialized role in the economy of the Continent, providing food and agricultural materials to the West. The ever-growing demand for agricultural products from the East resulted in the development of agriculture as a major capitalist industry there. As they rationalized their operations for increased efficiency and hence profitability, entrepreneurs recognized the degree to which they were hampered by the outmoded economic practices of serfdom, a system that prevented the mobility of labor and thus the formation of an effective agricultural work force. Serfdom was abolished in most parts of eastern and southern Europe by 1850, and in Poland and Russia in the 1860s.

The fact that industry continued to take a back seat to agriculture does not mean, however, that eastern Europe was without important manufacturing regions. By the 1880s, the number of men and women

Increased trade in raw materials

The slower pace of industrialization in eastern and southern Europe

Pockets of industrialization in the East

Women in a German Canning Factory. Not all industry took place in factories; much of it still required skilled handwork.

employed in the cotton industry in the Austrian province of Bohemia exceeded that in Saxony. In the Czechoslovakian region, textile industries, developed in the eighteenth century, continued to thrive. By the 1830s, there were machine-powered Czech cotton mills and iron works. In Russia, a factory industry producing coarse textiles—mostly linens—had grown up around Moscow. At mid-century, Russia was purchasing 24 percent of the total British machinery exports to mechanize its own mills. Many workers in Russian industry remained serfs until the 1860s—about 40 percent, a number of them employed in mines. Of the over 800,000 Russians engaged in manufacturing by 1860, however, most labored not in factories but in very small workshops, where average employment numbered about 40 persons.

Europe's economy within the world

By 1870 Europe was by no means a fully industrialized continent. Fifty percent of France's labor force remained on farms. Agricultural laborers were the single largest occupational category in Britain during the 1860s. Great stretches of the Continent—Spain, southern Italy, eastern Europe—were almost untouched by the Industrial Revolution. And in the industrialized countries, much work was still accomplished in tiny workshops or at home. Yet if Europe was by no means wholly industrial, it was far and away the most industrially advanced portion of the globe—and not by accident. In order to maintain its position of producer and seller to the world, Europe, and Britain particularly, made certain that no other areas stood a chance to compete. Europe used its economic and, when necessary, its military strength to ensure that the world remained divided between the producers of manufactured goods—Europe itself—and suppliers of the necessary raw materials and buyers of finished goods—everyone else. Often this arrangement suited those in other parts of the world who made their money by providing the raw materials that fueled the European economy. Cotton-growers in the southern United States, sugar-growers in the Caribbean, wheat-growers in the Ukraine—all remained content with arrangements as dictated by the industrialized West. Those countries that expressed their discontent—Egypt, for example, which in the 1830s attempted to establish its own cotton textile industry—were soon put in their place by a show of force. Western Europeans, believing in their right to industrial leadership in the world, saw nothing wrong with employing soldiers, if they had to, to make others understand their destiny.

SUMMARY POINTS

- The Industrial Revolution began in Great Britain around 1780 because Britain's economy was most advanced, in Britain there was a climate of respect for financial success, and Britain had developed extensive and expanding domestic and overseas markets. Britain also had an abundant supply of coal and a relatively advanced transportation network, which gave it an advantage over the rest of the Continent.

- Less-developed transportation networks, resistance to financial and manufacturing change, and the division of the Continent by wars and politics delayed the Industrial Revolution in Continental Europe until about 1830. Governments played a more direct role in industrialization on the Continent than in Britain.

- The massive construction of railways between 1840 and 1850 accelerated industrialization and allowed economies in America and on the Continent to become genuine competitors with the British.

SELECTED READINGS

Cameron, R. E., *France and the Industrial Development of Europe*, Princeton, 1968. Valuable material on the Industrial Revolution outside Britain.

Checkland, S. G., *The Rise of Industrial Society in England, 1815–1885*, New York, 1965. Emphasizes the economic organization of England.

Cipolla, Carlo M., ed., *The Industrial Revolution, 1700–1914,* New York, 1976. A collection of essays that emphasizes the wide range of industrializing experiences in Europe.

Deane, Phyllis, *The First Industrial Revolution,* 2d ed., Cambridge, Eng., 1979.

Goodman, Jordan, and Katrina Honeyman, *Gainful Pursuits: The Making of Industrial Europe, 1600–1914,* London, 1988. Stresses continuity.

Henderson, W. O., *The Industrialization of Europe, 1780–1914,* New York, 1969.

———, *The State and the Industrial Revolution in Prussia, 1740–1870,* Liverpool, 1958. A biographical approach. Good on technical education.

Hobsbawm, Eric, *Industry and Empire: The Making of Modern English Society, 1750 to the Present Day,* New York, 1968. A general survey of industrialization in Britain, written from a Marxist perspective.

Landes, David S., *The Unbound Prometheus: Technological Change and Industrial Development in Western Europe from 1750 to the Present,* London, 1969. An excellent treatment of the technological innovations and economic results of the Industrial Revolution.

McManners, John, *European History, 1789–1914: Men, Machines and Freedom,* New York, 1967.

Mathias, Peter, *The First Industrial Nation: An Economic History of Britain, 1700–1914,* 2d ed., London, 1988. An important general study of the industrialization process.

Price, Roger, *An Economic History of Modern France, 1730–1914,* New York, 1981. Stresses the importance of transportation and communications networks.

Schofer, Lawrence, *The Formation of a Modern Labor Force, Upper Silesia, 1865–1914,* Berkeley, 1975. Analyzes industrialization and its social consequences in Silesia.

Taylor, George Rogers, *The Transportation Revolution, 1815–1860,* Armonk, N.Y. 1989.

Trebilcock, Clive, *The Industrialization of the Continental Powers, 1780–1914,* New York, 1981. Emphasizes the relationship between politics and industrialization.

SOURCE MATERIALS

Dodd, George, *Days at the Factories; or the Manufacturing Industry of Great Britain Described, and Illustrated by Numerous Engravings of Machines and Processes,* Totowa, N.J., 1978. A reprint of the 1843 edition.

Mitchell, Brian R., and Phyllis Deane, *Abstract of British Historical Statistics,* Cambridge, Eng., 1962. The single best source for statistics on population, trade, manufacturing, etc.

Smith, Adam, *An Inquiry into the Nature and Causes of the Wealth of Nations,* Chicago, 1977. Written in 1776, this revolutionary work called for the end of mercantilism.

Ward, J. T., *The Factory System, 1830–1855,* New York, 1970. Excerpts from contemporary documents describing, defending, and criticizing the factory system and industrialization.

CHAPTER 21

CONSEQUENCES OF INDUSTRIALIZATION: URBANIZATION AND CLASS CONSCIOUSNESS (1800–1850)

What Art was to the ancient world, Science is to the modern: The distinctive faculty. In the minds of men the useful has succeeded the beautiful. Yet rightly understood, Manchester is as great a human exploit as Athens.

—BENJAMIN DISRAELI, *Coningsby*

THE INDUSTRIAL REVOLUTION was more than an important event in the economic and technological history of the West. It helped to reshape the patterns of life for men and women, first in Britain, then in Europe and America, and eventually throughout much of the world. By increasing the scale of production, the Industrial Revolution brought about the factory system, which in turn compelled the migration of millions from the countryside and small towns into cities. Once in those cities, men and women had to learn a new way of life, and learn it quickly: how to discipline themselves to the factory whistle and survive in a slum, if they were first-generation urban workers; how to manage a work force and achieve respectable prominence for themselves in the community, if they were businessmen and their wives. One particular lesson that industrialization and urbanization taught was that of class consciousness. Men and women, to a far greater degree than heretofore, began to perceive themselves as part of a class with interests of its own, and in opposition to the interests of men and women in other classes.

We shall examine this range of social and cultural changes as they occurred during the first fifty years or so of the nineteenth century, after looking briefly first at the condition of the bulk of the population, which, despite industrialization, remained on the land. Since the Industrial Revolution came first to Britain, our focus will be on that country. Yet the pattern set by the British was one that was repeated to a great extent in other European countries, as industrialization came to them in time.

Consequences of the Industrial Revolution

Consequences of Industrialization: Urbanization and Class Consciousness (1800–1850)

Population patterns

The dramatic story of the growth of industrialization and urbanization must not be allowed to obscure the fact that, in 1850, the population of Europe was still overwhelmingly a peasant population. While in Britain by 1830, a sizable minority lived in towns and cities, elsewhere society remained predominantly rural. In France and Italy, 60 percent lived in the country; in Prussia, over 70 percent; in Spain, over 90 percent; in Russia, over 95 percent. Demographic pressures, which helped produce chaos in the cities, likewise caused severe hardship in the countryside. The populations of the predominantly agricultural nations leapt forward with those that were industrializing. The population of Europe as a whole, estimated roughly at 205 million by 1800, had risen to 274 million by 1850, and to 320 million by 1870. In Britain, with its comparatively high standard of living, the numbers increased from 16 million to 27 million. Yet the rural Irish, despite their periodic famines, increased too, from 5.5 to 8 million, and the Russians from 39 to 60 million, in the same period.

Causes of continuing population expansion

The causes of this continuing population explosion remain obscure. The notion that the explanation can be traced to a desire on the part of parents in industrial countries to produce more family wage-earners is now downplayed by scholars, given the fact that increases occurred in rural regions as well. One contributing factor to this continued growth may have been a decline in the virulence of certain fatal diseases as a result of the cyclical potency of microbes. Certainly the curbing of cholera, through the adoption of sanitary reforms, and smallpox, as Edward Jenner's technique of vaccination gained gradual acceptance after 1796, help to explain the population trend. The increasing ability and desire of governments to monitor and improve the lives of their subjects had a direct effect on the decline of the death rate. At the same time the availability of less expensive foods of high nutritional value—most notably the potato—and the ability to transport foodstuffs cheaply by rail meant European populations would not suffer as much from undernourishment as in the past, and thus that they would be less susceptible to debilitating illness. Other plausible explanations suggest that the population increase was the result of rising birth rates caused by earlier marriages. As serfdom declined, peasants tended to set up households at a younger age. The spread of cottage industries also allowed more rural couples to marry and set up households even without the inheritance of land. This "proletarianization" of the countryside contributed not only to lowered age at marriage but also to a higher number of marriages. A relatively small expansion in the population of a region in one generation would result in a far greater one in the next. As the population grew, the number of young and fertile people grew faster, thereby significantly increasing the ratio of births to total population.

Wretched rural conditions

Whatever the reasons for the population increase, conditions remained such as to make the life of the poorer rural inhabitants of Europe

The Home of a Rural Laborer. This etching from the British magazine *Punch* portrays the hunger that came with a bad harvest, and that could lead to rural violence.

seldom more than bleak. Overpopulation brought underemployment, and hence poverty, in its train. Millions of tiny holdings produced a bare subsistence living, if that. Farmers still sowed and harvested by hand. Conditions in rural areas deteriorated sharply whenever there was a bad harvest. The average daily diet for an entire family in a "good" year might amount to no more than two or three pounds of bread—a total of about 3,000 calories. Hunger—often near-starvation—as well as epidemic disease were still common occurrences. The result was a standard of living—if one can dignify the condition with that name—that for many rural inhabitants of many areas in Europe actually declined in the first half of the nineteenth century, although not enough to reverse general population growth. Governments in some countries attempted to solve the related problems of population pressure and impoverishment by passing laws raising the age of marriage. In some of the states of southern and western Germany, as well as in Austria, men were forbidden to marry before the age of thirty, and were also required to prove their ability to support a family. Governments did their best to encourage emigration to ease the overcrowding, the majority of emigrants relocating in the Americas. Emigration from Britain rose from 57,000 in 1830, to 90,000 in 1840, to 280,000 in 1850. Ireland, in the early years of the nineteenth century, witnessed the departure of over 1.5 million before the great potato famine of 1846, when approximately three out of every four acres of

Agricultural capitalism

The legacy of manorialism

Rural societies and industrialization

potatoes were blighted. After the potato famine, the flow of emigrants increased to a flood.

Even had such policies acted as an effective curb on population growth—which, in the main, they did not—they would nevertheless have failed to prevent the rural stresses that resulted from the continuing spread of agricultural capitalism. The speed with which agricultural change occurred in various parts of Europe depended upon the nature of particular governments. Those more sympathetic to new capitalist impulses facilitated the transfer and reorganization of land by means of enabling legislation. They encouraged the elimination of small farms and an increase in larger, more efficient units of production. In Britain, over half the total area of the country, excluding waste land, was composed of estates of a thousand acres or more. In Spain, the fortunes of agricultural capitalism fluctuated with the political tenor of successive regimes: with the coming of a liberal party to power in 1820 came a law encouraging the free transfer of land; with the restoration of absolutism in 1823 came a repeal of the law. Russia was one of the countries least affected by agricultural change in the first half of the nineteenth century. There land was worked in vast blocks; some of the largest landowners possessed over half a million acres. Until the emancipation of the serfs in the 1860s, landowners claimed the labor of dependent peasant populations for as much as several days per week. But the system of serfdom gave neither landowners nor serfs incentive to improve farming or land-management techniques.

European serfdom, which bound hundreds of thousands of men, women, and children to particular estates for generations, prohibited the use of land as a negotiable commodity and therefore prevented the development of agricultural entrepreneurship. In France, despite the fact that manorialism had been abolished by the Revolution, there was no rapid movement toward large-scale capitalist farming. An army of peasant proprietors, direct beneficiaries of the Jacobins' democratic constitution, continued to work the small farms they owned. The fact that France suffered far less agricultural distress, even in the 1840s, than did other European countries, and the fact that there was less migration in France from the country to the city and overseas than there was in Germany and Britain, are marks of the general success of this rural lower-middle class in sustaining itself on the land. Its members were content to farm in the old way, opposed agricultural innovation, and, indeed, innovation generally. Despite their veneration of the Revolution, they were among the most conservative elements in European society.

Rural populations, though isolated from urban centers, found themselves directly affected by the events of the Industrial Revolution. Factories brought about a decline in cottage industry and a consequent loss of vital income, especially during winter months. Improved communication networks not only afforded rural populations a keener sense of events and opportunities elsewhere, but also made it possible for govern-

Agricultural Disturbances. Mob violence erupted in southern England in 1830 in protest against the introduction of threshing machines.

ments to intrude upon the lives of these men and women to a degree previously impossible. Central bureaucracies now found it easier to collect taxes from the peasantry, and to conscript its sons into their armies.

Country people responded with sporadic violence against these and other harsh intrusions upon their lives. In southern England in the late 1820s, small farmers joined forces to burn barns and hayricks in protest against the introduction of threshing machines, a symbol of the new agricultural capitalism. They masked and otherwise disguised themselves, riding out at night under the banner of their mythical leader, "Captain Swing." Their raids were preceded by anonymous threats such as the one received by a large-scale farmer in the county of Kent: "Pull down your threshing machine or else [expect] fire without delay. We are five thousand men [a highly inflated figure] and will not be stopped." Other major rural disturbances occurred in Ireland, Silesia, and Galicia in the 1830s and 1840s, and indeed, to a lesser degree, right across Europe. In Russia, serf uprisings were a reaction to continued bad harvests and exploitation rather than to agricultural innovation and displacement. In no country, however, was the agrarian population a united political force. Those who owned land, those who leased it as tenants, and those who worked it as laborers had interests as different from each other's as from those of the urban populations.

Rural disturbances

Manchester, England, at Mid-century. This powerful photograph evokes the dreary, prison-like atmosphere of the new industrial city.

URBANIZATION AND THE STANDARD OF LIVING

Reasons for the growth of cities

If the countryside continued to hold the bulk of Europe's population in the years between 1800 and 1850, the growth of cities nevertheless remains one of the most important facts in the social history of that period. Cities grew in size and number once the steam engine made it practical to bring together large concentrations of men, women, and children to work in factories. Steam engines freed entrepreneurs from their dependence on water power and allowed them to consolidate production in large cities. In cities, transportation was more accessible than in the countryside. Hence it was less costly to import raw materials and ship out finished goods. Workers were more readily available in cities, as well, attracted as they were in large numbers in the hope—often false—of finding steady work at higher wages than those paid agricultural laborers. Industrialization was not the only reason for the growth of cities in the early nineteenth century, however. General population increases combined with industrialization, forcing cities to expand at an alarming rate.

Urban population increases

In the ten years between 1831 and 1841 London's population grew by 130,000, Manchester's by 70,000. Paris increased by 120,000 between 1841 and 1846. Vienna grew by 125,000 from 1827 to 1847, into a city of 400,000. Berlin had as large a population by 1848, having increased by 180,000 since 1815. The primary result in these and other fast-growing centers was dreadful overcrowding. Construction lagged far behind population growth. In Vienna, though population rose 42 percent during the twenty years before 1847, the increase in housing was only 11.5 percent. In many of the larger cities, old and new, working men and women lived in lodging houses, apart from families left behind in the country. The poorest workers in almost all European cities dwelt in wretched basement rooms, often without any light or drainage.

With cities as overcrowded as they were, it is no wonder that they were a menace to the health of those who lived within them. The middle classes moved as far as possible from disease and factory smoke, leaving the poorest members of the community isolated and a prey to the sickness that ravaged working-class sections. Cholera, typhus, and tuberculosis were natural predators in areas without adequate sewerage facilities and fresh water, and over which smoke from factories, railroads, and domestic chimneys hung heavily. A local committee appointed to investigate conditions in the British manufacturing town of Huddersfield—not by any means the worst of that country's urban centers—reported that there were large areas without paving, sewers, or drains, "where garbage and filth of every description are left on the surface to ferment and rot; where pools of stagnant water are almost constant; where dwellings adjoining are thus necessarily caused to be of an inferior and even filthy description; thus where disease is engendered, and the health of the whole town perilled." Measures were gradually adopted by successive governments in an attempt to cure the worst of these ills, if only to prevent the spread of catastrophic epidemics. Legislation was designed to rid cities of their worst slums by tearing them down, and to improve sanitary

Cities as a health menace

Women and Boys Fetching Water from a Standpipe in Fryingpan Alley, London. Not until the beginning of the twentieth century did major European cities begin to provide poorer residents with an adequate water supply.

conditions by supplying both water and drainage. Yet by 1850, these projects had only just begun. Paris, perhaps better supplied with water than any European city, had enough for no more than two baths per capita per year; in London, human waste remained uncollected in 250,000 domestic cesspools; in Manchester, fewer than a third of the dwellings were equipped with toilets of any sort.

The standard-of-living debate

Conditions such as these are important evidence in the debate that has occupied historians for the past several decades. The question is: Did the standard of living rise or fall in Europe during the first half century of the Industrial Revolution? One school, the "optimists," argues that workers shared in the more general increase in living standards which occurred throughout Europe from 1800 onward. A variation on this optimistic theme maintains that whatever the hardships workers were compelled to suffer during the period of intense industrialization after 1800, they represent the necessary and worthwhile price society had to pay before it could "take off" into a period of "sustained economic growth." Sacrifices, in terms of standard of living, were required to permit accumulation of a capital base sufficient to guarantee economic expansion and an eventual level of general prosperity higher than any civilization had hitherto achieved. Other historians insist that such an analysis encourages one to ignore the evidence of physical squalor and psychological disruption that men, women, and children suffered as they provided the statistical "base" for future economic historians' abstract calculations.

Instability and unemployment

The debate is hampered by an absence of reliable evidence about wage levels, hours of work, and cost of living. Some skilled workers within the new factories, along with some artisans in older trades as yet unaffected by industrialization, appear to have benefited from a slight rise in wages and a decline in living costs. But regional variables, along with a constantly fluctuating demand for labor in all countries, suggest that the more lowly paid, unskilled worker, whether in Britain or on the Continent, led a thoroughly precarious existence. Textile workers in Britain, if

Soup Kitchen Run by Quakers, Manchester, England, 1862. Enterprises of this sort, which doled out charity "indiscriminately"—that is, without investigating the recipient's character—were condemned by many members of the middle class as encouraging the "worst" elements—idlers and loafers—among the poor.

guaranteed something like full employment, could theoretically earn enough to support a family. Such was not the case in Switzerland, however, where similar work paid only half what was necessary, or in Saxony, where a large portion of the population was apparently dependent upon either poor relief or charity. One of the most depressing features of working-class life in these years was its instability. Economic depressions were common occurrences; when they happened, workers were laid off for weeks at a time, with no system of unemployment insurance to sustain them. Half the working population of Britain's industrial cities was out of work in the early 1840s. In Paris, 85,000 went on relief in 1840. One particularly hard-pressed district of Silesia reported 30,000 out of 40,000 citizens in need of relief in 1844. Nor should one overlook the plight of those whose skills had been replaced by machinery—the hand-loom weavers being the most notable examples. In the British manufacturing town of Bolton, a hand-loom weaver could earn no more than about three shillings per week in 1842, at a time when experts estimated it took at least twenty shillings a week to keep a family of five above the poverty line. On that kind of pay, workers were fortunate if they did not starve to death. Forced to spend something like 65 percent of their income on food, the per capita meat consumption of the average worker declined to about forty pounds per year in the early nineteenth century.

Such figures make the optimists' generalizations hard to countenance. Figures of whatever sort fail to take into account the stress that urban factory life imposed upon the workers. Even workers making thirty shillings a week might well wonder if they were "better off," forced as they were to come to terms with the factory disciplines and living conditions imposed upon them. Of the more than three million men, women, and children living in Britain's sixty largest towns and cities in 1850, less than half had been born there. Though most migrated but a short distance from their place of birth, the psychological distance they traveled was tremendous. These qualitative factors, admittedly difficult to assess, must be weighed along with more easily quantifiable evidence before reaching any conclusion as to the increased standard of living in early-nineteenth-century cities. Whether or not life in cities was pleasant or ghastly, however, it was, for rapidly increasing numbers, a fact of life. Once we examine that life we will better understand the full impact of industrialization and urbanization upon those who first experienced it.

Stress of urban life

The Life of the Urban Middle Class

The urban middle class that emerged during this period was by no means one homogeneous unit, in terms of occupation or income. In a general category that includes merchant princes and humble shopkeepers, subdivisions are important. The middle class included families of industrialists, such as the Peels (cotton) in Britain and, at a later period, the Krupps (iron) in Germany. It included financiers like the internationally famed

The urban middle class

Isambard Kingdom Brunel. Behind him are lengths of anchor chain from the steamship *The Great Western.*

Movement from the middle class to the aristocracy

Self-help

Rothschilds, and, on a descending scale of wealth and power, bankers and capitalists throughout the major money markets of Europe: London, Brussels, Paris, Berlin. It included entrepreneurs like Thomas Brassey, the British railway magnate, and John Wilkinson, the British ironmaster, who had himself buried in an iron coffin, and technicians, like the engineer Isambard Kingdom Brunel, designer of the steamship *The Great Western.* It included bureaucrats, in growing demand when governments began to regulate the pace and direction of industrialization, and to ameliorate its harshest social and economic results. It included those in the already established professions—in law particularly, as lawyers put their expertise to the service of industrialists. It included the armies of managers and clerks necessary to the continuing momentum of industrial and financial expansion, and the equally large army of merchants and shopkeepers necessary to supply the wants of an increasingly affluent urban middle-class population. Finally, it included the families of all those who lived their lives in the various subcategories we have listed.

Movement within these ranks was often possible, in the course of one or two generations. Movement from the working class into the middle class, however, was far less common. Most middle-class successes originated within the middle class itself—the children of farmers, skilled artisans, or professionals. Upward mobility was almost impossible without education; education was an expensive, if not unattainable, luxury for the children of a laborer. Careers open to talents, that goal achieved by the French Revolution, frequently meant middle-class jobs for middle-class young men who could pass exams. The examination system was an important path for ascendancy within governmental bureaucracies.

If passage from working class to middle class was not common, neither was the equally difficult social journey from middle class to aristocratic, landed society. In Britain, mobility of this sort was easier than on the Continent. Children from wealthy upper-middle-class families, if they were sent, as occasionally they were, to elite schools and universities, and if they left the commercial or industrial world for a career in politics, might effect the change. William Gladstone, son of a Liverpool merchant, attended the exclusive educational preserves of Eton, a private boarding school, and Oxford University, married into the aristocratic Grenville family, and became prime minister of England. Yet Gladstone was an exception to the rule in Britain, and Britain was an exception to the Continent. Movement, when it occurred, generally did so in less spectacular degrees.

Nevertheless, the European middle class helped sustain itself with the belief that it was possible to get ahead by means of intelligence, pluck, and serious devotion to work. The Englishman Samuel Smiles, in his extraordinarily successful how-to-succeed book *Self Help* (1859), preached a gospel dear to the middle class. "The spirit of self-help is the root of all genuine growth in the individual," Smiles wrote. "Exhibited in the lives of many, it constitutes the true source of national vigor and strength." A corollary to Smiles's discussion was the moral obligation to use the fruits of success in accordance with middle-class notions of respectability. However, although Smiles's gospel declared that anyone willing to exert himself could rise to a position of responsibility and personal profit, and although some men actually did so, the notion remained no more than myth for the great majority.

Seriousness of purpose was reflected in the middle-class devotion to the ideal of family and home. A practical importance attached to the institution of the family in those areas in Britain, France, and Germany where sons, sons-in-law, nephews, and cousins were expected to assume responsibility in family firms when it came their turn. Yet the worship of family more often ignored those practical considerations and assumed the proportions of sacred belief. Away from the business and confusion of the world, sheltered behind solid masonry and amid the solid comfort of their ornate furnishings, middle-class fathers retired each evening to enjoy the fruits of their daily labors. Indeed, this retreat served as a reaffirmation of power and position for men whose success in the business world might be tenuous and insecure.

Inside the home, life was enclosed in a hierarchical and ritualistic system under which the husband and father was master. Wives and mothers were assigned to a "separate sphere" of life, in which they lived in subordination to their spouses. "Man for the field and woman for the hearth; man for the sword and for the needle she. . . . All else confusion." Thus wrote the British poet Alfred Lord Tennyson in 1847, and thus believed the vast majority of middle-class men and women. Boys were educated in secondary schools; girls at home. Men, soon after the revolutionary and Napoleonic period, began to dress in sober, practical clothing—discarding the tight breeches that had allowed them to advertise their masculinity. Women, however, continued to dress in a

Family and home

Separate spheres

Left: **A Salon in Vienna, 1830s.** Right: **A Victorian Family at Tea, 1860s.** Representations of middle-class home life on the Continent and in Britain.

Florence Nightingale

Middle-class women outside the home

George Sand

manner that proclaimed their feminine nature. The ideology of separate spheres was reflected in law; throughout Europe women were legally subjugated to their husbands. The Napoleonic Code, a model for other countries after 1815, classified women as legally incompetent, as it classified children and the insane. In Britain, a husband could lay absolute claim to his wife's property. Although unmarried women did enjoy a degree of legal independence in France and Austria, laws generally assigned them to the "protection" of their fathers. A middle-class wife was generally treated by her spouse as a kind of superior servant. Her task was to keep the household functioning smoothly and harmoniously. She maintained the accounts and directed the activities of the servants—usually two or three women. Called in Victorian Britain the "Angel in the House," the middle-class woman was responsible for the moral education of her children. Yet she probably spent no more than two or three hours a day at most with her offspring. Until sent to school, they were placed in the custody of a nursemaid or governess. Much of a middle-class woman's day was spent in the company of other women from similar households. An elaborate set of social customs involving "calls" and "at homes" was established in European middle-class society. Women were not expected to be the intellectual companions of their husbands. Rather, they were encouraged to be dabblers, education for them usually consisting of little beyond reading and writing, a smattering of arithmetic, geography, history, and a foreign language, embellished with lessons in drawing, painting in watercolors, singing, or piano-playing.

Very occasionally within the middle class, a wife served as shopkeeper or business associate with her husband. But women had very few respectable options for earning a living outside the home. Spinsters might act as companions or governesses—the British novelist Charlotte Bronte's heroine Jane Eyre did so, and led a generally miserable life until "rescued" by marriage to her not-altogether-pleasant employer. When married women ventured forth from their hearths for something beyond the society of friends and neighbors, it was to undertake voluntary charitable work, or to campaign for social reform. British women played an important role in the struggle to abolish the slave trade and then slavery in the British Empire. Throughout Europe, women worked hard and with great effect to improve conditions for the poor in schools, hospitals, and old-age homes. Florence Nightingale, who went out to the Crimean peninsula in Russia to nurse British soldiers fighting there in the 1850s, remains the most famous of those women whose determination to right social wrongs compelled them to ignore the doctrine of separate spheres. Equally famous—or infamous, at the time—was the French female novelist George Sand (1804–1876)—her real name, Amandine Aurore Dupin. She dressed like a man and smoked cigars. Her novels often told the tales of independent women thwarted by convention and unhappy marriage. Her notoriety gave rise to the expression "George Sandism," a term of opprobrium for those who defied middle-class convention.

Queen Victoria, who ascended the British throne in 1837, labored to make her solemn—occasionally almost stolid—public image reflect the feminine middle-class virtues of moral probity and dutiful domesticity. Her public reflection of private virtue emphasized the middle-class reliance upon image and appearance as an indicator of an underlying reality. Her court was eminently proper and preeminently bourgeois, a marked contrast to that of her uncle George IV, whose fleshly and unbuttoned ways had set the style for high life a generation before. Though possessing an imperious temper, Victoria trained herself to curb it in deference to her ministers and her public-spirited, ultra-respectable husband, Prince Albert of Saxe-Coburg. She was a successful queen because she embodied the traits dearest to the middle class, whose triumph she seemed to epitomize and whose habits of mind we have come to call Victorian.

Middle-class wives were indoctrinated to believe that they were superior to their husbands in one area only. A wife was "the better half" of a middle-class marriage because she was deemed pure—the untainted Vestal of the hearth, unsullied by cares of the world outside her home, and certainly untouched by those sexual desires that marked her husband, her natural moral inferior. A wife's charge was to encourage her husband's "higher nature." She must never respond to his sexual advances with equal passion; passion was, for her, a presumed impossibility. If she *was* passionate—and private diaries suggest, not surprisingly, that many middle-class women were—she would find it hard not to feel guilty

Queen Victoria as prototype

Sexuality

Prince Albert and Queen Victoria. In this photograph by Roger Fenton the royal couple is depicted not as monarch and consort but as a conventional upper-middle-class married couple.

Les Belles de la Nuit, by Jean Be-
raud. These "beauties of the night"
were clearly expensive prostitutes
displaying their wares before
middle-class gentlemen.

about the pleasures she was presumed too pure to taste. Contraception,
other than withdrawal, was not common practice among the middle
classes. The result was that for women, sexual intercourse was directly
related to the problems of frequent pregnancies. (Victoria, who had nine
children, declared that childbirth was "the shadow side" of marriage.)

The middle-class wife was expected to persuade her husband to seek,
through love of home and family, a substitute for the baser instincts with
which nature had unhappily endowed the male. Should she fail, she
must accept the fact of her "failure" as she was bound to accept the rest of
her life: uncomplainingly. That she often did fail was evidenced by the
brisk trade in prostitution that flourished in nineteenth-century cities. In
all European cities, prostitutes solicited openly. At mid-century the number of prostitutes in Vienna was estimated to be 15,000; in Paris, where
prostitution was a licensed trade, 50,000; in London, 80,000. London
newspaper reports of the 1850s catalogued the vast underworld of prostitutes and their followers: those who operated out of "lodging houses" run
by unsavory entrepreneurs whose names—Swindling Sal, Lushing Loo—
suggest their general character; the retinue of procurers, pimps, pander-
ers, and "fancy men" who made the lives of common prostitutes little
better than slavery; the relatively few "prima donnas" who enjoyed the
protection of rich, upper-middle-class lovers, who entertained lavishly
and whose wealth allowed them to move on the fringes of more respectable high society. The heroines of Alexandre Dumas's novel *La Dame
aux Camilles* and of Giuseppe Verdi's opera *La Traviata* ("The lost one")
were prototypes of women of this sort.

Prostitution

If a middle-class wife should herself succumb to "unwomanly desires" by taking a lover, and be discovered to have done so, she could expect nothing less than complete social banishment. The law tolerated a husband's infidelity and at all times respected a husband's rights both to his wife's person and to her property. It made quick work of an "unfaithful" wife, granting to her husband whatever he might desire in terms of divorce, property, and custody, to make amends to him for the personal wrongs and embarrassments he had suffered at the hands of his "unnatural" spouse.

Middle-class family rituals helped to sustain this hierarchy. Daily meals, with the father at the head of the table, were cooked and brought to each place by servants, who were a constant reminder of the family's social position. Family vacations were a particularly nineteenth-century middle-class invention. Thanks to the advent of the railways, excursions of one or two weeks to the mountains or to the seashore were available to families of even moderate means. Entrepreneurs built large, ornate hotels, adorned with imposing names—Palace, Beau Rivage, Excelsior—and attracted middle-class customers by offering them on a grander scale exactly the same sort of comfortable and sheltered existence they enjoyed at home.

The Middle Class at Leisure. The "morning lounge" at Biarritz, a French resort on the Atlantic coast.

Houses

The houses and furnishings of the middle class were an expression of the material security the middle class valued. Solidly built, heavily decorated, they proclaimed the financial worth and social respectability of those who dwelt within. In provincial cities they were often freestanding "villas." In London, Paris, Berlin, or Vienna, they might be rows of five- or six-story townhouses, or large apartments. Whatever particular shape they took, they were built to last a long time. The rooms were certain to be crowded with furniture, art objects, carpets, and wall hangings. Chairs, tables, cabinets, and sofas might be of any or all periods; no matter, so long as they were adorned with their proper complement of fringe, gilt, or other ornamentation. The size of the rooms, the elegance of the furniture, the number of servants, all depended, of course, on the extent of one's income. A bank clerk did not live as elegantly as a bank director. Yet in all likelihood both lived in obedience to the same set of standards and aspirations. And that obedience helped bind them, despite the differences in their material way of life, to the same class.

Cities and the middle class

The European middle class had no desire to confront the unpleasant urban by-products of its own success. Members of the middle class saw to it that they lived apart from the unpleasant sights and smells of industrialization. Their residential areas, usually built to the west of the cities, out of the path of the prevailing breeze, and therefore of industrial pollution,

Apartment Living in Paris. This print shows that on the Continent rich and poor often lived in the same buildings, the rich on the lower floors, the poor at the top. This sort of residential mixing was unknown in Britain.

The Paris Opera. An exterior view of the Opera. Designed by Charles Garnier, it was constructed between 1861 and 1875. This grandiose display of wealth and luxury epitomized the taste of the new industrial middle class.

were havens from the congestion for which they were primarily responsible. When the members of the middle class rode into the urban centers they took care to do so over avenues lined with respectable shops, or across railway embankments that lifted them above monotonous working-class streets en route to their destination. Yet the middle class, though it turned its face from what it did not want to see, did not turn from the city. Middle-class men and women celebrated the city as their particular creation and the source of their profits. They even praised its smoke—as a sign of prosperity—so long as they did not have to breathe it night and day. For the most part, it was they who managed their city's affairs. And it was they who provided new industrial cities with their proud architectural landmarks: city halls, stock exchanges, opera houses. These were the new cathedrals of the industrial age, proclamations of a triumphant middle class.

THE LIFE OF THE URBAN WORKING CLASS

Like the middle class, the working class was divided into various subgroups and categories, determined in this case by skill, wages, and workplace. The working class included skilled workers in crafts that were centuries old—glassblowing and cabinetmaking, for example. It included as well mechanics equally skilled in new industrial technology. It included the men who built textile machinery and the women and children who tended it. It included the men, women, and children who together worked in mines and quarries. And it included the

Ranks within the working class

Social mobility

Housing

countless millions who labored at unskilled jobs—dock workers, coal porters, cleaning women, and the like. The nature of workers' experiences naturally varied, depending upon where they worked, where they lived, and, above all, how much they earned. A skilled textile worker lived a life far different from that of a ditch digger, the former able to afford the food, shelter, and clothing necessary for a decent existence, the latter so busy trying to keep himself and his family alive that he would have little time to think about anything but the source of their next meal.

Some movement from the ranks of the unskilled to the skilled was possible, if children were provided, or provided themselves, with at least a rudimentary education. Yet education was considered by many parents a luxury, especially since children could be put to work at an early age to supplement a family's meager earnings. There was movement from skilled to unskilled also, as technological change—the introduction of the power loom, for example—drove highly paid workers into the ranks of the unskilled and destitute. Further variations within the working class were the result of the fact that though every year more men, women, and children were working in factories, the majority still labored either in workshops or at home. These variations mean that we cannot speak of a common European working-class experience during the years from 1800 to 1850. The life we shall be describing was most typical of British workers, during the first half-century of their exposure to industrialization. Only in the years 1850–1900 did most Continental workers undergo this harsh process of urban acclimatization.

Life in industrial cities was, for almost all workers, uncomfortable at best and unbearably squalid at worst. Workers and their families lived

Schools for the Poor. A rudimentary education could be the key to movement from unskilled to skilled worker.

Nineteenth-Century Working-Class Housing. Faced with insatiable demands for urban accommodations, developers responded in a variety of ways. In Oldham (top left), a textile manufacturing center in the north of England, the answer was street after street of row houses; in Glasgow, Scotland (top right), it was multistory tenements; and in the suburbs of Paris (lower right), it was shanties. In all three settings, the result was essentially the same: a bleak existence born of overcrowding and squalor.

in housing that failed to answer the needs of its inhabitants. In older cities single-family dwellings were broken up into apartments of often no more than one room per family. In new manufacturing centers, rows of tiny houses, located close by smoking factories, were built back-to-back, thereby eliminating any cross-ventilation or space for gardens. Whether housing was old or new, it was generally poorly built. Old buildings were allowed by landlords to fall into disrepair; new houses, constructed of cheap material, decayed quickly. Water often came from an outdoor tap, shared by several houses and adjacent to an outdoor toilet. Crowding was commonplace. Families of as many as eight lived in two or, at the most, three rooms. A newspaper account from the 1840s noted that in Leeds, a textile center in northern Britain, an "ordinary" worker's house contained no more than 150 square feet, and that in most cases those houses were "crammed almost to suffocation with human beings both day and night." When, after 1850, governments began to rid cities of some of their worst slums, many working-class men and women discovered that urban "improvement" meant relocation into dreary "model" tenements whose amenities were matched by their barracklike anonymity; or removal from one dilapidated structure to another in the wake of a clearance scheme—the nineteenth century called it "ventilation"—that replaced ancient, overcrowded housing with a more sanitary—and, for the landlord, more profitable—railway switching yard.

The life of women

The life of working-class wives and mothers was hard. Lack of cheap contraceptive devices and a belief that these devices were immoral helped to keep women pregnant through most of their childbearing years, thus endangering their general health and adding to the burden of their lives. Wives were usually handed a portion of the weekly wage packet by their husbands, and were expected to house, feed, and clothe the family on the very little they were given. Their daily life was a constant round of cooking, cleaning, shopping, and washing—in a tiny space and without enough money. Housewives could not rely, as in the country, on their own gardens to help supply them with food. Instead, they went to markets that catered to their needs with cheap goods, often stale or nearly rotten, or dangerously adulterated. Formaldehyde was added to milk to prevent spoilage. Pounded rice was mixed into sugar. Fine brown earth was introduced into cocoa. A woman's problems were compounded, of course, when she had to work, and therefore had far less time to accomplish the household tasks she was still expected to perform.

Women workers

Women were employed in growing numbers—along with children—in factories during the nineteenth century. Yet many more labored at home or in small workshops—"sweatshops," as they came to be called—for wretchedly low wages based not on the hours they worked but on the amount of work they did: so much per shirt stitched or matchbox glued. By far the greatest number of unmarried working-class young women worked as domestic servants, often a lonely occupation and one that occasionally trapped female servants into undesired sexual relationships with their male employers or their sons.

Sexuality

Female sexuality within the working classes of western Europe was acknowledged in a way that it was not within the middle class. Demographic evidence reveals a sharp rise in illegitimacy between 1750 and 1850. In Frankfurt, Germany, for example, where the illegitimacy rate had been a mere 2 percent in the early 1700s, it reached 25 percent in 1850. In Bordeaux, France, in 1840, one-third of the recorded births were illegitimate. Reasons for this increase are difficult to establish. Illegitimacy in Germany may have been the result of laws forbidding the poor to marry. Certainly, increased mobility meant weaker family ties, less parental supervision, and greater opportunity for an unrestricted life. This is not to say that the majority of working-class women were sexually promiscuous. Premarital intercourse was an accepted practice in preindustrial villages, but, because of the social controls that dominated village life, it was almost always a precursor to marriage. In the far more anonymous setting of a factory town, such controls often did not exist. In addition, the economic uncertainties of the early industrial age meant that a young workingman's promise of marriage based on his expectation of a job might frequently be difficult to fulfill. The same economic uncertainty led some young working-class women to careers—usually temporary—as prostitutes. The anonymity of city life encouraged prostitution. Middle-class men, prepared to postpone marriage until they could afford a house and furnishings reflecting the social position to which they aspired, turned to the sexual underworld to satisfy their desires. Class consciousness encouraged them to regard working-class women—prostitutes or not—as easy prey, possessed of coarser natures and therefore a lesser breed of womankind than the middle-class "ladies" they intended eventually to marry.

New cities could be lonely places, particularly for working-class men and women struggling to cope with an alien environment. If possible, they would live near relatives who had already made the transition and who could assist the newcomers in adjusting to their very different existence. In many cities working-class families lived in districts inhabited primarily by others working at the same trade—weavers in one place, miners in another—and in this way achieved some sense of commonality.

Loneliness

A Laundress and Her Children. Note the cramped and cluttered living quarters.

Conditions in factories and mines

Adjustment to the demands of the factory was every bit as difficult for workers as was acceptance of urban living patterns. The factory system, emphasizing as it did standard rather than individual work patterns, denied skilled laborers the pride in craft that had previously been theirs. Many workers found themselves stripped of the reassuring protection of guilds and formal apprenticeships that had bound their predecessors to a particular trade or place, and that were outlawed or sharply curtailed by legislation in France, Germany, and Britain in the first half of the nineteenth century. Factory hours were long; before 1850 usually twelve to fourteen hours a day. Conditions were dirty and dangerous. Textile mills remained unventilated, so that bits of material lodged in workers' lungs. Machines were unfenced and were a particular danger to child workers, often hired, because of their supposed agility, to clean under and around the moving parts. Manufacturing processes were unhealthy. The use of poisonous lead in the making of glazed pottery, for example, was a constant hazard to men and women workers in that industry. Surveys by British physicians in the 1840s catalogued the toll that long factory hours and harsh working conditions were taking, particularly on young workers. Spinal curvature and other bone malformations resulted from standing hour after hour in unnatural positions at machines. Varicose veins and fallen arches were also common. One concerned doctor stated his belief that "from what I saw myself, a large mass of deformity has been produced by the factory system." And what was true of factories was true as well of mines, in which over fifty thousand children and young people were employed in Britain in 1841. Children were used to haul coal to underground tramways or shafts. The youngest were set to work—often for as long as twelve hours at a stretch—operating doors that regulated the ventilation in the mines. When they fell asleep, which, because of long hours, they frequently did, they jeopardized the safety of the entire work force. Women—sometimes pregnant women—were employed to haul coal and perform other strenuous underground tasks. Lung diseases—popularly known as "black spittle"—and eye infections, not to mention the danger of explosions caused by trapped gas, were constant threats to life and limb in the mines.

Daily routine

As upsetting as the physical working conditions was the psychological readjustment demanded of the first-generation workers in the factories. Preindustrial laborers had to work long hours and for very little monetary reward. Yet, at least to some degree, they were free to set their own hours and structure their own activities, to move from their home workshops to their small garden plots and back again as they wished. In a factory, all "hands" learned the discipline of the whistle. To function efficiently, a factory demanded that all employees begin and end work at the same time. Most workers could not tell time; fewer possessed clocks. None was accustomed to the relentless pace of the machine. In order to increase production, the factory system encouraged the breaking down of the manufacturing process into specialized steps, each with its own assigned time, an innovation that upset workers accustomed to completing a task

CAPITAL AND LABOUR.

"Capital and Labour." In its earliest years, the British magazine *Punch*, though primarily a humorous weekly, manifested a strong social conscience. In this 1843 cartoon, the capitalists are seen reveling in the rewards of their investments while the workers—men, women, and children—who toil in the mines under cruel and dangerous conditions are found crippled and starving.

at their own pace. The employment of women and children was a further disturbing innovation. In preindustrial communities, women and children had worked, as well as men, but usually all together and at home. In factory towns women and children were frequently hired instead of men: they could be paid less and were declared to be easier to manage. When this happened, the pattern of family life was severely disrupted, and a further break with tradition had to be endured. It is no wonder that workers began to see machinery itself as the tyrant that had changed their lives and bound them to a kind of industrial slavery. A radical working-class song written in Britain in the 1840s expressed the feeling: "There is a king and a ruthless king;/ Not a king of the poet's dream;/ But a tyrant fell, white slaves know well,/ And that ruthless king is steam."

Faced with a drastic reordering of their lives, working-class men and women reacted in various ways. Some sought "the shortest way out of Manchester" by taking to drink (there were 1,200 public houses in that city in 1850). Many more men and women struggled to make some sort

Escape

of community out of the street where they lived or the factory where they worked. It was a long and discouraging process. Yet by mid-century their experiences were beginning to make them conscious of themselves as different from and in opposition to the middle class that was imposing a new way of life on them.

THE MIDDLE-CLASS WORLDVIEW

Uncertainty and the need for reassurance

The middle class was not unaware of the many social problems it was generating as it created an industrial society. Despite its confidence that the world was progressing—and at its own behest—the middle class was beset by uncertainties. Its belief in its own abilities was shadowed by concern as to whether its particular talents might ultimately prove irrelevant to the preservation of prosperity. Self-assurance could dissolve in the face of bankruptcy, and prosperity vanish in the abyss of economic catastrophe. Those who had risen by their own exertions might fall victim to someone else's ambitions. Nor was it always a simple matter for the middle class to reconcile its own affluence with the poverty of the thousands of workers exploited under its aegis. The middle class was responsible for having wrenched European society out of old patterns of living and thrust it into new ones. To those willing to acknowledge that responsibility, the realization was enough to temper confidence with apprehension. No one was certain what the factory system and urbanization might eventually produce. Evidence drawn from the reports of various official commissions and from the intentionally lurid writings of sensational journalists suggested that city life was already spawning an underclass of men and women who preferred a life of promiscuity and criminality to one of honest toil. French novelists began to use the sewers as a metaphor to describe the general condition of urban existence for what was assumed to be a vast number of Parisians. Poverty and crime were linked together in the public—middle-class—mind, until poverty itself began to be defined as criminal. All this was part of a middle-class compulsion to rationalize its own prosperity, and to legitimize its ascendancy over the urban working poor.

Classical economics

To assist themselves in constructing this congenial worldview, the members of the new industrial middle class made use of the theories of a number of political economists. It is important to recognize that a factory-owner or a banker was not likely to have read the works of these theorists. He might, however, have encountered popular journalistic condensations of their ideas, or have participated in discussions at which the conclusions, if not the reasoned arguments, of the economists were aired. Because those conclusions supported his own interests, he grew familiar with them, until, in time, he could talk of the ideas of these men as if they were his own. Because this new middle class—itself a loosely united collection of experiences, goals, and beliefs—was sailing uncharted waters, its members not infrequently employed chunks of seemingly contradictory theories to bolster its own often contradictory aims.

The Interior of the Crystal Palace. This building of iron and glass was constructed to house the Exhibition of the Works of Industry of All Nations, held in London in 1851. The exhibition celebrated the triumph of middle-class industrialization.

We have noted already the manner in which the ideas of the economist Adam Smith sustained middle-class respect for individual enterprise (see Chapter 18). Enlightenment thought in general had extolled the virtues of individualism. John Locke, for example, celebrated the reason in men and women that allowed them to make intelligent choices based upon their own enlightened self-interest. Arguments such as these were reinforced by a second generation of economists—particularly Thomas Malthus and David Ricardo of Britain—whose writings embodied principles appealing to businessmen who desired a free hand to remake the economies of their countries. The chief elements in the theories of these economists were:

The importance of individualism

(1) Economic individualism. Individuals are entitled to use for their own best interests the property they have inherited or acquired by any legitimate method. People must be allowed to do what they like so long as they do not trespass upon the equal right of others to do the same.

(2) Laissez-faire. The functions of the state should be reduced to the lowest minimum consistent with public safety. The government should

shrink itself into the role of a modest policeman, preserving order and protecting property, but never interfering with the operation of economic processes.

(3) Obedience to natural law. There are immutable laws operating in the realm of economics as in every sphere of the universe: the law of supply and demand, the law of diminishing returns, and so on. These laws must be recognized and respected; failure to do so is disastrous.

(4) Freedom of contract. Individuals should be free to negotiate the best kind of contract they can obtain from any other individual. In particular, the liberty of workers and employers to bargain with each other as to wages and hours should not be hampered by laws or by the collective power of labor unions.

(5) Free competition and free trade. Competition serves to keep prices down, to eliminate inefficient producers, and to ensure the maximum production in accordance with public demand. Therefore, no monopolies should be tolerated, nor any price-fixing laws for the benefit of incompetent enterprises. Further, in order to force each country to engage in the production of those things it is best fitted to produce, all protective tariffs should be abolished. Free international trade will also help to keep prices down.

Businessmen naturally warmed to theories so congenial to their own desires and intentions. But Malthus and Ricardo made further contributions to the middle-class worldview, based upon their perceptions of conflicting interests within society. Malthus, in his controversial *An Essay on the Principle of Population,* first published in 1798, argued that nature had set stubborn limits to the progress of mankind. Because of the voracity of the sexual appetite there was a natural tendency for population to increase more rapidly than the supply of food. To be sure, there were powerful checks, such as war, famine, disease, and vice; but these, when they operated effectively, further augmented the burden of human misery. It followed that poverty and pain were inescapable. Even if laws were passed distributing all wealth equally, the condition of the poor would be only temporarily improved; in a very short time they would begin to raise larger families, with the result that the eventual state of their class would be as bad as the earlier. In the second edition of his work, Malthus advocated postponement of marriage as a means of relief, but he continued to stress the danger that population would outrun any possible increase in the means of subsistence.

Malthus's arguments, with their emphasis on the inevitability of poverty and misery, allowed the middle class to acquiesce in the destruction of an older society that had made some attempt to care for its poor. In Britain, for example, officials in rural parishes had instituted a system of doles and subsidized wages to help sustain laborers and their families when unemployed. The attempt failed to prevent distress and was met with increasing resistance by taxpayers. Now Malthus told taxpayers that schemes designed to help the poor damaged both rich and poor alike. Poor relief took money, and therefore food, from the mouths of the more

Malthus on population

Thomas Malthus

The application of Malthusian doctrine

productive members of society and put it into the mouths of the least productive. Malthus helped shift the responsibility for poverty from society to the individual, a shift appealing to the middle class, which wished to be freed from the burden of supporting the urban unemployed. The private philanthropy that took the place of poor relief and was strongly influenced by an evangelical religious impulse, allowed charity to be dispensed solely to the "deserving" poor, often through the activities of middle-class women.

Malthusian assumptions played a large role in the development of the theories of the British economist Ricardo. According to Ricardo, wages seek a level that is just sufficient to enable workers "to subsist and perpetuate their race, without either increase or diminution." This Ricardo held to be an inescapable iron law, in much the same way that Malthus had seen the interplay between population growth and the means of subsistence. According to Ricardo, if wages should rise temporarily above the subsistence standard, men and women would be encouraged to marry earlier and produce more children, the population would increase, and the ensuing competition for jobs would quickly force the rate of pay down to its former level. Ricardo devised a law of rent as well as a law of wages. He maintained that rent is determined by the cost of production on the poorest land that must be brought under cultivation, and that, consequently, as a country's population increases and more land is cultivated and higher rents are charged for more productive land, an ever-increasing proportion of the national income is absorbed by landlords.

David Ricardo

Here again, a theorist provided arguments useful to the middle class in its attempt to define and defend itself within a new social order. The law of wages gave employers a useful weapon to protect themselves from their workers' petitions for higher pay. The "inevitability" of both population growth beyond the means of subsistence and the negative effects of overpopulation on wages and rent helped neutralize the middle class's sense of personal responsibility for the plight of the urban poor. In addition, Ricardo's law of rent justified middle-class opposition to the continuing power of landed interests: a class that derived its income not from hard work but simply from its role as rent-collector was profiting unfairly at the expense of the rest of society and deserved to have its profit-making curtailed.

The uses of theory

As soon as the middle class began to argue in this fashion, however, it betrayed its devotion to the doctrine of laissez-faire. Businessmen and entrepreneurs vehemently opposed to government intervention, which might deny them the chance to make as much money as they could, were nevertheless prepared to see the government step in and prevent profiteering landlords from making what *they* could from their property. How could this apparent inconsistency be justified? The answer lay in the theories of the Britisher Jeremy Bentham, without doubt among the most influential of middle-class apologists. Bentham, whose major work, *The Principles of Morals and Legislation,* was published in 1789, argued against the eighteenth-century notion that a satisfactory theory of social

Benthamite utilitarianism

Jeremy Bentham

Utilitarianism's appeal to the middle class

Individualism and intervention

order could be grounded in a belief in the natural harmony of human interests. Men and women were basically selfish beings. To suppose that a stable and beneficent society could emerge unassisted from a company of self-interested egos was, Bentham believed, to suppose the impossible. Society, if it was to function properly, needed an organizing principle that would both acknowledge humanity's basic selfishness and at the same time compel people to sacrifice at least a portion of their own interests for the good of the majority. That principle, called *utilitarianism,* stated that every institution, every law, must be measured according to its social usefulness. And a socially useful law was one that produced the greatest happiness of the greatest number. If a law passed this test, it could remain on the books; if it failed, it should be abandoned forthwith, no matter how venerable. A selfish man would accept this social yardstick, realizing that in the long run he would do himself serious harm by clinging to laws that might benefit him, but produce such general unhappiness as to result in disruptions detrimental to his own interests as well as to those of others.

In what ways did this philosophy particularly appeal to the industrial middle classes? First, it acknowledged the importance of the individual. The interests of the community were nothing more than the sum of the interests of those selfish egos who lived within it. Each individual best understood his or her own interests, and was therefore best left free, whenever possible, to pursue those interests as he or she saw fit. Only when they conflicted with the interests—the happiness—of the greatest number were they to be curtailed. Entrepreneurs could understand this doctrine as a license to proceed with the business of industrialization, since, they argued, industrialization was so clearly producing happiness for the majority of the world's population. At the same time, Bentham's doctrines could be used to justify those changes necessary to bring an industrial world into being. Was the greatest happiness produced, British factory-owners might ask, by an antiquated electoral system that denied representation to growing industrial cities? Obviously not. Let Parliament reform itself so that the weight of the manufacturing interests could be felt in the drafting of legislation.

Utilitarianism was thus a doctrine that could be used to cut two ways—in favor of laissez-faire, or in favor of governmental intervention. And the middle class proceeded to cut both ways at once. Benthamite utilitarianism provided the theoretical basis for many of the middle-class interventionist reforms, such as a revised poor law in Britain and an expanded educational system in France, achieved between 1815 and 1848 (see Chapter 22). At the same time utilitarianism, combined with the theories of Malthus and Ricardo, fortified the position of those businessmen who believed that unfettered individualism had produced the triumphs of the Industrial Revolution. To restrain that individualism was to jeopardize the further progress of industrialization and hence the greatest happiness of the greatest number.

Political economists and philosophers in France as well as in Britain helped provide the new middle class with a congenial worldview. Count Claude de Saint-Simon, while a proponent of utopian schemes for social reorganization, nevertheless preached the gospel of "industrialism" and "industrialists" (two words that he coined). Disciples of Saint-Simon were among the leading proponents in France of industrial entrepreneurship and a standardized and centralized financial system.

Far more generally influential was the positivist philosophy of Auguste Comte. Comte's philosophy, like utilitarianism, insisted that all truth is derived from experience or observation of the physical world. Comte rejected metaphysics as utterly futile; no one can discover the hidden essences of things—why events happen as they do, or what is the ultimate meaning and goal of existence. All one can really know is how things happen, the laws that control their occurrence, and the relations existing between them. *Positivism* derived its name from the assertion that the only knowledge of any current value was "positive," or scientific, knowledge. Comte argued that humankind's ability to analyze society scientifically and to predict its future had reached a point that would soon enable Europe to achieve a "positive" society, organized not in terms of belief but in terms of facts. Such an achievement would not be a simple matter, however; "positive" attitudes and institutions could not replace those of the "metaphysical" stage through which Europe had just passed without a struggle. By dividing the history of the world into progressive stages (a "religious" stage had preceded the "metaphysical"), and by declaring that the achievement of the highest stage was not possible without the turmoil of industrialization, Comte assured the middle class of its leading role in the better world that was to be.

Auguste Comte

EARLY CRITICS OF THE MIDDLE-CLASS WORLDVIEW

The middle-class worldview did not go unchallenged. Many writers deplored the social disintegration they saw as the legacy of the Industrial Revolution. Others criticized the materialism and hypocrisy they saw as the hallmarks of the middle class. The Scot Thomas Carlyle, though a defender of the French Revolution and a believer in the need for a new aristocracy of industrialists ("captains of industry"), had nothing but contempt for the theories of the utilitarians. In Carlyle's view, they did no more than excuse the greed and acquisitiveness of the new middle class. Equally scathing in his attacks on the middle class was the English novelist Charles Dickens. In such novels as *Oliver Twist, Hard Times,* and *Dombey and Son,* he wrote with sympathy of the tyrannization of industrial workers by the new rich. In France, the Abbé Felicité Lamennais, though preaching respect for private property, nevertheless attacked self-interest. He argued, in his *Book of the People,* that the "little people" of the

Challenges to the middle-class worldview

John Stuart Mill's criticisms of industrialization

John Stuart Mill

Art for the middle class

world enjoyed far too small a share in the direction of their lives. Honoré de Balzac wrote *The Human Comedy* to expose the stupidity, greed, and baseness of the middle class. Gustave Flaubert, in his foremost novel, *Madame Bovary,* depicted the banal, and literally fatal, nature of bourgeois existence for women.

One of the most trenchant critics of early industrialization was the English philosopher and economist John Stuart Mill. Mill's father had been a close disciple of Bentham, and his son began his adult life a convinced utilitarian. A severe psychological crisis in early manhood compelled him to modify his acceptance of classical economic theory. First, he rejected the universality of economic laws. Though he admitted that there are unchangeable laws governing production, he insisted that the distribution of wealth could be regulated by society for the benefit of the majority of its members. Second, he advocated radical departures from the doctrine of laissez-faire. He favored legislation, under certain conditions, for shortening the working day, and he believed that the state might properly take preliminary steps toward the redistribution of wealth by taxing inheritances and by appropriating the unearned increment of land. In the fourth book of his *Principles of Political Economy* he urged the abolition of the wage system and looked forward to a society of producers' cooperatives in which the workers would own the factories and elect the managers to run them. On the other hand, Mill was no socialist. He distrusted the state; his real reason for advocating producers' cooperatives was not to exalt the power of the workers but to give them the fruits of their labor. In 1859 he wrote what many consider the classic defense of individual freedom, *On Liberty,* in which he attacked what he called "the tyranny of the majority." Yet his ringing defense of individualism was as much a treatise against middle-class conformism as it was against the threat of state control. "If all mankind were of one opinion," Mill wrote, "and only one person were of the contrary opinion, mankind would be no more justified in silencing that one person than he, if he had the power, would be justified in silencing mankind." Those sentiments were not the sort to appeal to a society determined to define itself in accordance with rigid codes of conduct.

Artists, too, attacked the values of industrial society in their painting and sculpture. The art preferred by the European middle class in the nineteenth century was that which in some way either told a story or, better still, preached a message. Beauty was surface decoration, which could be admired for its intrinsic richness and for what it therefore declared about its owner's wealth. Or beauty was a moralism, easily understood and, if possible, reassuring. When the Great Exhibition of the Works of Industry in All Nations was held at the Crystal Palace in London in 1851 to celebrate the triumph of industrialism, one of the most popular exhibits was *The Greek Slave,* a statue by the American sculptor Hiram Powers. Depicting a young Christian woman stripped bare and standing, according to the catalogue, before the gaze of an Eastern potentate, the work allowed its Victorian male admirers a chance to relish its salaciousness while also profiting from its depiction of the woman's righteous disdain for her captor.

Some of the artists most critical of the middle class, while repudiating the artificial and decorative, nevertheless reflected the middle-class obsession with art as morality. The self-designated Pre-Raphaelite Brotherhood of British painters was a group of men and women, led by the painter-poet Dante Gabriel Rossetti, determined to express its disdain for contemporary values. They called themselves Pre-Raphaelites as a way of announcing their admiration for the techniques of early Renaissance artists, untainted, supposedly, by corrupted artistic taste. Yet the works of the leading members of the Brotherhood exuded a degree of sentimentality that compromised their rebel nature and rendered them conventionally pietistic and ultimately innocuous as social protest. The same can be said, to a lesser degree, of the work of the Frenchman Jean-François Millet. His *Man with the Hoe* is a stark, bitter statement about peasant life; his *The Angelus* softens the statement to sentiment. In both England and France, however, some of the most talented painters seriously questioned many of the values the middle class revered. Gustave Courbet and Honoré Daumier both expressed sympathy toward the plight of the French working class, contrasting scenes of rural and urban misfortune with unflattering caricatures of the bourgeoisie. Daumier, in particular, was a powerful satirist of social and political evils, ridiculing the corruption of petty officials and the hypocritical piety of the rich. There was a harsh bite to most of the work of Daumier and Courbet that proscribed sentimentalizing.

These writers and artists, while critical of the Industrial Revolution and middle-class values, proposed nothing very tangible in the way of radical reform. If they opposed the triumph of a materialistic middle class, they opposed, as well, the idea of complete democracy. Carlyle, in particular, criticized the present by comparing it with a rosy past that had never been. In this he was like one of the doughtiest critics of the new middle-class society, the Britisher William Cobbett. Cobbett, in his newspaper the *Political Register,* argued against industrialization itself as well as its effects. His propaganda mirrored the dilemma most critics had to face, in asking the question: Although industrialization has brought great social and economic hardship in its train, does this mean that we should try to return to the life of preindustrial society, also often harsh, and always confining, though probably more secure?

For some time, a small band of thinkers had been answering that question with a resounding "no." They argued that there could be no return to old times and old ways, but that society could be at the same time both industrial and humane. These radical thinkers were often explicitly utopian. Two of the most persuasive were the Scotsman Robert Owen and the Frenchman Charles Fourier. Owen, himself the proprietor of a large cotton factory at New Lanark in Scotland, argued against

The Greek Slave, by Hiram Powers (1805–1873). The art of the bourgeoisie: titillation combined with a moral lesson.

Utopian thinkers

The Angelus, by Jean-François Millet (1814–1875). The artist's peasants accept their humble lot in this sentimental portrayal.

The Third Class Carriage, by Honoré Daumier (1808–1879). Daumier's realism did not mask his sympathy with the condition of the common people of France.

the middle-class belief that the profit motive should be allowed to shape social and economic organization. Having reorganized his own mills to provide good housing and sanitation, good working conditions, free schooling, and a system of social security for his workers, he proceeded to advocate a general reorganization of society on the basis of cooperation, with communities rewarding workers solely as a result of their actual labor. Fourier urged an even more far-reaching reconstitution, including the abolition of the wage system, the division of work according to people's natural inclinations, and the complete equality of the sexes. The numerous followers of Owen and Fourier sought escape from the confusions of the contemporary world in idealist communities founded according to the principles of their leaders. All these attempts failed after a time, victims of faulty leadership and, in the case of Fourierist communities in France, of charges of moral turpitude resulting from Fourier's revolutionary sexual doctrines.

Less utopian radical theories were proposed during the 1840s, years that witnessed recurring economic depressions and their horrifying consequences. The French politician and journalist Louis Blanc stood, like many contemporary critics, against the competitiveness of the new industrial society and particularly opposed the exploitation of the working class. His solution was to campaign for universal male suffrage, which would give working-class men control of the state. Following their triumph, these workers would make the state the "banker of the poor" and institute "Associations of Production"—actually a system of workshops governed by workers—that would guarantee jobs and security for all. Once these associations became established, private enterprise would wither through competition, and with it the state, for which there would no longer be any need. As we shall see, these workshops were briefly instituted in Paris during the Revolution of 1848. Another Frenchman, Pierre Proudhon, condemned the profits accruing to employers at the expense of their employees. He, too, proposed new institutions, which he argued could be made to produce goods at a price fairer to the worker, a price based solely on the amount of labor devoted to the manufacture of any particular product.

The theories of the writers and thinkers whom we have been considering—both the defenders and the opponents of the middle-class industrial world—are historically important for two reasons. First, their ideas helped men and women better understand the new social order that had sprung up following the French and Industrial Revolutions, and the part they might play, as members of a class, in that new order. Second, the ideas themselves helped inspire the concrete political, social, and economic changes and events that are the subject of the next two chapters.

The theories of Blanc and Proudhon

Louis Blanc

The importance of theory

SUMMARY POINTS

● Between 1800 and 1850, the population of Europe, in both industrializing and nonindustrializing countries, grew rapidly. The
quality of life for poorer and low-skilled people, particularly in
rural areas, remained very low, and in some areas even declined.

● Industrialization and the concurrent growth of cities facilitated
the emergence of an urban middle class, which developed a complex code of social conduct.

● Urbanization and industrialization drastically altered the life of
the working class, who labored long hours in harsh factories, and
lived in overcrowded and unhealthy conditions.

● Theories developed by writers and thinkers enabled society to understand, and in some cases justify, the new social order that
sprang up with industrialization.

SELECTED READINGS

Banks, J. A., *Prosperity and Parenthood: A Study of Family Planning among the Victorian
Middle Classes,* London, 1954. Relates middle-class financial pressures to family limitation.

Beecher, Jonathan, *Charles Fourier: The Visionary and His World,* Berkeley, 1986. A
thorough examination of the reformer in the context of his times.

Bridenthal, Renate, Claudia Koonz, and Susan Stuard, eds., *Becoming Visible:
Women in European History,* 2d ed., Boston, 1987. Essays on the slowly changing role of women in society.

Briggs, Asa, *Victorian Cities,* New York, 1963. A survey of British cities, stressing
middle-class attitudes toward the new urban environment.

Burn, W. L., *The Age of Equipoise: A Study of the Mid-Victorian Generation,* New York,
1964. A charming account of the mid-Victorian years.

Chevalier, Louis, *Laboring Classes and Dangerous Classes During the First Half of the
Nineteenth Century,* New York, 1973. An intriguing though controversial study
of the quality of life in Paris between 1815 and 1848, which concludes that
social mobility was downward and that fear of crime dominated middle-class
social consciousness.

Davidoff, Leonore, and Catherine Hall, *Family Fortunes: Men and Women of the English Middle Class, 1780–1850,* Chicago, 1985. A study of the lives and ambitions of several English families.

Foster, John, *Class Struggle and the Industrial Revolution: Early Industrial Capitalism in
Three English Towns,* London, 1974. A Marxist social analysis of industry in
urban areas.

Halévy, Elie, *The Growth of Philosophic Radicalism,* rev. ed., London, 1949. The best
introduction to the thought of Malthus, Ricardo, Bentham, and their philosophical heirs.

———, *England in 1815,* London, 1949. The classic work by the greatest historian of nineteenth-century England.

Hammond, J. L., and Barbara Hammond, *The Town Labourer, 1760–1832,* London, 1917. An impassioned account of the economic changes that affected the quality of life of the English worker.

Heilbroner, Robert L., *The Worldly Philosophers,* 6th ed., New York, 1987. An introduction to the thought of economic liberals.

Hobsbawm, Eric, *The Age of Capital, 1848–1875,* London, 1975. A perceptive world survey that traces the global triumph of capitalism and its impact on the working class, written from a Marxist perspective.

———, *Labouring Men: Studies in the History of Labour,* London, 1964. A series of essays on workers and the working class in England.

Hobsbawm, Eric, and George Rudé, *Captain Swing: A Social History of the Great English Agricultural Uprising of 1830,* New York, 1975. Analyzes the formation of a rural working-class consciousness.

Houghton, Walter, *The Victorian Frame of Mind, 1830–1870,* New Haven, 1957. An outstanding synthesis of Victorian middle-class mentality.

Langer, William L., *Political and Social Upheaval, 1832–1852,* New York, 1969. Comprehensive survey of European history, with excellent analytical chapters and thorough bibliographies.

Lynch, Katherine A., *Family, Class and Ideology in Early Industrial France: Social Policy and the Working-Class Family, 1825–1848,* Madison, Wis., 1988. A study of attitudes toward social reform and the role of the state as a social welfare agency.

McLaren, Angus, *Sexuality and Social Order: The Debate over the Fertility of Women and Workers in France, 1770–1920,* New York, 1983. Examines the relationship between private and public morality.

Manuel, Frank E., *The Prophets of Paris,* Cambridge, Mass., 1962. An entertaining introduction to the philosophers of progress, from Turgot to Comte.

Rostow, W. W., *The Stages of Economic Growth,* 3d ed., Cambridge, Eng., 1990. A synthesis by the exponent of the "take-off" theory of economic development.

Rudé, George, *The Crowd in History, A study of popular disturbances in France and England 1730–1848,* rev. ed., London, 1981.

Sewell, William H., Jr., *Work and Revolution in France: The Language of Labor from the Old Regime to 1848,* Cambridge, Eng., 1980. Examines the mentalities of workers' organizations.

Smith, Bonnie G., *Changing Lives: Women in European History since 1700,* Lexington, Mass., 1989. Analysis of patterns in the domestic and working lives of women.

Taylor, Arthur J., *The Standard of Living in Britain in the Industrial Revolution,* New York, 1975. A good introduction to the debate on the effects of industrialization.

Thompson, E. P., *The Making of the English Working Class,* London, 1963. Argues that the coincidence of the French and Industrial Revolutions fostered the growth of working-class consciousness. A brilliant and important work.

Shorter, Edward, and Charles Tilly, *Strikes in France, 1830–1968,* New York, 1974. A valuable study of early Continental class consciousness.

Tilly, Louise A., and Joan W. Scott, *Women, Work and Family,* New York, 1978. Deals with women in nineteenth-century France and England.

Walker, Mack, *German Home Towns: Community, State and General Estate, 1648–1871,* Ithaca, N.Y., 1971. Attempts to explain the absence of a strong middle class in Germany.

Consequences of Industrialization: Urbanization and Class Consciousness (1800–1850)

Engels, Friedrich, *The Condition of the Working Class in England,* New York, 1958. A much criticized but reliable firsthand account by the later collaborator of Marx, written in 1844. Presents a devastating portrait of living and working conditions, especially in Manchester.

Malthus, Thomas R., *An Essay on the Principle of Population,* London, 1798 and 1803. Malthus's famous essay relating population growth and food production.

Mayhew, Henry, *London Labor and the London Poor,* New York, 1968. A reprint of the 1851 edition; provides a fascinating view of the population and trades of London. A good factual companion to Dickens.

Mill, John Stuart, *Autobiography,* London, 1873. The intellectual coming-of-age of one of England's major nineteenth-century figures.

———, *On Liberty,* London, 1859. The classic defense of individual freedom.

Murray, Janet H., *Strong-Minded Women and Other Lost Voices from Nineteenth-Century England,* New York, 1982. Discusses women's attitudes toward important political issues.

Owen, Robert, *A New View of Society,* London, 1813. A proposed utopian society based on cooperative villages by the founder of British socialism.

CHAPTER 22

THE RISE OF LIBERALISM
(1815–1870)

The general thought, the hope of France, has been order and liberty reuniting under constitutional monarchy.
—FRANÇOIS GUIZOT, "Speech on the State of the Nation," 1831

T HE HISTORY of nineteenth-century Europe was to a great extent shaped by the interplay of the forces of liberalism and nationalism. The middle classes of France and Britain, where liberalism was strongest, espoused a set of doctrines reflecting their concerns and interests. Liberalism to them meant (1) an efficient government prepared to acknowledge the value of unrestrained commercial and industrial development; (2) a government in which their interests would be protected by their direct representation in the legislature—in all probability, a constitutional monarchy, and most certainly not a democracy; (3) a foreign policy of peace and free trade; and (4) a belief in individualism and the doctrines of the classical economists.

The components of liberalism

Many middle-class men and women in other European countries shared these beliefs and assumptions, and worked diligently and with some success to carry through specific liberal reforms. But for them, an equally important and often more immediate objective was the achievement of some form of national unity. The middle classes in Germany, Italy, Poland, and the Austrian Empire, however dedicated they were to liberalism, believed that their chances of achieving liberal goals would be greatly enhanced if they could unify the patchwork of principalities that surrounded them into a vigorous, "modern" nation-state. In this chapter, we shall examine the phenomenon of liberalism, primarily as it affected the fortunes of France and Britain. In the following chapter, we shall describe the way in which liberalism combined with nationalism to reshape the history of central Europe.

The compulsion of nationalism

CONSERVATIVE REACTION, 1815–1830

The growth of liberalism occurred, in part, as a reaction to the conservative policies adopted by frightened aristocratic rulers anxious to restore domestic and international order following the Napoleonic wars. For a

The conservative restoration

period of about fifteen years after 1815 the governments of most European countries did their best to stem the advance of middle-class liberalism. In most instances, however, their repressive policies only made liberals more determined than ever to succeed. The primary concern of governments was to ensure that Europe would never again fall prey to the sort of revolutionary upheavals that it had experienced during the preceding quarter-century.

Following Napoleon's final defeat at Waterloo in 1815, the major powers reconfirmed the Vienna Settlement in the hope that their efforts might result in a permanently stable "Concert of Europe." To further ensure an end to revolutionary disturbances, they formed the Quadruple Alliance—Britain, Austria, Prussia, and Russia; when France was admitted as a fifth member in 1818 it became the Quintuple Alliance. Its members pledged to cooperate in the suppression of any disturbances that might arise from attempts to overthrow legitimate governments or to alter international boundaries. At the same time, Tsar Alexander I, his mystic nature now in the ascendant, persuaded the allies to join him in the declaration of another alliance—a "Holy Alliance"—dedicated to the precepts of justice, Christian charity, and peace. The only result of this second league was to confuse Europe's leaders as to Alexander's intentions. Was he a liberal—a Jacobin even, as the Austrian Klemens von Metternich feared—or a reliable conservative? The confusion was cleared away, as in one country after another, liberal uprisings were stifled by stern repressive policies of the allied governments, Alexander's among them.

Liberal rebellions in Naples and in Spain brought the allies scurrying to a conference at Troppau in Austria in 1820. Secret brotherhoods, many of them composed of young army officers, had spearheaded these revolts. These organizations, which originated in Italy, called themselves *carbonari*. They were an active counter-reactionary force whose influence spread throughout Europe in the early 1820s. In both Naples and Spain, they succeeded in forcing reactionary kings to take oaths to establish constitutions modeled on the liberal French constitution of 1789–1791. At Troppau, Austria, Prussia, and Russia reacted to these threats to international order and absolutism by pledging to come to each other's aid to suppress revolution. France and Britain declined to endorse the pledge, not so much because they opposed repression, but because they did not wish to curtail their freedom of action by binding themselves to detailed international treaties. Metternich nevertheless proceeded, with Russian and Prussian concurrence, in a repression of the *carbonari* rebels through imprisonment or exile.

Two years later, in 1822, another congress was convened at Verona, Italy, this one to deal with the continuing liberal threat to stability in Spain, with the series of revolutions occurring in Spanish colonies in South America, and with an insurrection in the Near East. To resolve the Spanish problem, the French dispatched an army of two hundred thousand men to the Iberian peninsula in 1823. Without much difficulty, this force put an end to the Spanish liberals, who opposed King Ferdinand

VII's attempt to undermine representative government. The French assisted Ferdinand in restoring his authority to rule as he pleased. Contrary to their experience in Spain, the defenders of the status quo were unable to succeed in stemming the move to independence and liberalism in the colonies of Central and South America. In 1823 President James Monroe of the United States issued the "Monroe Doctrine," which declared that attempts by European powers to intervene in the affairs of the New World would be looked upon as an unfriendly act by his government. Without British maritime support, the doctrine would have remained a dead letter. Britain was ready to recognize the independence of the South American republics, however, since as new countries they were prepared to trade with Britain instead of Spain. The British therefore used their navy to keep Spain from intervening to protect its vanishing empire.

In the Near East, in 1821, a Greek soldier, Alexander Ypsilanti, was attempting to encourage the formation of a Greek "empire," to be constructed on vaguely liberal principles. In doing so, he had engaged his band of armed followers in battles against the Turks who ruled over Greece. Though Ypsilanti was soon defeated, his movement lived on. Five years later its aims had been narrowed to the more accessible goal of an independent Greece. Supported for reasons of Mediterranean naval strategy by a joint Anglo-French-Russian naval intervention, and by a Russian invasion of the Balkans, the rebels this time succeeded. Their success signaled the extent of changes that had occurred since the Congress of Verona. No longer could Metternich and other reactionaries build alliances on the assumption that, for the powers of Europe, preservation of the status quo was the major goal.

Rebellion in Greece

LIBERAL GAINS IN WESTERN EUROPE, 1815–1832

For a time, the conservative reaction of 1815–1830 threatened the liberal revolutionary and Napoleonic heritage in France. The upper-middle class in France had remained generally content with the domestic settlement agreed upon by the major powers in 1814 and confirmed at the Congress of Vienna the following year. Louis XVIII, a clever yet self-indulgent man, had "granted" a "constitutional charter" upon his succession to the French throne. While refusing to deny himself absolute power in theory, in practice Louis XVIII had willingly enough agreed to support those principles most desired by French middle-class liberals: legal equality; careers open to talent; and a two-chamber parliamentary government, with the vote confined to property-holders. Yet by basing the franchise on age and property qualifications, which made it impossible for the vast majority of those born after 1789 to participate directly in the government of their country, Louis's charter divided France in a way that would contribute to eventual instability.

Louis XVIII and the French charter

Charles X and the threat to
liberalism

In 1824, Louis died and was succeeded by his brother Charles X (1824–1830). Charles was an honest, determined reactionary, who once declared that only he and Lafayette had not changed since 1789— Lafayette was still a liberal, Charles still a zealous absolutist. By his policies Charles immediately declared himself a foe of liberalism, modernization, and the general legacies of the revolutionary and Napoleonic eras. At his direction the French assembly voted indemnities to those aristocratic emigrés whose land had been confiscated by the state. The Church was allowed to reassert its traditionally exclusive right to teach in French classrooms. The upper-middle class, strengthened by its role within the country's growing industrial economy, reacted by heading a rebellion against Charles's reactionary policies. In March 1830, members of the Chamber of Deputies, led by bankers, passed a vote of no confidence in the government. Charles dissolved the chamber, as he was constitutionally empowered to do, and called new elections for deputies. When those elections went against his candidates, Charles further retaliated with a series of ordinances, issued on his own authority, which (1) again dissolved the newly elected chamber before it had even met; (2) imposed strict censorship on the press; (3) further restricted suffrage so as to exclude the upper-middle class almost completely; and (4) called for new elections.

The Revolution of 1830 in France

What Charles got in return for these measures was revolution. Led by republicans—workers, artisans, students, writers, and the like—Parisians took to the streets. For three days, in intense fighting behind hastily constructed barricades, they defied the army and the police, neither of which was anxious to fire into the crowds. Sensing the futility of further resistance, Charles abdicated. Those who had manned the barricades pressed for a genuine republic. But those with the power—bankers, merchants, and industrialists—wanted none of that. Instead they brought the duke of Orleans to the throne as King Louis Philippe (1830–1848) of *the French*—not of France—after extracting a promise from him to abide by the constitution of 1814, which had so suited their particular liberal needs. The franchise was extended, from about 100,000 to 200,000 males. But the right to vote was still based upon property ownership. The major beneficiaries of the change were members of the middle class, those whose interests the Revolution of 1830 primarily served. Even the monarch was to remain relatively weak. He was in the words of one French politician, "to reign but not to govern."

Tories and Whigs in Britain

Liberal gains in Britain came after an era of reaction that paralleled that which occurred on the Continent. The conservative Tory party enjoyed almost unbroken political supremacy between 1783 and 1832. Though William Pitt the younger had begun his career as something of a reformer, the French Revolution had turned him, along with his fellow Tories, into a staunch defender of the status quo. The Tories' political opponents, the Whigs, had throughout the long years of the revolutionary and Napoleonic conflicts remained to some degree conciliatory to the French. But Whigs were as unsympathetic as Tories to democratic notions and as defensive of their rights to the full fruits of their property.

The July Revolution of 1830 in Paris. Workers construct street barricades in the narrow streets of Paris to ward off government troops.

Hence when rioting broke out in England after 1815 as a result of depression and consequent unemployment, there was general support among the ruling class for the repressive measures adopted by the British government. Spies were hired to ferret out evidence against popular agitators and legislation was adopted to stifle workers' protests. In the industrial north, where conditions were particularly severe, radical members of the middle and working classes capitalized on the general unrest to press their demands for increased representation in Parliament. At Manchester in 1819 a crowd of 60,000, demonstrating for political reform in St. Peter's Field, was fired upon by soldiers. Eleven persons were killed and over 400 injured, including 113 women. The massacre was thereafter called "Peterloo" by British radicals: i.e., a domestic Waterloo. It was the first of several repressive measures taken by the government to stifle reform. Another was the legislation known as the Six Acts, which was passed by Parliament in 1819, and outlawed "seditious and blasphemous" literature, increased the stamp tax on newspapers, allowed the searching of houses for arms, and restricted the rights of public meeting.

Yet within a surprisingly short time British political leaders reversed their unyielding opposition to reform. Instead, they displayed an ability to compromise which kept their country free from revolution. George Canning, the foreign minister, and Robert Peel, the home secretary, son

"Peterloo" and the Six Acts

The liberalizing Tories

The Peterloo Massacre, 1819. A contemporary rendering of the riot. The cartoon's caption condemned the "wanton and furious attack by that brutal armed force The Manchester & Cheshire Yeomanry Cavalry."

of a rich cotton manufacturer, were both sensitive to the interests of Britain's liberal-minded capitalist entrepreneurs. Under their direction, the government retreated from its commitment to the intransigent Quintuple Alliance; it was Canning who took the lead in recognizing the new South American republics. At home, these same politicians began to make order out of the inefficient tangle of British laws; for example, they abolished capital punishment for about a hundred different offenses. And Canning liberalized, though he did not abolish, the Corn Laws. These laws levied a tariff on the importation of cheap foreign grain. As such, they benefited British landlords, but hurt manufacturers, who had to pay higher wages to enable their workers to purchase more expensive bread. These "liberalizers" among the still essentially conservative Tories went so far as to abolish the laws that had kept both dissenting Protestants (non-Anglican members of Protestant sects—Baptist, Congregationalist, Methodist) and Roman Catholics from full participation in public political life.

Parliamentary reform

What the conservatives would not do was reform the system of representation in the House of Commons, heavily weighted on the side of the landed interests. Here the Tories, the majority party in Parliament, drew the line and showed themselves still basically committed to the status quo. Yet members of the liberal middle class argued that such a reform was absolutely necessary before they could themselves play a constant and active role in shaping British policy to comply with their own interests. "Interest" was, indeed, the key word in the debate over parliamentary reform. For centuries Parliament had represented the interests of landowners, the major propertied class in Britain. About two-thirds of the members of the House of Commons were either directly nominated by or indirectly owed their election to the patronage of the richest landowners in the country. Many of the parliamentary electoral districts, or boroughs, which returned members to the House of Commons, were controlled by landowners who used the pressure of their local economic power—or, in many cases, outright bribery—to return candidates sympathetic to their interests. These were the "rotten" or "pocket" boroughs, so called because they were said to be in the pockets of those men who controlled them. Those who favored the system as it was argued that it mattered little that electoral politics was corrupt, that electoral districts represented unequal numbers, or that very, very few (about one in a hundred) were enfranchised. What did matter, they claimed, was that the interests of the nation at large, which they perceived to coincide with the interests of landed property, were well looked after by a Parliament elected in this fashion.

Of course the new industrial middle class did not agree with the arguments of the landowners. It is important to note, however, that the liberal middle class was *not* arguing in favor of reform on the basis of a belief in democracy. Some leaders within the emerging working class did make this argument—and, as we shall see, continued to make it after a reform bill was passed in 1832. Most of those who spoke in favor of reform declared that the middle class was capable of representing the interests of the working class, as well as of itself, in Parliament. Reformers took this position either because they believed it, or because they were afraid of working-class representatives, or because they realized that to favor direct representation for the working class would frighten the more timid reformers and hence defeat their whole campaign.

The middle class and reform

Spurred by the example of liberal reformers on the Continent and by the oratory and organizational abilities of middle-class and artisan radicals at home, the movement for reform intensified after 1830. It was strong enough to topple the Tories and to embolden the Whigs, under the leadership of Lord Grey, to make a party issue of reform by introducing a bill to modify the ancient electoral structure of the country. The government was clearly frightened. Revolution, if it were ever to come in Britain, would come as a result of the alliance now threatening between middle-class industrialists and the artisan/tradesman leadership of the emerging working class. In Birmingham, a middle-class banker, Thomas Attwood, organized a "Political Union of the Lower and Middle Classes of the People." By July 1830, there were similar organizations in Glasgow, Manchester, Liverpool, Sheffield, Newcastle, and Coventry, some willing to engage in bloody clashes with army units and police. Middle-class shopkeepers declared their determination to withhold taxes and, if necessary, to form a national guard. Plagued as well by an outbreak of cholera, the country appeared to be on the verge of serious general disorder, if not outright revolution. The king, William IV (1830–1837), wrote worriedly to Lord Grey that "miners, manufacturers, colliers, and labourers" appeared ready for some sort of open rebellion. Sensing the grave danger of a possible union of the working and middle classes, the governing class once more accommodated change, as it had in the 1820s.

Alliance of middle class with working class

The Reform Bill of 1832, however, was not a retreat from the notion of representation by interest. No attempt was made to create equal electoral districts. The franchise, though increased, extended the vote to no more than 3 percent of the total population. It was defined in terms of the amount of property owned and the length of time one had owned it. In other words, the vote was granted to the middle class, but to very few of the working class. Probably more significant than its extension of the franchise was the bill's scheme for a redistribution of seats. One hundred forty-three seats were reallocated, most of them from the rural south to the industrial north, thereby increasing the political power of the industrial middle classes. Though the bill was the product of change and itself brought change in its wake, it was understood as a conservative measure. It by no means destroyed the political strength of landed aristocratic interests, though it reduced that strength somewhat. And it preserved the notion of representation by interest. The liberal, industrial middle classes had been admitted into junior partnership with the landed oligarchy that had for centuries ruled Britain and was to rule it for at least one more generation.

Efforts to introduce liberal political reforms were not limited to France and Britain during this period. Across the world, in Russia, a group of army officers revolted following the death of Tsar Alexander in 1825, in hopes of persuading his liberally minded brother, Constantine, to assume the throne and guarantee a constitution. In this case, however, the attempt at reform failed. Constantine was unwilling to usurp power from the rightful heir, a third brother, Nicholas. The officers, called Decembrists (because of the month of their rebellion) came from noble families and were members of elite regiments. Learned in the ways of the West, they had obtained a taste of life outside Russia during the Napoleonic wars, when they imbibed the ideas of the Enlightenment and the French Revolution. Politically, they ranged from constitutional monarchists to Jacobin republicans. Their failure was the consequence not only of repression by the tsar but

Russian Revolt of 1825. This contemporary watercolor shows the formidable opposition the Decembrists faced in the disciplined troops of the government.

also of their inability to attract mass support from rank-and-file peasant soldiers. Nicholas I (1825–1855) continued to rule in the severely autocratic ways Alexander had adopted toward the end of his life, creating the Third Section, a political police force, to prevent further domestic disorder. Nicholas's proclaimed goal of "Orthodoxy, Autocracy, and Nationality" meant simply that he would serve as God's lieutenant in an army in which the rest of his countrymen would labor as obedient foot soldiers. Yet even under Nicholas, perhaps Europe's most unremitting conservative, Russia showed signs of modernization. Bureaucracy, less dependent than in the past on the aristocracy, grew more centralized and more efficient. Laws were systematically codified in 1832. Stimulated by European demand for Russian grain, estates were reorganized for more effective production, and railways built to transport the grain to Western markets.

Other countries in Europe caught the revolutionary fever in the early 1830s. In Belgium, an insurrection that combined elements of liberal and national sentiment put an end to the union of that country with the Dutch, instituted by the Congress of Vienna. The European powers strengthened Belgium's political structure, and hence its independence, by agreeing in 1831 to the accession as king of Leopold of Saxe-Coburg, uncle of the future Queen Victoria of Britain. Once again, a middle class had succeeded in establishing a constitutional monarchy to its liking, congenial to its liberal and entrepreneurial goals. No such fate awaited the liberal nationalists in Poland, who in 1830 moved at this time to depose their ruler, the Russian tsar Nicholas I, whose hegemony extended to Poland as a result of the Vienna Settlement of 1815. Western Europe did not intervene; Russian troops crushed the Polish liberal rebels, and Poland was completely merged into the tsarist empire.

Liberal revolts in Belgium and Poland

Liberal forces in Spain enjoyed a greater success. There, middle-class liberalism was linked to the attempts of Queen Maria Christina, widow of King Ferdinand VII, to secure the throne for her daughter, Isabella. Though no liberal herself, the queen was prepared to court the favor of urban middle-class elites to win her struggle against her late husband's brother, the reactionary Don Carlos. During the so-called Carlist Wars, which lasted from 1834 to 1840, liberals extracted from Isabella II (1833–1868) a constitution that ensured them a strong voice in the legislature, while restricting the franchise to keep the more radical lower-middle and artisan classes at bay. By mid-century, however, fear of these radicals led the middle class to acquiesce in a government that was nothing more or less than an authoritarian dictatorship, but that did not threaten directly their own economic interests.

Liberalism in Spain

LIBERALISM IN FRANCE AND BRITAIN, 1830–1848

The Revolution of 1830 in France and the Parliamentary Reform Bill of 1832 in Britain represented a setback for aristocratic power in both countries. Aristocrats and their supporters did not cease overnight to play an

Middle-class interests no longer ignored

active role in politics, however. Lord Palmerston, for example, was one of Britain's most influential prime ministers at mid-century and one of Europe's most authoritative arbiters. But no longer would it be possible for the legislatures of France and Britain to ignore the particular interests of the middle class. Henceforth representatives would include members from that class in sufficient numbers to press successfully for programs that accorded with liberal beliefs.

The pace of liberal reforms in France was slow for a number of reasons. Industrialization was at its early stages and, though the Chamber of Deputies contained representatives from the upper-middle class, they tended to be bankers and merchants generally uninterested in free trade. The principal liberal gains in France occurred in the area of education. Under the succession of governments dominated by France's leading politician of the period, François Guizot, the French expanded their educational system, thereby further underwriting their belief in the liberal doctrine of a meritocracy, or careers open to talent. A French law of 1833 provided for the establishment of elementary schools in every village. Children of indigent parents were to receive a free education; all others would pay a modest fee. In addition, larger towns were to provide training schools for trade and industry, and departments were to provide schools for teacher training. As a result, the number of pupils in France increased from about 2 million in 1831, to about 3.25 million in 1846.

Little else of lasting importance was accomplished during the regime of Louis Philippe. Guizot became more and more an apologist for the status quo. Everyone was free, he argued, to rise to the upper-middle class and thus to a position of political and economic power. His advice to those who criticized his complacency was "enrich yourselves." Politicians followed his advice, finding in schemes for the modernization of Paris and the expansion of the railway system ample opportunities for graft. Louis Philippe did little to counteract the lifelessness and corruption that characterized his regime. Although he had played a minor part in the Revolution of 1830, he was no revolutionary. He did not have the dash and glamour of a Napoleon. He was a paunchy, fussy, and undistinguished person, easily caricatured by his enemies. He appeared to most to be nothing more or less than a typically successful plutocrat. He amassed a fortune that, in characteristic bourgeois fashion, he claimed he had accumulated in order to provide for his five sons and three daughters. He enjoyed the company of bankers and businessmen, though he attempted to develop a reputation as the friend of the people. Rumor had it that when he stopped to shake hands with shopkeepers he wore a special pair of dirty gloves, which he would replace with white kid when hobnobbing with the rich. Louis Philippe was unable to rise above his stodgy public image. The German poet Heinrich Heine reported that the young people of France "yearned for great deeds and scorned the stingy small-mindedness and huckstering selfishness" that the king seemed to embody.

The slow pace of reform in France

The reign of Louis Philippe

Louis Philippe

Liberal reforms made significant headway in Britain during this period. There were several reasons for this. First, the Reform Bill of 1832 gave the middle class a share of political power. Second, and in part a consequence of reform, Parliament was generally sensitive to the needs of industrialists, above all their desire for policies of free trade. And third, rapid industrialization compelled legislative intervention on a number of fronts.

The nature of this intervention was mixed. In some cases, as with public health measures, it created government programs designed actively to improve the conditions of life. In others, it applied laissez-faire principles with little concern for human consequences. The principal example of the last type of legislation was the passage of a new law governing the treatment of paupers. In accordance with a law passed in 1598, each parish in England had been declared responsible for the maintenance of its own poor, either through accommodation in poorhouses, or through a system of doles, coupled with local public employment programs. This system, although it by no means eliminated the debilitating effects of poverty, did provide a kind of guarantee against actual starvation. But by 1830 the system had broken down. Population growth and economic depressions had produced a far larger number of underemployed men and women in Britain than had ever before existed, placing tremendous strain upon those funds, levied as taxes, which each parish used to provide relief. Industrialization also demanded that families move in search of employment from one part of the country to another; yet the law as it stood provided assistance only to those who applied in the parish of their birth. The old law did not accord with liberal notions of efficiency; the new Parliament set about to amend it. The result, drafted by Jeremy Bentham's former private secretary, Edwin Chadwick, and passed almost without dissent, clearly reflected the liberal, middle-class notion of how to achieve "the greatest happiness of the greatest number." Doles were to cease forthwith. Those who could not support themselves were to be confined in workhouses. Here conditions were to be made so severe as to all

Liberalism in France and Britain, 1830–1848

Liberal legislation in Britain: the new poor law

An English Workhouse for the Able-Bodied Poor. This workhouse in the county of Devon was built in the late 1830s.

but compel inmates to depart and accept either whatever work they might find outside, no matter how poorly paid, or whatever charity their friends and relatives might be able to provide them. Parishes were to be grouped together into more efficient unions; the law was to be administered by a central board of commissioners in London. Inspiring this new legislation were the liberal belief that poverty was a person's own fault and the liberal assumption that capitalism, though unregulated, was capable of providing enough jobs for all who genuinely wanted them. Economic depressions in the early 1840s proved that latter assumption false and wrecked the tidy schemes of the poor-law administrators. Doles were once more instituted, taxes once more increased. Yet the law's failure did not shake the liberal conviction that poverty was, in the end, an individual and not an institutional problem.

Even more symbolic of the political power of Britain's middle class than the new poor law was the repeal of the Corn Laws in 1846. These laws, even after their modification in the 1820s, continued to keep the price of bread artificially high, forcing employers, in turn, to pay wages high enough to allow workers to keep food on their tables. More than that, the Corn Laws symbolized to the middle classes the unwarranted privileges of an ancient and, to their minds, generally useless order: the landed aristocracy. The campaign to accomplish repeal was superbly orchestrated and relentless. The Anti–Corn Law League, an organization of middle-class industrialists and their supporters, held large meetings throughout the north of England, lobbied members of Parliament, and, in the end, managed to persuade Sir Robert Peel, now prime minister, of the inevitability of their goal. The widespread suffering caused by the potato famine in Ireland was a further argument for ending restrictions against the importation of cheap foodstuffs. That Peel was willing to split the Tory—or as it was now coming to be called, Conservative—party to introduce repeal suggests the power of the middle class and its belief in the gospel of free trade.

Legislation during this period reflected other middle-class concerns, and in some cases directly conflicted with the liberal doctrine of nonintervention. Many members of the urban middle class professed devotion to the tenets of Christianity, particularly the doctrine that argued that all human beings have within themselves a soul that they must work to preserve from sin for their eternal salvation. This belief in the ability of an individual to achieve salvation, which contradicted the older Calvinist doctrine of a predestined "elect," accorded well with more general middle-class notions about the importance of individualism and the responsibility of the individual for his or her own well-being. It produced legislation such as the abolition of the slave trade in British colonies (1833), and the series of Factory Acts, which set limits on the working hours for child labor and which, in 1847, culminated in the curtailment of the workday in some trades to ten hours.

The religious issue affected educational reform as well. Britain had no comprehensive system of state education before 1870. What state sup-

Repeal of the Corn Laws

Robert Peel

Reform and religious belief

Opposition to educational reform

port there was came, after the 1830s, in the form of government grants to schools managed by the Church of England. Any move to increase this support, however, met with the strong opposition of middle-class dissenters, who saw it as no more than an attempt by the religious Establishment to extend its influence over the young. Middle-class liberals thus found arguments for reform confusing. The laws of classical economics clashed with other prejudices and beliefs, pulling men and women in various directions at once. Their uncertainty mirrored the extent to which no one could discern a right course in this world of new difficulties and fresh options.

Meanwhile radical members of the French and British lower-middle and working classes who had assisted—if not propelled—the forces of liberalism to victory in 1830 and 1832 grew increasingly dissatisfied with the results of their efforts. In Britain they soon realized that the Reform Bill had done little to increase their chances for political participation. For a time they devoted their energies to the cause of trade unionism, believing that industrial, rather than political, action might bring them relief from the economic hardships they were suffering.

Growing dissatisfaction of radicals

Trade union organization had been a goal of militant workers since the beginning of the century. Among the first workers' campaigns in the nineteenth century were those often-riotous revolts organized both in Britain and, later, on the Continent against the introduction of machinery. In some instances, factories were attacked by workers and machines smashed, in the belief that machines, by replacing skilled workers, were producing widespread unemployment. In Britain, the rioters were called Luddites, after "Ned Ludd," the mythical leader of the movement. In other instances, the hostility of trade unionists was not directed so much toward machinery as toward those workers who refused to join in unions against their masters. Yet nowhere in Europe were trade unions able to organize themselves into effective bargaining agents before 1850. They came closest in Britain. There, artisans and skilled workers had banded together in the mid-1820s to form both Friendly Societies (mutual aid organizations) and cooperatives (communal stores that cut prices by eliminating the middlemen between producer and consumer).

Trade unionism

In 1834, a new and potentially far more radical organization, the Grand National Consolidated Trades Union of Great Britain and Ireland, was organized by a group of London artisans. Its leadership declared that only by bringing the country to a standstill with a general strike could workers compel the governing class to grant them a decent life. At that point, the government decided to put an end to unions. In 1834, six organizers for the Grand National were convicted of administering secret oaths (unions were not themselves illegal) and sentenced to transportation (forced emigration to penal colonies in Australia). Subsequently employers demanded that their workers sign a document pledging their refusal to join a union, thereby stifling opportunities for further organization.

Radical trade unionism

After the defeat of the Grand National, the efforts of radical democratic reformers in Britain turned back from trade union to political activity, centering on attempts to force further political reform upon the uninterested government through the device of the "People's Charter." This document, circulated across the country by committees of Chartists, as they were known, and signed by millions, contained six demands: universal male suffrage, institution of the secret ballot, abolition of property qualifications for membership in the House of Commons, annual parliamentary elections, payment of salaries to members of the House of Commons, and equal electoral districts.

The fortunes of the Chartist movement waxed and waned. In some areas its strength depended upon economic conditions: Chartism spread with unemployment and depression. There were arguments among its leaders as to both ends and means: Did Chartism imply a reorganization of industry or, instead, a return to preindustrial society? Were its goals to be accomplished by petition only, or by more violent means if necessary? The Chartist William Lovett, a cabinetmaker, for example, was as fervent a believer in self-improvement as any member of the middle class. He advocated a union of educated workers to acquire their fair share of the nation's increasing industrial bounty. The Chartist Feargus O'Connor, on the other hand, appealed to the more impoverished and desperate class of workers. He urged a rejection of industrialization, and the resettlement of the poor on agricultural allotments. These polarities and disagreements regarding the aims of the movement suggest the extent of the confusion within the working class, whose consciousness as a separate political force was only just beginning to develop. Events answered most of the

The Great Chartist Rally of April 10, 1848. Undiscovered in the royal archives until the 1970s, this early photograph draws attention to the respectable attire of working-class radicals.

Chartists' questions for them. Massive petitions calling for the Charter were presented to Parliament in 1839 and 1842, while in the north of England Chartists aided trade unionists in attacks on factories engaging in unfair practices. Still reform evaded the Chartists. In 1848 revolutionary outbreaks across the Continent inspired Chartist leaders to plan a major demonstration and show of force in London. A procession of five hundred thousand workers was called to bear to Parliament a petition containing six million signatures demanding the six points. Confronted once again with the spectre of open class conflict, special constables and contingents of the regular army were marshaled under the now-aged duke of Wellington, hero of the battle of Waterloo, to resist this threat to order. In the end, only a small delegation of leaders presented the petition to Parliament. Rain, poor management, and unwillingness on the part of many to do battle with the well-armed constabulary put an end to the Chartists' campaign. Increased prosperity among skilled workers disarmed the movement after mid-century.

In France, radical agitation produced very different results. There, those who had manned the barricades in 1830 soon grew disgusted with the liberalism for which they had risked their lives. In their minds they carried memories or myths of the years of the first French Republic—its domestic accomplishments, its foreign victories, if not its Reign of Terror. They were opposed to constitutional monarchy and unenthusiastic about parliamentary government, especially by a *nouveau riche* upper-middle class. They were prepared, if necessary, to use force in order to achieve their ends. Centered in an increasingly industrialized Paris, they were for the most part either writers, students, or working-class leaders. They met in secret, studied the works of the radical theorist Gracchus Babeuf (see p. 706), whose socialist *Conspiracy of Equals,* written during the French Revolution, became their Bible, and succeeded in making constant trouble for the liberal, middle-class governments of Louis Philippe. Their leading spokesman was the socialist Auguste Blanqui. He decried the victimization of the workers by the middle class and helped organize secret

Radical agitation in France

Rue Transnomain. A drawing by Honoré Daumier (1808–1879) to commemorate the victims of government repression in 1834.

Louis Philippe in Caricature. In contrast to the portrait of Louis Philippe as he wanted to appear, on page 794, these 1833 caricatures by Charles Philipon depict the king as he increasingly appeared to his subjects and suggest the degree to which Louis Philippe failed in his attempt to celebrate the supposed virtues of the bourgeoisie.

societies that were to become the instruments of eventual insurrection. Radicals waged some of their most successful campaigns in the press. Honoré Daumier's savage caricatures of Louis Philippe landed him in prison more than once. But campaigners took to the streets as well. In retaliation, the government in 1834 declared radical political organizations illegal. Rioting broke out in Lyons and Paris in protest, where for two days government troops massacred hundreds of insurgents and arrested some two thousand republican leaders. In 1835, following an attempt to assassinate Louis Philippe, the government passed a censorship law, which forbade the publication of articles attempting to inspire contempt for the king and which prohibited the printing of any drawing or emblem without prior governmental approval.

These repressive measures served only to increase dissatisfaction

Increasing disaffection

with the regime. Guizot was advised by more progressive members of the legislature to extend the franchise to professionals whose lack of wealth now denied them the vote, but whose general adherence to the doctrines of liberalism was unquestioned. Guizot unwisely refused, thereby driving these moderates into the camp of the more radical republicans. By 1847, various elements within the opposition were disaffected enough to instigate a general campaign of agitation throughout France. At political banquets, republicans such as the poet Alphonse de

Lamartine and socialist republicans such as Louis Blanc (see p. 781) preached drastic reform, though not outright revolution. Contrary to the expressed wishes of the king, a giant protest meeting was announced for February 22, 1848. The day before, the government forbade the meeting. Rioting and barricading during the following two days ended in the abdication of Louis Philippe and increased demands for a republic.

THE REVOLUTION OF 1848 IN FRANCE

The February revolution in France was a catalyst which, as we shall see, helped to produce uprisings in the succeeding months throughout much of Europe. Meanwhile, in Paris, a provisional government was established consisting of ten men, seven of whom, including Lamartine, were middle-of-the-road republicans; three of whom, including Blanc, were socialists. The tensions between middle-class republicans and radical socialists, which had been masked by a common disgust with the government of Louis Philippe, now emerged to shape the political events of the ensuing months in several specific ways. Blanc insisted upon the establishment of national workshops, institutions he had championed as a writer, which were to be organized by trades as producers' cooperatives, where men and women workers would be trained if necessary, put to work, and paid two francs a day when employed and a smaller stipend when unemployed. Instead, the government established what it called workshops, but what amounted to nothing more than a program of public works in and around Paris, where economic conditions had resulted in widespread unemployment. Initially, plans had called for the employment of no more than ten or twelve thousand in projects throughout the city. But with unemployment running as high as 65 percent in construction trades and 51 percent in textiles and clothing, workers began to flood into the government's so-called workshops, as many as 66,000 by April, and 120,000 by June.

> Republican-socialist split: Blanc's workshops

Paris meanwhile attracted radical writers, organizers, and agitators. The provisional government had removed all restrictions upon the formation of political clubs and the dissemination of political literature. As a result, 170 new journals and more than 200 clubs formed within weeks; the Central Republican Society, the club headed by the socialist Auguste Blanqui, boasted a membership of some 3,000. Delegations claiming to represent the oppressed of all European countries—Chartists, Hungarians, Poles—moved freely about the city, attracting attention, if not devoted followings, and contributing to tension that was convincing more and more members of the middle class that stern measures were needed to forestall further insurrectionary outbreaks. This sentiment was fortified as a result of elections held at the end of April. The provisional government had been pressured by Parisian radicals into decreeing universal male suffrage. But an extended electorate was no guarantee of radical success: the

> Moderates elected by universal suffrage

election returned only a small proportion of radical socialists. The largest blocs consisted of "true," or moderate, republicans and monarchists—this latter group divided, however, between supporters of the Bourbon dynasty and those of the Orleanist Louis Philippe.

By late spring, a majority of the assembly believed that the workshop system represented both an unbearable financial drain and a serious threat to social order. At the end of May, the workshops were closed to new enrollment as a first step toward barring membership to all who had resided for less than six months in Paris and sending all members between the ages of eighteen and twenty-five to the army. On June 21 thousands of workers lost their state-financed jobs, and with them their best chance for survival. Desperate, they and their supporters once more threw up barricades across Paris. For four days, June 23–26, they defended themselves in an ultimately hopeless military battle against armed forces recruited, in part, from willing provincials eager enough to assist in the repression of the urban working class. Whether or not the Parisian insurgents were fighting as members of a beleaguered class, or simply as men and women on the brink of starvation, is a matter that historians continue to debate. That they were taken seriously as a revolutionary threat can be seen by the ferocity with which they were hunted down once the street fighting had ceased. About 3,000 were killed and 12,000 more arrested, the majority of whom were deported to Algerian labor camps.

In the aftermath of the "June Days," the French government moved quickly to bring order to the country. Assembly members therefore arranged for the immediate election of a president. Their hope was that a strong leader might assist in bringing dissidents to heel. Four candidates stood: Lamartine, the moderate republican; General Louis Eugène Cavaignac, who had commanded the troops in June; Alexandre August Ledru-Rollin, a socialist; and Louis Napoleon Bonaparte, nephew of the former emperor, who polled more than twice as many votes as the other three candidates combined.

The Revolution of 1848 in France. A contemporary broadside celebrating the triumph of the people.

The astonishing upstart Louis Napoleon had spent most of his life in exile. Returning to France after the Revolution of 1830, he was imprisoned a few years later for attempting to provoke a local uprising. But in 1846 he escaped to England, where he was supplied with funds by both British and French reactionaries. By the summer of 1848 the situation in France was such that he knew it was safe to return. In fact, he was welcomed by members of all classes. Conservatives were looking for a savior to protect their property against the onslaughts of the radicals. Workers were beguiled by the glittering schemes for prosperity in his book, *The Extinction of Pauperism,* and by the fact that he had corresponded with Louis Blanc and with Pierre Proudhon, the anarchist. In between these two classes was a multitude of patriots and hero-worshipers to whom the name Napoleon was a symbol of glory and greatness. It was chiefly to this multitude that the nephew of the Corsican owed his astounding triumph. As one old peasant expressed it, "How could I help voting for this gentleman—I whose nose was frozen at Moscow?"

With dreams of emulating his uncle, Louis Napoleon was not long content to remain president of France. Almost from the first he used the power he already had to achieve the further power he desired. He enlisted the support of the Catholics by permitting them to regain control over the schools and by sending an expedition to Rome in 1849 to restore to the pope the temporal power denied him during the revolutionary struggles of 1848. He courted the workers and the middle class by introducing old-age insurance and laws for the encouragement of business. In 1851, alleging the need for extraordinary measures to protect the rights of the masses, he proclaimed a temporary dictatorship and invited the people to grant him the power to draw up a new constitution. In the plebiscite held on December 21, 1851, he was authorized by an overwhelming majority (7,500,000 to 640,000) to proceed as he liked. The new constitution, which he put into effect in January 1852, made the president an actual dictator. After one year Louis Napoleon Bonaparte ordered another plebiscite and, with the approval of over 95 percent of the voters, established the Second Empire and assumed the title of Napoleon III (1852–1870), emperor of the French.*

What is the significance of the French Revolution of 1848 and its political aftermath in the history of middle-class liberalism, which is our subject? Two points need particular emphasis. First, we must recognize the pivotal role of the liberal middle class. Under Louis Philippe, it increasingly perceived itself and its particular interests as neglected. Denied a direct political voice because of a severely limited franchise, it swung to the left, allying itself with radicals who, by themselves, would probably have stood no chance of permanent success. Yet no sooner had Louis Philippe abdicated than the liberal middle class began to wonder if

Louis Napoleon's appeal

The Barricade, by Ernest Meissonier (1815–1891). The despair felt by the revolutionaries who survived the Revolution of 1848 in France is portrayed in this contemporary painting. Note that the barricade has been reduced to rubble.

The implications of the French Revolution of 1848

*Napoleon I's son, Napoleon II, had died in Vienna in 1832.

AU NOM DU PEUPLE FRANÇAIS.

LE PRÉSIDENT DE LA RÉPUBLIQUE

DÉCRÈTE:

Art. 1.

L'Assemblée nationale est dissoute.

Art. 2.

Le Suffrage universel est rétabli. La loi du 31 mai est abrogée.

Art. 3.

Le Peuple français est convoqué dans ses comices à partir du 14 décembre jusqu'au 21 décembre suivant.

Art. 4.

L'état de siége est décrété dans l'étendue de la 1ʳᵉ division militaire.

Art. 5.

Le Conseil d'État est dissous.

Art. 6.

Le Ministre de l'intérieur est chargé de l'exécution du présent décret.

Fait au Palais de l'Élysée, le 2 décembre 1851.

LOUIS-NAPOLÉON BONAPARTE.

Le Ministre de l'Intérieur,
DE MORNY.

Napoleon III's Decree Dissolving the National Assembly

"success" was not about to bring disaster upon its heels. And so it swung again, this time to the right, where it found itself confronting the mysterious and yet not entirely unattractive prospect of Louis Napoleon. He, in turn, was clever enough to understand this first lesson of 1848, that in France no government could survive that did not cater to the interests of the middle class. By assisting it to achieve its liberal economic goals, the emperor helped it forget just how heavily he was trampling on its political liberties.

Yet 1848 proved that there was now in France another element—class consciousness may, at this point, not yet be the correct term—that governments ignored at their peril. If mid-nineteenth-century Europe saw the middle class closer than ever to the center of power, it saw the workers moving rapidly in from the edge. Their barricades could, if necessary, be destroyed, and their demands ignored, but only at an increasingly grave risk to the fabric of the state. Middle-class liberalism, if it was to thrive, would not only have to pay lip service to working-class demands, but in some measure accommodate them as well.

Working-class demands

LIBERALISM IN FRANCE AND BRITAIN AFTER 1850

Napoleon III recognized the vital role that public opinion had now assumed in the management of affairs of state. He labored hard and successfully to sell his empire to the people of France. He argued that legislative assemblies only served to divide a nation along class lines. With

Napoleon III as dictator

power residing in him, he would unite the country as it had not been for generations. The French, who craved order following their recent political misadventures, willingly bought the program he was selling. Napoleon III modeled his constitution upon that of his uncle. An assembly, elected by universal male suffrage, in fact possessed almost no power. It could do no more than approve legislation drafted at the emperor's direction by a Council of State. Elections were manipulated by the government to ensure the return of politically docile representatives. Control of finance, the army, and foreign affairs rested exclusively with the emperor. France was a democracy only in the sense that its people were periodically afforded a chance, through elections, to express their approval of Napoleon's regime.

In return for the gift of almost absolute power, Napoleon III gave the French what they appeared to want. For the middle class, he provided a chance to make a great deal of money. The device of the *Crédit Mobilier,* an investment banking institution, facilitated the expansion of industry by selling its shares to the public and using its income to underwrite various entrepreneurial schemes. In 1863 a limited liability law encouraged further investment by guaranteeing that stockholders could lose no more than the par value of their stock no matter how indebted the company in which they had invested. Railways, owned by the state, spread across the country and spurred further industrial expansion. So prosperous did the French economy appear that Napoleon was prepared to follow Britain's lead in pressing for tariff-free trade between the two countries. A treaty was signed in 1860. Though funds were set aside to compensate French industries for any loss they might suffer, they were never completely expended, suggesting that French manufacturers were now well enough established to meet the threat of British competition. The apparent satisfaction of the middle class with Napoleon's regime provides a measure with which to assess the state of liberalism in France after 1850. The fact that the country no longer enjoyed a free press, that universities were politically controlled, and that political opposition was repressed seemed to matter very little to most. Liberalism, if it existed at all, existed as the freedom to have one's own economic way.

Napoleon III, though he catered to the middle class, did not fail to court the favor of the workers as well. He encouraged the establishment of hospitals and instituted a program of free medical assistance. More important, he permitted, if he did nothing to encourage, the existence of trade unions and in 1864 introduced legislation to legalize strikes. Ultimately, he appealed to the workers much as he appealed to the middle class, as a glamorous, if not heroic symbol of his country's reemergence as a leading world power. The activities of his court, and of his stylish empress, Eugénie, were well publicized. The reconstruction of Paris into a city of broad boulevards and grand open spaces was calculated to provide appropriate scenery for the theater of empire—as well as to lessen the chances for successful proletarian barricade-building across narrow streets.

Napoleon III

French economic prosperity

Empress Eugénie

Paris under the Second Empire.
The Avenue de l'Imperatrice was designed for the enjoyment of the middle class.

Grandeur, however, appeared to Napoleon III to demand an aggressive foreign policy. Although early in his regime he declared himself in favor of that central liberal tenet—international peace—he was soon at war: first against Russia in the Crimea; then in Italy; then in Mexico, where he attempted to assist in the establishment of another empire; and finally and disastrously with Prussia. The details of these adventures are part of the subject of the following chapter. It is enough at this point to remark that Napoleon III's foreign policy reflects clearly how far he—and the rest of France with him—had subordinated the liberal heritage of the first French Revolution to that of another of its legacies: national glory.

What, meanwhile, of the liberal tradition in Britain? There the course of liberalism was altered by changes occurring within the working class. Industrialization had, by this time, begun to foster and sustain a growing stratum of labor "aristocrats," men whose particular skills, and the increasing demand for them, allowed them to demand wages high enough to ensure them a fairly comfortable standard of living. These workers— concentrated for the most part within the building, engineering, and textile industries—turned from the tradition of militant radicalism that had characterized the so-called hungry forties. Having succeeded within the liberal economic system imposed upon Britain by the middle class, they were now prepared to adapt many liberal, middle-class principles to their own ends. They believed in collective self-help, achieved by means of co-operative societies or through trade unions, whose major function was the accumulation of funds to be used as insurance against old age and unemployment. They believed in education as a tool for advancement, and

A foreign policy of national glory

Liberalism in Britain: the "labor aristocracy"

patronized the Mechanics Institutes and other similar institutions either founded by them or on their behalf.

Yet the labor aristocracy, as it came to appreciate its ability to achieve a decent life for itself within the capitalist system, grew all the more dissatisfied with a political system that excluded it from any direct participation in the governmental process. Although some pressed for extension of the franchise as democrats, as many argued for it on the same grounds the middle class had used in 1832. They were responsible workers, whose loyalty to the state could not be questioned. As such, they were a bona fide "interest," as worthy of the vote and of direct representation as the middle class. They were joined in their campaign by many middle-class reformers who continued to chafe at the privileged position of national institutions that they associated with the landed society and the old order. Many middle-class men and women, for example, were dissenters from the Church of England; yet they were forced to pay taxes to support a church that was staffed, in the main, by sons of the gentry. Their sons were denied the facilities of the nation's ancient universities, Oxford and Cambridge, unless those sons subscribed to the articles of faith of the Anglican Church.

Together with working-class leaders, these middle-class dissidents organized a Reform League to campaign across the country for a new reform bill and a House of Commons responsive to their interests. Though by no means revolutionary, the reformers made it clear by their actions that they were determined to press their case to the utmost. Politicians in Britain in the 1860s were confronted by a situation not unlike that which had faced Guizot in France in 1848: middle class, lower-middle class, and skilled workers discontented and demanding reform. Unlike Guizot, however, the leaders of both British political parties, Conservative (formerly Tory) and Liberal (formerly Whig), were prepared to concede what they recognized would be dangerous to withhold. Once convinced of this need, the Conservative leader of the House of Commons and future prime minister, Benjamin Disraeli, seized upon reform as an issue with

Dissatisfaction with the government

Reform Bill of 1867

The Labor Aristocracy. These men were founding members of an early trade union. Having achieved a comfortable standard of living from their skills, they soon came to demand political rights as well.

which to belabor the Liberals. In 1867 he steered a bill through Parliament more far-reaching than anything proposed by his political opponents. It doubled the franchise by extending the vote to any males who paid poor rates or rent of ten pounds or more a year in urban areas (this would mean, in general, the skilled workers), and to tenants paying rent of twelve pounds or more in the counties. Seats were again redistributed as in 1832, with large northern cities gaining representation at the expense of the rural south. The "responsible" working class had been deemed worthy to participate in the affairs of state. For the next twenty years it showed its appreciation by accepting its apprentice position without demur, and by following the lead prescribed by the middle class.

The triumph of British liberalism

The decade or so following the passage of the Reform Bill of 1867 marked the high point of British liberalism. The labor aristocracy was accommodated with an Education Act, virtually guaranteeing a primary education to all, with legalization of strikes, and with a series of measures designed to improve living conditions in the great cities; yet it was the middle class that set the governmental tone. Under Disraeli and his Liberal counterpart William Gladstone, and with the cooperation of the newly enfranchised skilled workers, Britain celebrated the triumph of the liberal principles of free trade, representative—but not democratic—government, and general prosperity.

SUMMARY POINTS

- The years 1815–1870 saw the rise among the middle class of liberalism, a set of political and economic doctrines that espoused unrestrained commercial and industrial development, government representation of middle-class interests, and free trade, among other things.

- In Britain, and to a lesser extent in France, liberal riots led the governments to institute moderate reforms at first, to placate the demands of the liberal middle class. In Belgium and Spain, too, the middle classes succeeded in winning increased political power. After 1830, the pace of reform in Britain began to increase.

- Dissatisfaction with the slow pace of reform brought on radical agitation, which in Britain led to two major political reforms. In France, however, radical agitators were placated with meaningless reform or suppressed.

- Resistance to reform on the part of the government of Louis Philippe in France led to the Revolution of 1848 and the rise to power of Louis Napoleon Bonaparte, who ruled as dictator for nearly twenty years, maintaining his popularity in part by initiating reforms that directly benefited both the middle and the working classes.

- The new "labor aristocracy" in Britain joined forces with middle-class activists to demand political reform, which came in the Reform Bill of 1867, doubling the electoral franchise and redistributing parliamentary seats to benefit the urban working-class population. The succeeding decade saw further liberal reforms enacted.

SELECTED READINGS

Agulhon, Maurice, *The Republican Experiment, 1848–1852,* New York, 1983. A full treatment of the revolution in France.

Anderson, R. D., *Education in France, 1848–1870,* Oxford, Eng., 1975. Covers every level of formal education and its practical and theoretical relationship to state and society.

Blake, Robert, *Disraeli,* London, 1966. A masterful biography.

Briggs, Asa, *The Age of Improvement, 1783–1867,* New York, 1979. A survey of England from 1780 to 1870, particularly strong on Victorian attitudes.

Colley, Linda, *Britons: Forging the Nation, 1707–1837,* New Haven, 1992. An important analysis of the manner in which Britain gained a national consciousness in the eighteenth and early nineteenth centuries.

Duveau, Georges, *1848: The Making of a Revolution,* New York, 1967. Focuses on the working class during the revolution in Paris: their unity at the outset, their division in the "June Days."

Harrison, Royden, *Before the Socialists: Studies in Labour and Politics, 1861–1881,* London, 1965. Examines the social and political background of franchise extension in Britain.

Hobsbawm, Eric, *The Age of Revolution: Europe 1789 to 1848,* New York, 1970. An enthusiastic account of the period by an enthusiastic Marxist.

Johnson, Douglas, *Guizot: Aspects of French History, 1787–1874,* London, 1963. Analytical essays about the leading politician of the July monarchy.

Magnus, Philip, *Gladstone: A Biography,* London, 1955. A readable and reliable biography.

Merriman, John M., ed., *1830 in France,* New York, 1975. Emphasizes the nature of revolution and examines events outside of Paris.

Pinkney, David, *Napoleon III and the Rebuilding of Paris,* Princeton, 1972. An interesting account of the creation of modern Paris during the Second Empire.

———, *The French Revolution of 1830,* Princeton, 1972. A reinterpretation, now the best history of the Revolution.

Raeff, Marc, *The Decembrist Movement,* New York, 1966. Examines the uprising in Russia; contains documents.

Roberts, David, *Victorian Origins of the British Welfare State,* New Haven, 1960. Examines various nineteenth-century reforms in England.

Robertson, Priscilla, *Revolutions of 1848: A Social History,* Princeton, 1952. Surveys the revolutions across Europe.

de Sauvigny, G. de Bertier, *The Bourbon Restoration,* New York, 1966. An outstanding work; the best history of a neglected period.

Saville, John, *1848: The British State and the Chartist Movement,* New York, 1987. A detailed account of the movement's limited successes and ultimate failure.

Stearns, Peter N., *1848: The Revolutionary Tide in Europe,* New York, 1974. Stresses the social background of the revolutions.

Thompson, J. L. *Louis Napoleon and the Second Empire,* Oxford, Eng., 1954. A good biography. Presents Louis Napoleon as a modern Hamlet.

Wright, Gordon, *France in Modern Times: From the Enlightenment to the Present,* 5th ed., New York, 1995. The best textbook on modern France.

Zeldin, Theodore, *The Political System of Napoleon III,* New York, 1958. Examines the processes by which Louis Napoleon maintained power as the first modern dictator.

———, *France, 1848–1945,* 2 vols., Oxford, Eng., 1973–77. A highly individualistic synthesis of French history, remarkable for its scope and insight.

SOURCE MATERIALS

Flaubert, Gustave, *L'Education Sentimentale,* London, 1961. Contains an unsympathetic but memorable portrait of the Revolution of 1848 and of the bourgeois style of life that contributed to its outbreak.

Marx, Karl, *The Class Struggles in France, 1848–1850,* Moscow, 1972. A contemporary account and an example of Marx's early theorizing and of his skill as a polemicist.

Price, Roger, ed., *1848 in France,* Ithaca, N.Y., 1975. An excellent collection of eyewitness accounts, annotated.

Stewart, John Hall, *The Restoration Era in France, 1814–1830,* Princeton, 1968. A brief narrative and a good collection of documents.

CHAPTER 23

NATIONALISM AND NATION-BUILDING (1815–1870)

The present problem, the first task . . . is simply to preserve the existence and continuance of what is German.

—JOHANN FICHTE, *Addresses to the German Nation*

The great questions of the day will not be decided by speeches or by majority decisions—that was the mistake of 1848 and 1849—but by blood and iron.

—OTTO VON BISMARCK, speech, 1862

I F THE HISTORY of nineteenth-century Britain and France can be studied against a general background of middle-class liberalism, that of much of the rest of Europe during the same period must be understood in terms of a more complex combination of the forces of liberalism, nationalism, and nation-building. We shall define *nationalism* as a sentiment rooted in broad historical, geographical, linguistic, or cultural circumstances. It is characterized by a consciousness of belonging, in a group, to a tradition derived from those circumstances, which differs from the traditions of other groups. *Nation-building* is the political implementation of nationalism, the translation of sentiment into power.

Nationalism and nation-building defined

Nationalism did not arise spontaneously from within the consciousness of nineteenth-century men and women; it was a sentiment created by political or cultural elites to serve their own particular purposes, usually the linking of the individual to the state. It might be implanted by youthful Italian *carbonari,* determined to put that sentiment to the service of their revolutionary cause: the identification of national purpose with the idea of equal citizenship, that potent legacy of the French Revolution. Or it might be imposed by conservative governments trying to counter the socially divisive forces of urbanization and industrialization with an appeal to a common culture. To the extent that nationalism was implanted or imposed, it was an artificial construct, and not, as its proponents then—and as some historians subsequently—liked to pretend, the sudden awakening of slumbering, atavistic feelings buried deep within the collective consciousness of a "German," an "Italian," a "French," or a "British" people.

Nationalism as invention

Given its artifical nature, nationalism depended for its existence upon an increasingly literate population. Thus a "national" language was

Nationalism and literacy

imposed by state-supported educational systems that consigned more traditional dialects to the cultural scrap heap. Italian became the national language of that country when it was unified after the middle of the nineteenth century, despite the fact that only 2.5 percent of the population spoke it. That tiny percentage, because of its dominant position, managed to define a "national" culture. The adoption of a national language assisted nation-builders in winning the allegiance of the increasingly populous lower-middle classes—teachers, clergy, shopkeepers, and artisans—men and women whose status depended upon the ability to speak and write a language fluently. Textbooks, newspapers, and journals, and the self-consciously nationalistic prose and poetry that appeared within them, encouraged citizens to believe in a heritage that was being invented for them.

Nationalism and liberalism

Neither nationalism nor nation-building were necessarily opposed to liberalism. In celebrating the achievements of common people over those of a cosmopolitan aristocratic elite, nationalism reflected liberalism's abhorrence of traditional privilege. Proponents of economic liberalism welcomed sentiments that encouraged the development of a national economy, a move from smaller, inward-turning communities to larger, homogeneous—that is, national—units of production and distribution. As industrialization uprooted people from their local traditions, nationalism provided them with a new identification, one less politically and socially threatening to established order than that of class. Liberals thus acknowledged that nationalism could assist in the achievement of their goals. Yet to liberalism's readiness to welcome the future, nationalism responded with an appreciation, if not veneration, of the past. And to the liberals' insistence upon the value and importance of individualism, nation-builders replied that their vital task might require the sacrifice of some measure of each citizen's freedom.

British and French nationalism

Liberal politicians in both Britain and France invoked nationalist imagery. When Britain's prime minister Lord Palmerston declared in 1850 that any British citizen in any part of the world had but to proclaim, like a citizen of the Roman Empire, *"civis Romanus sum"* (I am a citizen of Rome) to summon up whatever force might be necessary to protect him from foreign depradations, he was echoing his countrymen's pride in the powers of their nation. When the French rejoiced in 1840 at the return of the Emperor Napoleon's remains from St. Helena to an elaborate shrine in Paris, they were reliving triumphs that had become part of their nation's heritage. Palmerston's boast and Napoleon's bones were both artifacts of national traditions and sentiments bound up in the lives of the British and the French.

Nationalism elsewhere

Nineteenth-century nationalism in other areas of Europe was to be an even more assertive phenomenon than it was in Britain and France, which had for centuries existed as particular geographical, cultural, and political entities. Elsewhere, common traditions and language were more difficult to impose, because the political unity that might have defined them did not exist. East Prussians or Venetians had no difficulty in perceiving of themselves as such; history had provided them with those

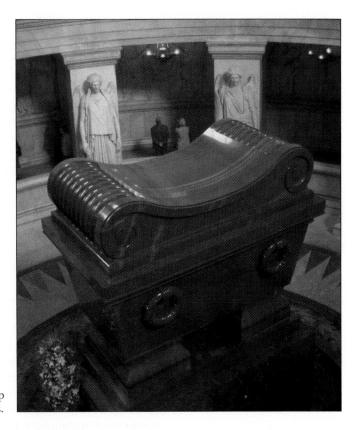

Napoleon's Tomb. The centerpiece of a group of buildings glorifying French military heroes.

identities. But history had not provided them, except in the most general way, with identities as Germans or Italians. They had to be compelled to think of themselves in those terms to a degree the British and French did not, before the terms themselves could have much reality.

In the Austrian Empire, nationalism asserted itself in a way that posed a constant threat to unification. The imposition of an Austrian national identity automatically called forth the counter-nationalism of Hungarians, Czechs, and others who quickly understood that assimilating into Austrian nationality would require an acknowledgment of their own cultural inferiority. The history of nineteenth-century Austria proved, in a specific instance, what the history of nineteenth-century Europe proved more generally: not all nationalisms could be accommodated, and nationalism, often seen as a sentiment guaranteeing order, might as easily produce disorder.

Nationalism in the Austrian Empire

The nation-building that was the political expression of nationalism, and that saw the unification of Germany and Italy, rested upon the foundation of a general balance of international power achieved by the European states during the half-century after 1815. The emergence of new nations would require readjustments in that balance. But accommodation remained possible, with only minor skirmishes marring the stability of the settlement achieved at the Congress of Vienna.

Nationalism and balance of power

Nationalism and Nation-Building (1815–1870)

Romanticism defined

As noted in Chapter 19, national sentiment was in part a child of the French Revolution. Nationalism was closely related, as well, to the intellectual movement that has been called "romanticism." Romanticism represented a reaction against the rationalism of the eighteenth-century Enlightenment. Where the eighteenth century relied on reason, the romantics put their faith in emotion. The eighteenth century understood the mind as a blank tablet, which received knowledge from impressions imprinted upon it through the senses by the external world. Romantics supplemented this reliance on sense experience with an insistence on the importance of the "soul"—that innate faculty that ordered sense experience within an emotional framework. One's individual soul mediated the sense experiences available to all, so that each person's response to the world was necessarily highly subjective, unique, and creative. At the same time, each individual was part of an organic whole, a nature that was unified, animate, and filled with "spirit."

Romanticism and individuality

One popular strand of romanticism was explicitly universal in its celebration of individual creativity. Men and women were declared free to interpret life in terms of their individual reactions to it, not simply as it might reflect a set of general rational precepts. The English poet Percy Shelley, the German poet Heinrich Heine, the Spanish painter Francisco Goya—all characteristic figures of the romantic movement—expressed in their works romanticism's concern for the experiences of human individuals. In addition romanticism encouraged women to make themselves heard: Madame Germaine de Staël, an emigré from France to Germany during the revolutionary period, whose essay *De l'Allemagne* (On Germany) was steeped in romanticism, and George Sand, whose novels and whose life proclaimed allegiance to the standards of radical individualism—these women exemplify romanticism's readiness to break with the past and its assumptions and stereotypes, if they stood in the path of individual expression.

Ludwig van Beethoven

Individual freedom and the problem of self-recognition were major themes in the works of two giants of the romantic movement, the composer Ludwig van Beethoven and the writer Johann Wolfgang von Goethe. The most remarkable quality about Beethoven's compositions is their romantic individuality. In the Fifth Symphony Beethoven reaches the summit of symphonic logic, the Sixth is a glorification of nature, the Seventh a Dionysian revelry. Goethe's dedication to the idea of individual freedom was, in part, the product of his having been born and raised in the free imperial city of Frankfurt. Frankfurt was an international center, a trading place open to intellectual winds from all quarters. The young Goethe published various romantically inclined works, including the immensely popular *The Sorrows of Young Werther,* a novel expressive of the author's early restlessness and emotionalism. The almost excessive sensitivity characteristic of Goethe's earlier writings gave way, in his middle years, to the search for a new individual spirit, equally free and yet more ordered.

An Illustration from Goethe's *Sorrows of Young Werther*

In 1790 Goethe published the first part of his masterpiece, *Faust,* a drama in verse, which he completed a year before his death in 1832. The play, in its retelling of the German legend of the man who sold his soul to the devil in return for universal knowledge, reflects the romantic unwillingness to restrain the spirit; it also expresses Goethe's own recognition of the magnitude of humanity's daring in its desire for unlimited knowledge and its own fulfillment.

Thus far, there would appear to be little linking romanticism, with its celebration of the individual, to nationalism, with its insistence upon the importance of community. Yet another strand within the romantic movement did forge just such a link. One of the earliest and most influential German nationalist romantics was Johann von Herder. A Protestant pastor and theologian, his interest in past cultures led him, in the 1780s, to set out his reflections in a lengthy and detailed treatise, *Ideas for a Philosophy of Human History.* Herder believed that civilization was not the product of an artificial, international elite—a criticism of Enlightenment thinking— but of the genuine culture of the common people, the *Volk.* No civilization could be considered sound which did not continue to express its own unique historical character, its *Volksgeist.* It was the particular genius not of one individual but of an entire people that Herder extolled as the *Volksgeist.* Herder did not argue that one *Volksgeist* was either better or worse than any other. He insisted only that each nation must be true to its own particular heritage.

Johann Wolfgang von Goethe

Herder and the *Volksgeist*

Johann von Herder

Georg Wilhelm Hegel

Fichte

Herder's intellectual heirs, men like the conservative German romantics Friedrich Schlegel and Friedrich von Savigny, condemned the implantation of democratic and liberal ideas—"foreign" to Germany—in German cultural soil. History, they argued, taught that institutions must evolve organically—a favorite word of the political romantics—and that proper laws were the product of national historical growth, not simply deductions from universal first principles. Thus the development of future laws and institutions must be predicated upon an understanding of a nation's past experience. This idea was not peculiar to German romantics. The English romantic poet and philosopher Samuel Taylor Coleridge argued against the utilitarian state and in favor of giving that ancient institution, the national church, a larger role in the shaping of society. The French conservative François Chateaubriand made much the same case in his treatise *The Genius of Christianity,* published in 1802. The past, and in particular the religious experiences of the national past, are woven into the present, he declared. They cannot be unwoven without destroying the fabric of a nation's society.

The theory of the organic evolution of national society and the state received its fullest exposition in the writings of the German metaphysician Georg Wilhelm Hegel, a professor of philosophy at the University of Berlin. Hegel wrote of history as development. Social and political institutions grew to maturity, achieved their purposes, and then gave way to others. Yet the new never entirely replaced the old, for the pattern of change was a "dialectic." When new institutions challenged established ones, there was a clash between what had been and what was becoming, producing a "synthesis," a reordering of society that retained elements from the past while adapting to the present. Hegel expected, for example, that the present disunity among the German states, which generated the idea of unity, would inevitably result in the creation of a nation-state. The institution of the national state was itself a natural historic organism; only within that institution, protected by its particular laws and customs from depradations, could men and women enjoy freedom, which Hegel defined not as the absence of restraint but as the absence of social disorder.

These theories of history and of historical development articulated by the romantics relate directly to the idea of nationalism formulated during the same period. The French Revolution provided an example of what a nation could achieve. Applying the historical lessons of the French Revolution and the theories of romantics, Germans were roused to a sense of their own historical destiny. The works of the philosopher J. G. Fichte are an example of this reawakening. As a young professor at the University of Jena, Fichte had at first advanced a belief in the importance of the individual spirit. Devoid of national feeling, he welcomed the French Revolution as an emancipator of the human spirit. Yet when France conquered much of Germany, Fichte's attitude changed dramatically. He adopted Herder's notion of a *Volksgeist;* what mattered was no longer the individual spirit, but the spirit of a whole people, expressed in its customs, traditions, and history. In 1808, Fichte delivered a series of

Addresses to the German Nation, in which he declared the existence of a German spirit to be, not just one among many such spirits, but superior to the rest. The world had not yet heard from that spirit; he predicted it soon would. Although the French military commander in Berlin, where Fichte spoke, believed the addresses to be too academic to warrant censorship, they expressed a sentiment that aided the Prussians in their conscious attempt to rally themselves and, as a political *Volk,* to drive out the French. One of the founders of the University of Berlin, the Prussian statesman Baron Karl Wilhelm van Humbolt, echoed Fichte's insistence on a special German *geist:* "Other nations do not love their country in the same way as we love Germany." That love, Humbolt insisted, was derived from "a longing for German feeling and German spirit." German nationalism insisted that romanticism's liberated individuals were, as individuals, unhappy and alienated. Only by fusing individuality with the collectivity of the German feeling and German spirit could they enjoy productive lives; and only through that fusion could the German nation assume its rightful place in history.

Nationalism was derived from varied romantic notions of historical development and destiny. The brothers Grimm, editors of *Grimms' Fairy Tales* (1812–1815), traveled across Germany to study native dialects, and collected folktales that were published as part of a national heritage. The poet Friedrich Schiller's drama of *William Tell* (1804), the Swiss hero, became a rallying cry for German national consciousness. In due course, the Italian composer Gioacchino Rossini turned Schiller's poem into an opera that was used to promote the cause of Italian nationalism. In Britain, Sir Walter Scott retold in many of his novels the popular history of Scotland, while the poet William Wordsworth consciously strove to express the simplicity and virtue of the English people in collections such as his *Lyrical Ballads* (1798). Throughout Europe, as governments began to impress a sense of nationality upon their people, they assiduously catalogued the relics of their historical past, as in the society for publishing the *Monumenta Germaniae Historica* (Monuments of German history), founded in 1819; the French École des Chartes (1821); and the English Public Records Office (1838). In France, the neoclassical style, typified by the paintings of Jacques Louis David and used by Napoleon to exalt his image, gave way to the turbulent romanticism of painters like Eugène Delacroix, whose *Liberty Leading the People* (1830) was a proclamation not only of liberty, but of the courage of the French nation. Music, too, reflected national themes, though not until a generation or so after 1815. Many of Giuseppe Verdi's operas, such as *Don Carlos,* contained musical declarations of faith in the possibility of an Italian *risorgimento:* a resurrection of the Italian spirit. The operas of Richard Wagner—in particular, those based on the German epic *Song of the Nibelungs*—managed to raise veneration for the myths of Nordic gods and goddesses to the level of pious exaltation. Architects, though they found it difficult to escape entirely from the neoclassicism of the eighteenth century, often tried to resurrect a "national" style in their designs. Sir Charles Barry, assigned the

An Illustration from *Grimms' Fairy Tales*

National themes in literature, art, music

Giuseppe Verdi

Raft of the Medusa (1818–1819), by Théodore Géricault. The painting itself became a political issue because the ill-fated ship was commanded by an incompetent loyalist to the Bourbon regime who owed his commission to political favoritism.

Execution of the Rebels on 3d May 1808, by Francisco Goya (1746–1828). Unlike most artists of his time, Goya dealt unflinchingly with suffering, violence, fear, and death. Depicting the execution of Spanish rebels by Napoleon's soldiers in 1808, this painting makes a powerful statement about the terror of authoritarian oppression.

The Massacre at Chios, by Eugène Delacroix (1798–1863). Delacroix was a romantic painter of dramatic and emotional scenes. Here he puts his brush to work for the cause of liberty, eulogizing the more than 20,000 Greeks slain by the Turks during the Greek war of independence in 1822. The painting is another example of the manner in which the emotionalism of romanticism came to the aid of reformist nationalism.

Liberty Leading the People, by Delacroix. In this painting Delacroix celebrates the triumph of the revolutionary principle of liberty in a tempestuous allegory that celebrates a national heritage as well.

Houses of Parliament, London. Redesigned by Sir Charles Barry with a Gothic facade after the earlier structure was destroyed by fire.

task of redesigning the British Houses of Parliament following their destruction by fire in 1836, managed to mask a straightforward and symmetrical classical plan behind a Gothic screen, intended to acknowledge the country's debt to its own past. All this creative activity was the spontaneous result of artists' and writers' enthusiastic response to the romantic movement. Yet politicians soon perceived how historical romanticism might serve their nationalist ends. They understood how an individual work of art, whether a painting, a song, a drama, or a building, could translate into a national symbol. And they did not hesitate to assist in that translation when they deemed it useful.

NATIONALISM AND NATION-BUILDING IN EUROPE, 1800–1848

Nationalism and reform in Prussia, 1806–1815

The humiliating French occupation of Prussia (1806–1815), combined with the growing sense of national destiny exemplified in Fichte's *Addresses* (1808), resulted in a drive on the part of Prussian intellectuals and political reformers to restore their country to its former position among European powers. Prussia's crushing defeat by the French in 1806 had been the logical outcome of the inertia that had gripped the country during the half-century or so since the aggressive achievements of Frederick the Great. Unlike the rest of the German states, however, which were allied directly with France in the Confederation of the Rhine, the separate kingdom of Prussia consciously avoided French "contamination," participating unwillingly in the Continental System and otherwise holding itself aloof.

Military reforms

The French invasion encouraged intellectuals like Fichte to make common cause with reform-minded soldiers and politicians. They labored to make Prussia into a power capable of defeating the hated French—evidence of the manner in which the existence of an external enemy can generate national sentiment. The reformers' major task was to rebuild the country's armies, since only by that means could Prussia reassert itself against Napoleon. To that end, two generals, Gerhard von Scharnhorst and August Gneisenau, instituted changes based on an essential lesson in nation-building they had learned from the French Revolution: that men were far more effective fighters if they believed themselves to have some direct stake in the wars they fought. A reconstituted national army, eventually based upon a system of universal military service, involved the country as a whole in its own defense and grew to become a far more consciously "Prussian" force than it had been before. Officers were recruited and promoted on the basis of merit, not birth, although the large majority continued to come from the Junker (aristocratic) class. This breach with tradition encouraged the Prussian middle class to take a more active and enthusiastic interest in its country's affairs. Old or inefficient officers, despite their social standing, were removed from positions of command; training at the royal cadet school in Berlin was modernized.

These reforms, which illustrate the way in which a liberal desire for modernization might combine with nationalism, paralleled similar changes instituted during the same period under the direction of Prussia's principal minister, Baron Heinrich Friedrich Karl vom und zum Stein, and his successor, Prince Karl August von Hardenberg. Stein was not himself a Prussian; he was initially less interested in achieving a Prussian nation-state than in uniting by some means or other all the various principalities of Germany. He had read Hegel and Fichte, and was convinced that a state must somehow make its citizens aware of their obligations to the national interest. Stein wrote that he hoped to bring about "the revival of patriotism and of a national honor and independence" so that Prussians would be willing "to sacrifice property and life" for king and fatherland. A sense of duty to the state could hardly be kindled, however, without first convincing men and women that loyalty meant reward as well as obligation.

Baron Heinrich Friedrich Karl vom und zum Stein

Stein's governmental reforms

Stein therefore labored to dismantle the caste system that had until that time characterized Prussia, in order to permit individuals to rise within society. The Edict of 1807 abolished serfdom and the estate system, ended the restrictions that kept nobles from selling their land to the middle class, and opened trades and professions to all classes. The Municipal Ordinance of 1808 was a conscious attempt to increase the middle-class Germans' sense of themselves as citizens—again, a goal shared by both liberals and nationalists. Cities and towns were henceforth required to elect their councilmen, while local justice and security continued to be administered by the central government in Berlin; all other matters, including finance, were left to individual communities. Education played a vital role in nation-building. Schools were ideal agencies for the dissemination of the doctrines of national duty. Recognizing this fact, the Prussian reformers expanded facilities for both primary and secondary education. The University of Berlin, founded in 1810, numbered among its faculty such ardent nationalists as Fichte and Savigny, and was the institutional embodiment of the new national spirit that contributed to Prussia's eventual victory over the French.

Economic nationalism

The history of Prussia between 1815 and 1850 can most easily be understood in terms of its continuing struggle to establish itself as the leading independent national power among the thirty-nine states that comprised Germany after 1806, and as a successful rival to Austrian domination. The most important Prussian victory in this respect was the establishment of the *Zollverein,* or customs union, which combined free trade within the German states and a uniform tariff against the rest of the world. By the 1840s, the union included almost all of Germany except German Austria, and offered manufacturers a market of almost 34 million people. The spread of the railways after 1835 provided easy access within this internal market. The writings of the economist Friedrich List justified this nationalist response to the internationalism of the liberal free-trade economists. List wrote that while free trade might suit the British, it did not suit a nation such as Prussia. Economics, he argued, far from being an abstract science equally applicable everywhere, was a discipline that must be grounded in the particular national experience of individual countries. Germany's, and therefore Prussia's, experience demanded not free trade but high tariffs. Only when sheltered behind a protectionist system could Prussia build the factories and manufacture the goods that would guarantee its economic health.

German liberalism thwarted

The events that had altered the political shape of Britain and France in the early 1830s—revolution in the latter and liberal reforms in both—had their counterparts in Germany. Liberals resented both Prussian dominance within the German Confederation and the conservatism of the ruling Habsburgs in the Austrian Empire. The governments of both Prussia and Austria were grounded in a combination of autocracy and bureaucracy that stifled the social and political goals of the liberals, who hoped for the achievement of both unity and freedom. The creation of a German nation would lead to the realization of liberal goals, while avoiding the particularism that had haunted Germany's political past and the domination by either Austria or Prussia that promised to blight its future. Student societies—*Burschenschaften*—had sprung up throughout Germany following the Napoleonic wars. At an assembly in 1817 at Wartburg Castle, where Martin Luther had three hundred years before proclaimed his ninety-five theses, these modern protestants on behalf of "the holy cause of union and freedom" marched to a bonfire upon which they placed the works of reactionary writers. Repressed for a time by Metternich, who was by now the Austrian chancellor, the *Burschenschaften* reappeared in the late 1820s and welcomed the 1830 revolution in France. Minor revolts occurred in Brunswick, Saxony, and Hesse-Cassel; unpopular monarchs were replaced by royal relatives more sympathetic to reform. In 1832 at an all-German festival held at Hambach, on the French border, twenty-five thousand men and women toasted Lafayette and denounced the Holy Alliance. The activities of the *Burschenschaften* bespoke a form of nationalism linked to the ideals of the French Revolution, and therefore anathema to the German and Austrian political establishment. "The holy cause of union and freedom" might be a rallying cry against Austrian domination of central Europe, but "freedom" was a slippery term, and, in the minds of conservatives, a signal that national sentiments might easily be joined with democratic aspirations. Once again, Metternich imposed a series of repressive reforms upon the German Confederation, which effectively stifled protest and thwarted youthful aspirations.

Prussia avoided revolution as a result of the reforms instituted a generation before by Stein and Hardenberg. In 1840 Frederick William IV (1840–1861) succeeded to the Prussian throne. Apparently devoted to liberal principles, he relaxed censorship laws and encouraged participation in the central government by provincial diets. It soon became apparent, however, that the king was no liberal, but some sort of romantic nationalist, and an authoritarian as well. He crushed the revolt of thousands of Silesian weavers in 1844, when they protested the importation of English yarn and cotton goods and their consequent unemployment and poverty. He further declared himself opposed to constitutionalism, that central doctrine in the liberal canon of beliefs. When Prussian liberals pressed, in 1847, for control over legislative and budgetary matters in the recently convened assembly of diets (the *Landtag*), the king saw to it that their request was denied. Frederick William then turned his attention to a scheme whereby Prussia might play a far larger role in the German Confederation. But before his plan could receive a hearing, it was overtaken by the revolutionary movement of 1848, which, as we shall see, engulfed central Europe as it had western Europe, though with different results.

Nationalist sentiment, the spirit that served to unite the Prussians against France, was at the same time operating to divide the heterogeneous elements within the Austrian Empire. Its people, who lived within three major geographical areas—Austria, Bohemia, and Hungary—were composed of a considerable number of different ethnic and language groups: Germans, Czechs, Magyars, Poles, Slovaks, Serbs, and Italians, to name the most prominent. In some parts of the empire, these people lived in isolation; elsewhere they dwelt in direct proximity, if not much harmony, with others. The Habsburgs' attempts to unite these groups failed increasingly, as a spirit of cultural nationalism grew persistently stronger in the years after 1815. In the Polish territories of the empire, where the gentry had for generations been conscious of themselves as Poles, the imperial government succeeded in stifling the sentiment by playing off the

The politics of Frederick William IV

Nationalism in the Austrian Empire

serfs against their masters, encouraging a class war as a means of preventing an ethnic one. Elsewhere within the empire they were less adroit. In Hungary, nationalism expressed itself in both cultural and political forms. In 1827, a Hungarian national theater was established at Budapest. The year before, Magyar was substituted for Latin as the official language of government. A political movement, whose most formidable leader was the radical nationalist Louis Kossuth, was at the same time seeking independence and a parliamentary government for Hungary.

Pan-Slavism

The most widespread of the eastern European cultural nationalist movements was Pan-Slavism. Slavs included Russians, Poles, Czechs, Slovaks, Slovenes, Croats, Serbs, and Bulgars. Before 1848 Pan-Slavism was an almost exclusively cultural movement, united by a generalized anti-Western, pro-Slavic sentiment, yet divided by a tendency to quarrel as to the primacy of this or that particular language or tradition. These divisions did not substantially lessen the effect of Pan-Slavism as a further problem of the Austrian Empire. The literature of the movement—for example, the historian Francis Palacky's *History of the Bohemian People* and the poetry of the revolutionary Pole Adam Mickiewicz—fed the desires of those who wished to rid themselves of what they considered a foreign yoke. In Russia, extreme nationalism had been held in check by the Western-looking Alexander I. After his death in 1825, however, the notion that the Russian people possessed a particular *Volksgeist* increased in general popularity. At the same time, the many ethnic minorities within Russia began pressing for their own recognition.

Nationalism in Italy

Two other nationalist movements were growing beyond infancy during the years before 1848: one in Italy, the other in Ireland. Italy, at the beginning of the nineteenth century, was a peninsula divided into a multitude of states, most of them poor and ineffectually governed. The most efficient governments in Italy after 1815 were those imposed by Austria on the northern territories of Lombardy and Venetia (see map, p. 836) and by the reform-minded king of Sardinia, Charles Albert (1831–1849). At the opposite pole were the Kingdom of the Two Sicilies and the Papal States, governed by equally obscurantist rulers, Francis I (1825–1830), a Bourbon, and thereafter by his son, Ferdinand II (1830–1859), and Pope Gregory XVI (1831–1846). Popular uprisings in Modena, Parma, and Bologna occurred in 1830, but with no lasting consequences, either for the initiation of local liberal reforms or for the cause of unification of the various disparate states into some sort of national whole. Among the pan-Italian organizations formed in the confused period at the end of the Napoleonic wars, none was louder in its nationalist proclamations than the Italian *carbonari*. One member of that group, Giuseppe Mazzini, founded a society of his own in 1831, Young Italy, which was dedicated to the cause of uniting the peninsula. In 1834, from Switzerland, Mazzini launched a totally unsuccessful verbal assault against the Kingdom of Sardinia, in the hope that the rest of Italy would join him. Mazzini subsequently contented himself with propagandizing for the cause of Italian nationalism and republicanism, attracting a devoted following, particu-

Giuseppe Mazzini

larly among British liberals. Liberals in Italy, however, mistrusted him. Although they too wished to see a united Italy, they were dismayed, as "good" liberals and members of the middle class, by Mazzini's insistence upon a republic; they hoped instead to merge existing principalities together into some sort of constitutional monarchy.

If Italian nationalism was primarily a middle-class liberal phenomenon at this time, the same was not true of the Irish movement to repeal the union with Britain. Headed by Daniel O'Connell, it derived its strength from the support of Irish peasants. O'Connell's remarkably successful appeal was based on the hatred all Irish felt for the British because of the centuries of oppression Irish Catholics had suffered under British Protestant rule. Both before and after the official union of 1801, the British had imposed on the Irish a foreign rule that had brought with it little but poverty and persecution. O'Connell's campaign for the repeal of the union was grounded in the hope that he would be able to negotiate some sort of moderate agreement with the British ruling class. The desires of his followers were far more radical. Neither the separatist hopes of O'Connell, called by the Irish the "Liberator," nor the more genuinely nationalist hopes of his followers, however, were to achieve realization. Unlike the nationalist movements of central Europe, nationalism in Ireland faced a powerful and determined adversary—Britain—which would for a century deny it victory.

NATIONALISM, LIBERALISM, AND REVOLUTION, 1848

The history of the revolutions of 1848 in central Europe can most easily be understood in terms of two major themes: the first, the struggle of various nationalities, particularly within the Austrian Empire, to assert their own autonomy; the second, the changing relationship between the forces of liberalism and nationalism in Germany.

News of the February revolution in France traveled quickly eastward. By the end of March the Austrian Empire was split apart. Hungary, with Kossuth in the lead, severed all but the most tenuous of links with the House of Habsburg and prepared to draft its own constitution. In Vienna, workers and students imitated their counterparts in Paris, erecting barricades and invading the imperial palace. A measure of the political chaos was the fact that Metternich, veteran of a score of threats to the precarious stability he had crafted, found the pressure this time too great, and fled in disguise to Britain. The feeble Habsburg emperor, Ferdinand II, once he had been deserted by Metternich, yielded to nationalist demands from Bohemia and granted that kingdom its own constitution as well. To the south, Italians launched attacks against the Austrian-held territories in Milan, Naples, Venetia, and Lombardy, where the forces of the Sardinian ruler, King Charles Albert, routed the Austrians.

Yet the forces of national sentiment that had brought Austria to its knees then succeeded in allowing the empire to recoup its fortunes. The

The "March Days" in Vienna. The revolutionary fervor of 1848 transcended class boundaries. In this watercolor a student leads armed railway workers to the center of Vienna.

paradox of nationalism in central Europe was that as soon as a cultural majority had declared itself an independent or semi-independent state, other cultural minorities within that new state complained bitterly about their newly institutionalized inferiority. This is precisely what happened in Bohemia. There the anti-German Czech majority refused to send delegates to an all-German assembly, which was meeting at Frankfurt in May 1848 to draft a German constitution. Instead, they summoned a confederation of Slavs to Prague. The delegates, most of them from within the boundaries of the old Austrian Empire, immediately recognized that the idea of a united Germany represented a far greater threat to their political and cultural autonomy than the fact of the empire ever had. The German minority in Bohemia, however, was naturally anxious to participate in discussions that might result in closer union with their ethnic counterparts. They resented the Bohemian government's refusal to do so. The resulting animosities made it all the easier for the Austrians to take advantage of a May 1848 insurrection in Prague, subdue the city, send the Slav congress packing, and reassert control in Bohemia. Although the Austrian government was at this time a liberal one, the product of the March revolution in Vienna, it was no less determined than its predecessor had been to prevent the total dismemberment of the empire, for economic as well as political reasons. Hence it was quick to restore Lombardy and Venetia to its realm when quarrels among the heretofore united Italian allies had sufficiently weakened their common stand against the Austrians.

Nationalism and counternationalism in Hungary set the stage for the final act of the restoration of Austrian hegemony. Kossuth's radical party was, above all, a Magyar nationalist party. Once in power, in early 1849 it moved the capital from Pressburg, near the Austrian border, to Budapest, and again proclaimed Magyar as the country's official language. These actions offended national minorities within Hungary, particularly the Croa-

Civil war in Hungary

tians, who prior to the revolution had enjoyed certain liberties under Austrian rule. The Croatians raised an insurgent army and launched a civil war. The Austrians, once more encouraging division along nationalist lines, named the Croatian rebel Josef von Jellachich their military commander against the Magyars. By this time the Viennese liberals began to recognize—too late—that their turn might come next. They were right. Despite a second uprising in Vienna in October, the revolution was spent. Forces loyal to the emperor, assisted by troops from Russia, descended upon Vienna. On October 31, the liberal government capitulated.

Once the imperial government had reasserted itself, it labored to suppress nationalist impulses as thoroughly as possible. Austria's ministers recognized that, though tactically advantageous at times, nationalist movements operated generally to the detriment of the empire's political and economic unity. The emperor's chief minister, Prince Felix von Schwarzenberg, and the minister of the interior, Alexander Bach, both nation-builders, together centralized the state within one united political system. Hungary and Bohemia no longer enjoyed separate rights. Peasants of all ethnic groups, liberated from serfdom as part of the general reform movement, were permitted to retain their freedom on the grounds of their loyalty to the empire. The law was reformed, again to achieve uniformity, and railways and roads were constructed to link the empire. Economic nationalism was encouraged through tariffs designed to exclude foreign manufactures, while a free trade area within the empire encouraged domestic industries. Having done all it could to eradicate separatist movements, the Austrian government thus moved to secure its advantage by engaging in a vigorous campaign of nation-building.

In Prussia, revolution ran a similar course. In March, King Frederick William IV found himself compelled to yield to demands for a popularly elected legislative assembly. When it met, the body proved particularly sympathetic to the plight of the Polish minority within Prussia, and antagonistic toward the Russians, whom radical legislators saw as the major threat to the spread of enlightened political ideas in central Europe. When the assembly's sympathy with Polish nationalism extended to the granting of self-government to Prussian Poland, however, it generated the same feelings among the German minority there that we have seen arousing minorities within the Austrian Empire. In so doing, it precipitated the same eventual results. Germans in Posen, the major city of Prussian Poland, revolted against the newly established Polish government; not surprisingly, Prussian army units on duty sided with the Germans and helped them crush the new government. Power, it now became clear, lay with the army, professionalized since the days of Gneisenau and Scharnhorst, yet still dominated by the Junkers. Against the armed authority of the military, the radical legislators of Berlin were no match; revolution ended in Prussia as quickly as it had begun.

Meanwhile, at Frankfurt, Germans engaged in the debate that provides the history of central Europe in these revolutionary years with its second theme: the shifting relationship between liberalism and nationalism.

Imperial nation-building

The failure of revolution in Prussia

The Frankfurt Assembly

Procession of the German National Assembly to Its Opening Session at St. Paul's Church, Frankfurt, May 1848

Delegates had been chosen from across Germany and Austria to attend the Frankfurt Assembly. They were largely from the professional classes—professors, lawyers, administrators—and generally devoted to the cause of middle-class liberalism. Many had assumed that their task would resemble that of the assembly that had met in 1789 to draft a constitution for the French: i.e., they would draft a constitution for a liberal, unified Germany. That former convocation, however, had been grounded in the simple but all-important fact that a French nation-state already existed. The French assembly had been elected to give the nation a new shape and new direction. But a centralized sovereign power was there to reshape; there was an authority that could be either commandeered or, if necessary, usurped. The Frankfurt Assembly, in contrast, was grounded upon nothing but its own words. It was a collection of thoughtful, well-intentioned middle-class liberals, committed to a belief that a liberal-national German state could somehow be constituted out of abstract principles.

Almost from the start, the assembly found itself tangled in the problems of nationality. Who, they asked, were the Germans? A majority of the delegates argued that they were all those who, by language, culture, or geography, felt themselves bound to the enterprise now underway at Frankfurt. The German nation that was to be constituted must include as many of those "Germans" as possible—a goal that seemed achievable in view of the disintegrating Habsburg Empire. This point of view came to be known as the "Great German" position. A minority called for a "Little Germany,"

Great Germans vs. Little Germans

one that excluded all lands of the Habsburg Empire. While Great Germans were a numerical majority, they found themselves stymied by the unwillingness of other nationalities to be included in their fold. The Czechs in Bohemia, as we have seen, wanted no part of Great Germany. In the end the Great Germans settled that the nation for which they were drafting a constitution should include, among other territories, all Austrian lands except Hungary. This decision meant that the crown of their new country might most logically be offered to the Habsburg emperor. As the Habsburg Empire began reasserting its strength, the Great German solution grew more impractical. At this point the voice of the Little Germans began to be heard, with the argument that Austria should be excluded altogether and the crown instead offered to King Frederick William of Prussia.

The liberalism of the assembly was put to the test by events in Austria and Poland in the fall of 1848. When the imperial forces crushed the Czech and Hungarian rebellions, when the Prussian Junkers put an end to Polish self-government, liberals found themselves forced to cheer. They were compelled to support the suppression of minority nationalities; otherwise there would be no new Germany. But their support was for the forces not only of German nationalism but of antiliberal authoritarianism. The assembly's most embarrassing moment occurred when it found itself compelled to take shelter behind the Prussian army. Riots broke out in Frankfurt protesting the assembly's willingness to withdraw from a confrontation with the Danes over the future of Germans in Schleswig, a Danish province. That particular area, which many considered to be part of Germany, had been annexed by the Danes in March 1848. The Frankfurters had been unable to do more than ask the Prussians to win Schleswig back for them, and the Prussians had refused. Hence the riots; hence a second request, this time heeded, for Prussian assistance.

Liberalism vs. nationalism

Fighting in Frankfurt, September 18, 1848. Note the contrast between the disciplined maneuvers of the troops and the guerrilla tactics of the rioting populace.

Reduced to the status of dependents, the Frankfurt delegates neverthe-less, in the spring of 1849, produced a constitution. By this time Austria, fearing its Prussian rival, had decided to have no more to do with Frank-furt. The Little Germans thus won by default and offered their constitu-tional monarchy to Frederick William of Prussia. Though tempted, he turned them down, arguing that their constitution was too liberal, em-bodying as it did the revolutionary notion that a crown could be offered to a monarch. Frederick wanted the crown, but on his own terms. The delegates went home, disillusioned by their experience, many of them convinced that their dual goal of liberalism and nationalism was an im-possible one. Some who refused to surrender that goal emigrated to the United States, where they believed the goal had already been achieved. Many of those who stayed behind convinced themselves that half the goal was better than none, and sacrificed the immediate achievement of liberal goals to the seemingly realistic goals of nationalism.

NATION-BUILDING IN EUROPE, 1850–1870

The twenty years between 1850 and 1870 were years of intense nation-building in the Western world. Of the master-builders, none was more ac-complished than the man who brought Germany under Prussian rule, Otto von Bismarck. Born into the Junker class, Bismarck had emerged during the revolutionary period of 1848 and 1849 as a defender of the monarchy. Bismarck was neither a liberal nor a nationalist; he was before all else a Prussian. When he instituted domestic reforms, he did so not be-cause he favored the "rights" of this or that particular group but because he thought that his policies would result in a more united, and hence more powerful, Prussia. When he maneuvered to bring other German states under Prussian domination, he did so not in conformity with a grand Germanic design but because he believed that some sort of union was almost inevitable and, if so, that it must come about at Prussia's be-hest. He prided himself on being a realist, and he became a first-rate prac-titioner of what has come to be called *Realpolitik*—the politics of what its practitioners claim to be hardheaded reality. Bismarck readily acknowl-edged his admiration of power. He at one point had considered a career in the military—not at all surprising in view of his Junker origins. He once wrote that he regretted that he was compelled to serve his country from behind a desk rather than at the front. But whatever his post, he in-tended to command. "I want to play the tune the way it sounds good to me or not at all," he declared. "Pride, the desire to command . . . I con-fess I am not free from these passions." Nor did he consider those pas-sions unworthy of the man who was to undertake the task of shaping the fortunes of the German state.

Bismarck came to power as minister-president of Prussia in 1862 at the behest of King William I (1861–1888), who required Bismarck's assistance in bringing a liberal parliament to heel. Its majority had been produced by an electoral system that was part of the constitution granted by Frederick William to Prussia in 1850, following the collapse of the assembly. The parliament was divided into two houses, the lower one elected by universal male suffrage. Votes were apportioned according to one's ability to pay taxes, however; those few who together paid one-third of the country's taxes elected one-third of the legislators. A large landowner or industrialist exercised about a hundred times the voting power of a poor man. Contrary to the king's expectations, however, under this constitution a liberal majority was succeeding in thwarting the plans of the sovereign and his advisers. Specifically, it had opposed since 1859 a proposed increase in military expenditures, despite pressure from the king. The liberals, having consolidated economic and political strengths gained during a decade of industrial growth, would not give way. In Bismarck the liberals more than met their match. When they refused to levy taxes, he dissolved the parliament and collected them anyway, claiming that the constitution, whatever its purposes, had not been designed to subvert the state. When liberals argued that Prussia was setting a poor example for the rest of Germany, Bismarck replied that Prussia was admired not for its liberalism but for its power.

Whether or not the Germans—or the rest of Europe—admired Prussia's power, they soon found themselves confronted by it. Bismarck proceeded to build a nation that in the short space of eight years came into being as the German Empire. Bismarck was assisted in his task by his readiness to take advantage of international situations as they presented themselves, without concerning himself particularly with the ideological or moral implications of his actions. He was aided as well by developments over which he had no initial control but which he was able to turn to his advantage. The first of these, the Crimean War, had occurred in 1854–1856, prior to his taking office. Russia and Turkey, perennial European squabblers, had precipitated the hostilities. Russia invaded the territories of Moldavia and Walachia (later Rumania) in an attempt to take advantage of the continuing political rot that made the Ottoman Empire an easy

The Crimean War

British Encampment near Sebastopol, 1854–1855. Photograph taken by Roger Fenton. The Crimean War was the first to be reported to the world by photograph as well as by news dispatch.

prey. Austria, in order to protect her border along the Danube, drove Russia out of these territories and garrisoned her own troops there. In 1854 France and then Britain came to the aid of the Turks by invading Russia's Crimean peninsula. These allies were soon joined by Sardinia. The quarrel had by this time enlarged to include the question of who was to protect the Christians in Jerusalem from the Turks; it was fueled from the start as well by Britain's continuing determination to prohibit a strong Russian presence in the Near East. The allies' eventual victory was primarily the result of a British blockade of Russia. The peace settlement was a severe setback for Russia, whose influence in the Balkans was drastically curbed. Moldavia and Walachia were united as Rumania, which, along with Serbia, was granted power as a self-governing principality. Austrian military resources had been severely taxed during the invasion and occupation of Moldavia and Walachia. And Austria's refusal to come to the aid of Russia lost her the support of that powerful erstwhile ally. It was the subsequent weakness of both Russia and Austria, the result of the Crimean War, that Bismarck used to his advantage in the 1860s.

Steps to German unification: (1) weakening of Austria

In consolidating the German states into a union controlled by Prussia, Bismarck first moved to eliminate Austria from its commanding position in the German Confederation. As a means to this end he inflamed the long-smoldering dispute with Denmark over the possession of Schleswig and Holstein. Inhabited by Germans and Danes, these two provinces had an anomalous status. Since 1815 Holstein had been included in the German Confederation, but both were subject to the personal overlordship of the king of Denmark. When, in 1864, the Danish king attempted to annex them, Bismarck invited Austria to participate in a war against Denmark. A brief struggle followed, at the end of which the Danish ruler was compelled to renounce all his claims to Schleswig and Holstein in favor of Austria and Prussia. Then the sequel for which Bismarck had ardently hoped occurred: a quarrel between the victors over division of the spoils. The conflict that followed in 1866, known as the Seven Weeks' War, ended in an easy triumph for Prussia over war-weakened Austria. Austria was forced to give up all claims to Schleswig and Holstein, to surrender Venetia, and to acquiesce in the dissolution of the German Confederation. Immediately following the war Bismarck proceeded to isolate Austria by uniting all of the German states north of the Main River into the North German Confederation.

(2) Courting the masses

Bismarck's adept use of the Prussian military was matched by his manipulation of public support and opinion. He willingly turned himself into a democrat to achieve the confederation. He saw that if he was to attain his end, which was a strong union with Prussia at its head, he would need to cultivate a constituency hitherto untapped by any German politicians: the masses. He appreciated the manner by which Napoleon III had reinforced his regime through plebiscites. And Bismarck understood that the majority of Germans were not particularly enthusiastic supporters of capitalist liberals, of the bureaucracies of their own small states, or of the Austrian Habsburgs. The constitution he devised for his confederation provided for two chambers: the upper chamber represented the individual states within the union, though not equally; the lower chamber was elected by universal male suffrage. The liberal middle class, to say nothing of the Junkers, was astonished and dismayed, as well they might be. Bismarck's intention was to use popular support to strengthen the hand of the conservative central government against the interests of both landlords and capitalists.

Bismarck's final step in the completion of German unity was the Franco-Prussian War of 1870–1871. He hoped that a conflict with France would kindle the spirit of German nationalism in Bavaria, Württemberg, and other southern states still outside the confederation; he understood, that is, how powerful a spur to national sentiment an enemy "other" could prove. Taking advantage of a diplomatic tempest concerning the right of the Hohenzollerns (Prussia's ruling family) to occupy the Spanish throne, Bismarck worked hard to foment a Franco-German misunderstanding. King William agreed to meet with the French ambassador at the resort spa of Ems in Prussia to discuss the Spanish succession. When William telegraphed Bismarck that the demands of the French for perpetual exclusion of the Hohenzollern family from the Spanish throne had been refused, Bismarck released portions of the message to the press so as to make it appear that King William had insulted the ambassador—which he had not done. Once the garbled report of what happened at Ems was received in France, the nation reacted with a call for war. The call was echoed in Prussia, where Bismarck published evidence that he claimed proved French designs upon the Rhineland. Upon the declaration of war, the south German states rallied to Prussia's side in the belief that it was the victim of aggression. The war was quickly fought. The French were no match for Prussia's professionally trained and superbly equipped forces. Nor did other European powers come to France's assistance. Austria, the most likely candidate, remained weakened by its recent war with Prussia. The Magyars, who at this time had assumed positions of influence within the Austrian government, were quite prepared to welcome a strengthened Prussia; Prussia's growing strength in Germany would further increase Austria's weakness there. And the weaker Austria was as a German power, the stronger would be the claims of the Magyars to predominance. Once more one nationalist consciousness was grinding against another. The war began in July; it ended in September with the defeat of the French and the capture of Napoleon III himself at Sedan in France.

Following the collapse of the French imperial government, insurrectionary forces in Paris continued to hold out against the Germans until the winter of 1871. Bismarck meanwhile proceeded to consummate the German union toward which he had worked so assiduously. On January 18, 1871, in the great Hall of Mirrors at Versailles the German Empire was proclaimed. All those states, except Austria, that had not already been absorbed into Prussia declared their allegiance to William I, henceforth emperor or kaiser. Four months later, at Frankfurt, a treaty between the French and Germans ceded the border region of Alsace to the new

Toward the Unification of Germany, 1740–1871

empire, condemned the French to an indemnity of five billion francs, and thereby broadcast to the world the remarkable success of Bismarck's nation-building.

Events in Italy ran a course almost parallel to that which had led to the unification of Germany. Italy before 1848, it will be recalled, was a patchwork of petty states. The most important of those possessing independence were the Kingdom of Sardinia in the north, the Papal States in the central region, and the Kingdom of the Two Sicilies in the south. The former republics of Lombardy and Venetia were held by Austria, while Habsburg dependents ruled in Tuscany, Parma, and Modena. As the revolutionary fervor of 1848 swept across the peninsula, one ruler after another granted democratic reforms. Charles Albert of Sardinia outdistanced all the others by guaranteeing civil liberties and granting a parliamentary form of government. It soon became evident, however, that the Italian political leadership was prey to the nationalist fervor that

Italian unification

had so much of Europe in its grip. For some years romantic patriots had been dreaming of a *risorgimento,* which would restore the nation to the position of glorious leadership it had held in Roman times and during the Renaissance. To achieve this, Italy must be welded into a single state. Opinions differed as to the form the new government should take. Young idealists for a time followed the leadership of the ultimately ineffectual Giuseppe Mazzini. Religious-minded patriots believed that the most practicable solution would be to federate the state of Italy under the presidency of the pope. The majority of the more moderate nationalists advocated a constitutional monarchy built upon the foundations of the Kingdom of Sardinia. The aims of this third group gradually crystallized under the leadership of a shrewd Sardinian nobleman, Count Camillo di Cavour. In 1850 he was appointed minister of commerce and agriculture of his native state and in 1852, premier.

The campaign for unification of the Italian peninsula began with efforts to expel the Austrians. In 1848 revolts were organized in the territories under Habsburg domination, and an army of liberation marched from Sardinia to aid the rebels. But the movement ended in failure. It was then that Cavour, as the new leader of the campaign, turned to less heroic but more practical methods. In 1858 he held a secret meeting with Napoleon III and prepared the stage for an Italian war of liberation. Napoleon agreed to cooperate in driving the Austrians from Italy for the price of the cession of Savoy and Nice by Sardinia to France. A war with Austria was duly provoked in 1859, and for a time all went well for the Franco-Italian allies. After the conquest of Lombardy, however, Napoleon III suddenly withdrew, fearful of ultimate defeat and afraid of antagonizing the Catholics in his own country by aiding the avowedly anticlerical government of Cavour. Thus deserted by its ally, Sardinia was unable to expel the Austrians from Venetia. Nevertheless, extensive gains were made; Sardinia annexed Lombardy and acquired by various means the duchies of Tuscany, Parma, and Modena, and the northern portion of the Papal States. Sardinia was now more than twice its original size and by far the most powerful state in Italy.

The second step in consolidating Italy was the conquest of the Kingdom of the Two Sicilies. This kingdom was ruled by a Bourbon, Francis II (1859–1860), who was thoroughly hated by his Italian subjects. In May 1860 a romantic adventurer, Giuseppe Garibaldi, set out with a regiment of one thousand "red shirts" to rescue his fellow Italians from oppression. Within three months he had conquered the island of Sicily and had then marched to the deliverance of Naples, where the people were already in revolt. By November the whole kingdom of Francis II had fallen to Garibaldi. He at first intended to convert the territory into an independent republic but was finally persuaded to surrender it to the Kingdom of Sardinia. With most of the peninsula now united under a single rule, Victor Emmanuel II, king of Sardinia, assumed the title of king of Italy (1861–1878). Venetia was still in the hands of the Austrians, but in 1866, following their defeat in the Seven Weeks' War, they were forced by the Prussians to cede it to Italy. All that remained to complete

Camillo di Cavour

Giuseppe Garibaldi

the unification of Italy was the annexation of Rome. The Eternal City had resisted conquest thus far, largely because of the military protection accorded the pope by Napoleon III. But in 1870 the outbreak of the Franco-Prussian War compelled Napoleon to withdraw his troops. In September 1870 Italian soldiers occupied Rome, and in July of the following year it was made the capital of the by now united kingdom.

The Unification of Italy

The occupation of Rome brought the kingdom of Italy into conflict with the papacy. During the first years of his reign, which began in 1846, Pope Pius IX instituted a series of "modern" improvements: gaslight, railways, vaccination. Yet Pius, who, like his reactionary predecessor, Gregory XVI, continued to rule over the Papal States in the manner of a secular prince, was no friend to either liberalism or nationalism. And no wonder: the movement that had brought Italian troops to Rome had from its inception expressed hostility to the Church as an impediment to unification. Following the occupation of Rome in 1870, an attempt was made to solve the problem of relations between the state and the papacy. In 1871 the Italian parliament enacted the Law of Papal Guaranties, purporting to define and limit the status of the pope as a reigning sovereign. At the same time, a Vatican council in 1870 had proclaimed the doctrine of papal infallibility in spiritual matters. The reigning pontiff, Pius IX, promptly denounced the secular law on the grounds that issues affecting the pope could be settled only by an international treaty to which he himself was a party. Whereupon he shut himself up in the Vatican and refused to have anything to do with a government that had so shamefully treated Christ's vicar on earth. His successors continued this practice of voluntary imprisonment until 1929, when a series of agreements between the Italian government and Pius XI effected settlement of the dispute.

Although Italy was now a unified state, it was hardly a nation. As already noted, fewer than 3 percent of the "Italian" population in fact spoke Italian; the rest used local and regional dialects so diverse that schoolmasters sent from Rome to Sicily following unification were, because of the "foreign" language they spoke, presumed to be British. As one politician remarked, "We have made Italy; now we must make Italians." That task did not prove an easy one. The gap between an increasingly industrialized North and a backward, rural South remained very wide. Cavour and those who succeeded him as prime minister battled not only against North-South disparities, but also against the tensions in rural regions between landlords and an increasingly embittered agricultural proletariat. Banditry in the territory of the former Kingdom of the Two Sicilies compelled the central administration to dispatch troops to quell serious uprisings, with the consequence that more people were killed at that time than in all the wars of unification. The history of Italy is proof that national spirit was a manufactured emotion, one that Italian politicians had to work hard, with limited success, to create and market.

The challenges of nationalism and nation-building also occupied the two countries to the east and west of Europe that were built upon systems of unfree labor: Russia and the United States. Serfdom in Russia, extended and formalized by Peter the Great in his dramatic empire-building (1689–1725), began to draw significant protest from the intelligentsia under the reign of Catherine the Great (1762–1796). Tied to the issue of serfdom was the question of how best to fulfill Russia's unique destiny, her *Volksgeist.* In the mid-nineteenth century two schools of thought emerged: the *slavophiles,* romantic nationalists who idealized traditional

Pope Pius IX. This contemporary cartoon lampoons the pope, shown as a conniving, worldly politician hiding behind the mask of Jesus. Pius IX, though in his early years something of a liberal, took an extreme reactionary political position in the wake of the revolutionary upheaval of 1848.

Post-unification problems

Russia: the abolition of serfdom

Jeffersonian principles

Thomas Jefferson, by Gilbert Stuart

Jacksonian democracy

Immigration

Russian culture, including the peasant commune, and rejected Western ideas and innovations; and the *westernizers,* who wished to raise Russia to the level of Europe by adopting the science, technology, and educational innovations they believed had shaped Europe's history. Both groups agreed that serfdom must be abolished. But not until 1861, under Alexander II, was emancipation effected—and then under a settlement that greatly favored landowners.

Alexander II (1855–1881) presented his reluctant nobles with emancipation from above as the only alternative to violent and protracted strife. In America, the eventual end of unfree labor came in the midst of a bloody civil war (1861–1865). But the American Civil War was not about the issue of slavery so much as it was about preserving the union of American states and territories. It was a union that had undergone tremendous stress as the original republic of thirteen states had grown into a huge amalgam of territories that stretched to the Pacific coast. Politically, the so-called Jeffersonian Revolution had moved the young country, founded upon the desire to protect the rights of private property against the leveling tendencies of majorities, toward a number of ultimately democratic objectives. Leaders of the movement under the Democratic-Republican president Thomas Jefferson supported a political system based on an aristocracy of "virtue and talent," in which respect for personal liberty would be the guiding principle. They were vigorous opponents of special privilege, whether of birth or of wealth. They worked for the abolition of established churches. They led the campaign for the addition of a Bill of Rights to the Constitution and were almost exclusively responsible for its success. Although professing devotion to the principle of the separation of powers, they actually believed in the supremacy of the representatives of the people and viewed with abhorrence the attempts of the executive and judicial branches to increase their power.

By 1820, with the growth of new urban centers as well as the "frontier democracy" that characterized life in the territories of the Louisiana Purchase (1803) and the Northwest Territory (western New York State and Ohio), the more circumscribed equality proposed by the Jeffersonians gave way to a new democratic spirit, shaped around the principle of equality and led by Andrew Jackson. The Jacksonian Democrats transformed the doctrines of liberalism into a more radical creed. They pronounced all (excluding slaves, American Indians, and women) politically equal, not merely in rights but in privileges. They were devoted adherents to the causes of suffrage for all white males; the election, rather than appointment, of all governmental officeholders; and the frequent rotation of men in positions of political power—a doctrine that served to put more Democratic politicians into federal office. These democratic beliefs helped encourage a spirit of unity within the United States during a period of rapid territorial expansion.

As the United States continued to acquire more territories in the West (the most notable addition resulting from the conquest of lands in the Southwest from Mexico in 1846), it also faced the problem of assimilating the thousands of immigrants who came to America from Europe in the first half of the century. Many were Scottish and English; for them the problems of adjusting to a new life in a new country were generally not difficult since they shared a common language with their fellow citizens. For others the problems were far greater. For the Irish, who immigrated in great numbers, particularly during the 1840s, there was the fact of their alien religion, Roman Catholicism. For Germans and others from the Continent, there was the language barrier. The United States's policy toward its immigrants was directed against the creation of any foreign nationalist enclaves apart from the main body of its citizenry. Although foreign-language newspapers were tolerated, and immigrants were free to attend churches and social gatherings as they chose, English remained the language of the public schools, the police, the law courts, and the government. To hold a job, a person was almost always forced to learn at least some English. In this way, the United States encouraged immigrants to shed their "foreign" ways and to commit themselves to their adopted nation.

If there was resistance to this emphasis on national identification, it could be found in the South, where the institution of slavery and the economic dependence of the planters upon Britain produced two distinct minorities, neither of which was to be assimilated without resort to war. During the nineteenth century, slavery had been abolished throughout

Slavery and the South

Slavery in the American South. Left: Slave pens at Pine, Birch & Co., a Virginia slave broker. Right: Cotton being prepared by slaves for the gin on a South Carolina plantation.

much of the Western world, for both economic and humanitarian reasons. Southern planters, like Russian serf-owners, continued to insist that without the slave system they would go bankrupt. To humanitarians they responded—just as their Russian counterparts had done—with arguments based upon theories of racial inferiority and upon their self-professed reputation as benevolent masters. The position of these Southern spokesmen grew increasingly distasteful and unconvincing to the North. As the country opened to the west, North and South engaged in a protracted tug-of-war as to which new states were to be "free" and which "slave." Northerners were motivated by more than concern for the well-being of blacks. The North was industrializing rapidly. Capitalists there were demanding protective tariffs to assist them in their enterprises. Southerners favored free trade, since they wished to import British goods in return for the cotton they sold to the manufacturers of Lancashire.

The Civil War

Thus, in 1861, President Abraham Lincoln undertook the war to defend the unity of the United States. European governments, while never recognizing the Confederacy officially, nevertheless remained sympathetic to its cause. They hoped that the fragmentation of the United States would result in the opening up of markets for their manufactured goods, much as the dissolution of the Spanish Empire had proved a boon to European commercial interests. The victory of the North in 1865, however, ensured the continued growth of the United States as a nation. The Fourteenth Amendment to the Constitution stated specifically that all Americans were citizens of the United States, and not of an individual state or territory. In declaring that no citizen was to be deprived of life, liberty, or property without due process of law, it established that "due process" was to be defined by the national, and not the state or territorial, government.

Nation-building and capitalism

The years following the American Civil War witnessed the binding together of the nation economically under the direction of Northern private enterprise. The symbol of the North's triumph as a nation-builder came with the driving of the final spike of the transcontinental Union Pacific railroad in 1869. Nation-building in Europe and the United States helped ensure the continuing expansion of capitalism. Liberalism had provided a general climate of opinion and a set of attitudes toward government that encouraged industrialization. Nation-building, in its turn, produced the necessary economic units—large enough to generate the wherewithal to sustain economic growth and confident enough to enter into competition with the British Goliath.

SUMMARY POINTS

- Nationalism, a sentiment of belonging to a community that shares a tradition of historical, geographic, linguistic, or cultural circumstances, was carefully cultivated by governmental and revolutionary elites during the nineteenth century to advance their own interests.

- The works of romantic writers, composers, and artists fueled the development of nationalism by idealizing the imagined characteristics specific to individual cultures. Works of art and literature were transformed from examples of their creators' talent into symbols of national culture.

- Although the forces of nationalism were used to great effect in the nation-building efforts of homogeneous and independent Prussia, nationalism threatened the survival of the heterogeneous Austrian Empire, because it tended to magnify the political and economic divisions among states.

- The revolutions of 1848 in central Europe saw various nationalities, facing the possibility of absorption into a Prussian or Austrian state, assert their own autonomy and thus undermine weak liberal governments.

- Otto von Bismarck in Prussia, and Camillo di Cavour and Giuseppe Garibaldi in Italy strategically used international politics, war, and internal revolt to forge a united Germany and a united Italy, respectively.

- In Russia and the United States, the conflicting forces of tradition and economic modernization led to modest reform in the former and civil war in the latter.

SELECTED READINGS

Alter, Peter, *Nationalism,* 2d ed., New York, 1994. Categorizes nationalisms and discusses them in political context.

Beales, Derek, *The Risorgimento and the Unification of Italy,* New York, 1971. Objective, concise survey of Italian unification.

Carr, Raymond, *Spain, 1808–1975,* 2d ed., Oxford, Eng., 1982. The standard survey.

Craig, Gordon, *The Politics of the Prussian Army, 1640–1945,* Oxford, Eng., 1964. Much more than the title implies. An excellent analysis of Prussian social structure and the role of the army in social reform and unification.

Deak, Istvan, *The Lawful Revolution: Louis Kossuth and the Hungarians, 1848–1849,* New York, 1979.

Epstein, Klaus, *The Genesis of German Conservatism,* Princeton, 1966. Provides excellent early-nineteenth-century background.

Eyck, Erich, *Bismarck and the German Empire,* 3d ed., London, 1968. The best one-volume study of Bismarck.

Eyck, Frank, *The Frankfurt Parliament, 1848–49,* New York, 1968. A detailed study of its composition and procedure.

Ford, Guy Stanton, *Stein: The Era of Reform in Prussia, 1807–1815,* New York, 1922. An old but still valuable work on a leading Prussian reformer.

Hamerow, Theodore S., *The Birth of a New Europe: State and Society in the Nineteenth Century,* Chapel Hill, N.C., 1983. A discussion of political and social change, and their relationship to industrialization and the increase in state power.

———, *The Social Foundations of German Unification, 1858–1871,* 2 vols., Princeton, 1969–1972. Concentrates on economic factors that determined the solution to the unification question. An impressive synthesis.

Hayes, C. J. H., *The Historical Evolution of Modern Nationalism,* rev. ed., New York, 1968. A valuable survey.

Hobsbawm, Eric J., *Nations and Nationalism since 1870: Programme, Myth, Reality,* 2d ed., Cambridge, Eng., 1992. A clear, concise analysis of the historical and cultural manifestations of nationalism.

Holborn, Hajo, *A History of Modern Germany,* Vols. II and III, Princeton, 1964. The best survey of German history in English.

Howard, Michael, *The Franco-Prussian War,* New York, 1981. The war's effect on society.

———, *War in European History,* Oxford, Eng., 1976. The best survey of international conflict sparked by European expansionism.

Kolchin, Peter, *Unfree Labor: American Slavery and Russian Serfdom,* Cambridge, Mass., 1987. Seminal comparative study.

Macartney, C. A., *The Habsburg Empire, 1790–1918,* London, 1968. A worthwhile survey.

Mack Smith, Denis, *Garibaldi: A Great Life in Brief,* New York, 1956. A useful account of the Italian hero's achievements.

———, *The Making of Italy, 1796–1870,* New York, 1968. A narrative with documents.

Mosse, George, *The Culture of Western Europe: The Nineteenth and Twentieth Centuries,* 3d ed., Boulder, Co., 1988. An overview that successfully combines compression with breadth of analysis.

Namier, Lewis B., *1848: The Revolution of the Intellectuals,* London, 1964. A controversial analysis, highly critical of the Frankfurt Assembly.

Noyes, P. H., *Organization and Revolution: Working-Class Associations in the German Revolutions of 1848–1849,* Princeton, 1966. An important monograph analyzing the degree of working-class consciousness at the time of the revolution.

Pflanze, Otto, *Bismarck and the Development of Germany,* 2d ed., 3 vols., Princeton, 1990. An impressive analysis of Bismarck's aims and policies.

Riasanovsky, Nicholas V., *Nicholas I and Official Nationality in Russia, 1825–1855,* Berkeley, 1959. Analyzes the way the tsar used nationalism to promote his conservative ends.

Rosenberg, Hans, *Bureaucracy, Aristocracy, and Autocracy: The Prussian Experience, 1660–1815,* Cambridge, Mass., 1958. A difficult but valuable book explaining the forces that molded the modern Prussian state.

Salvemini, Gaetano, *Mazzini,* London, 1956. Biography with excerpts from Mazzini's writings.

Sheehan, James J., *German Liberalism in the Nineteenth Century,* Chicago, 1978. Solid synthetic account.

Sperber, Jonathan, *Rhineland Radicals: The Democratic Movement and the Revolution of 1848–1849,* Princeton, 1993. Analyzes attitudes toward the revolution.

Taylor, A. J. P., *The Habsburg Monarchy, 1809–1918,* rev. ed., London, 1965. An idiosyncratic account by an eminent historian.

Bismarck, Otto von, *Bismarck, the Man and the Statesman, Written and Dictated by Himself,* London, 1899. Bismarck's memoirs, written after his fall from power.

Clausewitz, Karl von, *On War,* London, 1968. Published posthumously, this work, in reality a philosophy of war, was perceived by the Prussian military bureaucracy as a mandate for total war—for the subjugation of all interests of the state to war.

Fichte, Johann Gottlieb, *Addresses to the German Nation,* New York, 1968. Presented in 1808 while French armies occupied Prussia, these lectures helped stir a German nationalist spirit.

Schurz, Carl, *The Reminiscences of Carl Schurz,* 3 vols., New York, 1907–1908. Especially valuable is Vol. I. A young German liberal in 1848 and a delegate to the Frankfurt Assembly, Schurz spent the rest of his life as an exile in the United States.

PART SIX

THE WEST AT THE WORLD'S CENTER

THE YEARS BETWEEN 1870 and 1945 found the West at the center of global affairs. The industrial supremacy of western Europe and the United States gave them a combined power greater than that possessed by any nation or empire in previous times. Yet world domination was by no means accompanied by any sense of general world order. The economic might of the Western nations, while it resulted in their ability to dominate the less-developed quarters of the globe, resulted, as well, in their concern lest one of their number overpower the others. The old system of the balance of power, designed to preserve peace by ensuring that no one country achieved overwhelming predominance at the expense of its neighbors, was strained to the breaking point by economic rivalries that stretched around the world. Meanwhile, tensions mounted within each nation, as landed and middle classes, threatened by the possibility of social turmoil, tried to balance the mounting clamor for political concessions against their desire to retain power in their own hands. Twice during the period, in 1914 and 1939, international and domestic pressures exploded into global wars. Those wars and their results, generated by the rivalries and miscalculations of the Western nations, so sapped the strength of those nations as to depose them thereafter as the sole arbiters of the world's destinies.

Pan-American Unity, 1940. A fresco by Diego Rivera. The great Mexican painter Diego Rivera (1886–1957) created this immense, ten-panel mural for display at the newly opened City College of San Francisco. At once a historical panorama and a series of individually detailed scenes, it is a commentary that contrasts the darker forces plaguing Europe and the constructive effects of Pan-American cooperation.

THE WEST AT THE WORLD'S CENTER

	Politics	Science & Industry	Economics & Society	Arts & Letters
1840			Marx & Engels, *Communist Manifesto* (1848)	
	Anglo-Indian war (1857)	Darwin, *The Origin of Species* (1859)		
	Liberation of serfs, Russia (1861)			
				Tolstoy, *War and Peace* (1862–1869)
	Dominion of Canada established (1867)		Marx, *Capital* (1867)	
			Opening of Suez Canal (1869)	
1870		First commercially practical electrical generator (1870) Gilchrist-Thomas steel process (1870s)		Impressionism in art (1870–1900)
	Paris Commune (1871) *Kulturkampf,* Germany (1872) League of Three Emperors (1873)			
	Constitution for Third French Republic (1875) End of First International (1876) Congress of Berlin (1878) European scramble for Africa begins (1879)	Germ theory of disease (1875) Thomas Edison invents the light bulb (1879)		
			Growth of finance capitalism (1880s) Social welfare legislation, Germany (1882–1884)	Functionalism in architecture (1880–1890)
	British invasion of Egypt (1882) Triple Alliance formed (1882)			
				Nietzsche, *Thus Spoke Zarathustra* (1883) Émile Zola, *Germinal* (1885)
	Berlin conference on imperialism (1885)			
	Pan-Slavism (1890–1914)		Sherman Antitrust Act, United States (1890) Méline tariff (1892)	Henrik Ibsen, *Hedda Gabler* (1890)
	Dreyfus affair (1894–1899)			
	Spanish-American War (1898) Boer War (1899–1902)			

THE WEST AT THE WORLD'S CENTER

Politics	Science & Industry	Economics & Society	Arts & Letters	
		Women's suffrage movement, England (1900–1914)	Sigmund Freud, *The Interpretation of Dreams* (1900)	**1900**
N. Lenin, *What Is to Be Done?* (1902)				
Russo-Japanese War (1904–1905)	Ivan Pavlov, Nobel Prize for physiology (1904)	Social welfare legislation, France (1904; 1910)		
Revolution in Russia (1905)	Albert Einstein, development of relativity theory (1905–1910)	Weber, *The Protestant Ethic and the Spirit of Capitalism* (1905)	Cubism in art (1905–1930)	
		Social welfare legislation, England (1906–1912)		
Triple Entente formed (1907)				
Bosnian Crisis (1908)				
Revolt of the Young Turks (1908)				
Balkan Wars (1912–1913)				
			Stravinsky, *Rite of Spring* (1913)	
First World War (1914–1918)				
Easter Rebellion, Ireland (1916)				
U.S. enters World War I (1917)				
Russian Revolution (1917)				
			Oswald Spengler, *The Decline of the West* (1918)	
Treaty of Versailles (1919)			Bauhaus established (1919)	
Socialist revolution, Germany (1919)				
League of Nations (1920–1946)		German inflation (1920s)	Writers of the "Lost Generation" (1920–1930)	**1920**
		Soviet industrialization (1920s–1930s)	Surrealism and Dadaism (1920s)	
NEP, Russia (1921)			Ludwig Wittgenstein, *Tractatus Logico-philosophicus* (1921)	
Mussolini's march on Rome (1922)			T. S. Eliot, *The Waste Land* (1922)	
Hitler's attempted putsch (1923)			James Joyce, *Ulysses* (1922)	
New constitution, Soviet Union (1924)				
Locarno agreements (1925)				
Hitler, *Mein Kampf* (1925)				
		Great Depression (1929–1940)		

THE WEST AT THE WORLD'S CENTER

	Politics	Science & Industry	Economics & Society	Arts & Letters
1930		Discovery of viruses, sulfa drugs, and penicillin (1930s)		Neo-realism in art (1930s)
	Japan invades Manchuria (1931)			
	Hitler becomes chancellor of Germany (1933)		New Deal, United States (1933–1940)	
	Italy conquers Ethiopia (1935–1936) Rome-Berlin Axis (1936) Spanish Civil War (1936–1939)	National rearmament programs (1935)		
				Picasso, *Guernica* (1937)
	Germany annexes Austria (1938) Munich conference (1938) Nazi-Soviet pact (1939) Second World War (1939–1945)	Discovery of atomic fission (1939)		Steinbeck, *The Grapes of Wrath* (1939)
1940				
	United States enters war (1941)			
				Jean-Paul Sartre, *Being and Nothingness* (1943)
	Allied invasion of Normandy (1944) Bombing of Hiroshima and Nagasaki (1945) United Nations founded (1945) Yalta and Potsdam conferences (1945)	First atomic bomb test (1945)		
				Orwell, *Animal Farm* (1946)

CHAPTER 24

INTERNATIONAL INDUSTRIALIZATION AND IMPERIALISM (1870–1914)

We have conquered for ourselves a place in the sun. It will now be my task to see to it that this place in the sun shall remain our undisputed possession. . . .
—KAISER WILLIAM II, speech, 1901

F MOST HISTORIANS now speak of a second Industrial Revolution occurring during the years after 1870, they are quick to qualify the term. Whatever the changes in technique and in scope—and they were significant—they do not compare to those that characterized the first revolution—*the* Industrial Revolution. There is, however, good reason to distinguish a second period of industrial development and advance from the first. Successful nation-building meant that the years 1870–1914 would be characterized by sharply increased international political and economic rivalries, culminating in a scramble after imperial territories in Africa and Asia. Britain, if it did not actually surrender its industrial primacy during this period, failed to counter with any real success the energetic and determined challenges from Germany and the United States to its constantly decreasing lead. New technology, particularly in the fields of metals, chemicals, and electricity, resulted in new products. Larger populations and improving standards of living produced greater demand, which, in turn, increased the volume of production. And the need for increased production called forth significant reorganization to provide a freer supply of capital and to ensure a more efficient labor force. It is these changes that distinguish the second stage of industrialization from the first, and therefore warrant its separate treatment. Yet they must be perceived as stemming not only from those economic conditions that were the result of the first stage, but also from the more general political, social, and cultural climate whose history we have been tracing.

In analyzing the progress of industrialization, we shall deal with changes in three major areas: in technology, in scope and scale of consumption and production, and in the reorganization of the capitalist system. Finally we shall examine the phenomenon of late-nineteenth-century imperialism.

A second industrial revolution

Advantages of steel

A most important technological change in this period resulted in the mass production of steel. The advantages of steel over iron—a result of steel's lower carbon content—are its hardness, its malleability, and its strength. Steel can keep its cutting edge, where iron cannot; it can be worked more easily than iron, which is brittle and which, if it is to be used industrially, must almost always be cast (that is, poured into molds). And steel, because of its strength in proportion to its weight and volume, makes a particularly adaptable construction material. These advantages had been recognized by craftsmen for centuries. Until steel could be produced both cheaply and in mass, however, the advantages remained more theoretical than real.

Bessemer, Siemens-Martin, and Gilchrist-Thomas systems

Only with the invention of the Bessemer and Siemens-Martin processes could steel begin to compete with iron. In the 1850s, an Englishman, Henry Bessemer, discovered that by blowing air into and through the molten metal he could more exactly control the amount of carbon in the steel in much shorter time, and with far larger quantities of ore, than was possible with previous decarbonization methods. Bessemer soon found, however, that his "converters" were incapable of burning off sufficient quantities of phosphorous; and phosphorous in anything but the smallest quantities made the metal unworkable. This same problem plagued the German inventors Frederick and William Siemens, whose furnace made use of waste gases to increase heat. Not until Pierre Martin, a Frenchman, discovered that the introduction of scrap iron into the mix would induce proper decarbonization, could the Siemens furnace be used to make steel commercially. And not until the late 1870s was the problem of phosphoreting solved for both the Bessemer and the Siemens-Martin processes. The solution was a simple one, discovered by two Englishmen, a clerk and a chemist: Sidney Gilchrist Thomas and his cousin Sidney Gilchrist. They introduced limestone into the molten iron to combine with the phosphorus, which was then siphoned from the mix.

Increased steel production

Together, these three processes revolutionized the production of steel. Although the use of iron did not end overnight, steel soon moved into the lead. In the British shipbuilding industry, for example, steel had overtaken iron by 1890. In part because Siemens-Martin was particularly suited to the manufacture of steel plates used in shipbuilding, that process dominated the manufacture of steel in Britain, where shipbuilding was a major industry. Bessemer steel, which could be manufactured more cheaply and in larger plants, was more commonly produced on the Continent and in America. The result was a major increase in the production of German steel: by 1901, German converters were capable of pouring annually an average of 34,000 tons, compared to Britain's 21,750. By 1914 Germany was producing twice as much steel as Britain, and the United States twice as much as Germany.

The Rise of the Steel Industry. Bristling with massive machinery such as this steam hammer, the Krupp Works in Essen, Germany, was already a major force in steel production by the 1870s.

A second and equally important technological development resulted in the availability of electric power for industrial, commercial, and domestic use. Electricity's particular advantages result from the facts that it can be easily transmitted as energy over long distances, and that it can be converted into other forms of energy—heat and light, for example. Although electricity had, of course, been discovered prior to the first Industrial Revolution, its advantages could not have been put to general use without a series of inventions that occurred during the nineteenth century. Of these, some of the most important were the invention of the chemical battery by the Italian Alessandro Volta in 1800; of electromagnetic induction in 1831 and the electromagnetic generator in 1866 by the Englishman Michael Faraday; of the first commercially practical generator of direct current in 1870; and of alternators and transformers capable of producing high-voltage alternating current in the 1880s. These inventions meant that by the end of the century it was possible to send electric current from large power stations over comparatively long distances. Electric power could be manufactured by water—hence cheaply—and delivered from its source to the place where it was needed.

Increased availability of electricity

Once it had been delivered to its destination, the power was converted and put to use in myriad ways. Households quickly became one of the major users of electrical power. The invention in 1879 by Thomas Edison of the incandescent filament lamp—or light bulb—was crucial in this regard. As individual houses were electrified to receive the power that was to be transformed into light, consumer demand for electricity resulted in further expansion of the electrical industry. Demand for electrical power was increasing in the industrial sector as well. Electric motors soon began

The uses of electricity

New Technology: The Telephone. This 1885 photograph of a New York City telephone exchange bears witness to the transformation wrought by the dramatic expansion of the electrical industry. Note also the extent to which the position of operator has become the province of female employees.

to power subways, tramways, and, eventually, long-distance railways. Electricity made possible the development of new techniques in the chemical and metallurgical industries. Most important, electricity helped to transform the work patterns of the factory. Heavy steam engines had made equipment and machinery stationery; electric motors meant that comparatively lightweight power tools could be moved—often by hand—to the site of a particular piece of work. The result was far greater flexibility in terms of factory organization. Smaller workshop industries benefited as well; they could accommodate themselves to electrically powered motors and tools in a way they could not to steam.

Advances in chemical industry

Steel and electricity were only two of the most important areas where technological changes were taking place. The chemical industry was significantly advanced by developments in the manufacture of alkali and organic compounds. Demand for alkali had increased with the demand for soaps and textiles, and with the changes in the manufacturing process of paper, which required large amounts of bleach. An older, more expensive and wasteful technique used extensively by the British was superseded after 1880 by a new process perfected by the Belgian Ernest Solvay. The result was, again, a rapid overtaking of the British by the Germans in the production not only of alkalis but of sulfuric acid, a by-product recoverable in the Solvay process, and used in the manufacture of fertilizers, petroleum refining, iron, steel, and textiles. In the field of organic compounds, the impetus for further discovery came as a result of demand for synthetic dyes. Although the British and French were the first successful pioneers in this area, the Germans once more moved ahead to a commanding lead by 1900. At the turn of the century German firms controlled about 90 percent of the world market.

The need for more and more power to meet increasing industrial demands resulted not only in developments in the field of electricity, already noted, but in the improved design and expanded capacity of steam engines. The most noteworthy invention in this area was the steam turbine, which permitted engines to run at speeds heretofore unobtainable. Internal combustion engines made their appearance during this period as well. Their major advantage lay in their efficiency; i.e., they could be powered automatically, and did not need to be stoked by hand like steam engines. Once liquid fuels—petroleum and distilled gasoline—became available, as they did increasingly with the discovery of oil fields in Russia, Borneo, and Texas about 1900, the internal combustion engine took hold as a serious competitor to steam. By 1914 most navies had converted from coal to oil, as had domestic steamship companies. The automobile and the airplane, however, both still in their infancies, made little impact upon the industrial world before 1914.

Improved engines

CHANGES IN SCOPE AND SCALE

These technological changes must be understood as occurring against a background of—indeed in part as a result of—a constantly growing population and a generally increased standard of living for the majority of men and women in the Western world. Between 1870 and 1914, Europe's population increased from 295 million to 450 million. This was the case despite a declining birth rate in the more industrially advanced countries

Population increases

New Technology: The Elevated Train. This electric railway was erected in Paris in the 1880s.

The First Successful Airplane Flight. The brothers Orville and Wilbur Wright made history with their flight near Kitty Hawk, N.C., in 1903.

Louis Pasteur

of western Europe, where more and more middle- and working-class men and women were postponing marriage and limiting the number of their children, confident that those children they did have stood a fairly decent chance of survival. Population growth was primarily the result of a sharp decline in infant mortality, caused by improved sanitation and diet, and by the virtual elimination of diseases such as cholera and typhus. Increases were greatest in the areas of central and eastern Europe, where the birth rate did not drop as dramatically as in the West. Britain's population grew from 34.9 to 45.2 million between 1881 and 1911; France's from 37.4 to 39.1. But Germany's advanced during the same period from 45.2 to 64.9 million, and Russia's from 94 to an estimated 129 million.

The problems of public sanitation and health were slowly brought to heel by men and women working in the wake of scientific discoveries such as those by the Frenchman Louis Pasteur. By locating the source of bacteria, Pasteur's work opened the way for major improvements in the areas of public sanitation and health: among others, the process of ridding food of objectionable bacteria by sterilization—pasteurization—that was named for him. Pasteur, along with the German Robert Koch, also proved conclusively that germs were not, as was commonly supposed, the result but rather the cause of disease.

Declining death rates were an indicator of generally increasing material prosperity. There were, of course, still a great many very poor people, both in cities and in the country: casual laborers, the unemployed, those in declining industries and trades. Those skilled workers and their families whose real incomes did rise as a result of deflation and higher wage

Boulevard Montmartre, by Camille Pissarro (1830–1903). A reflection of the lively, consumer-oriented bourgeois urban life that characterized western Europe in the later nineteenth century.

The Railway Bridge at Argenteuil, by Claude Monet (1840–1926). Here the painter depicts the invasion of the countryside by the railways, suggesting how the sharp division between country and city had broken down by 1900.

rates did not experience anything like the rate of increase enjoyed by most of the middle class. Nor could they expect to avoid altogether the stretches of unemployment that made life so chaotic for so many of their unskilled co-workers. Yet despite these qualifications, it is fair to say that more people enjoyed a higher standard of living than ever before. And a higher standard of living produced the demand for an increase in consumer goods.

New consumers

Increased consumption of manufactured goods was by no means uniform; it was higher in urban and industrialized areas than in the country. But even in the country, traditional thrift was challenged as farmers and their wives journeyed by train into the cities, saw what they had not imagined they could have, and then decided they must spend their savings to have it. To accommodate the new and largely middle-class consumers, department stores and chain stores designed their products and their advertising to make shopping as easy and inviting as possible. Behind large plate-glass windows, goods were displayed attractively and temptingly; periodic sales encouraged householders to purchase "bar-

The Triumph of Middle-Class Consumerism. The interior of the Galeries Lafayette department store in Paris, c. 1890.

gains"; catalogues and charge accounts made it easy for customers to spend money without leaving home. The result was an enormous increase in the volume of manufactured goods produced for this rapidly expanding consumer market. Bicycles, clocks, appliances, furnishings—these and a great many other things were being made in large quantities, and with new materials (cheap steel) and new techniques (electrical power). Many of these products were designed according to the correct assumption that women were more and more responsible for household purchases. Therefore, goods were fashioned to appeal directly to women, or to the children for whom women were responsible. The foot-powered sewing machine was a particular case in point—the first domestic appliance. Isaac Singer, the American responsible for the development of the treadle and straight needle in the 1850s, was as much an entrepreneur as an inventor. He was a pioneer in the field of advertising and promotion, encouraging purchase on the installment plan and providing courses for would-be domestic seamstresses.

Sewing machines changed far more than the sewing habits of homemakers, however. They were inexpensive, lightweight tools, easily installed and easily operated. Workshop masters could set up several, employ a handful of young women at very low wages, and make a profit turning out cheap ready-made clothing in response to increasing demand. This was just one of the ways in which the scale of manufacturing was altered during the latter part of the nineteenth century, with both demand and technology conspiring to produce the change. The sewing machine also led to the development of other new tools that helped cut costs in the clothing industry: button-holers, lace-makers, leather-stitchers. Whereas it took one cobbler ten hours to make a pair of shoes in 1850 by hand, by the end of the century it took a team of cobblers but a few hours to produce ten pairs using machinery. In metal-working, hard-edged steel allowed for the rapid cutting of patterns, which reduced price, in turn encouraging the manufacture of a variety of inexpensive metal goods—kitchenware, for example. In textiles, improved engines doubled the pace of mules and looms. In heavy industry, steam hammers performed the work of many men more precisely and with greater speed than before. New equipment of this sort was expensive. As a result, in heavy industry, it was the larger companies that prospered, and in the course of their prosperity, they grew even larger.

> New tools affect scale of manufacturing

In all the countries of Europe, and in the United States, the pattern was one of expansion and consolidation. This was especially the case in Germany, where in the iron and steel industry nearly 75 percent of those employed worked in factories of a thousand or more, and where over 90 percent of the electrical equipment manufactured was made in factories with over fifty employees. Machinery was thus altering the scale of manufacturing in two directions at once. In the clothing industry, entrepreneurs could use inexpensive machines to make small workshops turn a profit. In steel foundries, the cost of new equipment forced small competitors to the wall, with the result that the foundries grew very much bigger.

> Industrial expansion and consolidation

Left: **Advertisement for a German Sewing Machine.** The company proclaims the machine's versatility: unsurpassed for use in the home as well as in the workshop or factory. Right: **Sweated Industry.** This British family is "manufacturing" cheap toys at home. While the scale of some industrial enterprises increased, others remained profitable through the employment of poorly paid home workers.

Effects of increase in scale on workers: (1) relearning

The increase in the scale of manufacturing had important and often disturbing consequences for workers. The most obvious was the need for men and women to relearn their trades. They were compelled to adapt their older skills to the new machines. Very often this adaptation resulted in a loss of either pay or prestige, or both. Most machine work was not skilled work. A trainee could "pick up" a trade in a week or so. Workers who had prided themselves on a particular skill and had been paid according to their ability to perform it, had to face the fact that industrial change was not only forcing them to relearn, but was compelling them to tell themselves that their new "skills"—if they could be called that—did not amount to very much. For example, when the machine itself could cut metal with infinitesimal accuracy, there was far less need than there had been previously for the skills of a human "fitter." Even if workers were not forced to relearn in these ways in order to adjust to increased scale, they often at least had to adjust to factory reorganization and rationalization. In workplaces where the hand-carrying of materials had been a major factor in their final cost, mechanization to reduce that cost would produce a bewildering series of changes. Electric cranes, used together with huge magnets in the iron and steel industries, increased the speed with which goods could be moved, and demanded that workers defer to whatever changes their introduction might entail.

(2) Efficiency

A second—and even more important—effect of the change in scale was the constant demand for further efficiency. The greater the scale of the operation, the more important it became to eliminate waste. One minute lost in the production of every ten pairs of shoes might not make much difference if only fifty pairs were produced in a day. But if hundreds were being made, it became crucial, in the eyes of management, to see that those minutes were no longer lost. In factories where large amounts of capital had been spent on new machinery, the owners, conscious of the cost of their investment, increased output in order to realize a profit on that investment. In factories where older machinery was still in use, owners believed that the only way they could remain competitive with modernized operations was by extracting all they could from their less productive equipment. In both cases, workers were pressed to produce more and more. One result of this drive for efficiency was a restructuring of wage scales. Prior to this period, although there had been serious wage disputes, both management and labor appeared content to bargain from the traditional notion of "a fair day's wage for a fair day's work." Definitions of what was fair naturally varied. But the level of individual performance was generally set by custom. What workers produced in the course of a day continued to determine what they were expected to produce. From about 1870 onward, however, expectations and procedures began to change. Periodic economic depressions in the last quarter of the nineteenth century saw profits fall before wages. This pattern caused employers to insist on greater individual productivity from their employees. It

Trade Union Certificate of Membership.
Trade unions helped workers as they adapted their skills to factory reorganization and modernization. The classical symbolism on the certificate helped ensure the union's respectability in the eyes of both its membership and the public.

BE UNITED AND INDUSTRIOUS

AMALGAMATED SOCIETY OF ENGINEERS, MACHINISTS, MILLWRIGHTS, SMITHS, AND PATTERN MAKERS.

FIRST · CAR

Henry Ford in His First Car. Ford was among the first to institute assembly-line efficiency in his factories.

was no longer enough to work at a job with customary speed. Workers were now asked to produce as much as the owners thought they were potentially capable of producing.

In order to encourage workers to accept these increased standards, factory-owners increasingly adopted piece rates (i.e., payment to workers according to the specific amount produced) rather than hourly or daily wages. Payment by piece rate was already a growing practice in many European and American factories. In theory, at least, workers were not opposed to this method of payment; they reasoned that their only hope for a share in increasing output lay in their chance to be paid directly for what they made. But when they were told that their pay would not increase unless they measured up to predetermined—and, to their mind, unrealistic—norms, they objected. They argued that rates were set according to the performance of the speediest workers. Even though workers might earn more money if they agreed to the new rates, they resented the intrusion of management upon their ability to control the pace of work.

THE NEW CAPITALISM

The growth of incorporation

Responding to increasing consumption and production and to the consequent pressures for further efficiency, the institutions of capitalism began to reorganize toward the end of the nineteenth century. Hitherto, most firms had been small or at most middle-sized; now, as firms grew and their need for capital increased, they began to incorporate. Limited liability laws, enacted by most countries in the course of the century, worked to encourage this incorporation. "Limited liability" meant that an individual owning stock in a particular corporation could be held liable only for the amount of his or her shares, should that corporation bankrupt itself. Once insured in this way, many thousands of middle-class men and women considered corporate investment a safe and financially promising way of making money for themselves. A stockholding, "rentier" class emerged, brought into existence by the willingness of governments to encourage capitalism through friendly legislation, and by the desire of capitalist businessmen to expand their industrial undertakings to meet increased demands.

More and more companies incorporated. In doing so, their management tended to be removed from the direct control of family founders or of company-based boards of directors. The influence of bankers and financiers, often situated in cities far removed from the factories they invested in, grew accordingly. These men were not investing their own money but the money of their clients; their power to stimulate or to discourage the growth of particular industries and enterprises encouraged a kind of impersonal "finance" capital. One consequence was a growing concern with cutting production costs, which, as we have seen, meant stricter control of labor.

Influence of bankers and financiers

Corporate organization on a large scale facilitated the spread of industrial unification. Some industries—steel, for example—combined vertically. Steel companies, to ensure uninterrupted production, acquired their own coal and iron mines. By doing so, they could guarantee themselves a supply of raw materials at attractive prices. Often the same steel

Vertical organization

companies would obtain control of companies whose products were made of steel: for example, shipyards or railway factories. Now they would not only possess a ready stock of raw materials but an equally ready market for their manufactured products—steel plates, steel rails, whatever they might be. Such vertical integration was possible only as a result of the money available for investment through the institutions of finance capital.

A second form of corporate organization was a horizontal formation: the cartel. These were combinations of individual companies producing the same kind of goods, joined for the purpose of controlling, if not eliminating, competition. Since their products were identical, an identical price could be charged. Companies involved in the production of coal and steel were especially suited to the organization of cartels because of the costs of initial capitalization. It is very expensive to build, equip, and man a steel foundry; thus there were relatively few of them. And because there were few, they were the more easily organized into a combine. Cartels were particularly strong in Germany; less so in France, where there was not as much heavy industry, where the tradition of the small family firm was particularly entrenched, and where there was longstanding opposition to competition in the form of price-cutting and general intra-industrial warfare. In Britain, though some cartels were formed, continuing subscription to the policy of free trade meant that companies would find it difficult to maintain fixed prices. How could they do so if they could not exclude, by means of a tariff, foreign competitors who wanted to undersell them? Germany had abandoned the policy of free trade in 1879; the United States, where cartels were known as trusts, did the same after the Civil War, though not all at once. Britain, because of its industrial lead and its reliance on foreign markets and imported raw materials, clung to free trade until well into the twentieth century.

Defenders of the cartel argued that the elimination of competition brought more stable prices and more continuous employment. They pointed out as well that cartels almost always reduced the cost of production. Opponents questioned, however, whether those reduced costs were reflected in lower prices, or, as they charged, in higher stockholder profits. Critics of cartels were vocal in the United States, where the so-called captains of industry, most prominently the financier J. P. Morgan, were attacked as a new breed of feudal barons. The Sherman Antitrust Act was passed by Congress in 1890 to curb the practice of industrial combination. It had little effect in retarding the process, however, until the trust-busting presidency of Theodore Roosevelt.

Elsewhere in the West at the end of the nineteenth century, governments and big business tended to develop close working relationships contrary to the laissez-faire theories of early industrial entrepreneurs. A significant manifestation of this new partnership was the appearance of businessmen and financiers as officers of state. Joseph Chamberlain, a Birmingham manufacturer, served as Britain's colonial secretary; the German banker Bernhard Dernburg was the German secretary of state for colonies; the Frenchman Charles Jonnart, president of the Suez Canal

Horizontal organization: cartels

J. P. Morgan

Big business and government

Company and the Saint-Étienne steel works, was later governor-general of Algeria; Guilio Prinetti, a northern Italian industrialist, was his country's foreign minister from 1901 to 1903. The interrelationship between government and industry, like the growth of cartels and combines, was seen as a natural development in the capitalist system, which, its defenders argued, was showering its benefits on all classes of society.

INTERNATIONAL COMPETITION: IMPERIALISM

As nations proceeded with the business of industrialization during the late nineteenth century, international competitiveness grew more intense. The search for markets brought the European nations into direct competition with one another. One result was that the dogma of free trade was abandoned by all save Britain. As we have seen, the Germans rejected the policy of low tariffs in 1879. Austria and Russia had already done so. Spain instituted new import duties in 1877 and again in 1891. In France, two decades of gradual abandonment were climaxed by the passage of the Méline Tariff in 1892. Although individual nations attempted to isolate themselves from each other in this way, developments in international economics mandated the continuing growth and development of an interlocking, worldwide system of manufacturing, trade, and finance. The general adoption by western Europe and the United States of the gold standard meant that the currencies could be readily exchanged with each other against the measure of a common standard—the international price of gold. Hence countries needing to import from the United States, for example, did not have to sell goods directly to that country. They could sell to South America, exchange the money they received for gold, and then buy from America.

A global economy

Almost all European countries, dependent on vast supplies of raw materials to sustain their rate of industrial production, imported more than they exported. To avoid the mounting deficits that would otherwise have resulted from this practice, they relied upon "invisible" exports: i.e., shipping, insurance, and interest on money lent or invested. The extent of Britain's exports in these areas was far greater than that of any other country. London was the money market of the world, to which would-be borrowers looked for assistance before turning elsewhere. By 1914, Britain had $20 billion invested overseas, compared with the $8.7 billion of the French and the $6 billion of the Germans. The insurance firm of Lloyds of London served clients around the world. The British merchant fleet transported the manufactured goods and raw materials of every trading nation. It was the volume of its "invisible" exports that permitted Britain to remain faithful to the doctrine of free trade while other European nations were forced to institute tariffs.

"Invisible" exports

The competition between the principal economic powers of this worldwide marketplace affected not only their relationships with each other but also with those less-developed areas upon which they were increasingly dependent for both raw materials and markets. Some of those areas,

Effects on Africa and Asia

such as India and China, were the seats of ancient empires. Others, such as central Africa, sheltered equally complex though less geographically expansive cultures. No matter what the nature of the indigenous civilization, the intrusion upon it of modern science and technology, systematic wage labor, and financial and legal institutions caused enormous disruption. Though drawn into the world economy, these areas did not draw from it the benefits that the West did. Native industries such as Indian textile spinning and weaving stood no chance in competition with the factory-made products of Manchester. African herdsmen and hunters endured the disruption of their living habits by the activities of European ranchers and miners. Men who had made their living as boatmen and carters lost their livelihood to the railways constructed by Western nations. New jobs there might be; but they were jobs worked according to a Western style, dictated by Western economic demands, and threatened by Western economic disorders. In great measure the workers of this emerging world were assuming the role of a global unskilled working class under the hegemony of Western capitalism.

Earlier imperialism

With this global background in mind, we can better understand the history of late-nineteenth-century imperialism—the subjugation by the European powers of vast tracts of land and indigenous populations, primarily on the continents of Africa and Asia. Imperialism was by no means a new phenomenon. During the eighteenth century, the French and British had colonized India. In other parts of the world, where Western powers did not govern directly, they often exercised an indirect influence so powerful as to shape the policies and dictate the activities of indigenous authorities. When the West "opened" China beginning in 1842, it left the Chinese in nominal charge of their state. But it ensured that affairs would be conducted to British advantage and within a British "sphere of influence." Britain added in this way to its "informal" empire, expanding into South America, Africa, and South and East Asia.

European views of overseas empire

As international rivalries increased, European powers moved with greater frequency and determination to control both the governments and economies of underdeveloped nations and territories. French politicians supported imperialism as a means of restoring national prestige and honor, lost in the humiliating defeat by the Germans in the Franco-Prussian War of 1870–1871. The British, on the other hand, looked with alarm at the accelerating pace of industrialization in Germany and France and feared losing their existing and potential world markets. The Germans, recently unified in a modern nation, viewed overseas empire as a "national" possession and as a way of entering the "club" of great powers.

Technology as a tool of imperialism

The West's inventions of the late eighteenth and nineteenth centuries provided the tools of imperialism. Metal-hulled steamships, widely used for trade with Africa from the 1850s, provided faster, cheaper transportation and allowed for the shipment of bulk cargoes such as unprocessed crops and heavy ores. Travel time between Liverpool and Cape Town was reduced from an average of three months to three weeks. Sail power quickly lost out to steam. By the same token, river and lake steamers overcame the problem of transportation in the African interior. Submarine

Dredges and Elevators at Work on the Construction of the Suez Canal, 1869. Imperial expansion depended to a great degree on technology.

telegraph cables also brought Africa closer to Europe; by 1885, western and southern Africa were linked to London and Paris. With the use of quinine, malaria became less threatening and Europeans were emboldened to penetrate the tropical rain forests. In military technology, the shift in Africa from muzzle-loading rifles to fast-firing breechloaders was completed by 1878. European armies gained an even greater advantage with the introduction in 1884 of the Maxim gun, a prototype of the modern machine gun, capable of firing eleven bullets a second. These and other inventions and scientific breakthroughs made imperialist conquest and resource exploitation vastly cheaper.

The scope, intensity, and long-range consequences of this so-called new imperialism of the late nineteenth century have generated a heated debate about its causes. One influential group of social critics and historians has argued that the causes were predominantly, if not exclusively, economic. As early as 1902, the English social reformer and theorist J. A. Hobson charged that what he called "the scramble for Africa" had occurred as a result of the economic interests of a small group of extremely rich and influential financiers throughout western Europe. Hobson declared that the colonization of Africa had produced little economic gain for the taxpayers whose countries had dispatched armies of conquest and occupation at the behest of international capitalists. Profits went only to the rich, who ventured beyond the bounds of economically stagnant western Europe in search of a higher return on their investments than could be realized at home. Hobson concluded that late-nineteenth-century imperialism was "a depraved choice of national life," appealing primarily to "the lusts of self-seeking acquisitiveness and forceful domination."

Hobson's analysis inspired a more influential critique of imperialism by the Russian communist and future revolutionary leader N. Lenin (see p. 930). Lenin agreed with Hobson that imperialism was an economic

Imperialism as economics: Hobson

Lenin

phenomenon. But, unlike Hobson, he saw it as an integral and inevitable phase of the capitalist system, as the title of his 1916 treatise, *Imperialism: The Highest Stage of Capitalism,* explicitly declared. Capitalist competition, Lenin argued, and the consequent monopolies that it had produced, had lowered domestic profits and thus compelled the owners of surplus capital to invest it overseas. The alternative, enlarging home markets by raising wages, would serve only to decrease profits further. Imperialism was thus the creature of the internal contradictions of industrial capitalism.

Limits to the economic argument

While most historians would agree that economic pressures were one important cause of imperialism, they have remained uncomfortable with analyses that ignore other factors they consider equally important. They remain prepared to acknowledge the role of economics when it seems to make sense to do so: in the case of Great Britain, for example, where about half its total of £4 billion in foreign investments was at work within its empire. In all western European countries, demand for raw materials made colonies a necessary investment and helped persuade governments that imperialism was a worthwhile policy. Yet the economic explanation begins to break down when one considers facts like the following: that colonial markets were generally too poor to answer the needs of European manufacturers; that Africa, the continent over which there was the greatest "scramble," was also the poorest and least profitable to investors; that only a very small portion of German capital was invested in German colonies before 1914; that only one-fifth of French capital was so invested; that, indeed, the French had more capital invested in Russia, hoping to stabilize that ally against the Germans, than in all their colonial possessions.

Imperialism and international politics

Imperial policy-making was both a response to political and economic considerations, and a corollary to the process of nation-building. National security and the preservation of a general balance of power were issues never far from the forefront of politicians' thinking and planning. Great-power interest in the eastern Mediterranean grew with the demise of the Ottoman Empire. At the Berlin Conference of 1878, France secured from Great Britain and Germany the assurance of a free hand in Tunisia as compensation for its acquiescence in the British annexation of Cyprus. This understanding breathed new life into the principle that remuneration of territorial claims in one region must be compensated for by concessions elsewhere.

British domination of Egypt

Britain's domination of Egypt in the 1880s was the result, in large measure, of its fear of what might occur in the Near East should large portions of the decaying Ottoman Empire fall into Russian hands. Britain had purchased 44 percent of the shares in the Suez Canal Company in 1875, and considered the waterway a strategic lifeline to the East. The canal had been built by the French under the direction of the engineer Ferdinand de Lesseps. Begun in 1859 and completed in 1869, it was expected to assist France in its bid for commercial expansion to the East. Britain obtained its shares in 1875 from the spendthrift khedive (viceroy) of Egypt at a time when he was threatened with bankruptcy. When, in 1882, nationalist rebels protested continuing British intervention in the internal affairs of Egypt, the British claimed they had no choice but to bombard the port of Alexandria and place the Egyptian ruler under their protection. A continuing British presence in Egypt, and the willingness of the British government to support Egyptian claims to the Upper Nile, worried the French, who were growing to fear Britain's political domination of the entire African continent. Moving to correct what they perceived as a severe political imbalance, the French challenged the British and at Fashoda, in the Sudan, came close to war in 1898. The British called the French bluff, however, and war was averted.

The power struggle over Suez, Egypt, and the Sudan provides an excellent example of the manner in which international politics was directly related to imperial advance. It suggests, as well, that what passed for "imperial policy" was less a matter of long-range planning than of a series of pragmatic and often spontaneous responses to particular colonial political and economic situations. Often those in charge of policy-making found themselves led beyond their original ambitions, not only by the demands of international rivalries, but by the actions of individual explorers and entrepreneurs who established claims to hitherto unknown territories that home governments then felt compelled to recognize and defend.

Imperialism must also be understood as something more than official policy, whether carefully conceived or accidental. A French diplomat once described the dynamic English imperial adventurer Cecil Rhodes as "a force cast in an idea"; the same might be said of imperialism itself. Imperialism as an idea excited the minds of explorers like the Scottish missionary David Livingstone, who believed that the British conquest of Africa would put an end to the East African slave trade, and "introduce the Negro family into the body of corporate nations." Rudyard Kipling, the English poet and novelist, wrote of "the white man's burden," of his mission to civilize the "half devil, half child" races that inhabited what most Europeans considered the "barbaric" and "heathen" quarters of the globe. To combat

Imperial policy-making

"The white man's burden"

A Traction Engine in Use during the Boer War. Imperial warfare was by 1900 an increasingly mechanized business.

slave-trading, famine, filth, and illiteracy seemed to many a legitimate reason for invading the jungles of Africa and Asia.

Imperialism as an idea was also of use to European governments at home. A populace could be encouraged to forget domestic hardships as it celebrated its country's triumphs overseas. Nationalism was stimulated by arguments such as that expressed by the German historian Heinrich von Treitschke in 1887: that "the colonizing impulse has become a vital question for a great nation"—the implication clearly being that a nation was not great unless it possessed colonies. Associations with a semi-official standing—the Deutsche Kolonialgesellschaft, the Comité de l'Afrique Française, the Royal Colonial Institute—propagandized on behalf of empire, as did newspapers, which recognized in sensational stories of overseas conquest a means of attracting a newly literate clientele. In these organizations and activities we discover further evidence of the way in which governments encouraged the nationalist sentiment to further state policy.

Imperial competition centered in Africa. In 1875, 11 percent of the continent was in European hands; by 1902, 90 percent. Germans pressed inward from the east; Frenchmen from the west. The Portuguese schemed to connect the ancient colonies of Angola, on the west, with Mozambique, on the east. Most active among the European powers during this initial period of late-nineteenth-century colonization was a privately financed group of Belgians under the leadership of that country's king, Leopold II (1865–1909). In association with H. M. Stanley, an American newspaperman and explorer, Leopold and a group of financiers founded the International Association for the Exploration and Civilization of the Congo in 1876, which negotiated treaties with chieftains that opened the Congo River basin to commercial exploitation. A conference, called in Berlin in 1884, was attended by most European nations and the United States and attempted to establish certain ground rules for the game of imperial acquisition. The Congo was declared a Free

Slaves in Chains, 1896. In Africa, native labor was exploited, sometimes by Europeans and often by other natives, as here.

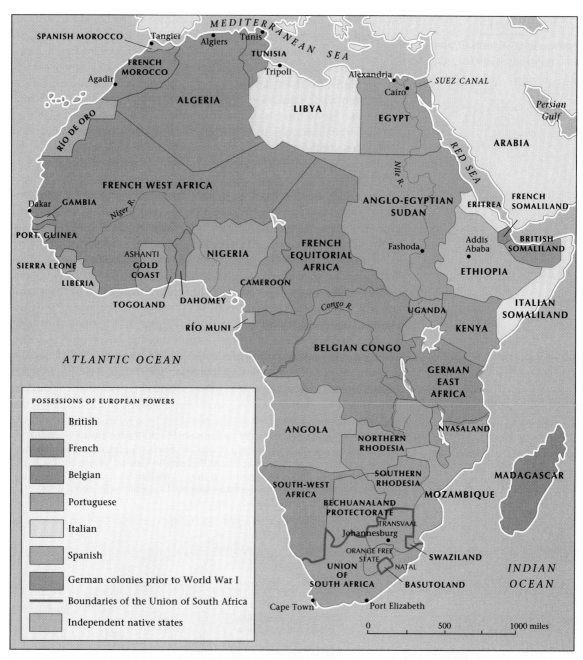

Imperialism in Africa to the Eve of World War I

State, under the trusteeship of Leopold (the first example of this later familiar device of protecting "backward" peoples). A European nation with holdings on the African coast was declared to have first rights to territory in the interior behind those coastal regions. Those rights, however, could be sustained only by what was termed "real" occupation—that is, the presence of either administrators or troops. The scramble was on! Occupation was accompanied by the exploitation of native labor. Agreements reached with local chieftains, whom the Europeans courted, authorized the employment of men and women as laborers under conditions little better than slavery. Often compelled to live in compounds apart from their families, Africans were victimized by a system that rooted out prevailing custom without attempting to establish anything like a new civilization in its place. In the Congo, the Arab slave trade was suppressed, replaced by a system of forced labor. Tribal lands were confiscated and rebellions brutally crushed.

The scramble for territory

The division of the geographical spoils accelerated after 1885. The Portuguese increased their hold in Angola and Mozambique. The Italians invaded Somaliland and Eritrea. They attempted to extend their controls to Ethiopia, but were repulsed in 1896 by an army of 80,000 Ethiopians, the first instance of a major victory by native Africans over whites. Germany came relatively late to the game. Bismarck was reluctant to engage in an enterprise that, he believed, would do little to profit the empire either politically or economically. Eventually concluding, however, that they could not afford to let other powers divide the continent among them, the Germans established colonies in German East Africa, in the Cameroons and Togo on the west coast, and in the desertlike territory of southwest Africa. The French controlled large areas in western Africa and, in the Red Sea, the port of Djibouti. It was to further their plan for an east-west link that the French risked challenging the British at Fashoda. That scheme, however,

Left: **"The Rhodes Colossus."** The ambitions of Cecil Rhodes, the driving force behind British imperialism in South Africa, are satirized in this cartoon, which appeared in *Punch*. Right: **"Now We Shant Be Long to Cairo."** So read the banner across Engine No. 1 taking the first train from Umtali to Salisbury, Rhodesia, reflecting Cecil Rhodes's vision of a Capetown-to-Cairo railway as a symbol of British domination of the African continent.

Boer Commandos under Louis Botha. Botha became the first prime minister of the Union of South Africa following the Boer War.

fell afoul of Britain's need to dominate Egypt, and of its plans for a north-south connection through the African continent.

Cecil Rhodes, the English entrepreneur and imperial visionary, promoted the notion of a Capetown-to-Cairo railway both before and after his assumption of the prime ministership of the Cape Colony in 1890. His plans were thwarted in the south, however, by the presence of two independent neighboring republics, the Transvaal and the Orange Free State, both inhabited by descendants of the original Dutch settlers in South Africa. These Boers—the Dutch word for "farmers"—had fled from the British in the Cape Colony and established themselves in their agricultural states in defiant opposition to the freebooting and exploitationist spirit of the British economic adventurers who had driven them from their original settlements. When diamonds and gold were discovered in the Transvaal in 1886, the tension between the British and the Boers grew. As British prospectors and entrepreneurs moved in, the Boers refused to pass laws permitting the exploitation of their resources by foreign firms. They also taxed the interlopers heavily. Rhodes retaliated by attempting to force a war with the republics. His first try, the dispatching of a force of irregular volunteers under the command of Dr. Leander Starr Jameson in 1895, failed to provoke a conflict, but precipitated general censure on the British for harassing a peaceful neighbor. Rhodes was forced to resign as prime minister of the Cape Colony in 1896. War broke out in 1899. Its course, however, did not run according to British plans. The Boers proved tough fighters. It took three years to

British Imperialism. Left: "The Execution of 'John Company.'" This 1857 *Punch* cartoon graphically depicts the abolition of the East India Company in the wake of the "Indian Mutiny." Above: A British officer in India, c. 1900.

secure an armistice; it took months more and resort to brutal policies such as detention camps and farm-burning to bring the resilient republicans to heel. The war cost the British their international prestige, and heightened the Anglo-German rivalry, the kaiser having publicly pronounced his sympathy with the Boer cause.

Britain managed to strengthen its hold on its prize imperial possession—India—throughout the nineteenth century. The "informal" rule of the commercially motivated British East India Company had proved ineffective in 1857, when native Indian troops and a large number of other disaffected elements within the subcontinent rebelled in what the British chose to call the "Indian mutiny" but which was in fact a far more serious and deep-seated challenge to foreign control. Thereafter the British government directly administered the subcontinent. But they decided to change their approach to colonial government in India, ruling through the Indian upper classes rather than in opposition to them. Although instruction in British-sponsored schools continued in English, Indian customs were tolerated as they had not been before, and princes and their bureaucracies were incorporated as protectorates into the general scheme of government. A class of westernized, and yet devotedly Indian, civil servants and businessmen thus emerged by the end of the nineteenth century, trained by the British yet burdened by no sense of obligation to their tutors. This group provided the leadership for the nationalist movement that was to challenge British rule in India during the mid-twentieth century.

The British in India

Imperialism. Germans traveling in East Africa, 1907.

Britain's aim in India was to promote order and stability. Civil servants administered justice even-handedly. They promoted improved sanitation, which, ironically, helped to increase the country's population beyond the point where it could sustain itself. But the vast majority of Indians remained desperately poor, victims in many cases of the importation of cheap manufactured goods that threatened indigenous industries and testified to Britain's willingness to subordinate its colonies' economic well-being to its own.

The consequences of British rule in India

The pattern of British imperialism differed throughout the world. In areas dominated by white settlers, home rule was introduced in hopes of preventing the sort of disaffection that had produced the American Revolution. Thus Australia was granted self-government in the 1850s, New Zealand in 1852. In 1867, a united Dominion of Canada, with its own federal government and legislature, was established.

From colonization to self-government

Elsewhere in the world, Western nations hastened to plant their colors upon those territories that promised rewards, either economic or strategic. Britain, France, Germany, and the Netherlands all staked claims in the East Indies; the Dutch achieved an overall hegemony there by 1900. China allowed itself to be victimized by a series of commercial treaties; among the predators was China's neighbor Japan, the only non-Western nation able to modernize in the nineteenth century.

Imperialism elsewhere

Russia was a persistently imperialist power throughout the nineteenth century. Its rulers championed a policy of annexation—by conquest, treaty, or both—of lands bordering on the existing Russian state. Beginning in 1813, with the acquisition of Georgia following a war with Persia, the tsars continued to press their expansionist quest. Bessarabia and Turkestan (from the Turks) and Armenia (from the Persians) vastly increased the empire's size. This southward colonization brought the Russians close to war with the British twice: first in 1881, when Russian

Russian imperialist advances

873

troops occupied territories in the Trans-Caspian region, and again in 1884–1887, when the tsar's forces advanced to the frontier of Afghanistan. In both cases the British feared incursions into areas they deemed within their sphere of influence in the Middle East. They were concerned, as well, about a possible threat to India. After mid-century, the Russians began to press east as well as south, wringing various commercial concessions from the Chinese and founding the Siberian city of Vladivostok in 1860. In 1875, the Japanese traded the southern half of Sakhalin Island for the previously Russian Kurile Islands. The tsars' eastward advance was finally halted in 1905, when in a war with the Japanese the imperial armies more than met their match.

Russian disunity

Although the vast Russian Empire was essentially of one geographical piece, it was by no means one nation. Racial, ethnic, and religious differences made any attempt at national unification all but impossible, and the task of governance complex. Whether under the nineteenth-century tsars or, later, under the dictatorship of the Soviet Union, powerful centrifugal forces pulled against genuine unification—a fact proven during the years immediately following the break-up of the Soviet Union in 1991.

U.S. imperialism

The United States played a double game. It acted as champion of the underdeveloped countries in the Western Hemisphere when they were threatened from Europe, yet was willing, whenever it suited the American government, to prey on its neighbors, either "informally" or formally. When, at the end of the century, Spain's feeble hold on its Caribbean and Pacific colonies encouraged talk of rebellion, the United States stepped in to protect its investments and guarantee its maritime security. It declared and won the Spanish-American War in 1898 on trumped-up grounds. In the same year the United States annexed Puerto Rico and the Philippines and established a "protectorate" over Cuba. When Colombia's colony Panama threatened to rebel in 1903, the Americans quickly backed the rebels, recognized Panama as a republic, and then proceeded to grant it protection while Americans built the Panama Canal on land leased from the new government. Intervention in Santo Domingo and in Hawaii proved that the United States was no less an imperial power than the nations of Europe.

By the end of the nineteenth century, Western imperialist powers had succeeded in binding the world together as it had never been before. The military and economic power with which they had accomplished this meant that, for the time being at any rate, they would be the world's masters.

SUMMARY POINTS

- Development of sophisticated technology, particularly in metals, chemicals, and electricity, accelerated after 1870. Iron was replaced by the much more versatile steel, and the convenience of electricity revolutionized travel, communication, industrial production, and commercial products.

- The ever-rising standard of living and a consequent dramatic increase in European consumerism stemmed from improvements in public sanitation, scientific discoveries about disease and health, and financial prosperity of families and businesses.

- Imperialism was integral to the worldwide system of manufacturing, trade, and finance. Both economic and cultural forces prompted European powers to occupy and control underdeveloped nations in Asia and Africa.

- Fierce international competition divided Africa, resulting in war and poverty for its inhabitants. Britain's monopoly of India promoted order and stability while fueling nationalist sentiments.

SELECTED READINGS

Ashworth, William, *A Short History of the International Economy since 1850,* 4th ed., New York, 1987. A good introduction.

Austen, Ralph A., *African Economic History,* Portsmouth, N.H., 1987. The first comprehensive examination of sub-Saharan Africa's economic history, focusing on internal development and external dependency.

Barkin, Kenneth D., *The Controversy over German Industrialization, 1890–1902,* Chicago, 1970. The political and social struggles between agricultural and industrial interests.

Cameron, Rondo E., *France and the Economic Development of Europe, 1800–1914,* Princeton, 1961. Emphasizes the export of French capital and skill in the economic growth of Europe.

Fieldhouse, D. K., *Economics and Empire, 1830–1914,* London, 1973. Argues against the primacy of economic factors in the spread of imperialism.

Gollwitzer, Heinz, *Europe in the Age of Imperialism, 1880–1914,* London, 1969. A brief survey with excellent illustrations.

Headrick, Daniel R., *The Tools of Empire: Technology and European Imperialism in the Nineteenth Century,* Oxford, Eng., 1981. A study of the relationship between technological innovation and imperialism.

Hobsbawm, Eric, *The Age of Empire, 1875–1914,* New York, 1987. Surveys the European scene at a time of apparent stability and real decline.

Kiernan, V. G., *Marxism and Imperialism,* New York, 1975. Argues the Marxist position effectively.

Kindleberger, C. P., *Economic Growth in France and Britain, 1851–1950,* Cambridge, Mass., 1963. A technical account.

Landes, David S., *The Unbound Prometheus: Technological Change and Industrial Development in Western Europe from 1750 to the Present,* London, 1969. Particularly good on the Anglo-German rivalry.

Langer, William L., *The Diplomacy of Imperialism, 1890–1902,* New York, 1960. A thorough, standard work, useful for its analysis of the intellectual as well as political origins of imperialism.

McLynn, Frank, *Hearts of Darkness: The European Exploration of Africa*, New York, 1992. An account of the Europeans who explored Africa, their backgrounds, motivations, strengths, and shortcomings.

Miller, Michael B., *The Bon Marché: Bourgeois Culture and the Department Store, 1869–1920*, Princeton, 1981. Explores the revolution in merchandising of the late nineteenth century.

Milward, Alan S., and S. B. Saul, *The Development of the Economies of Continental Europe, 1850–1914*, Cambridge, Mass., 1977. An excellent, comprehensive text, particularly good on the smaller European nations.

Moch, Leslie P., *Moving Europeans: Migration in Western Europe since 1650*, Bloomington, Ind., 1993. A survey of migratory patterns.

Moorehead, Alan, *The White Nile*, rev. ed., New York, 1971. Captures much of the excitement of imperial exploration.

Pakenham, Thomas, *The Scramble for Africa, 1876–1912*, London, 1991. A well-written and exhaustive exploration of the European scramble for Africa in the late nineteenth century.

Roberts, P. E., *History of British India under the Company and the Crown*, 3d ed., New York, 1952. An excellent political text.

Robinson, Ronald, and J. Gallagher, *Africa and the Victorians: The Official Mind of Imperialism*, London, 1961. Contains their famous thesis that imperialism was not deliberately pursued as a policy of state, but rather was a response to events in colonial areas. The modern debate over imperialism begins with this work.

Rotberg, Robert I., *The Founder: Cecil Rhodes and the Pursuit of Power*. New York, 1988. The author relies on psychology to assist in an analysis of the controversial imperialist.

Stolper, Gustav, et al., *The German Economy, 1870 to 1940*, New York, 1967. A good introduction.

SOURCE MATERIALS

Court, W. H. B., *British Economic History, 1870–1914; Commentary and Documents*, Cambridge, Eng., 1965. An excellent collection of documents.

Hobson, J. A., *Imperialism: A Study*, London, 1902.

Lenin, Vladimir, *Imperialism: The Highest Stage of Capitalism*, 1916. (Many English editions.) Lenin's most significant contribution to Marxist ideology. He saw the essence of imperialism as the export of capital rather than goods, which led to worldwide competition, of which World War I was an inevitable result.

Reitz, Deneys, *Commando: A Boer Journal of the Boer War*, London, 1929. A superb memoir of the Boer War.

CHAPTER 25

THE MIDDLE CLASS CHALLENGED

> The time of surprise attacks, of revolutions carried through by small conscious minorities at the head of unconscious masses, is past. Where it is a question of a complete transformation of the social organization, the masses themselves must also be in it, must themselves already have grasped what is at stake, what they are going in for, with body and soul.
>
> —FRIEDRICH ENGELS, Introduction to Karl Marx,
> *The Class Struggles in France*, 1848–50

CAPITALISM'S CONTINUING EXPANSION encouraged middle-class men and women at the end of the nineteenth century to consider themselves the necessary key to the progress of the human race. They believed that society would most successfully advance under their auspices and in accordance with their moral and economic precepts, grounded in a belief in the importance and inevitability of continued material progress. At the same time, however, that belief was being challenged from several directions. In each case, the challenges called into question assumptions close to the core of middle-class consciousness. Socialist doctrine, which was for the first time receiving a widespread hearing, pronounced capitalism a threat, rather than a boon, to society. New scientific theories—particularly the theory of evolution—declared that the key to progress was not the well-laid schemes of humanity, but chance. Psychologists posited the irrationality of human beings and philosophers their ultimate helplessness. Paintings, poetry, and music proclaimed an artists' revolution on behalf of the idea of art for its own sake, not for the edification of a middle-class public. Together, these various intellectual and cultural currents threatened notions of middle-class superiority.

THE CHALLENGE OF SOCIALISM

The history of socialism in the latter half of the nineteenth century is, to a great degree, the biography of its most famous propagandist and theoretician, the German Karl Marx. Marx was both a social thinker and a political leader. At certain times theory dictated his actions; at others, political events led him to alter doctrine. But always he was at the center of the socialist movement, his moral passion, as much as his scholarly research, shaping the course of its events. The fact of his widespread influence is

The influence of Karl Marx

Karl Marx

Marx's stages of history

Capital

particularly remarkable in light of his exile from the mainstream of Continental socialism. He lived from 1849 until his death in London, in a country whose toleration of socialists was a mark of its comparative immunity from their doctrines.

Like his friend and collaborator Friedrich Engels, Marx was the son of middle-class parents. After study at the University of Berlin, in 1842 he took a job as editor of the *Rhineland Gazette,* hoping to use that position to argue for the transformation of a society he was growing to despise. His radical politics soon put him at odds with his publishers, however. He moved first to Paris and then to Brussels, where he helped found the Communist League, a body whose declared aim was the overthrow of the middle class. While in Paris, Marx had renewed a former friendship with Engels. Engels, who lived in Manchester from 1842–1844 as part of his training for a position in the family firm, had just written *The Condition of the Working Class in England* (1845), in which he portrayed the misery of the recently industrialized urban masses. Together, during the late 1840s, the two men produced a theory of revolutionary change that was published by Marx at the request of the League in 1848, at the height of the struggles on the Continent, as *The Communist Manifesto.*

In the *Manifesto* Marx outlined a theory of history that owed a good deal to the German philosopher Hegel (see p. 816). Hegel, it will be recalled, had argued that ideas, the motive force of history, were in constant conflict with each other, and that this clash between ideas in turn would produce an eventual synthesis, representing an advance in the history of the human race. Marx adapted this particular progressive notion of history to his own uses. Whereas Hegel perceived conflict and resolution (a dialectic) in terms of ideas, Marx saw them in terms of economic forces. Society, he argued, was at any time no more than the reflection of a hierarchy of classes dictated by those who own the means of production and control the distribution of its material goods. As history had progressed, so had the means changed. Feudalism and manorialism were vanquished by capitalism. And capitalism, Marx declared, would be vanquished in turn by communism.

During the 1850s and 1860s Marx labored to produce his definitive analysis of capitalist economics. The first volume of *Capital* was published in 1867. The argument of *Capital* was grounded in that dialectical idealism and economic materialism that, as we have seen, shaped Marx's earlier thinking and writing. In *Capital* he synthesized ideas he and Engels had enunciated in their previous tracts. He described in detail the processes of production, exchange, and distribution as they operated within the capitalist system. He argued that under capitalism, workers were denied their rightful share of profits. The value of any manufactured item, Marx claimed, was determined by the amount of labor necessary to produce it. Yet workers were hired at wages whose value was far less than the value of the goods they produced. The difference between the value of workers' wages and the value of their work as sold was pocketed by members of the capitalist class, who, according to Marx, made off with far more than a justifiable portion of the sale price. This so-called labor theory of value, borrowed from a somewhat similar doctrine held by David Ricardo and other classical economists, was the basis for Marx's claim that the working class was compelled to suffer under the capitalist system. Because workers were forced to sell their labor they became nothing more than commodities in the economic market.

Marx predicted that capitalism would eventually do itself in. He argued that as time passed, market competition would compel the formation of ever-larger industrial and financial combinations. As the smaller entrepreneurial class—the petty bourgeoisie—was squeezed out by more powerful combines, its members would join with the proletariat, until society resembled a vast pyramid, with a much-enlarged proletariat at its base and an opposing force of a few powerful capitalists at its tip. At this point, Marx declared, the proletariat would rise in revolution against what was left of the bourgeoisie.

After capitalism had received its death blow at the hands of the workers, it would be followed by a socialist stage, characterized by the dictatorship of the proletariat; payment in accordance with work performed; and ownership and operation by the state of all means of production, distribution, and exchange. In time socialism would be succeeded by communism, the goal of historical evolution. The elimination of private property would also mean the elimination of the proletariat, which existed only in opposition to the property-owning class. Thus communism would bring with it a classless society. The essence of communism was payment in accordance with needs. The wage system would be abolished, and citizens would be expected to work in accordance with their abilities, entitled to receive from the total fund of wealth produced an amount in proportion to their needs. The state would now disappear, relegated to the museum of antiquities, "along with the bronze ax and the spinning wheel." Nothing would replace it except voluntary associations to operate the means of production and provide for social necessities.

In the ten years after its publication, *Capital* was translated into English (Marx had written it in German), French, Russian, and Italian. The book's widespread appeal was the result of its compelling deterministic certainty and of its vigorous crusading temper. Though most of what *Capital* predicted has failed to occur, middle- and working-class socialists reading it soon after its publication and measuring its pronouncements against the capitalistic world they knew had little difficulty in accepting Marx's reasoning. It seemed to them that he had constructed an objective science of society out of their own experiences. The book became the theoretical rallying point for a growing band of socialists who stood opposed to the world the middle class had made. For a time it breathed life into an organization of Continental and British workers that had been founded in London in 1864: the International Workingmen's Association, usually referred to as the International. This body had been formed with the declared purpose of forging an international working-class alliance to overthrow capitalism and abolish private property. Marx delivered its

Marx as prophet

The advent of communism

The International

Roadblocks to radicalism

Ferdinand Lassalle

Marx vs. Lassalle and Bakunin

Mikhail Bakunin

inaugural address, in which he preached that workers must win political power for themselves if they were ever to escape their industrial bondage.

Various difficulties had prevented the formation of a radically oriented workers' organization prior to this time. There was, first of all, fear of official reprisal. Second, the irregular pace of industrialization across Europe meant that workers in one country could have little understanding of the particular plight of their fellow workers elsewhere. Finally, the period after 1850 had witnessed an increase in general prosperity that encouraged the more highly skilled—and more politically conscious—workers to forsake revolutionary goals and to pursue the more immediate end of accommodation with middle-class politicians. The German socialists' dealings with Bismarck (see pp. 913–914), were a case in point. Meanwhile, however, the determination of a small band of dedicated radical socialists temporarily surmounted these problems to permit the formation of the first international workers' association.

Marx immediately assumed the direction of the International and labored to exclude both moderates and extreme radicals from its councils. He denounced the German socialists and their leader Ferdinand Lassalle for their failure to oppose Bismarck. Lassalle, a strong German nationalist, advocated democratic reform within a parliamentary framework. Marx, on the other hand, argued that the duty of socialists was not partnership with the state, but rather its overthrow. At the same time, Marx battled the doctrines of the Russian anarchist Mikhail Bakunin, who challenged the socialist notion that social evil was the product of capitalism. Bakunin argued that the state was the ultimate villain, and preached its immediate destruction through isolated acts of terrorism. He also opposed centralization within the International, urging instead a kind of federal autonomy for each national workers' group. To Marx, these individualist notions represented nothing more than reversion to a kind of primitive rebellion, heroic but ultimately fruitless. After years of conflict, he succeeded in having Bakunin banished from the International in 1872.

The International's successes were largely limited to the 1860s. Individual trade unions in various countries were persuaded to join in its united campaign, which preached revolution and, through the application of pressure both at the ballot box and in the factory, seemed to promise at least higher wages and shorter hours. Under Marx's direction the International was a highly organized and tightly controlled body, far more effective in this respect than any previous socialist organization.

Yet despite Marx's abilities as an authoritarian chief of staff, the International throughout its existence had to battle those same circumstances that had delayed its foundation. In addition, Marx's insistence upon control from the center thwarted a growing desire on the part of individual socialist organizations to pursue programs of immediate benefit to themselves. These factors weakened the International. What probably brought about its demise was its association with events occurring in Paris after the defeat of France by Germany in 1870 in the Franco-Prussian War.

Following the collapse of Napoleon III, a new republic, generally conservative in tone, had been established by the French. In March 1871, the government attempted to disarm the Paris National Guard, a volunteer citizen army with radical political sympathies. The guard refused to surrender, declared its autonomy, deposed officials of the new government, and proclaimed a revolutionary committee—the Commune—as the true government of France. Though this movement is commonly described as a rebellion of dangerous radicals intent upon the destruction of law and order, most of its members resembled the Jacobins of the first French Revolution and belonged largely to the lower-middle class. They did not advocate the abolition of private property but rather its wider distribution. Their respect for the deposits in the Bank of France was as scrupulous as any bourgeois financier might have wished. Their most radical political action was a symbolic one: the toppling of a statue of Napoleon I in the Place Vendôme. The movement was precipitated by bitterness over the defeat of Napoleon III and exhaustion by the long siege of Paris that followed. There were fears as well that the central government would be dominated by the rural population to the disadvantage of the urban masses in the capital. After several weeks of frustrating disputation, the conflict turned into a bloody civil war. The Communards killed about sixty hostages, including the archbishop of Paris. The government numbered its victims by the thousands. The courts-martial that were set up executed twenty-six. Thousands of others were sentenced to imprisonment or banishment in New Caledonia, in the South Pacific.

While middle-class Europe reacted in horror at what it mistakenly perceived as a second Reign of Terror, Marx, in the name of the International, extolled the courage of the Communards, who, he wrote, had fought the first pitched battle in the class war he had predicted. In a

The Paris Commune

The Commune and the International

A Symbol of the Paris Commune. The statue of Napoleon I in Roman garb, a symbol of imperial absolutism, is toppled from its base by the Communards.

Propaganda and the Paris Commune. This photograph, purporting to record the assassination of hostages by the radical Communards, was actually faked by their enemies in an effort to arouse anti-Communard sympathies.

pamphlet entitled *The Civil War in France* (1871), Marx claimed that the Commune was an example of the transitional form of government through which the working class would have to pass on its way to emancipation. Yet many of the less radical members of the International were frightened and disturbed, not only by the events of the Commune itself, but by the possibility of reprisals against members of an organization that openly praised men and women who were considered by the middle class to be little more than murderers. In 1872 Marx acknowledged defeat by moving the seat of the International's council to the United States, a country far removed from the organization's affairs and from the criticisms that had begun to be heaped upon Marx for his misdirection. In 1876, the International expired.

The spread of socialism
Although the International collapsed, socialism continued to gain ground as both a theory and a program—or rather, as several programs. As indicated by Marx's clashes with Lassalle and Bakunin, different Socialist parties could employ widely differing means toward similar ends, and as a result met with varied successes throughout Europe. The German Social Democratic party was founded in 1875; a Belgian Socialist party in 1879; and in France, despite the disasters of the Commune, a Socialist party was established in 1905. In England, although socialism was much debated and discussed, no party proclaiming itself socialist emerged. When the Labour party came into being in 1901, however, various social-

ist societies were represented on its executive council, along with less radical, nonsocialist trade union groups.

On the periphery of Europe—in Spain, Italy, and Russia—socialism made less headway. There the absence of widespread industrialization and the educational backwardness of large elements within the population retarded the development of a working-class consciousness, and of socialism as its political expression. Russian socialist thought was always the purview of a very small intelligentsia, and until 1905 was confined to expression through underground propagandizing and terrorist activity. Its strong flavor of agrarian idealism, based on the notion of the peasant commune as a rudimentary socialist institution that would allow Russia to bypass industrial capitalism on its way to socialism, differentiated Russian socialist thought from its Western counterparts. The Socialist Revolutionary party, formed clandestinely in 1901, continued to urge peasant socialism, while a more orthodox urban-based Marxism was advocated by the Social Democrat party after 1898.

During the years before the First World War, socialists continuously and often bitterly debated the course they should follow as they attempted to achieve their goal of radical change. One group, led by Marx himself until his death, urged socialists to avoid collaboration with other parties to achieve such immediate ends as higher wages, shorter working hours, and unemployment insurance. These reforms, the "purists" declared, were the means by which the bourgeoisie could buy off the proletariat and hence indefinitely postpone revolution. On the other hand, "revisionists" urged their followers to take advantage of the fact that many of them now could vote for socialist candidates in elections. They argued that those candidates, if elected, could help them obtain a better life in the immediate future. Socialist theory might proclaim a worldwide struggle of the proletariat against the bourgeoisie, but was this any reason to turn one's back on a chance to make real headway through the ballot box in achieving reforms that would put a better life within reach of workers and their families?

Another important point of disagreement centered on the relative importance of class versus gender. "Pure" socialist theory subsumed the special problems of working-class women under the more general problems of the class as a whole. Some "revisionists," on the other hand, argued that addressing problems specific to women would not dilute the socialist program as a whole and would in fact broaden its appeal. Finally, the problems of agricultural labor posed special challenges to socialists, as the example of Russia indicates. Because Marxism postulated an urban proletariat, many socialists split over the merits of incorporating large rural populations into a class struggle.

Revisionism spread despite efforts of the "purists" to put a stop to it. In Germany its most eloquent spokesman was Eduard Bernstein, a Social Democrat and a member of the German parliament, the Reichstag. Bernstein was among the first to question the predictions Marx had made in

Jean Jaurès

Radical socialists sharpen their attacks

Capital. In his appropriately titled book, *Evolutionary Socialism,* published in 1899, Bernstein pointed out that for most European workers the standard of living had risen since 1850, and that the lower-middle class showed no evidence that it wished to identify its interests with those of the proletariat. At the same time, increasingly wider franchises meant that workers had an excellent chance of achieving reform by means of the ballot box. The program of the future was not revolution, but democratic social reform. Bernstein's most outspoken opponent in Germany was his fellow socialist Karl Kautsky, an orthodox Marxist who warned that collaboration would end in the total corruption and demoralization of the proletariat. In France, the same battle was waged by the "purist" Jules Guesde, who preached that the Socialist party's primary goal should be the development of proletarian class consciousness, and Jean Jaurès, socialist leader in the Chamber of Deputies, who advocated a revisionist course. In both Germany and France, revisionists outnumbered purists by a wide margin. This was to an even greater degree the case in Britain. There, Fabian socialists—so named from their policy of delay, in imitation of the tactics of Fabius, a Roman general—preached what they called "the inevitability of gradualism." They believed their country would evolve toward socialism by means of parliamentary democracy. Prominent among the Fabians were the social investigators Sidney Webb and Beatrice Webb, the novelist H. G. Wells, and the playwright George Bernard Shaw.

The continued success of revisionism during the prewar years led its opponents to sharpen their attack and to advocate increasingly violent means to achieve their ends. Their campaigns, though they never managed to convince a majority of the working class, nevertheless attracted an increasing number of adherents. Some who had originally supported the revisionists grew disappointed when reforms did not come as quickly as expected. At the same time, in much of Europe, the cost of living began to rise for many workers. The comparative prosperity that some members of the working class had experienced vanished in the face of price rises that were not matched by wage increases. The result was a frustration that encouraged the adoption of a more militant stance. Germans rallied to the side of the radical socialists Rosa Luxemburg and Karl Liebknecht, while in France a new revolutionary Socialist party disowned the reformist leader Alexandre Millerand after he agreed to serve as a cabinet member in a nonsocialist government. The Second International, which had been founded in 1889, demanded at a conference in 1906 that affiliated parties declare their goal to be the destruction of the bourgeois order and the state that served its interests.

Anarchism and syndicalism

This militant mood encouraged acceptance of the doctrines of anarchists and syndicalists. *Anarchists* preached the overthrow of capitalism by violence. They differed from socialists, however, in their hatred of the machinery of the state or any government based upon coercion. Socialists argued that until the communist millennium promised by Marx, the state would remain a necessary means to the achievement of that eventual end. Anarchists worked to see the immediate abolition of a state bureaucracy that, no matter who controlled it, they believed would result in tyranny. Bakunin, whom Marx had succeeded in expelling from the First International, was anarchism's most popular propagandist. *Syndicalism,* like anarchism, demanded the abolition of both capitalism and the state. It resembled socialism in its demand that workers share in the ownership of the means of production. Instead of making the state the owner and operator of the means of production, however, the syndicalist would delegate these functions to syndicates of producers. The steel mills would be owned and operated by the workers in the steel industry, the coal mines by the workers in the coal industry, and so on. These associations would take the place of the state, each one governing its own members in their activities as producers.

Syndicalism received its most sympathetic hearing in France, where a General Confederation of Labour, after 1902, resolved to seek solutions to economic problems outside the legally constituted framework of French politics. The most effective spokesman for syndicalism was the Frenchman Georges Sorel. Sorel, in his *Reflections on Violence,* published in 1908, argued that workers should be made to believe in the possibility of a general strike by the proletariat that would result in the end of bourgeois civilization. The general strike might be nothing more than myth, Sorel acknowledged. Yet, as myth, it remained a powerful weapon in the hands of those whose goal was the destruction of society and who must not shy from the employment of violent means to achieve that end.

Georges Sorel

Socialism as a threat to the middle class

Socialism before the First World War, then, was not a unified force. It was divided by quarrels between purists and revisionists, and challenged by the even more radical proposals of anarchists and syndicalists. Socialists, intent on their goal of international solidarity among working classes, ignored the appeal that nationalism and imperialism might make to workers in France, Germany, and Britain. Yet despite its divisions and weaknesses, socialism appeared to the middle classes of Europe as a real threat to their continued prosperity. Capitalism had provided the machinery by which the bourgeoisie had achieved power. Socialism attacked capitalism and hence those who were its direct beneficiaries. Although most socialists disapproved of violence, violent acts were attributed by middle-class men and women to an amorphous, anticapitalist body easily labeled "socialist." Riots by trade unionists in Chicago's Haymarket Square in 1886 and in London's Trafalgar Square in 1887; the assassinations of President Sadi Carnot of France in 1894, of King Humbert of Italy in 1900, and of President William McKinley of the United States in 1901; strikes which grew in number and violence throughout Europe and America after 1900—all these events were perceived by members of the middle class as part of a larger movement whose professed goal was to tear from them their economic, political, and social security.

The Haymarket Riots, Chicago, 1886. A contemporary illustration depicting the results of attempts to unionize workers at the McCormick Harvester works.

THE CHALLENGE OF SCIENCE AND PHILOSOPHY

Science challenges notions of progress

While socialism grafted the middle-class belief in progress onto an apparently inevitable proletarian revolution, other forces were challenging the notion of "progress" altogether. Science, which had for decades appeared to bolster middle-class notions of progress, gradually undermined deeply held beliefs about man's place in the universe.

Lamarck and inheritance of acquired characteristics

Against the psychologically reassuring fortress of a harmonious universe, biological scientists hurled the bomb of evolutionary theory. This theory was at least as old as the sixth century B.C.E. and was accepted by many of the great minds of antiquity. It was revived in the eighteenth century by the scientists Buffon and Linnaeus (see Chapter 18). But neither of these men offered much proof or explained how the process of evolution might work. The first to develop a systematic hypothesis of evolution was the French biologist Jean Lamarck. The essential principle in Lamarck's hypothesis, published in 1809, was the inheritance of acquired characteristics. He maintained that an animal subjected to a change in environment acquired new habits, which in turn were reflected in structural changes. These acquired characteristics of body structure, he believed, were transmissible to the offspring, with the result that after a series of generations a new species of animal was eventually produced. Lamarck's hypothesis was widely attacked, raising as it did serious problems with the idea of nature as the unfolding of a divine plan.

Darwin and evolution

A much more convincing hypothesis of organic evolution was that of the English naturalist Charles Darwin, published in 1859. The son of a small-town physician, Darwin began the study of medicine at the University of Edinburgh, but soon withdrew and entered Cambridge to prepare for the ministry. Here he instead devoted most of his time to natural history. In 1831 Darwin obtained an appointment as naturalist without pay with a government-sponsored expedition aboard H.M.S. *Beagle,* which had been chartered for scientific exploration on a trip around the world. The voyage lasted nearly five years and gave Darwin an unparalleled opportunity to become acquainted at first hand with the manifold variations of animal life. He noted the differences between animals inhabiting islands and related species on nearby continents, and observed the resemblances between living animals and the fossilized remains of extinct species in the same locality. His knowledge of the popular hobby of pigeon-breeding, and the unique characteristics that breeders could select through controlled mating, prompted him to seek a "natural" mechanism for the selection of characteristics. After reading Thomas Malthus's essay on population upon his return to London, he was convinced he had found the mechanism he was seeking. Malthus argued that throughout the world of nature many more individuals are born than can survive, and that consequently the weaker ones must perish in the struggle for food. Competition for the means of survival was the "no miracles" mechanism Darwin sought. The fruits of his observations, research, and hypothesizing were eventually published in 1859, in the *Origin of Species.*

Charles Darwin

Darwin's hypothesis was that of natural selection. He argued that it is nature, or the environment, which selects those variants among offspring that are to survive and reproduce. Because no two offspring are exactly alike, some will have variations such as longer horns or sharper claws or body coloration that will enable them to win out in the struggle for existence and survive as the "fittest" of their generation; the others are eliminated generally before they have lived long enough to reproduce. Darwin regarded variation and natural selection as the primary factors in the origin of new species. He taught that individual plants and animals with favorable characteristics would transmit their inherited qualities to their descendants through countless generations, and that successive eliminations of the least fit would eventually produce a new species. Darwin applied his concept of evolution not only to plant and animal species but also to humans. In his second great work, *The Descent of Man* (1871), he attempted to show that the human race originally sprang from some apelike ancestor, long since extinct, but probably a common forebear of the existing anthropoid apes and humans.

The theory of natural selection

The two major scientific objections to the Darwinian hypothesis concerned the exact mechanism for the passing on of variations and the extremely long timespan needed for the evolution of actual new species through this incremental change. The German August Weismann flatly rejected the idea that acquired characteristics could be inherited. He conducted experiments to show that body cells and reproductive cells are entirely distinct, and that there is no way in which changes in the former can

Refinements of the Darwinian hypothesis

affect the latter. He concluded, therefore, that the only qualities transmissible to the offspring are those that have always been present in the reproductive cells of the parents. This seemed to deny any possibility of evolution from species to species, until in 1900 the Dutch botanist Hugo De Vries published his celebrated mutation hypothesis, based upon Darwin's original hypothesis and, in large part, upon laws of heredity discovered by the Austrian monk Gregor Mendel. De Vries asserted that evolution results not from minor variations, as Darwin had assumed, but from radical differences or mutations, which appear in a more or less definite ratio among the offspring. When any of these mutations are favorable to survival in a given environment, the individuals possessing them naturally emerge triumphant in the struggle for existence. Not only do their descendants inherit these qualities, but from time to time new mutants appear, some of which are even better adapted for survival than their parents. Thus in a limited number of generations a new species may be brought into existence.

Evolution and chance

The theory of evolution by natural selection clearly undermined a belief in an ordered, purposeful universe where progress through time was linear and goal-oriented, whether or not this belief was grounded in a literal interpretation of the Bible. A growing number of people regarded the Bible as containing a combination of myths, legends, history, and profoundly important moral truths. The work of the German theologian David Friedrich Strauss and of the French historian Ernest Renan had cast doubt on its historical accuracy, and dealt with its inconsistencies. These writers defended the intentions of the Bible's various authors, while firmly insisting upon their human fallibilities. Their searching, yet nevertheless sensitive, critiques helped people understand that they need not abandon their Christian faith simply because Darwin insisted that the world and all that lived within it had been created over millions of years and not in six days. Far more difficult to deal with was the notion, explicit in Darwin, that nature was not a changeless harmony, but instead a constant and apparently undirected struggle. Chance, and not order, ruled the universe. Nothing was fixed, nothing perfect; all was in a state of flux. Good and bad were defined only in terms of an ability to survive. The "best" of a species were those that triumphed over their weaker rivals. All of a sudden, the universe had become a harsh and uncompromising place, deprived of pre-Darwinian certainties; belief in a benevolent God was now much harder to sustain.

Thomas Henry Huxley

Darwin's most vigorous defender, the philosopher Thomas Henry Huxley, was one of those who could no longer reconcile science with a belief in God. Huxley earned himself the nickname of "Darwin's bulldog" because of his stout attacks upon orthodox Christians who refused to accept the implications of Darwinian theory. While he did not reject the possibility of a supernatural power, Huxley averred that "there is no evidence of the existence of such a being as the God of the theologians." He pronounced Christianity to be "a compound of some of the best and some of the worst elements of Paganism and Judaism, moulded in practice by the innate character of certain people of the Western World."

Huxley coined the word *agnosticism* to express his contempt for the attitude of dogmatic certainty symbolized by the beliefs of the ancient Gnostics. As propounded by Huxley, agnosticism was the doctrine that neither the existence nor the nature of God nor the ultimate character of the universe is knowable.

For those who could not sustain orthodox religious belief in light of these scientific and philosophical developments, the search for an ordering principle of human behavior took a number of forms. The so-called Social Darwinists, whose most famous proponent was the English philosopher Herbert Spencer, adapted Darwinian thought to the "science" of human society in a way that would have shocked Darwin himself. Spencer, who coined the phrase "survival of the fittest," grounded his defense of the virtues of competition in evolutionary theory. As a political philosopher, Spencer was a vigorous champion of individualism. He condemned collectivism as a relic of primitive society, as a feature of the earliest stage of social evolution. Any so-called assistance individuals might receive from the state, Spencer argued, would result not only in their own degeneration, but in that of society as well.

Spencer's followers, less subtly, argued that the apparent "success" of Western civilization was the result of its special fitness. The white race, they boasted, had proved itself superior to the black; non-Jews superior to Jews; rich superior to poor; the British Empire superior to the subject territories it controlled. If nature was a matter of competition, so was society, with the victory going to that race or nation that could demonstrate its fitness to survive by subduing others.

If Social Darwinists could reassure some by implying the biological right of Western civilization to survive as the "fittest" within the contemporary world, anthropologists—pioneers in what was essentially a new scientific discipline—argued, on the contrary, that no culture could be perceived as "better" than any other. All societies were adaptations to a particular environment. Each society produced its own customs, which could not be declared "good" or "bad," but only successful or unsuccessful, according to the degree to which they helped that society survive. This notion of cultural "relativism" was a theme in the influential work of the Scottish anthropologist Sir James Frazer, whose masterpiece, *The Golden Bough,* demonstrated the relationship of Christianity to primitive practices and magical rites. Similarly, other anthropologists showed that the notions of patriarchy and monogamy were culturally specific, not universal.

Other attempts to explore the various and sometimes contradictory implications of evolutionary theory helped to undermine the comforting notion of humankind's essential superiority to the rest of the animal kingdom. The work of the Russian psychologist Ivan Pavlov resulted in the discovery of the conditioned reflex, a form of behavior in which natural reactions are produced by an artificial stimulus. Pavlov showed that if dogs were fed immediately following the ringing of a bell, they would eventually respond to the sound of the bell alone and secrete

The Social Darwinists

Herbert Spencer

Anthropology and cultural relativism

Pavlov and the conditioned reflex

saliva exactly as if confronted by the sight and smell of the food. Because he insisted that his conclusions applied equally to human beings, Pavlov's discovery suggested the conclusion that the conditioned reflex is an important element in human behavior and encouraged psychologists to center their attention upon physiological experiment as a key to understanding the mind.

Pavlovians inaugurated a type of physiological psychology known as behaviorism. *Behaviorism* is an attempt to study the human being as a purely physiological organism—to reduce all human behavior to a series of physical responses. Such concepts as *mind* and *consciousness* are dismissed as vague and meaningless terms. For the behaviorist nothing is important except the reactions of muscles, nerves, glands, and visceral organs. There is no such thing as an independent psychic behavior; all that humans do is physical. Every complex emotion and idea is simply a group of physiological responses produced by some stimulus in the environment. Such was the mechanistic interpretation of human actions offered by followers of Pavlov.

In contradiction to this way of understanding human nature stood *psychoanalysis,* the other important school of psychology to make its appearance after the turn of the century. Founded by Sigmund Freud, an Austrian physician, psychoanalysis interprets human behavior mainly in terms of the unconscious mind. Freud admitted the existence of the conscious mind (the ego), but he avowed that the unconscious (the id) is much more important in determining the actions of the individual. He considered humans as creatures propelled by basic urges of power, self-preservation, and sex. These urges are much too strong to be overcome; but inasmuch as society (the superego) has branded their unrestrained fulfillment as sinful, they are commonly driven into the unconscious, where they linger indefinitely as suppressed desires. Yet they are seldom completely submerged; they rise to the surface in dreams, or they manifest themselves in lapses of memory, in fears and obsessions, and in various forms of abnormal behavior. Freud believed that most cases of mental and nervous disorder result from violent conflicts between natural instincts and the restraints imposed by an unfortunate environment. His dream theory for the first time grounded dreams in a "scientific" basis, ascribing them to the unconscious mind working through specific experiences of the conscious. Freud hoped that by elucidating his theory of the unconscious he could impose predictable patterns upon the irrationality that seemed to characterize so much human activity. His search for order, however, resembled that of the behaviorists by continuing to stress the extent to which men and women, like animals, were prey to drives, impulses, and reflexes over which they could exercise at best only minimal control.

Sigmund Freud

While Freud questioned the extent to which humans could gain control over their lives, the German philosopher Friedrich Nietzsche offered a way to increase that control—but only at the expense of characteristics traditionally exalted by Judaism and Christianity. For Nietzsche, accepted notions of good and evil merely trapped men and women in a fruitless search for security and "truth," which he denied existed. Instead, said Nietzsche, they must abandon the idea of service to society, which Nietzsche labeled the "slave morality" of Christianity, and instead master the world through the "will to power" that elevated individuals and their struggle against the chaos of the universe. The individual who abandoned the burden of convention was, for Nietzsche a "dionysian man," a "superman," who creates his own values based on moral courage and strength of character. Nietzsche here adapted the Darwinian notion of natural selection, with the "supermen" triumphing over the moral weaklings who lacked the strength and courage to face the chaos of the universe and overcome it. Before any such process of natural selection could operate, however, religious obstacles would have to be removed. Nietzsche therefore demanded that the moral supremacy of Christianity and Judaism be overthrown.

Friedrich Nietzsche

Nietzsche, whose philosophy is contained in such works as *Thus Spake Zarathustra* (1883), *Beyond Good and Evil* (1886), and *On the Genealogy of Morals* (1887), lapsed into permanent insanity in 1888 after a decade of agonizing ill-health. His broad-ranging critiques—of morals, music, academia, and democracy, to name but a few—were later adapted piecemeal by artists, students, and others who selected only those parts of Nietzsche's works that supported their own thought. Perhaps the most extreme example of this tendency was the use of Nietzschean philosophy to justify the politics of racism and virulent German nationalism advocated by Adolf Hitler and the National Socialist party in the 1930s.

Nietzsche's influence

Under the impact of these various scientific and philosophical challenges, the institutions responsible for the maintenance of traditional faith found themselves hard pressed. Protestantism had based its revolt against Roman Catholic orthodoxy upon the belief that men and women should seek to understand God with the aid of not much more than the Bible and a willing conscience. In consequence, Protestants had little in the way of authoritarian doctrine to support them when their faith was challenged. Some—the fundamentalists—chose to ignore the implications of scientific and philosophical inquiry altogether, and continued to believe in the literal truth of the Bible. Some were willing to agree with the school of American philosophers known as Pragmatists (Charles Peirce, William James), that if belief in a personal God produced mental peace or spiritual satisfaction, that belief must therefore be true. Truth, for the Pragmatists, was whatever provided useful, practical results. Other Protestants sought solace from religious doubt in religious activity, founding missions, and laboring among the poor. Many adherents to this "social gospel" were also "modernists," determined to accept the ethical teachings of Christianity while discarding belief in miracles and the doctrines of original sin and the Incarnation.

Effect of scientific and philosophical challenges

The Roman Catholic Church was compelled by its tradition of dogmatic assertion to assist its followers in their response to the modern world. In 1864 Pope Pius IX issued a *Syllabus of Errors* condemning what

Catholicism and the modern world

Pope Pius IX

Pope Leo XIII

The effect of scientific and philosophical changes

Schopenhauer's ideal world vs. the real world

he regarded as the principal religious and philosophical "errors" of the time. Among them were materialism, free thought, and "indifferentism," or the idea that one religion is as good as another. In 1869 he convoked a Church council, the first to be summoned since the Catholic Reformation. The most notable pronouncement of the Vatican Council was the dogma of papal infallibility. In the language of this dogma the pope, when he speaks *ex cathedra*—that is, in his capacity "as pastor and doctor of all Christians"—is infallible in regard to all matters of faith and morals. Though generally accepted by pious Catholics, the dogma of papal infallibility evoked a storm of protest in many circles. Governments of several Catholic countries denounced it, including those of France, Spain, and Italy. The death of Pius IX in 1878 and the accession of Pope Leo XIII brought a more accommodating climate to the Church. The new pope was ready to concede that there was "good" as well as "evil" in modern civilization. He added a scientific staff to the Vatican and opened archives and observatories. However, he made no concessions to "liberalism" or "anticlericalism" in the political sphere. He would go no farther than to urge capitalists and employers to be more generous in recognizing the rights of organized labor.

The effect of various scientific and philosophical challenges upon the men and women who lived at the end of the nineteenth century cannot be measured in any exact way. Millions undoubtedly went about the business of life untroubled by the implications of evolutionary theory, content to believe as they had believed. Certainly, for most members of the middle class, the challenge of socialism was understood as "real" in a way that the challenge of science and philosophy probably was not. Socialism was a threat to livelihood. Darwinism, relativism, and behaviorism, though "in the air" and troublesome to those who breathed that air, did not impinge upon consciousness to the same degree. Men and women can postpone thoughts about their origins and ultimate destiny in a way that they cannot postpone thoughts about their daily bread. And yet the impact of the changes we have been discussing was eventually profound. Darwin's theory was not so complicated as to prevent its popularization. If educated men and women had neither the time nor inclination to read the *Origin of Species,* they read magazines and newspapers that spelled out for them its implications. Those implications augmented an uncertainty that already tempered the optimism of capitalist expansion.

Men and women who had never read the German philosopher Arthur Schopenhauer might well have agreed with his assessment of this world as one condemned to witness the devouring of the weak by the strong. Yet their commitment to the ways of the world prevented their acceptance of Schopenhauer's particular remedy: an escape into a life of personal asceticism and self-denial. Like the English poet and essayist Matthew Arnold, sensitive men and women might feel themselves trapped in a world resembling no more than "a darkling plain," where there was "neither joy, nor love, nor light, nor certitude, nor peace, nor help for pain."

After 1850 a handful of artists and a greater number of writers continued to challenge the middle-class worldview, as had their predecessors, by drawing attention to the shortcomings of industrial society. As the century drew to a close, however, one of the major problems these critics now faced was the question of audience: not merely what to say, but whom to say it to. Before the middle of the eighteenth century, that audience had been primarily aristocratic. Between 1750 and 1870 it was both aristocratic and upper-middle class. Now, thanks to an increasingly literate general population, the potential audience appeared to have increased enormously. In 1850 approximately half the population of Europe had been illiterate. In subsequent decades, country after country introduced state-financed elementary and secondary education—as a device to provide citizens with an opportunity for social mobility, as a means of imposing a sense of nationality, as a preventive to the establishment of schools run by workers for workers, and as a measure to keep pace with changing technological knowledge. Britain instituted elementary education in 1870, Switzerland in 1874, Italy in 1877. France expanded its existing system between 1878 and 1881. After 1871 Germany instituted a state system modeled on Prussia's. By 1900, approximately 85 percent of the population in Britain, France, Belgium, the Netherlands, Scandinavia, and Germany could read. Elsewhere, however, the percentages were far lower, ranging between 30 and 60 percent.

The New Power of the Press. With the spread of literacy, newspapers adapted to the needs and desires of the new mass audience. Here British railway passengers scramble for the latest edition.

A new journalism

In those countries where literacy rates were highest, capitalist publishers such as Alfred Harmsworth in Britain and William Randolph Hearst in the United States hastened to serve the new reading public. Middle-class readers had for some time been well supplied by newspapers catering to their interests and point of view. The *Times* of London had a readership of well over 50,000 by 1850; the *Presse* and *Siècle* in France, a circulation of 70,000. By 1900, however, other newspapers were appealing to a different mass market—the newly literate—and doing so by means of sensational journalism and spicy, easy-to-read serials.

The distancing of art and literature from the public

These new developments encouraged writers and artists to distance themselves more and more from what seemed to them a vulgar, materialistic culture. They agreed with critics of the mid-century who had insisted that the purpose of art and literature was not to pander or sentimentalize. They went further, however, by declaring that art had no business preaching morality to a public that, in any event, had proved itself unwilling to heed the sermon. This generation of artists and writers argued that one did not look at a painting or read a poem to be instructed in the difference between good and evil, but to understand what was eternally true and beautiful—to appreciate art for its own sake. They were not so much interested in reaching a wider audience, whose standards of taste they generally deplored, as they were in addressing each other. This self-conscious desire not only to live apart but to think apart from society was reflected in their work. In 1850, educated men and women could read a Charles Dickens novel or examine an Honoré Daumier print and understand it, even if they did not admire it or agree with its message. In 1900, men and women found it much harder to understand, let alone admire, a painting by Paul Cézanne or a poem by Paul Valéry. Artists and public were ceasing to speak the same language, a fact that contributed, as did the ideas of Darwin and Nietzsche, Pavlov and Freud, to the further confusion and fragmentation of Western culture.

Realism

These new perceptions of the artist's relationship to society did not surface to any measurable degree before the very end of the century. Until that time, the arts were dominated by what has come to be called *realism*. Realists were predominantly critics of contemporary society. Swayed by a fervor for social reform, they depicted the inequities of the human condition against the sordid background of industrial society. Like the romantics, the realists affirmed the possibility of human freedom, although realists emphasized more than romantics the obstacles that prevented its achievement. Realists differed most markedly from romantics in their disdain of sentiment and emotional extravagance. Adopting from natural science the idea of life as a struggle for survival, they tried to portray human existence in accordance with hard facts, often insisting that their characters were the irresponsible victims of heredity, environment, or their own animal passions.

Literary realism in France

Realism as a literary movement made its initial appearance in France. Its leading exponents included the novelists Honoré de Balzac and Gus-

Balzac's Social Realism. In this frontispiece to Balzac's works, the author's muse holds a realist mirror before a bourgeois society not at all pleased by what it sees.

tave Flaubert, whose work, as we have already noted (see p. 778), contained a stinging assessment of the dullness and greed of modern life. Balzac's portrayal of the effects of social conditions upon the individual earned him a place as Marx's favorite novelist. Émile Zola, another Frenchman, is often called a naturalist rather than a realist, to convey the idea that he was interested in an exact, scientific presentation of the facts of nature without the intrusion of personal philosophy. Naturalism was expected to dismiss moral values in a way that realism was not. Zola did have a definite moral viewpoint, however. His early years of wretched poverty imbued him with a deep sympathy for the common people and with a passion for social justice. Though in novels such as *Nana* (1880) and *Germinal* (1885) he portrayed human nature as weak and prone to vice and crime, he was not without hope that a decided improvement might come from the creation of a better society. Many of his novels dealt with such social problems as alcoholism, poverty, and disease.

Realism in the writings of the Englishman Charles Dickens was overlaid with layers of sentimentality. Dickens was a master at depicting the evils of industrial society, but the invariably happy endings of his novels testify to his determined—and unrealistic—unwillingness to allow wrong to triumph over right. No such ambivalence marked the works of the later English novelist Thomas Hardy, however. In such well-known novels as *The Return of the Native* (1878), *Tess of the D'Urbervilles* (1891), and *Jude the Obscure* (1896), he expressed his conception that humans are the playthings of an inexorable fate. The universe was depicted as in no sense friendly, and the struggle of individuals with nature was a pitiable

Émile Zola

Literary realism in Britain

battle against almost impossible odds. If God existed, he watched with indifference while the helpless denizens of the human ant-heap crawled toward suffering and death. Yet Hardy pitied his fellow creatures, regarding them not as depraved animals but as the victims of cosmic forces beyond their control.

Pity for humanity was also a central theme in the work of the German dramatist Gerhart Hauptmann. Calling himself a naturalist, Hauptmann nevertheless reflected the realists' concern for suffering. His plays show the influence of Darwin in their emphasis upon determinism and environment. *The Weavers* (1892), which depicts the suffering of Silesian weavers in the 1840s, is probably his most outstanding work. Doubtless the most eminent playwright among realists and naturalists was the Norwegian Henrik Ibsen. The stark message of Ibsen's early dramas was not favorably received, and while still a young man he decided to abandon his native country. Residing first in Italy and then in Germany, he did not return permanently to Norway until 1891. His writings were characterized most of all by bitter rebellion against the tyranny and ignorance of society. In such plays as *A Doll's House* (1879), *An Enemy of the People* (1882), *The Wild Duck* (1884), and *Hedda Gabler* (1890), he satirized the conventions and institutions of respectable life, and showed, with great insight, how they oppressed women in particular. Along with his scorn for hypocrisy and social tyranny went a profound distrust of majority rule. Ibsen despised democracy as the enthronement of unprincipled leaders who would do anything for the sake of votes to perpetuate themselves in power. As one of his characters in *An Enemy of the People* says, "A minority may be right—a majority is always wrong."

The literature of the Russians, which flourished during the period of realism, comprises themes that are both romantic and idealist as well. Russia's three outstanding novelists of the late nineteenth century were Ivan Turgenev, Feodor Dostoevsky, and Leo Tolstoy. They were preceded by the equally talented Alexander Pushkin, who, between 1820 and his death in a duel seventeen years later, established himself as one of Russia's greatest writers. Though his early work was romantic in tone, his epic verse *Eugene Onegin* (1825–1831) demonstrated his sympathy with realistic themes.

Turgenev, who spent much of his life in France, was the first of the Russian novelists to become known to western Europe. His chief work, *Fathers and Sons* (1861), describes in brooding terms the struggle between the older and younger generations. The hero is a nihilist (a term first used by Turgenev), who is convinced that the whole social order has nothing in it worth preserving. The novel inspired a group of young Russian intellectuals, who sought to reform society by abandoning their parents' emphasis on status, wealth, and leisure and turning instead to service to "the people."

Dostoevsky was almost as tragic a figure as any he projected in his novels. Condemned at the age of twenty-eight on a charge of revolutionary

Realism in Germany and Scandinavia

Henrik Ibsen

Nineteenth-century Russian literature

Turgenev

Dostoevsky

activity, he was exiled to Siberia, where he endured four horrible years of imprisonment. His later life was harrowed by poverty, family troubles, and epileptic fits. As a novelist, he chose to explore the anguish of people driven to shameful deeds by their raw emotions and by the intolerable meanness of their lives. He was a master of psychological analysis, probing into the motives of distorted minds with an intensity that was almost morbid. At the same time he filled his novels with a broad sympathy and with a mystic conviction that humanity can be purified only through suffering. His best-known works are *Crime and Punishment* (1866) and *The Brothers Karamazov* (1879–1880).

As an earnest champion of the simple life of the peasant, Tolstoy was somewhat less deterministic than Dostoevsky. Yet in *War and Peace* (1862–1869), a majestic epic of Russian conditions at the time of the Napoleonic invasion, he expounds the theme that individuals are at the mercy of fate when powerful elemental forces are unleashed. His *Anna Karenina* (1873–1876) is a study of the tragedy that lurks in the pursuit of individual desire. As Tolstoy grew older he became more and more an evangelist preaching a social gospel. In such novels as *The Kreutzer Sonata* (1889) and *Resurrection* (1899–1900) he condemned most of the institutions of civilized society and called upon men and women to renounce selfishness and greed, to earn their living by manual toil, and to cultivate the virtues of poverty, meekness, and nonresistance. His last years were devoted to attacks upon such evils as war and capital punishment and to the defense of victims of political persecution.

The works of all these realists and naturalists, whatever their individual differences, shared two things in common: they contained vigorous moral criticism of present-day middle-class society, and they were written in direct and forceful language that the middle class could understand, if it chose to read or listen. The same can be said of realist painters such as Courbet and Daumier, discussed in Chapter 21, whose style and message were neither difficult to comprehend nor easy to ignore. Realist artists were still anxious to address the public, if only to attack its members for their shallowness and insensitivity. The advent of the impressionist movement in painting in the 1870s marks the first significant break in this tradition. At this point artists began to turn away from the public and toward each other. The movement started in France, among a group of young artists whose work had been refused a place in the annual exhibitions of the traditionally minded French Royal Academy. They had been labeled "impressionists" in derision by critics who took them to task for painting not an object itself, but only their impression of that object. The name in fact suited the personal, private nature of their work. They were painting to please themselves, to realize their own potential as artists.

In a sense, impressionists were realists, for they were determined to paint only what they saw, and they were vitally interested in the scientific

Leo Tolstoy

Realism vs. impressionism

Impressionist technique

Above: **The Birth of Venus,** by Alexandre Cabanel (1823–1889). Below: **Luncheon on the Grass,** by Edouard Manet (1823–1883). Cabanel's painting is a typical product of the fashionable French Salon, and was at one time owned by Napoleon III. It won the Salon prize in 1863 and was copied several times by the artist (as were other Salon paintings), emphasizing the fact that it was considered as much a piece of "decoration" as a piece of art. This sort of "bestseller" was exceedingly popular with upper-middle-class collectors, who felt no need to apologize for its semi-pornographic nature because of its classical subject matter. Manet's painting, done in the same year, created an enormous furor. Its style broke with the soft, painterly techniques of the Salon school; instead it was painted with broad, flat stokes that presaged the coming of impressionism. Its subject matter caused a sensation as well. Whereas voluptuous classical nudes were respectable art, a painting of a young woman seated without her clothing at a picnic with fully clothed gentlemen friends conveyed a sense of serious social impropriety to bourgeois viewers.

The Monarch of the Glen, by Sir Edwin Landseer (1802–1873). This was the sort of conventional, easy to comprehend art that appealed to the middle class and that brought forth the revolutionary impressionist movement in reaction.

interpretation of nature. But impressionist technique was different from that of the realist painters. Scenes from the world around them were not depicted as if the result of careful study. On the contrary, the works of impressionists sought to reveal immediate sense impressions, leaving it to the mind of the observer to fill in additional details. This often resulted in a type of work appearing at first glance to be nonnaturalistic. Figures were commonly distorted; a few significant details were made to represent an entire object; and dabs of primary color were placed side by side without a trace of blending. For example, the effect of the green in nature was achieved by placing daubs of pure blue and yellow side by side, allowing the eye to mix them.

Impressionism differed from realism in one other important respect. In these new paintings artists remained detached from their subject. They did not paint to evoke pity, or to teach a lesson. They painted to proclaim the value and importance of painting as *painting.* In doing so, the artist was not deliberately setting out to exclude the viewers. It was clear, however, that the viewer must not expect to understand a painting except on the artist's terms. Probably the greatest of the impressionists

Monet and Renoir

Realist paintings were not simply social critiques; they could, as these varied examples suggest, celebrate bourgeois virtue, or the beauties of nature.

A Woman Reading, by Camille Corot (1796–1875). Corot was a naturalist whose interest in the effects of light prefigured to a degree the work of the impressionists. Sentimentality and a preference for scenes of innocence and simplicity distinguished him from the realists.

The Last of England, by Ford Madox Brown (1821–1893). A haunting scene of a couple emigrating from England by one of the most noted pre-Raphaelites (see p. 779).

Public Notary Eltz and His Family, by Ferdinand Georg Waldmüller (1793–1865). Realism that is, at the same time, a celebration of the power and influence of the bourgeois bureaucrat.

Funeral at Ornans, by Gustave Courbet (1819–1877). Though a less strident realist than his contemporary Daumier, Courbet was concerned with expressing human nature as he found it—neither more handsome nor more ugly. This painting, in which he used men and women from his village as models, reflects his commitment to personal, as opposed to social, realism.

The Gleaners, by Jean François Millet (1814–1875). A realist, Millet remained fascinated with color and setting to a degree that often made his paintings something other than a record of social change.

The Movings, by Louis Léopold Boilly (1761–1845). Dating from 1822, this realist-allegorical painting depicts Parisians of various classes in the process of moving their household goods. By juxtaposing the buildings of contemporary Paris with the Church of Santa Maria de' Miracoli of Rome, the artist appears to suggest that for some, including the peasants in their wagon leaving the city and the corpse in the horse-drawn hearse heading for its grave, the idea of the metropolis as a place of promise and prosperity is an illusion.

Pink and Green, by Edgar Degas (1834–1917). Degas was an impressionist to the extent of his interest in fleeting motion. But as an admirer of the classicist Ingres, he emphasized line and careful composition.

Luncheon of the Boating Party, by Auguste Renoir (1841–1919). The impressionists enjoyed employing their revolutionary artistic techniques to portray the commonplace occasions of everyday outdoor life.

were the Frenchmen Claude Monet and Auguste Renoir. Monet was perhaps the leading exponent of the new mode of interpreting landscapes. His paintings have little structure or design in the conventional sense; they suggest, rather than depict, the outlines of cliffs, trees, mountains, and fields. Intensely interested in the problem of light, Monet would go out at sunrise with an armful of canvases in order to paint the same subject in a dozen momentary appearances. It has been said of one of his masterpieces that "light is the only important person in the picture." Renoir's subjects include not only landscapes but portraits and scenes from contemporary life. He is famous for his pink and ivory nudes, which, as expressions of frank sexuality, represented an additional threat to middle-class sensibilities.

The freedom explicit in the work of the impressionists encouraged other painters to pursue fresh techniques and to define different goals. The expressionists turned upon the impressionists, objecting to their preoccupation with the momentary aspects of nature and their indifference to meaning. Expressionists were not arguing for a return to meaning in the sense of "message." They were instead insisting that a painting must represent the artist's particular intellect. Here again, they were making art a private matter, removing it yet another step from the public. The artist who laid the foundations of expressionism was the Frenchman Paul Cézanne, who labored to express a sense of order in nature that he believed the impressionists had ignored. To achieve this end, he painted objects as a series of planes, each plane expressed in terms of a color change. While Cézanne was in this way equating form with color, he also began to reduce natural forms to their geometrical equivalents, hoping thereby to express the basic shapes of existence itself. He distorted form into geometrical regularity until abstraction became reality. In all this Cézanne was declaring the painter's right to recreate nature in such a way as to express an intensely personal vision.

Art as personal expression was the hallmark of two other painters in the so-called post-impressionist period, the Frenchman Paul Gauguin and the Dutchman Vincent Van Gogh. Both, by their life as well as their art, declared war on traditional nineteenth-century values. Dismayed by the artificiality and complexity of civilization, Gauguin fled to the South Sea Islands and spent the last decade of his life painting the hot and luscious colors of an unspoiled, primitive society. Van Gogh, whose passionate sympathy for the sufferings of his fellow humans led him to attempt the life of a minister to poor mining families and undoubtedly contributed to his eventual insanity and ultimate suicide, poured out the full intensity of his feelings in paintings such as *The Starry Night* (1889), which seems to swirl off the canvas.

In the years between 1900 and the First World War, art underwent still further revolutionary development. Henri Matisse greatly extended Cézanne's use of distortion, thereby declaring once again the painter's

Expressionism: the paintings of Cézanne

Van Gogh and Gauguin

Matisse and Picasso

The Card Players, by Paul Cézanne (1839–1906). Here are exemplified Cézanne's skill in composition, his discriminating sense of color, and the sculptured qualities of solidity and depth he gave to his figures.

Montagne Sainte-Victoire with Aqueduct, by Cézanne. Cézanne's post-impressionist insistence upon the reduction of the landscape to patterns of form and planes of color illustrates the manner in which his genius created the vital link between impressionism and cubism.

Ia Orana Maria, by Paul Gauguin (1848–1903). Gauguin's dissatisfaction with European life compelled his escape to Tahiti, where striking colors, bold patterns of light and shade, and local artistic tradition affected his style of painting.

The Starry Night, by Vincent van Gogh (1853–1890). Van Gogh's compulsive style and bold technique endow his compositions with a feverish rhythm that is both compelling and disturbing.

The Joy of Life, by Henri Matisse (1869–1954). The sensuous use of line and boldness of composition celebrate not only life but the artist's freedom to break from past convention.

Les Demoiselles d'Avignon, by Pablo Picasso (1881–1973). One of Picasso's most famous and most daring paintings from his cubist period.

The Scream (1893), by Edvard Munch, evokes fear and alarm in the viewer.

right to create according to an individual definition of aesthetic merit. This declaration was given its most ringing prewar endorsement by Pablo Picasso. Picasso, a Catalan Spaniard who came to Paris in 1903, developed a style, cubism, that takes its name from an attempt to carry Cézanne's fascination with geometrical form to its logical conclusion. Cubism results not only in distortion but in some cases in actual dismemberment. The artist may separate the various parts of a figure and rearrange them in other than their natural pattern. The purpose is to express defiance of traditional notions of form—to repudiate once and for all the conception of art as representational prettiness.

Symbolism was another artistic movement that flourished during the last decade of the nineteenth century and the beginning years of the twentieth. Its practitioners, both artists and writers, attempted to intensify personal experience and psychological perception, transcending reality in a way that, once again, challenged traditional notions of artistic purpose. Artists such as the Norwegian Edvard Munch and the Austrian Gustav Klimt painted in a manner that left viewers puzzled, if not disturbed. The French poets Paul Verlaine, Arthur Rimbaud, Stéphane Mallarmé, and Paul Valéry had much the same effect on their readers.

In music, as well, there was a break from the romantic tradition that had dominated the nineteenth century and that had been expressed in the works of composers such as Robert Schumann, Felix Mendelssohn, and Franz Liszt. Already the late romantic operas of Richard Wagner had taken vast liberties with harmony and departed from stereotypical melodic patterns, producing music that was not subject to the tyranny of form but was sensitive to personal expression. Now in the works of composers such as the Austrian Richard Strauss and the Frenchman Claude Debussy music moved even further in the direction of the intensely personal. Strauss's opera *Der Rosenkavalier* (1911), although based externally on the conventions of late-eighteenth-century plot, is nevertheless a musical expression of the inner realities of its characters, written to express those realities more directly than before. Both Strauss and Debussy were, like the impressionists, determined to convey atmosphere; Debussy's piano compositions and his symphonic sketch *La Mer* (1905) are musical manifestations of the impressionists' regard for association rather than formal structure.

Whether in painting, literature, or music, artists sought to escape to a position from which they could learn and then express what was closest to their own consciousness. Their direct, calculated dismissal of conventional form and content declared their fundamental disdain for the everyday. Their aloofness from the world served only to increase the general sense of a fragmented world that, despite its material prosperity, was at war with itself.

Judith II (Salomé) (1909), by Gustav Klimt (1862–1918). Symbolists were not afraid to address issues of sexuality in frank and often disturbing ways.

SUMMARY POINTS

- Socialism, according to Karl Marx's 1848 *Communist Manifesto,* would end capitalism and lead eventually to communism. This popular notion evolved into factions such as purism, revisionism, anarchism, and syndicalism, all of which espoused views that threatened the middle-class, capitalist state.

- Scientists and philosophers after 1859 challenged the middle-class assumption of a moral, orderly, Christian universe. They presented sound arguments for natural selection, agnosticism, social Darwinism, behavioralism, and psychoanalysis, among other theories.

- Realists and naturalists created books, paintings, and plays that reflected and criticized middle-class culture, using messages easy to understand and difficult to ignore. By contrast, impressionists, cubists, and symbolists launched "art for art's sake," refusing to attach moral lessons to their works on the grounds that moralizing hampered artists' freedom of expression.

SELECTED READINGS

SOCIALISM

Avineri, Shlomo, *The Social and Political Thought of Karl Marx,* London, 1968.

Berlin, Isaiah, *Karl Marx: His Life and Environment,* 4th ed., New York, 1996. The best short account.

Boxer, Marilyn, and Jean Quataert, eds., *Socialist Women: European Socialist Feminism in the Nineteenth and Early Twentieth Centuries,* New York, 1978. Stresses the ambivalence of socialist movements toward the role of women.

Cole, G. D. H., *A History of Socialist Thought,* Vols. I–III, London, 1953–1956. A comprehensive treatment of the period 1789–1914.

Derfler, Leslie, *Socialism since Marx: A Century of the European Left,* New York, 1973. Survey and analysis of Continental socialist movements.

Edwards, Stewart, *The Paris Commune of 1871,* London, 1971. Straightforward analysis.

Gay, Peter, *The Dilemma of Democratic Socialism: Eduard Bernstein's Challenge to Marx,* New York, 1962. A good study of German revisionism.

Goldberg, Harvey, *A Life of Jean Jaurès,* Madison, Wisc., 1962. A fine biography of the eminent French socialist.

Joll, James, *The Anarchists,* London, 1964. Survey of various radical European groups.

———, *The Second International, 1889–1914,* Boston, 1966. A general account of the socialist movement and its leaders.

Lichtheim, George, *A Short History of Socialism,* New York, 1970. Provides a useful overview.

Lidtke, Vernon, *The Alternative Culture: Socialist Labor in Imperial Germany,* New York, 1985. The relationship between politics and working-class culture.

——, *The Outlawed Party: Social Democracy in Germany, 1878–1890,* Princeton, 1966. Deals with German socialists from 1878 to 1890.

McBriar, A. M., *Fabian Socialism and English Politics, 1884–1918,* Cambridge, Eng., 1966. An extensive study of this important circle: their composition, their ideology, their methods.

Mehring, Franz, *Karl Marx: The Story of His Life,* New York, 1976. A well-done recounting of Marx's life.

Noland, Aaron, *The Founding of the French Socialist Party, 1893–1905,* Cambridge, Mass., 1956. Primarily a narrative account of the translation of ideology into political reality.

Schorske, Carl E., *German Social Democracy, 1905–1918,* Cambridge, Mass., 1955. A magnificent study of the problems of the Social Democrats in a time of imperialism and war.

SCIENTIFIC THOUGHT

Butterfield, Herbert B., *The Origins of Modern Science, 1300–1800,* rev. ed., New York, 1957. A standard survey.

Eiseley, Loren C., *Darwin's Century: Evolution and the Men Who Discovered It,* New York, 1961. The history of evolution after Darwin.

Gay, Peter, *Freud, Jews, and Other Germans: Masters and Victims in Modernist Culture,* New York, 1978. Essays on end-of-the-century German culture.

Gillespie, Charles C., *The Edge of Objectivity,* Princeton, 1960. A history of scientific ideas.

Hughes, H. Stuart, *Consciousness and Society,* New York, 1958. Examines the reaction to Positivism and the growing interest in the irrational by considering the work of Freud, Max Weber, and others.

Jones, Ernest, *The Life and Work of Sigmund Freud,* 3 vols., New York, 1953–1957. The official biography, by a close collaborator and eminent psychoanalyst.

Rieff, P., *Freud: The Mind of the Moralist,* 3d ed., Chicago, 1979. A useful, one-volume discussion.

Stocking, George W., Jr., *Victorian Anthropology,* London, 1975. Ties together science and culture.

THE ARTS AND PHILOSOPHY

Clark, T. J., *The Painting of Modern Life: Paris in the Art of Manet and His Followers,* New York, 1985. Argues for seeing impressionism as a critique of French society.

Evenson, Norma, *Paris: A Century of Change, 1878–1978,* New Haven, Conn., 1979.

Jelavich, Peter, *Munich and Theatrical Modernism: Politics, Playwriting, and Performance, 1890–1914,* Cambridge, Mass., 1985. The interrelationship of popular culture and political attitudes.

Kaufmann, Walter A., *Nietzsche: Philosopher, Psychologist, Anti-Christ,* 4th ed., Princeton, 1975. A superb intellectual biography.

Lang, Paul Henry, *Music in Western Civilization,* New York, 1940. Useful survey and reference.

Masur, Gerhard, *Prophets of Yesterday: Studies in European Culture, 1890–1914,* New York, 1961. A broad survey of nineteenth-century European thinkers.

Mosse, George L., *The Culture of Western Europe: The Nineteenth and Twentieth Centuries,* 3d ed., Boulder, Co., 1988. Thoughtful analysis and overview.

Schorske, Carl, *Fin-de-Siècle Vienna: Politics and Culture,* New York, 1980. Essays on Vienna's cultural impact on the West.

Shattuck, Roger, *The Banquet Years: The Arts in France, 1885–1918,* New York, 1958. The emergence of modernism in French art, literature, and music.

Silverman, Debora L., *Art Nouveau in Fin-de-Siècle France: Politics, Psychology, and Style,* Berkeley, 1989. The relationship between psychological and artistic change.

SOURCE MATERIALS

Arnold, Matthew, *Culture and Anarchy,* New York, 1971. Originally published in 1867. A perceptive criticism of English society and a call for an authoritarian principle in an increasingly democratic society.

Darwin, Charles, *The Descent of Man,* Cambridge, Mass., 1964. See especially chapter XXI.

———, *Origin of Species,* Cambridge, Mass., 1964. See especially chapters IX, XV.

Edwards, Stewart, ed., *The Communards of Paris, 1871,* New York, 1976. Annotated eyewitness reports, documents, and accounts of the Paris Commune.

Gosse, Edmund, *Father and Son,* New York, 1963. A moving autobiography by a distinguished Victorian literary critic, this work reveals the conflict between the religious fundamentalism of the father and the skepticism of the son in the wake of Darwinian theory.

Kohn, Hans, *The Mind of Russia,* New Brunswick, N.J., 1955. An edited collection of historical, literary, and philosophical works of nineteenth- and twentieth-century Russian authors, designed to reveal the conflict between traditional and Western thought in Russia.

Marx, Karl, *Capital,* intro. by G. D. H. Cole, New York, 1974. A good edition of the classic.

Marx, Karl, and Friedrich Engels, *The Marx-Engels Reader,* 2d ed., ed. R. C. Tucker, New York, 1978. Reprints the basic texts.

Thompson, D. M., ed., *Nonconformity in the Nineteenth Century,* London, 1972. Superb collection of documents.

Webb, Beatrice, *My Apprenticeship,* London, 1926. Beatrice Webb was one of the leading Fabian socialists, and in this first volume of her autobiography she explains how she, as a member of one of England's wealthier families, was converted to a socialist creed.

Zola, Émile, *L'Assommoir,* London, 1970. Written in 1877 and set in the Paris of the 1860s, this bitterly realistic novel portrays the brutalization of the French working class by the forces of industrial change, poverty, and alcohol.

CHAPTER 26

A DELICATE EQUILIBRIUM
(1870–1914)

Ah! What a seething there has been, . . . customs worthy of the inquisition
and despotism, the pleasure of a few gold-braided individuals setting their
heels on the nation, and stifling its cry for truth and justice, under the menda-
cious and sacrilegious pretext of the interest of the State!

—ÉMILE ZOLA, "J'accuse"

BETWEEN 1870 and 1914, the major powers of Europe balanced between stability and strife. Domestic and international uncertainty
was caused by continuing industrialization. Periodic trade depressions tempered the optimism accompanying general prosperity. Almost
all classes of society shared in the expansion of material production at
least until 1900. Prosperity helped to produce stability, allowing for
the establishment in many countries of social welfare systems designed
to benefit workers and their families, and thus to gain their political
allegiance.

> Continuing prosperity

At the same time, various factors operated to make the achievement of
a generally stable Western world difficult, and ultimately impossible.
First, the process of nation-building, which had resulted in the dramatic
creation of a modern Germany and Italy, left potential conflict in its
wake. Second, although the majority of citizens in most western European countries participated at least indirectly in the governance of their
country and enjoyed certain guaranteed rights, heated debate continued
as to the political usefulness of such arrangements. In France, monarchists threatened the republic; in Germany, democrats battled imperial
and bureaucratic oligarchy; in Russia, liberals rose against tsarist autocracy. And across Europe, socialists contended against the political
strength of the middle classes.

> The roots of instability

Internal tension was resulting as well from shifts in class structure and
class consciousness. One of the most dramatic occupational changes to
occur in late-nineteenth-century Europe was the rapid growth of a lower-
to middle-level, "white-collar" class of bureaucrats, employed in commerce and industry and in expanding government departments. The post
office, the railways, the police, and the bureaus charged with administering various social welfare and insurance programs, all demanded growing
numbers of recruits. In Germany, for example, by 1914 there were more

> Shifts in class and class
> consciousness

911

than two million white-collar employees in private firms and two million lower- or middle-range civil servants. Members of this new class were particularly anxious to give sharp definition to the line separating them from skilled "labor aristocrats," who might earn as much money as they did, but whose blue collars were, in the eyes of the white-collar brigades, a badge of their inferior status. Those same "aristocrats," as we have seen, however, often found their skills made obsolete by technological change, with the result that they showed themselves more willing than in the past to make common cause with their unskilled fellow workers against the middle class.

International rivalries

One further important source of European instability during this period lay in the international rivalries that grew between nations as they reached out to build empires. Nations grouped into alliances, hoping that a balance between power blocs might continue to provide the international stability that Europe had enjoyed since 1815, and that had prevented general war. Instead, the alliances produced only further tensions, and ultimately general world conflict.

GERMANY: THE SEARCH FOR IMPERIAL UNITY

The structure of the German Empire

During the years immediately following the foundation of the German Empire, Otto von Bismarck was particularly anxious to achieve imperial unity under Prussian domination. In this he was aided by the economic and military predominance of the Prussian state, by his willingness to appropriate imperial prerogatives for his own ends, and by the organizational framework upon which the empire had been constructed. All powers not granted to the central government were reserved to the individual states. Each state had control over its own form of government, public education, highways, police, and other local agencies. Even the enforcement of the laws was left primarily in the hands of the state governments, since the empire had no machinery for applying its laws against individuals. Despite their apparent autonomy, however, the states were in fact subordinate to the empire, and to the emperor himself, the Prussian William I. The German imperial units were once described as comprised of "a lion, a half-dozen foxes, and a score of mice." The Prussian "lion" exercised authority through the person of the emperor and his chancellor. The empire was not governed by a cabinet system, in which ministers of state were responsible to a popularly elected legislature. Instead, ministers were responsible to the chancellor, and the chancellor was responsible solely to the emperor. William was no mere figurehead; the emperor was vested with extensive authority over the army and navy, over foreign relations, and over the general enactment and execution of imperial laws. He had the authority to declare war if the coasts or territory of the empire were attacked. And as king of Prussia, he controlled that country's delegation in the generally conservative upper house, or Bundesrat, of the imperial parliament, commanding enough votes to veto any bill submitted.

William I of Germany

The chairman of the Bundesrat, charged with the control and supervision of the federal administration, was also the Prussian prime minister, appointed by the king of Prussia.

The parliament was no rubber stamp, however. Money for the imperial treasury had to be voted by the lower house, the Reichstag, which was elected by universal male suffrage, and whose membership was primarily middle class. Yet the Reichstag's powers were essentially negative. Although the parliament could veto proposals of the kaiser (emperor) and his ministers, it could not initiate legislation on its own. Moreover, the monarchy could bypass the legislature by working with a previous year's budget when no new one was formulated. Hence, although Bismarck often found himself temporarily stymied by the activities of an unsympathetic legislature, he could expect, in the end, to have his way. That way was directed toward the goal of a unified Germany under Prussian domination: essentially conservative; antisocialist, though not necessarily opposed to social welfare schemes; protectionist, and thus sympathetic to the interests of German industrialists; and, in foreign affairs, anti-French, standing firm against any threat from that longtime antagonist.

Bismarck's first campaign on behalf of imperial unity was launched against the Roman Catholic Church. Called the *Kulturkampf,* or "struggle for civilization," the attack was initiated, with some help from intellectual liberals, in 1871. Bismarck's motives were almost exclusively nationalistic. He perceived in some Catholic activities a threat to the power and stability of the empire, particularly the support Catholic priests continued to give to the states'-rights movement in southern Germany and to the grievances of Alsatians and Poles. Bismarck was alarmed also by recent assertions of the authority of the pope to intervene in secular matters and by the promulgation in 1870 of the dogma of papal infallibility. For these reasons he resolved to deal such a blow to Catholic influence in Germany that it would never again be a major factor in national or local politics. His weapons were a series of laws and decrees issued between 1872 and 1875, designed to curb the independent power of the Church. Bismarck's campaign backfired, however. The Catholic Center party appealed to the electorate so effectively on behalf of the persecuted clergy, while adopting an economic policy attractive to the upper-middle class, that it won fully one-quarter of the seats in the Reichstag in 1874. Recognizing that he needed Catholic support for other elements of his program, Bismarck took the occasion of the election of the more conciliatory Pope Leo XIII to make his peace with the Vatican and to negotiate an alliance of convenience with the Catholic Center party. By 1886 almost all of his anticlerical legislation either had been permitted to lapse or had been repealed.

Having forged a new political combination in 1878, Bismarck shifted the focus of his attacks to German socialism, now perceived by him as a far more immediate threat to the empire than Catholicism. The Social Democratic party, under the reformist leadership of the politician Wilhelm Liebknecht, successor to Ferdinand Lassalle, was building a substantial

The *Kulturkampf*

Bismarck and the socialists

following. Bismarck, his memory of the Paris Commune (see p. 881) still fresh, feared socialism as anarchy, and therefore as a direct challenge to the stability and unity he was attempting to achieve within the empire. Forgetting for the moment the manner in which he had courted the socialists when he needed their support in the 1860s, Bismarck now appeared determined to extinguish them. His attack was motivated not only by his personal perception of the socialist threat but also by his continuing need to secure the favor of industrialists whom he had won to his side through his policy of protective tariffs. In 1878, two separate attempts were made by unbalanced zealots on the life of the emperor. Although neither would-be assassin had anything but the most tenuous connection with the socialists, Bismarck used their actions as an excuse to secure legislation abolishing workers' rights to meet and to publish. The legislature also agreed to a law that gave the government the right to expel socialists from major cities, as was later done in Berlin, Breslau, and Leipzig. These laws in effect dissolved the Social Democratic party until after 1890, although individual socialist candidates continued to be elected to the Reichstag.

Social welfare legislation

Bismarck was too clever a politician to suppose that he could abolish socialism solely by means of repression. He was prepared to steal at least a portion of the socialists' thunder by adopting parts of their legislative program as his own. In a speech in the Reichstag he frankly avowed his purpose of insuring the worker against sickness and old age so that "these gentlemen [the Social Democrats] will sound their bird call in vain." In addition, he had military purposes in mind. He hoped to make the German worker an effective potential soldier by safeguarding his health in some measure from the debilitating effects of factory labor. Bismarck's program of social legislation was initiated in 1883–1884 with the adoption of laws insuring workers against sickness and accidents. These acts were followed by others providing for rigid factory inspection, limiting the employment of women and children, fixing maximum hours of labor, establishing public employment agencies, and insuring workers against incapacity on account of old age. By 1890, Germany had adopted nearly all the elements, with the exception of unemployment insurance, in the matrix of social legislation that later became familiar in the majority of Western nations.

William II's politics

In that same year the Iron Chancellor was dismissed by the young emperor William II (1888–1918), following the four-month reign of his father, Frederick III. Bismarck's loss of power was to a degree the result of a personality clash between the two men. William's father had remarked that his son had "a tendency to overestimate himself"; his tutor noted that he "imagined he knew everything—without having learned anything." William's arrogance was encouraged by the cult of imperial family worship that had by this time become part of the nationalistic creed that was imposed by the state upon its citizens. Yet the quarrel between the young kaiser and his chancellor was a matter of substance as well as personality, involving policies directed at curbing the activities and popular-

Left: **William II of Germany.** Right: **Dropping the Pilot.** This cartoon appeared in the British magazine *Punch* on March 29, 1890, after the inexperienced but ambitious young emperor dismissed Bismarck as chancellor and personally assumed the helm of the ship of state. Note that Bismarck appears stripped of the insignia of office.

ity of the socialists. Bismarck's dismissal came in part over William's insistence that the antisocialist legislation of the past decade had achieved very little, and his mistaken belief that socialists would respond positively to his determination to rule in his own right and to create a more unified, stable, and powerful reich. Within a few years, however, William was arguing a line that appealed to the landowners, military leaders, and industrialists, whom he continued to court throughout his reign. He wooed the landowners by embarking on a policy of agricultural protection as a means of recovering from the depression brought on by inexpensive imports. And he wooed the military and the industrialists with a vast program of naval rearmament.

Despite his decision to end the ban against the Social Democrats, William did all he could to undermine their growing political strength. State schools were instructed to teach the dangers of socialism by stressing the virtues of patriotism and piety. Admission to the civil service was almost impossible unless one was an officer in the military reserve; and admission to that very influential body was not open to socialists—or to Jews. Stealing a leaf from Bismarck's text, William authorized the extension of earlier programs of social insurance, hoping to dampen enthusiasm for the Social Democrats by granting some of the reforms for which they continued to campaign. But William steadfastly refused to extend any sort of meaningful political participation beyond the powerful industrial, military, and agricultural classes. The country was administered efficiently, but not democratically. With the exception of Count Leo von Caprivi, a military officer, all his chancellors were civil servants, a fact that underscored his determination to keep the administration of the country as far removed as possible from democratic control.

Growing opposition to these policies brought the Social Democrats increasingly impressive electoral victories. In 1912 they polled a third of the

Combating the socialists

Social Democrats and the political stalemate

votes cast, and elected 110 members—the largest single bloc—to the Reich-stag. Yet they were thwarted, not only by William's determination to ignore his parliament, but by their inability to resolve the conflict within their own ranks between purist and revisionist theory (see p. 883). The party continued to profess itself devoted to the principles of socialist purity, yet the need to cultivate mass electoral support pushed it in the direction of piecemeal reformist legislation. And even with their large bloc of Reichstag votes, the Social Democrats could not command a majority there unless they formed a coalition with conservative center parties. By 1914, German politics was approaching stalemate. The country was spared a domestic constitutional crisis only by the infinitely more profound international crisis of the First World War.

FRANCE: THE EMBATTLED THIRD REPUBLIC

Politically divided France

Although in 1870 France was not a newly constructed nation like the German Empire, it was a nation sorely in need of reunification and dedication to a common set of political purposes. Its history for the past century had left it torn between various factions; the ease with which the German Army had conquered them shook the self-confidence of all French citizens. The conflicts experienced after 1870 tended to be more ideological than social, a reflection not only of France's tumultuous political past, but of its comparatively slow rate of industrialization. Monarchists were divided between supporters of the Bourbon and Orleanist dynasties, their allegiance sustained by loyalties either to the descendants of Louis XVIII or to those of Louis Philippe. Bonapartists looked for political salvation to Napoleon III's son and heir Louis Napoleon. Republicans recalled the short-lived triumphs of their revolutionary ancestors. Socialists called down plagues on all political houses but their own. The result of this deep division was that not until 1875 did France have a constitution under which it could function.

The formation of the Third Republic

Following the collapse of Napoleon III's empire a provisional government was organized to rule the country until a new constitution could be drafted. Elections held in 1871 for a national constituent assembly resulted in the choice of some 500 monarchists and only about 200 republicans. Conservative political sentiment was further reinforced by the events of the Paris Commune, which occurred during the period immediately following the elections. But the apparent winners, the monarchists, could not agree among themselves as to whether their king should be a Bourbon or an Orleanist. This stalemate led to the eventual passage in 1875—by one vote—of a series of constitutive laws that made France a republic. These laws established a parliament with a lower house elected by universal male suffrage (the Chamber of Deputies) and an upper house elected indirectly (the Senate), a cabinet of ministers presided over by a premier, and a president. Although at first the relative powers of president and premier were not clearly established, within two years the nation had declared itself in favor of a premier at the head of a government answerable to the Chamber of Deputies. An early president, Marshal Marie-Edmé MacMahon, attempted in 1877 to dismiss a premier with whom he disagreed but who was supported by a majority in the chamber. When new elections were held, MacMahon's policy was repudiated. Henceforth, premiers of the Third Republic were answerable to the chamber and not to the president, who became a figurehead. Yet the resolution of this constitutional question failed to produce political stability, since the premier had no authority to dissolve the legislature. This meant that members of the chamber could vote a premier and his fellow ministers out of office at will, with no risk of being forced to stand for reelection. If defeated on a vote, the premier and his colleagues had no alternative but to resign. The result was no fewer than fifty ministries in the years between 1870 and 1914. The Third Republic, for all its constitutional shortcomings, nevertheless managed to last until 1940—far longer than any other system of French government since 1789. Its longevity was due, as much as anything, to the stability of other French institutions—the family, the law courts, and the police, for example. And its stability was attested to by the willingness of French men and women to invest their savings in state loans, rather than in industrial enterprises that appeared far less secure to them.

In the years after 1875, the republicans, who had been feared at first as dangerous radicals, proved themselves to be generally moderate. It was the discontented monarchists and authoritarian sympathizers within the army, the Roman Catholic Church, and among the families of the

Radical reactionaries

Turn-of-the-Century Paris Streets. Left: The Avenue de l'Opéra, c. 1880. Right: The Rue Mouffeta, 1910. These photos illustrate the degree to which Paris, like all major European cities, was divided into districts of rich and poor.

aristocracy who took to plotting the overthrow of duly constituted governmental authority. Much of the time of successive republican governments was taken up defending the country from these reactionary radicals. In the late 1880s, a general, Georges Boulanger, gathered a following not only of Bonapartists, monarchists, and aristocrats, but of working people who were disgruntled with their lot and who believed, with Boulanger, that a war of revenge against Germany would put an end to all their troubles. Thanks to the general's own indecisiveness, the threatened coup d'état came to nothing. But the attempt was a symptom of deep discontents; Boulanger appealed, like Napoleon III, to disparate groups of disenchanted citizens, promising quick, dramatic solutions to tedious problems.

The Dreyfus affair

One further symptom of the divisions that plagued the republic during the later years of the nineteenth century was the campaign of anti-Semitism that the reactionaries adopted to advance their aims. The fact that certain Jewish bankers were involved in scandalous dealings with politicians lent color to the monarchist insistence that the government was shot through with corruption and that Jews were largely to blame. An anti-Semitic journalist, Édouard Drumont, insisted that "Jews in the army" were subverting the national interest. In 1889 he and others founded the Anti-Semitic League. This ugly and heated campaign furnished the background of the famous Dreyfus affair. In 1894 a Jewish captain in the French general staff, Alfred Dreyfus, was accused by a clique of monarchist officers of selling military secrets to Germany. Tried by court-martial, he was convicted and sentenced for life to Devil's Island, a ghastly prison camp in the Caribbean. At first the verdict was accepted as the merited punishment of a traitor, but in 1896 Colonel Georges Picquart, a new head of the Intelligence Division, announced his conclusion that the documents upon which Dreyfus had been convicted were forgeries. A movement was launched for a new trial, which the War

Alfred Dreyfus Leaving His Court Martial

Department promptly refused. Soon the whole nation was divided into friends and opponents of Dreyfus. On his side were the radical republicans, socialists, people of liberal and humanitarian sympathies, and such prominent literary figures as Anatole France and Émile Zola, the latter achieving fame with his pamphlet defending Dreyfus, "J'accuse." The anti-Dreyfusards included monarchists, clerics, anti-Semites, militarists, and a considerable number of conservative working people. A Roman Catholic newspaper insisted that the question was not whether Dreyfus was guilty or innocent, but whether Jews and unbelievers were not the secret masters of France. Dreyfus was finally set free by executive order in 1899, and in 1906 was cleared of all guilt by the Supreme Court and restored to the army. He was immediately promoted to the rank of major and decorated with the emblem of the Legion of Honor.

The history of the Dreyfus affair gave the republicans the solid ground they had lacked in order to end the plottings of the radical reactionaries once and for all. The leaders of the republic chose to attack their enemies by effectively destroying the political power of the Roman Catholic Church in France. The anticlericalism expressed in this campaign was probably in part the product of a materialistic age, and of a longstanding mistrust by French republicans of the institution of the Church. Its main source, however, was the nationalism that we have already seen fueling Bismarck's *Kulturkampf.* In 1901 the government passed a law prohibiting the existence of religious orders not authorized by the state; in 1904 another law forbade members of religious orders to teach in either public or private schools. Finally, in 1905, the union of Church and state was dissolved, thereby prohibiting payment of the clergy from public funds. For the first time since 1801 the adherents of all creeds were placed on an equal basis.

Legislation to curb the Church

The republic was, during these years, pressed from the Left as well as the Right. Socialism was a political force in France, as it was in Germany. Yet the response of republicans in France to socialist pressure differed markedly from that of Bismarck. There was no antisocialist legislation. Indeed, a law was passed in 1881 abolishing "crimes of opinion," thereby extending the freedom of the press considerably. In the same year, another law authorized public meetings without prior official approval. But if there was no attempt at repression, there was little positive social reform. The largest single party in the republic, the Radicals or Radical Socialists, was really a party representing small shopkeepers and lesser propertied interests. The Radicals were willing to found and maintain a democratic compulsory educational system, but they were reluctant to respond to demands for social legislation such as had been instituted in Germany. Those laws that were passed—establishing a ten-hour workday in 1904 and old-age pensions in 1910—were passed grudgingly and only after socialist pressure. The result was a growing belief among socialists and other workers that parliamentary democracy was worthless, that progress, if it was to be made, would be made only as a result of direct industrial action: the strike.

Pressure from the Left

Conflicts and Contrasts in Working-Class Life. Left: In this cartoon tighter work controls led a working-class French woman to complain to her father that "all day long, it's against the rules to sit down." He responded, "Do as we do! Ditch them." Right: At the same time, as this scene of workers on day-holiday at Yarmouth Sands in Britain suggests, workers enjoyed greater opportunities for at least some leisure time than ever before. These contrasts helped to produce the class conflicts that characterized European politics before the First World War.

Socialist strikes and debates

In response to this growing sentiment came a wave of strikes that swept the country for several years before 1914, including one by postal workers in 1909 and by teachers and railway workers in 1910. The government suppressed these actions by ruthless intervention. Tension increased after 1910 during debates over the extension of military conscription from two to three years, opposed by the socialists, and over the institution of an income tax, favored by the socialists as a way of financing social programs threatened as a result of increased military spending. By 1914, the republic, though hardly on the brink of revolution, remained divided. If the threat from the radical Right had been quelled, the challenge from the Left was only just being faced.

BRITAIN: FROM MODERATION TO MILITANCE

Reform legislation in Britain

During the half-century before 1914, the British prided themselves on what they believed to be a reasonable, orderly, and workable system of government. Following the passage of the Second Reform Bill in 1867, which extended suffrage to more than a third of the nation's adult males, the two major political parties, Liberal and Conservative, vied with each other in adopting legislation designed to provide an increasingly larger proportion of the population the chance to lead fuller and healthier lives. Laws that recognized the legality of trade unions, allowed male religious dissenters to participate fully in the life of the ancient universities of Oxford and Cambridge, provided elementary education for the first time to all children, and facilitated the clearance and rebuilding of large urban areas, were among those placed on the books during this period. In 1884, suffrage was once more widened, to include more than three-fourths of adult males, and to allow rural workingmen the chance to vote for the first time. Coupled with a previous act that instituted the secret ballot, this electoral reform bill brought Britain nearer to representative democracy.

Politics was dominated by two figures, the Conservative Benjamin Disraeli and the Liberal William Gladstone. Disraeli, a converted Jew and popular novelist, and Gladstone, a devout Anglican and moral reformer, were remarkably different men. Disraeli was a pragmatist who remarked upon becoming prime minister that he had at last climbed to "the top of the greasy pole," while Gladstone devised political programs on the basis of his moral convictions. Despite this personality conflict, however, British political parties adopted a similar overall approach to policy-making. Managed by cabinet ministers drawn from either the upper-middle class or landed society, they offered moderate programs that appealed to the widening electorate. Cabinet ministers sought to impose a legislative program on the House of Commons but, acknowledging its ultimate authority as duly elected representative of the people, resigned if their program was rejected. The result was political stability. And if differences of opinion did arise—as they did over imperialism, for example—both parties generally agreed upon a course steered by men whose similar backgrounds promised a moderation that suited the electorate.

Not everyone was content, however. Prosperity, though widespread enough, did not extend to the unskilled: dock workers, transport workers, and the like. These groups formed trade unions to press their claims. Their determination encouraged other unions to assume a more militant and demanding stance. In the 1890s this activity produced a reaction in

Benjamin Disraeli

Liberal reforms, 1906–1914

William E. Gladstone Campaigning, 1885. Perhaps the first politician to make effective use of the railway in his campaigns, Gladstone took advantage of the mobility it provided to reach out to the electorate.

David Lloyd George and Winston Churchill on their way to the House of Commons in 1910

the form of anti–trade union employers' associations and a series of legal decisions limiting the right of unions to strike. Workers, in turn, reacted by associating with middle-class socialist societies to form an independent Labour party, which was born in 1901 and five years later managed to send twenty-nine members to the House of Commons. Sensitive to this pressure from the Left, the Liberals, during a ministry that began in 1906, passed a series of reforms they hoped would ensure a minimum standard of living for those who had heretofore known little security. Sickness, accident, old-age, and unemployment insurance schemes were adopted. A minimum wage was decreed in certain industries. Labor exchanges, designed to help unemployed men and women find new jobs, were established. Restrictions on strikes and on the right of trade unions to raise money for political purposes were relaxed.

Much of this legislation was the work of David Lloyd George, a radical lawyer from Wales, much feared by many within the political establishment. Lloyd George was chancellor of the exchequer (finance minister) in the Liberal cabinet of Prime Minister Herbert Asquith. Together with another young Liberal, Winston Churchill, he hammered together legislation that was both a reflection of his own political philosophy and a practical response to the growing political power of the working class. To pay for these programs—and for a larger navy to counter the German buildup—Lloyd George proposed a budget in 1909 that included progressive income and inheritance taxes, designed to make wealthier taxpayers pay at higher rates. His proposals so enraged the aristocratic members of the House of Lords that they declared themselves prepared to throw out the budget, an action contrary to constitutional precedent. Asquith countered with a threat to create enough new peers (titled noblemen) sympa-

Lloyd George's budget

922

London Dock Strike, 1911. Police move to clear demonstrators from shops where they have taken refuge after having been fired upon.

thetic to the budget to ensure its passage.* The House of Lords eventually surrendered; the result of the crisis was an act of Parliament in 1911 that provided that the House of Lords could not veto legislation passed by the House of Commons.

The rancor aroused by this constitutional conflict was intense. Self-proclaimed defenders of the House of Lords screamed threats in a chamber unused to anything but gentlemanly debate. Angry threats were by no means confined to Parliament during these years, however. Throughout Britain, men and women threw moderation to the winds as they disputed issues in an atmosphere little short of anarchic. The reasons for this continued agitation were various. A decline in real wages after 1900 kept the working class in a militant mood despite Liberal reforms and produced an unusually severe series of strikes in 1911 and 1912. A Liberal plan to grant Home Rule (self-government) to Ireland produced not only panic in the Protestant-majority counties of the north (Ulster) but arming and drilling of private militias with an intensity that seemed to forecast civil war.

Perhaps the most alarming—because the most unexpected—of the militant revolts that seized Britain in the years before 1914 was the campaign for women's suffrage. The middle-class women who engaged in this struggle enjoyed more freedom of opportunity than their mothers had

Increased militance

Suffragettes

*In Britain the monarch had the authority to elevate an unlimited number of men to the peerage. But since the crown acts only on the advice of the prime minister, it is this official who had the actual power to create new members of the House of Lords. If necessary, he could use this power to pack the upper house with his own followers.

Violent Suffragette Protest.
Emmeline Pankhurst is arrested
during a violent demonstration
at Buckingham Palace in 1911.

Britain prey to instability

known. Laws had been passed easing the process of divorce and permitting married women control of their own property. Some universities had started to grant degrees to women. Contraceptive devices—and feminist propaganda defending their use—had begun to result in changed attitudes toward sexuality within the middle class. Perhaps because of these gains, many women felt their lack of the vote all the more acutely. Although the movement began among middle-class women, it soon included some female members of the working class and the aristocracy. Agitation reached a peak after 1900, when militant suffragettes—under the leadership of Emmeline Pankhurst, her daughters Christabel and Sylvia, and others—resorted to violence in order to impress upon the nation the seriousness of their commitment. Women chained themselves to the visitors' gallery in the House of Commons; slashed paintings in museums; invaded that male sanctum, the golf course, and inscribed "VOTES FOR WOMEN" in acid on the greens; disrupted political meetings; burned politicians' houses; and smashed department store windows. The government countered violence with repression. When women, arrested for their disruptive activities, went on hunger strikes in prisons, wardens proceeded to feed them forcibly, tying them down, holding their mouths open with wooden and metal clamps, and running tubes down their throats. When hunger strikes threatened to produce deaths and thus martyrs for the cause, the government passed the constitutionally dubious "Cat and Mouse" Act, which sanctioned the freeing of prisoners to halt their starvation and then, once they had regained their health, authorized their rearrest. The movement was not to see the achievement of its goal until after the First World War, when reform came largely because of women's contributions to the war effort.

Whether Britain's militant mood might have led to some sort of general conflict if the war had not begun in 1914 is a question historians

Militant Actions for Women's Suffrage. Left: Emily Davison threw herself under the king's horse at the Derby in 1913. Right: This suffragette was arrested after having joined an attack on Buckingham Palace in 1914. Women resorted to violence to show the nation the seriousness of their commitment to gaining the vote. Attitudes toward the suffragettes were typified by the response of Britain's monarchy to the trampling of Emily Davison—the queen inquired about the woman, the king about his horse.

continue to debate. Suffice it to say that national sentiment in the last few years before the outbreak of general hostilities was far different from that of the 1870s. Britain, so confident of itself and of its moderation, was proving no less a prey to instability than other European nations.

RUSSIA: THE ROAD TO REVOLUTION

In only one European country, Russia, did conditions pass from instability to active insurrection during these prewar years. The early-twentieth-century Russian revolutionary movement had numerous forerunners. Waves of discontent broke out several times during the nineteenth century. Threatened uprisings between 1850 and 1860, partly a consequence of Russia's defeat in the Crimean War, persuaded Tsar Alexander II (1855–1881) to liberate the serfs, to modernize the military establishment, to reform the judicial system, and to grant local self-government.

Reform and reaction in nineteenth-century Russia

The law of 1861 granted legal rights to some 22 million serfs and authorized their title to at least a portion of the land they had worked. Yet the pattern of rural life in Russia did not change drastically. Large-scale landowners managed to retain the most profitable acreage for themselves, and vastly inflated the prices they charged the state for land surrendered to emancipated serfs. Newly liberated serfs, in turn, faced the need to pay the state for the land they received—which, in addition to being of generally poor quality, was often insufficient to sustain themselves and their families. The overall result of emancipation was to compel peasants to return to work as agricultural laborers for their previous masters.

Liberation of the serfs

The military reform of 1874 was designed to broaden the ranks to include all males, not just conscripted peasants serving under an officer elite open only to the nobility. The period of active duty was reduced from twenty-five to six years. Schooling was provided for draftees and corporal punishment was abolished.

Military reform

Russia's judicial system, heretofore secret, corrupt, and tied to a rigid class system that ensured legal inequality, was reformed so as to make the courts for the first time independent of the central administration. All Russians were declared equal before the law, and trial by jury was introduced for most criminal cases, although crimes against the state remained the province of secret courts under the Ministry of the Interior. Whereas formerly evidence could be presented only in written form, oral testimony was now permitted, thereby making trials far more public in character. A tiered system of courts, rising from local justices of the peace, provided the right to appeal.

Judicial innovations

The structure of local government instituted in 1861 placed responsibility in the hands of the *mir,* or village commune, which had traditionally regulated the lives of peasants and serfs. Its officials assigned land and collected taxes. They were also able to restrict the movement of residents in and out of their community, a regulation used by the state to ensure that peasants could not escape their obligation to pay for the land they

Local government reform

now occupied as free men. At a higher level, district councils were authorized to administer their own courts and tax collection. In 1864, indirectly elected provincial councils—*zemstvos*—were empowered to manage local welfare and educational programs.

Though only moderately reformist, these *zemstvos* provided forums for the debate of political issues and, along with the extension of educational opportunities, encouraged middle-class Russians to suppose themselves on the way to some sort of liberalized state. The government, however, grown fearful of the path it was treading, called a halt to reform and substituted repression in its place. By 1875, censorship had been extended not only to the *zemstvos,* which were forbidden to discuss general political issues, but to the press and to schools as well. The result of suppression was, not surprisingly, further discontent and active subversion. Middle-class Russians and disaffected students argued privately the virtues of utopian socialism, liberal parliamentarianism, and Pan-Slavism. A growing number, calling themselves nihilists, espoused the doctrines of the anarchist Bakunin (see p. 880). Terrorism became the preferred course of action for the student revolutionaries of the People's Will, which had begun as an agrarian socialist party. Increased government repression and failure of peaceful political activity convinced them that assassination of the tsar was the only solution to oppression. They achieved their goal in 1881, when a bomb killed Alexander II.

The most important radical political element in late-nineteenth-century Russia was a large, loosely knit group of men and women who called themselves populists. They believed that although their country must Westernize, it could not expect to do so according to examples set elsewhere. They proclaimed a new Russia, yet one based upon the ancient institution of the village commune, which was to serve as a model for the socialist society they hoped to create. Populism sprang primarily from the middle class; a majority of its adherents were young, many of them students; and about 15 percent were women, a significantly large proportion for the period. They formed secret cadres, plotting the overthrow of tsarism by terror and insurrection. They dedicated their lives to "the people" (hence their name), attempting wherever possible to live among common laborers so as to understand and express the popular will. Populism's historical importance lies not so much in what it accomplished, which was little, but in what it promised for the future. A movement that marked the beginning of organized revolutionary agitation in Russia, it was the seedbed for thought and action that would in time produce general revolution. Populists read Marx's *Capital* before it was translated into Russian; they tested and revised his ideas and those of other major revolutionaries of the nineteenth century so as to produce a doctrine suited to Russia's particular destiny.

The activities of populists and anarchists triggered a floodtide of reaction against the entire policy of reform. Alexander III (1881–1894) governed under the theory that Russia had nothing in common with western Europe, that its people had been nurtured on despotism and mystical piety for centuries and would be utterly lost without them. With this doctrine as his guiding principle, Alexander III enforced a regime of stern repression. He curtailed in every way possible the powers of the local assemblies, increased the authority of the secret police, and subjected villages to government by wealthy nobles selected by the state. These policies were continued, though in somewhat less rigorous form, by his son Nicholas II (1894–1917), a much less effective ruler. Both tsars were ardent proponents of Russification, a more ruthless counterpart of similar nationalistic movements in various countries. Its purpose was to extend the language, religion, and culture of Great Russia, or Russia proper, over all of the subjects of the tsar and thereby to simplify the problem of governing them. It was aimed primarily at Poles, Finns, and Jews, since these were the nationalities considered most dangerous to the stability of the state. Russification meant repression. The Finns were deprived of their constitution; the Poles were compelled to study their own literature in Russian translations; and high officials in the tsar's government connived at *pogroms,* i.e., wholesale massacres, against the Jews. Other groups whose repression by the state led to long-lasting undercurrents of non-Russian nationalism included the Georgians, Armenians, and Azerbaijanis of the Caucasus Mountains. Tensions between Christians and Muslims within these groups augmented inter-ethnic tensions, which even a common hatred of forced Russification could not defuse.

Despite these attempts to turn Russia's back to the West, however, the nation was being drawn more closely than it had ever been before into the European orbit. Russia was industrializing, and making use of European capital to do so. Economic policies during the 1890s, when Count Sergei Witte was the tsar's leading minister, resulted in the adoption of the gold standard, which made Russian currency easily convertible. Railways and telegraph lines were constructed; exports and imports multiplied by factors of seven and five respectively from 1880 to 1913. In addition, Russian writers and musicians contributed in a major way to the enriching of Western culture. We have already noted the singular contributions of Tolstoy, Turgenev, and Dostoevsky. The musical works of Peter Tchaikovsky and Nikolai Rimsky-Korsakov, while expressing a peculiarly Russian temperament and tradition, were recognized as important additions to the general body of first-rate contemporary composition.

With Westernization came the growth of a new wage-earning class. Most of Russia's workers were recruited from the countryside. We have seen that regulations made migration outside the *mir* difficult if not impossible. To live permanently in cities meant surrendering all claim to one's land. The result was that many peasant factory workers lived away from their villages only temporarily, returning to attend to farming's seasonal demands. Consequently, these workers could not easily master a trade, and were forced to take unskilled jobs at extremely low wages. They lived in large barracks; they were marched to and from factories, where conditions were as unsafe and unhealthy as they had been in British factories in the early years of industrialization. An average working

Westernization

A new working class

day in a textile mill was from twelve to fourteen hours long. This sudden and extremely harsh transition from country to city living instilled deep discontent and divisiveness in Russian workers. Those who renounced their village ties and adopted the life of the city tended to be skilled workers who could command higher wages and better working conditions than the unskilled. Workers thus tended to be divided along lines of skill as well as by trade, defusing the development of a uniform working-class consciousness for many years. The heavy concentration of workers in urban areas, however, introduced many, especially the generally better-educated skilled workers, to political organizers seeking reform or revolution.

The dilemma of modernization

Industrialization and modernization compelled Russia's autocratic rulers to face a dilemma they could never hope to resolve satisfactorily. If they refused to modernize they doomed their country as a great power. Yet by modernizing, they sealed their own fate, for modernization demanded that they not only recondition their country economically, but effect vast changes in those social and legal systems upon which the autocracy itself rested. Legal codes, for example, were incapable of recognizing institutions such as trade unions or workers' councils. Laws were drawn, instead, with reference to the ancient social subdivisions of nobility, peasant, clergy, and town dweller. How were workers to seek legal relief? As "peasants"? As "town dwellers"? Neither category corresponded to the new facts of an industrializing class-divided society. Yet to redraw legal boundaries threatened directly the stability of the tsarist regime. Middle classes, too, suffered as a consequence of outdated banking and financial laws that bore little relevance to rapidly changing economic circumstances. Meanwhile, of course, the traditional orders understood modernization as a challenge to their very existence and grew

A Railroad Yard in Eastern Russia, 1896. Evidence of the degree to which Russia was industrialized at the end of the century.

Worker's Quarters in St. Petersburg, c. 1900. These buildings, in which workers from the country were housed temporarily while they labored in factories, were breeding grounds for class consciousness.

increasingly restive with changes that they found hard to accept, or indeed to comprehend.

New social tensions and new class divisions brought the emergence of new political parties. The famine of 1891 encouraged this, as private relief workers saw that agricultural capitalism had made deep inroads into the traditional structure of the *mir*. For the first time it appeared that the rural commune might not be the uniquely Russian answer to the problems of unequal distribution, leading some to develop urban-based political responses to Russian conditions.

The heavy involvement of the state in the rapid industrialization of the 1890s in general wedded industrialists and capitalists to the autocracy for the short term. Other members of the middle class, however, primarily enterprising landowners, came together in 1905 to form a Constitutional Democratic party, whose program included the creation of a nationally elected parliament, or Duma, to determine and carry out policies that would further the twin goals of liberalization and modernization. Meanwhile, the Social Revolutionaries and the Social Democrats began to agitate for far more radical solutions to the problems of Russian autocracy. The Social Revolutionaries concerned themselves with the onerous plight of the peasants, burdened with land purchase and high taxes. The Social Revolutionaries wanted to equalize the landholdings of peasants within their *mirs,* and to increase the power of the *mirs* in their continuing competition with large landowners. The Social Democrats, on the other hand, concentrated their efforts on behalf of urban workers. They were Marxists, who saw themselves as westerners and as part of the international working-class movement. In 1903 the leadership of the Social

Bolsheviks vs. Mensheviks

Democratic party split in an important disagreement over revolutionary strategy. One group, which achieved a temporary majority (and thus called itself the Bolsheviks—"majority group"), favored a strongly centralized party of active revolutionaries, and opposed the notion of a postrevolutionary transitional bourgeois state, insisting instead that revolution be succeeded immediately by a socialist regime. The Mensheviks ("minority group"), whose position resembled that of other European revisionist socialists, soon managed to regain control of the party. The Bolshevik splinter party remained in existence, however, under the leadership of the young, dedicated revolutionary Vladimir Ilyich Ulanov, who wrote under the pseudonym of N. Lenin.

Lenin was a member of the middle class, his father having served as an inspector of schools and minor political functionary. He had been expelled from the University of Kazan for engaging in radical activity, following the execution of his elder brother for his involvement in a plot to assassinate Alexander III. Lenin spent three years as a political prisoner in Siberia; from 1900 until 1917 he lived as an exile in western Europe. His zeal and abilities as both a theoretician and a political activist are evidenced by the fact that he retained leadership of the Social Democrats even while residing abroad. Lenin continued to preach the gospel of Marxism and of a relentless class struggle. He argued the need for a coordinated revolutionary socialist movement throughout Europe. He believed that Russia was passing into a capitalist stage that might soon allow for revolution there. To effect that revolution, it was the Bolsheviks' responsibility to organize on behalf of workers who, without the party's disciplined commitment, could not accomplish change of the necessary magnitude. Lenin's vision of Russia's special destiny was reflected in his treatise *What Is to Be Done?* (1902), a stinging response to revisionists who were urging collaboration with less radical parties. Revolution was what was to be done, Lenin argued, revolution "made" as soon as possible by an elitist group of agitators working through the agency of a disciplined party. Lenin and his followers, by merging the tradition of Russian revolutionism with Western Marxism, and by endowing the result with a sense of immediate possibility, fused the Russian situation in such a way as to make eventual explosion almost inevitable.

The revolution that came in 1905, however, took even the Bolsheviks by surprise. Its unexpected occurrence was the result of an imperial war between Russia and Japan, which broke out in 1904, and in which the Russians were soundly beaten. Both countries had conflicting interests in Manchuria and Korea; this fact was the immediate cause of the conflict. On land and sea the Japanese proved themselves the military superiors of the Russians. As dispatches continued to report the defeats of the tsar's army and navy, the Russian people were presented with dramatic evidence of the inefficiency of autocracy.

Just as defeat in the Crimean War had spurred the movement for reform in Russia, so now members of the middle class who had hitherto refrained from association with the revolutionists joined in the clamor

Lenin

The Young Lenin, 1897

The Russo-Japanese War

Bloody Sunday

for change. Radical workers organized strikes and held demonstrations in every important city. Led by a priest, Father Gapon, a group of 200,000 workers and their families went to demonstrate their grievances at the tsar's winter palace in St. Petersburg on January 22, 1905—known ever after as Bloody Sunday. The demonstrators were met by guard troops; many of them were shot dead. The massacre removed the last vestiges of "naive monarchism," the belief that the tsar sincerely loved his subjects and was prevented from gratifying their needs only through the machinations of his evil councillors. By the autumn of 1905 nearly the entire urban population had enlisted in a strike of protest. Merchants closed their stores, factory-owners shut down their plants, lawyers refused to plead cases in court. It was soon evident to Tsar Nicholas that the government would have to yield. On October 30, he issued a manifesto, pledging guarantees of individual liberties, promising a moderately liberal franchise for the election of a Duma, and affirming that henceforth no law would be valid unless it had the Duma's approval. This was the high-water mark of the revolutionary movement. During the next two years Nicholas issued a series of sweeping decrees that negated most of the promises made in the October Manifesto. He deprived the Duma of many of its powers, and decreed that it be elected indirectly on a class basis by a number of electoral colleges. Thereafter the legislative body contained a majority of obedient followers of the tsar.

There were several reasons for the setback to this movement for major political reform. In the first place, the army remained loyal to its commander-in-chief. Consequently, after the termination of the war with Japan in 1905, the tsar had a large body of troops that could be counted upon if necessary to decimate the ranks of the revolutionists. An even more important reason was the split in the ranks of the revolutionists themselves. After the issuance of the October Manifesto, large

The reasons for setback

Bloody Sunday. Demonstrating workers who sought to bring their grievances to the attention of the tsar were met and gunned down by government troops, January 1905.

numbers of the bourgeoisie became frightened at threats of the radicals and declared their conviction that the revolution had gone far enough. Withdrawing their support altogether, they became known henceforth as Octobrists. The more radical merchants and professional men, organized into the Constitutional Democratic party, maintained that opposition should continue until the tsar had been forced to establish a government modeled after that of Great Britain. This fatal division rendered the middle class politically impotent. Finally, disaffection appeared within the ranks of the workers. Further attempts to employ the general strike as a weapon against the government ended in disaster.

Gains from the revolutionary movement

But the Russian revolutionary movement of 1905 was not a total failure. Many retrospectively viewed it as a "dress rehearsal" for the Revolution of 1917. The tsar's vengeance convinced many people that their government was not a benevolent autocracy, as they had been led to believe, but a stubborn and brutal tyranny. The uprising revealed the ability of working-class leaders to control the destiny of Russia. The general strike had proved a valuable revolutionary tool, as had workers' councils, elected from the factory floor and briefly operating as the only effective government in some areas. In addition, the revolt of 1905 persuaded some of the more sagacious advisers of the tsar that last-ditch conservatism was none too safe. The result was the enactment of a number of conciliatory reforms. Among the most significant were the agrarian programs sponsored by the government's leading minister, Peter Stolypin, between 1906 and 1911. These included transfer of five million acres of royal land to the peasants for a price; the granting of permission to peasants to withdraw from the *mir* and set up as independent farmers; and cancellation of the remaining installments owed by the peasants for their land. Decrees were issued permitting the formation of labor unions, providing for a reduction of the working day (to not more than ten hours in most cases), and establishing sickness and accident insurance. Yet the hopes of some liberals that Russia was on the way to becoming a progressive nation on the Western model proved illusory. The tsar remained stubbornly autocratic. Few peasants had enough money to buy the lands offered for purchase. In view of the rising cost of living, the factory workers considered their modest gains insufficient. A new revolutionary outbreak merely awaited a convenient spark.

Revolutionary Poster. "The Revolution of 1905 united the workers and Lenin in its gunpowder smoke."

The Search for Equilibrium Elsewhere in the West

Problems in Italy

Other European countries generally found it just as difficult to attain internal stability between 1870 and 1914 as did those whose history we have already surveyed. Italy was burdened with the problems of a rapidly increasing population, the need to industrialize quickly, and a stark disparity between a relatively prosperous industrial north and an impoverished agricultural south. As the population increased, so did the stream of rural migration into cities, where there were few jobs available. In its drive to create jobs and to industrialize, the government intervened directly in the economy by placing large orders for military equipment and by undertaking an ambitious program of railway construction. By the First World War the share of industrial production in the national economy had risen to 25 percent.

These strides were largely the result of policies instituted by Giovanni Giolitti, who was prime minister for almost the entire period between 1900 and 1914. Yet his efforts to spur industrialization widened the division between north and south. Relying on opportunistic maneuvering, which he called *trasformismo,* and which argued the pointlessness of party politics, Giolitti rewarded the support of southern politicians for his program of industrial expansion by allowing the south to remain under the domination of the great landowners, the Church, and—in Sicily—the Mafia, none of which was interested in furthering the economic well-being or political consciousness of the average citizen. Thus whereas illiteracy was reduced in northern Italy to about 11 percent, in the south it remained at 90 percent. By failing to address the desperate economic conditions in the south, *trasformismo* denied the country an opportunity to develop a much needed internal market for its goods.

Trasformismo

Hoping to gain support for his program from the socialists, Giolitti engineered passage of laws legalizing trade unions, improving factory conditions, and extending the suffrage to virtually all males over thirty. But attempts to satisfy the Left did not sit well with more conservative elements in Italian society, who remembered bread riots in Milan in 1896, the assassination of King Humbert by radicals in 1900, and widespread strikes in 1902 and 1904. Meanwhile, socialists in Italy were as divided on the matter of strategy as they were elsewhere in Europe. Reformists competed with radicals, organized into chambers of labor—local trade union councils with a revolutionary outlook—which assisted in the takeover of the Socialist party by a militant left wing in 1912.

Socialist split

Nationalist aspirations continued to be a major problem in eastern Europe. In 1867 an attempt had been made to resolve national differences in Austria by dividing the empire in two—an Austrian empire west of the Leitha River, and a kingdom of Hungary to its east. Each of the two components in this so-called Dual Monarchy was to be the equal of the other, though the two were joined by the same Habsburg monarch, by several common ministries, and by a kind of superparliament. This solution failed to put an end to nationalist divisions, however.

Nationalism in Austria-Hungary

The Austrian portion of the monarchy was composed not only of a German-speaking majority, but of Czechs, Slovaks, Slovenes, and Ruthenians as well. Without concessions to these nationalities the government could expect little peace. Yet to give in to their aspirations was to antagonize the German majority, a group constantly wary of any move that appeared to threaten its predominance. During the 1890s, an attempt to pacify the Czechs by requiring all officials in areas of mixed German and Czech populations to speak both languages infuriated the Germans, who staged violent demonstrations proclaiming the superiority of their culture

Nationalist tensions in Austria

and forced the government to back down. By this time the Czech middle class had asserted its opposition to German hegemony by founding a Czech bank and a national theater in Prague. Cultural organizations such as gymnastic clubs, whose gatherings had an unquestionably political undertone, and mass political rallies throughout Czech territories attended in some cases by tens of thousands made it increasingly difficult for the government of Vienna to withstand the centrifugal force of particularist nationalist fervor.

Anxious to promote industrial development, the Vienna bureaucracy recognized that to introduce the requisite economic and financial measures, a Reichstag more sympathetic to modernization and to the needs of diverse imperial constituencies would be necessary. To that end, the Austrians introduced universal male suffrage in 1907, in the belief that newly enfranchised peasants recognized a primary allegiance to the emperor, rather than to any one particular nationality. Because the new

Austrian electoral reforms

Europe after the Congress of Berlin, 1878

Vienna, 1873. Despite the fact that Vienna was the capital of an empire that straddled eastern and western Europe, it was by this date clearly a stylish and Westernized metropolis.

electoral laws continued to specify quotas for each ethnic minority in the parliament, however, they strengthened the hand of the various national groups in the legislature, encouraging them to demand still further autonomy.

The major issue in the Hungarian half of the monarchy was a proposal to separate out the Hungarian regiments in the imperial army, allowing them their own insignia and requiring that they be commanded in their native language. The emperor, Francis Joseph, rejected these demands, countering with a threat to introduce male suffrage in empire-wide elections, a move the Magyars correctly saw as a challenge to their supremacy, as it had been to the Germans in Austria. The result was a standoff, part of the continuing desperate attempt on the part of the central government to play one side off against the other in order to maintain a shaky *status quo*.

In southeastern Europe nationalist agitation continued to rend the ever-disintegrating Ottoman Empire. Before 1829 the entire Balkan peninsula—bounded by the Aegean, Black, and Adriatic Seas—was controlled by the Turks. But during the next eighty-five years a gradual dismemberment of the Turkish Empire occurred. In some instances the slicing away of territories had been perpetrated by rival European powers, especially by Russia and Austria; but generally it was the result of nationalist revolts by the sultan's Christian subjects. In 1829, at the conclusion of a war between Russia and Turkey, the Ottoman Empire was compelled to acknowledge the independence of Greece and to grant autonomy to Serbia and to the provinces that later became Rumania. As the years passed, resentment against Ottoman rule spread through other Balkan

Nationalist tensions in Hungary

The disintegrating Ottoman Empire

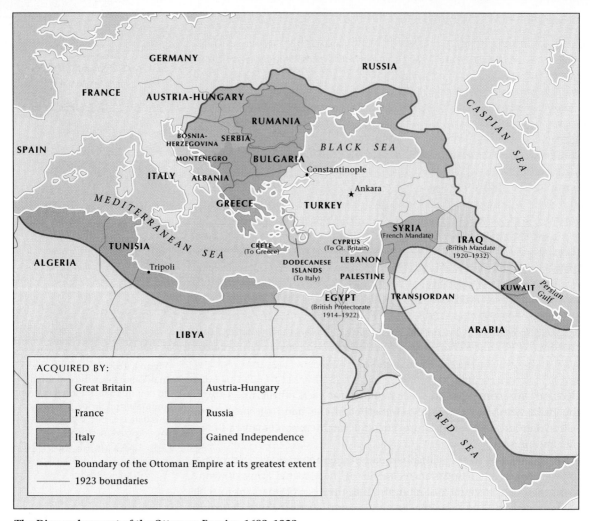

The Dismemberment of the Ottoman Empire, 1683–1923

territories. In 1875–1876 there were uprisings in Bosnia, Herzegovina, and Bulgaria, which the sultan suppressed with effective ferocity. Reports of atrocities against Christians gave Russia an excuse for renewal of its age-long struggle for domination of the Balkans. In this second Russo-Turkish War (1877–1878) the armies of the tsar won a smashing victory. The Treaty of San Stefano, which terminated the conflict, provided that the sultan surrender nearly all of his territory in Europe, except for a remnant around Constantinople. But at this juncture the great powers intervened. Austria and Great Britain, especially, were opposed to granting Russia jurisdiction over so large a portion of the Near East. In 1878 a congress of the great powers, meeting in Berlin, transferred Bessarabia to Russia, Thessaly to Greece, and Bosnia and Herzegovina to the control of Austria. Montenegro, Serbia, and Rumania were recognized as independent states. Seven years later the Bulgars, who had been granted some degree of autonomy by the Congress of Berlin, seized the province of Eastern Rumelia from Turkey. In 1908 they established the independent Kingdom of Bulgaria.

In the very year when this last dismemberment occurred, Turkey itself was engulfed by a tidal wave of nationalism. For some time the more enlightened Turks had grown increasingly disgusted with the weakness and incompetence of the sultan's government. Those who had been educated in European universities were convinced that their country should be rejuvenated by the introduction of Western ideas of science, patriotism, and democracy. Organizing themselves into a society known as the Young Turks, they forced the sultan in 1908 to establish constitutional government. The following year, in the face of a reactionary movement, they deposed the reigning sultan, Abdul Hamid II (1876–1909), and placed on the throne his brother, Mohammed V (1909–1918), as a titular sovereign. The real powers of government were now entrusted to a grand vizier and ministers responsible to an elected parliament. This revolution did not mean increased liberty for the non-Turkish inhabitants of the empire. Instead, the Young Turks launched a vigorous movement to Ottomanize all of the Christian subjects of the sultan. At the same time the disturbances preceding and accompanying the revolution opened the way for still further dismemberment. In 1908 Austria annexed the provinces of Bosnia and Herzegovina, which the Treaty of Berlin had allowed it merely to administer, and in 1911–1912 Italy entered into war with Turkey for the conquest of Tripoli.

Of all the major nations of the West, the United States probably underwent the least domestic turmoil during the several decades before 1914. The Civil War had exhausted the country; until the end of the century the ever-expanding frontier provided an alternative for those discontented with their present lot. Yet the United States also felt, to some degree, the pressures that made stability so hard to sustain in Europe. Though the Civil War had ended, the complex moral problem of racism continued to block all attempts to heal the nation. Severe economic crises, particularly an economic depression in the 1890s, accompanied by the collapse of agricultural prices and the closing of factories, caused great suffering and aroused anger at capitalist adventurers who seemed to be profiting at the expense of the country as a whole. Many grew convinced that a restricted money supply had produced the depression. Demand for the issuance of paper money and the increased coinage of silver were at the heart of the programs of the Greenback and the Populist parties, which attracted large followings, and which campaigned as well for an income tax and government ownership of railways and telephone and telegraph lines. Socialism of a reformist brand was espoused by Eugene V. Debs, leader of a mildly Marxist Socialist party. It failed to appeal to the generally un-class-conscious American worker, who continued to have faith in the dream of economic mobility. More radical was the membership of the Industrial Workers of the World (also known as the Wobblies), a general union whose goal was to organize the unskilled and immigrant

The Young Turk revolution

Unrest in the United States

Eugene Debs

Emblem from a United Mine Workers of America Poster, 1890.

worker. Perceived as a device of foreign agitators, the IWW was repressed both by the government and by industrial management. Characteristic of the generally moderate tone of American reformism, the Progressive movement captured both the imagination and votes of a vocal minority of middle-class Americans whose hostility over the accumulation of private economic power and the political corruption of urban "bosses" was balanced by its belief in the democratic process and in the possibility of continuing progress. The movement, many of whose ideas were embodied in the programs of Presidents Theodore Roosevelt and Woodrow Wilson, was curtailed by the new realities that emerged with the advent of the First World War.

INTERNATIONAL RIVALRIES: THE ROAD TO THE FIRST WORLD WAR

The end of a century of peace

Despite the domestic instabilities and uncertainties that characterized the Western world in the years before 1914, a great many men and women retained a faith in the notion of peaceful progress. There had been an absence of multinational armed conflict—with the exception of the Crimean War—for a century. European countries—even autocratic Russia—had been moving gradually toward what most agreed was the worthy goal of democracy. Indeed, instability could be understood as the result of either an overzealous or an overdelayed movement in that direction. Above all, industrialization seemed to be providing a better standard of living for all—or at least all within the Western world. There is little wonder, therefore, that men and women reacted with disbelief as they saw their world crumbling during the days of frantic diplomatic maneuvering just prior to the outbreak of war in August 1914.

The balance of power

The key to understanding the coming of the First World War lies in an analysis of international diplomacy during the years after 1870. Europe had prided itself on the establishment of a balance of power, which had kept any one nation from assuming so predominating a position as to threaten the general peace. During his years as chancellor, Bismarck played a diplomatic variation upon this general theme in order to ensure that France would not engage in a war of revenge against the German victors of 1870. There was little prospect that the French would attempt war singlehandedly. Therefore, Bismarck determined to isolate France by attaching all of its potential allies to Germany. In 1872 he managed to form an alliance with both Austria and Russia, the so-called Three Emperors' League, a precarious combination that soon foundered. Bismarck then cemented a new and much stronger alliance with Austria. In 1882 this partnership was expanded into a Triple Alliance with Italy. The Italians joined out of fear of the French. They resented the French occupation of Tunisia (1881), a territory that they regarded as properly theirs. Moreover, Italian politicians, still at odds with the Roman Catholic Church, feared that supporters of the papacy in France might gain the upper hand and send a

French army to defend the pope. In the meantime, the Three Emperors' League had been revived. Though it lasted officially for only six years (1881–1887), Germany managed to hold the friendship of Russia until 1890 by means of a Reinsurance Treaty (1887) providing for the neutrality of either power if the other went to war.

Thus after more than a decade of diplomatic maneuvering, Bismarck had achieved his ambition. By 1882 France was cut off from nearly every possibility of obtaining aid from powerful friends. Austria and Italy were united with Germany in the Triple Alliance, and Russia after a three-year lapse was back once more in the Bismarckian camp. The only conceivable quarter from which help might come to the French was Great Britain; but, with respect to Continental affairs, the British were maintaining a policy of "splendid isolation." Therefore, so far as the danger of a war of revenge was concerned, Germany had little to fear. Bismarck's complicated structure of alliances appeared to answer the purpose for which he claimed it had been built—to keep the peace. But the alliance system was a weapon that could cut two ways. In Bismarck's hands, it kept the peace. In hands less diplomatically capable, it might become less an asset than a liability, as was the case after 1890.

During the years between 1890 and 1907, European nations, competing across the globe for trade and territory, became more suspicious of each other. This general international insecurity produced a diplomatic realignment that obliterated Bismarck's handiwork and threatened Germany. The Germans retained the support of Austria, but they lost the friendship of both Russia and Italy, while Britain abandoned its isolation to enter into agreements with Russia and France. This shift in the balance of power had fateful results. It helped convince the Germans that they were surrounded by a ring of enemies, and that consequently they must do everything in their power to retain the loyalty of Austria-Hungary.

The first of the major results of this diplomatic revolution was the formation of the Triple Entente between Russia, France, and Great Britain. William II of Germany, mistrustful of Russian ambitions in the Balkans, refused to renew the Reinsurance Treaty following Bismarck's dismissal in 1890. A growing coolness between the two countries led to Russia's political flirtation with France. Secret military conventions signed by the two countries in 1894 provided that each would come to the aid of the other in case of an attack by Germany, or by Austria or Italy supported by Germany. This Dual Alliance of Russia and France was followed by an Entente Cordiale between France and Great Britain. During the last two decades of the nineteenth century, the British and the French had been involved in frequent altercations over colonies and trade, as in the Sudan, for example. By 1904, however, France, fearing Germany, had buried its differences with Britain and in that year signed the Entente. This was not a formal alliance but a friendly agreement covering a variety of subjects. The final step in the formation of the Triple Entente was the conclusion of a mutual understanding between Great Britain and Russia in 1907. Again there was no formal alliance, but the ability of the two powers to

Bismarck's diplomatic success

A diplomatic realignment

The Triple Entente

reconcile their ambitions in Asia suggested a willingness to ally in case of war.

Thus by 1907 the great powers of Europe were arrayed in two opposing combinations, the Triple Alliance of Germany, Italy, and Austria-Hungary, and the Triple Entente of Britain, France, and Russia. Nevertheless, these new groupings were not without internal strains. Italy and Austria, though allied, were bitterly at odds over the disposition of territory in the Adriatic region—Trieste in particular, which the Austrians held and which the Italians claimed as *Italia Irredenta* (unredeemed Italy). The Italians had designs on portions of Africa as well. In the 1890s, under the premiership of Francesco Crispi, a hero of the *Risorgimento,* they had attempted to establish a protectorate over the Ethiopians, only to suffer a devastating loss at Aduwa in 1896. Now the Italians coveted Tripoli in North Africa, which they believed they might more easily obtain, over the objections of Turkey, if they supported the Moroccan claims of their French adversaries. Strains within the Entente were equally apparent. Britain viewed Russia's growing determination to control the Dardenelles as a threat to its supply routes to the East.

The generally fragile state of international relations was certainly one of the important causes of the First World War. Yet it was by no means the only one. The German historian Fritz Fischer and other scholars ignited a controversy in the 1960s by insisting that the paramount reason was Germany's internally generated drive to power, its compulsion to aggrandize itself at the expense of the rest of Europe—not simply to achieve what the emperor had called its "place in the sun," but to see to it that the sun shone no more than fitfully on anyone else. Scholars of this persuasion, writing against the view that all nations must share the blame, point to Germany's rapid commercial expansion, the growth, in particular, of its coal and steel industries, and its dockyards and overseas shipping as indications of its intentions. German capitalists financed the construction of a Berlin-to-Baghdad railway, as part of a concerted *drang nach osten* (drive to the East). At the same time, the Germans launched a massive campaign to increase the size of their navy, a prospect particularly pleasing to the industrial bourgeoisie, who would profit directly from the new construction, and whose sons, excluded from the aristocratically based army, manned the naval officer corps. The naval buildup was accompanied by a brash and effective propaganda campaign—perhaps the first of its kind—directed by the secretary of the navy, Admiral Alfred von Tirpitz, and concerted through "navy leagues," organizations devoted to trumpeting Germany's intention of matching the strength of the British navy.

Others have taken issue with the notion that Germany faced the prospect of a preemptive war with equanimity, as it ignores the fact that many German industrialists did not want war since they had heavy investments in the economies of both Russia and France. They further argue that it is a mistake to view the problem of the war's outbreak through the single lens of Germany. They maintain that Britain's rapprochement with Russia and France, and France's aggressive pursuit of an alliance against Germany, for example, reflected demands that were more than a defensive response to overweening German ambition.

In canvassing reasons for the outbreak of the First World War, we must revisit once again the phenomenon of nationalism. The ethnic rivalries that tore at central Europe throughout the nineteenth century undoubtedly played their part. From the beginning of the twentieth century, Serbia moved to extend its jurisdiction over all those alleged to be similar to its own citizens in ethnicity and in culture. Some of these peoples inhabited what were then two Turkish provinces, Bosnia and Herzegovina. Others included Croatians and Slovenes in the southern provinces of Austria-Hungary. After 1908, when Austria suddenly annexed Bosnia and Herzegovina, Serbian activity was directed exclusively against the Habsburg Empire. It took the form of agitation to provoke discontent among the Slav subjects of Austria, in the hope of drawing them away and uniting the territories they inhabited with Serbia. It resulted in a series of dangerous plots against the peace and integrity of the Dual Monarchy.

Nationalism's contribution to the outbreak of war was not limited to the desperate quarrels of fanatical central Europeans. In a larger sense, nationalism, as preached by governments throughout the West, encouraged a kind of patriotism that led men and women to believe their country's cause, whatever it might be, was a righteous one. After 1870, it became clear to politicians throughout Europe that changing circumstance—in particular the extension of the franchise to lower-middle- and working-class men—required new methods of ruling. The state was replacing the traditional, localized institutions, such as church, guild, and agricultural estate, that had hitherto engaged the loyalty of men and women. Yet without traditions, how could the state expect to extract such loyalty? The answer: by inventing traditions of its own.

During the period from 1870 to 1914, governments provided their citizens with remodeled capital cities, featuring broad avenues suitable for military parades with flags, national anthems, and uniforms—all of which encouraged the populace to understand citizenship in terms of patriotism. The French Third Republic used a sanitized revolutionary tradition to inspire patriotic nationalism, erecting statues of the mythic Marianne, revolutionary symbol of the French people. Bastille Day, commemorating the prison's fall in July 1789, was first celebrated in 1880. The Germans, lacking an appropriate historical reference point, called upon the very recent past to encourage patriotic devotion to the state. Monuments celebrating the 1871 victory over the French and the subsequent unification of Germany sprang up throughout the Empire.

The emotions these invented symbols and traditions evoked encouraged, in whatever country they appeared, a kind of self-righteous superiority over an enemy "other." In consequence, they helped fuel feelings of national rivalry and superiority, feelings that proved particularly powerful among newly enfranchised, socially insecure lower-middle-class men and women who, with little more than meager salaries and frayed white collars, needed a reason to feel important. This brand of nationalism in

Ethnic rivalries as a cause of war

National patriotism

The invention of national traditions

National self-righteousness

turn encouraged militarism, as all major European countries came to deploy massive "war machines." Serbia and Rumania possessed armies of over 400,000 troops each. In 1913, Russia embarked on a program of military expansion that bolstered its army by 500,000, to over 2,000,000 men, making it roughly equivalent in size to that of Germany. Nation after nation followed the German example by establishing a general staff, an institution one historian has called "the greatest military innovation of the nineteenth century." Problems of supplying and deploying mass armies had compelled governments to create a cadre of high-level planners, professional military advisers who were increasingly heeded by the civilian politicians to whom they reported.

Social impact of militarism

Reliance upon mass armies fostered a preoccupation with national birth rates, public health, and literacy. France regarded its declining birth rate after 1870 with alarm partly because it foretold a diminishing capacity to field a modern world-class army. If birth rates reflected a nation's long-term prospects for military manpower, the physical well-being of draft-age civilians was of immediate concern and encouraged reforms in health care and housing. A report on "physical deterioration" in Britain after the Boer War profoundly disturbed both military and civilian planners by demonstrating that in industrial cities such as Manchester as many as 8,000 out of 11,000 volunteers had been turned away by the army as unfit for military service. And, of course, with the introduction of increasingly sophisticated weaponry that required mastery of technological detail, noncommissioned officers and enlisted men could not function without the ability to read and to figure. The new armies had to be literate armies.

Notions of the therapeutic value of war

General European militarism was fed by notions of war as a therapeutic exercise. The French historian Ernest Renan had justified armed conflict as a condition of progress, "the sting which prevents a country from going to sleep." Middle-class citizens, anxious to prove themselves as patriotically aggressive as aristocrats, joined in the clamor to establish that the counting house was as much the seat of national fervor as the country estate. People began to speak increasingly of the "just" war. The British politician David Lloyd George praised the formation of a Balkan Alliance to fight the Turks in 1912 as "enlarging the boundaries of freedom."

Increasing tension: Morocco

All these factors—diplomatic instability, nationalism, and international militarism—combined to produce a series of crises between 1905 and 1913. In some cases hostilities were averted only because one of the parties was too weak at the time to offer resistance. The result was a sense of humiliation, a smoldering resentment that was almost bound to burst into flame in the future. Two of the crises were generated by disputes over Morocco. Both Germany and France wanted to control Morocco; in 1905 and 1911 the two powers stood on the brink of war. Each time the dispute was smoothed over, but not without the usual legacy of suspicion.

The Bosnian crisis

In addition to the clash over Morocco, two flare-ups occurred in the Near East, the first in Bosnia in 1908. At the Congress of Berlin in 1878 the two Turkish provinces of Bosnia and Herzegovina had been placed under the administrative control of Austria, although actual sovereignty was still to be vested in the Ottoman Empire. Serbia also coveted the territories; they would double the size of its kingdom and place it within striking distance of the Adriatic. Suddenly, in October 1908, as we have seen, Austria annexed the two provinces, in flat violation of the Treaty of Berlin. The Serbs were furious and appealed to Russia for support. The tsar's government threatened war, until Germany addressed a sharp note to St. Petersburg announcing its firm intention to back Austria. Since Russia had not yet fully recovered from its war with Japan and was plagued by internal troubles, Russian intervention was postponed but not renounced. The tsar's government resolved never to let itself be humiliated again.

Still more bad blood between the nations of eastern Europe was created by the Balkan Wars. In 1912 Serbia, Bulgaria, Montenegro, and Greece, with encouragement from Russia, joined in a Balkan League for the conquest of the Turkish province of Macedonia. The war started in October 1912; in less than two months the resistance of the Turks was shattered. Then came the problem of dividing the spoils. In secret treaties negotiated before hostilities began, Serbia had been promised Albania, in addition to a generous slice of Macedonia. But now Austria, fearful as always of any increase in Serbian power, intervened at the peace conference and obtained the establishment of Albania as an independent state. For the Serbs this was the last straw. It seemed to them that at every turn their path to western expansion was certain to be blocked by the Habsburg government. From this time on, anti-Austrian agitation in Serbia and in the neighboring province of Bosnia became ever more venomous.

Balkan Wars

The Iron Fist of the Kaiser Strikes Agadir. This British cartoon depicts the Germans' use of gun-boat diplomacy in Morocco in 1911 to secure colonial concessions from the French as an overtly hostile and sinister act. In precipitating this second Moroccan crisis the Germans hoped to drive a wedge between Britain and France but succeeded only in drawing the Entente powers closer together.

It was the assassination of the Austrian archduke Francis Ferdinand by a Serbian sympathizer on June 28, 1914, that ignited the conflict. The four-year war that ensued altered the Western world immeasurably. Yet many changes that came either during or after the First World War were the result, not of the war itself, but of pressures and forces we have seen at work during the prewar years, when European power, at its height, was challenged by forces which that power had unleashed and which it proved unable to contain.

SUMMARY POINTS

- In Germany, Otto von Bismarck and Emperor William II simultaneously attacked Social Democrats and coopted their social programs as part of their attempts to unify the new empire.

- Deep divisions in French society were evidenced in the Dreyfus affair (1894–1899), which revealed an ugly seam of anti-Semitism that would surface again in the twentieth century.

- In Britain, political militance on the part of the working class and women caused unrest and instability as Liberals and Conservatives drafted legislation to address the concerns of larger portions of the population.

- The 1905 Revolution in Russia involved protests and strikes that were harshly suppressed by the tsarist government, yet in many ways cleared the path for the Revolution of 1917.

- The First World War has its roots in the combination of international rivalries, flagrant nationalism, and widespread militarism that developed in the four decades preceding the war.

SELECTED READINGS

Balfour, Michael, *The Kaiser and His Times*, London, 1964. An excellent biography of William II.

Barrows, Susanna, *Distorting Mirrors: Visions of the Crowd in Late Nineteenth-Century France*, New Haven, 1981. A study of crowd psychology.

Berghahn, Victor, *Germany and the Approach of War in 1914*, 2d ed., New York, 1993. Examines the domestic background of German foreign policy, especially the naval program.

Berlanstein, Lenard R., *The Working People of Paris, 1871–1914*, Baltimore, 1984. The changing nature of the workplace, and the effect of those changes on the lives of men and women.

Blum, J., *Lord and Peasant in Russia from the Ninth to the Nineteenth Century*, Princeton, 1961. Contains a thorough discussion of emancipation.

Brogan, D. W., *France under the Republic, 1870–1930*, New York, 1940. An excellent survey, comprehensive and analytical.

Dangerfield, George, *The Strange Death of Liberal England,* Stanford, 1997. Examines England's three major crises of the prewar period: women's suffrage, labor unrest, and Irish home rule.

Evans, Richard J., *The Feminist Movement in Germany: 1894–1933,* Newbury Park, Calif., 1976. The relationship between the movement and more general politics.

Fischer, Fritz, *Germany's Aims in the First World War,* New York, 1967. An extremely controversial study that seeks to lay major blame for the coming of the First World War on Germany.

Gatrell, Peter, *The Tsarist Economy, 1850–1917,* London, 1986. Discusses population growth and the labor market, and surveys the agricultural, manufacturing, and commercial sectors of the Russian economy during the period of modernization.

Gay, Peter, *The Education of the Senses,* New York, 1984. A discussion of nineteenth-century European and American sexuality, arguing that women were not as sexually repressed as is generally believed. Written from a Freudian perspective.

Haimson, L., *The Russian Marxists and the Origins of Bolshevism,* Cambridge, Mass., 1955. Analyzes the revolutionaries as part of the Russian radical tradition.

Hale, Oron J., *The Great Illusion, 1900–1914,* New York, 1971. A general synthetic treatment of the period that is particularly concerned with mood and spirit.

Jenks, William A., *Austria under the Iron Ring, 1879–1893,* Charlottesville, Va., 1965. An examination of Austria's attempts at political and social reform, set in the context of a struggle for autonomy from German domination.

Johnson, Douglas, *France and the Dreyfus Affair,* London, 1966. A good survey, with breadth.

Jones, Gareth Stedman, *Outcast London,* Oxford, 1971. Examines the breakdown in the relationship between classes in London during the latter half of the nineteenth century.

Mack Smith, Denis, *Italy: A Modern History,* rev. ed., Ann Arbor, Mich., 1969. An excellent survey.

McManners, John, *Church and State in France, 1870–1914,* New York, 1972. Particularly good on the question of education and the final separation of Church and state.

May, Arthur J., *The Hapsburg Monarchy, 1867–1914,* Cambridge, Mass., 1951. A detailed narrative of the period.

Moses, Claire, *French Feminism in the Nineteenth Century,* Albany, N.Y., 1984. The particular nature of the movement in France.

Mosse, W. E., *Alexander II and the Modernization of Russia,* New York, 1958. Brief but useful biography.

Neuberger, Joan, *Hooliganism: Crime, Culture and Power in St. Petersburg,* Berkeley, 1994. The importance of a particular working-class subculture to the history of the revolutionary movement in Russia.

Pulzer, Peter, *The Rise of Political Anti-Semitism in Germany and Austria,* New York, 1964. An excellent study of the roots of anti-Semitism and the part it played in shaping politics.

Ralston, David B., *The Army of the Republic: The Place of the Military in the Political Evolution of France, 1871–1914,* Cambridge, Mass., 1967. Useful for background to the Dreyfus affair.

Rémond, René, *The Right Wing in France: From 1815 to De Gaulle,* rev. ed., Philadelphia, 1969. Traces the survival of royalism and Bonapartism in French thought and politics.

Seton-Watson, Hugh, *The Russian Empire, 1801–1917,* Oxford, 1967. Standard survey.

Stavrianos, Leften S., *The Balkans, 1815–1914,* New York, 1963. Surveys domestic and international affairs within the entire troubled region.

Taylor, A. J. P., *Bismarck: The Man and the Statesman,* New York, 1955. A deft and penetrating analysis of the Prussian statesman.

——, *The Struggle for Mastery in Europe, 1848–1918,* Oxford, 1971. An excellent diplomatic history.

Thayer, John A., *Italy and the Great War: Politics and Culture, 1870–1914,* Madison, Wisc., 1964. Written to explain Italian policy and its origins in the prewar period.

Ulam, Adam, *Russia's Failed Revolutions: From the Decembrists to the Dissidents,* New York, 1981. Activities of revolutionary societies before 1917.

Vicinus, Martha, ed., *A Widening Sphere: Changing Roles of Victorian Women,* Bloomington, Ind., 1977. Essays that trace the slow emancipation of Victorian women.

Weber, Eugen, *Peasants into Frenchmen: The Modernization of Rural France, 1870–1914,* Stanford, 1976. Argues that the great achievement of the Third Republic was the consolidation of France, accomplished by bringing rural areas into the mainstream of modern life.

Wehler, Hans-Ulrich, *The German Empire, 1871–1918,* Dover, N.H., 1985. Revisionist study of political policy under Bismarck and William II.

Williams, Roger L., *The French Revolution of 1870–1871,* New York, 1969. A good narrative account.

Zelnik, Reginald E., *Labor and Society in Tsarist Russia: The Factory Workers of St. Petersburg, 1855–1870,* Stanford, 1971. The growth of class consciousness in tsarist Russia.

SOURCE MATERIALS

Childers, Erskine, *The Riddle of the Sands,* New York, 1978. A bestseller in England in 1903, this novel concerns a future war between England and Germany. Its reception gives evidence of the rise of anti-German sentiment prior to the First World War.

Hamerow, Theodore S., ed., *The Age of Bismarck: Documents and Interpretations,* New York, 1973.

Lenin, Nikolai, *What Is To Be Done?* London, 1918. Written in 1902, this is Lenin's most famous pamphlet. In it he called for the proletarian revolution to be led by elite cadres of bourgeois intellectuals like himself.

Mackenzie, Midge, ed., *Shoulder to Shoulder,* New York, 1975. A richly illustrated documentary history of the British movement for women's suffrage.

Pankhurst, Emmeline, *My Own Story,* New York, 1914. The memoirs of one of the leaders of England's militant suffragettes.

Turgenev, Ivan, *Fathers and Sons,* New York, 1966. Turgenev's greatest novel is set in Russia in the 1860s and portrays the ideological conflict between generations at the time of the emancipation of the serfs and the rise of nihilism.

Zola, Émile, *Germinal,* New York, 1964. Zola's realistic novel describes class conflict in France's coal-mining region.

CHAPTER 27

THE FIRST WORLD WAR

Nevertheless, except you share
With them in hell the sorrowful dark of hell
Whose world is but the trembling of a flare
And heaven but as the highway for a shell
You shall not hear their mirth:
You shall not think them well content
By any jest of mine. These men are worth
Your tears. You are not worth their merriment.
—WILFRED OWEN, "Apologia
Pro Poemate Meo"

THE WAR THAT BROKE OUT in 1914 was not really the "first world war." The wars against Napoleon at the beginning of the nineteenth century had extended beyond the European continent. Yet the war that took place between 1914 and 1918 had an impact that far exceeded any ever fought before. Colonies supported their imperial centers while trading partners were often forced to side with the Allies (initially the Triple Entente) or the Central Powers (initially the Triple Alliance). The scale of the war was such that it quickly became a "people's war," to which civilians as well as soldiers and sailors were directly and totally committed. War bore fruit in revolution, and sowed the seeds of new and even more deadly conflicts in the future. It set the pattern for an age of violence that has continued through most of the twentieth century.

PRELUDE TO WAR

The assassination of the Austrian archduke was the immediate cause of the First World War. Francis Ferdinand was soon to become emperor of Austria-Hungary. The reigning monarch, Francis Joseph (1848–1916), had reached his eighty-fourth year, and his death was expected soon. The murderer of Francis Ferdinand was a Bosnian student, Gavrilo Princip, the tool of Serbian nationalists. The murder, though committed in Sarajevo, the capital of Bosnia, was the result of a plot hatched in Belgrade, the Serbian capital.

Der Bombenwer

The Assassination at Sarajevo. Left: The Archduke Francis Ferdinand greets Bosnian notables a few hours before his death. Right: The police seize Princip after he had killed the heir to the Habsburg monarchy.

Austrian ultimatum to Serbia

The Austrians were immediately convinced that the Serbian government was behind this violent act. Austria waited for more than three weeks before acting on its suspicions and seizing the opportunity to extract a high price from Serbia for its transgressions. The delay was due in part to Austria's inability to decide how to proceed and in part to its unwillingness to mobilize its forces until after the harvest. On July 23, 1914, the Austrian government dispatched a severe ultimatum to the Serbians consisting of eleven demands: among them Serbia was to suppress anti-Austrian newspapers, to crush secret patriotic societies, to eliminate from the government and from the army all persons guilty of anti-Austrian propaganda, and to accept the collaboration of Austrian officials in stamping out the subversive movement against the Habsburg Empire. Two days later the Serbian government transmitted its reply. Of the total of eleven demands, only one was emphatically refused, and five were accepted without reservations. The Austrians, however, pronounced the Serbian reply unsatisfactory, severed diplomatic relations, and mobilized parts of their army. The Serbs themselves had been under no illusions about pleasing Austria, since, three hours before transmitting their reply, they had issued an order to mobilize their troops.

The attitude of Germany

The attitude of Germany in these critical days was ambiguous. Although the kaiser was shocked and infuriated by the assassination, his government did not make any threats until after the actions of Russia gave cause for alarm. Yet both William II and the chancellor, Theobald von Bethmann-Hollweg, adopted the premise that stern punishment must be meted out to Serbia without delay.

948

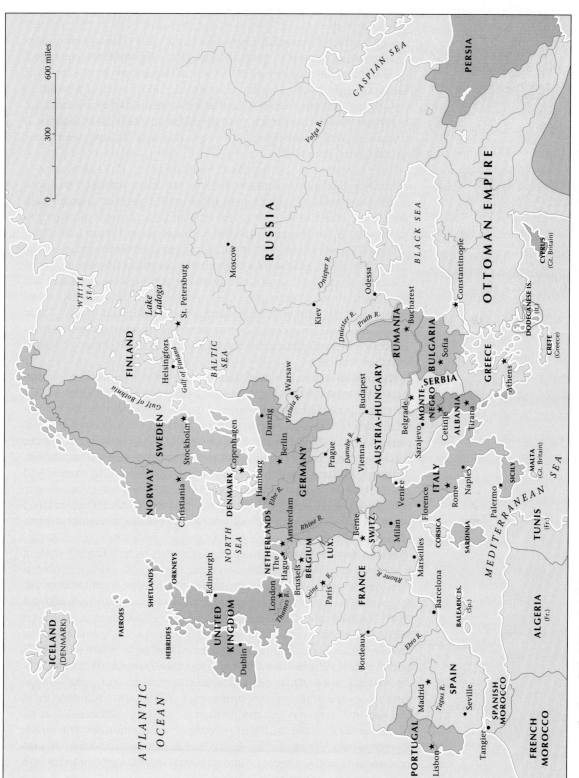

Europe on the Eve of World War I, 1914

Full mobilization in Russia

Austria declared war against Serbia on July 28, 1914. For a fleeting, anxious moment there was a possibility that the conflict might be contained. But it was quickly transformed into a war of larger scope by the action of Russia. On July 24 the Russian government had decided to respond to any Austrian military initiative against Serbia with a partial mobilization. By July 30, however, a prowar military clique persuaded Tsar Nicholas II to issue an order mobilizing all troops, not only against Austria but against Germany as well.

The German ultimatums to Russia and France

There was now no drawing back from the abyss. The Germans were alarmed by Russian preparations for war. The latest action by the tsar's government made the situation far more critical, since in German military circles, and also in French and Russian ones, general mobilization meant war. Upon learning that the tsar's decree had gone into effect, William II's government sent an ultimatum to St. Petersburg demanding that mobilization cease within twelve hours. On the afternoon of August 1, the foreign minister refused. Meanwhile, the kaiser's ministers had also dispatched an ultimatum to France demanding that its leaders make known their intentions. Premier René Viviani replied on August 1 that France would act "in accordance with her interests," and immediately ordered a general mobilization of the army. On August 3 Germany declared war upon France.

The British position

These grim timetables had doomed the efforts of Britain's foreign secretary, Sir Edward Grey, to convene a conference to settle the Austro-Serbian dispute. Perhaps if Britain had declared its readiness to go to war on the side of France and Russia earlier, that declaration would have compelled Germany and Austria to draw back. Yet Grey was not certain enough of his country's willingness to fight to make such a commitment. Although military conversations between the British and French had bound the former to an expeditionary force on French soil in case of war, the British public did not know this. Opinion was divided: Conservatives generally favored war; the Liberals, still in power, disagreed among themselves; Labour was opposed.

Britain enters the war

Fortunately for Grey and the prime minister, Herbert Asquith, both of whom wanted a British declaration of war, Germany's invasion of neutral Belgium brought together parliamentary and public support for intervention. In 1839, along with the other great powers, Britain had signed a treaty guaranteeing the neutrality of Belgium. Moreover, it had been British policy for a century or more to try to prevent domination of the Low Countries, lying directly across the Channel, by any powerful Continental nation. The Germans planned to attack France through Belgium. Accordingly, they demanded of the Belgian government permission to send troops across its territory, promising to respect the independence of the nation and to pay for any damage to property. When Belgium refused, the kaiser's legions began pouring across the frontier. The British foreign secretary immediately went before Parliament and urged that his country rally to the defense of international law and to the protection of

August 1, 1914. A German officer hands out the declaration of war in the streets of Berlin.

small nations. The next day, August 4, 1914, the cabinet sent an ultimatum to Berlin demanding that Germany respect Belgian neutrality, and that the Germans give a satisfactory reply by midnight. The kaiser's ministers offered no answer save military necessity, arguing that it was a matter of life and death for Germany that its soldiers reach France by the quickest route. As the clock struck twelve, Great Britain and Germany were at war.

Other nations were quickly drawn into the struggle. On August 7 the Montenegrins joined with the Serbs in fighting Austria. Two weeks later the Japanese declared war upon Germany, partly because of their alliance with Great Britain, but mainly for the purpose of conquering German possessions in the Far East. On August 1 Turkey negotiated an alliance with Germany, and in October began the bombardment of Russian ports on the Black Sea. Italy, though still technically a member of the Triple Alliance, proclaimed neutrality. The Italians insisted that the Germans were not fighting a defensive war, and that consequently they were not bound to go to their aid. Italy remained neutral until May 1915, when it entered the war on the side of the Triple Entente.

Other nations join the combat

The diplomatic maneuvers during the five weeks that followed the assassination at Sarajevo have probably best been characterized as "a tragedy of miscalculation." Because the war brought such disaster in its train, debate about immediate responsibility for its outbreak has been

The question of "war guilt"

Allied Propaganda Posters.
During the war, governments,
confronted with the bitter fruit
of prewar militarism and nationalist rivalry, resorted to using
any image that seemed likely to
stir the passions of their populations against their foes. Top:
U.S. poster exhorts citizens to
join up and "Treat 'Em Rough."
Bottom: British poster depicts
the Kaiser as Satan.

Propaganda efforts

continual and often acrimonious. The eventual victors—Britain, France,
the United States, and their allies—insisted at the war's end that Germany
assume that responsibility, and wrote German war "guilt" into the postwar settlement. Historians during the 1920s and 1930s challenged that
harsh assessment, arguing instead that all the major European nations—
and the alliance systems they had constructed—had driven the world
into conflict in those fatal weeks during the summer of 1914. In the
1960s, the historian Fritz Fischer insisted that William II and Bethmann-
Hollweg did everything they could to encourage the Austrians to go to
war against Serbia, knowing that such a war would almost certainly engage the Russians on the side of the Serbians and the French on the side
of the Russians. There were those in positions of power in Germany arguing that war was inevitable, that to wait until Russia had fully recovered
from its war with Japan, and until France's armies had been strengthened
by its three-year conscription law, was to invite defeat. Better to do battle
now, from a position of strength. Bethmann-Hollweg had succumbed to
such fatalism by July 1914.

THE ORDEAL OF BATTLE

Because the war soon demanded the wholehearted support of entire civilian populations, national leaders felt compelled to depict it as a noble
conflict rather than a widespread quarrel between imperialist powers or
the unexpected outcome of nationalist jealousies. The socialist Second International had declared that workers should respond to a call to arms
with a general strike. Although none of the European Socialist parties
heeded that call, governments continued to fear subversion of the war effort from "below," and attempted to head off any such movement by
ceaseless appeals to patriotism. Propaganda became as important a
weapon as the machine gun. The task of the Allies was at first made easier
by Germany's treatment of the neutral Belgians: their execution of civilian hostages, destruction of the ancient library at Louvain, and massacre
of over six hundred civilians at Dinant.

On August 6, 1914, Prime Minister Asquith declared that Britain had
entered the conflict to vindicate "the principle that smaller nationalities
are not to be crushed by the arbitrary will of a strong and overmastering
Power." Across the Channel, President Raymond Poincaré was assuring
his fellow citizens that France had no other purpose than to stand "before
the universe for Liberty, Justice and Reason." Later, as a consequence of
the writings of individuals such as H. G. Wells and Gilbert Murray, and
the pronouncements of the American president, Woodrow Wilson, the
crusade of the Allied powers became a war to redeem mankind from the
curse of militarism. In the opposing camp, the subordinates of the kaiser
were doing all in their power to justify Germany's military efforts. The
struggle against the Allied powers was represented to the German people

German Propaganda Poster. As in the British propaganda poster, the foes of the Germans are shown as evil—e.g., Wilson as a serpent—thereby justifying the death and destruction caused by the fighting.

as a crusade on behalf of a superior *Kultur* and as a battle to protect the fatherland against the wicked encirclement policy of the Allied nations. German socialist politicians were persuaded to vote for the war on the grounds that a German war with Russia would help liberate the Russian people from the tsarist yoke.

The First World War fooled military experts who believed it would end quickly. Open warfare soon disappeared from the Western Front—the battle line that stretched across France from Switzerland to the North Sea, where the fighting was concentrated for four years. Germany's initially successful advance into France followed war plans drawn up by General Alfred von Schlieffen and adopted in 1905. Schlieffen's strategy called for Austria to hold against the Russians while Germany dealt a quick blow to the French, knocking them out of the war. Germany was then to turn, with Austria, to the major task of defeating the Russians. Contrary to expectation, however, the advance to the west, which brought German troops to within thirty miles of Paris, was halted. A series of flanking maneuvers by both sides ended in the extension of the battle lines in a vast network of trenches.

Open warfare disappears from Western Front

Attacks to dislodge the enemy from their positions on the line failed to achieve more than very limited gains. Protected by barbed wire and machine guns—both making their first major appearance in a European war—defenders had the advantage. The one weapon with the potential to break the stalemate, the tank, was not introduced into battle until 1916, and then with such reluctance by tradition-bound commanders that its half-hearted employment made almost no difference. Airplanes were used almost exclusively for reconnaissance, though occasional

Stalemate

953

"dog-fights" did occur between German and Allied pilots. The Germans sent Zeppelins to raid London, but they did little significant damage. On more than one occasion those in charge of the war attempted to end the stalemate by opening military fronts in other areas of the world. In 1915, Britain and France attempted a landing at Gallipoli, in Asia Minor, in the hope of driving Turkey from the war. The campaign was a disaster for the Allied powers, however, failing, as did others, to refocus the fighting or to free it from the immobility of the trenches.

Life for the common soldier on the Western Front alternated between the daily boredom and extreme unpleasantness of weeks spent in muddy and vermin-ridden trench communities, and the occasional and horrifying experience of battle, a nightmare not only of artillery, machine guns, and barbed wire, but of exploding bullets, liquid fire, and poison gas. Morale among most troops remained remarkably steady, given the dreadful conditions in the trenches and the endless series of battles fought without significant gain to either side. Mutinies did occur among French troops in 1917, when soldiers moved forward in attack bleating like sheep, their pathetic way of protesting their commanders' continued willingness to lead them like lambs to the slaughter. Meanwhile, conditions within Germany worsened, as an Allied blockade slowly reduced the country's raw materials and food supply.

By 1916 the war, which appeared to have settled into an interminable stalemate, had extracted a fearful cost. Commanders on both sides embarked on a war of attrition. Only by battering their enemies first with artillery and then with thousands of men armed with rifles, grenades, and bayonets did they believe they could achieve the always-elusive "breakthrough." These assaults produced high casualties and a few extra yards of mud. More than 600,000 were killed and wounded when the Germans unsuccessfully besieged the French stronghold of Verdun, near France's eastern border, in the spring of 1916. The Germans acknowledged that

Gallipoli Campaign. Allied troops land at Gallipoli on the Turkish peninsula in the summer of 1915.

Trench Warfare. Left: Trenches were dug for protection against tanks and artillery. Here a tank is shown after having crashed into such a trench. Right: After the first few battles, the war on the Western Front settled into static, or position, warfare. During the four-year period, veritable cities of mud, stone, and timber sprang up behind the trenches.

their aim was not so much to take the fortified city, which they knew the French would defend with desperation, but to "bleed France white of all able-bodied men"; yet the Germans lost as many men as the French. In July 1916 the British launched an enormous attack along the Somme River to ease the pressure on Verdun. Lasting from July to November, the battle cost the Germans 500,000, the British 400,000, and the French 200,000 in return for an Allied advance of seven miles across the front. On the first day of fighting alone, more than 57,000 British troops were killed or wounded.

In time such losses fueled an unsuccessful move on the part of a minority on both sides to press for a negotiated peace. But in the minds of those who were making decisions, both military and civilian, the immediate effect of the carnage was to reinforce determination to press ahead for total victory. This intransigence led, in turn, to changes in leadership. In Britain, the ineffectual prime minister Asquith was replaced by David Lloyd George, the buccaneer politician behind many of Britain's prewar social reforms. If Lloyd George had little new to propose, he nevertheless projected a properly fervent public image. In France, the following year, Georges Clemenceau assumed the premiership, again with a mandate to counter a growing defeatist attitude within the military high command. And in Germany, control passed into the hands of Generals Paul von Hindenburg and Erich Ludendorff, the men responsible as well for the overall military strategy of the Central Powers.

Changes in leadership

As the conflict dragged on, other countries were drawn into the war. Italy was bribed by the Allies with a promise of Austrian territories and a generous slice of the eastern shore of the Adriatic. Bulgaria joined the Central Powers in October 1915, and Rumania sided with the Allies a year later. It was the intervention of the United States on the Allied side, however, in April 1917, that tipped the balance. The United States entered the war vowing, in the words of its president, Woodrow Wilson, to "make the world safe for democracy," to banish autocracy and militarism, and to establish a league or society of nations in place of the old diplomatic maneuvering. Undoubtedly the primary reason for the American decision to enter the war, though, was the government's concern to maintain the international balance of power. For years it had been a cardinal doctrine in American diplomatic and military circles that the security of the United States depended upon a balance of forces in Europe. So long as Britain was strong enough to prevent any one nation from achieving supremacy in Europe, the United States was safe. American officials had grown so accustomed to thinking of the British navy as the shield of American security that they found it difficult to contemplate any different situation. Germany, however, presented not merely a challenge to British naval supremacy; it threatened to starve the British nation into surrender and to establish a hegemony over all of Europe.

The direct cause of United States participation in the First World War was the U-boat, or submarine, warfare of the Germans. Once it became clear that the war would be one of attrition, the Germans recognized that unless they could break the Allies' stranglehold on their shipping, they would be defeated. In February 1915, the kaiser's government announced that neutral vessels headed for British ports would be torpedoed without warning. President Wilson replied by declaring that the United States would hold Germany to a "strict accountability" if any harm should come to American lives or property. The warning caused Germany to discontinue the campaign, but only temporarily. The Germans were convinced that the U-boat was one of their most valuable weapons, and they considered themselves justified in using it against the British blockade. They also believed, correctly, that the British were receiving war matériel clandestinely shipped aboard passenger ships from the United States, and therefore continued to sink them, thus appearing to violate U.S. neutrality. When the kaiser's ministers announced that, on February 1, 1917, they would launch a campaign of unrestricted submarine warfare, Wilson cut off diplomatic relations with the Berlin government. On April 6 he went before Congress and requested and received a declaration of war.

The immediate result of U.S. entry was an increase in the amount of war matériel and food—later, in the number of troops—shipped unmolested in armed convoys across the Atlantic. New ship construction overcame earlier losses; submarine warfare, Germany's most effective weapon against the Allies, had been neutralized.

The *Lusitania*. In February 1915 the *Lusitania* was torpedoed and sunk by a German U-boat. Among the 1,200 people drowned were 119 Americans. The disaster was one step in the chain of events that led to the entry of the United States into the war on the side of Britain and France.

REVOLUTION IN THE MIDST OF WAR

In the midst of world war came revolution. Russia, already severely weakened by internal conflicts before 1914, found itself unable to sustain the additional burden of continuous warfare. In a nation ruled as autocratically as was Russia, a successful war effort depended greatly on the ability of its ruler to command and sustain cooperation across the political and social spectrum. But Tsar Nicholas II had seriously undermined his own limited capabilities to enlist support by his actions after the October Revolution of 1905, especially in his determined efforts to erode the minimal political power he had been forced to grant to the Duma. Further mistrust centered on the irrationality of his wife Alexandra, a religious fanatic, and her spiritual mentor, the monk Rasputin. The latter had gained the tsarina's sympathy by his ability to alleviate the sufferings of her hemophiliac son, and used his influence over her to shape policy to his own self-aggrandizing ends.

Tsar Nicholas II loses support

Although the outbreak of war temporarily united Russia against a common enemy, Russia's armies proved incapable of sustained success in the field. In 1914 they managed to advance against the Austrians into Galicia in the south, but suffered two stunning defeats in the north, at Tannenberg and the Masurian Lakes, losing almost 250,000 men in the process. In some instances soldiers were sent to the front without rifles; clothing

The collapse of Russia's war effort

The Last of the Romanovs. Tsar Nicholas II and his family on the eve of the Revolution.

Gregory Rasputin

The March 1917 Revolution

supplies were inadequate; medical facilities were scarce; and the railway system broke down, producing a shortage of food not only in the army but in cities as well. A major offensive in the summer of 1916, to coincide with the campaign along the Somme in the west, was initially successful. It turned into a humiliating retreat, however, thanks to transportation breakdowns and a lack of ammunition. By the end of 1916, Russia's power to resist a foreign invader had all but collapsed.

So also had its power to override domestic resistance and rebellion. The disaster of the 1916 campaign touched off waves of increasing unrest at home, where a rebellious urban population grew more and more impatient with inflation and shortages of food and fuel. Demands for a popularly elected, broad-based government were met by the tsar's determination to retain power in his own hands, until bread riots in Petrograd (St. Petersburg, whose "Germanic" name had been changed at the beginning of the war) precipitated his forced abdication in March 1917. The bread riots, led by women workers, were merely the latest in a wave of strikes and demonstrations that had crippled Petrograd for months. This particular demonstration, however, moved spontaneously from a protest by women in bread lines into a mass movement that filled the streets and converged on the city center. Troops summoned to quell the uprising broke ranks and joined the protesters, further evidence of the collapse of both civilian and military order. Nicholas tried to put down the uprising by force and to dissolve the Duma, but the Duma refused to obey and the insurgents took over Petrograd. Within five days armed insurrection had forced the end of the tsarist government.

Scenes from the Russian Revolution. Top left: Mass demonstration sponsored by the First All-Russian Congress of Soviets in which Bolshevik banners far outnumber the rest, spring 1917. Top right: Street fighting in Petrograd, summer 1917. Bottom right: Russian soldiers join the Bolsheviks in front of the Winter Palace, fall 1917.

With the overthrow of the tsar, the authority of the government passed into the hands of a provisional ministry organized by leaders in the Duma in conjunction with representatives of workers in Petrograd, calling themselves a *soviet,* or government council. With the exception of Alexander Kerensky, who was a member of the rurally based Socialist Revolutionary party, nearly all of the ministers were middle-of-the-road bourgeois liberals, many of whom had served in the *zemstva,* or provincial governing bodies. The ministry's primary responsibility was to prepare for national elections to a constituent assembly; it also acted to grant and secure civil liberties, release political prisoners, and redirect power into the hands of local government officials.

Provisional ministry

Alexander Kerensky (second from right) **and His Aides in the Winter Palace.** This is the last known photograph of Kerensky in Petrograd.

The Petrograd soviet, on the other hand, consisted largely of moderate socialists. It was responsible for coordinating the other soviets formed throughout Russia, and retained most of the real power of the provisional government.

Conflict between the two groups soon arose over control of the army and foreign policy. The increasingly powerful soviets of workers and soldiers pressed for social reform, the redistribution of land, and a negotiated settlement with the Central Powers. Yet ministers of the provisional government insisted that demands for domestic change must be subordinated to the war effort, which they defined in terms of previously declared imperialistic aims. They argued that basic governmental and economic reform should await the convening of the constituent assembly. Because the provisional ministers could not govern without the cooperation of the soviets, Kerensky, vice-chairman of the Petrograd soviet, entered the ministry in March as minister of war, leading the coalition government under Prince Georgi Lvov. In July 1917 Kerensky replaced Lvov as prime minister and organized a government that managed to retain power for several months.

The Kerensky government

The Bolsheviks, who had failed to gain leadership positions in the provisional government, emerged as an increasingly formidable opposition party, as conflicts between ministers and soviets increased. On April 16, 1917, they gathered at Petrograd's Finland Station to welcome back Lenin, smuggled into Russia by Germans who welcomed his potential as a troublemaker for Kerensky's government. Throughout the spring and summer of 1917, while Kerensky was struggling to hold his government together, Lenin led the Bolsheviks on a bolder course that shunned all

Lenin and the Bolsheviks

collaboration with the bourgeoisie and condemned their war policies. He soon became the leader of a vast popular uprising of workers, soldiers, and peasants; the Bolsheviks at this time clearly spoke to the people's needs as no other party did.

Meanwhile, opposition to the growing radicalization of the ministry—reflected in Kerensky's elevation to prime minister—encouraged conservatives and liberals to make common cause and to mount a military action led by General Lavr Kornilov, the commander-in-chief of the army, against the government. The attempted coup in September 1917 was crushed. Yet Kerensky's own position had been undermined, his enemies on the Left arguing that Kornilov's ability to mount a counter-revolutionary effort was a sign of Kerensky's ineffectual leadership and willingness to compromise revolutionary aims. Although Lenin had been forced to seek refuge in Finland in mid-summer to escape prosecution as a German agent, he retained control of his party's activities. After Kornilov's failure, Lenin determined to seize power from Kerensky. In October he moved to Vyborg and concentrated on consolidating the Bolsheviks' agenda and support base. When the second All-Russian Congress of Soviets convened on November 6, Lenin was ready.

On November 6, a coup d'état centered in Petrograd and directed by Lenin's ally Leon Trotsky succeeded in overturning the provisional government. Lenin immediately proceeded to issue decrees that would give substance to the Bolsheviks' slogan of "Peace, Bread, and Land." "People's Commissars" (ministers) ordered the partition of land and its distribution to peasants, without compensation to former owners; nationalized banks, confiscating private accounts in the process; handed factory control over to workers; and began to negotiate a treaty with the Germans to end the war. The resulting agreement, signed at Brest-Litovsk in March 1918, surrendered Poland, Finland, and the Ukraine to the Germans. The treaty aroused the fury of Lenin's political enemies, both moderates and reactionaries, who were still a force to be reckoned with and who were prepared to plunge Russia into civil war rather than accept the revolution.

Yet another outbreak of revolution in this period was the so-called Easter Rebellion in Ireland. At the beginning of the world war, Irish nationalists, who resented the rule of their country by the British, were ripe for revolt. They had been promised self-rule on the eve of the war, but the British later reneged on the grounds that a national emergency must take preeminence over domestic politics. This greatly angered the Roman Catholic majority of southern Ireland. They scheduled Easter Sunday, 1916, as a day for revolt. British forces quelled the uprising, but not until a hundred people had been killed. Sporadic outbreaks kept the island in turmoil for years thereafter, but were finally brought to a temporary end by an agreement constituting southern Ireland as a free republic. The northern counties, or the province of Ulster, were to continue subject to the British crown.

Attempted coup undermines Kerensky

Death to the Capitalists. A Soviet propaganda poster from 1918.

The overthrow of Kerensky

The Easter Rebellion in Ireland

The Irish Rebellion, 1916. Dubliners gather among the ruins of Sackville Street.

ARMISTICE AND PEACE

Peace proposals

While the fighting raged on for four years, various attempts were made to bring about peace negotiations. In the spring of 1917, Dutch and Scandinavian socialists summoned an international socialist conference to meet at Stockholm to draft plans to end the fighting that would be acceptable to all the belligerents. The Petrograd soviet embraced the idea and on May 15 issued an appeal to socialists of all nations to send delegates to the conference and to induce their governments to agree to a peace "without annexations and indemnities, on the basis of the self-determination of peoples." The socialist parties in all the principal countries on both sides of the war accepted this formula and were eager to send delegates to the conference. When the British and French governments refused to permit any of their subjects to attend, however, the project was abandoned. The rulers of the Allied states did not reject these proposals because they emanated from socialists; indeed, a similar formula suggested by the pope was just as emphatically rejected. Nowhere was there a disposition to take peace proposals seriously. Woodrow Wilson, as spokesman for the Allies, declared that negotiation of peace under any conditions was impossible so long as Germany was ruled by the kaiser. The Central Powers regarded the general import of the papal suggestions with favor, but they refused to commit themselves on indemnities and restorations, especially the restoration of Belgium.

The best known of all the peace proposals was President Wilson's program of Fourteen Points, which he incorporated in an address to Congress on January 8, 1918. Summarized as briefly as possible, this program included: (1) "open covenants openly arrived at," i.e., the abolition of secret diplomacy; (2) freedom of the seas in peace and war; (3) removal of economic barriers between nations; (4) reduction of national armaments "to the lowest point consistent with safety"; (5) impartial adjustment of colonial claims, with consideration for the interests of the peoples involved; (6) evacuation of Russia by foreign armies and general restoration of conquered territories in Russia; (7) restoration of the independence of Belgium; (8) restoration of Alsace and Lorraine to France; (9) a readjustment of Italian frontiers "along clearly recognizable lines of nationality"; (10) autonomous development for the peoples of Austria-Hungary; (11) restoration of Rumania, Serbia, and Montenegro, with access to the sea for Serbia; (12) autonomous development for the peoples of Turkey, with the straits from the Black Sea to the Mediterranean "permanently opened"; (13) an independent Poland, "inhabited by indisputably Polish populations," and with access to the sea; and (14) establishment of a League of Nations. On several other occasions Wilson reiterated in public addresses that his program would be the basis of the peace for which he would work. Thousands of copies of the Fourteen Points were scattered by Allied planes over the German trenches and behind the lines, in an effort to convince both soldiers and civilians that the Allied nations were striving for a just and durable peace.

> The Fourteen Points

With Russia now no longer a combatant, Germany appeared to have gained an advantage that would almost guarantee ultimate victory. Yet by the late spring of 1918 the Germans were suffering acutely, not only because of the continued effectiveness of the Allied blockade, but because of a growing domestic conflict over war aims. German socialists attacked expansionist goals—control of the steel- and coal-producing areas of Belgium and of the agricultural regions in eastern Europe—which conservatives continued to urge and which the government endorsed. Socialists were alarmed as well by the reactionary administration imposed upon the territories taken from Russia at Brest-Litovsk. By the fall of 1918, Germany was a country on the verge of civil war.

> Domestic conflict in Germany

Meanwhile, fighting continued as it had for four years on the Western Front. A great offensive launched by the British, French, and United States forces in July dealt one shattering blow after another to the German battalions and forced them back almost to the Belgian frontier. By the end of September the cause of the Central Powers appeared hopeless. Bulgaria withdrew from the war on September 29. Early in October the new chancellor of Germany, the liberal Prince Maximilian of Baden, appealed to President Wilson for a negotiated peace on the basis of the Fourteen

> The collapse of the Central Powers

Points. But the fighting went on, Wilson now demanding that Germany agree to depose the kaiser. Germany's remaining allies tottered on the verge of collapse. Turkey surrendered at the end of October. The Habsburg Empire was cracked open by rebellions on the part of the empire's subject nationalities. A German-Austrian offensive in Italy in October 1917 had gained them a major victory at Caporetto, where Italian military police were ordered to shoot their own soldiers, if necessary, to stem the retreat. Yet a year later, the Italians responded to a similar attack with a counter-offensive that cost Austria the city of Trieste and 300,000 prisoners. On November 3, 1918, the Emperor Charles, who had succeeded Francis Joseph in 1916, signed an armistice that took Austria out of the war.

Germany was now left with the impossible task of carrying on the struggle alone. The morale of its troops was rapidly breaking. The Allied naval blockade was causing such a shortage of food that there was real danger of starvation. Revolutionary tremors that had been felt for some time swelled into an earthquake. On November 8 a republic was proclaimed in Bavaria. The next day nearly all of Germany was in the throes of revolution. A decree was published in Berlin announcing the kaiser's abdication, and early the next morning he was moved across the frontier into Holland. In the meantime, the government of the nation had passed into the hands of a provisional council headed by Friedrich Ebert, leader of the socialists in the Reichstag. Ebert and his colleagues immediately took steps to conclude negotiations for an armistice. The terms as now laid down by the Allied powers provided for acceptance of the Fourteen Points with three amendments. First, the item on freedom of the seas was to be stricken (in accordance with the request of the British). Second, restoration of invaded areas was to be interpreted in such a way as to include reparations, that is, payment to the victors to compensate them for their losses. Third, the demand for autonomy for the subject peoples of Austria-Hungary was to be changed to a demand for independence. In addition, troops of the Allied nations were to occupy cities in the Rhine valley, and the blockade was to

The signing of the armistice

German Supplies Moving toward the Somme during the Last German Offensive in 1918

be continued in force. The Germans could do nothing but accept these terms. At five o'clock in the morning of November 11, 1918, two delegates of the defeated nation met with the commander of the Allied armies, Marshal Ferdinand Foch, in the Compiègne forest and signed the papers officially ending the war. Six hours later the order "cease fire" was given to the troops. That night thousands of people danced through the streets of London, Paris, and Rome in the same delirium of excitement with which they had greeted the declarations of war four years before.

The peace concluded at the various conferences in 1919 and 1920 more closely resembled a sentence from a court than a negotiated settlement. Propaganda had encouraged victorious soldiers and civilians to suppose that their sacrifices to the war effort would be compensated for by payments extracted from the "wicked" Germans. The British prime minister, David Lloyd George, campaigned during the election of 1918 on the slogan "Hang the Kaiser!", while one of his partisans demanded "Squeeze the German lemon until the pips squeak!" In all the Allied countries nationalism and democracy combined to make compromise impossible and to reassert the claim that the war was a crusade of good against evil. The peace settlement drafted by the victors inevitably reflected these feelings.

A harsh peace

The conference convoked in Paris* to draft a peace with Germany was technically in session from January until June of 1919, but only six plenary meetings were held. The final character of the Treaty of Versailles was determined almost entirely by the so-called Big Three—Wilson, Lloyd George, and Clemenceau. These men were as different in personality as any three rulers who have ever come together for a common purpose. Wilson was an inflexible idealist, accustomed to dictating to subordinates and convinced that the hosts of righteousness were on his side. Lloyd George, the canny Welshman, possessed cleverness and Celtic humor that enabled him to succeed, on occasions, where Wilson failed; he was above all a politician—shifty, and not particularly sympathetic to problems such as nationalism. The third member of the triumvirate was the aged and cynical French premier, Georges Clemenceau. Twice in his lifetime he had seen France invaded and its existence gravely imperiled. Now the tables were turned, and the French, he believed, should take full advantage of their opportunity. Only by keeping a strict control over a prostrate Germany could the security of France be preserved.

The Big Three: Wilson, Lloyd George, and Clemenceau

From the beginning a number of embarrassing problems confronted the chief architects of the Versailles treaty. The most important was what to do about the Fourteen Points. There could be no doubt that they had been the basis of the German surrender on November 11. It was beyond question also that Wilson had represented them as the Allied program

Gutting the Fourteen Points

*The conference did most of its work in Paris. The treaty of peace with Germany, however, takes its name from Versailles, the suburb of Paris in which it was signed.

The Council of Four. Meeting to draft a peace treaty in Paris were Lloyd George of Britain, Orlando of Italy, Clemenceau of France, and Wilson of the United States.

for a permanent peace. Consequently there was every reason for the peoples of the world to expect that the Fourteen Points would be the model for the Versailles settlement—subject only to the three amendments made before the armistice was signed. In actuality, however, no one among the highest dignitaries at the conference, with the exception of Wilson himself, gave more than lip service to the Fourteen Points. In the end, the American president was able to salvage, in unmodified form, only four parts of his famous program: point seven, requiring the restoration of Belgium; point eight, demanding the return of Alsace and Lorraine to France; point ten, providing for independence for the peoples of Austria-Hungary; and the final provision calling for a League of Nations. The others were ignored or modified to such an extent as to change their original meanings.

The main provisions of the Treaty of Versailles

The provisions of the Treaty of Versailles can be outlined briefly. Germany was required to surrender Alsace and Lorraine to France, northern Schleswig to Denmark, and most of Posen and West Prussia to Poland. The coal mines of the Saar Basin were to be ceded to France, to be exploited by the French for fifteen years. At the end of this time the German government would be permitted to buy them back. The Saar territory itself was to be administered by the League of Nations until 1935, when a plebiscite would be held to determine whether it should remain under the league, be returned to Germany, or be awarded to France. Germany's province of East Prussia was cut off from the rest of its territory, and the port of Danzig, almost wholly German, was subjected to the political control of the League of Nations and the economic domination of Poland. Germany was disarmed, surrendering all its submarines and surface vessels, with the exception of six small battleships, six light cruisers, six destroyers, and twelve torpedo boats. The Germans were forbidden to possess an air force; their army was limited to 100,000 officers and men, to be recruited by voluntary enlistment. To make sure that Germany would not launch any new attack upon France or Belgium, it was forbidden to keep soldiers or maintain fortifications in the Rhine valley. Last, Germany and its allies were held responsible for all the loss and damage suffered by the Allied governments and their citizens, "as a consequence of the war imposed upon them by the aggression of Germany and her allies." This was the so-called war-guilt provision of the treaty (Article 231), and also the basis for German reparations. The exact amount that Germany should pay was left to a Reparations Commission. In 1921 the total was set at $33 billion.

For the most part, the Treaty of Versailles applied only to Germany. Separate pacts were drawn up to settle accounts with Germany's allies—Austria-Hungary, Bulgaria, and Turkey. The final form of these treaties was determined primarily by a Council of Five, composed of Clemenceau as chairman and one delegate each from the United States, Great Britain, France, and Italy. The treaties reflected a desire on the part of their drafters to recognize the principle of national self-determination. The experience of the prewar years convinced diplomats that they must draw

The goal of self-determination

Crowds Greet President Wilson in Paris after the War. Despite public demonstrations of this sort, Wilson's attempt to shape the peace was a failure.

national boundaries to conform as closely as possible to the ethnic, linguistic, and historical traditions of the people they were to contain. Yet practical, political difficulties made such divisions impossible.

The settlement with Austria, completed in September 1919, was known as the Treaty of St. Germain. Austria was required to recognize the independence of Hungary, Czechoslovakia, Yugoslavia, and Poland, and to cede to them large portions of its territory. In addition, Austria had to surrender Trieste, the south Tyrol, and the Istrian peninsula to Italy. Altogether the Austrian portion of the Dual Monarchy was deprived of three-fourths of its area and three-fourths of its people. Contrary to the principles of self-determination, in several of the territories surrendered the inhabitants were largely German-speaking—for example, in the Tyrol, and the region of the Sudeten mountains awarded to Czechoslovakia. The Austrian nation itself was reduced to a small, land-locked state, with nearly one-third of its population concentrated in the city of Vienna.

The second of the treaties with lesser belligerents was that with Bulgaria, which was signed in November 1919 and called the Treaty of Neuilly. Bulgaria was forced to give up nearly all of the territory it had gained since the First Balkan War. Land was ceded to Rumania, to the new kingdom of Yugoslavia, and to Greece.

The settlement with Turkey was a product of unusual circumstances. The secret treaties had contemplated the transfer of Constantinople and Armenia to Russia and the division of most of the remainder of Turkey between Britain and France. But Russia's withdrawal from the war after the Bolshevik Revolution, together with insistence by Italy and Greece upon fulfillment of promises made to them, necessitated considerable revision of the original scheme. Finally, in August 1920, a treaty was signed at Sèvres, near Paris, and submitted to the government of the sultan. It provided that Armenia be organized as a Christian republic; that most of Turkey in Europe be given to Greece; that Palestine and Mesopotamia become British "mandates," i.e., to remain under League of Nations control but to be administered by Britain; that Syria become a mandate of France; and that southern Anatolia be set apart as a sphere of influence for Italy. About all that would be left of the Ottoman Empire would be the city of Constantinople and the northern and central portions of Asia Minor. The decrepit government of the sultan, overawed by Allied military forces, agreed to accept this treaty. But a revolutionary government of Turkish nationalists, which had been organized at Ankara under the leadership of Mustapha Kemal (later called Atatürk), determined to prevent acceptance of the settlement of Sèvres. The forces of Kemal obliterated the republic of Armenia, frightened the Italians into withdrawing from Anatolia, and conquered most of the territory in Europe that had been given to Greece. At last, in November 1922, they occupied Constantinople, deposed the sultan, and proclaimed Turkey a republic. The Allies now consented to a revision of the peace. A new treaty was concluded at Lausanne in Switzerland in 1923, which permitted the Turks to retain practically all of the ter-

Kemal Atatürk

ritory they had conquered. Though much reduced in size compared with the old Ottoman Empire, the Turkish republic still had an area of about 300,000 square miles and a population of 13 million.

Incorporated in each of the five treaties that liquidated the war with the Central Powers was the Covenant of the League of Nations. The establishment of a league in which the states of the world, both great and small, would cooperate for the preservation of peace had long been the cherished dream of President Wilson. Indeed, that had been one of his chief reasons for taking the United States into the war. He believed that the defeat of Germany would mean the deathblow of militarism, and that the road would thenceforth be clear for setting up the control of international relations by a community of nations instead of by the cumbersome and ineffective balance of power. But to get the league accepted he found himself compelled to make numerous compromises. He permitted his original idea of providing for a reduction of armaments "to the lowest point consistent with domestic safety" to be changed into the altogether different phrasing of "consistent with national safety." To induce the Japanese to accept the league he allowed them to keep former German concessions in China. To please the French, he sanctioned the exclusion of both Germany and Russia from his proposed federation, despite his long insistence that it should be a league of *all* nations. These handicaps were serious enough. But the league received an even more deadly blow when it was repudiated by the very nation whose president had proposed it. The United States Congress, citing longstanding national preferences for isolation, refused to ratify American entry into the league.

Established under such unfavorable auspices, the league never achieved the aims of its founder. In only a few cases did it succeed in allaying the threat of war, and in each of these the parties to the dispute were small nations. But in every dispute involving one or more major powers, the league failed. It did nothing about the seizure of Vilna by Poland in 1920, because Lithuania, the victimized nation, was friendless, while Poland had the powerful backing of France. When, in 1923, war threatened between Italy and Greece, the Italians refused to submit to the intervention of the league, and the dispute was settled by direct mediation of Great Britain and France. Thereafter, in every great crisis the league was either defied or ignored. Its authority was flouted by Japan in seizing Manchuria in 1931 and by Italy in conquering Ethiopia in 1936. By September 1938, when the Czechoslovakian crisis arose, the prestige of the league had sunk so low that scarcely anyone thought of appealing to it. Yet the league justified its existence in other, less spectacular, ways. It reduced the international opium traffic and aided poor and backward countries in controlling the spread of disease. Its agencies collected invaluable statistics on labor and business conditions throughout the world. It conducted plebiscites in disputed areas, supervised the administration of internationalized cities, helped find homes for racial

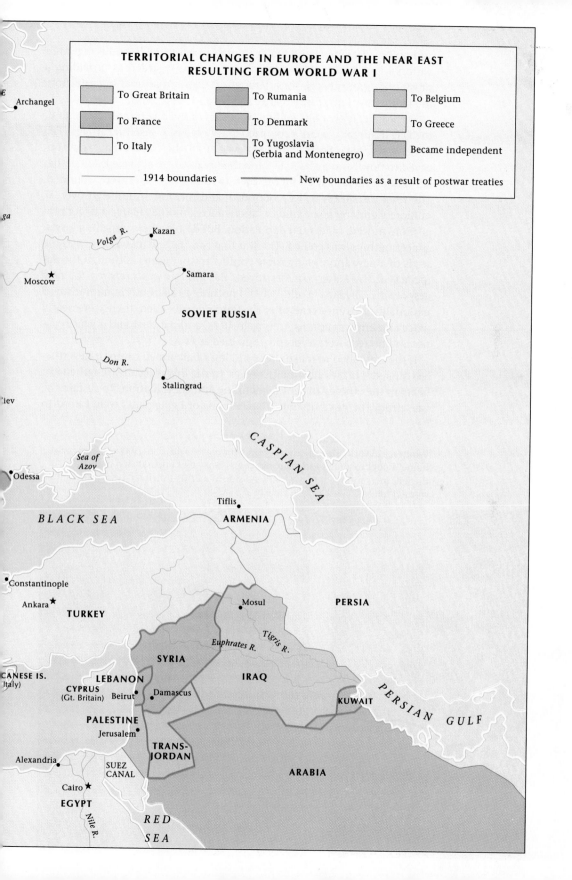

TERRITORIAL CHANGES IN EUROPE AND THE NEAR EAST RESULTING FROM WORLD WAR I

☐ To Great Britain	☐ To Rumania	☐ To Belgium
☐ To France	☐ To Denmark	☐ To Greece
☐ To Italy	☐ To Yugoslavia (Serbia and Montenegro)	☐ Became independent

—— 1914 boundaries   ══ New boundaries as a result of postwar treaties

Archangel

Volga R.

Kazan

Moscow ★

Samara

SOVIET RUSSIA

Don R.

Kiev

Stalingrad

CASPIAN SEA

Sea of Azov

Odessa

Tiflis

BLACK SEA

ARMENIA

Constantinople

Ankara ★

PERSIA

TURKEY

Mosul

Tigris R.

Euphrates R.

SYRIA

DODECANESE IS. (Italy)

LEBANON

CYPRUS (Gt. Britain)

Beirut

Damascus

IRAQ

KUWAIT

PERSIAN GULF

PALESTINE

Jerusalem

TRANS-JORDAN

Alexandria

SUEZ CANAL

ARABIA

Cairo ★

EGYPT

Nile R.

RED SEA

and political refugees, and made a notable beginning in codifying international law. Such achievements may well be regarded as providing a substantial groundwork for a later effort at international organization, the United Nations, formed after the Second World War.

The league, with all its failings, was seen as the one promising result of the war that many soon recognized as a hideously wasteful carnage. The price would have been enormous even if all the results that were supposed to flow from an Allied victory had really been achieved. Altogether 8.5 million men died and more than twice that number were wounded. The total casualties—killed, wounded, and missing—numbered over 37 million. Germany lost 6 million and France almost as many, a larger proportion, indeed, of its total population. But despite these appalling losses, almost nothing was gained. The war that was to "end all wars" sowed the seeds of a new and more terrible conflict in the future. Although the autocracy of the kaiser was destroyed, the ground was prepared for new despotisms. The First World War did nothing to abate either militarism or nationalism. Twenty years after the fighting had ended, there were nearly twice as many men under arms as in 1913, and national and ethnic rivalries and hatreds were as deeply ingrained as ever.

If the war failed to make the world less of an armed camp, it nevertheless altered it drastically in other ways. In the first place, it strengthened a belief in the efficacy of central planning and coordination. To sustain the war effort, the governments of all the major belligerents were forced to

Women at Work. The all-out war effort combined with a manpower shortage at home brought women into factories across Europe in unparalleled numbers. On the left, men and women work side-by-side in a British shell factory. At the right, women toil in a German gun factory.

manage their economies by regulating industrial output, exercising a close control over imports and exports, and making the most effective use of manpower—both civilian and military. Second, the war upset the world trade balance. With few manufactured goods coming from Europe, Japanese, Indian, and South American capitalists were free to develop industries in their own countries. When the war was over, Europe found it had lost many of its previously guaranteed markets and that it had become a debtor to the United States, which, throughout the war, had lent large sums to the Allies. Third, while war was altering the patterns of world trade, it was also producing worldwide inflation. To finance their fighting, governments resorted to policies of deficit financing (spending above their income) and increased paper money that, with the shortage of goods, inflated their price. Inflation hit hardest at the middle class, those men and women who had lived on their income from invested money, and now saw that money worth far less than it once had been. Fourth, the war, while it brought hardships to most, brought freedom to many. Women were temporarily emancipated by their governments' need for them in factories and on farms. The contribution of women to the war effort undoubtedly explains the granting of female suffrage in both Great Britain and the United States in 1918 and 1920. Finally, despite this legacy of liberation, the war's most permanent contribution to the spirit of the postwar years was disillusion—particularly within the middle classes. A generation of men had been sacrificed—"lost"—to no apparent end. Many of those left alive were sickened by the useless slaughter, to which they knew they had contributed and for which they believed they must share at least part of the guilt. They were disgusted by the greedy abandonment of principles by the politicians at Versailles. Hatred and mistrust of the "old men" who had dragged the world into an unnecessary conflict, who had then mismanaged its direction with such ghastly results, and who had betrayed the cause of international peace for national gain soured the minds of many younger men and women in the postwar period. The British poet Edmund Blunden expressed this profound disillusionment when he took as the title for a poem, written to celebrate New Year's Day 1921, this biblical verse: "The dog is turned to his own vomit again, and the sow that was washed to her wallowing in the mire."

Women in the War. A World War I poster encouraging British women to work in munitions factories.

SUMMARY POINTS

- The assassination of Austria's Archduke Ferdinand by a Bosnian led to military threats to Serbia by Austria, to Germany/Austria by Russia, to France and Belgium by Germany, and to Germany by Britain. The Allies (Russia, France, Britain) and the Central Powers (Germany, Austria) thus began World War I.

- World War I was a war of slow attrition. New technology such as machine guns and barbed wire proved effective, but tanks and airplanes were rarely used in battle, and most battles resulted in heavy casualties but limited gains.

- The Irish staged the Easter Rebellion in 1916, an unsuccessful attempt to win self-rule from the British. The Russian Revolution of 1917 first ended the tsarist regime and later brought down Alexander Kerensky's provisional government, making way for Lenin's Bolshevik regime, which drew support from workers, soldiers, and peasants.

- Germany surrendered on the basis of Wilson's Fourteen Points in 1918. The Treaty of Versailles provided for the settlement of Germany's debts to the Allied nations.

- Despite the creation of the League of Nations, World War I produced little other than 37 million casualties and a foundation for World War II.

Selected Readings

THE WORLD WAR AND THE PEACE SETTLEMENT

Albrecht-Carré, Rene, ed., *The Meaning of the First World War,* Englewood Cliffs, N.J., 1965. The war's consequences for both soldiers and civilians.

Carsten, F. L., *Revolution in Central Europe, 1918–1919,* London, 1972. A useful study of the uprising that followed the war.

Eksteins, Modris, *Rites of Spring: The Great War and the Birth of the Modern Age,* New York, 1989. The roots of the war are seen in the art and culture of pre-war years.

Falls, Cyril, *The Great War,* New York, 1961. A military history.

Feldman, Gerald D., *Army, Industry, and Labor in Germany, 1914–1918,* Princeton, 1966. The effect of war on the domestic economy.

Ferro, Marc, *The Great War, 1914–1918,* London, 1973. Social and economic developments receive particular treatment.

Fischer, Fritz, *War of Illusions,* New York, 1975. Deals with Germany within the context of internal social and economic trends.

Fussell, Paul, *The Great War and Modern Memory,* New York, 1975. A brilliant examination of British intellectuals' attitudes toward the war.

Hardach, Gerd, *The First World War, 1914–1918,* Berkeley, 1977. An excellent economic history of the war.

Horne, Alistair, *The Price of Glory: Verdun, 1916,* New York, 1963. A devastating account of the ten-month siege of Verdun and its consequences.

Hynes, Samuel, *A War Imagined: The First World War and English Culture,* New York, 1991. The war as perceived on the home front.

Jelavich, Barbara, *History of the Balkans: Twentieth Century,* New York, 1983. Useful for an understanding of the continuing conflict in Eastern Europe.

Lafore, Laurence D., *The Long Fuse: An Interpretation of the Origins of World War I,* 2d ed., Philadelphia, 1971. Argues that the war was the result of obsolete institutions and ideas.

Mayer, Arno, *Politics and Diplomacy of Peacemaking: Containment and Counterrevolution at Versailles, 1918–1919,* New York, 1967. Emphasizes the role of the Russian Revolution in the peacemaking process.

Moorehead, Alan, *Gallipoli,* London, 1956. A study of the British campaign.

Nicolson, Harold, *Peacemaking, 1919,* Boston, 1933. Written by a participant, provides a good account of the atmosphere of Versailles.

Smith, Leonard, *Between Mutiny and Obedience: The Case of the French Fifth Infantry Division During World War I,* Princeton, N. J., 1994. An account of mutiny and the reasons behind it.

Steiner, Zara S., *Britain and the Origins of the First World War,* New York, 1977. Argues that external rather than internal strains brought Britain into the war.

Taylor, A. J. P., *English History, 1914–1945,* New York, 1965. Contains an excellent treatment of the war and its impact on British society.

Tuchman, Barbara, *The Guns of August,* New York, 1962. A popular account of the outbreak of war.

Wheeler-Bennett, J. W., *Brest-Litovsk: The Forgotten Peace, March 1918,* London, 1939. An excellent study of personalities involved in the Russo-German peace treaty.

Williams, John, *The Home Fronts: Britain, France and Germany, 1914–1918,* London, 1972. A survey of life away from the battlefield and the impact of the war on domestic life.

Winter, J. M., *The Experience of World War I,* New York, 1989. Comprehensive illustrated history viewing the war from different perspectives.

Winter, J. M., and Richard Wall, *The Upheaval of War: Family, Work and Welfare in Europe, 1914–1918,* Cambridge, 1988. A comparative social history of European home fronts.

Wohl, Robert, *The Generation of 1914,* Cambridge, Mass., 1979. Uses generational analysis to explain attitudes toward the war.

THE RUSSIAN REVOLUTION

Deutscher, Isaac, *The Prophet Armed: Trotsky,* New York, 1954. The first volume of a magnificent biography of Trotsky; covers the years 1879–1921.

Fischer, Louis, *The Life of Lenin,* New York, 1964. A lengthy, somewhat popularized biography by a journalist who was present during the revolution.

Keep, John L. H., *The Russian Revolution,* New York, 1977.

Pares, Bernard, *A History of Russia,* rev. ed., New York, 1953. A useful, straightforward survey.

Pipes, Richard, *The Formation of the Soviet Union,* New York, 1964. A solid, reliable study.

Rabinowitch, Alexander, *The Bolsheviks Come to Power,* New York, 1976. A well-researched and carefully documented account.

Stites, Richard, *Revolutionary Dreams: Utopian Visions and Experimental Life in the Russian Revolution,* New York, 1989. The influence of Utopian thinking on the revolution.

Ulam, Adam, *The Bolsheviks,* New York, 1965. Analysis of both ideas and events.

Wolfe, Bertram D., *Three Who Made a Revolution,* rev. ed., New York, 1964. A study of Lenin, Trotsky, and Stalin.

Brittain, Vera, *Testament of Youth,* London, 1933. An Englishwoman's autobiographical account of her experiences as a nurse during the war.

Carnegie Foundation, Endowment for International Peace, *The Treaties of Peace, 1919–1923,* 2 vols., New York, 1924.

Gooch, G. P., and H. Temperley, eds., *British Documents on the Origins of the War, 1898–1914,* London, 1927.

Keynes, John Maynard, *The Economic Consequences of the Peace,* London, 1919. A contemporary attack upon the peace settlement, particularly the reparations agreements, by the brilliant economist who served on the British delegation to the peace conference.

Owen, Wilfred, *Collected Poems,* London, 1963. Moving evidence of the horror of life at the front by Britain's most talented war poet.

Reed, John, *Ten Days That Shook the World,* New York, 1919. (Many editions.) A contemporary account by a sympathetic American journalist of the Bolshevik Revolution.

Remarque, Erich Maria, *All Quiet on the Western Front,* 1929. (Many editions.) A famous novel describing the war on the Western Front.

CHAPTER 28

TURMOIL BETWEEN THE WARS

Democracy of the West today is the forerunner of Marxism, which would be inconceivable without it. It is democracy alone which furnishes this universal plague with the soil in which it spreads. In parliamentarianism, its outward form of expression, democracy created a monstrosity of filth and fire. . . .
—ADOLF HITLER, *Mein Kampf*

MONG THE CLAIMS MADE by the Allied Powers during the First World War was that an Allied victory would make the world "safe for democracy." The boast was grounded in a belief in the inevitability of progress, fostered by a century of growing material prosperity and by a habit of mind that found it all but impossible to equate the events of history with something other than the "advance" of civilization. The history of Europe in the 1920s and 1930s, however, would make it increasingly difficult for men and women to believe in progress as they had, or to assume that war might prove of ultimate benefit to mankind. These were decades of disillusionment and desperation, a circumstance brought about not only by the war itself but by the events that followed in the wake of war. Rather than encourage the growth of democracy, those events often caused its decline and fall. A number of Western nations remained democracies—Great Britain, France, and the United States being the most notable cases—yet they nevertheless experienced the same pressures and strains that in other countries resulted in the demise of democracy altogether.

Although the reasons for the decline of democracy in the West varied according to particular national circumstances, its failure can be attributed to several major causes. The foremost was a series of continuing disruptions in the world economy. These were brought about by dislocations that followed in the wake of the First World War and the Versailles reparations settlements, and by a worsening agricultural crisis that, in turn, helped precipitate the Great Depression after 1929. A second cause of democracy's decline was increased class conflict, often rooted in harsh economic realities. A major issue in most parts of Continental Europe was whether control of governments and economic systems would remain in the hands of industrialists and financiers, unwilling to surrender more than a fraction of their considerable power to the less-privileged majorities which, at great sacrifice, had made major contributions to the war effort. The common people expected and had been promised that those

Decline of democracy

Reasons for the decline

contributions would be rewarded by greater attention to their political rights and economic needs. When they were ignored, they were naturally embittered, and hence prey to the blandishments of political extremists. Finally, nationalist sentiment encouraged discontent among minorities in the newly established states of central Europe. Countries weakened by conflicts between national minorities were an unlikely proving ground for democracy, a political system that functions best in an atmosphere of unified national purpose.

Rise of authoritarian dictatorships

The political history of the interwar years must be understood not only in terms of the decline of democracy, however, but also against the background of the rise of authoritarian dictatorships in three major European nations—the Soviet Union, Italy, and Germany. As we shall see, the experiences of those three countries differed significantly, as a result of varying historical circumstances and personalities. Yet in each case, citizens of those countries allowed themselves to be persuaded—or bullied into accepting—that nothing short of radical measures would suffice to bring society to rights. Those measures included the use of violent force, intimidation, and propaganda to divert men and women from the pursuit of their individual interests and to deny them an increasingly large measure of human freedom. Their willingness to accept this sacrifice was a measure of their desperation.

THE SOVIET EXPERIENCE AND THE RISE OF STALIN

Lenin

Soon after the 1917 Revolution in Russia, the country's desperate plight—a result of wartime devastation and tsarist corruption and mismanagement—compelled the Bolshevik leaders to exercise bold and often ruthless leadership. During this traumatic period, Lenin showed himself as capable a revolutionary administrator and politician as he had been a strategist. He commanded the respect and loyalty of his fellow Bolshevik ministers and won the confidence of the Russian people as well by speaking frankly to them of the dangers and difficulties inherent in a revolution as bold and all-consuming as theirs was. He was what he appeared to be: a selfless man, unwilling to claim special privileges for himself, wholly dedicated to the revolution that he had done so much to bring about. He cared nothing for luxury or personal glory, living an almost monklike existence in two rooms in the Kremlin, and dressing little better than an ordinary worker.

Trotsky

Lenin's ablest and most prominent lieutenant was Leon Trotsky. Originally named Lev Bronstein, Trotsky was born into a family of prosperous farmers in the Ukraine. Before the Revolution he had refused to identify himself with any particular faction, preferring to remain an independent Marxist. For his part in the revolutionary movement of 1905 he was exiled to Siberia; he escaped, and for some years led a roving existence in

Lenin Speaking to Crowds in Moscow. To the right of the platform, in uniform, is Trotsky.

various European capitals. He was expelled from Paris in 1916 for pacifist activity and took refuge in the United States. Upon learning of the overthrow of the tsar, he attempted to return to Russia. Captured by British agents at Halifax, Nova Scotia, he was eventually released through the intervention of Alexander Kerensky. He arrived in Russia in April 1917 and immediately began plotting the overthrow of the provisional government and later of Kerensky himself. He became minister of foreign affairs in the government headed by Lenin, and later, commissar for war.

Scarcely had the Bolsheviks concluded the war with the Central Powers than they were confronted with a desperate civil war at home. The struggle was, in part, a battle between those who welcomed the Revolution and those who did not. Reactionary tsarists, disaffected liberals, Social Revolutionaries, Mensheviks, and peasants were assisted for a time by an expeditionary force of British, French, American, and Japanese troops— hoping to defeat the Bolsheviks in order to bring Russia back into the war against Germany. At the same time, however, the Soviet government faced serious insurrections in parts of the former Russian Empire that had never lost their own nationalist affections and aspirations. Much of the most severe fighting occurred in the Ukraine, Georgia, and the North Caucasus regions.

The civil war

Under the direction of Trotsky, who appealed to the Russian people both in the name of revolution and the fatherland, the "Red" army was mobilized to a degree that allowed it to withstand both the foreign invaders and the Russian insurgents. By 1922, the Bolsheviks had managed to stabilize their boundaries, although to do so they were forced to cede former Russian territory to the Finns, to the Baltic states of Latvia and

"Red" vs. "White" Russians

The Soviet Union, 1918–1945

The Union of Soviet Socialist Republics in 1939

Annexed 1940–45

ARCTIC OCEAN

SEA OF OKHOTSK

SAKHALIN I.

JAPAN

SEA OF JAPAN

Vladivostok

KOREA

Khabarovsk

MANCHURIA

Amur R.

Yakutsk

Lena R.

Chita

Ulan-Bator

Lake Baikal

MONGOLIA

Irkutsk

CHINA

1000 miles

500

0

Krasnoyarsk

Novosibirsk

Yenisei R.

RUSSIAN SOVIET FEDERATED SOCIALIST REPUBLIC

Ob R.

Omsk

URAL MTS.

Sverdlovsk

Chelyabinsk

KAZAKH S.S.R.

SINKIANG

Alma-Ata

Frunze

KIRGIZ S.S.R.

TADZHIK S.S.R.

Murmansk

Archangel

FINLAND

Helsinki

Kropstadt

Leningrad

ESTONIAN S.S.R.

LATVIAN S.S.R.

LITHUANIAN S.S.

Tallinn

Riga

Kaunas

Minsk

BELORUSSIAN S.S.R.

Gomel

Orekhovo

Yaroslavl

Ivanovo

Moscow

Gorki

Kazan

Perm

Kuibyshev

Saratov

Orenburg

Dushanbe

Ashkabad

UZBEK S.S.R.

Tashkent

TURKMEN S.S.R.

ARAL SEA

Kama R.

Volga R.

Don R.

Stalingrad

Rostov

Kharkov

UKRAINIAN S.S.R.

Kiev

Odessa

Kishinev

MOLDAVIAN S.S.R.

RUMANIA

HUNG.

CZECHOSLOVAKIA

POLAND

Brest-Litovsk

Bobruisk

Grodno

Warsaw

Kalinin

Danzig

NORWAY

SWEDEN

Gulf of Bothnia

Krasnodar

Novorossisk

Pyatigorsk

CAUCASUS MTS.

BLACK SEA

GEORGIAN S.S.R.

Tiflis

ARMENIAN S.S.R.

Yerevan

AZER-BAIDZHAN S.S.R.

Baku

CASPIAN SEA

IRAN

TURKEY

SYRIA

IRAQ

AFGHANISTAN

Estonia, to Poland, and to Rumania. Internally, the Bolsheviks responded to the "White" counter-revolution by instituting a "terror" far more extensive than the repression that had earned that name during the French Revolution. A secret police force shot thousands of suspects and hostages. The tsar and tsarina and their children were executed by local Bolsheviks in July 1918 as White forces advanced on the town of Ekaterinburg, where the family had been held prisoner. That same year "enemies of the state" were hunted down in large numbers following the attempted assassination of Lenin. The terror abated when the regime had satisfied itself that it had destroyed its internal opposition.

The civil war was accompanied by an appalling economic breakdown. In 1920 total industrial production was only 13 percent of what it had been in 1913. To alleviate the shortage of goods, the government abolished the payment of wages and distributed supplies among urban workers in proportion to their need. All private trade was prohibited; everything produced by the peasants above what they required to subsist was requisitioned by the state. This system was an expedient to crush bourgeois opposition to the revolutionary regime and to obtain as much food as possible for the army in the field. In 1921 it was superseded by the New Economic Policy (NEP), which Lenin described as "one step backward in order to take two steps forward." The NEP authorized private manufacturing and private trade on a small scale, reintroduced the payment of wages, and permitted peasants to sell their grain in the open market. In 1924 a constitution was adopted, replacing imperial Russia with the Union of Soviet Socialist Republics. The union represented an attempt to unite the various nationalities and territories that had constituted the old empire. Each separate republic was, in theory,

Economic and constitutional changes

The Red Army, 1919. This scene near the southern front shows the celebration of victory over counter-revolutionary forces.

granted certain autonomous rights. In fact, government remained centralized in the hands of a few leaders. Further, central authority was maintained by means of the one legal political party—the Communist party—whose Central Committee was the directing force behind both politics and government, and whose organizational apparatus reached out into all areas of the vast country.

The philosophy of Bolshevism, now known as communism, was developed primarily by Lenin during these years. It was proclaimed not as a new body of thought, but as a strict interpretation of Marx's writings. Nevertheless, from the beginning it departed at several important points from Marx's teachings. Lenin emphasized the revolutionary character of socialism much more than did its original founder. Marx did believe that in most cases revolution would be necessary, but he was inclined to deplore the fact rather than to welcome it. Communism differed from Marxism as well in its conception of proletarian rule. When Marx spoke of the "dictatorship of the proletariat," he meant by this a dictatorship of the whole working class over the remnants of the bourgeoisie. Within the ranks of this class, democratic forms would prevail. Lenin, however, was persuaded by the desperate circumstances attendant upon the birth of the Soviet Union to proclaim the need for a dictatorship by the party elite, wielding supremacy not only over the bourgeoisie but over the bulk of the proletariat.

The death of Lenin in January 1924 precipitated a struggle among various factions to inherit his mantle of power. Outside of the Soviet Union it was generally assumed that Trotsky would succeed the fallen leader. But the fiery commander of the Red army had a formidable rival in the tough and mysterious Joseph Stalin. The son of a peasant shoemaker in the province of Georgia, Stalin received part of his education in a theological

The tenets of communism

The struggles between Trotsky and Stalin

Left: **Lenin's Casket Is Carried through the Streets of Moscow.** It was not known with certainty until 1956 that, prior to his death, Lenin had discredited Stalin. Right: **Lenin and Stalin.** Under Stalin this picture was used to show his close relationship with Lenin. In fact, the photograph has been doctored.

seminary. Expelled at the age of seventeen for "lack of religious vocation," he thereafter dedicated his career to revolutionary activity.

In 1922 Stalin assumed the secretary-generalship of the Communist party, which, in the years that followed, became the heart of the government. Theoretically, the Soviet Union was ruled by a Central Executive Committee, which in turn represented local, provincial, and regional Councils of Workers and Peasants. Because the Central Executive did not remain in continuous session, however, power increasingly fell into the hands of that body responsible for day-to-day operations and decisions: the Council of the People's Commissars—that is, the various departmental ministers. These commissars were nominated by, and were themselves members of, the Communist party. In his position as the party's secretary-general, Stalin was ultimately able to control nominations to the Council of Commissars, and thus to fill the government with party members loyal to him.

Stalin and the party

The battle over Lenin's succession was not simply a struggle for personal power; fundamental issues of political policy were also involved. Trotsky maintained that socialism in the Soviet Union could never be entirely successful until capitalism was overthrown in surrounding countries. Therefore, he insisted upon a continuous crusade for world revolution. Once European governments appeared to stabilize, as they did after 1924, that goal seemed increasingly unrealistic to many. Trotsky's enemies, most notably Nikolai Bukharin, argued in favor of a program that would expand the revolution within the Soviet Union by transferring wealth from the agricultural to the industrial sector of society. Stalin came to accept this view, preaching the goal of "socialism in one country." His advocacy of forced collectivization of peasant farms and of a crash program of industrialization won him further support within the party, since it was clearly the party that would spearhead this drastic change. Stalin's essentially nationalistic strategy had triumphed by the end of the decade. His rivals—most notably Trotsky—were officially disgraced. In 1927 Trotsky was expelled from the Communist party, and two years later he was driven from the country. In 1940 he was murdered in Mexico City by Stalinist agents. Others, including Gregory Zinoviev and Lev Kamenev, were convicted of crimes against the state in public trials and executed in the 1930s.

The question of world revolution

Once Stalin consolidated his power, he reinforced the role of the party as a state within a state, with its own bureaucrats—the *apparatchiki*—assuming ever-increasing influence in the administration of the country and in the determination of its fortunes. He insisted that the Soviet Union's first priority was economic well-being. His major reform was the introduction of the so-called five-year plan, based on the conviction that the Soviet Union had to take drastic steps to industrialize and thereby achieve economic parity among the nations of the world. The plan instituted an elaborate system of priorities. It decreed how much of each major industrial and agricultural commodity the nation should produce, the wages workers should receive, and the prices that should be charged

The party and the state: five-year plan

СО ЗНАМЕНЕМ ЛЕНИНА ПОБЕДИЛИ МЫ В БОЯХ ЗА ОКТЯБРЬСКУЮ РЕВОЛЮЦИЮ.
СО ЗНАМЕНЕМ ЛЕНИНА ДОБИЛИСЬ МЫ РЕШАЮЩИХ УСПЕХОВ В БОРЬБЕ ЗА ПОБЕДУ
СОЦИАЛИСТИЧЕСКОГО СТРОИТЕЛЬСТВА.
С ЭТИМ ЖЕ ЗНАМЕНЕМ ПОБЕДИМ В ПРОЛЕТАРСКОЙ РЕВОЛЮЦИИ ВО ВСЕМ МИРЕ-
(Сталин. Политический отчет ЦК XVI съезда ВКП(б).)

"The Five-Year Plan in Four Years." Stalin faces down reactionary capitalist enemies in this Soviet propaganda poster of the 1930s.

for goods sold at home and abroad. The first plan, instituted in 1928, was succeeded by others during the 1930s. In some areas goals were met, in a few they were exceeded, in some they fell short. One of the major results of the five-year plans was the creation of an extensive state bureaucracy, charged with the task of organization and supervision at all levels.

Included in the first plan was a program for agricultural collectiviza-

Agricultural collectivization

tion. The scheme was designed to bring rural farms together into larger units of several thousand acres, under the communal proprietorship of peasants. Only with this sort of reorganization, the Soviet Union's rulers declared, could the new and expensive processes of mechanization be introduced, and the country's agricultural yield thereby increased. Not surprisingly, the argument failed to win the support of the more prosperous farmers—the *kulaks*—who had been allowed to retain ownership of their land. Their opposition led to another terror, made all the more deadly by a famine that occurred in the Ukraine in 1932 as a result of the government's grain-allocation policies. The kulaks were liquidated, either killed or transported to distant labor camps; the rural bourgeoisie was eliminated, to be replaced by a rural proletariat. Collectivization was an accomplished fact by 1939. To a vast number of Russians it represented a revolution far more immediate than that of 1917. Twenty million people were moved off the land, which, once it had been reorganized into larger units, and production had been mechanized, required fewer laborers. They were sent to cities, where most went to work in factories. Although agricultural output did not increase during the early years of collectivization, the scheme was nevertheless of benefit to the government. By controlling production, the central bureaucracy was able to regulate the distribution of agricultural products, allocating them for export, where necessary, to pay for the importation of much-needed industrial machinery.

As part of Stalin's campaign to put the interests of the Soviet Union ahead of those of international communism, the Bolshevik regime adopted a new and more conservative foreign policy during the 1930s. Its international goals contradicted the militant socialist internationalism of the 1920s. Lenin had supported revolutionary leftist movements in Europe, sending money and lending moral support to the radical German Marxists Karl Liebknecht and Rosa Luxemburg in 1919 (see p. 991), and to the short-lived Soviet regime of the Bolshevik Béla Kun in Hungary in the same year. Shortly thereafter, the Third International—later called the Comintern—was formed. It declared its allegiance to international communism; its policy was to oppose cooperation or collaboration with the capitalist governments of the West and to work for their overthrow.

With Stalin's suppression of the internationalism advocated by Lenin and Trotsky, however, came a change in tactics and the revival of an interest in playing the game of power politics. The Soviet army was more than doubled in size and was reorganized in accordance with the western European model. Patriotism, which strict Marxists despised as a form of capitalist propaganda, was exalted into a Soviet virtue. When Germany once again appeared to threaten Soviet security, as it did in the 1930s, the Soviet leadership looked abroad for allies. Along with their efforts to build up a great army and to make their own country self-sufficient, they adopted a policy of cooperation with the western European powers. In 1934 they entered the League of Nations, and in 1936 they ratified a military alliance with France.

In June 1936, the Soviets adopted a new constitution, some of whose provisions suggested the possibility of a more liberal regime. Power continued to reside in a governing body (the Presidium) and an administrative agency (the Council of Ministers), both of which were chosen by a two-chamber parliament, the Supreme Soviet, which was elected, in turn, by universal suffrage. This pyramidal structure was not unlike that which it superseded and which, because of the dominant position of the Communist party, had resulted in the concentration of power in the person of Stalin. Now, however, the constitution provided citizens with a bill of rights guaranteeing freedom of speech, of assembly, and of religion. In addition, they were promised the right to employment, the right to leisure, and the right to maintenance at the expense of the state in case of old age or disability.

These guarantees meant little, however, so long as all aspects of life in the Soviet Union continued to be dominated by the Communist party, whose membership of about 1 million in 1930 was but a small fraction of the total population of 150 million. That the new "bill of rights" was a sham was quickly proved by a series of purges that began shortly after the constitution was adopted. In August 1936, the first of several "show trials" occurred, at which persons alleged to be "Trotskyites" and spies were publicly condemned and either imprisoned, executed, or exiled to Siberia. Although the accused for the most part confessed to their "crimes," those confessions were obtained by physical and psychological torture.

Stalin's victims—almost 9 million imprisoned, banished, or killed—were people at all levels who had opposed his personal rule, men such as Bukharin, now editor of the newspaper *Izvestia,* who had spoken out against the elimination of the kulaks; Karl Radek, a leading political theorist; and a number of "old" Bolsheviks, who had been unwilling to acquiesce in Stalin's refusal to debate policy, who had opposed his increasingly nationalistic foreign policy, or who had hoped that revolution did not mean the complete suppression of personal liberty.

The results of the Soviet revolution were profound. No other regime in the history of western Europe had ever attempted to reorder completely the politics, economy, and society of a vast nation as the Soviets had in the short space of twenty years. By 1939 private manufacturing and trade had been almost entirely abolished. Factories, mines, railroads, and public utilities were exclusively owned by the state. Stores were either government enterprises or cooperatives in which consumers owned shares. Agriculture had been almost completely socialized. In the area of social reform, illiteracy was reduced from at least 50 percent to about 20 percent, and higher education was made available to increasingly large numbers. Government assistance for working mothers and free hospitalization did a great deal to raise the national standard of health. Probably the greatest Soviet achievement of the 1920s and 1930s was the transformation of the nation into a modern industrial giant. The state was able to achieve or exceed targets in various sectors: iron and steel, oil and electricity, chemicals, and in the manufacture of heavy equipment such as tractors. At the same time that depression was inhibiting industrial development in the West, the Soviet economy enjoyed a growth rate of 27 percent. By 1932, over 70 percent of the Soviet Union's national product was industrial in origin.

But those achievements were purchased at a very high price. In addition to the liquidation of millions of kulaks and political dissidents and the internment of millions of others in slave-labor camps, the Soviet people were subjected to an unrelenting campaign of indoctrination that encompassed every aspect of their lives. Subtle forms of persecution were implemented to discourage religious orthodoxy, while the nation's youth were inculcated with the new Soviet ideals of steadfast loyalty to the Soviet state and unquestioning obedience to the Communist party. Over time, experiments in the arts and literature, which had been promoted during the early years of the revolution under Lenin, gave way to the culture of authoritarian bureaucracy. The composers Sergei Prokofiev and Dmitri Shostakovich, the poet Vladimir Mayakovsky, the writer Maxim Gorky and his protégé Isaac Babel, the filmmaker Sergei Eisenstein, and other creative men and women flourished in the Soviet Union during the 1920s. Although most of them continued to work through the following decade and after, those who remained in official favor were compelled to compromise their art to conform to the dictates of Stalin's Soviet Union.

Education became a tool of the revolution, much as violence and intimidation had. Control of the minds of the populace was regarded as a prerequisite to building a new society in which individual interests would be sacrificed to those of the state. The communist revolution ultimately succeeded because Stalin's government was able to convince Soviet citizens that they were engaged upon a glorious historical mission, the building of a genuine socialist state. When barely literate peasants and workers were placed in charge of farms and factories they could not help but understand as progress the tremendous changes they and their country were undergoing. What those enthusiasts were willing to overlook, if they were aware of it, was the fact the after two decades of revolutionary change, the Stalinist regime had fastened upon the Soviet people a tyranny as heavy as any imposed by the tsars.

THE EMERGENCE OF FASCISM IN ITALY

That Italy turned its back on democracy may at first seem surprising, in view of the fact that the Italians emerged as victors after the First World War. Yet Italy's difficulties were rooted in longstanding problems that the war had done little to resolve. Italy continued to be divided into two sharply contrasting halves: a relatively prosperous industrialized north, and a wretchedly poor agrarian south. In addition to the problems the country faced as a result of that unhealthy economic split, it was also the victim of an unrequited imperialist impulse that had existed since the 1890s. Its unsuccessful attempts to establish itself as a power in North Africa had left the country with a sense of frustration and humiliation. Before the war, the ruling class was held in public contempt by a younger generation anxious to cleanse the nation of rulers widely perceived to be at once cynical and corrupt, vaccilating and defeatist.

Yet the establishment of a dictatorship in Italy would never have been possible without the demoralizing and humiliating effects of the First World War. The chief business of the Italian armies had been to keep the Austrians occupied on the Southern Front while the British, French, and Americans hammered Germany into submission along the battle lines in the west. To accomplish this assignment, Italy had mobilized more than 5,500,000 men; of these nearly 700,000 were killed. The direct financial cost of Italian participation in the struggle was over $15 billion. These sacrifices were no greater than those made by the British and the French, but Italy was a poor country. Moreover, in the division of the spoils after the fighting, the Italians got less than they expected. While Italy did receive most of the Austrian territories promised in the secret treaties, the Italians maintained that these were inadequate rewards for their sacrifices and for their valuable contribution to an Allied victory. At first the nationalists vented their spleen for the "humiliation of Versailles" upon President Wilson, but after a short time they returned to castigating their own rulers. They alleged Premier Vittorio Orlando had been so cravenly weak and inept that he and those who governed with him had allowed their country to be cheated of its just deserts.

Italy's long-term problems

The demoralizing and humiliating effects of the war

Inflation, radicalism, and
economic chaos

The war contributed to the revolutionary mood in a multitude of other ways. It resulted in inflation of the currency, with consequent high prices, speculation, and profiteering. Normally wages would have risen also, but the postwar labor market was glutted by the return to civilian life of millions of soldiers. Furthermore, business was demoralized, owing to extensive and frequent strikes and to the closing of foreign markets. In the minds of the upper and middle classes the most ominous consequence of the war was the growth of socialism. As hardship and chaos increased, the Italian socialists embraced a philosophy akin to Bolshevism. They voted as a party to join the Third International. In the elections of November 1919, they won about a third of the seats in the Chamber of Deputies. During the following winter socialist workers took over about a hundred factories and attempted to run them for the benefit of the workers. Radicalism also spread through rural areas, where so-called Red Leagues organized to break up large estates and to force landlords to reduce their rents. Two large political parties with mass appeal, the Socialists and the Catholic People's party, drained strength from other parties of the Center and moderate Left. Neither preached revolution, yet both urged far-reaching social and economic reforms. Industrialists and landowners were badly frightened and were therefore ready to accept totalitarianism as a less dangerous form of radicalism that might save at least part of their property from confiscation.

The career of Mussolini

How much the Fascist movement depended for its success upon the leadership of Benito Mussolini is difficult to say. Mussolini was the son of a socialist blacksmith. His mother was a schoolteacher, and in deference to her wishes he eventually became a teacher. But he was restless and dissatisfied, soon leaving Italy for further study in Switzerland. Here he gave part of his time to his books and the rest to writing articles for socialist newspapers. He was eventually expelled from the country for fomenting strikes. Returning to Italy, he became a journalist, and eventually editor of *Avanti,* the leading socialist daily. His ideas in the years before the war were a contradictory mixture of radicalisms. He professed to be a Marxist socialist, but he mingled his socialism with doctrines adapted from the French syndicalists.

Mussolini's contradictory ideas

Mussolini in fact believed in no particular set of doctrines. No man with a definite philosophy could have reversed himself so often. When war broke out in August 1914, Mussolini insisted that Italy should remain neutral. He had scarcely adopted this position when he began urging participation on the Allied side. Deprived of his position as editor of *Avanti,* he founded a new paper, *Il Popolo d'Italia,* and dedicated its columns to arousing enthusiasm for war. He regarded the decision of the government the following spring to go in on the side of the Allies as a personal victory.

The evolution of fascism

The word "fascism" derives from the Latin *fasces,* the ax surrounded by a bundle of sticks representing the authority of the Roman state; the Italian *fascio* means "group" or "band." *Fasci* were organized as early as October 1914, as units of agitation to drive Italy into the war. Their

Left: **Mussolini Reviews a Fascist Youth Parade.** Totalitarianism demanded the capture of youthful minds. Right: **Mussolini Addressing a Crowd of his Followers from the Balcony of the Palazzo Venezia in Rome**

members were young idealists, fanatical nationalists, and frustrated white-collar workers. The original platform of the Fascist party was drafted by Mussolini in 1919. It was a surprisingly radical document, which demanded universal suffrage, abolition of the conservative Senate, the establishment by law of an eight-hour workday, a heavy capital levy, a heavy tax on inheritances, confiscation of 85 percent of war profits, acceptance of the League of Nations, and "opposition to all imperialisms." This platform was accepted more or less officially by the movement until May 1920, when it was supplanted by another of a more conservative character. Indeed, the new program omitted all reference to economic reform. On neither of these platforms did the fascists achieve much political success.

The fascists made up for their initial lack of numbers by disciplined aggressiveness and strong determination. As the old regime crumbled, they prepared to take over the government. In September 1922, Mussolini began to talk openly of revolution. On October 28 an army of about 50,000 fascist militia, in blackshirted uniforms, marched into Rome and occupied the capital. The premier resigned, and the following day the king, Victor Emmanuel III, invited Mussolini to form a cabinet. Without firing a shot the blackshirts had gained control of the Italian government. The explanation of their success is to be found not in the strength of fascism, but in the chaos created by the war and in the weakness and irresolution of the old ruling classes. By the end of the next three years Mussolini's revolution was virtually complete.

The march on Rome

Italian fascism embodied a variety of doctrines that were an expression of its authoritarian nature:

(1) Statism. The state was declared to incorporate every interest and every loyalty of its members. There was to be "nothing above the state, nothing outside the state, nothing against the state."

(2) Nationalism. Nationhood was the highest form of society. It had a life and a soul of its own apart from the lives and souls of the individuals who composed it. Yet there could be no real harmony of interests between two or more distinct nations. Hence internationalism was a perversion of human progress.

(3) Militarism. Strife was the origin of all things. Nations that did not expand would eventually wither and die. War exalted and ennobled man and regenerated sluggish and decadent peoples.

Declaring his allegiance to these principles, Mussolini began to rebuild Italy in accordance with them. He abolished the cabinet system and all but extinguished the powers of the Parliament. He made the Fascist party an integral part of the Italian constitution. The king was compelled to select a prime minister from a list compiled by the party's Great Council. Voters, as well, were left with no real choice; they were forced to select their candidates from lists prepared by the party. Within a few years, there were no other political parties left in Italy. Mussolini assumed the dual position of prime minister and party leader (*duce*). A potent and effective mechanism of political discipline was the party's militia, which Mussolini used to eliminate his enemies by violent means. Police supervision and censorship of the press and of academic life were soon imposed upon the Italian people by the party.

Mussolini reorganized the economy while preaching the end of class conflict as fascist doctrine. He secured worker support by instituting massive public works and building projects, along with state-sponsored programs of library-building, vacations, and social security. He won further popular acclaim when, in 1929, he settled Italy's sixty-year-old conflict with the Roman Catholic Church by a treaty granting independence to the papal residence in the Vatican City and restitution for expropriations that had occurred at the time of Italian unification. The treaty established Roman Catholicism as the official religion of the state, guaranteed religious education in the nation's schools, and made religious marriage ceremonies mandatory.

At the same time that Mussolini was attempting to pacify the Italian working class, he was pulling the teeth of the country's labor movement. The Italian economy was placed under the management of twenty-two corporations, each responsible for a major industrial enterprise. In each corporation were representatives of trade unions, whose members were organized by the Fascist party, the employers, and the government. Together, the members of these corporations were given the task of determining working conditions, wages, and prices. In fact, however, the decisions of these bodies were closely managed by the government and favored the position of management.

Mussolini's fascism did not truly revolutionize government, economy, and society. Party officers exercised a degree of political supervision over bureaucrats, yet did not infiltrate the bureaucracy in significant numbers. Mussolini remained on friendly terms with the wealthy industrialists and bankers who had assisted his rise to power, insuring that whatever he might proclaim about the distinctions between fascism and capitalism, the economy of Italy would remain dependent upon private enterprise. Further evidence of Mussolini's conservatism was his concordat with the Church—this despite his earlier declarations of allegiance to atheism.

The Italian dictator enjoyed boasting that fascism had pulled the country back from economic chaos. The economy did improve somewhat—along with the economies of other European countries—in the late 1920s, yet fascism did little to lessen Italy's plight during the years of worldwide depression that occurred in the 1930s. Although he managed to make his country appear more efficient—his admirers often bragged that he had at last "made the trains run on time"—Mussolini failed to solve its major problems, particularly those of the peasantry, whose standard of living remained desperately low. Mussolini's fascism was little more than illusion. It is a measure of the Italians' disgust with their past leaders that they were so ready to be taken in by him.

THE RISE OF NAZI GERMANY

For a brief period following the First World War, events seemed to be moving Germany significantly to the Left. Most of the leading politicians in the immediate post-armistice government were socialists, members of the Social Democratic party. Their reformist policies, which had seemed radical enough to many prior to the war, now appeared too mild to a group of extreme Marxists who had been encouraged by the revolution in Russia. Calling themselves Spartacists,* and led by Rosa Luxemburg and Karl Liebknecht, they attempted an uprising in 1919 designed to bring the proletarian revolution to Germany. Despite assistance from the Russian Bolsheviks, the rebellion was crushed; Liebknecht and Luxemburg were killed by soldiers while being taken to prison. In engineering the Spartacists' defeat, the German government had recourse to private vigilante groups headed by disillusioned former army officers, men whose true sympathies lay no more with democratic socialism than with Russian communism, and whose discontent would soon focus on the government they had helped to salvage.

With the Spartacist revolt only just behind them, the leaders of a coalition of socialists, Catholic centrists, and liberal democrats in 1919 drafted a constitution for the new German republic reflecting a generally progressive political and social philosophy. It provided for universal suffrage, for

Mussolini's conservatism

Fascism fails to solve Italy's problems

Karl Liebknecht and Rosa Luxemburg

*After the Roman Spartacus who led a slave revolt.

The German Election of 1919. Here German women line up to vote for the first time.

women as well as men; for a cabinet system of government; and for a bill of rights, guaranteeing not only civil liberties but the right of the citizen to employment, to an education, and to protection against the hazards of an industrial society. The republic established under this constitution was beset with troubles from the start. Reactionaries and other extremists plotted against it. Moreover, the German people had had little experience with democratic government. The Weimar Republic (named for the city where its constitution was drafted) did not spring from the desires of a majority of the nation. It was born of change forced upon Germany in its hour of defeat. Its instability made it a likely victim of the forces it was desperately attempting to tame.

Various factors led to the eventual demise of democracy in Germany. First was the sense of humiliation arising from defeat in the war. Between 1871 and 1914, German universities, science, philosophy, and music were known and admired all over the world. The country had likewise attained a remarkable prosperity, by 1914 surpassing Britain and the United States in several fields of industrial production. Then came the defeat of 1918, with Germany left to the mercy of its powerful enemies. It was too much for the German people to understand. They found it difficult to believe that their invincible armies had really been worsted in battle. Quickly the legend grew that the nation had been "stabbed in the back" by socialists and Jews in the government. Though there was no truth in this charge, it helped to salve the wounded nationalistic pride of German patriots. Those in search of a scapegoat also blamed the laxity and irresponsibility that appeared to distinguish the republican regime. It was alleged that Berlin had displaced Paris as the most frivolous and decadent city of Europe. What the country seemed to need was authoritative leadership to spearhead a campaign to regain the world's respect.

The sense of humiliation was increased by two of the provisions imposed on the Germans in the Versailles treaty. First, Germany was compelled to reduce its army to 100,000 men, a requirement that produced bitter discontent among the politically powerful corps of officers that remained at the head of its ranks. Second, the enormous burden of reparations payments continued to arouse the anger of the Germans. Opponents of the reparations settlement urged an obstructionist policy of nonpayment, arguing that the sum of $33 billion demanded would doom the German economy for the foreseeable future. German politicians of all persuasions agreed that the sum was impossibly large. Yet Weimar's foreign minister in the early 1920s, Walter Rathenau, opposed the obstructionists, and attempted to reach a compromise with the former Allied powers. Rathenau's assassination in 1922, by a secret organization of army officers, produced a reaction that led to the German government's refusal to make further payments. The result was French occupation of the Ruhr valley in early 1923, in a fruitless attempt to compel German miners there to produce for France. The ensuing stalemate, which lasted for several months, was ended by the German chancellor, Gustav Stresemann, who recognized the futility of obstructionist tactics. His success in persuading the Germans to accept his point of view was aided by an international agreement to renegotiate reparations under the guidance of a committee of experts headed by the American Charles G. Dawes. Crisis was temporarily averted, but the psychological wounds caused by the reparations controversy did not heal.

Another major reason for democracy's collapse in Germany was the inflation the country suffered in the 1920s. Inflation had plagued the country during the war years. Now the government further increased the supply of money in a desperate effort to finance social welfare programs in the face of rising unemployment and to buy gold with which to make reparations payments. The result was a period of further and more severe inflation, particularly demoralizing to the middle class. Salaries could not keep up with the vast increase in the cost of living. Farmers were angered by the collapse of agricultural prices and by their burden of debts and taxes. University students saw little prospect of gaining a place in already overcrowded professions. Those who existed on fixed incomes—pensioners, stockholders—watched their security vanish. As they lost their faith in the ability of the government to come to their aid, these men and women began, as well, to lose whatever faith they may have had in the republic. The middle class, traumatized by inflation, continued its search for a government that promised attention to its needs and sympathy with its problems. That search intensified with the advent of the Great Depression of 1929. As we shall see, the depression was a major disaster for most of the world. In few countries, however, were its effects more keenly felt than in Germany. Six million workers were unemployed. Once again the middle class saw its savings vanish.

For a brief period in the late 1920s, however, it had appeared that the German economy, and the Weimar Republic with it, might recover.

Inflation and the German Mark. As German inflation gained momentum and the value of the mark plummeted, suitcases were pressed into service to transport money from place to place.

Weimar's later years

Borrowed money meant that the country was able to make its reparations payments, scaled down in accordance with the Dawes Committee recommendations, and to earn money abroad with cheaply priced exports. Building programs, sponsored by socialist municipal governments in large cities such as Frankfurt, Düsseldorf, and Berlin—schools, hospitals, and low-cost worker housing—suggested that the country was both politically and economically healthier than it actually was. In fact the Dawes Plan, by stressing the need for immediate increases in production, ensured that the economy would remain in the hands of the country's leading industrialists whose tendency to overcapitalize their enterprises impaired their ability to cut costs once the depression struck. These were very conservative men, some of whom sympathized with the restoration of a more authoritarian form of government than Weimar represented. They were allied with equally conservative landowners, bound together by their mutual desire for a protective economic policy that would stimulate the sale of domestically produced goods and foodstuffs. These conservative forces were augmented by the army and civil service, staffed with men opposed to the traditions of parliamentary democracy and international cooperation embodied in the republic.

Political polarization

By the end of the decade, party politics had polarized much as they had in Italy. The moderate parties attracted diminishing support while candidates for the Communist party on the Left and the monarchist German People's party on the Right were enjoying increased success. In 1932 discontent with the republic manifested itself in the national elections, which resulted in the continued presidency of the war hero Marshal Paul von Hindenburg. What was significant, however, was not Hindenburg's return to power, but the fact that the Communists polled about five million votes, and that the candidate of the radical Right, Adolf Hitler, received over eleven million votes, more than one-third of those cast. The Weimar Republic was doomed. And Hitler was its logical nemesis.

Adolf Hitler was born in 1889, the son of a petty customs official in the Austrian civil service. He was a failure in school, decided that he would become an artist, and went to Vienna in 1909, where he unsuccessfully attempted to enroll in the Academy. He eked out a dismal existence as a casual laborer and a painter of watercolors during his last eighteen months in Vienna. Meanwhile he developed violent political prejudices. He became an ardent admirer of certain vociferously anti-Semitic politicians in Vienna; and since he associated Judaism with Marxism, he learned to despise that philosophy as well. When war broke out, Hitler was living in Munich. Though an Austrian citizen, he immediately enlisted in the German army. Following the war, he joined with other disaffected Germans to denounce the Weimar Republic, choosing as the vehicle to express his alienation the newly formed National Socialist Workers' Party (whose name was soon abbreviated in popular usage to Nazi). Originally a party of the Left, addressing itself primarily to working-class discontents, the Nazis under Hitler's direction in the mid-1920s broadened their appeal to attract disaffected members of the middle class as well. Nazism's doctrines

One Step Away from Power.
President Hindenburg followed by Adolf Hitler.

derived in large part from a rambling treatise by Hitler entitled *Mein Kampf* (My struggle), which he wrote while in prison following an attempt by the Nazis' private army to stage a *putsch,* or sudden overthrow of the government, in Munich in 1923. In *Mein Kampf,* Hitler expressed his hatred of Jews and communists, his sense of Germany's betrayal by its enemies, and his belief that only with strong leadership could the country regain its rightful place within the European concert of nations.

Hitler's message appealed to an ever-growing number of his disillusioned and economically threatened countrymen and women. In the election of 1928 the Nazis won 12 seats in the Reichstag. In 1930 they won 107 seats, their popular vote increasing from 800,000 to 6,500,000. During the summer of 1932 the parliamentary system broke down. No chancellor could retain a majority in the Reichstag; the Nazis declined to support any cabinet not headed by Hitler, and the communists refused to collaborate with the socialists. In January 1933, a group of reactionaries prevailed upon President Hindenburg to designate Hitler as chancellor, in the mistaken belief that they could control him. It was arranged that there should be only three Nazis in the cabinet, and that Franz von Papen, a Catholic aristocrat, should hold the position of vice-chancellor. The sponsors of this plan failed to appreciate the tremendous popularity of the Nazi movement, however. Hitler was not slow to make the most of his new opportunity. He persuaded Hindenburg to dissolve the Reichstag and to order a new election on March 5. When the new Reichstag assembled, it voted to confer upon Hitler practically unlimited powers. Soon afterward the flag of the Weimar Republic was lowered and replaced by the swastika banner of the National Socialists. The new Germany was proclaimed to be the Third Reich, the successor of the Hohenstaufen Empire of the Middle Ages and of the Hohenzollern Empire of the kaisers.

During the next few months, other sweeping changes converted Germany from Bismarck's federalized state into a highly centralized regime. As both chancellor and leader of the Nazi party, Hitler was in a unique position to put the powers of the state to the purposes of the party. To this end, all other political parties were declared illegal. Nazi party luminaries were appointed heads of various government departments, and party *gauleiters,* or regional directors, assumed administrative responsibility throughout the country. Hitler made use of paramilitary Nazi "storm troopers" (the S.A.) to maintain discipline within the party and to impose order on the populace through calculated intimidation and violence. Not even the S.A. itself was immune to the imperatives of terror: when the aspirations of the S.A. leadership to supplant the established army hierarchy threatened to undermine Hitler's support within the military in June 1934, he unleashed a bloody purge in which more than a thousand high-ranking S.A. officials were summarily executed. Hitler and his associates would brook no interference with their plans to achieve absolute power. During the late 1930s, a second paramilitary organization, the *Schutzstaffel* (bodyguard), or S.S., became the most dreaded arm of Nazi oppression and terror. Headed by the fanatical Heinrich Himmler, the S.S. exercised

An Anti-Nazi Poster Employed by the Social Democrats in 1932

"Our Last Hope: Hitler." A pro-Nazi poster from the election of 1932.

Nazis on Parade, 1933. Politics as theater.

sovereign power over the lives of all Germans, arresting, detaining, imprisoning, and murdering anyone who appeared to stand in the path of Nazi domination.

Nazi ideology and ruralism

Although Germany was one of the most highly industrialized countries in the world, National Socialist ideology had a peculiarly peasant flavor. The key to Nazi theory was contained in the phrase *Blut und Boden* (blood and soil). The word *soil* reflected not only a deep reverence for the homeland but an abiding affection for the peasants, who were said to embody the finest qualities of the German race. This high regard for country folk came partly, no doubt, from the fact that they had the highest birth rate of the nation's citizens and therefore were most valuable for military reasons. It was explainable also by the reaction of the Nazi leaders against everything that the city stood for—not only intellectualism and radicalism but high finance and the complicated problems of industrial society.

Rearmament and pro-industrial economic policy

Despite these sentiments, however, the Nazis did little to restructure the economy of Germany. Although they came to power promising to tax department stores heavily so as to benefit the small shopkeeper, they succumbed to pressure from bankers to mitigate those plans. Indeed, they encouraged heavy industry as part of their program of rearmament, forming what amounted to partnerships with such giants as I. G. Farben, the chemical concern, which worked closely with the government on the development of synthetic fuels. Like other Western nations, the Germans battled unemployment with large state-financed construction projects: highways, public housing, and reforestation. Late in the decade, rearma-

996

Nazism and the Rural Myth. Left: To stress the rural strength of Aryan Germany, Hitler appeared in lederhosen in the 1920s. Right and center: During the 1930s the Nazi artist W. Willrich painted sober, healthy peasant-types, the ideal Hitler professed to admire and to cultivate.

ment and a substantial increase in the size of the military establishment all but ended the German unemployment problem—much as the same policies and programs were ending it elsewhere.

Germany's social structure remained relatively untouched by Nazi rule. Government policy encouraged women to withdraw from the labor force, both to ease unemployment and to conform to Nazi notions of a woman's proper role. "Can woman," one propagandist asked, "conceive of anything more beautiful than to sit with her husband in her cozy home and listen inwardly to the loom of time weaving the weft and warp of motherhood . . .?" Like Mussolini, Hitler moved to abolish class conflict by robbing working-class institutions of their power. He outlawed trade unions and strikes, froze wages, and organized workers and employers into a National Labor Front, while at the same time increasing workers' welfare benefits. Class distinctions were to some degree blurred by the regime's insistence on infusing a new national "spirit" into the entire society. Organizations like the Hitler Youth, a sinister variant on the Boy Scout movement, and National Labor Service, which drafted students and others for a term to work on various state-sponsored building and reclamation projects, cut across, but did not abolish, class lines.

Social structure

For the National Socialists, the great social dividing line was race; its most degrading tenet, anti-Semitism. Anti-Semitism was a centuries-old phenomenon, a part of Catholic Christian doctrine from the Middle Ages on. It manifested itself throughout Europe in the nineteenth century—in the Dreyfus affair in France, for example, and in the Russian pogroms. In

Anti-Semitism in nineteenth-century Germany

Germany, anti-Semitism flourished as a kind of perverted stepchild of nationalism. Jews were perceived as an alien race, and as such, forever incapable of assimilation into the German *Volksgeist.* Johann Fichte, whose *Addresses to the German Nation* had aroused Germans to the idea of a national destiny (see pp. 816–817), declared forthrightly that "the only way I can see to give the Jews civil rights is to cut off their heads in a single night and equip them with new ones devoid of every Jewish idea." Jews were outsiders, without roots in any national culture, and therefore destructive of German racial "purity." The only culture to which Jews were attached, anti-Semites argued, was the culture of the marketplace. The composer Richard Wagner concluded that "the Jew will rule as long as money remains the power before which all our doings and our dealings lose their force."

Anti-Semitism, urbanism, and capitalism

Jews were a threat to those who feared urbanization and reform. The majority of Jews lived in cities. They were in the forefront of scientific, cultural, and political innovation. Sigmund Freud was a Jew, as, of course, was Karl Marx. By attacking Jews, anti-Semites could simultaneously attack the modern institutions that they saw as part of a "conspiracy" to deprive civilization of its reassuring base in tradition and authority. Lower-middle-class men and women, uneasy in a society that appeared to ignore them, believed conservative party leaders who blamed "Jewish capitalists" for the demise of small businesses, for the replacement of corner shops by department stores, and for the periodic economic swings that threatened their precarious livelihoods with depression or inflation. In Vienna, middle-class voters supported the anti-Semitic Christian Democrats. It was that party's poison that Hitler swallowed with satisfaction during the years before 1914. In Germany, in 1893, sixteen avowed anti-Semites were elected to the Reichstag, and the Conservative party made anti-Semitism part of its official program. Large numbers of Germans would have agreed with the historian Heinrich von Treitschke, who lamented in 1879 that "the Jews are our national misfortune."

Nazi persecution of the Jews

Given that legacy, it is no surprise that Germans in the 1920s and 1930s subscribed willingly to Hitler's fanatical anti-Semitism. The Nazis argued that the so-called Aryan race, which was supposed to include the Nordics as its most perfect specimens, was the only one ever to have made any notable contributions to human progress. They contended further that the accomplishments and mental qualities of a people were determined by blood. Thus the achievements of the Jew forever remained Jewish, no matter how long he or she might live in a Western country. It followed that no Jewish science or Jewish literature or Jewish music could ever truly represent the German nation. A series of laws passed in 1935 deprived Jews and people of Jewish blood of their German citizenship, and prohibited marriage between Jews and other Germans. Eventually, between four and five and a half million Jews were rounded up, tortured, and murdered in concentration camps. Other representatives of "imperfect" racial and social groups—homosexuals, gypsies, and anti-Nazi intellectuals—met a similar fate. The extremism of Hitler's anti-Semitic cam-

The Nazi Party Congress in Nuremburg, 1934. The Nazis were masters of the use of humanity *en masse* as propaganda. Hitler stands at attention in the center.

paigns underscores the fact that National Socialism was more fanatical than Italian fascism. It was a new religion, not only in its dogmatism and its ritual, but in its fierce intolerance and its zeal for expansion.

If Nazism was a form of perverted religion, Hitler was its high priest. His appeal was based in part on his ability to give the German people what they wanted: jobs for workers, a productive economy for industrialists, a bulwark against communism for the still-influential Junker class. But more important, he preached what the German people wished to hear. His power lay not so much in the programs he championed, many of which were ill-thought-out or contradictory, but in his talent for responding to the sentiments of his fellow Germans, and for turning those sentiments into holy writ. As one of his early followers remarked, "Hitler responds to the vibrations of the human heart with the delicacy of a seismograph. . . . His words go like an arrow to their target; he touches each private wound on the raw, liberating the mass unconscious, expressing its innermost aspirations, telling it what it most wants to hear." That so many wanted most to listen to the poisonous dogmas of Adolf Hitler is a depressing commentary on the state of the Western world in the 1930s.

The significance of German Nazism and Italian fascism remains a subject of controversy among students of modern history. Some argue that they reflected the enthronement of force by capitalists in an effort to save their dying system from destruction. And it is true that the success of both movements in gaining control of the government depended on

The power of Adolf Hitler

The significance of German Nazism and Italian fascism

support from great landowners and captains of industry. Others explain Nazism and fascism as a reaction of debtors against creditors, of farmers against bankers and manufacturers, and of small businessmen against high finance and monopolistic practices. Still others interpret them as a reaction to communist threat, a reversion to primitivism, a result of the despair of the masses, a protest against the weaknesses of democracy, or a supreme manifestation of nationalism. Undoubtedly they were all of these things combined. One further argument holds that fascism and Nazism were extreme expressions of tendencies prevalent in all industrialized countries. If official policies in most Western countries in the 1930s took on more and more of an authoritarian semblance—a tightly controlled economy, limitation of production to maintain prices, and expansion of armaments to promote prosperity—it was because nearly all nations in that period were beset with similar problems and, in varying degrees, were frightened of their implications.

THE DEMOCRACIES BETWEEN THE WARS

Class conflict in France

The histories of the three major Western democracies—Great Britain, France, and the United States—run roughly parallel during the years after the First World War. In all three countries there was an attempt by governments to trust in policies and assumptions that had prevailed before the war. The French, not surprisingly, continued to fear Germany and to take whatever steps they could to keep their traditional enemy as weak as possible. Under the leadership of the moderate conservative Raymond Poincaré, who held office from 1922 to 1924, and again from 1926 to 1929, the French pursued a policy of deflation, which attempted to keep the prices of manufactured goods low by restraining wages. This policy pleased businessmen, but was hard on the working class. Édouard Herriot, a Radical Socialist who served as premier from 1924 to 1926 was, despite his party's name, a spokesman for the small businessman, farmer, and lower-middle class. Herriot declared himself in favor of social reform, but refused to raise taxes in order to pay for it. Class conflict lay close to the surface of French national affairs throughout the 1920s. While industries prospered, employers rejected trade unionists' demands to bargain collectively. A period of major strikes immediately after the war was followed by a sharp decline in union activity. Workers remained dissatisfied, even after the government passed a modified social insurance program in 1930, insuring against sickness, old age, and death.

Class conflict in Britain

Class conflict flared in Britain as well. Anxious to regain its now irretrievably lost position as the major industrial and financial power in the world, Britain, like France, pursued a policy of deflation, designed to lower the price of manufactured goods and thus make them more attractive on the world market. The result was a reduction in wages that undermined the standard of living of many British workers. Their resentment helped to elect the first Labour party government in 1924, and elected one again in 1929. But its minority position in Parliament left it little chance to accomplish much of consequence, even had its leader, Prime Minister J. Ramsay MacDonald, been a more adventurous socialist than he was. In 1926 British trade unions grew increasingly militant because of the particularly distressing wage levels in the coal mining industry, and because the Conservative government, returned to power under Stanley Baldwin in 1925, refused to be deflected from its deflationary stance. The unions staged a nationwide general strike which, though it failed as an industrial strategy, turned the middle class more than ever against the workers.

The United States was undoubtedly the most impregnable fortress of conservative power among the democracies. The presidents elected in the 1920s—Warren G. Harding, Calvin Coolidge, and Herbert Hoover— upheld a social philosophy formulated by the barons of big business in the nineteenth century, while the Supreme Court used its power of judicial review to nullify progressive legislation enacted by state governments and occasionally by Congress.

Conservatism in the U.S.

The course of Western history was dramatically altered by the advent of worldwide depression in 1929. We have already seen the way in which depression contributed to the rise of Nazism. But all countries were forced to come to terms with the economic and social devastation it produced. The Great Depression had its roots in a sluggish economic growth rate, which had plagued the West throughout the 1920s, and which was the result, in part, of competition from the economies of non-European nations. In addition, a significant worldwide drop in agricultural prices meant that the peasant countries of southern and eastern Europe, where farm production was geared to small-scale, high-cost agriculture, could not sell their crops profitably on the international market. Their ability to purchase foreign-made manufactured goods thus declined; and that decline seriously affected industrial productivity throughout Europe. Meanwhile, in response to shrinking markets, countries were imposing trade barriers to protect their own domestic manufacturers from foreign competitors, thereby further crippling the economy of the West as a whole.

Roots of the Great Depression

This crisis in production was compounded by the collapse of prices on the New York Stock Exchange in 1929. With a drop in the value of stocks, banks found themselves short of capital and forced to close. International investors called in their debts. Industries, unable to sell their products, stopped manufacturing and started laying off workers. Unemployment further contracted markets—fewer people had money with which to buy goods or services—and that contraction led to more unemployment.

Crash of New York Stock Exchange

The results of the depression took varied forms throughout the West. In 1931 Great Britain abandoned the gold standard; the government of the United States followed suit in 1933. By no longer pegging their currencies to the price of gold, these countries hoped to make money cheaper, and thus more available for programs of public and private economic recovery. This action was the forerunner of a broad program of

Results of depression: economic nationalism

Left: **U.S. Farmers on Their Way West in the 1930s.** Forced from their land by depression debts and by drought, thousands of farmers and their families headed to California, Oregon, and Washington in search of employment. Right: **The Stock Market Crash, October 24, 1929.** Crowds milling outside the New York Stock Exchange on the day of the big crash.

currency management, which became an important element in a general policy of economic nationalism. As early as 1932 Great Britain abandoned its time-honored policy of free trade. Protective tariffs were raised in some instances as high as 100 percent.

Domestically, Britain moved cautiously to alleviate the effects of the depression. A national government, which came to power in 1931 with a ministry composed of members from the Conservative, Liberal, and Labour parties, was reluctant to spend beyond its income, as it would have to in order to underwrite effective programs of public assistance. Of the European democracies, France adopted the most advanced set of policies to combat the inequalities and distress that followed in the wake of the depression. In 1936, responding to a threat from ultraconservatives to overthrow the republic, a Popular Front government, under the leadership of the socialist Léon Blum, was formed by the Radical, Radical Socialist, and Communist parties, and lasted for two years. The Popular Front nationalized the munitions industry and reorganized the Bank of France so as to deprive the 200 largest stockholders of their monopolistic control over credit. In addition, it decreed a forty-hour week for all urban workers and initiated a program of public works. For the benefit of the farmers it established a wheat office to fix the price and regulate the distribution of grain. Although the threat from the political Right was for a time quelled by the Popular Front, conservatives were generally uncooperative and unimpressed by its attempts to ameliorate the conditions of the French

Policies to alleviate effects of depression

Léon Blum

working class. The anti-Semitism that had appeared at the time of the Dreyfus affair resurfaced; Blum was both a socialist and a Jew. Businessmen saw him as the forerunner of a French Lenin, and were heard to opine, "better Hitler than Blum." They got their wish before the decade was out.

The most dramatic changes in policy occurred not in Europe but in the United States. The explanation was twofold. The United States had clung longer to the economic philosophy of the nineteenth century. Prior to the depression the business classes had adhered firmly to the dogma of freedom of contract and insisted upon their right to form monopolies and to use the government as their agent in frustrating the demands of both workers and consumers. The depression in the United States was also more severe than in the European democracies. Industrial production shrank by about two-thirds. The structure of agricultural prices and of common stocks collapsed. Thousands of banks were forced to close their doors. Unemployment rose to one-third of the total labor force. An attempt to alleviate distress was contained in a program of reform and reconstruction known as the New Deal. The chief architect and motivator of this program was Franklin D. Roosevelt, who succeeded Herbert Hoover in the presidency on March 4, 1933.

The aim of the New Deal was to preserve the capitalist system, by managing the economy and undertaking programs of relief and public works to increase mass purchasing power. Although the New Deal did assist in the recovery both of individual citizens and of the country, through programs of currency management and social security, it left the crucial problem of unemployment unsolved. In 1939, after six years of the New Deal, the United States still had more than 9 million jobless workers—a

Severity of depression in the U.S.

Achievements of the New Deal

The New Deal. After 1935 the Works Progress Administration (WPA) put to work unemployed Americans who erected and repaired buildings, roads, and bridges throughout the United States.

figure that exceeded the combined unemployment of the rest of the world. Ironically, only the outbreak of a new world war could provide the full recovery that the New Deal had failed to assure, by directing millions from the labor market into the army and by creating jobs in the countless factories that turned to the manufacture of war matériel.

INTELLECTUAL AND CULTURAL TRENDS IN THE INTERWAR YEARS

Philosophy: the Logical Positivists

The First World War, which proved so disillusioning to so many, and the generally dispiriting political events that followed in its train, made it difficult to hold fast to any notion of a purposeful universe. Philosophers, to a greater degree than their predecessors, declared that there was little point in attempting to discover answers to questions about the nature of ultimate reality. These antimetaphysicians broke dramatically with the philosophers of the past century, who had grounded their speculations in a belief in progress and in a search for all-encompassing explanations of human behavior. Probably the most influential of these new thinkers was the Viennese Ludwig Wittgenstein, founder, with the Englishman Bertrand Russell, of the school of Logical Positivism. Developed further by the so-called Vienna Circle, whose leader was Rudolf Carnap, Logical Positivism emerged as an uncompromisingly scientific philosophy. It is not concerned with values or ideals except to the extent that they may be demonstrable by mathematics or physics. In general, the Logical Positivists reject as "meaningless" everything that cannot be reduced to a "one-to-one correspondence" with something in the physical universe. They reduce philosophy to a mere instrument for the discovery of truth in harmony with the facts of the physical environment. They divest it almost entirely of its traditional content and use it as a medium for answering questions and solving problems. They are concerned especially to attack political theory, regarding that subject as particularly burdened with unproved assumptions and questionable dogmas.

Bertrand Russell

Religion and charismatic leadership as cultural forces

Sociologists reinforced philosophers in denying the value of metaphysics. One of the most important was the German Max Weber, who in his book *The Protestant Ethic and the Spirit of Capitalism* (1905) argued that religion must be understood as a cultural force, in this case assisting directly in the spread of capitalism. By making work a cardinal virtue and idleness a supreme vice, Protestantism had encouraged the work ethic, which in turn had fueled the energies of early capitalist entrepreneurs. When he turned to a study of the contemporary world, Weber concluded that societies would inevitably fall more and more under the sway of ever-expanding and potentially authoritarian bureaucracies. Recognizing the extent to which such a development might threaten human freedom, Weber posited the notion of "charismatic" leadership as a means of escaping the deadening tyranny of state control. A term derived from the Greek word for gift, "charisma" was, according to Weber, an almost magic quality that could induce hero worship and that, if properly directed by its possessor, might produce an authority to challenge bureaucracy. Weber himself recognized the dangers as well as the attractions of charismatic authority, dangers that the careers of Stalin, Hitler, and Mussolini soon made all too apparent. Another thinker who treated religion as a powerful social and psychological force, rather than as a branch of metaphysics, was the Swiss psychologist Carl Jung. Originally a student and disciple of Sigmund Freud, Jung broke with his intellectual mentor by proclaiming the existence of a force behind individual id, ego, and superego: the "collective unconscious." Jung's literary background and his personal penchant for mysticism helped persuade him of the enduring psychological and therapeutic value of myth and religion, something Freud refused to acknowledge.

The writings of some philosophers during the interwar years not only reflected a sense of crisis and despair but, because of the influence of those works, contributed to it as well. Foremost among these were the Italian Vilfredo Pareto and the German Oswald Spengler, who agreed in their contempt for the masses, in their belief that democracy was impossible, in their anti-intellectual viewpoint, and in their admiration for strong and aggressive leaders. Spengler was, in many respects, more extreme than Pareto. In his *Decline of the West,* completed in 1918, and even more in his later writings, he expressed attitudes that reflect the extent to which authoritarianism might appeal to an "anti-intellectual" intellectual. In his *Hour of Decision,* published in 1933, he fulminated against democracy, pacifism, internationalism, the lower classes, and nonwhite peoples. He sang the praises of those "who feel themselves born and called to be masters," of "healthy instincts, race, the will to possession and power." Spengler despised the analytical reasoning of urban intellectuals and called upon men to admire the "deep wisdom of old peasant families." Human beings, he maintained, are "beasts of prey," and those who deny this conclusion are simply "beasts of prey with broken teeth."

Further confusion and uncertainty were encouraged by the pioneering work of the German physicist Albert Einstein, whose theorizing and experiments were revolutionizing the way in which men and women perceived the universe. In 1905 Einstein began to challenge not merely the older conceptions of matter but the entire structure of traditional physics. The doctrine for which he is most noted is his principle of relativity. He maintained that space and motion, instead of being absolute, as previously believed, are relative to each other. Objects have not merely three dimensions but four. To the familiar length, breadth, and thickness, Einstein added a new dimension of *time* and represented all four as fused in a synthesis that he called the *space-time continuum.* In this way he sought to explain the idea that mass is dependent upon motion. Bodies traveling at high velocity have proportions of extension and mass different from those they would have at rest. Einstein also posited the conception of a finite universe—that is, finite in space. The region of matter does not extend into infinity; the universe has limits. While these are by no means

Antirationalist and antidemocratic philosophies

Albert Einstein

Releasing the energy within the atom

definite boundaries, there is at least a region beyond which nothing exists. Space curves back upon itself so as to make of the universe a gigantic sphere within which are contained galaxies, solar systems, stars, and planets.

The Einstein theories had a major influence in precipitating another revolutionary development in physics: the splitting of the atom to release the energy contained within it. As early as 1905 Einstein became convinced of the equivalence of mass and energy and worked out a formula for the conversion of one into the other, which he expressed as $E = mc^2$, where E represents the energy in ergs, m the mass in grams, and c the velocity of light in centimeters per second. In other words, the amount of energy locked within the atom is equal to the mass multiplied by the square of the velocity of light. But no practical application of this formula was possible until after the discovery of the neutron by the Englishman Sir James Chadwick in 1932. Since the neutron carries no charge of electricity, it is an ideal weapon for bombarding the atom. It is not repelled by the positively charged protons or by the negatively charged electrons. Moreover, in the process of bombardment it produces more neutrons, which hit other atoms and cause them in turn to split and create neutrons. In this way the original reaction is repeated in an almost unending series.

Laying the groundwork for the atomic bomb

In 1939 two German physicists, Otto Hahn and Fritz Strassman, succeeded in splitting atoms of uranium by bombarding them with neutrons. The initial reaction produced a chain of reactions, in much the same way that a fire burning at the edge of a piece of paper raises the temperature of adjoining portions of the paper high enough to cause them to ignite. Scientists in Germany, Great Britain, and the United States were spurred on by governments anxious to make use of these discoveries for military purposes during the Second World War. The first use made of the knowledge of atomic fission was in the preparation of an atomic bomb—a device that would further heighten and perpetuate the anxieties of the era.

Literary movements during the interwar period showed tendencies similar to those in philosophy. Like the philosophers, the major novelists, poets, and dramatists were disillusioned by the brute facts of world war and by the failure of victory to fulfill its promises. Many were profoundly affected also by revolutionary developments in science, such as the theories of Einstein, and especially by the probings of the new science of psychoanalysis into the hidden secrets of the mind. Much of the literature of the interwar period reflected themes of frustration, cynicism, and disenchantment. The general mood of the era was expressed individually by different writers; for example, by the early novels of the American Ernest Hemingway, by the poetry of the Anglo-American T. S. Eliot, and by the plays of the German Bertolt Brecht. In *The Sun Also Rises* (1926), Hemingway gave the public a powerful description of the essential tragedy of the so-called lost generation and set a pattern that other writers, like the American F. Scott Fitzgerald, were soon to follow. In his poem *The Waste Land* (1922), Eliot presented a philosophy that was close to despair: life is

T. S. Eliot

a living death, to be endured as boredom and frustration. Brecht, in plays written to be performed before the proletarian patrons of cabarets, proclaimed the corruption of the bourgeois state and the pointlessness of war.

The works of many writers in the interwar period reflected to an increasing extent the isolation of self-conscious intellectuals and the constricting of their audience that characterized the years before the First World War. While Brecht carried his revolutionary messages into the streets of Berlin, others wrote primarily for each other or for the small elite group who could understand what they were saying. Eliot crammed his poetry with esoteric allusions. The Irishman James Joyce, whose ability to enter his characters' minds and to reproduce their "stream of consciousness" on paper made him a writer of the very first order, nevertheless wrote with a complexity that relatively few could appreciate. The same was true, though to a lesser extent, of the novels of the Frenchman Marcel Proust and the Englishwoman Virginia Woolf. In her novels and essays, Woolf was, as well, an eloquent and biting critic of the ruling class of Britain, focusing in part on the enforced oppression of women even in that class.

The depression of the 1930s forced a reexamination of the methods and purposes of literature. In the midst of economic stagnation and threats of totalitarianism and war, literature was politicized. Authors came to believe that their work must indict meanness, cruelty, and barbarism, and point the way to a more just society, that it should also be a literature addressed not to fellow intellectuals, but to common men and women. The American John Steinbeck, in *The Grapes of Wrath* (1939), depicted the sorry plight of impoverished farmers fleeing from the "dust bowl" to California only to find that all the land had been monopolized by companies that exploited their workers. Pervading the novels of the Frenchman André Malraux was the strong suggestion that the human struggle against tyranny and injustice is that which gives meaning and value to life. Young British writers such as W. H. Auden, Stephen Spender, and Christopher Isherwood declared, as communist sympathizers, that artists had an obligation to politicize their art for the benefit of the revolution. They rejected the pessimism of their immediate literary forebears for the optimism of political commitment to a common cause.

In this they differed radically from their French contemporary, Jean-Paul Sartre, whose pessimistic philosophy of existentialism was receiving its first hearing at this time. Sartre was a teacher of philosophy in a Paris *lycée* and subsequently a member of the French Resistance movement against the Germans during the Second World War. His philosophy takes its name from its doctrine that the *existence* of human beings as free individuals is the fundamental fact of life. But this freedom is of no help to humanity; instead it is a source of anguish and terror. Realizing, however vaguely, that they are free agents, morally responsible for all their acts, individuals feel themselves strangers in an alien world. They can have no confidence in a benevolent God or in a universe guided by purpose, for, according to Sartre, all such ideas have been reduced to fictions by

Virginia Woolf

The influence of worldwide depression

Jean-Paul Sartre

George Orwell

Keynes and the economy

John Maynard Keynes

Trends in art

modern science. The only way of escape from despair is the path of "involvement," or active participation in human affairs.

Another writer who refused to allow himself the luxury of political optimism was the Englishman George Orwell. Although sympathetic to the cause of international socialism, Orwell continued to insist that all political movements were to some degree corrupted. He urged writers to recognize a duty to write only on the basis of what they had themselves experienced. Above all, writers should never simply parrot party propaganda. Orwell's last two novels, *Animal Farm* (1946) and *Nineteen Eighty-Four* (1949), written during and immediately after the Second World War, are powerful expressions of his mistrust of political regimes—whether of the Left or the Right—that profess democracy but in fact destroy human freedom.

Optimism during the 1930s was generally the property of those writers who were prepared to advocate a violent change in the social order, most notably men and women sympathetic to the doctrines of communism and the achievements of Soviet Russia. An exception to this rule was the British economist John Maynard Keynes, who argued that capitalism could be made to work if governments would play a part in its management, and whose theories helped shape the economic policies of the New Deal. Keynes had served as an economic adviser to the British government during the 1919 treaty-making at Paris. He was disgusted with the harsh terms imposed upon the Germans, recognizing that they would serve only to keep alive the hatreds and uncertainties that breed war. Keynes believed that capitalism with its inner faults corrected could provide a just and efficient economy. First, Keynes abandoned the sacred cow of balanced budgets. He did not advocate continuous deficit financing. He would have the government deliberately operate in the red whenever private investment was too scanty to provide for the economic needs of the country. When depression gave way to recovery, private financing could take the place of deficit spending for most purposes. He favored the accumulation and investment of large amounts of venture capital, which he declared to be the only socially productive form of capital. Finally, Keynes recommended monetary control as a means of promoting prosperity and full employment. He would establish what is commonly called a "managed currency," regulating its value by a process of contraction or expansion in accordance with the needs of the economy. Prosperity would thus be assured in terms of the condition of the home market, and no nation would be tempted to "beggar its neighbor" in the foolish pursuit of a favorable balance of trade.

Trends in art tended to parallel those in literature. For much of the period, visual artists continued to explore aesthetic frontiers far removed from the conventional taste of average men and women. Picasso followed his particular genius as it led him further into cubist variations and inventions. So did others, such as the Frenchman Fernand Léger, who combined devotion to cubist principles and a fascination with the artifacts of industrial civilization. A group more advanced, perhaps, than the cubists,

"Tie Yourself to the Fatherland, Dear Fatherland," by George Grosz (1893–1959). Grosz's attacks on unfeeling capitalism during the Weimar years undoubtedly served to weaken the political center during the 1930s.

the expressionists argued that since color and line express inherent psychological qualities that can be represented without reference to subject matter, a painting need not have a "subject" at all. The Russian Wassily Kandinsky carried the logic of this position to its conclusion by calling his untitled paintings "improvisations," and insisting that they meant nothing. A second group of expressionists rejected intellectuality for what they called "objectivity," by which they meant a candid appraisal of the state of the human mind. Their analysis took the form of an attack upon the greed and decadence of postwar Europe. Chief among this group was the German George Grosz, whose cruel, satiric line has been likened to a "razor lancing a carbuncle." Another school expressed its disgust with the world by declaring that there was in fact no such thing as aesthetic principle, since aesthetic principle was based on reason and the world had conclusively proved by fighting itself to death that reason did not exist. Calling themselves *dada-ists* (after a name picked at random, allegedly, from the dictionary) these artists, led by the Frenchman Marcel Duchamp, the German Max Ernst, and the Alsatian Jean Hans Arp, concocted "fabrications" from cutouts and juxtapositions of wood, glass, and metal, and gave them bizarre names: *The Bride stripped bare by her Bachelors, even* (Duchamp), for example. These works were declared by critics, however, to belie their professed meaninglessness, to be, in fact, expressions of the subconscious. Such certainly were the paintings of the surrealists, artists such as the Italian Giorgio de Chirico and the Spaniard Salvador Dali, whose explorations of the interior of the mind produced irrational, fantastic, and generally melancholy images.

For a time in the 1930s artists, like writers, responded to the sense of international crisis by painting to express their pain and outrage directly to a mass audience. Among the chief representatives of the new movement were the Mexicans Diego Rivera and José Clemente Orozco, and the Americans Thomas Hart Benton and Reginald Marsh. The fundamental aim of these artists was to depict the social conditions of the modern world and to

Art as social commentary

1009

Panel (3) of Painting Number 198 (1914), by Wassily Kandinsky (1866–1944). The expressionist painters carried their explorations of the psychological properties of color and line to the point where subject matter was deemed unnecessary and even undesirable.

Nude Descending a Staircase, by Marcel Duchamp (1887–1968). An example of the impact of film on painting. The effect is that of a series of closely spaced photographs coalescing to create motion.

The Funeral Procession, by Grosz. Painted in the late stages of the First World War, this portrayal of a funeral procession gone mad shows death triumphant as humanity is swept into a hell of its own making. The work expresses an anger and a loathing felt by an entire generation.

The Persistence of Memory, by Salvador Dali (1904–1989). The Spaniard Dali is the outstanding representative of the surrealist school. Many objects in his paintings are Freudian images.

Mystery and Melancholy of a Street, by Giorgio de Chirico (1888–1978). Employing perspective to fashion familiar components into dreamscapes fraught with anxiety and loneliness, de Chirico had a profound effect on the surrealists.

Barricade (1931), by José Clemente Orozco (1883–1949). The Mexican muralist Orozco was one of the most celebrated of contemporary painters with a social message. His themes were revolutionary fervor, satire of aristocracy and the Church, and deification of the common man.

Around the Fish (1926), by Paul Klee (1879–1940). Klee is recognized as the most subtle humorist of twentieth-century art. The central motif of a fish on a platter suggests a banquet, but many of the surrounding objects appear to be products of fantasy.

The Table, by Georges Braque (1881–1963). An example of later cubism showing the predominance of curvilinear form and line instead of geometric structure.

I and the Village, by Marc Chagall (1887–1985). The subject refers to the artist's childhood and youth in Vitebsk, Russia. The profile on the right is probably that of the artist himself.

Mural of Kansas City, Missouri, by Thomas Hart Benton
(1889–1975). The mural protests the corruption of American
politics and the depression, misery, and degradation of farm
workers and industrial laborers. The man in the armchair is the
political boss of Kansas City in the 1930s, Tom Pendergast.

Detroit Industry (detail), by Diego Rivera (1886–1957). Painted between 1931
and 1933, this work aimed to depict the social conditions of the modern world,
especially the struggles and triumphs of the working class.

Igor Stravinsky

Polytonality

Development of functional architecture

present in graphic detail the hopes and struggles of peasants and workers. While they scarcely adhered to the conventions of the past, there was nothing unintelligible about their work; it was intended to be art that anyone could understand. Much of it bore the sting or thrust of social satire. Orozco, in particular, delighted in pillorying the hypocrisy of the Church and the greed and cruelty of plutocrats and plunderers.

Music, along with the rest of the arts, continued its movement away from nineteenth-century form and intentions. Impressionists, such as Debussy, were succeeded by expressionists, whose work is concerned more with form than with sensuous effects and tends toward abstraction. Expressionism, more radical and more influential than impressionism, comprises two main schools: atonality, founded by the Viennese Arnold Schoenberg, and polytonality, best typified by the Russian Igor Stravinsky. Atonality abolishes key. In this type of music, dissonances are the rule rather than the exception, and the melodic line commonly alternates between chromatic manipulation and strange unsingable leaps. In short, the ordinary principles of composition are reversed. The atonalists attempt, with some success, to let musical sound become a vehicle for expressing the inner meaning and elemental structure of things.

Polytonality is essentially a radical kind of counterpoint, deriving its inspiration partly from baroque practices of counterpoint that were placed in the service of new ideas. However, it does not simply interweave independent melodies, but undertakes to combine separate keys and unrelated harmonic systems, with results that are highly discordant. While the atonalists have retained elements of romanticism, the polytonalists have tried to resurrect the architectural qualities of pure form, movement, and rhythm, stripping away all sentimentality and sensuous connotations.

Architects during this period were also intent upon denying sentimentality. Between 1880 and 1890 designers in Europe and America announced that the prevailing styles of building construction were out of harmony with the facts of modern civilization, and declared as well their intention of restoring that harmony. The chief pioneers of this "functionalism" were Otto Wagner in Austria; Charles Édouard Jeanneret, known as Le Corbusier, in France; and Louis Sullivan and Frank Lloyd Wright in the United States. The basic principle of functionalism is the idea that the appearance of a building should proclaim its actual use and purpose. True beauty consists in an honest adaptation of materials to the purpose they are intended to serve. Functionalism also embodies the notion that architecture should express either directly or symbolically the distinguishing features of contemporary culture. Ornamentation must therefore be restricted to such elements as will reflect an age of science and machines. A leading European practitioner of functionalism was the German Walter Gropius, who in 1919 established a school—the *Bauhaus*—in Dessau to serve as a center for the theory and practice of modern architecture. Gropius and his followers declared that their style of design, which in time came to be called "international," was the only one that permitted an honest application of new material—chromium, glass, steel, and concrete.

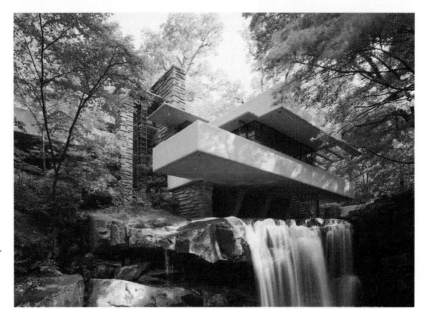

Fallingwater, by Frank Lloyd Wright (1867–1959). This most famous example of Wright's "organic architecture" is perched atop a waterfall. The pattern of the house conforms to the natural surroundings.

Gropius was one of the multitude of German intellectuals—both Jewish and non-Jewish—to leave their country after Hitler's rise to power. Nazism had its own cultural aesthetic. Functionalism, which celebrated the qualities of material, line, and proportion, had no place in a Nazi regime, where the arts were obliged to advertise the virtues of the state, its tradition, and the aspirations of its people. Instead of Gropius, Hitler had Albert Speer, an architect of unimpressive talents, who produced for him grandiose designs whose vacuous pretentiousness was an unconscious

Contrasting Architectural Styles in Germany between the Wars. Left: The Bauhaus, by Walter Gropius (1883–1969). This school in Dessau, Germany, is a starkly functional prototype of the interwar "international style." Right: The Chancellery in Berlin, by Albert Speer (1905–1981). Note the massive qualities of the Nazi state style.

parody of Nazi ideology. Atonality in music was banished along with functionalism in architecture, to be replaced by a state-sponsored revival of the mystical and heroic nationalism of Wagner.

Art was an important part of the new and cultural arm of the regimes of Soviet Russia, Italy, and Germany: propaganda, the practice of indoctrinating populations to believe only what governments wished them to believe. It mattered not at all that belief was based on falsehood, as in the "superiority of the Aryan race," for example. If it served the interest of the state, it was disseminated as truth. Never before had so many of the world's people been able to read. Nineteenth- and twentieth-century governments had encouraged literacy, fearing an ignorant working class as a revolutionary threat. Now authoritarian regimes used education unashamedly as a means of propagating a party line. "All effective propaganda has to limit itself to a very few points and to use them like slogans," Hitler wrote in *Mein Kampf.* "It has to confine itself to little and to repeat this eternally." Books critical of the state were banned, their places on school and library shelves taken by others specifically written to glorify the present leadership. Youth programs instructed children in the virtues of discipline and loyalty to the state. Mass gymnastic displays suggested the ease with which well-trained bodies could be made to respond to the military needs of the nation. Propagandizing was made more effective by the advent of mass-circulation publishing, the radio, and the motion picture. Newspapers, which printed only what the state wanted printed, reached a wider audience than ever before. Party political broadcasts, beamed into homes or blared through loudspeakers in town squares, by their constant repetitiveness made people begin to accept—if not believe—what they knew to be untrue. Films could transform German youths into Aryan gods and goddesses, as they could Russian collective farms into a worker's paradise. Sergei Eisenstein, the Russian director, rewrote Russian history on film to serve the ends of the Soviet state. Hitler commissioned the filmmaker Leni Riefenstahl to record a political rally staged by herself and Speer. The film, entitled *Triumph of the Will,* was a visual hymn to the Nordic race and the Nazi regime. And the comedian Charlie Chaplin riposted in his celebrated lampoon *The Great Dictator* (1940) an enormously successful parody of Nazi pomposities.

In Western democracies, although the media were not manipulated by the state as they were elsewhere, their effectiveness as propagandizers was nevertheless recognized and exploited. Advertising became an industry when manufacturers realized the mass markets that newspapers, magazines, and radio represented. Much that was printed and aired was trivialized by writers and editors who feared that serious or difficult material would antagonize the readers or listeners upon whom they depended for their livelihood. This is not to say that the new media were uniformly banal, or that artists and performers were unable to use them to make thoughtful protests. The film version of Steinbeck's *Grapes of Wrath,* directed by John Ford, though an exception to the normal run of escapist Hollywood comedies and adventures, was perhaps as stinging an indictment of capitalism as the novel, and it reached far more people. During these years popular culture, whatever else it was, remained a powerful and alarming new fact of life: powerful in terms of its vast audience; alarming because of its particular applicability as a means of controlling the minds of men and women.

SUMMARY POINTS

- In 1924 Lenin's Communist party established the USSR. To abolish capitalism and impose socialism Lenin's successor, Stalin, forcibly reorganized the Soviet economy, politics, and society, using violence, intimidation, and nationalist education.

- Italian fascism arose from the discontent with the outcome of World War I, and was dependent on Mussolini for leadership. Its doctrines were statism, nationalism, and militarism.

- The humiliation felt by Germany after World War I turned the population toward authoritative leadership to regain the world's respect. In Germany the discontented lower and middle classes rallied around Hitler, who glorified the homeland and the common folk, and stigmatized Jews, homosexuals, and political dissidents.

- In France, Britain, and the United States, conflicts between large businesses and the working class escalated, and the Great Depression (1929) caused even greater social unrest. Even the New Deal programs in the United States could not solve the unemployment crisis.

- Post–World War I intellectuals presented the world with troubling new theories. Scientists presented new evidence of a finite, fragmented universe, dividing even the atom; philosophers developed the lonely notion of existentialism; and writers and artists expressed alienation, cynicism, and depression, creating works that jarred middle-class assumptions about the meaning of art.

SELECTED READINGS

GENERAL

Cohen-Solal, Annie, *Sartre: A Life,* New York, 1987. An excellent biography of the French existentialist.

Collaer, P., *A History of Modern Music,* Cleveland, Oh 1961.

Galbraith, John Kenneth, *The Great Crash, 1929,* Boston, 1955. An entertaining and informative account by the celebrated economist.

Gamow, George, *Thirty Years That Shook Physics,* Mineola, N.Y., 1966. Deals with the Einstein revolution.

Hamilton, George H., *Painting and Sculpture in Europe, 1880–1940,* Baltimore, 1967. An accounting of the major artistic movements of the first half of the twentieth century.

Hartnack, Justus, *Wittgenstein and Modern Philosophy,* Garden City, N.Y., 1965. Clear introduction to a difficult subject.

Hitchcock, H. R., *Architecture: 19th and 20th Centuries,* London, 1958. Thorough and well-written survey.

Kahler, Erich, *The Tower and the Abyss,* New York, 1957. A survey of the arts in the context of contemporary culture.

Kindleberger, C. P., *The World in Depression, 1929–1939,* Berkeley, 1973. A first-rate study of the worldwide aspects of the slump.

Laqueur, Walter, and George L. Mosse, eds., *The Left-Wing Intellectuals between the Wars, 1919–1939,* New York, 1966. Essays by modern historians.

Masur, Gerhard, *Prophets of Yesterday,* New York, 1961. A useful intellectual history of the interwar period.

Shapiro, Theda, *Painters and Politics: The European Avant-Garde and Society, 1900–1925,* New York, 1976. An analysis of the political and social attitudes of a revolutionary generation in the arts.

Sontag, Raymond V., *A Broken World, 1919–1939,* New York, 1971. A fine detailed survey of interwar Europe.

THE SOVIET UNION

Carr, E. H., *The Russian Revolution: From Lenin to Stalin,* New York, 1979. A distillation from his ten-volume *History of Soviet Russia.* A fine starting point for the general reader.

Conquest, Robert, *The Great Terror,* New York, 1968. Analysis of the Stalin purges.

Daniels, Robert V., *The Conscience of the Revolution,* Cambridge, Mass., 1960. Discusses the opposition to Bolshevism in the 1920s.

Deutscher, Isaac, *The Prophet Armed,* London, 1954; *The Prophet Unarmed,* London, 1959; *The Prophet Outcast,* London, 1963. A superb three-volume biography of Leon Trotsky.

Fitzpatrick, Sheila, *The Cultural Front: Power and Culture in Revolutionary Russia,* Ithaca, N.Y., 1992. Focuses on the relationship between the Communist party and the Russian intelligentsia over three decades.

Hosking, Geoffrey, *The First Socialist Society: A History of the Soviet Union from Within,* 2d ed., Cambridge, Mass., 1993. Deals with the Soviet leadership, but also with the interaction of various social, religious, and national groups during the Stalinist era and after.

Tucker, Robert C., *Stalin as Revolutionary, 1879–1929: A Study in History and Personality,* New York, 1973. An excellent account of Stalin's rise to power, and of the change from revolution to dictatorship in Russia.

GERMANY AND ITALY

Bessel, Richard, *Life in the Third Reich,* New York, 1987. Essays analyzing various aspects of life under Nazi rule.

Bracher, Karl Dietrich, *The German Dictatorship: The Origins, Structure, and Effects of National Socialism,* New York, 1970. A penetrating and exhaustive study of the Nazi state by a political scientist.

Bridenthal, Renate, ed., *When Biology Becomes Destiny: Women in Weimar and Nazi Germany,* New York, 1984. Analysis of the position of women, particularly their progressive subjugation to national ideals.

Bullock, Alan, *Hitler: A Study in Tyranny,* rev. ed., New York, 1971.

Carsten, F. L., *Revolution in Central Europe, 1918–1919,* London, 1972. A useful treatment of the postwar revolts.

Eyck, Erich, *History of the Weimar Republic,* 2 vols., Cambridge, Mass., 1962. A sympathetic account by a prominent German liberal.

Gay, Peter, *Weimar Culture: The Outsider as Insider,* New York, 1970. Examines the failure of commitment to the Weimar Republic by German intellectuals.

Hale, Oron J., *The Captive Press in the Third Reich,* Princeton, 1964. Examines the manner in which totalitarianism invades journalism.

Koonz, Claudia, *Mothers in the Fatherland: Women, the Family, and Nazi Politics,* New York, 1987. Demonstrates the degree to which Nazi policies were shaped with regard to women and their role.

Lyttelton, Adrian, *The Seizure of Power: Fascism in Italy, 1919–1929,* 2d ed., London, 1988. An excellent introduction.

Mack Smith, Denis, *Mussolini's Roman Empire,* New York, 1976. An able treatment of Italian fascism by the foremost English scholar of Italy.

Payne, Stanley G., *Fascism: A Comparative Approach toward a Definition,* Madison, Wisc., 1980. A balanced review of various European fascist movements.

Rogger, Hans, and Eugen Weber, eds., *The European Right: A Historical Profile,* Berkeley, 1965. A country-by-country survey.

Rothschild, Joseph, *East Central Europe between the Two World Wars,* Seattle, 1975. An authoritative survey; does not include Austria.

Schoenbaum, David, *Hitler's Social Revolution: Class and Status in Nazi Germany, 1933–39,* Garden City, N.Y., 1966. Hitler's impact upon the various social and economic classes in Germany.

Stern, Fritz, *The Politics of Cultural Despair: A Study in the Rise of Germanic Ideology,* Berkeley, 1961. Assesses the way in which cultural beliefs influence politics.

Tannenbaum, Edward R., *The Fascist Experience: Italian Society and Culture, 1922–1945,* New York, 1972. A thorough discussion and analysis of the effect of fascism on Italian society.

Zeman, Z. A. B., *Nazi Propaganda,* New York, 1973. Examines an important bulwark of the authoritarian state.

THE DEMOCRACIES

Bullock, Alan, *The Life and Times of Ernest Bevin: Trade Union Leader, 1881–1940,* London, 1960. An excellent study of the British trade unionist and the political and social history of Britain between the wars.

Burns, James M., *Roosevelt: The Lion and the Fox,* New York, 1956.

Colton, Joel, *Léon Blum: Humanist in Politics,* New York, 1966. A first-rate biography that illuminates the history of the Popular Front.

Graves, Robert, and Alan Hodge, *The Long Weekend: A Social History of Great Britain, 1918–1939,* London, 1940. A striking portrait of England in the interwar years.

Greene, Nathanael, *From Versailles to Vichy: The Third Republic, 1919–1940,* Arlington Heights, Ill., 1970. Valuable survey.

Hughes, H. Stuart, *The Obstructed Path: French Social Thought in the Years of Desperation, 1930–1960,* New York, 1968. Analysis of major French thinkers.

Jackson, Julia, *The Popular Front in France: Defending Democracy, 1934–1958,* New York, 1988. The anti-fascist alliance of the Left, its policies, and culture.

Kent, Susan, *Making Peace: The Reconstruction of Gender in Postwar Britain,* Princeton, 1993. The effect of the war on women and their position in society.

Leuchtenburg, W. E., *Franklin Roosevelt and the New Deal, 1932–1940,* New York, 1964. A good introduction.

Mowat, Charles L., *Britain between the Wars, 1918–1940,* Chicago, 1955. A detailed political and social history, especially valuable for its extensive bibliographical footnotes.

Skidelsky, Robert, *John Maynard Keynes,* vol. 1 & 2, New York, 1986. The most recent and best account of Keynes's life and work.

Taylor, A. J. P., *English History, 1914–1945,* New York, 1965. The best survey of the period; witty, provocative, insightful.

Weber, Eugen, *Action Française: Royalism and Reaction in Twentieth Century France,* Stanford, 1962. The best study of this protofascist movement.

SOURCE MATERIALS

Cole, G. D. H., and M. I. Cole, *The Condition of Britain,* London, 1937. A contemporary analysis by English socialists.

Ehrenburg, Ilya, *Memoirs, 1921–1941,* New York, 1964. The intellectual at work within the Stalinist regime.

Greene, Nathanael, comp., *European Socialism since World War I,* Chicago, 1971. A collection of contemporary accounts.

Gruber, H., *International Communism in the Era of Lenin: A Documentary History,* Greenwich, Conn., 1967. A very useful collection of primary materials.

Hitler, Adolf, *Mein Kampf,* New York, 1962. Hitler's 1925 autobiography. Contains his version of history and his vision for the future. Especially important for his insight into the nature of the masses and the use of propaganda.

Noakes, Jeremy, and Geoffrey Pridham, *Documents on Nazism, 1919–1945,* New York, 1975. An excellent sourcebook; comprehensive and annotated.

Orwell, George, *The Road to Wigan Pier,* New York, 1972. Vivid description of Britain's interwar poverty and class system by an independent-minded socialist.

Scott, John, *Behind the Urals: An American Worker in Russia's City of Steel,* ed. Stephen Kotkin, Bloomington, Ind., 1989. An account by a sympathetic U.S. citizen, written in the early 1940s, of his experience in the recently founded industrial city of Magnitogorsk.

Silone, Ignazio, *Bread and Wine,* rev. ed., tr. H. Ferguson, New York, 1965. A moving account of the effects of Italian fascism.

Speer, Albert, *Inside the Third Reich,* New York, 1964. The self-serving but informative memoirs of one of the leaders of Nazi Germany.

Tucker, Robert C., ed., *The Great Purge Trial,* New York, 1965. An annotated edition of the transcript of one of the Soviet "show-trials" that so puzzled Western observers.

CHAPTER 29

THE SECOND WORLD WAR

The President [Roosevelt] and the Prime Minister [Churchill], after a complete
survey of the world situation, are more than ever determined that peace can
come to the world only by a total elimination of German and Japanese war
power. This involves the simple formula of placing the objective of this war in
terms of an unconditional surrender by Germany, Italy, and Japan.
—FRANKLIN D. ROOSEVELT, Casablanca, January 24, 1943

I N SEPTEMBER 1939, Europe was drawn again into a general war.
The peace of 1919–1920 proved to be no more than an armistice; once
more millions of people were locked in a conflict whose devastation
surpassed any that had occurred before. As had happened in 1914–1918,
the new struggle soon became worldwide. Although the Second World
War was not merely a continuation of, or a sequel to, the First, the simi-
larity in causes and characteristics was more than superficial. Both were
precipitated by threats to the balance of power, and both were conflicts
between peoples, entire nations, rather than between governments. On
the other hand, there were notable differences between the two conflicts.
The methods of warfare in the Second World War had little in common
with those of the earlier conflict. Trench warfare was superseded by bombing and by sudden aerial (blitzkrieg) attacks, with highly mobile armies,
on both civilian populations and military installations. Because whole
populations were now vulnerable to the ravages of warfare, the distinction between those on the battlefield and those at home was more completely obliterated in the Second World War than it had been in the First.
Finally, this war was not greeted with the almost universal, naïve enthusiasm that had marked the outbreak of the other. Men and women still remembered the horrors of the First World War. They entered the Second
with determination, but also with a keener appreciation of the frightful
devastation that war could bring than their predecessors had possessed.

A comparison of the two world wars

THE CAUSES OF THE WAR

The causes of the Second World War related to the failure of the peace
terms of 1919–1920. Those terms, while understandable in view of the
passions and hatreds engendered by the First World War, created almost
as many problems as they solved. By yielding to the demands of the

Defects of the peace treaties

victors for annexation of territory and the creation of satellite states, the peacemakers sowed new seeds of bitterness and conflict. By proclaiming the principle of self-determination while acquiescing in the distribution of national minorities behind alien frontiers, the treaties raised expectations while at the same time frustrating them. Perhaps most important, by imposing harsh terms on Germany and undermining German autonomy, the treaty-makers gave the Germans what seemed to many to be legitimate grievances by depriving them of their rightful share of international power and saddling them with the entire burden of war "guilt."

Power politics were a second cause of war. Although Woodrow Wilson and other sponsors of the League of Nations had acclaimed the league as a means of eliminating power struggles, it did nothing of the sort. It merely substituted a new and more precarious balance for the old. The signatures on the peace treaties had scarcely dried when the victors began to construct new alliances to maintain their supremacy. A neutralized zone consisting of the Baltic states, Poland, and Rumania was created as a buffer against the Soviet Union. A "Little Entente" composed of Czechoslovakia, Yugoslavia, and Rumania was established to prevent a revival of Austrian power. These combinations, together with Franco-Belgian and Franco-Polish alliances, isolated Germany. Even the league itself was fundamentally an alliance of the victors against the vanquished. That there would be fears and anxieties over a disturbance of the new power arrangement was natural. The first sign of such a disturbance appeared in 1922 when Germany and the Soviet Union negotiated the Treaty of Rapallo. Though disguised as a trade agreement, it opened the way for political and, according to some accounts, even military collaboration between the two states.

Diplomats made various attempts to preserve or restore international amity during the 1920s and 1930s. Some saw in disarmament the most promising means of achieving their purpose. Accordingly, a succession of conferences was called in the hope of at least limiting a race to rearm. In 1925 representatives of the chief European powers met at Locarno and acted on the suggestion of the German and French foreign ministers, Gustav Stresemann and Aristide Briand, that Germany and France pledge themselves to respect the Rhine frontiers as established in the Versailles treaty. They agreed also that they would never go to war against each other except in "legitimate defense." More widely celebrated than the Locarno agreements was the Pact of Paris, or Kellogg-Briand Pact of 1928. Its purpose was to outlaw war as an international crime. Eventually, nearly all the nations of the world signed this agreement renouncing war as "an instrument of national policy" and providing that the settlement of international disputes "of whatever nature or of whatever origin" should never be sought "except by peaceful means." Neither the Locarno Agreements nor the Pact of Paris was much more than a pious gesture. The signatory nations adopted them with so many reservations and exceptions in favor of "vital interests" that they could never be effective instruments for preserving peace. Had the League of Nations been better organized, it might have relieved some of the tensions and prevented clashes between nations still unwilling to relinquish their absolute sovereignty. Yet it was not a league of all nations, since both Germany and the Soviet Union were excluded for much of the interwar period, and the United States was not a member.

Economic conditions were a third important cause of the outbreak of war. The huge reparations imposed upon the Germans, and the French occupation of much of Germany's industrial heartland, helped, as we have seen, to retard Germany's economic recovery and bring on the debilitating inflation of the 1920s. The depression of the 1930s contributed to the coming of the war in several ways. It intensified economic nationalism. Baffled by problems of unemployment and business stagnation, governments resorted to high tariffs in an attempt to preserve the home market for their own producers. The depression was also responsible for a marked increase in armaments production, which was seen as a means of reducing unemployment. Despite the misgivings of some within the governments of Britain and France, Germany was allowed to rearm. Armaments expansion, on a large scale, was first undertaken by Germany about 1935, with the result that unemployment was substantially reduced and business boomed. Other nations followed the German example, not simply as a way of boosting their economies, but in response to Nazi military power. The depression helped as well to produce a new wave of militant expansionism directed toward the conquest of neighboring territories as a means of solving economic problems. Japan took the lead in 1931 with the invasion of Manchuria. The decline of Japanese exports of raw silk and cotton cloth meant that the nation did not have adequate foreign currency holdings to pay for needed imports of coal, iron, and other minerals. Japanese militarists were thus furnished with a convenient pretext for seizing Manchuria, where supplies of these commodities could then be purchased with Japanese, rather than foreign, currency. Mussolini, in part to distract Italians from the domestic problems brought on by economic depression, invaded and annexed Ethiopia in 1935–1936. Finally,

Economic conditions

The Krupp Shipworks in Germany. Seen here are German submarines in the final stages of assembly.

the depression was primarily responsible for the triumph of Nazism, whose expansionist policies contributed directly to the outbreak of war.

Nationalism was a further cause of the general discontent that helped increase the chances for world war. In eastern Europe, national and ethnic minorities remained alienated from the sovereign states into which the treaty-makers had placed them. This was particularly the case for the Sudetenland Germans, who had been included in the newly created state of Czechoslovakia. That country could in fact boast no national majority, including as it did Czechs, Slovaks, Poles, Ruthenians, and Hungarians, as well as Germans. Although it possessed an enlightened policy of minority self-government, the patchwork state of Czechoslovakia remained unstable. And its instability was to prove a key factor as the tensions mounted in the late 1930s.

A final cause of war was the policy of "appeasement" that was pursued by the Western democracies in the face of German, Italian, and Japanese aggression. The appeasers' strategy was grounded in three commonly held assumptions. The first was that the outbreak of another war was unthinkable. With the memory of the slaughter of 1914–1918 fresh in their minds, many in the West embraced pacifism, or at any rate adopted an attitude that kept them from realistically addressing the implications of Nazi and fascist policies and programs. Second, many in Britain and the United States argued that Germany had been mistreated in the Versailles treaty, that the Germans had legitimate grievances that should be acknowledged and resolved. Finally, the appeasers were, for the most part, staunch anticommunists. They believed that by assisting Germany to regain its former military and economic power, they were constructing a bulwark to halt the westward advance of Soviet communism. When Japan invaded Manchuria, the West refused to impose sanctions against the Japanese through the League of Nations, arguing that Japan, too, could serve as a counterweight to the Soviet Union.

Hitler took advantage of this generally tolerant attitude to advance the expansionist ambitions of Germany. As the country rearmed, Hitler played upon his people's sense of shame and betrayal, proclaiming their right to regain their former power within the world. In 1933, he removed Germany from the League of Nations (it had been admitted in 1926) and thus from any obligation to adhere to its declarations. In 1935 Hitler tore up the disarmament provisions of the Treaty of Versailles, announcing the revival of conscription and the return to universal military training. In 1936 he repudiated the Locarno agreements and invaded the Rhineland. Britain and France did nothing to stop him, as they had done nothing to prevent Mussolini's invasion and conquest of Ethiopia the previous year. Hitler's move tipped the balance of power in Germany's favor. While the Rhineland remained demilitarized and German industry in the Ruhr valley unprotected, France had held the upper hand. Now it no longer did so.

In 1936 civil war broke out in Spain; a series of weak republican governments had proved unable to prevent the country's political disintegration. Although they had signed a pact of nonintervention with the other

Guernica (1937), by Pablo Picasso (1881–1973). This painting, a protest against the bombing of an undefended city during the Spanish Civil War, has come to be recognized as one of the century's most profound antiwar statements.

Western powers, Hitler and Mussolini both sent troops and equipment to assist the forces of the rebel fascist commander, Francisco Franco. The Soviet Union countered with aid to the communist troops serving under the banner of the Spanish republic. Again, Britain and France failed to act decisively. The Spanish Civil War lasted three years, with the forces of the fascists finally victorious over those of the republicans. The conflict engaged the commitment of many young European and American leftists and intellectuals, who saw it as a test of the West's determination to resist authoritarian dictatorships. The fighting was brutal; aerial bombardment of civilians and troops was employed for the first time on a large scale. Because of this, the Spanish Civil War has often been seen as a "dress rehearsal" for the much larger struggle that was shortly to follow. The war also served to confirm Hitler's belief that if Britain, France, and the Soviet Union did decide to attempt to contain fascism, they would have a difficult time concerting their policies—another reason, indeed, why Britain and France remained content to do nothing.

In March of 1938, Hitler annexed Austria, declaring it his intention to bring all Germans into his Reich. Once more, there was no official reaction from the West. Hitler's next target was the Sudetenland in Czechoslovakia, which had a large ethnically German population. With Austria now a part of Germany, Czechoslovakia was almost entirely surrounded by its hostile expansionist neighbor. Hitler declared that the Sudetenland was a natural part of the Reich and that he intended to occupy it. The British prime minister, Neville Chamberlain, decided to negotiate, but on Hitler's terms. On September 29, Hitler agreed to meet with Chamberlain, Premier Édouard Daladier of France, and Mussolini in a four-power conference in Munich. The result was another capitulation by France and Britain. Ignoring the vital interests of a nation whose territory

Munich and after

Europe on the Eve of World War II, September 1, 1939

Axis-aligned
Allies-aligned
Neutral

ATLANTIC OCEAN

ICELAND (Denmark)

FAEROES (Denmark)

SHETLANDS

ORKNEYS

HEBRIDES

SCOTLAND

Edinburgh

NORTHERN IRELAND

Belfast ★

IRELAND

Dublin ●

Liverpool ●

Manchester ●

WALES

ENGLAND

London ★

UNITED KINGDOM

English Channel

NORTH SEA

NETHER-LANDS

Amsterdam ★

Brussels ★

BELGIUM

LUXEMBURG

Paris ★

FRANCE

Seine R.

Loire R.

Rhône R.

Garonne R.

BAY OF BISCAY

Bordeaux ●

Lyons ●

Marseilles ●

ANDORRA

Ebro R.

Barcelona ●

BALEARIC IS. (Spain)

Madrid ★

SPAIN

Seville ●

Algeciras ●

Tagus R.

Douro R.

Lisbon ★

PORTUGAL

Strait of Gibraltar

Tangier

SPANISH MOROCCO

MOROCCO (France)

ALGERIA (France)

Algiers ●

TUNISIA (France)

Tunis ●

MEDITERRANEAN

SARDINIA (Italy)

CORSICA (France)

Geneva ●

SWITZ.

Berne ★

Milan ●

Venice ●

ITALY

Rome ★

Tiber R.

MALTA (Br.)

SICILY (Italy)

ADRIATIC SEA

ALBANIA

Tirana ★

YUGOSLAVIA

Belgrade ★

HUNGARY

Budapest ★

AUSTRIA

Vienna ●

Munich ●

Danube R.

GERMANY

Prague ●

Berlin ★

Cologne ●

Hamburg ●

Elbe R.

Oder R.

Rhine R.

SLOVAKIA

Warsaw ★

POLAND

Vistula R.

EAST PRUSSIA (Germany)

Danzig ●

Memel ●

LITHUANIA

Kaunas ★

LATVIA

Riga ★

ESTONIA

Tallinn ★

BALTIC SEA

Gulf of Finland

Leningrad ●

Lake Ladoga

FINLAND

Helsinki ★

Gulf of Bothnia

SWEDEN

Stockholm ★

NORWAY

Oslo ★

Skagerrak

Kattegat

DENMARK

Copenhagen ★

WHITE SEA

Archangel ●

Moscow ★

Volga R.

UNION OF SOVIET SOCIALIST REPUBLICS

Kharkov ●

Don R.

Stalingrad ●

CASPIAN SEA

Kiev ●

Dnieper R.

Odessa ●

Dniester R.

RUMANIA

Bucharest ★

Danube R.

BULGARIA

Sofia ★

BLACK SEA

Sea of Azov

TURKEY

Ankara ★

Istanbul ●

AEGEAN SEA

GREECE

Athens ★

CRETE (Greece)

DODECANESE IS. (Italy)

CYPRUS (Gt. Britain)

SYRIA (Fr.)

LEBANON (Fr.)

Damascus ●

PALESTINE (Br.)

ARMENIA

IRAN

IRAQ

Baghdad ●

0   200   400 miles

The Munich Conference, 1938. Left: Prime Minister Chamberlain of Britain and Hitler during the Munich conference. Right: Chamberlain addressing a crowd on his return from the Munich conference.

the Treaty of Versailles had guaranteed, the four negotiators bargained away a major slice of Czechoslovakia, while that country's representatives were left to await their fate outside the conference room. Chamberlain returned to England proclaiming "peace in our time." Hitler soon proved that fatuous boast untrue. In March 1939 he invaded what was left of Czechoslovakia and established a puppet regime in its capital, Prague, the first occupation by Hitler's Germany of a non-German territory. This action convinced British public opinion of the foolhardiness of appeasement. Chamberlain, compelled to shift his policies dramatically, guaranteed the sovereignty of the two states now directly in Hitler's path: Poland and Rumania. France followed suit.

Meanwhile, the appeasement policies of Britain and France had fueled Stalin's fears that the Western democracies might strike a deal with Germany at Soviet expense by diverting Nazi expansion eastward. This, along with the suspicion that they might make unreliable allies, convinced Stalin that he must look elsewhere for security. Tempted by the traditional Soviet desire for territory in Poland, and promised a share of both Poland and the Baltic states by Hitler, Stalin signed a nonaggression pact with the Nazis in August 1939. In going to Munich, Britain and France had put their interests first; the Soviet Union would now look after its own.

> Nazi-Soviet pact

THE OUTBREAK OF HOSTILITIES

Following the takeover of Czechoslovakia, and despite Chamberlain's guarantee, Hitler demanded the abolition of the Polish Corridor, a narrow strip of territory connecting Poland with the Baltic Sea and dividing East Prussia from the rest of Germany. The corridor contained a large

> Beginning of the war

The Beginning of the Second World War. A German armored division invades Poland.

German population, which Hitler declared must be reunited with the Fatherland. Judging Britain and France by past performance he believed their pledges to Poland worthless. With the Soviets now in his camp, he expected that Poland would quickly capitulate, and that the Western allies would back down once more as they had done at Munich. When Poland stood firm, Hitler attacked. On September 1, 1939, German tanks crossed the Polish border. Britain and France sent a joint warning to Germany to cease its aggression. There was no reply; on September 3, Britain and France declared war against Germany.

The blitzkrieg

The conquest of Poland was sharp and quick. In less than four weeks the Polish armies had been routed by combined air and tank attacks, Warsaw had been captured, and the chiefs of the Polish government had fled to Rumania. For some months after that the war resolved itself into a kind of siege, a "phony war" or "sitzkrieg," as it was sometimes called. Such fighting as did occur was largely confined to submarine warfare, aerial raids on naval bases, and occasional battles between naval vessels. In the spring of 1940 the sitzkrieg was suddenly transformed into a blitzkrieg, or "lightning war." The Germans struck blows at Norway, Denmark, Luxembourg, Belgium, the Netherlands, and France, conquering them in short order and driving the British and French forces back against the English Channel at Dunkirk in Belgium. Despite heavy German air attacks, the British were able to evacuate more than 300,000 troops, many of them in commercial and pleasure boats that had been pressed into emergency service. Northern France, including Paris, was occupied by the Germans. In the south, a puppet government loyal to the

Germans was established at Vichy under the leadership of the aged First World War hero, Marshal Henri Philippe Pétain.

Before launching an invasion across the Channel, the Nazis decided to reduce Britain's military strength and civilian will by air raids. From August 1940 to June 1941, in the so-called Battle of Britain, thousands of planes dropped millions of tons of bombs on British ports, industrial centers, and air defenses throughout the country. Despite the fact that whole sections of cities were laid in ruins and more than 40,000 civilians killed, the British held firm. Winston Churchill had by this time succeeded Neville Chamberlain as prime minister of Britain. A maverick Conservative who had served in Britain's First World War government as a Liberal, Churchill was not trusted by his party's leadership, particularly since he had been one of the few who had spoken out in favor of British rearmament during the years of appeasement. Now that his warnings had proved true, he was given direction of the war as head of a national government composed of ministers from the Conservative, Liberal, and Labour parties. Churchill, an exceedingly compelling orator, used the radio to persuade his countrymen and women—and the rest of the free world—that Britain must not, and would not, surrender to the Nazis. His friendship with President Roosevelt, and the latter's conviction that the United States must come to Britain's aid, resulted in the shipment of military equipment and ships to the British under the Lend-Lease Act passed by the U.S. Congress in 1941.

Meanwhile, Germany moved eastward into the Balkans, subduing the Rumanians, Hungarians, Bulgarians, and Yugoslavs. The Italians, less successful in their campaigns in Greece and North Africa, required German assistance to accomplish their missions. Scornful of Mussolini's military inadequacies, Churchill called him Hitler's "jackal." Frustrated in his

The German invasion of Russia

Left: **London during the Blitz.** A vivid impression of the devastation that the British capital suffered during the Battle of Britain, which lasted from August 1940 to June 1941. Right: **French Refugees.** These French refugees were driven from their homes during the early years of the Nazi occupation.

Pearl Harbor, December 7, 1941. This photo shows an aerial view of the harbor following the Japanese raid on what President Franklin D. Roosevelt declared was "a date that will live in infamy."

attempt to subjugate Britain, Hitler broke with his erstwhile ally the Soviet Union and turned eastward, on June 22, 1941, with a massive invasion. Before the end of the year his armies had smashed their way to the gates of Moscow but never actually succeeded in capturing it. The defense of Moscow by the Soviet armies marked one of the war's important early turning points.

The war was converted into a global conflict when Japan struck at Pearl Harbor in Hawaii on December 7 of the same year. The Japanese had been involved in a costly war with China since 1937. To wage it successfully they needed the oil, rubber, and extensive food resources of the Netherlands Indies, the Malay Peninsula, and Southeast Asia. They had allied with Germany in 1940. (Germany, Italy, and Japan were together known as the Axis powers, a name derived from the Rome-Berlin diplomatic axis formed in the 1930s.) Now, before attacking south, they considered it necessary to secure their position to the rear by crushing American naval and air power on the base of Pearl Harbor. The next day the United States Congress (as well as Canada and Great Britain) recognized a state of war with Japan, and on December 11 Germany and its allies also declared war upon the United States.

This second global war was a total war to an even greater extent than was the case in the First World War. Entire populations were mobilized as

Pearl Harbor

Total war

part of the war effort: governments imposed the rationing of food and clothing and the regulation of manpower and production quotas demanded that factories produce around the clock. In the Soviet Union, all men between the ages of sixteen and fifty-five and all women between the ages of sixteen and forty-five were pressed into service, either in the armed forces or on the home front. The Germans destroyed much of the Soviet Union's industrial plant and existing war matériel in the early months of the war—over 90 percent of the Soviet Union's tanks, for example. To produce what was necessary, factories were rebuilt in the security of the Ural mountain region, and whole populations moved there to work in them.

In countries conquered and occupied by the Germans and Italians, the Axis powers installed administrations willing to follow their commands without question. (Vidkun Quisling, the Norwegian Nazi leader, made his name synonymous with the word "traitor.") Life for civilians was harsh at best. Rations in occupied France, for example, were less than half the amount considered to be a healthy minimum. Civilians from occupied countries were transported to Germany to work there in factories and labor battalions. In France and elsewhere, Resistance movements emerged, composed of men and women of various political persuasions united in their determination to assist the Allies in driving the Axis powers from their native lands. By transmitting intelligence reports, aiding prisoners to escape, distributing newspapers to counter official propaganda, and undertaking acts of direct sabotage of military and industrial targets, these groups helped the Allied cause immeasurably. The success of the Normandy invasion was in part the result of information concerning German military emplacements sent to Britain by the French Resistance.

The Resistance

The war brought devastation in the form of street fighting and air bombardment to most of the major urban centers of Europe. The Allies proved to be fully as ruthless and even more efficient than the Axis powers in this regard. After some debate, British and American strategists abandoned pinpoint bombing in favor of the nighttime aerial bombardment of entire cities. The result was the deliberate fire-bombing of civilian populations, climaxing in Europe in early 1945 with the brutal obliteration of Dresden, a German city without significant industry and filled with refugees. These attacks were equaled by the German bombing of French, Belgian, Dutch, Russian, and British cities and civilian populations.

Bombing of cities

Ghastly as was the destruction meted out by the armed forces to each other and to civilians, none of it matched in premeditated, obscene horror the systematic persecution by the Nazis of whole Jewish populations, not only in Germany itself but in occupied countries as well. At first, Jews were part of a larger array of victims—particularly in Poland, where clergy, homosexuals, gypsies, and others were either systematically murdered and buried in mass graves, or drafted into battalions of slave laborers to produce war matériel. More than 30,000 civilians, mostly Jews, were slaughtered in the Soviet Union after the fall of Kiev in 1941.

Nazi persecution of Jews

Polish Jews, evicted from the Warsaw Ghetto, on their way to a concentration camp.

The concentration camps

By 1942, however, a new policy, reflecting Hitler's increasingly furious anti-Semitism, proposed a "final solution" to the "problem" of Jewish populations throughout Germany and its conquered territories. Prior to the war, in the name of social improvement, Nazi doctors had participated in the so-called T4 project, which resulted in the killing of more than 200,000 elderly and handicapped people by means of carbon monoxide and other poisons. Those methods were now brought to bear on a far larger scale to exterminate the Jews. Camps were set up in Germany, Austria, Czechoslovakia, and Poland, to which hundreds of thousands of Jews were sent. Children—and the mothers who chose to remain with them—were automatically doomed. Others were permitted to remain alive to labor in prison factories, until illness or exhaustion condemned them to death as well. Auschwitz, one of the most notorious of the camps, had the capacity to cremate as many as 1.7 million bodies per year. Those who remained alive did so despite all but impossible odds, living on less than 500 calories per day, prey to sadistic medical "experiments" and brutalization by prison personnel. And yet, despite their treatment, many inmates managed to retain the spark of humanity that distinguished them from their captors.

The Holocaust

Ultimately, six million men, women, and children lost their lives in what has come to be known as the Holocaust. Although the Allies knew of the existence of the death camps, they refused to bomb them, for reasons that have never been made entirely clear. Equally unresolved is the frightening question of why the population of an apparently highly civilized nation such as Germany either actively participated or knowingly acquiesced in the terrifying and grisly extermination of its fellow citizens.

Allied victories in North Africa and Italy

After the United States entered the war, events turned slowly but inexorably against the forces of Germany, Italy, and Japan. Churchill and Roosevelt, meeting shortly after the United States's entry into the war, agreed that victory in the West would be their first priority. As an initial step toward that goal, the British succeeded in halting the North African advance of Germany's brilliant tank commander General Erwin Rommel, who had driven the British back across the Sahara to the Egyptian border. That victory was the prelude to a joint Anglo-American invasion of North Africa in November 1942. The success of this first major combined Allied offensive led in turn to further Mediterranean campaigns in 1943, first in Sicily and then in Italy. Mussolini's government was overthrown, and his successors sued for peace. The Germans, however, sent troops into Italy and resurrected Mussolini as the ruler of a puppet state in the north, where he remained a virtual prisoner of the Nazis until his death at the hands of his countrymen at the time of the general defeat of the Axis powers in Europe. Despite Allied attempts to break the German grip on the peninsula, the Nazi forces continued to hold central and northern Italy until the spring of 1945.

In eastern Europe, meanwhile, the Germans had continued to press the war against the Soviets, turning in 1942 to the south and the rich agricultural and industrial areas of the Ukraine, the Donets Basin, and the Caucasus oilfields. The German advance was stopped at Stalingrad, in a military struggle of great strategic and symbolic importance for both sides. The battle saw 300,000 Germans for a time in control of the city, then enclosed by the counterattacking Soviets in a pincers movement, and eventually, by the time of their surrender in February 1943, reduced to fewer than half their original number. The loss of the battle of Stalingrad compelled the Germans to undertake a general retreat. By the spring of 1943, they were no further east than they had been the previous year.

> The battle of Stalingrad

Stalin continued to pressure his allies to open a second front in the west to relieve the concerted Nazi drive against the Soviet Union. The North African and Italian campaigns were a response to that plea. But not until June 1944 did Allied troops invade France. On June 6 (D-Day) a massive invasion force landed on the Normandy coast. Air superiority, plus a tremendous buildup of matériel and manpower, produced a series of successful advances and the liberation of Paris on August 25. Despite a final German assault in December 1944, the Allied armies penetrated deep into Germany itself by the early spring of 1945.

> The D-Day invasion

At the same time, Soviet troops were approaching from the east. On April 21, 1945, they hammered their way into the suburbs of Berlin. During the next ten days a savage battle raged amid the ruins and heaps of rubble. Adolf Hitler killed himself in the bomb-proof shelter of the Chancellery on April 30. On May 2 the heart of the city was captured, and the Soviet red banner flew from the Brandenburg Gate. On May 7 representatives of the German High Command signed a document of unconditional surrender, which was ratified in Berlin the next day.

> End of the war in Europe

The war in the Pacific came to an end four months later. Important victories won by the United States Navy against the Japanese at the battles of the Coral Sea and Midway in the spring of 1942 forestalled Japanese attempts to capture Australia and the Hawaiian Islands so as to deprive the United States of advance bases for a counteroffensive against Japan. Final

> The Pacific war

Left: **D-Day.** Cargo ships are seen pouring supplies ashore during the invasion of France on June 6, 1944. Balloon barrages float overhead to protect the ships from low-flying enemy planes. Right: **The German Surrender.** British Field Marshal Bernard Montgomery (seated, in beret) accepts the surrender of Germany's northern forces on May 4, 1945. Three days later, the entire German army surrendered.

Allied victory followed further naval battles, island assaults, and land battles in Southeast Asia. In June 1945, the Japanese island of Okinawa was taken, after eighty-two days of desperate fighting. The American forces now had a foothold less than 500 miles from the Japanese mainland. The government in Tokyo was anticipating an invasion and calling upon its citizens for supreme endeavors to meet the crisis.

The Holocaust. These German civilians were compelled to view the bodies of concentration camp victims at the Landesburg camp in 1945 as an American army officer lectures them on the horrors of the Nazis' "final solution."

View of Hiroshima after the First Atom Bomb Was Dropped, August 6, 1945.
This photo, taken one month later, shows the utter devastation of the city. Only a few steel and concrete buildings remained intact.

On July 26 the heads of the United States, British, and Chinese governments issued a joint proclamation calling upon Japan to surrender or be destroyed. In the absence of a reply the United States resolved to make use of a new and revolutionary weapon to end the war quickly. This was the atomic bomb, which could destroy entire cities and their inhabitants, a weapon developed in secrecy in the United States by scientists from Europe and America, some of whom were exiles from Nazi or fascist oppression.

Many high military and naval officers contended that use of the bomb was not necessary, on the assumption that Japan was already beaten. Harry Truman, who had succeeded Roosevelt following the latter's death in April 1945, decided otherwise. On August 6, a single atomic bomb was dropped on Hiroshima, completely obliterating about 60 percent of the city. Three days later a second bomb was dropped, this time on Nagasaki. President Truman warned that the United States would continue to use the atom bomb as long as might be necessary to bring Japan to its knees. On August 14, Tokyo transmitted to Washington an unconditional acceptance of Allied demands.

The atomic bomb

The atomic bomb and the war's end

THE PEACE SETTLEMENT

During the war the Allied leaders had come together on several occasions to discuss war aims and postwar goals. The public rhetoric of government propaganda spoke of the need for a world without conflict and of the right of all people to political self-determination, objectives expressed in the "Atlantic Charter" issued by Roosevelt and Churchill in August 1941, and in a declaration signed by twenty-six nations, including Britain, the United States, the Soviet Union, and China, the following year. Yet those

The question of war aims

worthy goals, like Wilson's earlier Fourteen Points, fell victim to the realities of international politics.

Stalin, Churchill, and Roosevelt met in two conferences that were of major importance in determining the shape and political complexion of postwar Europe. In both cases, tensions between the three major participants were to some degree glossed over in their desire to present a united front to the world. Yet those tensions were real. The focus of disagreement was central Europe, and particularly the future of Germany and Poland. Stalin insisted that the Soviet Union retain the Polish territory annexed in 1939 at the time of the Nazi-Soviet pact, an expression of his understandable desire to build a bulwark against any future German aggression, and a reflection of his unwillingness to see postwar Western influence extended too far in the Soviet Union's direction. His memories of Anglo-American participation in the attempt by White Russians to overthrow the newly created communist regime in 1919 (see p. 979) were matched by American perceptions of the Soviet Union as an expansionist and politically alien and dangerous regime. All three leaders were also confronted by conflicting plots and aspirations on the part of governments-in-exile from Nazi-occupied countries, and of extra-governmental Resistance groups—often led by communists—whose struggles to retain or to assume leadership in their homelands were exceeded only by their determination to oust the Germans.

When the three leaders met in Teheran in December 1943, they managed to put forward a declaration of unified purpose only by postponing the really knotty problems that confronted them. The invasion of France was agreed to for the following year; Stalin undertook to enter the war against Japan following the defeat of Germany. But on the question of Poland, only the most tentative agreement was reached regarding boundary lines, while the nature of the postwar Polish government was left for further negotiation.

By the time Stalin, Churchill, and Roosevelt met again, in February 1945 at Yalta, the military situation favored the Soviet Union's position. Soviet troops had occupied Poland the previous spring; they now held part of Czechoslovakia as well, and were poised to invade Germany. Once more the matter of Poland's future arose, as well as that of the composition of postwar regimes. A general declaration outlined plans for Soviet expansion westward into Poland, and the compensation of Poland with territory taken from the Germans. As to Poland's government, though communiqués spoke of the need for free elections there and elsewhere among the occupied countries, the fact remained that the Soviets had already established a communist government in Warsaw, and were unlikely to tolerate its replacement by an anticommunist faction still in London, whatever the results of an election. Yalta produced accord on several important issues: the establishment of a United Nations organization to keep the peace; the terms for Soviet entry into the Japanese war; the positioning of zones of Allied occupation in Germany and Austria; and agreement in principle to a policy of German reparation payments—though in

The Yalta Conference, 1945. From the left, Winston Churchill, Franklin Roosevelt, and Joseph Stalin, gathered for a press conference.

goods, production, and equipment rather than in gold, as had been the case after the First World War.

Little more than two months after Germany's surrender, the Allies met again, this time at Potsdam, a suburb of Berlin and the former residence of Prussian kings. Roosevelt had died shortly before the German surrender; his place at the conference was taken by his successor, Harry Truman. Churchill represented Britain until replaced, as the result of elections at home, by the new prime minister and Labour party leader, Clement Attlee. Stalin remained to negotiate for the Soviets. As at past conferences, less was settled than was allowed to remain unresolved. Peace treaties were to be prepared with the "recognized democratic governments" of previously occupied lands. Yet the question as to whether those governments set up by the Soviets in Poland and—by this time—elsewhere in eastern Europe were truly democratic was not settled. Polish boundaries were redrawn to conform to the general agreement reached at Yalta. An inter-Allied war tribunal was established to try major Nazi leaders for "war crimes." In November 1945, the trials began in Nuremberg, Germany. The following September, eighteen of the twenty-two defendants were found guilty and received sentences ranging from ten years' imprisonment to death.

The Potsdam conference

The Potsdam conference was shadowed by the East-West conflict that had darkened all the wartime meetings and was to do the same to international politics in the immediate postwar years. The division of Germany into four occupied zones—American, British, French, and Soviet—and the agreement to structure reparations payments on the basis of those zones rather than on a united Germany, forecast the unwillingness of either the Soviet Union or the Western powers to trust each other, or to

East-West tensions

The Potsdam Conference.
Churchill, a cigar in his mouth, is
seated in the back to the left; Stalin
is at the right; Truman is seated
with his back to the camera.

tolerate the extension of the other's influence in that country which, though devastated, still remained vital to the security and peace of Europe as a whole.

The treaty with Japan

The treaty with Japan, though it too produced disagreement between the Soviet Union and the West, did not reflect conflicts as immediate as those that characterized the European negotiations. The treaty deprived the Japanese of all the territory they had acquired since 1854—their entire overseas empire. They surrendered the southern half of Sakhalin Island and the Kuril Islands to the Soviet Union, and the Bonin and Ryukyu Islands to control by the United States. They also renounced all rights to Formosa, which was left in an undefined status. They yielded as well to the United States the right to continue maintaining military installations in Japan until the latter was able to defend itself. Despite opposition from the Soviets, who feared a U.S. military presence in the Far East, military occupation under the command of U.S. General Douglas MacArthur continued until a peace treaty went into effect in April 1952, restoring full sovereignty to Japan.

Establishment of the United Nations

As in the case of the Versailles treaty one of the most significant elements in the settlements was their provision for an international organization. The old League of Nations had failed to avert the outbreak of war in 1939; in April 1946 it was formally dissolved. Yet Allied statesmen continued to recognize the need for some international organization. In February 1945, they agreed at Yalta that a conference to respond to that need should be convoked the following April. Despite the sudden death of Roosevelt two weeks earlier, the conference met in San Francisco as scheduled. A charter was adopted on June 26, providing for a world organization to be known as the United Nations (U.N.) and to be founded upon the principle of "the sovereign equality of all peace-loving states." Its important agencies were to be (1) a General Assembly composed of representatives of all the member states; (2) a Security Council composed of representatives of the United States, Great Britain, the Soviet Union, the Republic of China, and France, with permanent seats, and of ten other states chosen by the General Assembly to fill nonpermanent seats; (3) a Secretariat consisting of a secretary-general and a staff of subordinates; (4) an Economic and Social Council composed of eighteen members chosen by the General Assembly; (5) a Trusteeship Council; and (6) an International Court of Justice.

Although the United Nations has failed to live up to the hopes of its founders, it continues to function as the world's longest-lived international assembly of nations. By far the most important functions of the new organization were assigned by the charter to the Security Council. This agency has the "primary responsibility for the maintenance of international peace and security." It has authority to investigate any dispute between nations, to recommend methods for settlement, and, if necessary to preserve the peace, to employ diplomatic or economic measures against an aggressor. If, in its judgment, these have proved, or are likely to prove, inadequate, it may "take such action by air, naval, or land forces" as may be required to maintain or restore international order. The member states are required by the charter to make available to the Security Council, on its call, armed forces for the maintenance of peace.

> The Security Council

The Security Council was so organized as to give almost a monopoly of authority to its permanent members, since no action of any kind could be taken without the unanimous consent of Great Britain, France, the United States, the Republic of China, the Soviet Union, and four other members besides. This absolute veto given to each of the principal states, instead of bolstering the peace of the world, potentially crippled the council and rendered it helpless in the face of many emergencies.

> The veto power of the Big Five

The remaining agencies of the U.N. were given a wide variety of functions. The Secretariat, composed of a secretary-general and a numerous staff, is chiefly an administrative authority. Its duties, though, are by no means routine, for the secretary-general may bring to the attention of the Security Council any matter that, in his opinion, threatens international peace. The functions of the Economic and Social Council are the most varied of all. Composed of eighteen members elected by the General Assembly, it has authority to initiate studies and make recommendations with respect to international social, economic, health, educational, cultural, and related matters, and may perform services within such fields at the request of U.N. members.

> Other agencies of the U.N.

During its first half-century the work of various U.N. agencies helped the organization achieve a modestly impressive record of accomplishment. But against its successes must be recorded major failures as well. The United Nations was unable to establish control of nuclear weapons. And it was powerless in the face of any determined effort by a major power to have its own way, as in the case of the Soviet suppression of a

> Record of the U.N.

revolt in Hungary in 1956; or the massive intervention by the United States in Vietnam in the 1960s and early 1970s. If the United Nations acted upon occasion to defuse potentially explosive world situations, as it did in Korea, it failed to achieve the lofty peacemaking and peacekeeping goals set for it by its founders.

SUMMARY POINTS

- The harsh terms of the Versailles Treaty and the worldwide depression in the 1930s facilitated the rise of nationalistic and authoritarian leadership in Germany and Italy, and also led those powers, as well as Japan, to pursue a policy of militant expansionism.

- The expansionist policies of the Axis powers went unchallenged by other European powers, who preferred to "appease" rather than confront Germany.

- The German invasion of Poland in September 1939 began World War II. The war became a global conflict when Japan attacked Pearl Harbor in Hawaii in December 1941 and the United States then entered the conflict.

- Germany surrendered in May 1945; Japan surrendered after atomic bombs were dropped at Hiroshima and Nagasaki in August 1945.

- The peace settlements acquiesced in the division of Europe into East and West, providing the basis for forty years of cold war conflict. They also led to the creation of the United Nations, which was given responsibility for the maintenance of international peace and security.

SELECTED READINGS

Carr, Raymond, *The Spanish Tragedy: The Civil War in Perspective,* London, 1977. A thoughtful introduction to the Spanish Civil War and the evolution of Franco's Spain.

Collins, Larry, *Is Paris Burning?* New York, 1965. A highly readable account of the liberation of Paris.

Dawidowicz, Lucy S., *The War against the Jews, 1933–1945,* New York, 1975. A full account of the Holocaust.

Divine, Robert A., *Roosevelt and World War II,* Baltimore, 1969. A diplomatic history.

Feis, Herbert, *Churchill, Roosevelt, Stalin: The War They Waged and the Peace They Sought,* Princeton, 1957. A standard survey.

Géraud, André, *The Gravediggers of France,* Garden City, N.Y., 1944. A critical and impassioned account of the fall of France.

Gilbert, Martin, and Richard Gott, *The Appeasers,* Boston, 1963. Excellent study of British pro-German sentiment in the 1930s.

———, *The Second World War: A Complete History,* rev. ed., New York, 1991. The most up-to-date general account.

Hilberg, Raul, *The Destruction of the European Jews,* 2d ed., 3 vols., New York, 1985. Another excellent treatment of the Holocaust, its origins, and consequences.

Michel, Henri, *The Shadow War: The European Resistance, 1939–1945,* New York, 1972. Thoroughly researched and compelling reading.

Milward, Alan S., *War, Economy, and Society, 1939–1945,* Berkeley, 1977. Analyzes the impact of the war on the world economy and the ways in which economic resources of the belligerents determined strategies.

Nash, Gerald D., *World War II and the West: Reshaping the Economy,* Lincoln, Nebr., 1990. Well-argued discussion of the development of an international economy after 1945.

Overy, Richard, *Why the Allies Won,* New York, 1996. A concise, compelling analysis.

Paxton, Robert O., *Vichy France: Old Guard and New Order, 1940–1944,* New York, 1982. A bitter account.

Taylor, A. J. P., *The Origins of the Second World War,* New York, 1962. A controversial but provocative attempt to prove that Hitler did not want a world war.

Thomas, Hugh, *The Spanish Civil War,* 3d ed., New York, 1986. A thorough and balanced account.

Wheeler-Bennett, J. W., *Munich: Prologue to Tragedy,* London, 1966. A sensitive treatment of prewar diplomatic negotiations, outdated to some extent, but still evocative.

Wilkinson, James D., *The Intellectual Resistance in Europe,* Cambridge, Mass., 1981. A comparative study of the movement throughout Europe.

Wright, Gordon, *The Ordeal of Total War, 1939–1945,* New York, 1968. Particularly good on the domestic response to war and the mobilization of the resources of the modern state.

SOURCE MATERIALS

Bloch, Marc, *Strange Defeat: A Statement of Evidence Written in 1940,* New York, 1968. An analysis of the fall of France, written by one of France's greatest historians, who later died fighting for the Resistance.

Churchill, Winston S., *The Second World War,* 6 vols., London, 1948–1954. The war as Churchill saw it and as he wanted history to see it. Especially useful is the first volume on the 1930s, *The Gathering Storm.*

De Gaulle, Charles, *The Complete War Memoirs,* New York, 1964. De Gaulle's apologia.

Hersey, John, *Hiroshima,* New York, 1946. A moving account of the aftermath of the U.S. atomic bombing written very soon after the event.

Noakes, Jeremy, and Geoffrey Pridham, *Documents on Nazism, 1919–1945,* New York, 1975. A helpful collection.

Vassiltchikov, Marie, *Berlin Diaries, 1940–1945,* New York, 1988. A compelling firsthand account of daily life during the war by a woman close to a group that attempted to assassinate Hitler.

Wiesel, Elie, *Night,* New York, 1960. A moving Holocaust document written by one of its most famous survivors.

PART SEVEN

THE EMERGENCE OF A WORLD CIVILIZATION

WESTERN CIVILIZATION, as we have described and analyzed it, no longer exists today. Instead, we speak in terms of a world civilization, one that owes much of its history and many of its most perplexing problems to the West, but one that is no longer shaped by those few nations that for so many centuries dominated the globe.

The great powers of the nineteenth century—Britain, France, and Germany—are powers now only insofar as they have agreed to pool their interests in an all-European Union. The mid-twentieth-century powers—the United States and the Soviet Union—after four decades of confrontation no longer dominate the world as they did in the years immediately after the Second World War. The former Soviet Union is now a collection of weakened, semiautonomous states, struggling to find enough food to feed their deprived and disgruntled populations, prey, like much of the rest of eastern Europe, to serious nationalistic tensions. The United States, plagued by political gridlock, no longer commands the obedience of nations once its willing allies.

Power, and with it the attention of the world, is shifting from the West to the emerging nations of Asia, Africa, the Middle East, and Latin America. Their vast natural resources are affording many of them the chance to play the old Western game of power politics, and in a world arena wider than ever before. The equally vast dimensions of their internal problems—economic, ethnic, nutritional, and political—suggest that their solution will have to be worldwide as well. We are all, as the American designer Buckminster Fuller has said, partners for better or worse on "spaceship earth."

The Earth, Viewed from a Satellite. Saudi Arabia, Africa, and Antarctica are visible through the clouds.

THE EMERGENCE OF WORLD CIVILIZATION

	Politics	Science & Industry	Economics & Society	Arts & Letters
	Stalin's dictatorship, U.S.S.R. (1927–1953)			
	Second World War (1939–1945)			
1940				Richard Wright, *Native Son* (1940) Abstract expressionism in art (mid-1940s) Jackson Pollock's abstract expressionism (1943–1956)
	Communist regimes established in Eastern Europe (1945–1948) Independence of India and Pakistan (1947) Truman Doctrine (1947) Vietnam War, French phase (1947–1954) State of Israel proclaimed (1948) Yugoslavia breaks with Soviet Union (1948) Berlin blockade (1948–1949) Division of Germany (1949) NATO formed (1949) Communist regime in China (1949–)		Marshall Plan (1948) Apartheid policy in South Africa (1948–1991) High rates of growth in Western Europe (late 1940s–1960s)	Simone de Beauvoir, *The Second Sex* (1949–1950)
1950	Korean War (1950–1953)		European Coal and Steel Community created (1951)	
	Egypt becomes a republic (1952–1953) Khrushchev leader of U.S.S.R. (1953–1964) Independence begins for British colonies in Africa (1954) Algerian war of independence (1954–1962) Warsaw Pact formed (1955) Hungarian revolt (1956) Suez crisis (1956)	Hydrogen bomb (1952) Discovery of polio vaccine (1953) Discovery of DNA (1953)		Samuel Beckett, *Waiting for Godot* (1952) Ilya Ehrenburg, *The Thaw* (1954)
		Sputnik launched (1957)	European Common Market established (1958)	Boris Pasternak, *Doctor Zhivago* (1957)
	Establishment of Castro regime in Cuba (1959)			Günter Grass, *The Tin Drum* (1959)

THE EMERGENCE OF WORLD CIVILIZATION

Politics	Science & Industry	Economics & Society	Arts & Letters	
Conflict in the Congo (1960) Independence of French colonies in Africa (1960)		Black civil rights movement, U.S. (1960–1968) Youth "revolution" (1960s) Women's liberation movement (1960s–1970s)	Andy Warhol introduces "pop art" (1960s)	**1960**
Berlin Wall built (1961) Independence struggle in Portuguese Africa (1961–1974) Cuban missile crisis (1962) Vietnam War, American phase (1963–1975) Era of military rule begins in Africa (1964) Brezhnev leader of U.S.S.R. (1964–1982)			François Truffaut, *Jules and Jim* (1961) James Baldwin, *The Fire Next Time* (1963)	
Six-Day War (1967) Civil war, Nigeria (1967–1970) Czechoslovakian revolt (1968)		Student riots in Paris (1968) Martin Luther King, Jr., assassinated (1968)	Arthur Penn, *Bonnie and Clyde* (1967)	
	Manned spacecraft lands on moon (1969) Advent of automation (1970s)			**1970**
India-Pakistan War (1971) Republic of Bangladesh (1972) First SALT agreements signed (1972) Watergate scandal, U.S. (1972–1974)			Bernardo Bertolucci, *Last Tango in Paris* (1972)	
Civil war in Angola (1975–1994)		OPEC oil embargo (1973)	Aleksandr Solzhenitsyn, *The Gulag Archipelago* (1974)	
Revolution in Iran (1979) Soviet military intervention in Afghanistan (1979–1989)		Worldwide inflation and unemployment (late 1970s and early 1980s) World Bank's Structural Adjustment Programs in Africa launched (1979)		

THE EMERGENCE OF WORLD CIVILIZATION

	Politics	Science & Industry	Economics & Society	Arts & Letters
1980	Solidarity movement organizes strikes in Poland (1980) Iraq-Iran war (1980–1988) U.S. rejection of SALT II agreement (1981)			
		Toxic gas leak in Bhopal, India (1984)		
	Gorbachev leader of U.S.S.R. (1985–1991)			
		AIDS virus found outside Africa (1986) Explosion of U.S. space shuttle *Challenger* (1986) Nuclear accident at Chernobyl, U.S.S.R. (1986)		
			Stock market crash, U.S. (1987)	
	Solidarity leaders elected to run Poland (1989) Fall of Berlin Wall (1989)	Exxon *Valdez* oil spill (1989)		
1990	Germany reunited (1990) Iraqi invasion of Kuwait (1990) Nelson Mandela freed (1990) Government-ANC talks begin in South Africa (1990) Persian Gulf War (1991) Dissolution of U.S.S.R. (1991) War in Bosnia (1992–1995)	Rio summit on environment (1992)	Eastern European countries restore market economies (1990s)	
	End of colonial era in Africa (1993) Genocide in Rwanda (1994) African majority rule in South Africa (1994–)		NAFTA passed (1993)	

CHAPTER 30

THE POSTWAR YEARS: RIVALRY AND RECOVERY

This conjunction of an immense military establishment and a large arms industry is new in American experience. The total influence—economic, political, even spiritual—is felt in every city, every statehouse, every office of the federal government.... We must guard against the acquisition of unwarranted influence, whether sought or unsought, by the military-industrial complex. The potential for the disastrous rise of misplaced power exists and will persist.
—DWIGHT D. EISENHOWER, "Farewell Address"

IN APRIL 1945, European men and women, surveying the devastation that their countries had brought down upon each other during the preceding six years, found it all but impossible to imagine their continent arising from the ashes of total conflict. As in the First World War, both victors and vanquished had endured punishing destruction. Between 1914 and 1918, 8 million had died. Now the total was four times as great. Although France and Britain had suffered fewer casualties in the Second than in the First World War, loss of life elsewhere had been cataclysmic. Poland's population was reduced by 20 percent (in part as a consequence of the Nazis' ruthless destruction of the Jews); losses in the Soviet Union were close to 15 million; in Germany, they were 5 million.

Across Europe, cities lay in ruins. Hitler had boasted in 1935 that in ten years Berlin would be transformed so that no one could recognize it. His prophecy came true, though in a grisly fashion he had not intended. Industrial and commercial centers in France, the Low Countries, Italy, and in the wasted territories of central Europe and Russia were largely rubble. Housing was scarce everywhere—in some areas it was practically nonexistent. Food remained in dangerously short supply, a consequence of the violation of agricultural lands and people, the lack of farm machinery and fertilizer, and a severe drought in the summer of 1945. A year later, about 100 million people in Europe still existed on less than 1,500 calories per day—not enough to sustain working adults in a healthy state. Food rationing remained a dreary fact of life everywhere, for without it a large portion of the Continent's population would have starved to death. During the winter of 1945–1946, many regions had little or no fuel for heat and what coal there was (less than half the prewar supply) could not be transported to those areas most in need of it.

The extent of the destruction

Berlin, 1945. The rubble from which the German "miracle" was created.

No wonder Europeans were initially dazed by the trauma they had inflicted upon themselves. The wonder, indeed, was that the period of trauma lasted such a relatively short time. Ten years later, Europe had been transformed—though not restored. Two all-important changes had occurred by then. The first, reflecting an altered balance of international power, resulted in a divided continent, with Eastern Europe under the control of the Soviet Union, and Western Europe dominated by the military and diplomatic presence of the United States. The second change, a consequence of human determination and favorable economic trends, produced in the West a buoyant, lively, and creative civilization, more expansive and up-to-date than even the most optimistic forecaster might have deemed possible in 1945.

A DIVIDED CONTINENT

During the decade after the Second World War the world of nations assumed a bipolar character, in large measure the result of mutual mistrust and increasing hostility between the Soviet Union and the United States. The Soviet Union had insisted during the negotiations at Teheran and Yalta that it had a legitimate claim to hegemony over Eastern Europe, a claim that Western leaders willingly acknowledged. When visiting Moscow in 1944, Churchill and Stalin had bargained like two Old World power brokers over the fate of several supposedly free nations. Churchill proposed a 90 percent preponderance of Soviet influence in Rumania, countered by 90 percent for the West in Greece; Yugoslavia, 50–50; and so on. Stalin, however, increasingly mistrustful of Western leadership, believed that bargains with the West, no matter how attractive they might appear on paper, were really worth little. "Churchill," he remarked, "is the kind who, if you don't watch him, will slip a kopek out of your pocket. . . . Roosevelt . . . dips in his hands only for bigger coins." Stalin's authoritarian domestic regime was motivated by a siege mentality that saw almost everyone as an enemy or, at best, a threat. Not surprisingly, his foreign policy was dictated by that same state of mind.

Yet Stalin's anti-Western policy was based upon more than personal paranoia. It was a reflection of traditional fears that had characterized Russia's attitudes toward its European neighbors for centuries, of ambivalence toward Western ways that had marked Russia during the regimes of Peter the Great, at the beginning of the eighteenth century, and of Alexander III at the end of the nineteenth. Stalin's mistrust of the United States in particular stemmed as well from the prewar years when the Americans had never hesitated to express their antagonism to Soviet communism. U.S. mistrust was matched by Soviet leaders' escalating fear of American-inspired military and economic encirclement.

Winston Churchill Denounces Soviet Tyranny. In a speech at Fulton, Missouri, in March 1946, Churchill coined the phrase "Iron Curtain" to characterize the Soviets' partitioning of Eastern from Western Europe.

The Soviet Union in Eastern Europe

Because of the need to recoup their enormous industrial losses and their fears of further invasion, the Soviets were determined to maintain political, economic, and military control of those countries in Eastern Europe that they had liberated from Nazi control. They employed diplomatic pressure, political infiltration, and military terrorism to establish "people's republics" in Eastern Europe sympathetic to the Soviet regime. In country after country the process repeated itself: at first, all-party coalition governments from which only fascists were excluded; then further coalitions, in which communists predominated; and finally, one-party states. By 1948, governments that owed allegiance to Moscow were established in Poland, Hungary, Rumania, Bulgaria, and Czechoslovakia. The nations of Eastern Europe did not all succumb without a struggle. Greece, which the Soviets wished to include within their sphere of influence, was torn by civil war until 1949, when with Western aid its monarchy was restored. A direct challenge to the Yalta guarantee of free, democratic elections occurred in Czechoslovakia, where in 1948 the Soviets crushed the coalition government of liberal leaders Eduard Beneš and Jan Masaryk.

The most important check the Soviets received at this time to their campaign for Eastern European hegemony also occurred in 1948, when the Yugoslavian government of the wartime hero Marshal Tito declared its independence of Moscow and its determination to steer a course unallied to either East or West. Tito, the only Eastern European "satellite" communist leader who had risen to power on his own and not as a Soviet puppet, possessed political authority rooted within his own country, and this secured his position from reprisals once he had established Yugoslavia's freedom from Soviet hegemony. Events in Czechoslovakia and

Yugoslavian resistance

Europe during the Cold War

Yugoslavia inspired a series of Soviet-directed purges within the political hierarchies of the various satellite governments, a measure of Stalin's continuing fear of opposition.

The United States countered these moves with massive programs of economic and military aid to Western Europe. In 1947, President Harry Truman proclaimed the Truman Doctrine, which provided assistance programs to prevent further communist infiltration into the governments of Greece and Turkey. The following year, the European Recovery Program, or Marshall Plan, named for Secretary of State George Marshall, who first proposed it, provided funds for the reconstruction of Western European industry.

At the same time, the United States moved to shore up the military defenses of the West. In April 1949, a group of representatives of Western European states, together with Canada and the United States, signed an agreement providing for the establishment of the North Atlantic Treaty Organization (NATO). Subsequently Greece, Turkey, and West Germany were added as members. The treaty declared that an armed attack against any one of the signatory parties would be regarded as an attack against all, and that they would combine their armed strength to whatever extent necessary to repel the aggressor. The joint military command, or NATO army, established in 1950, was increased from thirty to fifty divisions in 1953, with a rearmed West Germany contributing twelve of the divisions.

The Soviets reacted with understandable alarm to the determination of the United States to strengthen Western Europe. In 1947 they organized an international political arm, the Cominform (Communist Information Bureau), responsible for coordinating worldwide communist policy and programs. In addition the Soviets rejected an original offer of Marshall Plan aid, and instead organized an Eastern European counterpart for economic recovery, the Council for Mutual Economic Assistance, or Comecon. They responded to NATO with the establishment of their own military alliances, confirmed by the Warsaw Pact of 1955. This agreement set up a joint armed forces command among its signatories, and more important, authorized the continued stationing of Soviet troops in Albania, Bulgaria, Czechoslovakia, Hungary, Poland, Rumania, and the eastern portion of Germany, which had remained under Soviet domination since the end of the war.

Germany was, in fact, the focal point of East-West tensions during these years. By 1946 the joint administration of Germany by the four former Allied powers had collapsed. The Soviet Union remained in control of the eastern portion, which eventually became the nominally independent German Democratic Republic (East Germany), while the Western powers continued to support the industrial recovery of the area under their control—in its turn to emerge as the Federal Republic of Germany (West Germany). A crisis arose in 1948 when, in retaliation for the reunification of the western zones of control under one authority, the Soviets closed down road, rail, and water access from the west to Berlin. Berlin,

The Truman Doctrine and Marshall Plan

George Marshall

Cominform and Warsaw Pact

The Berlin blockade

Crises in Berlin. Left: The Berlin Airlift, 1948. For eight and a half months the United States, Britain, and France airlifted over two million tons of supplies into West Berlin, around which the Russians had imposed a land blockade. Right: The Berlin Wall, 1961. Thirteen years after the blockade, the East German government constructed a wall between East and West Berlin to stop the flow of escapees to the West. This manifestation of the "Iron Curtain" was dismantled in 1989.

though within the territory of East Germany, was administered by all four powers. The Western powers countered with an airlift of food and other necessary supplies, which prevented the collapse of the city into Soviet hands. After more than eight months the Soviets lifted the blockade. For many years to come, however, Berlin was to remain one of the hottest spots in the ongoing "cold war," as it came to be called, between the Soviet Union and the West. The city symbolized the determination of the Western powers to ensure West Germany's economic recovery, as well as their opposition to what they continued to see as communist aggression.

The tensions that produced the cold war were the result of misperceptions on both sides. Americans, who had been persuaded by wartime government propaganda to admire the Soviets as stalwart anti-fascists, were naively disillusioned when they discovered that their erstwhile allies were in fact not democrats. Concerned about the economic weakness throughout postwar Western Europe, U.S. leaders believed that the Soviets were hatching a vast plan to take advantage of that weakness by establishing communist regimes throughout the West, as they had in the East.

Scholars have recently argued convincingly that there was no grand Soviet strategy of this sort. The Soviets were not willing to undertake any

The cold war: U.S. attitudes

Soviet attitudes

such campaign, primarily because they were economically and militarily incapable of doing so. Since the Soviets had long feared encirclement by hostile capitalist powers, however, they saw the Truman and Marshall programs as a direct form of neoimperialism, an American plot to subject Western Europe to the economic hegemony of the United States.

Stalin himself remained deeply suspicious, not only of the West, but of any power or personality that he perceived to be a threat to his dictatorial rule. He convened neither party congress, the assembly of representatives from local, regional, and organizational-level subgroups of the Communist party, nor central committee, the smaller group of high-level party officials that was supposed to decide policy issues. He relied on a handful of political allies to carry out the business of government, among them Vyacheslav Molotov, the Soviet foreign minister; Lavrenty Beria, head of the powerful secret police; and Andrei Zhdanov, secretary of the party central committee. Zhdanov was charged with the task of devising a new communist gospel, one prescribed by Stalin, which tended to ignore the earlier doctrines of Marx, Engels, and Lenin, and amounted to little more than an apologia for Stalin's repressive personal despotism. Party propaganda preached Soviet superiority to the West. Soviet writers and artists were attacked for imitating their Western counterparts. Economists were taken to task for suggesting that European industry might succeed in recovering from the damages it had sustained. In the realm of science, accepted genetic theory was supplanted by that of Trofim Lysenko, whose work implied the inheritance of acquired characteristics; Einstein was vilified; and Freud was pronounced a decadent charlatan.

Only with Stalin's death in 1953 did this relentless barrage of anti-Western propaganda begin to abate somewhat. Although relations between East and West remained wary, tensions eased considerably during the late 1950s and 1960s. The United States, it is true, continued to adhere to a policy of Soviet "containment," seeking as allies those most willing to oppose by military force, if necessary, the spread of international communism. By the mid-1950s, however, Western European nations had begun to wonder whether U.S. intervention in their affairs might not, in fact, represent as much an American power play as an attempt to protect the West from Soviet aggression. American claims to the role of "protector of the free world" began to sound hollow, particularly after U.S. Secretary of State John Foster Dulles negotiated a diplomatic and military understanding with the aging Spanish dictator Francisco Franco in 1955.

In the Soviet Union, a change of direction was signaled by the accession to power in 1953 of Nikita Khrushchev. Khrushchev possessed a kind of earthy directness which, despite his hostility to the West, nevertheless helped for a time to ease tensions. Abandoning the seclusion of the Kremlin, where Stalin had immured himself, he traveled throughout the world. On a visit to the United States in 1959, he traded quips with Iowa farmers and was entertained at Disneyland.

As testimony to his desire to reduce international conflict, Khrushchev soon agreed to the first of a series of summit meetings with the

Stalinism

After Stalin

Khrushchev to power

Khrushchev's goals and policies

Nikita Khrushchev. Premier (1958–1964) and First Secretary of the Communist party (1953–1964) of the Soviet Union, Khrushchev visited the United States in 1959. Here he is shown joking with an Iowan farmer.

leaders of Britain, France, and the United States. This new Soviet determination to lower international tensions grew out of Khrushchev's need to consolidate his regime at home and to prevent the threatened crumbling of the communist bloc in Eastern Europe. The harsh demands of the Stalin regime had generated discontent among the Soviet people. Dissenters, their voices no longer silenced by the Stalinist police, began to demand a shift from the production of heavy machinery and armaments to the manufacture of consumer goods, and, in the arts, a return to at least a measure of freedom. Their voices were heard in essays and in novels such as Ilya Ehrenburg's *The Thaw* (1954), by which name this period became known.

Challenges in Eastern Europe: Poland and Hungary

Meanwhile, throughout the other communist states, growing resentment of Soviet demands for rapid industrialization and collectivization generated arguments for easing the restrictions Stalinism had imposed. In response to these pressures the Soviet leaders altered their economic goals and began preaching that there was more than one road to socialism. The Soviet Union's new posture toward its client states in Eastern Europe received its severest test in 1956 when Poland and Hungary demanded greater autonomy in the management of their domestic affairs. In Poland, the government at first responded to major strikes with military repression and then with a promise of liberalization. The anti-Stalinist Polish leader Wladyslaw Gomulka was able to win Soviet permission for his country to pursue its own "ways of socialist development" by pledging Poland's continued loyalty to the terms of the Warsaw Pact. Events in Hungary produced a different result. There, protests against Stalinist policies developed into a much broader anti-communist struggle and attempted secession from the Warsaw Pact. If the Soviets were prepared to entertain a liberalization of domestic policy, they would not tolerate a repudiation of the Warsaw Pact. On November 4, 1956, Soviet troops occupied Budapest; leaders of the Hungarian liberation were taken prisoner and executed.

Despite these events, Khrushchev held to his policy of "peaceful coexistence" with the West. Though he did not renounce his ultimate belief in the triumph of communism, he argued that victory could be achieved by other than military means. Yet Soviet leaders remained unyielding in their determination to reduce any possible German military threat to Eastern Europe. They continued to nurture the fear that Germany might launch a new war, abetted by its capitalist allies. For this reason, they staunchly opposed the reunification of the country. In 1961 the East German government built a high wall separating the two sectors of Berlin in order to cut off the escape of thousands of East Germans to West Berlin and thence to West Germany. For almost thirty years, until 1989, the wall remained a potent symbol of Soviet determination to prevent the formation of a united Germany.

The limits of coexistence: the Berlin Wall

Khrushchev eventually fell prey to political rivals and was deposed in 1964. The reins of Soviet power passed to Leonid Brezhnev as secretary of the Communist party. The Soviets continued to hold the governments of Eastern Europe in check. In 1968 they sent tanks and troops into Czechoslovakia after the Czech leadership under Alexander Dubček had attempted to meet criticisms by decentralizing the administration, democratizing the Communist party, pursuing an independent foreign policy, and permitting a brief flowering of intellectual life called the "Prague Spring."

The Czech revolt of 1968

Western leaders remained concerned about a divided Europe and sought ways to bring the two halves into closer association with each other. Despite evidence to the contrary in Hungary and Czechoslovakia, Soviet leaders also perceived a need to relax their hold on the satellite nations of the East. Following the Czech invasion in 1968, they proclaimed the so-called Brezhnev Doctrine, which stated that no socialist state should permit itself to adopt policies detrimental to the interests of international socialism and that the Soviet Union could intervene in the

The Brezhnev Doctrine

The Occupation of Czechoslovakia. In 1968 the liberalized regime of Alexander Dubček was suppressed by the Soviets. The violent response by the citizens was put down by military force.

The policies of Willy Brandt

**West German Chancellor
Willy Brandt**

Solidarity in Poland and Soviet
threat

domestic affairs of any Soviet-bloc nation if communist rule was threatened. But it also asserted that each state might proceed to determine the most appropriate path for its own development.

The politician most effective in bridging the gap between East and West was the West German Willy Brandt, chancellor of West Germany in the early 1970s. Brandt, in his youth an outspoken enemy of Hitler, had fled Germany in the 1930s to Norway, where he joined the anti-Nazi resistance movement in the Second World War. His wartime record increased his credibility with Eastern Europeans, who, if they were not pleased to be subject to the Soviet Union, had as much historical reason to fear Germany as they did the Soviet Union. Brandt recognized the need to accept the division of Germany into two nations. Accordingly his government initiated a policy to regularize relations with West Germany's eastern neighbors (*Ostpolitik*). A complex series of diplomatic negotiations with the Soviet Union, East Germany, and Poland resulted in treaties that established East and West Germany as separate states within one nation, guaranteed unimpeded Western access to Berlin, and recognized Poland's claim to a western frontier along the Oder and Neisse Rivers as established originally after the Second World War.

Tensions between East and West, which eased during the 1960s and 1970s, arose once more in the next decade, in response to the Soviet Union's meddling in Poland's internal affairs. In 1980, calling their movement "Solidarity," Polish workers had organized strikes that brought the government of the country to a standstill. The strikers were objecting to working conditions imposed by the government to combat a severe

Defiance in Poland. Thousands of striking workers take part in religious services in the Lenin Shipyards in Gdansk on August 24, 1980. This was the scene of the first in a series of strikes that paralyzed an already troubled economic and political system and challenged Soviet domination of Polish governmental policy.

economic crisis that had produced high prices. They were led by an electrician from the Gdansk shipyards, Lech Walesa, whose charismatic personality appealed not only to the Polish citizenry but to sympathizers in the West. Again the Soviets assisted a puppet military regime in reimposing authoritarian rule. Though the Soviet Union did not intervene directly, the implied threat that it might do so, reinforced by the presence of increasing numbers of Soviet troops near the Polish border, reemphasized Soviet unwillingness to permit its Eastern European neighbors autonomy over their internal affairs.

ECONOMIC RENAISSANCE

The end of World War II brought not only the tensions of a global superpower rivalry but also the makings of a remarkable recovery in Western Europe. In thinking of their successful postwar economic recovery as a "miracle," Western Europeans ignored the degree to which human agencies and predictable economic forces precipitated change. First, the war had encouraged a variety of technological innovations with direct and important peacetime applications: improved communications (the invention of radar, for example), the manufacture of synthetic materials, the increasing use of aluminum and alloy steels, and advances in the techniques of prefabrication. Secondly, through wartime manufacturing, nations had added significantly to the sum of their productive capital during the war. Despite the wartime devastation, capital invested in European plants that were easily damaged but difficult to destroy survived to sustain a postwar boom grounded in the recovery initiated by the Marshall Plan. This boom was fueled by a third set of factors: the continued buoyancy of consumer demand and the consequent high level of employment throughout the 1950s and 1960s. These in turn encouraged continued capital investment and technological innovation. Finally, brisk foreign demand for goods convinced Europeans of the need to remove obstacles to international trade and payments. This fortuitous combination of circumstances made possible a remarkable period of dynamic economic growth.

Reasons for postwar boom

Governments resorted to a variety of devices to facilitate economic expansion: West Germany provided tax breaks to encourage business investment; Britain and Italy offered investment allowances to their steel and petroleum industries. Virtually all of Western Europe experimented with the nationalization of industry and services in an effort to enhance efficiency and productivity. The result was a series of "mixed" economies combining public and private ownership. France, Britain, Italy, and Austria took the lead in the move toward state-controlled enterprise. In France, where public ownership was already well advanced in the 1930s, railways, electricity and gas, banking, radio and television, and a large segment of the automobile industry were brought under state management.

Movement toward "mixed" economies

In Britain, the list was equally long: coal and utilities; road, railroad, and air transport; and banking. Though nationalization was less common in West Germany, the railway system (state-owned since the late nineteenth century); some electrical, chemical, and metallurgical concerns; and the Volkswagen company—the remnant of Hitler's attempt to produce a "people's car"—were all in state hands, though the latter was largely returned to the private sector in 1963.

These government policies and programs contributed to astonishing growth rates. Between 1945 and 1963 the average yearly growth of gross domestic product (gross national product minus income received from abroad) in West Germany was 7.6 percent; in Austria, 5.8 percent; in Italy, 6 percent; in Holland, 4.7 percent; and so on. This was a remarkable reversal of the economic patterns of an interwar period that had been beset by slack demand, overproduction, and insufficient investment. In the face of reconstruction and recovery, production facilities were hard pressed to keep up with soaring demand.

West Germany's recovery was particularly noteworthy. Production increased sixfold between 1948 and 1964. Unemployment fell to record lows, reaching 0.4 percent in 1965, when there were six jobs for every unemployed person. Though prices rose initially, their subsequent leveling off provided an opportunity for most citizens to participate in a domestic buying spree that caused production to soar. In the 1950s, an average of half a million housing units were constructed annually to accommodate those whose homes had been destroyed, an influx of new resident-refugees from East Germany and Eastern Europe, and transient workers from Italy, Spain, Greece, and elsewhere who were attracted by West Germany's demand for labor.

In France the major economic problem following the war was the need to modernize the nation's industries, many of which remained small family enterprises resistant to technological change. Under the direction of a minister for planning, Jean Monnet, a special office—the General Commissariat for Planning—was established to initiate and execute a program for national economic recovery. Using money provided by the Marshall Plan, the French government played a direct and active role in industrial revival and reform, contributing not only capital but expert advice, and facilitating shifts in the national labor pool to place workers where they were most needed. The plan gave priority to basic industries, with the result that the production of electricity doubled, the steel industry was thoroughly modernized, and the French railway system became the fastest and most efficient on the Continent. Other sectors of the economy tended to stagnate, however, while agriculture remained in the hands of a peasant class loathe to avail itself of government incentives intended to foster productivity through mechanization. Nevertheless, the French gross national product (GNP) increased at the creditable rate of about 5 percent per year in the 1950s.

Italy's industrial "miracle" was even more impressive than those of West Germany and France, given the woeful state of the nation's econ-

Economic growth rates

West German resurgence

France's program of national economic recovery

Italy's industrial "miracle"

Modernization in France. Technological advancement may be slowed by people reluctant to abandon the old ways of doing things. Modern trains often traverse routes where farms remain small and unmechanized. Left: a modern train traveling over a route in Normandy. Right: Herding livestock in Normandy.

omy immediately following the war. Stimulated by infusions of capital from the government and from the Marshall Plan, Italian companies soon began to compete with other European international giants. The products of Olivetti, Fiat, and Pirelli became familiar in households across the world to an extent that no Italian goods had in the past. Electric power production—particularly important in Italy because of its lack of coal—had by 1953 increased 100 percent over that in 1938. By 1954 real wages were 50 percent higher than they had been in 1938. Yet Italy's success was marred by the enduring poverty of the country's southern regions, where illiteracy remained high and land continued to be held by a few rich families.

Elsewhere on the Continent, nations with little in common in terms of political traditions or industrial patterns all shared in the general prosperity. Spain's economy changed markedly in the late 1950s, when a combination of rising foreign investment and the lifting of government controls spurred higher levels of production. Tourism was for Spain, as for all European countries, an increasingly important industry. Seventeen million visitors came to Spain in 1966, making it second only to Italy as a tourist attraction. Holland, Belgium, Austria, Greece, and the Scandinavian countries all enjoyed booms in the late 1950s. Though each country succeeded in increasing its GNP significantly, however, there remained marked differences in the levels of prosperity across the Continent. The per capita GNP in Sweden, for example, was almost ten times that of Turkey.

Britain throughout remained a special case. Although it shared in the economic prosperity of the postwar years, it did so to a lesser extent than

Shared prosperity elsewhere on the Continent

Britain as a special case

Heating Fuel Shortage in Great Britain. This scene of British householders queuing for coal during the severely cold winter of 1948 provides a measure of the degree to which "winners" as well as "losers" suffered in the immediate aftermath of the Second World War.

The Common Market

Success of the European Economic Community

other European countries. The British rise in GNP averaged 2.5 percent per year between 1948 and 1962—a respectable enough figure when compared with past performance but nothing like the spectacular achievements recorded during the same period across the Channel. The Conservative prime minister Harold Macmillan campaigned successfully for reelection in 1959 with the slogan "You've never had it so good"—an accurate enough boast. Yet the British economy remained sluggish. The country was burdened with obsolete factories and techniques, the legacy of its early industrialization. It was plagued as well by a series of balance-of-payments crises precipitated by an inability to sell more goods abroad than it imported.

The Western European renaissance was achieved by more than the efforts of individual nations. From the late 1940s on, they took steps to bind themselves together as an effective economic third force between the superpowers. In 1951 the European Coal and Steel Community was created, which placed the management of those industries in France, West Germany, Belgium, Holland, and Luxembourg under a joint High Authority. Consisting of experts from each of the participating countries, the Authority possessed the power to regulate prices, to increase or limit production, and to impose administrative fees. Britain declared itself unwilling to participate, fearing the effects of European economic union on its declining coal industry and on its relationship with longtime trading partners such as Australia, New Zealand, and Canada.

During the mid-1950s, further steps toward transnational economic integration were taken—the establishment of Euratom, for example, a research organization in the field of nuclear development—culminating in 1958 with the founding of the European Economic Community (EEC), or Common Market. The EEC declared its goals to be the abolition of all trade barriers between the initial six members: France, West Germany, Italy, Belgium, Holland, and Luxembourg. In addition, the organization pledged itself to common external tariffs, the free movement of labor and capital among the member nations, and the establishment of uniform wage structures and social security systems, so as to foster similar working conditions throughout the EEC. A commission with headquarters in Brussels was charged with the administration of this ambitious program.

Despite inevitable difficulties, particularly in the area of agricultural policy and prices, the European Economic Community was a remarkable success. By 1963, it had become the world's largest importer. Its steel production was second only to that of the United States, and total industrial production was over 70 percent higher than it had been in 1950. Even critics who complained about constant interference of EEC "Eurocrats"—more than 3,000 in Brussels by 1962—conceded that centralized European planning and decision-making had brought the Continent extraordinary and unheralded prosperity. The Common Market operated increasingly as a semiautonomous political unit, and in 1972 citizens of member nations voted directly for representatives to an EEC parliament.

Although economic development in Eastern Europe was not nearly as dramatic as that of the West, significant advances occurred there as well. National income rose and output increased. Poland and Hungary, in particular, strengthened their economic connections with the West, primarily with France and West Germany. By the 1970s, commerce outside the Soviet bloc accounted for about 30 percent of Eastern Europe's volume of trade. Nevertheless, the Soviet Union required its satellites to design their economic policies to serve more than their own national interests. Regulations governing the Eastern European equivalent of the Common Market—Comecon—insured that the Soviet Union could sell its exports at prices well above the world level, while other members were compelled to trade with the Soviet Union to their disadvantage. Emphasis initially was on heavy industry and collectivized agriculture, though political tension in countries such as Hungary and Poland compelled the Soviets eventually to moderate their policies so as to permit the manufacture of more consumer goods and the development of a modest trade with the West. As with the Western nations, those in the East demonstrated a continuing determination to free themselves from economic dependence upon a single power.

Behind the drive for economic growth in Western Europe lay the determination of individual men and women to improve their standard of living and quality of life. To this end, they demanded more from their governments in the form of social services. Governments, in turn, relied on their generally robust economies to provide for their citizens to a greater degree than ever before. State welfare programs had, of course, existed throughout the twentieth century, their roots extending back to the insurance schemes for old age, sickness, and disability introduced by Bismarck in Germany in the late 1880s. Postwar Western Europe saw the expansion of such programs based on assumptions of state support that were hardly less compelling than the obligation to keep the peace, nowhere stated more clearly than in the preamble of the French constitution: "The nation guarantees the condition necessary for the development of the individual and the family. It guarantees every individual . . . the protection of health, material security, rest and leisure." A survey in 1957 found that public expenditure on health, pensions, family allowances and assistance (excluding housing and education), accounted for 20.8 percent of the national income in West Germany, 18.9 percent in France, and 12.1 percent in Britain. In Sweden, money spent on social services was six times higher in 1957 than in 1930; in Italy, it was fourteen times higher.

THE POLITICS OF EUROPEAN RECOVERY

The governments responsible for these remarkable economic and social changes were ideologically almost uniformly middle-of-the-road. Yet unlike the situation after 1918, when the "old men" resumed power throughout Europe, new men who were unwilling to see Europe return to business as usual moved into positions of authority after 1945. In Britain the Labour party, led by middle-class, mild-mannered socialist Clement Attlee, enacted the social legislation that produced a welfare state. The Labour government gave way in 1951 to the Conservatives who, led most notably by Harold Macmillan from 1957 to 1963, proved more than willing to embrace the promise of economic growth and a continuation of welfare policies. The Labour party returned to power in the mid-1960s, under the prime ministership of Harold Wilson, who pledged to forge a more prosperous nation in the "white heat" of a new technological revolution. Although Labourites and Conservatives fought partisan campaigns, they appeared to agree upon fundamentals: a mixed economy and an extended program of welfare benefits. Labourites still called themselves socialists, but most defined socialism, as the party's mainstream always had, as centralization, rather than as worker control of the means of production.

The triumph of moderation on the Continent

Moderates dominated the politics of continental Europe as well. In Germany, France, and Italy, centrist parties affiliated with the Roman Catholic Church held power throughout most of the two decades after 1945: the German Christian Democratic Union; the French Mouvement Républicain Populaire (the M.R.P., initially more popular than it would be in the mid-1950s); and the Italian Christian Democrats. The leaders responsible for the direction of European political affairs during the immediate postwar period were no-nonsense men, committed to the achievement of practical economic and social agendas: Robert Schuman, for a time the French premier and the man most responsible for the establishment of the European Coal and Steel Community; Alcide De Gasperi, Italian premier from 1948 to 1953; and Konrad Adenauer, West German chancellor from 1949 to 1963. Adenauer was a former mayor of

Alcide De Gasperi of Italy Electioneering during His 1948 Campaign

Cologne, a devout Roman Catholic who, though he despised the traditions of Prussian militarism that had contributed to the rise of Hitler, was apprehensive about the consequences of parliamentary democracy for Germany, and thus tended to govern in a paternalistic if not authoritarian manner. His determination to see an end to the centuries-old hostility between France and Germany contributed significantly to the movement toward economic union. De Gasperi, too, was not particularly enamored of democracy and thwarted attempts by Italian socialists and communists immediately after the war to institute radical reforms.

Yet neither Adenauer nor De Gasperi aroused much real political enmity. Socialists throughout Western Europe, recognizing the political popularity of economic prosperity, toned down their rhetoric and their demands, speaking far less about the inevitability of class war and more often about the contributions workers were making to the European postwar renaissance. The program adopted by the German Socialist party (the Social Democrats) in 1959, for example, abandoned orthodox Marxism by declaring the need to leave economic planning as much as possible to individual enterprise, rather than in the hands of the state.

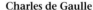

Moderated socialism

France's political situation during the early 1950s was tangled in a way that West Germany's and Italy's were not. Party strength was fragmented. Twenty-five percent of the voting population regularly supported the French Communist party, not so much from commitment to its current policies as from a traditional proletarian habit of mind. Several conservative or reactionary parties of the Right existed as well. The political middle, strong in other countries and initially strong in France, gradually eroded after 1945. Matters reached a crisis when successive centrist governments found it increasingly difficult to resolve a seemingly intractable political problem borne of an independence movement in the French colony of Algeria. In May 1958 a revolt of French nationals in Algeria and disgruntled French army officers, both at home and in the colony, threatened to topple the French government. In desperation, the political leadership stepped down in favor of the Resistance hero General Charles de Gaulle, who had played a brief role in French politics immediately after the war and then retired.

French political fragmentation and de Gaulle

De Gaulle accepted office on the condition that he be permitted to rule by decree for six months and to draft a new constitution for France. This document, adopted by referendum in September 1958 and ushering in France's Fifth Republic, strengthened the executive branch of the government as a means of avoiding the parliamentary deadlocks that had so weakened France earlier in the decade and, indeed, throughout much of the preceding century. The president was granted power to appoint the premier and dissolve the National Assembly. And the assembly's powers to dismiss a premier were considerably weakened. Thus armed with new authority, de Gaulle set out to restore France to power and prestige. "France is not really herself unless in the front rank," he wrote in his memoirs. "France cannot be France without greatness." De Gaulle assumed that Algeria would have to be granted independence, which in due course it was, in 1963. Concerned about U.S. influence in Europe, he

Charles de Gaulle

withdrew French troops from NATO in 1966. He cultivated better relations with the Soviet Union and, with Adenauer, he worked toward closer cooperation between France and West Germany. He accelerated the pace of France's economic and industrial expansion by building a modern military establishment, complete with atomic weapons—a nuclear "force de frappe," an independent nuclear strike force whose objectives were primarily political and diplomatic, part of de Gaulle's effort to reclaim France's great power status. De Gaulle's independent stand was largely based upon his belief that invasion of the West was far from the minds of the Soviet leadership.

Other countries and other courses

Like De Gasperi and Adenauer, de Gaulle was not by nature a democrat but was committed to a centrist course. Such a policy entailed avoiding extremism and working hard to produce "practical" solutions to vexing political problems, thereby undermining radical sentiments of the sort that had produced fascism in Italy and Nazism in Germany. Most other Western European nations followed suit. Holland, Belgium, and the Scandinavian countries initiated economic and social policies that echoed those of the British, French, Germans, and Italians. In Spain and Portugal, however, different political, economic, and social agendas were pursued under the dictatorships of General Francisco Franco and António Salazar. And in Greece, political instability in the 1950s and early 1960s opened the way for a coup by conservative right-wing generals in 1967. Yet these were exceptions to a two-decade history of domestic tranquility and economic prosperity—a sharp contrast to the tragic failures of the 1920s and 1930s.

INTELLECTUAL AND CULTURAL PATTERNS

Growing gulf between avant-garde and the educated layman

Intellectual life in the West after 1945 was patterned broadly, as it had been in the interwar years. The gulf remained wide between the avant-garde and the generally educated public—the latter larger than ever before thanks to burgeoning universities. If attendance at museums increased—as it did dramatically—more often than not it was because people were attracted by exhibits of treasures from the distant past—from King Tutankhamen's tomb or from the Renaissance collections of the Vatican Museum. Audiences who welcomed a chance to hear the works of long-dead composers—Mozart and Verdi—sung by internationally acclaimed "stars"—the soprano Maria Callas, the tenor Luciano Pavarotti—rejected as pointless the puzzling works of composers such as John Cage, whose "silent sonata" entitled "4.33" consisted of a pianist seated at the piano for precisely four minutes, thirty-three seconds, but who never once actually struck a note. Intellectuals, on the other hand, railed against the increasing vapidity of mass culture and in particular of television, the "idiot box" that by 1965 had found its way into 62 million homes in the United States, 13 million in Britain, 10 million in West

Germany, and 5 million each in France and Italy. They also objected to the promotion of art and music as big business. Jam-packed "blockbuster" art exhibits attracted tens of thousands; opera tickets sold at prices approaching $100 apiece. New York's Metropolitan Museum merchandised reproductions of its treasures on television; an elegant shopping mall opened beneath the Louvre Museum in Paris.

The work of many of the West's leading writers reflected the dilemmas of the human condition that prevailed throughout the years after 1945. During the immediate postwar period novelists concerned themselves with the horrors of war and of the totalitarian systems that had spawned the conflict of the 1940s. The American Joseph Heller in *Catch-22* (1961) portrayed the coarseness and cruelty of military life with ruthless realism. The German Günter Grass's first and probably most important novel, *The Tin Drum* (1959), depicted the vicious and politically diseased life of Nazi Germany in the 1930s. In France, Jean-Paul Sartre, as a result of his own and his country's wartime experiences, recommitted himself in his novels, plays, and other writings to a life of active political involvement as a Marxist. Whereas he had previously defined hell in terms of individual hostilities, he now defined it in terms of class inequality. Unlike Sartre, his compatriot Albert Camus was unable to construct a secular faith from his own perceptions of the world and its apparent absurdities. Though idealistic enough to participate in the French resistance movement in the Second World War, and though proclaiming the virtues of rebellion, Camus remained tortured in novels such as *The Stranger* (1942), *The Plague* (1947), and *The Fall* (1956) by the problem of humanity's responsibility for its own miserable dilemma and by the limitations placed upon the ability of men and women to help each other.

Marxism continued to attract European intellectuals, both as a recipe for changing the world and as a way of explaining it. Historians, economists, and sociologists focused their attention more frequently on the writings of the young Marx, less on his economic theories, more on his perceptions of alienation and class consciousness. The writings of the Italian Antonio Gramsci and the Hungarian Georg Lukács, both concerned with these particular matters, attracted widespread attention. Claude Lévi-Strauss, a French sociologist who considers himself a Marxist in contemporary matters, nevertheless applied a different model than Marx's essentially idealist and value-laden dialectic to the study of society. A leading exponent of the so-called structuralist school, Lévi-Strauss subjected all elements of the primitive societies he studied—kinship, rituals, and traditions—to analysis in terms of thought structures, which though unconscious were nevertheless said to possess an objective reality. He argued that his method proved the intrinsic value of every society and that there was rationality where many had previously seen only the irrational or the absurd. It is worth noting that these reinterpretations of Marx came from outside the Soviet Union. Inside, genuine philosophical debate was repressed by the government until the 1980s, when political reforms enabled Soviet intellectuals to speak out.

Postwar literature

Shifting focus on Marx in the West

Boris Pasternak

Aleksandr Solzhenitsyn

The theme of individual alienation and helplessness, a reflection of the problems arising from the growth of state power, was one to which writers addressed themselves with increasing frequency in the 1960s and 1970s. The Russian Boris Pasternak, in his novel *Dr. Zhivago* (1957), indicted the Soviet campaign to shape all its citizens to the same mold. His countryman Aleksandr Solzhenitsyn attacked the brutal methods employed by the Soviet Union in its rapid climb to world power. His *Gulag Archipelago,* published in 1974, is a fictionalized account of the fate of those whose willingness to stand in the way of Soviet "progress" sentenced them to life in Siberian labor camps. Both Pasternak and Solzhenitsyn were awarded the Nobel Prize for literature, the former in 1958 and the latter in 1970. Herbert Marcuse, a naturalized American, charged that authoritarianism was just as much a fact of life under capitalism as under communism. He argued that industrial capitalism had produced a "one-dimensional" society, in which the interests of individual citizens had been ruthlessly subordinated to those of the powerful corporate interests that were the true governors of the world.

Some authors, although they agreed with indictments of contemporary civilization, believed the human condition too hopeless to warrant direct attack. They expressed their despair by escaping into the absurd and fantastic. In such plays as *Waiting for Godot* (1953) by Samuel Beckett, an Irishman who wrote in French, and *The Caretaker* (1960) and *Homecoming* (1965) by the Englishman Harold Pinter, nothing happens. Characters speak in the banalities that have become the hallmark of modern times. Words that are meaningless when spoken by human beings nevertheless take on a logic of their own; yet they explain nothing. Other authors, less willing, perhaps, to attempt to make a statement out of nothingness, invaded the realms of hallucination, science fiction, and fantasy. The novels of the Americans William Burroughs and Kurt Vonnegut convey their readers from interior fantasizing to outer space. Similarly the writings of the Czech author Milan Kundera—who fled the repressive Czech government to live in Paris—portray the senselessness of resisting the human condition. Significantly one of the most popular books among the young people of the sixties and seventies was *The Lord of the Rings* (1954–1955), a pseudo-saga set in the fantasy world of "Middle Earth," written before the Second World War by the Englishman J. R. R. Tolkien.

In the decades after the Second World War, filmmakers made films that mirrored the problems and concerns of society, with a depth and artistic integrity seldom attempted or achieved previously. The Swede Ingmar Bergman, the Frenchmen Jean-Luc Godard and François Truffaut, the Italians Federico Fellini and Michelangelo Antonioni, to name but a few of the most gifted directors, dealt in their films with the same themes that marked the literature of the period: loneliness, war, oppression, and corruption. One important factor facilitating the achievement of artistic quality was the general willingness on the part of censors—state- or industry-sponsored—to reflect public taste by permitting filmmakers great license in the handling of themes such as racism, violence, and sexuality. While there is no question that this relaxation led to exploitation, it cleared the way for extraordinarily powerful film statements, such as the American Arthur Penn's *Bonnie and Clyde* (1967) and the Italian Bernardo Bertolucci's *Last Tango in Paris* (1972), shocking declarations about humanity made possible by explicit depictions of violence and sex. Yet film, while gaining a general maturity it had heretofore lacked, did not abandon its role as entertainment. The international popularity of the British rock-and-roll group the Beatles was translated, for example, into equally successful films—charming, slapstick escapism that nevertheless proclaimed the emancipation of youth from the confining formalities and conventions of their elders.

Fine arts

Unlike writers or filmmakers, the majority of postwar artists did not use their work as a vehicle to express either ideological commitment or a concern for the human situation. Following trends established by the impressionists and cubists, they spoke neither about the world nor to the world, but instead to each other and to the extremely small coterie of initiates who understood their artistic language. Foremost among the postwar schools of art was abstract expressionism, whose chief exponents were the American painters Jackson Pollock, Willem de Kooning, and Franz Kline. Their interests lay in further experimentation with the relationship between color, texture, and surface, to the total exclusion of "meaning" or "message" in the traditional sense. Jasper Johns's painting of the American flag demanded that the viewer see it not as *a* painting—that is, something to be interpreted—but instead as painting, the treatment of canvas with paint. Robert Rauschenberg, in revolt against the abstract expressionists, exhibited blank white panels, insisting that by so doing he was pressing art to the ultimate question of a choice of medium. Painters fought the notion that their work in some way expressed disgust with an empty civilization. "My paintings are based on the fact that only what can be seen is there," declared the American Frank Stella, who painted stripes on irregularly shaped canvases. "Pop" art, a phenomenon of the late sixties associated with the work of Americans Andy Warhol and Roy Lichtenstein, took as its subject everyday objects such as soup cans and comic-strip heroes. According to its practitioners, it was not a protest against the banality of industrialism but another experiment in abstractions. Even the remote and yet extraordinarily compelling abstractions of Mark Rothko, glowing or somber rectangles of color imposed upon other rectangles, were said by the artist himself to represent "nothing but content—no associations, only sensation."

Art in the age of AIDS

The coming of the so-called hyper-realists in the 1970s marked a significant change from the abstract expressionists and pop art movements of the 1940s, 1950s, and 1960s. Increasingly, artists used their work to comment directly upon alienation, pain, and the despair they observed in Western life. The American sculptor Duane Hanson, for example, who recreates his invariably depressing human subjects in plastic down to the last eyelash, made a statement about what he perceives to be the vacuity of life. Since the outbreak of the AIDS epidemic in the early 1980s, which

Two Women's Torsos, by Willem de Kooning (1904–1997). A work representative of the abstract expressionists's desire to explore the varieties of light, texture, color, and surface.

Four Darks in Red, by Mark Rothko (1903–1970). Rothko became obsessed with the need to reduce both color and form, achieving thereby a kind of gloomy mysticism.

Abstract Expressionism. *Sea Change,* by Jackson Pollock (1912–1956), explores texture and surface to the exclusion of meaning in the traditional sense.

Three Flags, by Jasper Johns (1930–). Painted with absolute objectivity Johns's objects, in this case three American flags, cease to be mere reproductions and take on distinctive identities of their own.

Gran Cairo, by Frank Stella (1936–). The artist employs absolute symmetry and a rectilinear pattern with compelling effect.

Woman with Dog, by Duane Hanson (1925–1996). Hanson recreates the human artifacts of middle-American culture as symbols of a hollow society.

Grief, by Eric Fischl (1948–). Fischl takes art in a new direction, beyond abstract expressionism but also beyond the realism depicted in the sculptures of Duane Hanson.

has taken scores of internationally regarded painters, sculptors, and performers as its victims, artists have engaged in a battle against indifference to human suffering and to human sexuality. They have done this with work that has shocked, because it has threatened, the values of a predominantly conservative middle class—much as the impressionist and post-impressionist painters challenged those values a hundred years before.

SUMMARY POINTS

- During the decade after the Second World War, Europe was divided in two, with Eastern Europe coming under the political and economic control of the Soviet Union, and Western Europe falling under the military and diplomatic sway of the United States. Mistrust and misperception produced tension between both sides.

- The years 1945–1970 saw a tremendous economic recovery in Western Europe, fueled by technological and capital improvements developed during the war, high levels of consumer demand, and government attempts to encourage investment. The major European countries combined public and private ownership to varying degrees in "mixed economies."

- The major European powers elected politically centrist governments during the decades after the war, which fostered economic growth and international cooperation.

- While many postwar writers, thinkers, and filmmakers tended to reflect upon the dilemmas of the human condition in modern society, the work of artists became increasingly focused on experimentation with material and technique. More recently, however, some artists have returned to social commentary.

SELECTED READINGS

Allsop, Kenneth, *The Angry Decade: A Survey of the Cultural Revolt of the 1950s,* 3d ed., London, 1969. An essay on postwar disillusionment that traces the roots of the revolt that flourished in the 1960s.

Ardagh, John, *The New French Revolution: A Social and Economic Survey of France, 1945–1967,* New York, 1969. The social impact of economic change.

Aron, Raymond, *The Imperial Republic: The United States and the World, 1945–1973,* Lanham, Md., 1974. World analysis by a leading French political theorist.

Crouzet, Maurice, *The European Renaissance since 1945,* New York, 1971. Optimistic appraisal of Europe's postwar recovery.

Daalder, Hans, and Peter Mair, eds., *Western European Party Systems: Continuity and Change,* Beverly Hills, Calif., 1983. Fine overview of political developments at the national level.

Dahrendorf, Ralf, *Society and Democracy in Germany,* New York, 1971. The extent of the change from fascism to democracy.

Ehrmann, Henry W., *Politics in France,* Boston, 1968. Detailed treatment of politics in the decade after 1958.

Gaddis, John Lewis, *The United States and the Origins of the Cold War, 1941–1947,* New York, 1972. Focuses on the United States. A balanced account.

Garton Ash, Timothy, *The Polish Revolution: Solidarity,* rev. ed., New York, 1991. The best account.

Gilbert, Felix, with David Clay Large, *The End of the European Era, 1890 to the Present,* 4th ed., New York, 1991. Comprehensive overview of political developments.

Hough, Jerry F., and Merle Fainsod, *How the Soviet Union Is Governed,* Cambridge, Mass., 1979. An analysis of postwar Soviet politics.

Kolko, Gabriel, *The Politics of War: The World and United States Foreign Policy 1943–1945,* New York, 1990. Argues that the blame for the cold war rests with the Western Allies.

Lapidus, Gail, *Women in Soviet Society: Equality, Development and Social Change,* Berkeley, 1978. The history of women's lives in the postwar years.

Laqueur, Walter, *Europe since Hitler,* rev. ed., New York, 1982. A useful, thorough survey.

Medvedev, Roy, *Khrushchev,* New York, 1983. A perceptive biography of the Soviet leader by a Soviet historian.

Milward, Alan S., *The Reconstruction of Western Europe, 1945–1951,* Berkeley, 1984. The "miracle," which the author argues took place in the years immediately after the war.

Postan, M. M., *An Economic History of Western Europe, 1945–1964,* London, 1967. A lively account of a lively period.

Sampson, Anthony, *The Changing Anatomy of Britain,* New York, 1982. A sharp critical dissection of British society.

Turner, Henry Ashby, Jr., *The Two Germanies since 1945,* New Haven, 1987. Examines the effect of the political division on German people and institutions.

Wheeler, Daniel, *Art since Mid-Century, 1945 to the Present,* New York, 1991. A thorough examination of recent trends.

Wright, Gordan, *Rural Revolution in France: The Peasantry in the Twentieth Century,* Stanford, 1964. The effect of social change on a firmly entrenched peasantry.

Source Materials

Adenauer, Konrad, *Memoirs, 1945–1953,* Chicago, 1966. Adenauer served as chancellor of the Federal Republic of Germany from 1949 to 1963 and sought both American support and the reunification of dismembered Germany.

Barnes, Thomas G., and Gerald D. Feldman, eds., *Breakdown and Rebirth: 1914 to the Present,* Boston, 1972. An excellent documentary collection of contemporary history, primarily European.

Beauvoir, Simone de, *The Mandarins,* New York, 1956. The politics and intellectual life of postwar France.

De Gaulle, Charles, *Memoirs of Hope: Renewal and Endeavor,* New York, 1971.

Kennan, George F., *Memoirs, 1925–1950,* New York, 1967. Kennan, a career diplomat, was America's leading expert on Russia and instrumental in the formation of the containment policy.

Pasternak, Boris, *Dr. Zhivago,* New York, 1958. Banned by the Soviets, a novel describing the political and social turmoil of the Soviet period.

Servan-Schreiber, J. J., *The American Challenge,* New York, 1968. A Frenchman's assessment of the impact of American economy and technology on Europe.

CHAPTER 31

FRAGMENTATION AND CHANGE: THE END OF POSTWAR CERTAINTIES

The end of Communism is, first and foremost, a message to the human race. It is a message we have not yet fully deciphered and comprehended. In its deepest sense, the end of Communism has brought a major era in human history to an end. It has brought an end not just to the 19th and 20th centuries, but to the modern age as a whole.
—VACLAV HAVEL, president of Czechoslovakia, 1991–1992

WHILE 1960 SEEMED both golden and full of promise, thirty years later Western Europeans were no longer so certain of their prosperity or of their leaders' abilities to provide them with the sort of life they had come to take for granted. From the mid-1960s, social and economic tensions ate away at the consensus that postwar prosperity had created in the West. Societies fragmented in new and confusing ways. Governments were baffled about how to deal with the demands of newly politicized groups. Their problems were compounded after 1975 by a continuing economic crisis that threatened the security a generation had labored so hard to achieve. The problems generated by stagnation and protest that plagued the West throughout the 1970s and 1980s, however, were overshadowed during the early 1990s by an extraordinarily rapid and surprising series of events in Eastern Europe: the collapse of communist rule and the introduction of democracy in those countries hitherto dominated by the Soviet Union; the astonishing disintegration of the Soviet Union itself; and the consequent destabilization of a vast region stretching from the borders of China in the east to the borders of Poland in the west.

| The onset of new crises |

PATTERNS OF SOCIAL CHANGE AND SOCIAL PROTEST

Across Europe, the major economic changes that occurred during the decades after the Second World War brought social change as well. Prosperity brought with it population shifts. The population of Western Europe in 1940 was 264 million; in 1982 it was 320 million. This increase was the result of an increase in the birthrate. Population growth was

| Population growth |

sustained by social welfare policies such as family allowances, which encouraged parents to have children and enabled them to care adequately for them, and by health programs, which extended longevity considerably. As populations increased they also shifted across the Continent. Both West Germany and France found it necessary to import workers in order to sustain their production booms. By the mid-1960s, there were 1.3 million foreign workers in West Germany and 1.8 million in France. Most came from the south, particularly from the agrarian areas of southern Italy, where unemployment remained high, while workers from former colonies emigrated to Britain, often to take low-paid, menial jobs and encounter pervasive discrimination at work and in the community. Migrations of this sort, not to mention the movement of political refugees that occurred during and immediately after the war, contributed to a breaking down of national barriers that was accelerated by the advent of the Common Market.

The rise of a managerial class

Economic resurgence also altered patterns and perceptions of class. Commentators were quick to perceive a marked growth in the number of middle-class, white-collar employees, the result, in part, of the bureaucratic expansion of the state. By 1964, the total number of men and women employed in government service in most European states exceeded 40 percent of the labor force, significantly higher than the number in the 1920s and 1930s. In business and industry, the number of "middle-management" employees grew as well. This "managerial class" tended to be more innovative and adventurous than were the owner-managers of business in previous generations. More often than not, these managers possessed university degrees. In the mid-1950s, for example, over 72 percent of a sample of 5,000 French industrialists were university graduates, more than half of them with degrees in engineering. This stood in marked contrast to the prewar situation, when managers far more frequently moved directly from secondary education into family-run concerns. What was true of the West was true of the Soviet Union as well, where, following educational reforms instituted by Nikita Khrushchev in 1958, programs encouraged bright children to pursue a course of study leading eventually to managerial positions. This new class was not "bourgeois" in the Marxist sense of that term. The technocrats were not "owners of the means of production" or capitalist tycoons. To some degree they saw themselves less as the servants of the company that employed them than as servants of the general public who purchased the goods or services they were providing.

The changing working class

If the nature of the middle class was changing, so was that of the working class. The introduction of complex machinery effectively altered the shape of the factory work force. The proportion of salaried employees—supervisors, inspectors, technicians, and draftsmen—grew significantly. In West Germany, for example, the number of such workers increased between 1950 and 1961 by 95 percent. And manual labor tended to mean something far different from what it had in the nineteenth century. Skills were specialized to a greater degree than ever, based on technological expertise rather than custom and routine. "Skill" meant the ability to monitor automatic controls, to interpret abstract signals, and to make precise, mathematically calculated adjustments.

All of these changes, suggesting a merging of the interests of working class and middle class, led some observers in the mid-1960s to declare class consciousness and its associated fierce antagonisms at an end. In fact, however, events in the late 1960s and 1970s reopened class conflicts, as we shall see. Although men and women earned more money than ever before, performing less physically yet more mentally demanding jobs and living more secure lives, they did not entirely lose their sense of themselves as workers. Trade unions remained powerful institutions: the largest of the French general unions had a membership of 1.5 million; of the Italian, 3.5 million; of the German, 6.5 million. Britain's Trades Union Congress, an affiliation of separate unions, boasted close to 8 million members.

Continuing class consciousness

Unquestionably, workers tended to lead lives that more closely resembled those of the prewar middle class than of their own parents and grandparents. They and their children went to school longer. All European countries passed laws providing for the extension of compulsory secondary education—up to the age of sixteen in France, West Germany, and Britain. As a consequence of new legislation and increased birthrates, school populations increased dramatically. Secondary school enrollment in France, Holland, and Belgium doubled between 1950 and 1960. In England and West Germany it grew by more than 50 percent. Higher education was used in the Soviet Union as a means of unifying a nation that remained culturally heterogeneous. Turks and Slavs constituted sizable minorities in the Soviet Union. Concern lest the pull of ethnic "nationality" tear at the none-too-solid fabric of the Soviet "union" increased the government's desire to impose one unifying culture by means of education, not always with success.

The leveling effect of education

Educational reforms were accompanied by a communications revolution. In both Western and Eastern Europe the paperback book, the long-playing record, radio, television, and a variety of computerized information-storing devices brought knowledge—of varying degrees of quality—to millions who heretofore had had neither the time nor the money to acquire it. Workers in the West for the first time found it possible to take inexpensive holidays, often in their own automobiles. Between 1948 and 1965 car ownership increased in Western Europe from 5 million to 44 million. The work week contracted from forty-eight hours to about forty-two. In most countries, workers received over thirty days of paid vacation per year. Britain's prime minister Harold Macmillan was not alone in his belief that "we've never had it so good!"

Communications, transportation, and leisure

Despite evidence suggesting a social complacency based upon increased material prosperity, the years from 1960 to 1975 were marked by protests in Western Europe and the United States that signaled significant social change. Young people had, of course, revolted in previous generations—indeed, revolt has always been considered a prerogative of youth. Yet in the past, leadership had come from an older generation. Now it was to come from men and women in their twenties.

Protest and upheaval among the young

Universities as breeding grounds
of unrest

Products of the baby boom of the immediate postwar period, young people were jammed into recently expanded universities whose conservative, authoritarian traditions made intellectual reform all but impossible. University enrollment tripled in France, Italy, and Britain between 1938 and 1960; in West Germany, the university population increased from 110,000 in 1950 to 280,000 in 1960. Members of this new generation sought a more permissive society where premarital sex and liberation from traditional patterns of middle-class behavior would become the norm. As students they had little use for the disciplines of the past. Science antagonized them because of its association with warmaking—in particular with the unpopular war the United States waged in Southeast Asia during the 1960s and early 1970s. Knowledge that was not perceived as relevant to the world's problems was challenged as worthless.

Violent student protest

The most serious outbreak of student unrest in Europe occurred in Paris in the spring of 1968. Inspired in part by the role young people had played in the revolt against Soviet oppression in Czechoslovakia that same year, French students at the University of Paris demanded reforms that would modernize their university. Confrontation with authorities precipitated riots, which in turn brought police interference. Sympathy with the students' cause expanded to encompass opposition to President de Gaulle's regime, leading to massive trade union strikes. By mid-May, 10 million French workers had walked off their jobs. The government was able to satisfy the strikers by acquiescing to wage increases, thereby isolating the students, who grudgingly agreed to resume university life. De Gaulle had no sympathy for the students: "Reform, yes—bed messing, no," he is said to have declared at the height of the confrontation. Yet events of May and June 1968 undoubtedly helped weaken de Gaulle's position as president and contributed to his retirement from office in the following year. Young people elsewhere staged protests as well. Students in Berlin rioted at the appearance there of the autocratic shah of Iran and

Student Uprising at the University of Paris, May 1968. Following demonstrations calling for sweeping reforms at the university, French students took to the streets to make their case more forcefully and violently at the barricades.

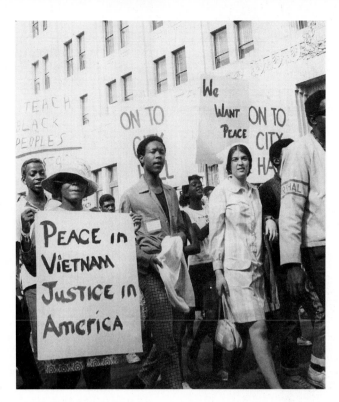

American Demonstration for Social Change.
Young activists in Norfolk, Virginia, demand social
equality for blacks and an end to the Vietnam War.

against newspapers critical of the revolt of the young. In Italy, undergrad-
uates staged a lengthy series of riots to draw attention to university overcrowding. And in the United States, serious protests against the Vietnam
War continued into the early 1970s.

Women, like young people, began to assert themselves during the
1960s and 1970s. As was the case with the youth rebellion, the women's
movement first emerged from the middle class and mainly addressed
the problems of middle-class women. By the mid-1970s the movement
had spread worldwide and was no longer limited to the middle class.
Women's position within society had changed dramatically since the
nineteenth century. The assumption that the middle-class woman's
place was in the home had been challenged by the ever-increasing demand for women workers and by the need experienced by more and
more women to hold a job—either for financial reasons or because
housework was for a growing number an unfulfilling occupation. The
increased availability and social acceptance of birth-control devices
meant that women were having fewer children and that they could
begin to exercise more control over the pattern of their lives.

Yet society seemed unwilling to acknowledge the implication of these
changes: that women are equal to men. Women were paid less than men
for similar work. Women with qualifications no different from those of
men were turned down because of their gender when they applied for
jobs. Women with excellent employment records were forced to rely on

The women's movement

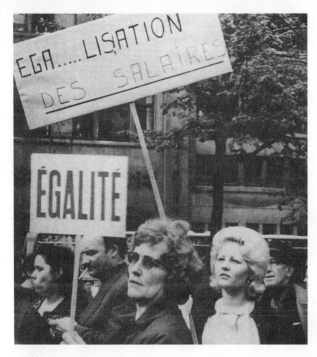

The Women's Movement in France. French women demand equal pay for equal work.

their husbands to establish credit. Political action helped alleviate some of these inequities in the late 1960s and the 1970s. The U.S. government instituted programs of "affirmative action," which mandated the hiring of qualified women as well as members of racial minority groups. In Britain an Equal Pay Act, passed in the late 1960s, established that wages for women should be equal to those of men holding the same job. In France a ministry for the status of women was created in the mid-1970s, and in Germany government agencies were established to deal with family and youth affairs. By 1990, despite the failure in the United States to pass a constitutional "Equal Rights Amendment," the campaigners for women's equality had a good many successes to their credit.

A particularly volatile subject in the area of women's rights was abortion. Feminists argued that women must enjoy the freedom to plan for their future unencumbered by the responsibilities of motherhood if they chose, and that their bodies were theirs to govern. Their opponents, who included members of the so-called right-to-life movement, countered with the argument that abortion encouraged sexual irresponsibility; some declared abortion to be the equivalent of murder. Legislation throughout most of Western Europe legalized abortion. Yet its opponents, many of them in the United States, continued to protest the practice.

The specific issues that drove women in Western Europe and America to committed action in the mid-1960s compelled writers to take sides as well. Women authors described not only the general loneliness of the human condition, but the particular plight of women trapped in a world not of their own making. The Frenchwoman Simone de Beauvoir in *The Second Sex* (1949), an influential study of the female condition, denounced the male middle class for turning not only workers but also

Simone de Beauvoir

women into objects for its own ends. Writers like Germaine Greer, Betty Friedan, and the poet Adrienne Rich helped define the politics and culture of the women's movement in its early years.

One further protest producing significant social change, particularly within the United States, was that of African Americans, who struggled in the 1960s to combat racial discrimination and to campaign for their civil rights. The liberation of colonial peoples in the decades following the Second World War heightened racial consciousness and racial conflict, not only in Africa and Asia but in the West as well. Newly independent black nations, on guard against real or perceived threats of neocolonialism, remained understandably sensitive to the fact of their economic dependence upon the predominantly white nations of Western Europe and America. Black and Asian immigration into those nations produced tension and frequent violence. And indigenous black populations in the West, particularly in the United States, derived a sense of both their present social and economic inferiority and their potential strength as a political force from the independence movements occurring elsewhere in the world.

Betty Friedan

The growth of insurgency among American blacks paralleled the rise of black nations in Africa and the Caribbean. The Second World War saw a major influx of blacks into northern U.S. cities, and intensified a drive for dignity and independence that had been fueled during the pre-war era by organizations such as the National Association for the Advancement of Colored People (NAACP) and the National Urban League. By 1960, various civil rights groups, led by the Congress of Racial Equality (CORE), had begun organizing boycotts and demonstrations directed at private businesses and public services that discriminated against blacks in the South. The leader of these protests, and the undoubted leader of the black movement in the United States in the 1960s, was Martin Luther King, Jr., a Baptist minister. King embraced the philosophy of nonviolence promoted by the Indian social and political activist Mohandas Gandhi. King's personal participation in countless demonstrations, his willingness to go to jail for a cause that he believed to be just, and his ability as an orator to arouse both blacks and whites with his message led to his position as the most highly regarded—and widely feared—defender of black rights. His inspiring career was tragically ended by assassination in 1968.

U.S. blacks after the Second World War

The goal of King and of organizations like CORE was a fully integrated nation. That of other charismatic black leaders was complete independence from white society. One such separatist was Malcolm X, who assumed the "X" after having discarded his "white" surname. For most of his adult life a spokesman for the Black Muslim movement, Malcolm X urged blacks to renew their commitment to their own heritage—the Muslim religion, for example—and to establish black businesses as a way of maintaining economic and psychological distance from white domination. Like King he was assassinated, in 1965 while addressing a rally in Harlem.

Black independence: Malcolm X

Civil rights laws enacted under the administration of President Lyndon B. Johnson in the 1960s brought African Americans some measure of

Limited gains against racism

equality with regard to voting rights—and, to a much lesser degree, school desegregation. In other areas, such as housing and job opportunities, blacks continue to suffer disadvantage and discrimination as a result of white racism, which often lies beneath arguments that blacks should be satisfied with the gains they have made, and the general recalcitrance of administrations following Johnson's domestically innovative one. These problems are not confined to the United States. Immigrants to Britain from former colonies in the West Indies and from India and Pakistan, for example, have met with discrimination in jobs and housing, with the result that racial disturbances are not an uncommon occurrence in major British cities. France has witnessed hostility toward Algerian immigration, Germany toward the importation of cheap Turkish labor. In Western Europe, as in the United States, there appears to be no immediate hope for genuine racial and ethnic integration.

ECONOMIC STAGNATION: THE PRICE OF SUCCESS

The 1960s roots of 1970s economic stagnation

Economic as well as social problems plagued Europe in the 1970s and 1980s. The stagnation that overtook the Continent was the product of trends that had their roots in the prosperous 1960s. By the middle of that decade, for example, the West German growth rate had slowed. Demand for manufactured goods declined and in 1966 the country suffered its first postwar recession. Volkswagen, that mythic symbol of the German "miracle," introduced a shortened work week; almost 700,000 West Germans were thrown out of work. In France a persistent housing shortage increased the cost of living. While new industries continued to prosper, the basic industries—coal, steel, and railways—began to run up deficits. Unemployment was rising in tandem with prices. Prime Minister Harold Wilson's pledge to revive Britain's economy by introducing new technology foundered on balance-of-payment crises. The Common Market, expanded in 1973 to include Britain, Ireland, and Denmark, and again in the early 1980s to admit Greece, Spain, and Portugal, struggled to overcome problems stemming from the conflict between the domestic economic regulations characteristic of many European states and the free-market policies that prevailed among the EEC countries.

OPEC, inflation, and competition

All these difficulties were compounded by the dramatic rise in the price of oil that occurred once the Arab-dominated Organization of Petroleum Exporting Countries (OPEC) instituted an oil embargo against the Western powers for economic and political reasons in 1973. By 1975 the cost of one barrel of oil had risen to $10.46, as compared with $1.73 two years before, and it continued to rise to over $30 by the early 1980s. This increase produced an inflationary spiral; interest rates rose and with them the price of almost everything else Western consumers were used to buying. Wage demands calculated to meet rising costs produced strikes. The placid industrial relations that had characterized the 1950s and early

1960s were a thing of the past. At the same time, European manufacturers encountered serious competition, not only from highly developed countries like Japan but also from the increasingly active economies of Asia and Africa, in which the West had invested capital eagerly in the previous decades. By 1980 Japan had captured 10 percent of the automobile market in West Germany and 25 percent in Belgium. By 1984, unemployment in Western Europe had reached about 19 million. The lean years had arrived.

Meanwhile the Soviet Union and its satellites were also experiencing the stagnation that accompanies the maturing of an economy. The Soviet Communist party proclaimed in 1961 that by 1970 the U.S.S.R. would exceed the United States in per capita production. By the end of the 1970s, however, Soviet per capita production was not much higher than in the less industrialized countries of southern Europe. During the same period its rate of economic growth was on a sluggish par with that of other Western nations.

Following an impressive economic performance during the early 1970s, the Eastern European nations encountered serious financial difficulties. Their success had rested in part on capital borrowed not from the Soviet Union but from the West. By 1980 those debts had become serious burdens to their national economies. Poland's hard-currency indebtedness to Western countries, for example, was almost four times as great as its annual exports. The solution to this problem, attempted in Poland and elsewhere, was to cut back on production for domestic consumption in order to increase exports. Yet this policy encountered strong popular opposition. Although there was virtually no unemployment in Eastern Europe, men and women were by no means happy with their economic situation. Working hours were longer than in Western Europe, and goods and services, even in prosperous times, remained far from abundant.

Western governments also found it difficult to react effectively to the abrupt change in their economic circumstances. Politicians of both the Right and the Left struggled to rediscover the magic that had produced prosperity, but with little success. In Britain, the Labour and Conservative parties alternately governed through the 1970s, unable to meet the demands of trade unionists who were angry as they saw their real wages eroded by inflation, or of international bankers who were impatient with Britain's inability to bring its trade figures into balance. The new, radically conservative leader of the Conservative party, Margaret Thatcher, claimed to have the answer, and was elected in 1979—and reelected in 1983 and 1987—on the basis of that claim. Yet despite curbs on trade union power, tax cuts designed to stimulate the economy, and the return of many publicly owned enterprises to private hands, the economy remained weak, with close to 15 percent of the work force unemployed by 1986.

West Germany, like Britain, veered to the Right in the 1980s. The Social Democratic party, headed in the late 1960s and early 1970s by Willy Brandt, had remained in power after Brandt's resignation as chancellor in 1974 under the leadership of his less charismatic successor, Helmut

Soviet economic stagnation

Eastern European economic malaise in the 1970s

Margaret Thatcher, Prime Minister of Great Britain, 1979–1990

Helmut Kohl, Chancellor of the Federal Republic of Germany, 1982–1991

François Mitterrand, French President, 1981–1995

The Hard Ecu. The proposed single currency of the EC.

Schmidt. Schmidt's coalition government attempted in the early 1980s to combat economic recession with job-training programs and tax incentives, both financed by higher taxes. These programs did little to assist economic recovery, and Schmidt was replaced in 1982 by the Christian Democrat Helmut Kohl, who, like Margaret Thatcher in Britain, proposed cuts in social programs and unemployment compensation.

France fared little better than its neighbor in the struggle to maintain economic momentum. De Gaulle resigned in 1969, his prestige eroded by the protests and strikes of the previous year. His successors in the 1970s, Georges Pompidou and Valéry Giscard d'Estaing, pursued a middle course that did no more than keep the country on an even keel. In 1981, Giscard was ousted by a socialist, François Mitterrand, whose record as an escaped prisoner of war and Resistance fighter in the Second World War made him a popular figure (a record challenged by evidence of collaboration just before his death), and whose public visit to the tomb of the French socialist hero Jean Jaurès was meant to symbolize his intention to govern in accordance with Marxist ideals. Among the array of reforms promptly undertaken by the new government was the further nationalization of major industries and private financial institutions, including the famed 150-year-old Rothschild bank, Pompidou's former employer. Yet these bold moves, bitterly opposed by conservative interests, did not resolve the nation's economic malaise. Inflation and unemployment rose, along with budget and balance-of-trade deficits. Newly nationalized enterprises drained government resources. These difficulties led to a devaluation of the franc, a temporary freeze on wages and prices, and in 1986 to a return to power of more conservative political forces committed to a policy of "privatization" of companies and industries that had been nationalized under the socialists.

Spain and Italy moved Left in the early 1980s. Spain, freed from the rule of General Franco by his death in 1974, and under the nominal rule of his hand-picked successor King Juan Carlos, saw the Socialist Workers party score a major upset in 1982. Intent on modernizing rather than radicalizing Spain, the socialists eschewed widespread government ownership of industry in favor of selective nationalization, which included the nation's electric-power grid. Similarly, Italy for a time witnessed increasing victories by parties of the Left at the expense of the previously indomitable Christian Democratic party.

The fact that governments of Right and Left were unable to recreate the sort of economic climate that had characterized Europe's unprecedented postwar prosperity suggests the degree to which economic forces remain outside the control of individual states, prey to the far-from-predictable vagaries of international finance, trade cycles, and human miscalculation. The economic malaise afflicting Europe led to renewed efforts to address common problems through the increasingly dominant organization of European states. By the end of the 1980s, the EEC, today known as the European Union (EU), embarked on an ambitious program of integration. Long-term goals, agreed upon in 1991, include a monetary union, with a central European bank and a single currency, and unified social policies to reduce poverty and unemployment. Whether the community can overcome the claims of national sovereignty and the logistical problems associated with conducting business in ten official languages remains to be seen.

EUROPE RECAST: THE COLLAPSE OF COMMUNISM AND THE END OF THE SOVIET UNION

One of history's fascinations is its unpredictability. There has been no more telling example of this than the sudden collapse of the Eastern European communist regimes in the early 1990s, and the simultaneous disintegration of the once-mighty Soviet Union.

The beginning of the end came with the accession of Mikhail Gorbachev to the leadership of the Soviet Communist party in 1985. In his mid-fifties, Gorbachev was significantly younger than his immediate predecessors and less prey to the habits of mind that had shaped Soviet domestic and foreign affairs. He was frankly critical of the repressive aspects of communist society as well as its sluggish economy, and he did not hesitate to voice those criticisms openly. His twin policies of *glasnost* (intellectual openness) and *perestroika* (economic restructuring) held out hope for a freer, more prosperous Soviet Union. Under Gorbachev, a number of imprisoned dissidents were freed, among them Andrei Sakharov, the scientist known as "the father of the Soviet hydrogen bomb."

Gorbachev: the beginning of the end

The policies of *perestroika* took aim at the privileges of the political elite and the immobility of the state bureaucracy by instituting competitive elections to official positions and limiting terms of office. Economically, Gorbachev's program of *perestroika* called for a shift from the centrally planned economy instituted by Stalin to a mixed economy combining planning with the operation of market forces. In agriculture, *perestroika* accelerated the move away from cooperative production and instituted incentives for the achievement of production targets. Gorbachev called for the integration of the Soviet Union into the international economy by participation in organizations such as the International Monetary Fund.

Perestroika

Even these dramatic reforms, however, were proving to be too little too late by the late 1980s. Ethnic unrest, a legacy of Russia's nineteenth-century imperialism, threatened to split the Soviet Union apart, while secession movements gathered steam in the Baltic republics and elsewhere. From 1988 onward, fighting between Armenians and Azerbaijanis over an ethnically Azerbaijani region located inside Armenia threatened to escalate into a border dispute with Iran; only the presence of Soviet troops temporarily quelled the conflict.

Ethnic unrest

Spurred on by these events in the Soviet Union, the countries of Eastern Europe began to agitate for independence from Moscow. Gorbachev

Glasnost

Gorbachev and the Old Guard. Gorbachev is pictured here at the height of his power in 1986, with KGB chief Victor Chebrikov, President Andrei Gromyko, and Premier Nikolai Rzyhkov. *Perestroika* aimed at the privileges of the political elite and would eventually lead to the fall from power of all these men.

Old Opponents Meet in Poland, 1989. Lech Walesa, head of Solidarity, and General Wojciech Jaruzelski, who imposed martial law on Poland in 1981, are pictured here after the government agreed to hold open elections.

Czech resistance

encouraged open discussion—*glasnost*—not only in his own country but also in the satellite nations. He revoked the Brezhnev Doctrine's insistence on single-party socialist governments and made frequent and inspiring trips to the capitals of neighboring satellites. *Glasnost* rekindled the flame of opposition in Poland, where Solidarity had been defeated but not destroyed by the government in 1981. In 1988 the union launched a new series of strikes. These disturbances culminated in an agreement between the government and Solidarity that legalized the union and promised open elections. The results, in June 1989, astonished the world: virtually all of the government's candidates lost and the Citizen's Committee, affiliated with Solidarity, won a sizeable majority in the Polish parliament.

In Hungary and Czechoslovakia, events followed a similar course during 1988 and 1989. As a result of continuing demonstrations, Janos Kadar, the Hungarian leader since the Soviet crackdown of 1956, resigned in May 1988 and was replaced by the reformist government of the Hungarian Socialist Workers' party. By the spring of 1989 the Hungarian Politburo had been purged of Communist party supporters. At the same time, the government had begun to dismantle its security fences along the Austrian border. A year later the Hungarian Democratic Forum, proclaiming its dedication to the reinstatement of full civil rights and to the restructuring of the economy, secured a plurality of seats in the National Assembly.

The Czechs, too, staged demonstrations against Soviet domination in late 1988. Brutal beating of student demonstrators by the police in 1989 led to the radicalization of the nations' workers and to mass demonstrations. Civic Forum, an opposition coalition, called for the installation of a coalition government to include non-communists, for free elections, and for the resignation of the country's communist leadership. It reinforced its demands with continuing mass demonstrations and threats of a general strike that resulted in the toppling of the old regime and the election of the playwright and Civic Forum leader Vaclav Havel as president.

Undoubtedly the most significant political change in Eastern Europe during the late 1980s was the collapse of communism in East Germany and the reunification of East and West Germany. Although long considered the most prosperous of the Soviet satellite countries, East Germany suffered from severe economic stagnation and environmental degradation. Waves of East Germans registered their discontent with worsening conditions by massive illegal emigration to the West. This movement combined with evidence of widespread official corruption to force the resignation of East Germany's longtime hard-line premier, Erich Honecker. His successor, Egon Krenz, promised reforms, but he was nevertheless faced with continuing protests and continuing mass emigration. On November 4, 1989, the government, in a move that acknowledged its powerlessness to hold its citizens captive, opened its border with Czechoslovakia. This move effectively freed East Germans to travel to the West. In a matter of days, the Berlin Wall, embodiment of the cold war, the Iron Curtain, and the division of East from West, was demolished. Jubilant throngs from both sides walked through the gaping holes that now permitted men, women, and children to take the few steps that symbolized the return to freedom and a chance for national unity. Free elections were held throughout Germany in March 1990, resulting in a victory for the "Alliance for Germany," a coalition allied with West German chancellor Helmut Kohl's Christian Democratic Union. With heavy emigration

Europe Recast: The Collapse of Communism and the End of the Soviet Union

Vaclav Havel, President of Post-communist Czechoslovakia

The Fall of the Berlin Wall, 1989. When East German officials announced that citizens could leave the country through any border crossing, rendering the Berlin Wall obsolete, people gathered at the wall to celebrate and to tear it down with picks and axes and small hammers.

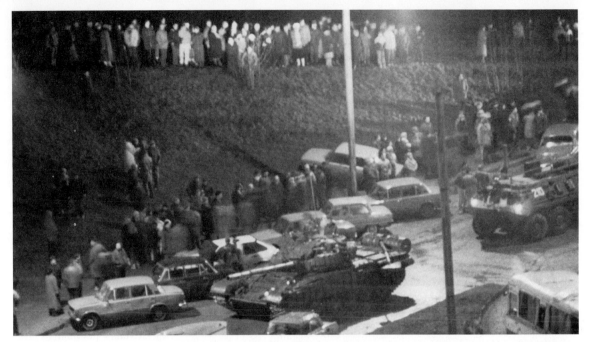

Soviet Forces Seizing Control of Lithuania's Main Television Broadcast Station in January 1991. By fall 1991 Lithuania, Estonia, and Latvia had successfully seceded from the Soviet Union.

continuing, reunification talks quickly culminated in the formal proclamation of a united Germany on October 3, 1990.

Lithuanian, Latvian, and Estonian independence

Throughout the rest of Eastern Europe, single-party governments in the countries behind what was left of the tattered Iron Curtain—Albania, Bulgaria, Rumania, and Yugoslavia—collapsed in the face of democratic pressure for change. Meanwhile, in the Soviet Union itself, inspired by events in Eastern Europe, the Balkan republics of Lithuania and Latvia strained to free themselves from the Soviet yoke. In 1990 they unilaterally proclaimed their independence from the Soviet Union, throwing into sharp relief the tension between "union" and "republics." Gorbachev reacted with an uncertain mixture of armed intervention and promises of greater local autonomy. In the fall of 1991 Lithuania and Latvia, along with the third Baltic state of Estonia, won international recognition as independent republics.

Failure of *perestroika*

The Soviet Union's unproductive economy continued to fuel widespread dissatisfaction. With the failure of *perestroika*—largely the result of a lack of resources and an inability to increase production—came the rise of a powerful political rival to Gorbachev, the latter's erstwhile ally Boris Yeltsin. The reforming mayor of Moscow, Yeltsin was elected president of the Russian Federation—the largest Soviet republic—on an anti-Gorbachev platform in 1990. Pressure from the Yeltsin camp weakened Gorbachev's ability to maneuver independently of reactionary factions in the Politburo and the military, undermining his reform program and his ability to remain in power.

The Soviet Union's increasingly severe domestic problems led to mounting protests in 1991, when Gorbachev's policies failed to improve—indeed diminished—the living standard of the Soviet people. Demands increased that the bloated government bureaucracy respond with a dramatic cure for the country's continuing economic stagnation. Gorbachev appeared to lose his political nerve, having first ordered and then cancelled a radical "500 day" economic reform plan, while at the same time agreeing to negotiations with the increasingly disaffected republics within the union, now clamoring for independence. Sensing their political lives to be in jeopardy, a group of highly placed hard-line Communist party officials staged an abortive coup in August 1991, incarcerating Gorbachev and his wife and declaring a return to party-line orthodoxy. In response, the Soviet citizenry defied their self-proclaimed saviors. Led by Boris Yeltsin, who at one point mounted a tank in a Moscow street to rally the people, they successfully called the plotters' bluff. Within two weeks, Gorbachev was back in power, and the coup leaders were in prison.

Gorbachev's power was diminished by the August events, however, while Yeltsin's was dramatically increased. Throughout the fall of 1991, as Gorbachev struggled to hold the nation together, Yeltsin capitalized on the discontent throughout the union, which was no longer united by the force of a powerful one-party state. On December 8, 1991, the presidents of the republics of Russia, Ukraine, and Belorussia (now called Belarus) declared that the Soviet Union was no more: "The U.S.S.R. as a subject of international law and geopolitical reality is ceasing to exist." Though the

Abortive hard-line coup

Dissolution of the Soviet Union

Boris Yeltsin Faces Down the Coup, August 1991. Russian president Boris Yeltsin stood his ground at the Russian parliament building against the hard-liners who attempted to overthrow Mikhail Gorbachev. Here Yeltsin is encouraging the people to fight the takeover of the central government.

The Post–Cold War West, 1992

BARENTS SEA

KARA SEA

WHITE SEA

RUSSIA

COMMONWEALTH OF INDEPENDENT STATES

KAZAKHSTAN

Alma Ata

Bishkek
KYRGYZSTAN

TAJIKISTAN
Dushanbe

Tashkent

UZBEKISTAN

TURKMENISTAN
Ashkhabad

ARAL
SEA

CASPIAN
SEA

Baku

AZERBAIJAN

GEORGIA
Tbilisi

ARMENIA
Yerevan

TURKEY

Ankara

Yalta

BLACK SEA

Istanbul

Moscow

Kiev

UKRAINE

Kishinev
Odessa

MOLDOVA

Bucharest

ROMANIA

BULGARIA
Sofia

GREECE

Athens

Minsk

BELARUS

St. Petersburg

FINLAND

Helsinki

Tallinn
ESTONIA

Riga
LATVIA

Vilnius
LITHUANIA

Warsaw

POLAND

Gdansk

BALTIC
SEA

Stockholm

SWEDEN

Copenhagen

DENMARK

Berlin

GERMANY
Bonn

Prague
CZECH
REPUBLIC

Bratislava
SLOVAKIA

Budapest

HUNGARY

Belgrade

YUGOSLAVIA
Sarajevo

BOSNIA
HERZE-
GOVINA

Skopje
MACEDONIA

Titana
ALBANIA

ADRIATIC SEA

ITALY

Rome

MEDITERRANEAN
SEA

Vienna
AUSTRIA

Ljubljana
SLOVENIA

Zagreb
CROATIA

Berne
SWITZ.

NORWAY

Oslo

Post-Cold War West, 1992

prose was flat, the message was momentous. The once-mighty Soviet Union, founded seventy-five years before in a burst of revolutionary fervor and violence, had evaporated nearly overnight, leaving in its wake a collection of eleven far-from-powerful nations loosely joined together as the "Commonwealth of Independent States." On December 25, 1991, Gorbachev resigned the leadership of the now nonexistent union, as the Soviet flag—the hammer and sickle that had symbolized the nation that for fifty years had kept half of Europe in thrall—was lowered for the last time over the Kremlin.

The mighty fall left mighty problems in its wake. Food shortages worsened during the winter of 1992. The value of the ruble plummeted. The republics could not agree on common military policies, or resolve difficult and dangerous questions concerning the control of nuclear warheads. Yeltsin's pleas for economic assistance from the West resulted in massive infusions of private and public capital, which nevertheless failed to prevent serious economic hardship and dislocation. Free enterprise brought with it unemployment and encouraged profiteering and crime. Yeltsin's determination to press ahead with his economic program met with stiff resistance from a parliament and citizenry alarmed by the ruthlessness and rapidity of the change they were experiencing. When the parliament balked at Yeltsin's proposals in September 1993, he dissolved it. Elections in the fall of 1995 were a measure of continuing discontent. The resurgent Communists captured the largest block of parliamentary seats—roughly one-third; Yeltsin's party, though second in terms of representation, could claim no more than 10 percent. The president's position was also threatened from the right. Vladimir Zhirinovsky, a xenophobic nationalist, played upon the anxieties of a populace increasingly willing to blame the West for its country's difficulties.

> Economic hardship in the wake of collapse

Meanwhile, ethnic and religious conflict plagued the republics. In the first years following the dissolution of the Soviet Union, warfare flared in Georgia, Armenia, and Azerbaijan. The most serious conflict arose in the predominately Muslim area of Chechnya, bordering Georgia in the Caucasus, which had declared its independence from Russia in late 1991. Three years later the Russian government, weary of this continuing challenge to its shabby authority, launched a concerted effort to quash resistance. The attempt failed, exposing Russia's military ineptitude to the world in a conflict that saw the commission of atrocities on both sides. A truce signed on July 30, 1995, was short-lived. Continuing warfare suggested that stability within the borders of the former Soviet Union was an elusive goal under present political and economic circumstances.

> Conflict in the republics

Despite the high hopes spawned by the upheavals in central and eastern Europe, these countries face continuing difficulties as well. The achievement of genuine reunification in Germany will take considerable time. Economic development in the east has been slow and uneven, as explicitly racist political movements once again surface, with massive dislocations caused by the shift from central planning to a free-market economy. As much of the initial euphoria regarding Germany's future

> Realities of German reunification

Free market in Eastern Europe

evaporates, it is unclear whether the mild malaise the country continues to suffer will lead to more serious unrest.

Adapting to change has been difficult throughout eastern Europe. Attempts to create free-market economies have brought inflation, unemployment, and—in their wake—anti-capitalist demonstrations. Inefficient industries, a work force resistant to change, energy shortages, lack of venture capital, and a severely polluted environment have combined to hinder progress and to sour hopes. Uprisings against governments in Bulgaria and Albania in early 1997 were fueled by the inability of governments to resolve basic economic and social problems. In addition, racial and ethnic conflicts have continued to divide newly liberated democracies, recalling the divisions that led to the First World War and that have plagued eastern Europe throughout its history. Minorities have waged often violent campaigns for autonomous rights—or outright secession. In Czechoslovakia, for example, the election of deputies calling for Slovakian independence resulted in Havel's resignation and the dissolution of the tight federal union between Czechs and Slovaks.

Yugoslavia fragments

In Yugoslavia, fierce fighting broke out both before and after the interior states of Croatia and Slovenia declared their independence from the Serbian-dominated central government in June 1991. By the spring of 1992, Croatia, Slovenia, Bosnia-Herzegovina, and Macedonia had seceded from Yugoslavia. The situation in Bosnia posed the most serious threat to regional stability. A Serbian minority, under the leadership of Radovan Karadzic, challenged the regime of Muslim president Alia Izetbegovic by proclaiming a Serbian republic within the borders of Bosnia-Herzegovina. An all-out civil war commenced in April 1992. The Bosnian capital of Sarajevo was besieged by rebels. Although the Bosnians outnumbered their Serbian foes, they were poorly equipped, whereas Yugoslavian Serbs, led by Slobodan Milosevic, ensured that their Serbian allies in Bosnia were well supplied.

Ethnic cleansing and genocide in Bosnia

Alarm spread throughout the West as the fighting continued. Yet the European Union, NATO, and the United Nations failed to coordinate their efforts to impose peace on the warring factions. The conflict was ethnic and religious, reflecting centuries of bitter animosities that survived the postwar years of Marshal Tito's communist centralization. By mid-1993, Bosnian Croats, Muslims, and Serbs were all engaged in the grisly, inhumane business of "ethnic cleansing"—that is, purging their particular regions of religious and ethnic minorities, either by forced emigration, imprisonment, or the method often deemed most effective—mass slaughter. The failure of UN-imposed sanctions to end the conflict led NATO to begin bombing raids against Serbian positions in May of 1994. When Croatian forces entered the battle on the side of the Bosnians, in July 1995, the international community stood aghast, fearing the spread of the war into Yugoslavia and Macedonia.

An uneasy peace

Finally, for no other apparent reason than that all sides were exhausted by the conflict, Izetbegovic, Milosevic, and the Croatian leader Franjo Tudjman met in Dayton, Ohio, in December 1995, to agree on an accord that partitioned Bosnia into two areas, a Muslim-Croat–controlled west

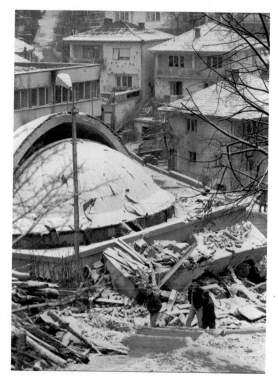

Civil War in Bosnia. Residents of Bosnia face the tremendous task of reconstructing their lives and cities after the devastating civil war that ripped their country apart from 1992–1995. The mosque shown in this photograph was destroyed during the three-year-long siege of Srebenica by Serbian forces.

and a Serbian-controlled east. An international army of 60,000, under UN command and including U.S. troops, was given the unenviable and perhaps impossible task of enforcing a peace that many Bosnians of all persuasions remained unwilling to accept. Each side continued to blame the others for the deaths of 250,000 men, women and children, the forced migration of more than three million, the rapes, and the wholesale burnings. If the world needed evidence that life after the collapse of communism would continue for many eastern Europeans to be a brutish business, the fate of Yugoslavia proved it in abundant measure.

SUMMARY POINTS

- Beginning in the mid-1960s social and economic tensions eroded the consensus that postwar prosperity had brought about in the West. Youth protests, the women's movement, and ethnic and racial conflicts forced governments to adopt policies aimed at promoting equality and improving the lives of workers.

- The West in the 1970s and 1980s saw economic growth slow, energy prices rise drastically, and international competition increase, leading governments of both Left and Right to try unsuccessfully to recapture the economic prosperity of the preceding decades.

- The political changes of *glasnost* and *perestroika* inititated by Mikhail Gorbachev resulted in the defeat of communist governments in Eastern Europe and the Soviet Union. Ethnic and nationalistic tensions caused the Soviet Union to break up in 1990–1991.

- Since 1990, the countries of the former Soviet bloc have experienced severe economic problems, while ethnic conflict has plagued several former Soviet republics and, most notably, Bosnia-Herzegovina in the former Yugoslavia.

SELECTED READINGS

Beschloss, Michael, and Strobe Talbott, *At the Highest Levels: The Inside Story of the End of the Cold War,* Boston, 1993. An analysis of the relationships between Presidents Gorbachev and Bush, and their determination to ignore hard-liners.

Garton Ash, Timothy, *In Europe's Name: Germany and the Divided Continent,* New York, 1993. An analysis of the effect of German reunification on the future of Europe.

Hosking, Geoffrey, *The Awakening of the Soviet Union,* Cambridge, Mass., 1990. The factors that led to the end of the Soviet era.

Hughes, H. Stuart, *Sophisticated Rebels: The Political Culture of European Dissent, 1968–1987,* Cambridge, Mass., 1990. The nature of dissent on both sides of the disintegrating Iron Curtain in the years 1988–1989.

Hulsberg, Werner, *The German Greens: A Social and Political Profile,* New York, 1988. The origins, politics, and impact of environmental politics.

Jarausch, Konrad, *The Rush to German Unity,* New York, 1994. The problems of reunification analyzed.

Kennedy, Paul, *Preparing for the Twenty-First Century,* New York, 1993. A critical and generally pessimistic appraisal of the current state of world politics.

Lewin, Moshe, *The Gorbachev Phenomenon,* exp. ed., Berkeley, 1991. Written as a firsthand account, tracing the roots of Gorbachev's successes and failures.

Pinder, John, *European Community: The Building of a Union,* 2d ed., New York, 1995. Analyzes the chances for the Community's success in the 1990s.

Wright, Patrick, *On Living in an Old Country: The National Past in Contemporary Britain,* New York, 1986. The culture of Britain in the 1980s.

Young, Hugo, *One of Us: A Biography of Margaret Thatcher,* New York, 1989. A perceptive, thorough examination of Britain's first woman prime minister, her character, and her policies.

SOURCE MATERIALS

Garton Ash, Timothy, *The Magic Lantern: The Revolution of 1989 Witnessed in Warsaw, Budapest, Berlin, and Prague,* New York, 1990. Eyewitness accounts of the end of the Soviet era.

Philipsen, Dirk, *We Were the People: Voices from East Germany's Revolutionary Autumn of 1989,* Durham, N.C., 1993. A collection of interviews.

CHAPTER 32

PROBLEMS OF WORLD CIVILIZATION

Our species has not won its independence from nature, and we cannot do all that we can dream. Or at least we cannot do it at the rate required to avoid tragedy, for we are not unbounded from time.
—STEPHEN JAY GOULD, "The Terrifying Normalcy of AIDS,"
New York Times Magazine, April 19, 1997

THE WRITING OF A FINAL CHAPTER in a textbook of this sort is a difficult task. It demands not only an instant analysis of contemporary society but also an attempt to discern in present events patterns that will continue to be of some consequence five to ten years hence. Human idiosyncrasies make prediction a tricky business, and historians are particularly loath to single out this movement or that trend and to pronounce it "significant" in terms of the future. We shall therefore content ourselves with a discussion of some of the most serious problems confronting society at the end of the twentieth century, calling attention at the outset to the fact that the problems are rooted in historical developments—industrialization, urbanization, and international competition, for example, that we have traced in the preceding chapters.

The present as history

DECOLONIZATION AND THE EMERGENCE OF THE DEVELOPING WORLD

As significant as any trend in world politics since the end of the Second World War has been the decline of the Western imperial powers and the concurrent emergence of the developing world—newly independent states in Africa and Asia, along with older nations there as well as in South America. Many of these countries have established themselves in territories that were formerly parts of European empires. Others—China and the various nations of the Middle East and South America, for example—while nominally independent of both the West and the Soviet Union before 1945, nevertheless existed under European hegemony and were forced to acquiesce to European demands. Such is the case no longer. Although many of these so-called emerging nations are poor, and

The emergence of the developing world

although the people of developing nations are by no means a united block, they represent an increasingly independent factor in the world power equation.

Many of these countries are rich in natural resources. Nations in the Middle East, South America, and Africa possess oil in quantities sufficient to make their every move of vital importance to the West. Other African nations, such as the Congo (formerly Zaire) and Angola, are immensely rich in mineral resources. Population resources serve as both liability and asset in developing countries. The people of China or India, for example, by their sheer numbers, can have a significant impact on the world at all times. Every area in the developing world is a potential "trouble spot," and the history of developing countries since 1945 is often a history of violent internal dissent. This is so not only because the problems of racism, ethnicity, tribalism, poverty, hunger, and overpopulation make them particularly vulnerable to violent civil conflicts, but also because the United States, the former Soviet Union, the European nations, and China itself were until recently prepared to engage each other through the medium of adversaries in the developing world, thus increasing the possibility of conflict by their willingness to encourage it. To protect themselves from direct confrontation with each other, these powerful nations interfered in the civil wars of others, on opposite sides and with an intensity that frequently belied their declared interest in avoiding general world war.

The governments of most developing countries have attempted with varying degrees of success to pursue the twin goals of industrialization and modernization. In this they have been encouraged by the governments of the West. Transnational corporations with headquarters in western Europe or the United States have also been more than willing to invest capital in parts of the world where manufacturing costs can be kept to a minimum because labor is cheap, or where valuable natural resources can be extracted and processed profitably for the same reason. Such practices have brought prosperity to an increasingly large middle class in countries such as Indonesia, South Korea, and Venezuela, but at considerable cost. In 1984, for example, a gas plant owned by the U.S. chemical company Union Carbide in Bhopal, India, leaked toxic material that killed more than 8,000 people and injured a further 150,000. As a consequence of the North American Free Trade Agreement (NAFTA), signed in 1993 by Canada, the United States, and Mexico, factories financed by transnationals sprang up in northern Mexico, where demand for employment guaranteed a low wage scale. The rapid construction of those factories was not matched, however, by the timely provision of adequate environmental safeguards, or decent accommodation, health, and educational facilities for workers or their families. International oil and mining corporations have not hesitated to destroy vast areas of tropical rain forest or to threaten the very existence of ancient tribal civilizations as they have moved into parts of the world hitherto untouched by the West.

Bhopal. This Union Carbide factory in Bhopal, India, was the site of a catastrophic poisonous-gas leak in 1984.

In one area of manufacture, the developing world has continued to respond to a steady and immensely profitable market in the West: the production of opium, heroin, and cocaine is a thriving industry in countries such as Colombia, Myanmar (formerly Burma), Afghanistan, and Malaysia. Though the trade in drugs is illegal, the fragile economies of those countries where they are produced have encouraged governments to turn a blind eye to the global devastation such multi-billion-dollar trafficking brings in its wake.

The international drug trade

The twin policies of industrialization and modernization have not gone unchallenged. In the spring of 1979, for example, the extremely repressive regime of one of the developing world's most devoted "Western-

Iran's attack on Western "progress"

Environmental Degradation. Intentional flooding makes it easier for rainforest trees to be felled and logged, but causes severe environmental damage.

The Ayatollah Ruhollah Khomeini of Iran

Revolution in China

izers," the shah of oil-rich Iran, was overthrown by the revolutionary forces of an equally repressive Islamic fundamentalist, the Ayatollah Khomeini, whose explicit policy was to turn his country's back not only on the West but on "progress" as the West has defined that term for the past two hundred years. Internal conflicts over intercourse with the West have continued to surface since Khomeini's death in 1989.

The most radical change in the developing world resulting from the events of the Second World War was the Chinese Revolution. A civil war had raged in China since 1926, when the forces of the nationalists under Chiang Kai-shek had engaged in battle first in the south, then in the north, with communist insurgents under the leadership of Mao Zedong, a former teacher and union organizer. A truce in 1937 had allowed both sides to wage common battle against the Japanese. At the end of the war, however, the communists, still led by Mao Zedong, refused to surrender the northern provinces under their control, and civil war broke out again. The United States intervened, first as mediator and then with massive military assistance, as an ally of Chiang—all to no avail. The nationalists, corrupt and unrepresentative of the people, surrendered in 1949 to the communists and decamped to the island of Taiwan. Intensely hostile to the capitalist West, the Chinese communists soon found themselves engaged, as well, in a series of skirmishes, verbal and otherwise, with their erstwhile Marxist co-revolutionaries, the Soviets. The Sino-Soviet rivalry, the willingness of the United States in the 1970s to reach an accommodation with the Chinese in order to capitalize on that rivalry, and the willingness of Mao's successors, Deng Xiaoping and Jiang Zemin, to encourage Western capitalist investment, suggest that however much power shifted after the Second World War, power politics remained a game

Left: **A Red Guard Demonstration.** Middle-school students display their solidarity with Mao Zedong's revolution by waving copies of a book of his quotations. The slogan proclaims, "Not only are we able to destroy the old world, we are able to build a new world instead—Mao Zedong." Below: **Chairman Mao Zedong.**

Leaders of Indian Nationalism—Nehru and Gandhi. Mohandas Gandhi was assassinated in 1948. Jawaharlal Nehru served as prime minister of India from 1947 to his death in 1964.

nations believed themselves compelled to play—if necessary, in opposition to their professed ideological commitments.

The Second World War, which had assisted the course of Chinese revolution by dissolving older power structures, served the same purpose within the colonial empires of the West. The first major British colony to establish self-government after the war was India. Rebel movements had harassed the representatives of Britain in India throughout the nineteenth century. By 1945 anti-British sentiment had reached such a pitch that the country was ripe for revolution. Resolutions by nationalist bodies such as the Indian National Congress called upon Britain to "quit India." The foremost Indian nationalist leader, Mohandas K. Gandhi, did not approve of armed attacks on rulers and their institutions, however. His methods were noncooperation and civil disobedience. By 1947 he and his comrade and disciple Jawaharlal Nehru had gained such widespread support that the British found it expedient to grant autonomy to India and its neighboring area, Pakistan. In 1950 both countries organized themselves as independent republics. Disorders, stemming largely from religious conflicts between Hindus, Muslims, and Sikhs, continued to plague the two countries, however, resulting in a bloody war in 1971. An important outcome of this conflict was the establishment of the independent republic of Bangladesh, formerly East Pakistan.

> Self-government for India

Important as India was to Britain, it was only the first and largest of the colonies surrendered by colonial powers following the war. Vast areas of Africa achieved independence as well after 1945. In 1951 nationalists compelled the British to withdraw their troops from Egyptian territory. A year later a group of nationalist army officers seized control of the government.

> Egyptian nationalism

Riot in Calcutta, 1946. A dead Hindu surrounded by armed Muslims. Such scenes were not uncommon on the eve of Indian independence, when extreme tension developed between Hindu and Muslim segments of the population.

Gamal Abdel Nasser, dynamic Arab nationalist and president of Egypt, 1956–1970

The British withdrawal from Africa

They deposed the playboy king, Farouk, alleged to be subservient to the British, and proclaimed the state a republic. Shortly thereafter an Egyptian colonel, Gamal Abdel Nasser, assumed the presidency of the country. When Nasser nationalized the Suez Canal Company in 1956 in order to finance the construction of the Aswan dam on the Nile, the British and French, dependent on the canal as their major trade route to the East, interpreted the Egyptian action as a direct threat to their economic security. Together with the newly created country of Israel—itself a by-product of British decolonization—Britain and France launched an abortive, ill-fated invasion of the canal zone. World opinion—led by the United States—turned against the invaders, who were forced to withdraw.

The British gradually departed from sub-Saharan Africa as well, beginning with Ghana (formerly called the Gold Coast), which was granted self-government in 1954 and independence in 1957. Apologists for British colonial rule claimed that by training indigenous elites and gradually transferring to them responsibility for local administration, British colonies would make the transition to independence more smoothly than would the colonies of other European states, where self-government came with less preparation. Despite such protestations, the British colonies' emergence into independence and political and economic stability proved no less difficult than it was for their neighbors. Even in resource-rich Nigeria the euphoria of independence (gained in 1960) fell prey in 1966 to charges of government corruption and inefficiency, political assassinations, the overthrow of the government, the secession of the eastern region of the country, and a devastating thirty-one-month civil war in which more than a million people perished in battle and of starvation. Kenya, as poor as Nigeria was rich, was beset by tribal rebellion in 1952, more than a decade before independence. Although driven in part by racial and ethnic antipathies, the uprising was essentially a nationalistic movement dedicated to achieving African self-determination over questions of land and governance, a goal realized in 1965 with the election of Jomo Kenyatta, a proponent of African socialism, to the presidency in 1964.

In Rhodesia, race was the dominant issue. White Rhodesians had long denied the inevitability of black rule, instituting a system of rigid racial segregation. In 1965 they unilaterally declared their independence from Britain. The white government held firm in its determination to resist black rule until 1977 when the cumulative effect of U.S. and British pressure, economic sanctions, fierce guerrilla warfare, and the withdrawal of South African assistance caused the government to open negotiations that eventually led in 1980 to the creation of a state named Zimbabwe, which was dominated by black nationalists and presided over by Robert Mugabe.

Undoubtedly the most explosive area of conflict on the African continent was the former British colony of South Africa, whose all-white minority government continued to oppose appeals and pressures from all quarters to relax its racial policy of *apartheid*. This policy enforced a separate and desperately inferior existence for the country's black and mixed-race population. Initially, the nonwhites responded to apartheid with campaigns of passive resistance. Government-sponsored repression and violence, however, drove the African National Congress (ANC),

> Rhodesian independence

Police Action in Johannesburg. In downtown Johannesburg the authorities disperse a group of black and white demonstrators who were protesting police actions in the huge Soweto ghetto. Over 1,000 blacks were killed by police in Soweto in June 1976.

Pieter W. Botha, president of South Africa from 1984 to 1989 and prime minister from 1978 to 1984

Change in South Africa. President F. W. de Klerk of the Republic of South Africa and Nelson Mandela, deputy president of the African National Congress, as they meet in May 1990 to open negotiations on the future of South Africa

Strife in the Congo

led by Nelson Mandela, to adopt a more radical and violent strategy after 1960. The government responded by banning the ANC as a terrorist organization, hunting down and prosecuting militants, imprisoning Mandela in 1962, and legislating further curbs on the personal liberties of nonwhites.

Seeking ways to defuse domestic tensions and improve the South African image abroad, the government of Pieter W. Botha took steps in the early 1980s to liberalize the country's social and economic policies toward the nonwhite population by authorizing African labor unions to bargain collectively, desegregating some public facilities, and raising wages. At the same time, however, nearly three million blacks were deprived of citizenship and sent to live in overcrowded "ethnic homelands." A new constitution adopted in 1984 conferred near-dictatorial powers on the president and, while creating a tricameral legislature with separate chambers for whites, "colored," and Asians, totally excluded blacks from political participation. Angry blacks became more violent still in their opposition to the white regime and Botha declared a state of emergency in mid-1985. By 1986 a wide range of nations, fearing a cataclysmic confrontation between the white minority and the black majority, joined in imposing severe economic sanctions upon South Africa in hopes of persuading the government to come to terms peacefully with the black population. Mandela's release from prison in 1990 (after more than twenty-seven years of imprisonment) by Botha's successor, F. W. De Klerk, prompted the lifting of some of these sanctions. In March 1992 De Klerk and Mandela began the process of negotiating an end to apartheid. In May 1994, following elections in which all races participated, Mandela was chosen South Africa's first black president.

This outline of the British experience of disengagement illustrates the difficulties besetting the transition from colonialism to independence. Other European countries fared no better than Great Britain in this enterprise. For France, the most protracted withdrawal occurred in Algeria, where approximately one million mainly French immigrants lived within a population of over ten million. In 1954 nationalists' demands for equal status with the immigrants were denied, triggering a seven-year war. During the course of the war, Algeria's European settlers grew to fear the French government—and its desire for a resolution of the conflict even at the cost of granting independence to Algeria—almost as much as they feared the Algerian nationalists. Charles de Gaulle's promise of self-determination put an end to the fighting and led to independence in 1962. In the meantime the French extricated themselves from other portions of their North African empire with less difficulty. In 1955 they withdrew their protectorate over Morocco, and a short time later they renounced their protectorate over Tunisia; both countries were granted independence in 1956.

Belgium, yet another colonial power, made the precipitous decision to grant independence to the Congo (later Zaire) in 1960, starting a civil war that raged for more than five years between the newly formed central government and the southeastern, mineral-rich province of Katanga

Algerian Soldiers Protecting Shopping Areas in Algiers during Fight for Independence from France, 1963

(later known as Shaba) and continued to smolder into the 1980s with assistance from Angolan-based Katangan refugees.

Political turmoil in Africa was compounded by the onset of a massive economic decline in the 1970s after the global escalation of petroleum prices and the attendant inflation in prices for Western technology, seed, and fertilizer. Recurring droughts in the 1980s and 1990s struck nearly every part of the continent, impairing agricultural development and bringing starvation to many areas. African states were compelled to divert currency from development projects to import goods for their swelling populations at the very time that falling world prices for agricultural commodities and metals diminished the market value of Africa's major exports and the sources of foreign currency. The severity of the famine exacerbated existing tensions within these drought-stricken areas, and the distribution of famine relief became a frequent arena for political struggle. In addition, in the growing number of African states whose leaders espoused various brands of socialism, many government-sponsored corporations were inefficiently managed and became financial liabilities. This made it all the more difficult for these nations to maintain payments to Western financial institutions on debts incurred for development projects during the 1960s; defaulting in turn limited their access to further loans.

Africa and the world economy

As a consequence of these and other factors, Africa was, at the end of the twentieth century, an impoverished and strife-torn continent. Conflicts erupted in the Sudan and Chad between a Muslim north and a Christian/animist south, in Ethiopia between the Marxist central government and the Islamic Eritreans, and in Angola and Zimbabwe between the government and ethnic and regional revolutionary movements that had participated in the struggle for independence but not in the subsequent regime. The early 1990s witnessed the further weakening of states

Ethnic warfare

Civil War in Chad. Chad has been in the throes of internal strife, born of ethnic, religious, and regional disputes, for decades. Light-skinned Muslim Arabs from the north are at odds with dark-skinned Christian sub-Saharan Africans from the south. Here southern troops guard the perimeter of a political stronghold.

collapsed under the weight of failed economies and ethnic and clan warfare. In Somalia the fall of the dictatorship of Siad Barre plunged the country into anarchy and civil war. By mid-1992, more than 300,000 Somalians had died of starvation or war wounds. Similar political chaos prevailed in Liberia, where civil war claimed 150,000 lives, and many more fled the country. In Rwanda and Burundi, ethnic slaughter left nearly a million dead. Those who fled to hoped-for safety in neighboring Zaire (now called the Congo) were confronted in early 1997 by the collapse of

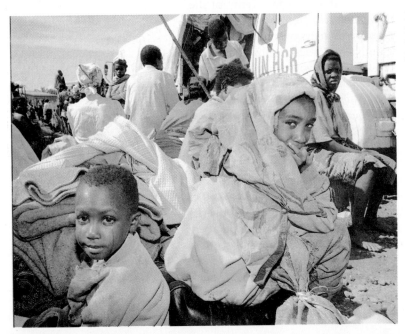

Hutu Refugees. Thousands of Hutu refugees had to be repatriated by the U.N. from politically unstable Zaire, where they fled during the 1994 genocide in Rwanda.

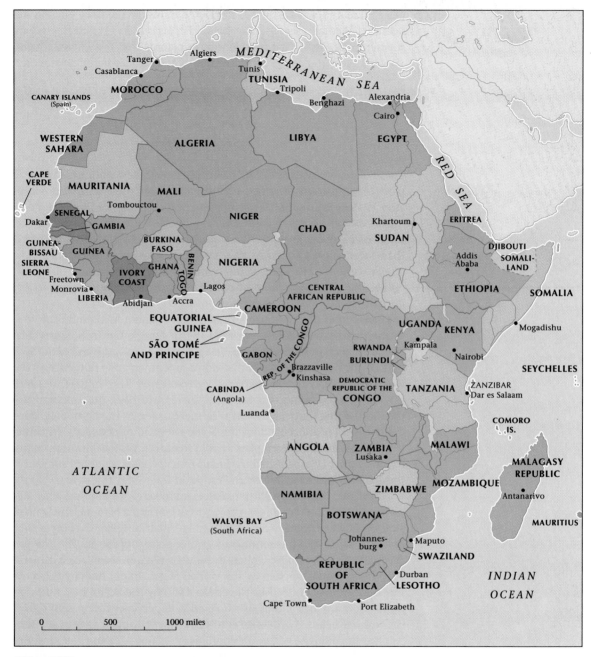

Africa, 1997

that country's social and economic structure as well, and by political instability following the forced resignation of long-time dictator Sese Seko Mobuto.

Although the history of decolonization in Africa was probably grimmer than in any other part of the world, it was almost nowhere an easy or

The consequences of decolonization

1105

peaceful matter, whether it was the Dutch in Indonesia, the French in Indochina (Vietnam, see p. 1107), or the Portuguese in Goa on the Indian subcontinent. The detritus of European colonialism and of subsequent Western economic intervention was too frequently economic chaos and political bloodshed.

WARMAKING AND PEACEKEEPING IN THE NUCLEAR AGE

The fragility of peacekeeping efforts

The violence attendant upon the emergence of new nations was but a part of the pattern of armed confrontations imposed across the globe after 1945 by international rivalries and tensions. The conflicts that have intruded with agonizing consistency upon the world were frequently the result of local circumstance. Yet almost always they produced far more than local consequences. As they unfolded, they proved not only how fragile were the processes of international peacekeeping, but also how vulnerable even the mightiest nations were to circumstances that frequently lay beyond their limited control.

The Korean War

The most serious clash between communist and noncommunist forces in the first postwar decade occurred not in Europe but in Korea, where armed conflict broke out in 1950. Treaties with Japan at the end of the Second World War had provided that Korea, under Japanese rule since 1910, would become an independent and united country. The United States and the Soviet Union left occupying forces there until 1949, the Americans to the south of the thirty-eighth parallel, the Russians to the north of it. During this period of occupation, the Soviets refused to cooperate with the United Nations–sponsored plan to hold free elections for the entire country. Instead, they established in the north a "people's republic" similar to those they had erected in Eastern Europe. In June 1950, troops from North Korea crossed the thirty-eighth parallel and invaded the south. Taking advantage of a temporary Russian boycott of the United Nations, the United States was able to avoid a Soviet veto of an American plan to counter this invasion by sending a contingent of troops to oppose it. The troops, though nominally under United Nations command, were largely American, directed and supplied by the United States. Initial military gains by this force were countered in November 1950 by the influx into Korea of troops from the newly established People's Republic of China, sent to aid the North Koreans. A stalemate ensued, President Truman and his advisers being as unwilling to widen the conflict into China—fearing a third world war—as they were to abandon their South Korean allies. After two years of military and diplomatic deadlock, a peace was concluded in July 1953, recognizing the existence of both North and South Korea and abandoning any scheme for their reunion. As in the case of Germany, the limited ability of major powers to achieve their goals completely resulted in a divided settlement—and a divided nation.

The Vietnam War

Vietnam also produced the same lesson, in a war far more devastating than that in Korea. After the defeat of Japan in 1945, France had sought to recover its lost empire in the Far East. Vietnam declared its independence from France, and French attempts to reassert control sparked a rebellion of Vietnamese nationalists under the communist leadership of Ho Chi Minh. The rebels, known as the Viet Minh, resorted to guerrilla warfare and inflicted such costly defeats upon the French that the latter decided to abandon the struggle. An agreement was signed at Geneva in 1954 providing for the division of Vietnam into two zones, pending elections to determine the future government of the entire country. Ho Chi Minh became president of North Vietnam and established his capital at Hanoi. Had elections been held as provided by the Geneva Agreement, Ho Chi Minh would probably have been elected president of all of Vietnam. But the government of South Vietnam, backed by the United States, refused to permit elections to be held. As a result, the Viet Cong, communist insurgents aided by Ho Chi Minh, stepped up guerrilla warfare against the government and its troops in South Vietnam.

By the mid-1960s, the United States had become directly involved in the conflict. President Lyndon Johnson sent a force of 100,000 troops into battle, hoping it would be sufficient to defeat the Viet Cong. Little consideration was given to the fact that the Viet Cong were solidly entrenched in South Vietnam, and that they had been waging a bitter national struggle for upward of eighteen years. They had succeeded in driving out the French in 1954 and were not likely to surrender to a new invader, as they conceived the Americans to be. The Viet Cong and the North Vietnamese, though less well equipped, nevertheless fought the South Vietnamese and their American allies to a standstill on several occasions. Exasperated by failure to win an easy victory in South Vietnam, the American civilian and military chiefs quickly expanded the U.S. presence there. Ultimately, as much tonnage in non-nuclear bombs was dropped on tiny Vietnam as was unloaded by the Allied forces on all of Germany in the Second World War. As the struggle entered its fifth year, with no end in sight, disillusionment spread throughout the United States. Criticism of President Johnson was so harsh in 1968 that he was forced to abandon his plans to run for a second term. Johnson's successor, Richard M. Nixon, elected on the strength of promises to end the war, instead continued its escalation. Following further stalemate, however, negotiations for a U.S. withdrawal commenced in late 1972. A cease-fire early the following year did no more than postpone the inevitable. Two years later, South Vietnam fell to the Viet Cong and the North Vietnamese. The massive intervention had proved a ghastly failure.

The lesson of Vietnam—that in a nuclear age there are limits to national power—was one that the United States, the former Soviet Union, and other countries have continued to find hard to learn. Beginning in the 1950s the U.S. government attempted to contain or destroy communist or other leftist regimes in Central America, most notably in the case of Cuba, whose president, Fidel Castro, was to remain a thorn in the side of successive American presidents despite attempts to undermine Castro's regime with economic sanctions. In Nicaragua and El Salvador as well, the United States government failed to achieve its objectives, even

Ho Chi Minh

The fiasco of U.S. involvement

Fidel Castro

though it gave support to anticommunist rebels. American intervention in those two countries, as elsewhere, was limited by an unwillingness to engage directly in conflicts there, and to this extent expressed a realization that even a superpower could not expect to shape the world to its own ends.

The Cuban missile crisis

During the same period the former Soviet Union was forced to come to terms with this lesson as well. Having arranged to supply their Cuban ally Castro with nuclear missiles and other war matériel, the Soviets were confronted by a U.S. naval blockade of the island designed to prevent delivery of the promised equipment in October 1962. The Soviet government, alarmed by the threat of war, agreed to withdraw and to remove the bombers and missiles already on Cuban soil. The incident posed an extremely difficult question for the superpowers: how could one nation convince another of its determination to brook no further interference with its plans, if its adversary could be fairly certain that because of the fear of nuclear war the threat was no more than a bluff?

Soviet failure in Afghanistan

In deciding to invade Afghanistan in 1979 in support of a recently installed pro-Soviet regime, the Soviet Union seemed to repeat the experience of the French and the Americans in Vietnam. Ten years later, a force of 100,000 Soviet troops had been unable to quell Afghan guerrilla resistance, and Soviet troops were recalled. This retreat left the field open for continuing internal warfare fueled by religious conflict.

Conflict over Israel

To achieve regional order was a seemingly impossible task in the most persistent trouble spot in the post–Second World War era: the Middle East. Here the major conflict centered on the presence of the Jewish state of Israel, which declared its independence in 1948, following twenty-six years as a mandated protectorate of Britain. Despite continued wars with its Arab neighbors, Israel embarked on a concerted program of industrialization to strengthen its economy. Large sums of money flowed into the country, mainly from the United States, Britain, and West Germany, as restitution for the outrages of Nazi persecution. Yet Israel's conflict with its Arab neighbors continued unabated, fueled by Israel's inability to resolve the question of the rights of Palestinian Arabs who still claim the territory of Israel as their homeland and by the Arabs' refusal to recognize Israel as a legitimate state.

The wars of the 1960s and 1970s

These tensions were exacerbated by a series of conflicts between Israel and its neighbors in the decades following independence. War with Egypt in 1967 and with other neighbors in 1973, and a continuing Palestinian insurgency over Israeli occupation of lands claimed by the Palestinians made prospects for peace less than promising. Negotiations continued into the late 1990s between Israel's prime minister Yitzhak Rabin and his successor, Benjamin Netanyahu, and the leader of the Palestinians' political arm, the Palestine Liberation Organization (PLO), Yassar Arafat. But there appears to be little indication of an easy or early settlement.

Iranian and Iraqi threats to peace

The issue of Israel's place among the nations of the Middle East was by no means the sole cause of that area's political volatility. The revolutionary government of Iran, following the overthrow of the shah in 1979,

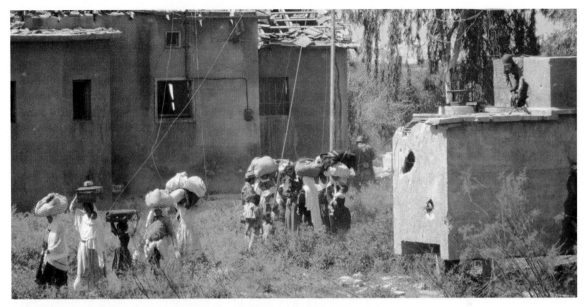

Palestinian Refugees. After the Six-Day War in 1967, more than 1.5 million Palestinians came under Israeli rule. Some refugees are seen here trying to escape the fighting, carrying whatever belongings they can.

Checkpoint on the West Bank. Controlled by Jordan before passing to Israel after the Six-Day War, the West Bank is occupied primarily by Palestinians. Travel between the West Bank and Israel proper is limited by Israeli checkpoints.

charted an erratic course that further jeopardized the stability of the region. In 1980 war broke out between Iran and Iraq, ultimately spilling into the Persian Gulf, where it threatened to disrupt vital oil-shipping lanes in international waters. A cease-fire declared in 1988 formally ended overt hostilities between Iran and Iraq, although peace talks continued for well over a year. The tenuous peace was broken in August 1990 when the Iraqi dictator, Saddam Hussein, ordered an invasion of oil-rich Kuwait, claiming the principality as part of "greater Iraq" in an effort to bolster his country's economy, weakened by the war with Iran. A coalition of twenty-nine countries led by the United States declared war on Iraq. The brief, intense war in early 1991 decimated Iraqi forces and forced Iraq's withdrawal from Kuwait. The war's aftermath produced severe internal disorder, especially regarding the fate of the ethnic Kurds in Iraq.

The Persian Gulf War

The 1991 Persian Gulf War heightened the theme that has characterized relationships between Middle Eastern and other countries since the 1960s: Western dependence on Arab oil. The Organization of Petroleum Exporting Countries (OPEC), formed in 1960 to regulate the production and pricing of crude oil, assumed an increasingly militant posture in the 1970s under the leadership of its Middle Eastern Arab members. For a time a majority appeared willing to follow the lead of militant Middle

The Iraqi Threat to Stability in the Middle East: The Case of Jordan. Left: In the wake of the Iraqi invasion and occupation of Kuwait, thousands of refugees fled from Kuwait to Jordan where they were stranded in tent cities. Added to the existing Palestinian refugee problem, this latest wave of displaced people placed an enormous burden on Jordan's fragile economy. Right: Large numbers of Jordanians and Palestinians rallied to Saddam Hussein's call for a "holy war" to free Arab soil of Western imperialists and their agents. Caught between Iraq and an international force led by a U.S. army of over 400,000 men and women, the government of King Hussein of Jordan faced the specter of revolution.

Eastern nationalists such as Moammar Qaddafi, the Libyan chief of state, in attempting to extract a high price—both economic and political—from the West. Western powers tempered their support of Israel and designed their policies toward the PLO at least in part on the basis of their continuing need for oil. In the mid-1980s overproduction and a decrease in the demand for oil brought about by economic recession in Western Europe and the United States made it far more difficult for the OPEC countries to keep the price of oil uniformly high. Yet the resulting price reductions were not an unalloyed boon to Western economies. Many oil-producing nations in the developing world had borrowed large sums of money from Western financial institutions in the 1970s using their "black gold" as collateral. When reduced oil prices resulted in financial crisis for some of those nations—as in Mexico, for example—Western lenders were threatened with default. The problems of oil production and pricing illustrate convincingly the way in which the problems of the world economy and of international peacekeeping are interlocked.

Even without the dangerous conflicts that have scarred global trouble spots since 1945, the world would not be at peace. Terrorism, a plague of apparently senseless acts of human destruction, though often related to larger events and causes, has over the past several decades emerged as a frightening and thus far insolvable threat to world stability. Terrorism was employed by separatist or nationalist movements, such as the Palestinians (the PLO) in the Middle East, the Basques in northern Spain, or the Catholic (Irish Republican Army, or IRA) and Protestant extremists in Northern Ireland. It has also been the tactic of radical national leaders such as the Ayatollah Khomeini of Iran and Qaddafi of Libya. Terrorist outrages in the 1970s and 1980s were frequently the work of radicals: the incendiary attacks and bank robberies of the so-called "Red Army

Terrorism

Terrorism. Members of the Red Army Faction, a German terrorist group, used a car bomb to kill a German banker in 1989.

Faction" in Germany in the 1970s, which were launched to arouse revolutionary sentiment among frustrated youth; the PLO murder of Israeli athletes at the 1972 Olympics in Munich; the kidnapping and murder of the Italian politician Aldo Moro by the Italian "Red Brigade" in 1978; the murder of Israel-bound passengers in the Rome airport in 1985; the repeated hijacking of passenger planes, and indeed, on one occasion in 1985, of a Mediterranean cruise ship, the *Achille Lauro*; and the bombing of a Pan American Airlines jet over Lockerbie, Scotland, in 1988. The bombing of the World Trade Center in New York City in 1993 and of the Federal Building in Oklahoma City in 1995 proved to Americans that their country was by no means immune to attack. In Britain the continuing conflict in Northern Ireland has resulted in fresh outbreaks of terrorism, despite the existence of a cease-fire and attempts by the Irish and British governments to construct a peace.

The threat of nuclear destruction

Looming above all the other issues and circumstances we have surveyed has been the continuing threat of nuclear destruction. During the 1960s and 1970s, both the United States and the Soviet Union vacillated in their willingness to discuss arms control, let alone to move toward actual reduction of their arsenals. Henry Kissinger, U.S. secretary of state under Presidents Richard Nixon and Gerald Ford in the 1970s, proclaimed détente with the Russians as his goal, and devoted much time to negotiations aimed at defusing potentially explosive areas of conflict between the two nations. Both countries hoped to curb the spread of nuclear weapons and to limit, if possible, the expansion of their own stockpiles. The Strategic Arms Limitation Treaty (SALT) talks, in which the Russians and Americans engaged during the 1970s and early 1980s, were an indication of mutual willingness to recognize and tackle a problem of awesome dimensions. Yet the talks produced little in the way of concrete agreement. President Ronald Reagan, who took office in 1981, denounced a second stage of the SALT negotiations during his campaign and subsequently continued to press for dramatic increases in his military budgets for sophisticated armaments, even as he proclaimed his devotion to the cause of disarmament. Yet in December 1987, despite continuing disagreement on other issues, Soviet leader Mikhail Gorbachev and Reagan signed a treaty in Washington eliminating all short- and medium-range nuclear missiles from the European arsenals of both East and West.

President Ronald Reagan of the United States and Mikhail Gorbachev of the Soviet Union at a Summit Meeting on Arms Control in December 1987

An increasing global arsenal

The nuclear threat did not disappear with the breakup of the Soviet Union, although both the United States and the former Soviet states began to reduce significantly their nuclear arms stocks as a result of agreements negotiated in 1991 and 1992. Yet countries as diverse as Iraq, Pakistan, and China continued to develop nuclear technology that further threatened stability across the globe. Besides threatening a nuclear doomsday the steadily expanding manufacture of armaments has produced huge stockpiles of highly toxic radioactive waste. While the manufacture of substances that will retain their toxicity for thousands of years continues, no reliable plan for disposing of or storing these wastes has yet been devised.

Pessimism about the human condition in the 1990s stems from more than the problems of the present. It derives as well from a fear about the future, the future of the earth's human beings, and of the earth itself. This concern arises from assessments of the environmental damage that industry and development have wrought. These environmental violations consist not merely of poisoning the atmosphere and contaminating oceans, rivers, and lakes by dumping wastes into them, but of any assault upon them that makes them less valuable for human survival. The excessive construction of dams, for example, causes the silting of rivers and the accumulation of nitrates at a faster rate than the surrounding soil can absorb. The Aswan High Dam of Egypt, undoubtedly valuable for increasing the water supply of that country, has at the same time cut down the flow of algal nutrients to the Mediterranean, with damaging effects on the fishing industry of various countries. From the ecological standpoint the rapid development of industry in modern times is an almost unmitigated disaster. For thousands of years the human race introduced into the environment no more waste substances than could easily be absorbed by the environment. But modern technology has introduced a variety of wastes never abundant before. Among them are carbon monoxide, sulfur dioxide, and nitrogen oxide. And this is to say nothing of the discharge into nature of pesticides, the great host of synthetic products that are not biologically degradable, and the fallout of nuclear weapons testing. As the nature and gravity of these problems have become apparent, governments have been pressured to take preventive and remedial action.

In 1986, a nuclear power station at Chernobyl, near Kiev in the Soviet Union, exploded, producing highly dangerous radioactive fallout not only in the vicinity of the accident but, because of prevailing winds, across the continent of Europe. Affected countries protested, while citizens increased the pressure on their governments to curtail the manufacture of such lethal industrial and military by-products. The political abuses of natural resources received attention in the 1991 Persian Gulf War, when between five million and ten million barrels of oil were spilled into the Persian Gulf. Both Iraqi and coalition forces accused the other of causing the spill. The devastation it wrought rivaled that resulting from the 1989 grounding of the Exxon Corporation's *Valdez* oil tanker, in which eleven million gallons of crude oil were spilled into Alaskan waters.

Environmental problems are caused not simply by the dumping of harmful and nondegradable products. They are also the result of wastage of land as our most valuable natural resource. In many parts of the world rivers run brown because they are filled with earth washed from the fields bordering them. Each year 24 billion tons of the earth's topsoil are lost, largely through erosion. Forests are disappearing, not only from

Assaults upon nature

Chemical leaks and oil spills

Erosion and land wastage

The Exxon *Valdez* Oil Spill, Prince William Sound, 1989. Left: the contents of 270,000 barrels of crude oil coat the water and shoreline of southern Alaska. Above: a loon, smothered by oil.

overcutting but from the effects of "acid rain" produced by the millions of tons of sulfur dioxide spewed into the air by utilities and other soft-coal-burning plants.

Other environmental issues commanding attention in the 1990s include the continued destruction of global rain forests, with the threatened extinction of plant and animal species, and the problem of global warming due to depletion of the ozone layer of the atmosphere. The so-called greenhouse effect could eventually melt the polar icecaps. In May 1990 a panel of thirty-nine nations concluded that, if the warming trend is not checked, rising sea levels will inundate Bangladesh, the Netherlands, and numerous other coastal areas and islands. This slow but detectable climatic change is directly linked to the accumulation of carbon dioxide gas. Some 5.6 billion tons of CO_2 are discharged into the atmosphere every year as a result of the burning of fossil fuels and of the annual destruction of more than forty million acres of tropical forest. A parallel hazard lies in the depletion of the ozone layer through chemical reaction with chlorofluorocarbons (CFCs), used in aerosol sprays and in refrigerants. Destruction of the ozone would expose living creatures to damaging radiation from the sun's ultraviolet rays. Environmentally induced changes in wind patterns have also produced catastrophic effects. New transatlantic stratospheric currents annually dump millions of tons of rich West African topsoil in Brazil. This uncontrollable phenomenon is enlarging the desert area of West Africa. Despite an international conference on such issues in June 1992 in Rio de Janeiro, international response to these problems continues to be tentative and conservative.

A close link exists between the problems of environment and the population explosion that is occurring throughout the world. Indeed, if pop-

Destruction of rain forests and global warming

Environment and the population explosion

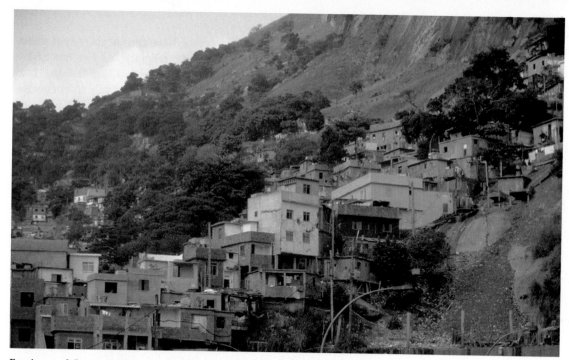

Erosion and Overpopulation in Brazil. The houses and shacks crammed together on this hillside not only are overcrowded with families, but also are causing the soil to erode. Neither humans nor wildlife can survive long under such precarious conditions.

ulation had not increased alarmingly in recent years, environmental problems might well have passed unnoticed. Calcutta now has a population of 12.9 million, compared with 3 million in 1961. Tokyo has grown from 5 million to over 28.5 million in little more than thirty years. The total population of the earth at the beginning of the common era was about 250 million. More than sixteen centuries passed before another quarter-billion had been added to the total. Not until 1860 did the population of the globe approximate 1 billion. From then on the increase was vastly more rapid. The sixth half-billion, added about 1960, required scarcely more than ten years. By 1997 the earth's population had reached 5.8 billion.

What have been the causes of this demographic revolution overturning the ancient balance between births and deaths, which had long kept the population on a stationary or slowly rising level? Fundamentally, the world has experienced a decrease in the death rate and an increase in the birth rate. Infant mortality rates have markedly declined except in the developing world, where 40,000 infants die each year from malnutrition and disease. Deaths of mothers in childbirth have also diminished. The great plagues, such as cholera, typhus, and tuberculosis, take a much smaller toll than they did in earlier centuries. Wars and famines still number their victims by the millions, yet such factors are insufficient to counteract an uncurbed rate of reproduction. Though the practice of contraception has been approved by the governments of such nations as India,

Causes of the demographic revolution

China, and Japan, only in the last decade have the effects of that policy been noticeable. In some countries poverty, religion, and ignorance have made the widespread use of contraceptives difficult. Leaders in Third World countries charge that attempts by Western powers to encourage them to limit population growth, either by contraceptive devices or by sterilization, is a not-so-subtle form of genocide. Even in the West, attitudes toward birth control are ambivalent. The Roman Catholic Church remains an implacable opponent of birth control and family planning.

Uneven effects of the demographic revolution

The effects of the demographic revolution have been most conspicuous in the underdeveloped nations of Central and South America, Africa, and Asia. Whereas the population of the world as a whole will double, at present rates of increase, in thirty-five years, that of Central and South America will multiply twofold in only twenty-six years. The population of Asia (excluding the U.S.S.R.) grew from 813 million in 1900 to approximately 2.9 billion in 1986—approximately 60 percent of the world's population. A situation in which the poorest nations are also the most overpopulated does not argue well for the future of world stability.

THE ACHIEVEMENTS AND LIMITATIONS OF SCIENCE AND TECHNOLOGY

Inventing solutions

For solutions to many of these problems, men and women have, paradoxically, turned to those agencies responsible, in many cases, for the creation of the problems: science and technology. Scientists and technicians invented and perfected the internal combustion engine and chemical insecticides. Now other scientists and technicians are seeking ways to combat their deleterious effects. Scientific research has been responsible for the medical advances that have helped to produce worldwide population increase. No one would argue, of course, that the research should not have taken place, or that the continuing battle against disease is not one of humanity's most worthwhile engagements. Most would agree, however, that science must move as quickly as possible to come up with a safe and simple method of controlling birth, as it continues to fight to prolong life.

The discovery of viruses; DNA

The achievements of science in the field of health during the past half-century have been truly remarkable. Two discoveries of great importance have enabled scientists to understand more clearly the ways in which the human body receives and transmits disease. The discovery of viruses was the result of experimentation conducted chiefly by the American biochemist Wendell Stanley in the 1930s. Viruses are microscopic organisms that show signs of life—including the ability to reproduce—only when existing inside living cells. They are the cause of many human diseases, including measles, poliomyelitis (infantile paralysis), and rabies. Not until the nature of viruses was understood could scientists begin to develop means of treating and preventing the virus-produced illnesses in

The Decoding of DNA. Left: F. H. C. Crick and James D. Watson discuss their efforts to analyze the molecular structure of DNA. Right: A model of the molecular structure of DNA. The dual spiral chains are called a double helix.

human beings. The second most important discovery increasing our understanding of human life occurred in 1953, when the Englishman F. H. C. Crick and the American James D. Watson further unlocked the mysteries of genetic inheritance that had been explored by Gregor Mendel at the end of the nineteenth century. Crick and Watson successfully analyzed deoxyribonucleic acid, or DNA, the chemical molecular structure that occurs in the nuclei of gene cells. They discovered that DNA is composed of smaller molecules of four different kinds, linked together in spiral chains. The arrangement of these molecules in each cell forms a distinct chemical message that determines the character of the genes and therefore of the human organism of which they are a part. The knowledge gained through analysis of DNA has enabled scientists and doctors to understand the causes of hereditary disease and also, by altering a patient's body chemistry, to prevent it. Despite the great benefits that have resulted from this recent discovery, scientists and others have warned that an understanding of the workings of DNA could lead to dangerous tampering with the genetic processes, as, for example, in attempts to produce artificially a breed of more "perfect" human beings. Indeed, in 1997 scientists in Scotland revealed the successful cloning of a sheep.

Experimentation based upon a fuller understanding of the causes of disease has led to the discovery of new medicines to treat it. About 1930, the Englishman Sir Alexander Fleming discovered the first of the antibiotics, penicillin. Antibiotics are chemical agents produced by living organisms and possessing the power to check or kill bacteria. Many have their origin in molds, fungi, algae, and in simple organisms living in the soil. Penicillin was eventually found to be a drug that could produce spectacular results in the treatment of pneumonia, syphilis, peritonitis,

Medical advances: antibiotics

**Dr. Jonas Salk in His
Laboratory**

**Infant with AIDS, Bombay,
India.** Although AIDS is slowly
responding to treatment in the
West, it remains a scourge
throughout the world.

Space exploration

tetanus, and numerous other maladies hitherto frequently fatal. Yet new bacterial strains have proved resistant to treatment; tuberculosis has resurfaced as a major world health threat, for example, and the Ebola virus has thus far been immune from effective treatment.

As important as the discovery of new drugs to treat disease has been the development of new means of preventing it. Edward Jenner discovered the first successful vaccine, used to prevent smallpox, in 1796. But not until the 1950s were vaccines found that could protect people from diseases such as mumps, measles, and cholera. One of the most exciting breakthroughs occurred with the development of an inoculation against poliomyelitis by the American Dr. Jonas Salk in 1953. Still to be discovered are effective agents for the successful treatment of two of the world's most deadly killers, heart disease and cancer, and of a recent and potentially more dangerous worldwide plague, Acquired Immune Deficiency Syndrome (AIDS), a virus that attacks the body's immune system, thus making it prey to any number of deadly diseases and infections. Unlike the victims of heart disease and cancer, no AIDS patient has ever been cured.

Attempts to cure a variety of mental illnesses such as schizophrenia and bipolar depression have met with measured success, as scientists have discovered the chemical basis for such disorders. Antidepressants and antipsychotics have allowed many to live comparatively normal lives. Yet the overprescription of some antidepressants, such as Valium and Prozac, has brought further problems, including addiction and ethical questions about how we view and value personality. Addiction to prescription drugs is in many countries a serious problem as well, comparable to the increasing dependency of millions on alcohol and cigarettes.

Few would today oppose continued campaigns by scientists intent upon eradicating disease. Governments have found it increasingly difficult, however, to justify spending vast sums of public money on programs designed to facilitate the exploration of outer space. At first these programs resembled international competitions between the United States and the Soviet Union as much as scientific and technological investigations. On October 4, 1957, the government of the Soviet Union rocketed the first artificial satellite into space at a speed of about 18,000 miles an hour. Though it weighed nearly 200 pounds, it was propelled upward higher than 500 miles. This Soviet achievement gave the English language a new word—*Sputnik*, the Russian for "satellite" or "fellow traveler." In April 1961, the Soviets succeeded in sending the first man, Yuri Gagarin, into orbit around the earth. Meanwhile, scientists and military specialists in the United States had been competing to match the Soviets' achievements. They launched the first American manned spaceship into orbit around the earth on February 20, 1962, with John Glenn circling the earth three times. Their successes were climaxed in July 1969 when Neil Armstrong, a civilian astronaut, left his lunar landing module and became the first man to walk on the moon's surface. These voyages and those that followed were hailed as events of capital importance. They promised an extension of our knowledge of outer space and could doubtless prepare the way for exploration of the moon and eventually of distant planets. But by the mid-1970s, both the United States and the Soviet Union had drastically cut back their space programs in response to demands on their economies from other quarters. A space "shuttle" and laboratory, plus continuing experiments that resulted in the landing of a satellite on Mars in 1997, proved to most the value of space exploration, despite its heavy costs.

Undoubtedly it was in the area of nuclear science that the largest and most troubling questions arose as to the capabilities, limitations, and implications of science and technology. Even more powerful than the nuclear bombs dropped on Japan at the end of the Second World War was the hydrogen bomb, first tested by the United States in November 1952. The tests were conducted in the South Pacific, where an entire island disappeared after burning brightly for several hours. The hydrogen bomb, or H-bomb, is based upon fusion of hydrogen atoms, a process that requires the enormous heat generated by the splitting of uranium atoms to start the reaction. The fusion results in the creation of a new element, helium, which actually weighs less than the sum of the hydrogen atoms. The "free" energy left over provides the tremendous explosive power of the H-bomb. The force of hydrogen bombs is measured in *megatons,* each of which represents one million tons of TNT. Thus a five-megaton H-bomb would equal 250 times the power of the A-bombs dropped on Hiroshima and Nagasaki.

Governments experimented with schemes to harness nuclear energy for peaceful purposes. Some progress has been made in the development of atomic power as an alternative source of domestic and industrial fuel. But

The First Lunar Landing. Astronaut Edwin E. Aldrin, Jr., photographed walking near the lunar module of Apollo 11. Astronaut Neil Armstrong, who took the picture, and part of the lunar module are reflected in Aldrin's face plate.

The uses of atomic energy

A Protest in Japan against Nuclear Power and Weaponry, Early 1980s

the dangers of radiation as a by-product suggest that this scheme may prove of limited value. During the late 1970s, when the West's supplies of oil were threatened, heated debate continued between proponents of atomic power and those who argued in favor of other energy forms—among them solar—as safer and cheaper alternatives.

Meanwhile, scientists working for private industry made use of discoveries in atomic physics to pioneer the field of electronics. Electronics derives from that branch of physics which deals with the behavior and effects of electrons, or negatively charged constituents within the atom. Electronic devices have multiplied in staggering profusion since the Second World War. Among them are devices to measure the trajectory of missiles, to give warnings of approaching missiles or aircraft, to make possible "blind" landings of airplanes, to store and release electrical signals, to amplify and regulate the transmission of light and sound images, and to provide the power for photoelectric cells that operate various automatic machines.

The use of electronic devices for radio reception led to initial progress in automation. Automation means a close integration of four elements: (1) a processing system, (2) a mechanical handling system, (3) sensing equipment, and (4) a control system. Though all of these elements are necessary, the last two are the most significant. Sensing equipment performs a function similar to that of the human senses. It observes and measures what is happening and sends the information thus gained to the control unit. A control system receives information from a sensing element, compares this information with that required by the "program," and then makes the necessary adjustments. This series of operations is continuous, so that a desired state is constantly maintained without any human intervention, except for that initially involved in "programming." This revolution has been greatly extended by the invention of lasers. A laser is a device for amplifying the focus and intensity of light, in which high-energy atoms are stimulated by light to amplify a beam of light. Lasers have demonstrated their value most promisingly in medicine. They have been used effectively in arresting hemorrhaging in the retina in eye afflictions, for example.

Undoubtedly the electronic invention that has produced the greatest change in the everyday lives of men and women around the world has been the personal computer. Increasingly sophisticated, these machines now bring people into instant communication with each other across continents in an efficient manner that rivals that of the telephone and appears to be relegating the writing and sending of letters through the mails to the past. Electronic communications by means of the Internet and the World Wide Web have given a compelling new meaning to the term "global village." When Chinese demonstrators rallied against the repressive Chinese regime in Tiananmen Square in 1989 they learned of the global response to their heroic efforts by means of fax machines. In addition, material stored in computers facilitates access to an extraordinary variety of information: entire library catalogues, for example, are now available to users in their own homes and offices. Here again, however, questions have been raised about the implications of the computer revolution. Will it, perhaps, result in a dangerous privatization of life, as people spend more and more of their time by themselves, communicating with each other not face to face, but through the isolating and distancing glare of their computer screens?

As such a question suggests, these communications and information systems have raised important cultural issues and generated considerable debate. Two influential French philosophers, for example, examined the new technologies and arrived at very different conclusions about their social and cultural impact. Jean Baudrillard analyzed the growth of mass media, particularly television, and argued that far from encouraging communication, they isolated people and hindered meaningful interaction. Jean-François Lyotard, on the other hand, saw in computers a cause for optimism. He asserted that computerized knowledge held out the promise of open access to information, and with it complete freedom of thought and creativity. Lyotard did not overlook the problems of access to information, a subject his fellow countryman Michel Foucault analyzed in great detail. Foucault wrote extensively on subjects as diverse as prison reform and the "genealogy" of human society. If there is a central theme in his writings, it is that the ability to control access to information and to define the limits of knowledge is itself power. He showed that without information, physical force is useless in the modern world.

Electronic inventions will undoubtedly prove no more an unmixed blessing than have the other discoveries and developments of scientists and technicians. One obvious problem generated by devices that can do the work of humans is that they put humans out of work. Technological unemployment has become an important problem for the modern world. Though new industries absorbed many workers, others were bound to be displaced by automation. While the demand for skilled labor remained high, the so-called entry jobs performed by the unskilled were fast disappearing. Mechanization of agriculture also eliminated thousands of jobs for unskilled and uneducated workers. In those industries where human beings were still required—clothing, furniture, and the assembling and packaging of machinery, for example—transnational corporations continued to shift their operations to countries of the developing world, where labor was cheap, thus creating unemployment and consequent worker resentment in the traditional manufacturing centers of western Europe and North America. At the same time, corporations channelled profits into more technology, rather than increased pay for their employees.

Science and technology provide no panaceas for the problems of the world. If those problems are to be solved, men and women, not machines, will have to do the work. They will be better equipped to do so if they possess some sense of their own past. The lesson of history is not that it repeats itself. The lesson is, rather, that the present can be clearly perceived, and the future intelligently planned for, only when those responsible for the world's destiny understand the workings of human nature. And for knowledge of that extraordinarily complicated and fascinating mechanism, there is no better source than history.

SUMMARY POINTS

- Political, ethnic, tribal, and religious strife has followed the decolonization of Asia and Africa. Rising energy prices in the 1970s and 1980s compounded the problems of developing countries.

- Revolutions and civil wars in developing countries brought East and West into conflict on the Korean peninsula, in Vietnam, and in Cuba. Far from resolving conflict, however, such confrontations only demonstrated the limits of national power in the nuclear age.

- The most persistent trouble spot in the world since the mid-1960s has been the Middle East, where religious conflicts, wars, and terrorism have thwarted hopes for peace.

- Modernization, the endless quest for natural resources, and population growth pose serious problems for the entire world, problems for which the great leaps in science and technology made since the twentieth century provide no panacea.

SELECTED READINGS

American Friends Service Committee, *A Compassionate Peace: A Future for the Middle East,* New York, 1981. An examination of the problems and proposals for their solution.

Bates, Robert H., *Essays on the Political Economy of Rural Africa,* Cambridge, Eng., 1983. An excellent study of the problems of food production in contemporary Africa.

Baudrillard, Jean, *Selected Writings,* ed. Mark Poster, Stanford, 1988. Essays and extracts by one of France's leading cultural theorists.

Bhatia, Krishan, *The Ordeal of Nationhood: A Social Study of India since Independence, 1947–1970,* New York, 1971. Informed and objective account of India's problems.

Butterfield, Fox, *China, Alive in the Bitter Sea,* rev. ed., New York, 1990. Poignant and critical.

Caputo, Philip, *A Rumor of War,* New York, 1977. The best memoir of the American experience in the Vietnam War.

Coetzee, J. M., *Waiting for the Barbarians,* London, 1980. A searing critique of South Africa by a brilliant Afrikaner novelist.

Cornish, Edward, *The Study of the Future: An Introduction to the Art and Science of Understanding and Shaping Tomorrow's World,* Washington, D.C., 1977. An introduction to the world of the "futurists."

Ellul, Jacques, *The Technological Society,* New York, 1964. A contemporary attack on the purposes and effects of technology.

Ehrlich, Paul R., *The Population Bomb,* New York, 1968. Discusses the threat of overpopulation.

Fanon, Frantz, *The Wretched of the Earth,* New York, 1968. A polemical delineation of the oppression of developing-world peoples.

Foucault, Michel, *Discipline and Punish: The Birth of the Prison.* New York, 1977. Accessible introduction to Foucault's thought.

Gamow, George, *Thirty Years that Shook Physics,* New York, 1966. A lucid account by a physicist.

Heilbroner, Robert L., *An Inquiry into the Human Prospect,* New York, 1980. Optimistic assessment of the durability of Western cultural values.

Laqueur, Walter, *The Age of Terrorism,* Boston, 1987. A look at the way terrorism spread across the world in the 1970s and 1980s.

Lukacs, John, *The End of the Twentieth Century and the End of the Modern Age,* New York, 1991. Populism, nationalism, and state authority as they clash in contemporary society.

Lyotard, Jean-Francois, *The Postmodern Condition: A Report on Knowledge,* Minneapolis, Minn., 1984. Important analysis of the effects of communications technology.

Medvedev, Zhores, *The Legacy of Chernobyl,* New York, 1990. A study of the disaster and its aftermath.

Myrdal, Gunnar, *Against the Stream: Critical Essays on Economics,* New York, 1972. Offers pertinent comments on the problems of the developing world.

Nelson, Nici, ed., *African Women in the Development Process,* London, 1981. A useful collection of essays.

Ngugi wa Thiong'o, *Petals of Blood,* New York, 1977. A scathing critique of neo-colonialism in Kenya by Africa's best-known novelist.

Penley, Constance, and Andrew Ross, eds., *Technoculture,* Minneapolis, Minn., 1991. Essays on the technological world of the 1980s and 1990s.

Proctor, Robert, *Cancer Wars: The Politics Behind What We Know and Don't Know about Causes and Trends,* New York, 1994. The relationship among industrialism, the environment, politics, and disease.

Rubin, Barry, *Paved with Good Intentions: The American Experience and Iran,* New York, 1980. Reliable account of U.S.-Iranian diplomacy.

Servan-Schreiber, J. J., *The World Challenge,* New York, 1981. Analyzes problems of distribution of world resources.

Shilts, Randy, *And the Band Played On: Politics, People, and the AIDS Epidemic,* New York, 1987. An impassioned attack on the individuals and governments that refused to come to grips with the AIDS epidemic.

THE CAROLINGIAN DYNASTY

Pepin of Heristal, Mayor of the Palace, 687–714
Charles Martel, Mayor of the Palace, 715–741
Pepin III, Mayor of the Palace, 741–751; King, 751–768
Charlemagne, King, 768–814; Emperor, 800–814
Louis the Pious, Emperor, 814–840

Middle Kingdoms

Lothair, Emperor, 840–855
Louis (Italy), Emperor, 855–875
Charles (Provence), King, 855–863
Lothair II (Lorraine), King, 855–869

West Francia

Charles the Bald, King, 840–877; Emperor, 875–877
Louis II, King, 877–879
Louis III, King, 879–882
Carloman, King, 879–884

East Francia

Ludwig, King, 840–876
Carloman, King, 876–880
Ludwig, King, 876–882
Charles the Fat, Emperor, 876–887

HOLY ROMAN EMPERORS

Saxon Dynasty

Otto I, 962–973
Otto II, 973–983
Otto III, 983–1002
Henry II, 1002–1024

Franconian Dynasty

Conrad II, 1024–1039
Henry III, 1039–1056
Henry IV, 1056–1106
Henry V, 1106–1125
Lothair II (Saxony), 1125–1137

Hohenstaufen Dynasty

Conrad III, 1138–1152
Frederick I (Barbarossa), 1152–1190
Henry VI, 1190–1197
Philip of Swabia, 1198–1208 ⎫
Otto IV (Welf), 1198–1215 ⎬ Rivals
Frederick II, 1220–1250
Conrad IV, 1250–1254

Interregnum, 1254–1273
Emperors from Various Dynasties

Rudolf I (Habsburg), 1273–1291
Adolf (Nassau), 1292–1298

Albert I (Habsburg), 1298–1308
Henry VII (Luxemburg), 1308–1313
Ludwig IV (Wittelsbach), 1314–1347
Charles IV (Luxemburg), 1347–1378
Wenceslas (Luxemburg), 1378–1400
Rupert (Wittelsbach), 1400–1410
Sigismund (Luxemburg), 1410–1437

Habsburg Dynasty

Albert II, 1438–1439
Frederick III, 1440–1493
Maximilian I, 1493–1519
Charles V, 1519–1556
Ferdinand I, 1556–1564
Maximilian II, 1564–1576
Rudolf II, 1576–1612
Matthias, 1612–1619
Ferdinand II, 1619–1637
Ferdinand III, 1637–1657
Leopold I, 1658–1705
Joseph I, 1705–1711
Charles VI, 1711–1740
Charles VII (not a Habsburg), 1742–1745
Francis I, 1745–1765
Joseph II, 1765–1790
Leopold II, 1790–1792
Francis II, 1792–1806

RULERS OF FRANCE FROM HUGH CAPET

Capetian Dynasty

Hugh Capet, 987–996
Robert II, 996–1031
Henry I, 1031–1060
Philip I, 1060–1108
Louis VI, 1108–1137
Louis VII, 1137–1180
Philip II (Augustus), 1180–1223
Louis VIII, 1223–1226
Louis IX (St. Louis), 1226–1270
Philip III, 1270–1285
Philip IV, 1285–1314
Louis X, 1314–1316
Philip V, 1316–1322
Charles IV, 1322–1328

Valois Dynasty

Philip VI, 1328–1350
John, 1350–1364
Charles V, 1364–1380
Charles VI, 1380–1422
Charles VII, 1422–1461
Louis XI, 1461–1483
Charles VIII, 1483–1498
Louis XII, 1498–1515
Francis I, 1515–1547

Henry II, 1547–1559
Francis II, 1559–1560
Charles IX, 1560–1574
Henry III, 1574–1589

Bourbon Dynasty

Henry IV, 1589–1610
Louis XIII, 1610–1643
Louis XIV, 1643–1715
Louis XV, 1715–1774
Louis XVI, 1774–1792

After 1792

First Republic, 1792–1799
Napoleon Bonaparte, First Consul, 1799–1804
Napoleon I, Emperor, 1804–1814
Louis XVIII (Bourbon dynasty), 1814–1824
Charles X (Bourbon dynasty), 1824–1830
Louis Philippe, 1830–1848
Second Republic, 1848–1852
Napoleon III, Emperor, 1852–1870
Third Republic, 1870–1940
Pétain regime, 1940–1944
Provisional government, 1944–1946
Fourth Republic, 1946–1958
Fifth Republic, 1958–

RULERS OF ENGLAND

Anglo-Saxon Dynasty

Alfred the Great, 871–899
Edward the Elder, 899–924
Ethelstan, 924–939
Edmund I, 939–946
Edred, 946–955
Edwy, 955–959
Edgar, 959–975
Edward the Martyr, 975–978
Ethelred the Unready, 978–1016
Canute, 1016–1035 (Danish Nationality)
Harold I, 1035–1040
Hardicanute, 1040–1042
Edward the Confessor, 1042–1066
Harold II, 1066

House of Normandy

William I (the Conqueror), 1066–1087
William II, 1087–1100
Henry I, 1100–1135
Stephen, 1135–1154

House of Plantagenet

Henry II, 1154–1189
Richard I, 1189–1199
John, 1199–1216
Henry III, 1216–1272
Edward I, 1272–1307
Edward II, 1307–1327
Edward III, 1327–1377
Richard II, 1377–1399

House of Lancaster

Henry IV, 1399–1413
Henry V, 1413–1422
Henry VI, 1422–1461

House of York

Edward IV, 1461–1483
Edward V, 1483
Richard III, 1483–1485

House of Tudor

Henry VII, 1485–1509
Henry VIII, 1509–1547
Edward VI, 1547–1553
Mary, 1553–1558
Elizabeth I, 1558–1603

House of Stuart

James I, 1603–1625
Charles I, 1625–1649

Commonwealth and Protectorate, 1649–1659

House of Stuart Restored

Charles II, 1660–1685
James II, 1685–1688
William III and Mary II, 1689–1694
William III alone, 1694–1702
Anne, 1702–1714

House of Hanover

George I, 1714–1727
George II, 1727–1760
George III, 1760–1820
George IV, 1820–1830
William IV, 1830–1837
Victoria, 1837–1901

House of Saxe-Coburg-Gotha

Edward VII, 1901–1910
George V, 1910–1917

House of Windsor

George V, 1917–1936
Edward VIII, 1936
George VI, 1936–1952
Elizabeth II, 1952–

RULERS OF AUSTRIA AND AUSTRIA-HUNGARY

*Maximilian I (Archduke), 1493–1519
*Charles V, 1519–1556
*Ferdinand I, 1556–1564
*Maximilian II, 1564–1576
*Rudolf II, 1576–1612
*Matthias, 1612–1619
*Ferdinand II, 1619–1637
*Ferdinand III, 1637–1657
*Leopold I, 1658–1705
*Joseph I, 1705–1711
*Charles VI, 1711–1740
Maria Theresa, 1740–1780
*Joseph II, 1780–1790

*also bore title of Holy Roman Emperor

*Leopold II, 1790–1792
*Francis II, 1792–1835 (Emperor of Austria as Francis I after 1804)
Ferdinand I, 1835–1848
Francis Joseph, 1848–1916 (after 1867 Emperor of Austria and King of Hungary)
Charles I, 1916–1918 (Emperor of Austria and King of Hungary)
Republic of Austria, 1918–1938 (dictatorship after 1934)
Republic restored, under Allied occupation, 1945–1956
Free Republic, 1956–

RULERS OF PRUSSIA AND GERMANY

*Frederick I, 1701–1713
*Frederick William I, 1713–1740
*Frederick II (the Great), 1740–1786
*Frederick William II, 1786–1797
*Frederick William III, 1797–1840
*Frederick William IV, 1840–1861
*William I, 1861–1888 (German Emperor after 1871)
Frederick III, 1888

*Kings of Prussia

*William II, 1888–1918
Weimar Republic, 1918–1933
Third Reich (Nazi Dictatorship), 1933–1945
Allied occupation, 1945–1952
Division into Federal Republic of Germany in west
    and German Democratic Republic in east,
    1949–1991
Federal Republic of Germany (united), 1991–

RULERS OF RUSSIA

Ivan III, 1462–1505
Vasily III, 1505–1533
Ivan IV, 1533–1584
Theodore I, 1584–1598
Boris Godunov, 1598–1605
Theodore II, 1605
Vasily IV, 1606–1610
Michael, 1613–1645
Alexius, 1645–1676
Theodore III, 1676–1682
Ivan V and Peter I, 1682–1689
Peter I (the Great), 1689–1725
Catherine I, 1725–1727
Peter II, 1727–1730

Anna, 1730–1740
Ivan VI, 1740–1741
Elizabeth, 1741–1762
Peter III, 1762
Catherine II (the Great), 1762–1796
Paul, 1796–1801
Alexander I, 1801–1825
Nicholas I, 1825–1855
Alexander II, 1855–1881
Alexander III, 1881–1894
Nicholas II, 1894–1917
Soviet Republic, 1917–1991
Russian Federation, 1991–

RULERS OF SPAIN

Ferdinand { and Isabella, 1479–1504
{ and Philip I, 1504–1506
{ and Charles I, 1506–1516
Charles I (Holy Roman Emperor Charles V),
    1516–1556
Philip II, 1556–1598
Philip III, 1598–1621
Philip IV, 1621–1665
Charles II, 1665–1700
Philip V, 1700–1746
Ferdinand VI, 1746–1759
Charles III, 1759–1788
Charles IV, 1788–1808

Ferdinand VII, 1808
Joseph Bonaparte, 1808–1813
Ferdinand VII (restored), 1814–1833
Isabella II, 1833–1868
Republic, 1868–1870
Amadeo, 1870–1873
Republic, 1873–1874
Alfonso XII, 1874–1885
Alfonso XIII, 1886–1931
Republic, 1931–1939
Fascist Dictatorship, 1939–1975
Juan Carlos I, 1975–

RULERS OF ITALY

Victor Emmanuel II, 1861–1878
Humbert I, 1878–1900
Victor Emmanuel III, 1900–1946
Fascist Dictatorship, 1922–1943 (maintained in northern Italy until 1945)

Humbert II, May 9–June 13, 1946
Republic, 1946–

PROMINENT POPES

Silvester I, 314–335
Leo I, 440–461
Gelasius I, 492–496
Gregory I, 590–604
Nicholas I, 858–867
Silvester II, 999–1003
Leo IX, 1049–1054
Nicholas II, 1058–1061
Gregory VII, 1073–1085
Urban II, 1088–1099
Paschal II, 1099–1118
Alexander III, 1159–1181
Innocent III, 1198–1216
Gregory IX, 1227–1241
Innocent IV, 1243–1254
Boniface VIII, 1294–1303
John XXII, 1316–1334
Nicholas V, 1447–1455
Pius II, 1458–1464

Alexander VI, 1492–1503
Julius II, 1503–1513
Leo X, 1513–1521
Paul III, 1534–1549
Paul IV, 1555–1559
Sixtus V, 1585–1590
Urban VIII, 1623–1644
Gregory XVI, 1831–1846
Pius IX, 1846–1878
Leo XIII, 1878–1903
Pius X, 1903–1914
Benedict XV, 1914–1922
Pius XI, 1922–1939
Pius XII, 1939–1958
John XXIII, 1958–1963
Paul VI, 1963–1978
John Paul I, 1978
John Paul II, 1978–

ILLUSTRATION CREDITS

Volume Two

Frontispiece, **ii**, *The Arrival* (1913–1914), by Christopher Nevinson. Courtesy of the Tate Gallery, London/Art Resource, NY.

Chapter 15: 502, François Dubois, La St. Barthélemy, 1572, oil on wood. 94 × 154 cm. photo: J.-C. Ducret, Musée des Beaux-Arts, Lausanne; **506**, Giraudon/Art Resource, NY; **507**, Photo Bulloz, Musée Carnavalet; **508 (top)**, Museo del Prado, Madrid; **508 (bottom)**, Courtesy of the Hispanic Society of America, New York; **510**, The New York Public Library: Astor, Lenox, and Tilden Foundations; **511 (left)**, National Maritime Museum, London; **511 (right)**, By courtesy of the National Portrait Gallery, London; **513 (both)**, John R. Freeman & Co.; **514**, The Hulton Deutsch Collection; **516**, Museo del Prado, Madrid; **517**, Ampliaciones Y Reproducciones, MAS; **519**, Giraudon/Art Resource, NY; **520**, By courtesy of the National Portrait Gallery, London; **522**, Photo Bulloz, Coll. Privée; **523**, Scala/Art Resource, NY; **525**, Bibliothèque Royale, Brussels; **526**, The Mansell Collection, London; **527 (top)**, Photo Bulloz, Chantilly; **527 (bottom)**, Urb. Lat. 276, fol. 41r, Foto Biblioteca Apostolica Vaticana; **529**, cliché Bibliothèque Nationale de France, Paris; **530**, Photo Bulloz, Versailles; **531**, Art Resource, NY; **532**, By permission of the Folger Shakespeare Library; **533**, The Warder Collection, NY; **534 (top)**, The Metropolitan Museum of Art. Bequest of Mrs. H. O. Havemeyer, 1929. The H. O. Havemeyer Collection (29.100.16) Photograph © 1990 The Metropolitan Museum of Art; **534 (bottom)**, Isaac Sweetser Fund/Courtesy Museum of Fine Arts, Boston; **535 (top)**, Erich Lessing/Art Resource, NY; **535 (bottom)**, Museo del Prado, Madrid; **536**, El Greco, Laocoön, Samuel H. Kress Collection, © Board of Trustees, National Gallery of Art, Washington; **537**, The Metropolitan Museum of Art, H.O. Havemeyer Collection, Bequest of Mrs. H. O. Havemeyer, 1929. (29.100.6) Photograph © 1992 The Metropolitan Museum of Art; **538 (all)**, Scala/Art Resource, NY; **539**, Scala/Art Resource, NY; **540 (top left)**, Scala/Art Resource, NY; **540 (top right)**, Museo del Prado, Madrid; **540 (bottom)**, Museo del Prado, Madrid; **541 (top)**, Erich Lessing/Art Resource, NY; **541 (bottom)**, The Metropolitan Museum of Art, Rogers Fund, 1919. (19.164) Photograph © The Metropolitan Museum of Art; **542**, Art Resource, NY; **543 (top)**, Nimatallah/Art Resource, NY; **543 (bottom)**, Museo del Prado, Madrid; **544 (top)**, © The Frick Collection, New York; **544 (bottom)**, The Metropolitan Museum of Art, Purchase, special contributions and funds given or bequeathed by friends of the Museum, 1961. (61.198) Photograph © The Metropolitan Museum of Art; **545**, Gift of Mr. and Mrs. Robert Woods Bliss, © 1997 Board of Trustees, National Gallery of Art, Washington, c. 1630, oil on canvas, .746 × .657 (29⅜ × 25⅞); framed: .975 × .876 × .092 (38⅜ × 34½ × 3⅝)

Chapter 16: 551 (left), Negativ aus dem Bildarchiv der Österreicheschen Nationalbibliothek, Wien; **551 (right)**, Inv. nr. HB 13157, Germanisches Nationalmuseum, Nürnberg; **552 (top)**, Bridgeman Art Library; **552 (bottom)**, St. Bartholomew's Hospital, London; **555**, Routledge, Inc.; **557**, The New York Public Library: Astor, Lenox, and Tilden Foundations; **559 (left)**, Bridgeman Art Library; **559 (right)**, Staatliche Museen zu Berlin—Preußischer Kulturbesitz, Gemäldgalerie; **561**, Bridgeman Art Library; **562**, John R. Freeman & Co.; **566**, Giraudon/Art Resource, NY; **568**, cliché Bibliothèque Nationale de France, Paris; **573**, John R. Freeman & Co.; **574**, Victoria & Albert Museum, London/Art Resource, NY; **576 (top)**, The Warder Collection, NY; **576 (bottom)**, The Hulton Deutsch Collection; **578**, Roger-Viollet; **579**, Erich Lessing/Art Resource, NY; **581**, Giraudon/Art Resource, NY; **582**, Giraudon/Art Resource, NY; **583**, Courtesy of the British Museum; **585**, The New York Public Library: Astor, Lenox, and Tilden Foundations; **587**, Giraudon/Art Resource, NY; **588**, Victoria & Albert Museum, London/Art Resource, NY; **589**, cliché Bibliothèque Nationale de France, Paris

Chapter 17: 596, Erich Lessing/Art Resource, NY; **597**, Giraudon/Art Resource, NY; **598**, Giraudon/Art Resource, NY; **599**, Erich Lessing/Art Resource, NY; **601**, The Metropolitan Museum of Art, Gift of the Wildenstein Foundation, Inc., 1951. (51.34) Photograph © 1979 The Metropolitan Museum of Art; **603**, by Friedrich Wilhelm Kurfürst von Brandenburg/Ullstein; **605 (top)**, Erich Lessing/Art Resource, NY; **605 (bottom)**, Staatliche Museen zu Berlin—Preußischer Kulturbesitz; **606**, By permission of the British Library; **608 (left)**, Society for Cultural Relations with the Soviet Union; **608 (right)**, Roger-Viollet; **609**, Victoria & Albert Museum, London/Art Resource, NY; **610**, Bridgeman Art Library; **612**, Bridgeman Art Library; **613**, Photo Bulloz, Valenciennes; **618**, Photo Bulloz, Petit Palais; **619**, Bridgeman Art Library; **620**, cliché Bibliothèque Nationale de France, Paris; **621**, Erich Lessing/Art Resource, NY; **622**, Erich Lessing/Art Resource, NY; **623 (top)**, Giraudon/Art Resource, NY; **623 (bottom)**, The Warder Collection, NY; **624**, By courtesy of the National Portrait Gallery, London; **625**, By courtesy of the National Portrait Gallery, London; **626 (left)**, Courtesy of the British Museum; **626 (right)**, Victoria & Albert Museum, London/Art Resource, NY; **629**, Courtesy of the Director, National Army Museum, London; **631**, Giraudon/Art Resource, NY

Chapter 18: 637 (top), By permission of the British Library; **637 (bottom)**, Photo Bulloz, Versailles; **638**, The Warder Collection, NY; **639**, Giraudon/Art Resource, NY; **641**, The New York Public Library: Astor, Lenox, and Tilden Foundations; **643**, Giraudon/Art Resource, NY; **645 (top)**, Giraudon/Art Resource, NY; **645 (bottom)**, The New York Public Library: Astor, Lenox, and Tilden Foundations; **646**, Photo Bulloz, Louvre; **647**, Giraudon/Art Resource, NY; **649**, The Mansell Collection, London; **650 (top)**, Historisches Museum der Stadt Wien; **650 (bottom)**, The New York Public Library: Astor, Lenox, and Tilden Foundations; **651**, Image Select/Art Resource, NY; **653**, Philadelphia Museum of Art: Mr. and Mrs. Wharton Sinkler Collection; **654**, The Warder Collection, NY; **656**, © Photo RMN, Paris; **657 (top)**, Erich Lessing/Art Resource, NY; **657 (bottom)**, French Embassy Press and Information Bureau; **658 (top left)**, Alinari/Art Resource, NY; **658 (top right)**, The Warder Collection, NY; **658 (bottom)**, Bridgeman Art Library; **659 (top)**, Reproduced by courtesy of the Trustees, the National Gallery, London. Photograph © The National Gallery, London; **659 (bottom)**, Kunsthistorisches Museum, Vienna; **661 (top)**, The Metropolitan Museum of Art, Munsey Fund, 1934. (34.138) Photograph © 1988 The Metropolitan Museum of Art; **661 (bottom)**, Photo Bulloz, Louvre; **662**, Reproduced by courtesy of the Trustees, The National Gallery, London. Photograph © The National Gallery, London; **663 (top left)**, Reproduced by permission of the Trustees of the Wallace Collection; **663 (top right and bottom left)**, Scala/Art Resource, NY; **663 (bottom right)**, The Warder Collection, NY; **667 (top)**, Erich Lessing/Art Resource, NY; **667 (bottom)**, Scala/Art Resource, NY; **668 (both)**, Erich Lessing/Art Resource, NY; **669**, Giraudon/Art Resource, NY; **670**, The Warder Collection, NY

Part Five: 674, The Granger Collection, New York
Chapter 19: 681, The New York Public Library: Astor, Lenox, and Tilden Foundations; **683 (both)**, cliché Bibliothèque Nationale de France, Paris; **684**, Photo Bulloz, Versailles; **687**, Photo Bulloz, Louvre; **688**, Giraudon/Art Resource, NY; **689**, Giraudon/Art Resource, NY; **690**, Giraudon/Art Resource, NY; **691**, cliché Bibliothèque Nationale de France, Paris; **695 (top)**, By courtesy of the National Portrait Gallery, London; **695 (bottom)**, The Granger Collection, New York; **697**, Giraudon/Art Resource, NY; **698**, Giraudon/Art Resource, NY; **700**, The Hulton Deutsch Collection; **701 (both)**, Giraudon/Art Resource, NY; **702**, Giraudon/Art Resource, NY; **703 (top)**, cliché Bibliothèque Nationale de France, Paris; **703 (bottom)**, The Hulton Deutsch Collection; **705**, Giraudon/Art Resource, NY: Musée de la Ville de Paris, Musée Carnavalet, Paris, France; **707**, Photo Bulloz, Versailles; **709**, Photo Bulloz, Louvre; **713 (top)**, cliché Bibliothèque Nationale de France, Paris; **713 (bottom)**, Giraudon/Art Resource, NY; **714**, © Photo RMN, Paris; **715**, Giraudon/Art Resource, NY; **717 (both)**, cliché Bibliothèque Nationale de France, Paris; **718**, Giraudon/Art Resource, NY; **719 (top)**, The Warder Collection, NY; **719 (bottom)**, Erich Lessing/Art Resource, NY

Chapter 20: 727, The Hulton Deutsch Collection; **729**, The Granger Collection, New York; **731 (both)**, The Granger Collection, New York; **732**, The Granger Collection, New York; **733 (top)**, Image Select/Art Resource, NY; **733 (bottom)**, The Hulton

Deutsch Collection; **734**, John R. Freeman & Co.; **738**, Staatliche Museen zu Berlin—Preußischer Kulturbesitz; **739**, City Archives of Lyons; **740 (left)**, The Warder Collection, NY; **740 (right)**, The New York Public Library: Astor, Lenox, and Tilden Foundations; **741 (top)**, The New York Public Library: Astor, Lenox, and Tilden Foundations; **741 (bottom)**, Scala/Art Resource, NY; **742**, Giraudon/Art Resource, NY; **743 (both)**, The Warder Collection, NY; **744**, The Warder Collection, NY; **746**, Erich Lessing/Art Resource, NY

Chapter 21: 751, The Hulton Deutsch Collection; **753**, The Hulton Deutsch Collection; **754**, Edward Piper/The Warder Collection, NY; **755**, Wellcome Institute Library, London; **756**, The Warder Collection, NY; **758**, International Museum of Photography; **759 (left)**, Historisches Museum der Stadt Wien; **759 (right)**, The Hulton Deutsch Collection; **760 (top)**, The Granger Collection, New York; **760 (bottom)**, Erich Lessing/Art Resource, NY; **761**, Victoria & Albert Museum, London/Art Resource, NY; **762**, Giraudon/Art Resource, NY; **763**, The New York Public Library: Astor, Lenox, and Tilden Foundations; **764**, cliché Bibliothèque Nationale de France, Paris; **765**, Art Resource, NY; **766**, The Hulton Deutsch Collection; **767 (top left)**, Corbis-Bettmann; **767 (top right)**, The Mansell Collection, London; **767 (bottom)**, Giraudon/Art Resource, NY; **769**, The Warder Collection, NY; **771**, The Granger Collection, New York; **773**, The Mansell Collection, London; **774**, The Granger Collection, New York; **775**, The Granger Collection, New York; **776**, Corbis-Bettmann; **777**, The Granger Collection, New York; **778**, The Granger Collection, New York; **779**, Hiram Powers, Greek Slave. Marble. In the Collection of the Corcoran Gallery of Art. Gift of William Wilson Corcoran.; **780 (top)**, Giraudon/Art Resource, NY; **780 (bottom)**, Honoré Daumier, Third-Class Carriage, 1863–65 (M. I-165). Oil on canvas, 65.4 × 90.2 cm (25¾ × 35½ in.). New York, The Metropolitan Museum of Art, H. O. Havemeyer Collection, Bequest of Mrs. H. O. Havemeyer, 1929; **781**, The Granger Collection, New York

Chapter 22: 789, Giraudon/Art Resource, NY; **790**, Manchester and Cheshire Library; **792**, Josse/Art Resource, NY; **794**, Roger-Viollet; **795**, The Warder Collection, NY; **796**, The Warder Collection, NY; **798**, Reproduced by the Gracious Permission of Her Majesty the Queen; **799**, Philadelphia Museum of Art: Bequest of Fiske and Marie Kimball; **800**, cliché Bibliothèque Nationale de France, Paris; **802**, Giraudon/Art Resource, NY; **803**, Giraudon/Art Resource, NY; **804**, cliché Bibliothèque Nationale de France, Paris; **805 (both)**, Giraudon/Art Resource, NY; **806**, Roger-Viollet; **807**, The Hulton Deutsch Collection

Chapter 23: 813, Owen Franken/Corbis; **814**, Erich Lessing/Art Resource, NY; **815 (top)**, The Warder Collection, NY; **815 (bottom)**, Giraudon/Art Resource, NY; **816 (top)**, The Warder Collection, NY; **816 (bottom)**, The Mansell Collection, London; **817 (top)**, Bridgeman Art Library; **817 (bottom)**, Giraudon/Art Resource, NY; **818 (top)**, Scala/Art Resource, NY; **818 (bottom)**, Museo del Prado, Madrid; **819 (both)**, © Photo RMN, Paris; **820**, SEF/Art Resource, NY; **821**, The Warder Collection, NY; **824**, Scala/Art Resource, NY; **826**, Erich Lessing/Art Resource, NY; **828**, Staatliche Museen zu Berlin—Preußischer Kulturbesitz; **829**, Stadtarchiv, Frankfurt; **831**, Roger-Viollet; **835 (top)**, Giraudon/Art Resource, NY; **835 (bottom)**, Scala/Art Resource, NY; **837**, MAS Photo Agency; **838**, Bowdoin College Museum of Art, Brunswick, Maine. Bequest of the Honorable James Bowdoin III; **839 (both)**, Library of Congress

Part Six: 844, City College of San Francisco. © 1998 Institute Nacional de Bellas Artes, Mexico City. Photo: © Dirk Bakker, Photographer
Chapter 24: 851, Krupp/Warder Collection, NY; **852**, Corbis-Bettmann; **853**, Library of Congress/Corbis; **854 (top)**, National Archives; **854 (bottom)**, Erich Lessing/Art Resource, NY; **855 (top)**, Hermitage Museum, St. Petersburg/Art Resource, NY; **855 (bottom)**, Scala/Art Resource, NY; **856**, The Warder Collection, NY; **858 (left)**, The Warder Collection, NY; **858 (right)**, Institute of Agricultural History and Museum of English Rural Life; **859**, The Hulton Deutsch Collection; **860**, Hulton Deutsch Collection/Corbis; **861**, The Warder Collection, NY; **862**, The New York Public Library: Astor, Lenox, and Tilden Foundations; **865**, The Warder Collection, NY; **867**, Courtesy of the Director, National Army Museum, London; **868**, The Hulton Deutsch Collection; **870 (left)**, The Warder Collection, NY; **870 (right)**, Corbis-Bettmann; **871**, The New York Public Library: Astor, Lenox, and Tilden Foundations; **872 (left)**, From

Punch magazine, 1857/Warder Collection, NY; **872 (right)**, The Hulton Deutsch Collection; **873**, Ullstein Bilderdienst

Chapter 25: 878, Corbis-Bettmann; **880 (top)**, Hulton Deutsch Collection/Corbis; **880 (bottom)**, The Hulton Deutsch Collection; **881**, Gernsheim Collection, University of Texas/Warder Collection, NY; **882**, Staatliche Museen zu Berlin—Preußischer Kulturbesitz; **884**, Roger-Viollet; **885**, Roger-Viollet; **886**, Library of Congress/Corbis; **887**, The Warder Collection, NY; **888**, Hulton Deutsch Collection/Corbis; **889**, Hulton Deutsch Collection/Corbis; **890**, Library of Congress/Corbis; **891**, The Hulton Deutsch Collection; **892 (both)**, Archivo Iconografico, S.A./Corbis; **893**, The Warder Collection, NY; **895 (top)**, The New York Public Library: Astor, Lenox, and Tilden Foundations; **895 (bottom)**, Corbis-Bettmann; **896**, Library of Congress/Corbis; **897**, Scala/Art Resource, NY; **898 (both)**, © Photo RMN, Paris; **899**, BAL 3435 Monarch of the Glen by Sir Edwin Landseer (1802–73), United Distillers Ltd., London/Bridgeman Art Library Int'l Ltd., London/New York; **900 (top left)**, Ford Madox Brown, The Last of England, 1852–55, oil on panel, 32½ × 29½ inches. By permission of Birmingham Museum and Art Gallery; **900 (top right)**, The Metropolitan Museum of Art, Gift of Louise Senff Cameron in memory of Charles H. Senff, 1928. (28.90) Photograph © 1990 The Metropolitan Museum of Art; **900 (bottom)**, Österreichische Galerie, Vienna; **901 (top and center)**, © Photo RMN, Paris; **901 (bottom)**, Giraudon/Art Resource, NY; **902 (top)**, The Metropolitan Museum of Art, H. O. Havemeyer Collection, Bequest of Mrs. H. O. Havemeyer, 1929. (29.100.42) Photograph © 1986 The Metropolitan Museum of Art; **902 (bottom)**, Giraudon/Art Resource, NY; **904 (top)**, Giraudon/Art Resource, NY; **904 (bottom)**, The Metropolitan Museum of Art, H. O. Havemeyer Collection, Bequest of Mrs. H. O. Havemeyer, 1929. (29.100.64) Photograph © 1984 The Metropolitan Museum of Art; **905 (top)**, The Metropolitan Museum of Art, Bequest of Sam A. Lewisohn, 1951. (51.112.2) Photograph © 1986 The Metropolitan Museum of Art; **905 (bottom)**, Vincent van Gogh, The Starry Night. 1889. Oil on canvas. 29 × 36¼" (73.7 × 92.1 cm). The Museum of Modern Art, New York. Acquired through the Lillie P. Bliss Bequest. Photograph © 1997 The Museum of Modern Art, New York.; **906 (top)**, Photograph © The Barnes Foundation. All Rights Reserved; **906 (bottom left)**, Pablo Picasso, Les Demoiselles d'Avignon, 1907. Oil on canvas. 8' × 7'8" (243.9 × 233.7 cm). The Museum of Modern Art, New York. Acquired through the Lillie P. Bliss Bequest. Photograph © 1997 The Museum of Modern Art, New York. © 1998 Estate of Pablo Picasso/Artists Rights Society (ARS), New York; **906 (bottom right)**, National Gallery, Oslo. Photograph by J. Lathion; **907**, Cameraphoto/Art Resource, NY

Chapter 26: 912, Staatliche Museen zu Berlin—Preußischer Kulturbesitz; **915 (left)**, Christel Gerstenberg/Corbis; **915 (right)**, The New York Public Library: Astor, Lenox, and Tilden Foundations; **917 (both)**, cliché Bibliothèque Nationale de France, Paris; **918**, cliché Bibliothèque Nationale de France, Paris; **920 (both)**, The New York Public Library: Astor, Lenox, and Tilden Foundations; **921 (top)**, Staatliche Museen zu Berlin—Preußischer Kulturbesitz; **921 (bottom)**, Gernsheim Collection/Warder Collection, NY; **922**, The Mansell Collection, London; **923**, The Warder Collection, NY; **924 (all)**, The Hulton Deutsch Collection; **928**, The Warder Collection, NY; **929**, From Heinz Bergschicker's "Leningrad"/Warder Collection, NY; **930**, The Warder Collection, NY; **931**, Staatliche Museen zu Berlin—Preußischer Kulturbesitz; **932**, Corbis-Bettmann; **935**, Museen der Stadt Wien; **937**, The Warder Collection, NY; **938**, Corbis-Bettmann; **943**, The Warder Collection, NY

Chapter 27: 948 (both), Staatliche Museen zu Berlin—Preußischer Kulturbesitz; **951**, Corbis-Bettmann; **952 (top)**, The National Archives/Corbis; **952 (bottom)**, By permission of the British Library; **953**, The Imperial War Museum, London; **954**, The Hulton Deutsch Collection; **955 (both)**, The Imperial War Museum, London; **957**, Hulton Deusch Collection/Corbis; **958 (top)**, The Warder Collection, NY; **958 (bottom)**, Hulton Deutsch Collection/Corbis; **959 (top left and right)**, Staatliche Museen zu Berlin—Preußischer Kulturbesitz; **959 (bottom right)**, The Warder Collection, NY; **960**, The Hulton Deutsch Collection; **961**, Snark/Art Resource, NY; **962**, Hulton Deutsch Collection/Corbis; **964**, The Imperial War Museum, London; **966**, The National Archives/Corbis; **967**, The National Archives; **968**, The Warder Collection, NY; **972 (left)**, The Imperial War Museum, London; **972 (right)**, The Warder Collection, NY; **973**, Hulton Deutsch Collection/Corbis

Chapter 28: 979, The Warder Collection, NY; **981**, The Warder Collection, NY; **982 (left)**, The Warder Collection, NY; **982 (right)**, Staatliche Museen zu Berlin—Preußischer Kulturbesitz; **984**, The Fotomas Index, London/The Warder Collection, NY; **989 (left)**, Brown Brothers; **989 (right)**, International News Photo/The Warder Collection, NY; **991**, Ullstein Bilderdienst; **992**, Stefan Lorant/The Warder Collection, NY; **993**, The Warder Collection, NY; **994**, The Warder Collection, NY; **995 (top)**, The New York Public Library: Astor, Lenox, and Tilden Foundations; **995 (bottom)**, Christel Gerstenberg/Corbis; **996**, The Hulton Deutsch Collection; **997 (left)**, Stefan Lorant/The Warder Collection, NY; **997 (center and right)**, The New York Public Library: Astor, Lenox, and Tilden Foundations; **999**, Ullstein Bilderdienst; **1002 (top left)**, Library of Congress; **1002 (top right)**, UPI/Corbis-Bettmann; **1002 (bottom)**, Hulton Deutsch Collection/Corbis; **1003**, AP/Wide World Photos; **1004**, Hulton Deutsch Collection/Corbis; **1005**, UPI Photo; **1006**, The Warder Collection, NY; **1007 (top)**, The Bettmann Archive; **1007 (bottom)**, The Warder Collection, NY; **1008 (both)**, AP/Wide World Photos; **1009**, © Estate of George Grosz/Licensed by VAGA, New York, NY From George Grosz, Abrechnung folgt! © 1984 by Allison and Busby; **1010 (top left)**, Kandinsky, Painting for Edwin R. Campbell No. 198. 1914. Oil on canvas, 64" × 36½" (162.5 × 80 cm). The Museum of Modern Art, New York. Mrs. Simon Guggenheim Fund. Photograph © 1997 The Museum of Modern Art, New York. © 1998 Artists Rights Society (ARS), New York/ADAGP, Paris; **1010 (top right)**, Philadelphia Museum of Art: Louise and Walter Arensberg Collection © 1998 Artists Rights Society (ARS), New York/ADAGP, Paris/Estate of Marcel Duchamp; **1010 (bottom)**, © Estate of George Grosz/Licensed by VAGA, New York, NY. Photograph Erich Lessing/Art Resource, NY; **1011 (top)**, Dali, The Persistence of Memory. 1931. Oil on canvas, 9½" × 13" (24.1 × 33 cm). The Museum of Modern Art, New York. Given anonymously. Photograph © 1997 The Museum of Modern Art, New York. © 1998 Demart Pro Arte (R), Geneva/Artists Rights Society (ARS), New York; **1011 (center)**, Orozco, Barricade. 1931. Oil on canvas, 55" × 45" (139.7 × 114.3 cm). The Museum of Modern Art, New York. Given anonymously. Photograph © 1997 The Museum of Modern Art, New York. © Estate of José Clemente Orozco/Licensed by VAGA, New York, NY; **1011 (bottom)**, © Foundation Georgio de Chirico/Licensed by VAGA, New York, NY. Photograph by Boltin Picture Library; **1012 (top left)**, Klee, Around the Fish. 1926. Oil on canvas, 18⅜" × 25⅛" (46.7 × 63.8 cm). The Museum of Modern Art, New York. Abby Aldrich Rockefeller Fund. Photograph © 1997 The Museum of Modern Art, New York. © 1998 Artists Rights Society (ARS), New York/VG Bild-Kunst, Bonn; **1012 (bottom left)**, Chagall, I and the Village. 1911. Oil on canvas, 6' 3⅝" × 59⅝" (192.1 × 151.4 cm). The Museum of Modern Art, New York. Mrs. Simon Guggenheim Fund. Photograph © 1997 The Museum of Modern Art, New York. © 1998 Artists Rights Society (ARS), New York/ADAGP, Paris; **1012 (right)**, Braque, The Table. 1928. Oil and sand on canvas, 70¾" × 28¾" (179.7 × 73 cm). The Museum of Modern Art, New York. Acquired through the Lillie P. Bliss Bequest. Photograph © 1997 The Museum of Modern Art, New York. © 1998 Artists Rights Society (ARS), New York/ADAGP, Paris; **1013 (top)**, © T.H. Benton and R.P. Benton Testamentary Trusts/Licensed by VAGA, New York, NY; **1013 (bottom)**, Gift of Edsel B. Ford. © 1998 Institute Nacional de Bellas Artes, Mexico City. Photograph © The Detroit Institute of Arts; **1014**, Hulton Deutsch Collection/Corbis; **1015 (top)**, Western Pennsylvania Conservancy/Art Resource, NY; **1015 (bottom left)**, The Museum of Modern Art, New York. Photograph Courtesy The Museum of Modern Art, New York; **1015 (bottom right)**, The Warder Collection, NY

Chapter 29: 1023, The Imperial War Museum, London; **1025**, Giraudon/Art Resource, NY. © 1998 Estate of Pablo Picasso/Artists Rights Society (ARS), New York; **1027 (left)**, The National Archives/Corbis; **1027 (right)**, AP/Wide World Photos; **1028**, Library of Congress/Corbis; **1029 (left)**, Hulton Deutsch Collection/Corbis; **1029 (right)**, The National Archives; **1030**, The National Archives/Corbis; **1032**, The Warder Collection, NY; **1034 (top left)**, The National Archives/Corbis; **1034 (top right)**, The Imperial War Museum, London; **1034 (bottom)**, AP/Wide World Photos; **1035**, Hulton Deutsch Collection/Corbis; **1037**, Snark/Art Resource, NY; **1038**, The Imperial War Museum, London

Part Seven: 1042, U.S. Dept. of the Interior, U.S. Geological Survey, ESIC
Chapter 30: 1048, UPI/Corbis-Bettmann; **1049**, AP/Wide World Photos; **1051**, Library of Congress/Corbis; **1052 (left)**, UPI/Corbis-Bettmann; **1052 (right)**, German

Information Center/The Warder Collection, NY; **1054**, AP/Wide World Photos; **1055**, Hulton Deutsch Collection/Corbis; **1056 (top)**, Hulton Deutsch Collection/Corbis; **1056 (bottom)**, UPI/Corbis-Bettmann; **1059 (left)**, French National Railways/The Warder Collection, NY; **1059 (right)**, Lee Snider/Photo Images/The Warder Collection, NY; **1060**, AP/Wide World Photos; **1062**, AP/Wide World Photos; **1063**, AP/Wide World Photos; **1066 (both)**, Hulton Deutsch Collection/Corbis; **1068 (top)**, © 1998 Willem de Kooning Revocable Trust/Artists Rights Society (ARS), New York. Francis G. Mayer/Corbis; **1068 (bottom)**, © 1998 Kate Rothko Prizel & Christopher Rothko/Artists Rights Society (ARS), New York. Photograph © The Whitney Museum of American Art, New York; **1069**, © 1998 Pollock-Krasner Foundation/Artists Rights Society (ARS), New York. Seattle Art Museum/Corbis; **1070 (top)**, © Jasper Johns/Licensed by VAGA, New York, NY. Photograph © The Whitney Museum of American Art, New York; **1070 (bottom)**, © 1998 Frank Stella/Artists Rights Society (ARS), New York. Photograph © The Whitney Museum of American Art, New York; **1071 (top)**, © The Whitney Museum of American Art, New York; **1071 (bottom)**, Cincinnati Art Museum, Gift of the RSM Company. © 1998 Eric Fischl

Chapter 31: 1078, Roger-Viollet; **1079**, New York Free Press/Corbis-Bettmann; **1080 (top)**, Niépce-Rapho/The Warder Collection, NY; **1080 (bottom)**, Hulton Deutsch Collection/Corbis; **1081**, Shelly Gazin/Corbis; **1083**, Adam Woolfitt/Corbis; **1084 (top)**, Ronald Reagan Library/Corbis; **1084 (center)**, Owen Franken/Corbis; **1084 (bottom)**, MTB Banking Corporation/Warder Collection, NY; **1086 (both)**, AP/Wide World Photos; **1087 (top)**, UPI/Corbis-Bettmann; **1087 (bottom)**, © Alexandra Avakian/Woodfin Camp; **1088**, AP/Wide World Photos; **1089**, AP/Wide World Photos; **1093**, AP/Wide World Photos

Chapter 32: 1097 (top), Chris Rainier/Corbis; **1097 (bottom)**, Ecoscene/Corbis; **1098 (top)**, AP/Wide World Photos; **1098 (bottom left)**, Sovfoto/Eastfoto; **1098 (bottom right)**, Hulton-Deutsch Collection/Corbis; **1099**, The Warder Collection, NY; **1100 (top)**, Hulton Deutsch Collection/Corbis; **1100 (bottom)**, UPI/Corbis-Bettmann; **1101**, AP/Wide World Photos; **1102 (top)**, Consulate General of the Republic of South Africa; **1102 (bottom)**, AP/Wide World Photos; **1103**, Corbis-Bettmann; **1104 (top)**, UPI/Corbis-Bettmann; **1104 (bottom)**, AP/Wide World Photos; **1107 (top)**, Hulton Deutsch Collection/Corbis; **1107 (bottom)**, The Warder Collection, NY; **1109 (top)**, Tim Page/Corbis; **1109 (bottom)**, Howard Davies/Corbis; **1110 (left)**, Reuters/Corbis-Bettmann; **1110 (right)**, Reuters/Corbis-Bettmann; **1111**, AP/Wide World Photos; **1112**, AP/Wide World Photos; **1114 (left)**, Natalie Fobes/Corbis; **1114 (right)**, © Kennan Ward Photography/Corbis; **1115**, Dave G. Houser/Corbis; **1117 (both)**, The Warder Collection, NY; **1118 (top)**, The Warder Collection, NY; **1118 (bottom)**, Jeffrey Rotman/Corbis; **1119 (top)**, NASA; **1119 (bottom)**, Nik Wheeler/Corbis

INDEX

GUIDE TO PRONUNCIATION

The sounds represented by the diacritical marks used in this Index are illustrated by the following common words:

āle   ēve   ıce   ōld   ūse
ăt   ĕnd   ĭll   ŏf   ŭs   foŏt
câre   fôrm   ûrn
ärm

Vowels that have no diacritical marks are to be "neutral," for example: Aegean = ȧ-je′an, Basel = bäz′ el, Basil = ba′ zil, common = kŏm′ on, Alcaeus = ăl-sē′ us. The combinations *ou* and *oi* are pronounced as in "out" and "oil."